CapStg By weekend 2?

W9-BLL-032

JAPAN

A Short Cultural History

decrease if full
House preference —
Increase Rent
type lease
Want something for little sis please
How much in dues owed

JAPAN

A Short Cultural History

G. B. SANSOM

STANFORD UNIVERSITY PRESS

STANFORD, CALIFORNIA

Stanford University Press, Stanford, California
©1931, 1943, 1952 by G. B. Sansom
Originating publishers: D. Appleton (New York),
Cresset (London), 1931. Second edition published in 1943 in New York,
in 1946 in London; revised in 1952
Stanford University Press edition published in 1978
Printed in the United States of America
Cloth ISBN 0-8047-0952-1   Paper ISBN 0-8047-0954-8
Last figure below indicates year of this printing:
87   86   85   84   83   82

PUBLISHER'S NOTE

Japan: A Short Cultural History was first published in 1931 by the Cresset Press in London and D. Appleton in New York. A revised edition, without the original plates and with the revisions indicated in the Preface, was issued in New York in 1943 and went out of print in the United States in 1977; an essentially identical edition, retaining the plates, was published in England in 1946. Further minor revisions were made by the author in 1952.

The present Stanford edition, the first to appear in paperback in the United States, is reproduced photographically from the British edition except in two particulars: eight of the original twenty plates have been dropped, and the maps have been redrawn by Margaret Kays. In redrawing the maps, it was decided to retain the author's terminology, orthography, and dating even where these have been discarded or superseded by more recent scholarship.

PREFACE

THIS BOOK was first published in 1931. In a revised edition, prepared in wartime and published in 1946, only a few changes were made. Some obvious errors were corrected; the first chapter was rewritten; and at the end of most chapters some notes were added for the benefit of students.

There were still omissions which I wished to repair and themes which I might have developed. Thus, although I paid special attention to the plastic arts I did not bring out clearly enough the important part played by aesthetic feeling in the enrichment of Japanese life. Among Japanese of all classes an instinctive awareness of beauty seems to compensate for a standard of material well-being which to Western judgment seems poor and bleak. Their habit of finding pleasure in common things, their quick appreciation of form and colour, their feeling for simple elegance, are gifts which may well be envied by us who depend so much for our pleasures upon quantity of possessions and complexity of apparatus. Such happy conditions, in which frugality is not the enemy of satisfaction, are perhaps the most distinctive feature in the cultural history of Japan. They are conditions likely to disappear, being incompatible with modern industrial society; but it is worth while to mark and learn a lesson in the art of living, even if only from the past of a people among whom there once flourished a great refinement and virtuosity, coupled with superb accomplishment in the arts and crafts.

Another shortcoming is perhaps more pardonable. I tried to chart the main intellectual currents in Japanese history, but I fear I did not succeed in showing the characteristic attitude of the Japanese towards moral and philosophical problems—their intuitive, emotional approach and their mistrust of logic and analysis. Yet perhaps I may be excused for this failure, seeing that the quintessence of Japanese thought is to be found in Zen Buddhism or in other philosophical systems whose doctrines are by definition incommunicable by the written word and can be made clear only by some inner illumination. This is a state of things which one cannot explain but can only record, observing that it accounts for a number of religious and political beliefs that to the Western mind may seem to have no rational foundation but are none the less genuine sources of behaviour.

But to deal fully with these and other neglected topics would have impeded the flow of a narrative already none too brisk, or it would have called for a complete rewriting of the book. This I could not face; and so I decided to make only a few minor changes. The work as it appears in this edition remains substantially as it was when first written more than twenty years ago.

A thoughtful reviewer of the first edition suggested that in my treatment of Japanese history, by omitting such episodes as the feudal wars of the twelfth century I neglected those romantic or dramatic elements which would have invested it with "the colour and music of a pageant". I have some sympathy with that point of view, since I have a taste for dynastic quarrels, political strife, treason, conspiracy, plots, battles, murders and other public and private adventures and crimes. Though they went out of fashion some decades ago, I think they are as much the proper stuff of history as economic discourse and description of cultural trends. But once you have said something about panache and pointed out the current methods of slaughter, one feudal war seems very like another and romantic incidents begin to pall. Moreover, I do not, like my friendly critic, see history as a pageant, but rather as a motley procession, with some bright banners but many dingy emblems, marching out of step and not very certain of its destination.

It has been pointed out to me by several readers that they are left in the air by the last chapter, which comes to a sudden end without explaining the steps by which Japan emerged from seclusion and entered the modern world. This phase I have since treated in considerable detail in a recent volume (also in the Cresset Historical Series) entitled *The Western World and Japan*, which is in part an expansion and continuation of the last hundred pages of the present work.

For their assistance in preparing the revised edition for the press I am much indebted to my friends and colleagues at Columbia University, in particular to Mr. Harold G. Henderson; to Mr. R. Tsunoda; and to Mr. Eliot Sarasohn, who generously undertook to compile the index.

I should like to repeat here the thanks which I expressed in the Preface of the first edition to the late Professor C. Seligman, F.R.S., whose death, in 1940, was a sore loss to learning and to friendship.

G. B. S.

Columbia University
New York, 1952

NOTE ON PERIODS IN JAPANESE HISTORY

THE periods usually distinguished by historians of Japan are fairly well marked and correspond well enough to phases in political and cultural development. They are of course arbitrary divisions, but most Japanese scholars agree with them and they can be defended on grounds of convenience.

As to periods of Art History, there is less uniformity among specialists, and in this book I have therefore confined myself to a very general treatment of the progress of the arts during each political period. But I take this opportunity of recommending the following classification, which has been adopted by the Art Research Institute of Tokyo and other authorities.

Art Period					Date, A.D.
Asuka	..	..	..	..	552–646
Nara, Early	..	..	..	..	646–710
„ Late	..	..	..	..	710–794
Kōnin	..	..	..	..	794–897
Fujiwara, Main	..	..	..	..	897–1086
„ Late	..	..	..	..	1086–1185
Kamakura, Early	..	..	..	..	1185–1249
„ Late	..	..	..	..	1249–1392
Ashikaga	..	..	..	..	1392–1568
Momoyama	..	..	..	..	1568–1615
Tokugawa	..	..	..	..	1615–1867

CONTENTS

LIST OF PLATES

LIST OF ILLUSTRATIONS

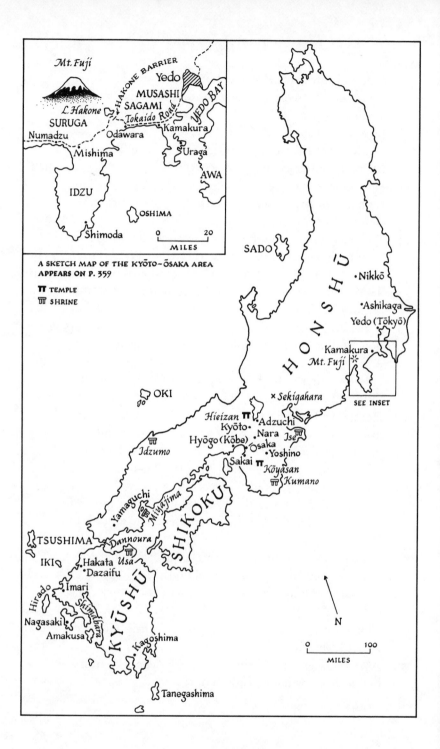

Mt. Fuji
HAKONE BARRIER
Yedo
MUSASHI
SAGAMI
L. Hakone
Tokaido Road
SURUGA
Numadzu
Odawara
Kamakura
Mishima
Uraga
AWA
IDZU
OSHIMA
Shimoda
0   20
MILES

A SKETCH MAP OF THE KYŌTO~ŌSAKA AREA
APPEARS ON P. 359

☖ TEMPLE
☖ SHRINE

SADO

HONSHŪ

• Nikkō

• Ashikaga
Yedo (Tōkyō)

Kamakura •
Mt. Fuji
SEE INSET

OKI

× Sekigahara

Hieizan •
Kyōto • • Adzuchi
Hyōgo (Kōbe) Nara
Idzumo   Ise
        Ōsaka
        • Yoshino
Sakai •
        • Kōyasan
        Kumano

SHIKOKU

Yamaguchi
Miyajima
TSUSHIMA
Dannoura
IKI
Hakata Usa
• Dazaifu
Hirado
Imari
Shimabara
Nagasaki •
Amakusa Kagoshima

KYŪSHŪ

N

0   100
MILES

Tanegashima

PART ONE—EARLY HISTORY

Chapter I—THE ORIGINS

THE origins of the Japanese are still in dispute, but *a priori* reasoning in the light of known facts of geography and history leads to the conclusion that the Japanese race is a compound of elements drawn in prehistoric times from different parts of the Asiatic mainland. The order in which these elements arrived and the proportions in which they are mixed cannot be definitely stated, but it seems probable from the position of the Japanese archipelago, lying in a curve across the coast of north-eastern Asia, and almost touching it at two points, that there is a strong if not a predominant northern strain, and that shores adjacent to the mainland were peopled in neolithic times by Mongol tribes arriving through Korea. At the same time there are reasons for supposing that some features of early Japanese civilisation, notably the wet method of rice culture, originated in South China; and there is nothing improbable in the belief that the Japanese race includes elements from that region. As to the Ainu, a people who now inhabit the northern island of Japan (the Hokkaidō), philological and other evidence shows that they were at one time spread over the whole archipelago. There is some disagreement about their origins, but modern anthropologists regard them as of early Caucasic stock.

The archæological evidence so far collected, while furnishing a picture of prehistoric culture in Japan, does not throw any direct light on the problem of racial origins, but it is worth reviewing briefly because it gives colour to certain plausible conjectures as to the peopling of the Japanese islands.

No traces of a palæolithic culture have yet been found in Japan, but two main types of neolithic culture are distinguished. One is known as the Jōmon ("rope-pattern") type, because the pottery which characterises it was made by coiling or has a coil as conventional decoration. The other is known as the Yayoi type, because of certain characteristic pottery first found in a neolithic site at a place of that name.

Both types are found in neolithic sites all over Japan, but Jōmon

pottery is more frequent in the North and East, where Yayoi
pottery is relatively scarce. Where they occur together, Jōmon
pottery is generally below Yayoi pottery and is therefore thought
to be older. Technically it is inferior to Yayoi pottery and yet it is
artistically more advanced, showing much greater freedom of
design and variety of shape. Also the stone artifacts which occur
with Jōmon pottery are on the whole more advanced than those

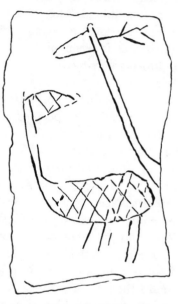

FIG. 1. *Picture incised on Yayoi
neolithic pottery found in Japan.
Represents a man standing in
a boat.*

FIG. 2. *Picture incised on Yayoi
neolithic pottery found in Yamato.
Represents deer.*

which occur with Yayoi pottery. From these and other data it is
inferred that the neolithic culture represented by Jōmon pottery,
after a long development in isolation, was gradually displaced by
the later (Yayoi) culture in Southern and Western Japan and
reached its zenith in the North and East. The Yayoi culture on
the other hand was, perhaps already by the time when the two
cultures came into contact, declining as a neolithic culture and
about to pass into a metal phase, as is shown by the occurrence in
many sites of bronze articles associated with Yayoi pottery.

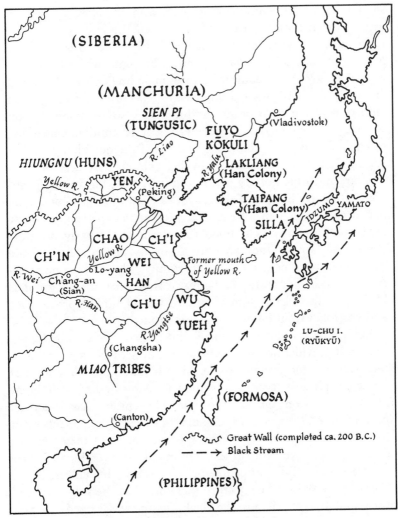

FIG. 3. *Japan and the mainland.*

The archæological evidence cited above bears only upon the
nature of prehistoric culture in Japan. It does not tell us where
its component elements originated and still less does it tell us
whence the people came who inhabited Japan in neolithic times.
But it is improbable that the neolithic culture of an island country

should be an autochthonous growth, and therefore it may be
assumed that both the early (Jōmon) and the late (Yayoi) neolithic cultures were of continental origin. The Jōmon culture
extends to the Luchu Islands but not to Formosa, which belongs to
a separate group of neolithic cultures including South China and
Indo-China. It is thus reasonable to conjecture that the Jōmon
culture is of northern origin; and if that is so, we might expect
to find somewhere on the northern Asiatic continent neolithic
remains showing a resemblance to those of the neolithic period in
Japan. Such a resemblance is in fact exhibited by certain rudimentary neolithic pottery discovered in Korea; but it is a resemblance to early pottery of the Yayoi rather than the Jōmon type
and it cannot therefore be said at present that pottery or other
artifacts throw any light upon the origin of the early neolithic
culture of Japan. One can only argue by analogy that, if the
Yayoi culture came (as it almost certainly did) from the northern
Asiatic continent by way of Korea, it is on geographical grounds
likely that the earlier Jōmon culture was of similar provenance
and possible that it followed the same route.

The study of human remains found in neolithic sites in Japan,
though it provides no positive evidence, at least gives a hint as to
the origins of the Jōmon people, since it shows that they were of
the same physical type as the modern Ainu and of a different
physical type from the Yayoi people. This opinion has, it is true,
been attacked by reputable scholars; but even its opponents seem
to be prepared to recognise the existence of what they style an
Ainoid people, who spread the Jōmon culture over Japan before
the arrival of a different people or peoples bringing culture of the
Yayoi type. We may conjecture therefore that the substratum of
the population of Japan in the Neolithic Age was formed by a race
sprung from those early Caucasic people who spread over northern
Europe and Asia from homelands which are not so far determined. Their survivors in the modern world are the Ainu of the
Hokkaidō and Sakhalin and, in much diluted form, people like
the Gilyaks in eastern Siberia.

The neolithic culture which they developed in Japan reached,
as we have seen, a very high level. Some Japanese scholars assert
that it was one of the most advanced neolithic cultures in the

world, in point of skill in the manufacture of weapons and tools and originality in the design and ornament of pottery. This view is in part confirmed by one European authority (Dr. N. G. Munro, in *Prehistoric Japan*), who says of the early pottery that "it roams into lavish conceptions of form and decoration probably unsurpassed in any place or time." He adds the opinion that "the

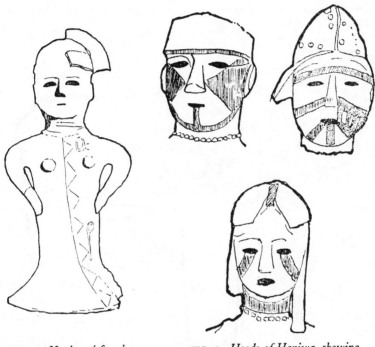

FIG. 4. *Haniwa (female figure). The original has a cinnabar pattern on face and neck.*

FIG. 5. *Heads of Haniwa, showing patterns on the face (red).*

artistic talent of later Japan was rooted in the prehistoric past." This early culture, in order to reach such a degree of perfection, must have gone through a very long development in Japan, and it is possible that during its course more than one wave of migration came from the mainland, whether from the Korean peninsula or from the regions now known as the Maritime Province of Siberia and Kamchatka. Indeed the possibility of movements in

the reverse direction should not be excluded. But all this is conjecture about a very misty past, and it is not until we approach
the Christian era that we find more dependable evidence of
relationship with the mainland of Asia.

When we come to inquire into the origins of the later (Yayoi)
neolithic culture of Japan, ample if not conclusive evidence is
furnished by the results of archæological research in Korea, where
several types of neolithic remains occur, marking fairly well

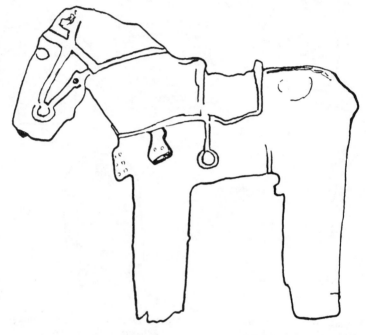

FIG. 6. *Haniwa representing a horse.*

differentiated cultural phases for each of which a corresponding
Yayoi type can be distinguished in Japan. A detailed study of this
question would be out of place here, and we may content ourselves with noticing that the evidence points to an early neolithic
culture common to Manchuria, Korea and the Maritime Province, which had its counterpart in Japan in the earliest forms of
Yayoi culture. Korea was thereafter, it seems, subjected to successive new cultural influences from outside, and these influences

were in turn transmitted—no doubt by the agency of immigrants from Korea—to Japan, where, as the technical improvement in some Yayoi artifacts testifies, they raised the general cultural level and enabled the Yayoi people to displace or absorb the Jōmon people.

The various phases of culture exhibited by neolithic remains in Korea are characterised by three types of pottery which are thought by some Japanese scholars to correspond with

FIG. 7. *Haniwa repre-senting an armed man. "Yamato" Dolmen Per-iod. (From Imperial Mu-seum Collection, Tokyo.)*

FIG. 8. *Detail of Chinese stone monument of North-ern Wei dynasty. Compare the dress with that of the Haniwa of an armed man.*

neolithic pottery found respectively in: Siberia, Northern Russia, Finland and Sweden; Western China, Manchuria and Inner Mongolia; and Southern China. It should be noted, however, that this view, though it raises presumptions as to the origin of the later phases of neolithic culture in Japan, does not by itself justify any dogma as to the origins of the Yayoi people. All that we can say is that probably the population of the Japanese archipelago during the Stone Age included people of Mongol stock. There are many features of early Japanese culture as reconstructed from folk-lore and other survivals which point to an affinity with Mongol peoples. Thus, for example, the earliest Japanese religion has much in common with the Shamanism prac-

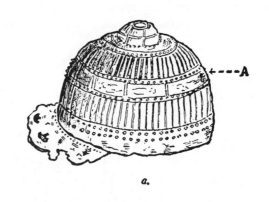

a.

b.

FIG. 9 (a). *Portion of helmet—iron and bronze, gilt. Unearthed in Eastern Japan. Conjectured date, circa A.D. 400.*
(b). *The pattern chiselled at* A.

tised in north-eastern Asia: primitive Japanese weapons resemble the weapons of north-eastern Asia rather than those of the Oceanic islands; and the dominant Japanese physical type is Mongoloid in so far as it is broad-skulled, somewhat prognathic, yellow-skinned and straight-haired, while the eyelid presents the characteristic "Mongol fold" and the so-called "Mongol spot" is general in Japanese babies.

As to the presence of other than northern elements in the population of Japan, there can be little doubt; but whence they came we do not know. If, as modern anthropologists say, there is a proto-Malay constituent in the Mongol stock, then the Japanese may have derived a southern strain from this source. There is little or nothing to support any of those hypotheses which assume direct migrations to Japan from Indonesia, Malaysia or Polynesia. It is much more likely that it was diffusion from a common centre on the Asiatic mainland which at the same time peopled the islands of the south and furnished the southern strain in the people and culture of Japan. A good deal of evidence has been collected, which tends to show that this centre was in southern China or Indo-China. But all this is in the realm of conjecture.

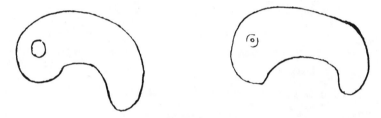

FIG. 10. *Magatama from Sepulchral Mound, actual size.*

The archæological evidence proves only that there was a fairly uniform civilisation in Japan prior to the Christian era. The ethnical fusion which produced the Japanese race goes back to a remoter antiquity, of which we have no knowledge, and the most that we can safely say is that the Japanese from the end of the Stone Age onward exhibit a blend of many ethnic features. The historian should resist the temptation of easy analogies, yet there is no harm in comparing the situation of the British Isles, lying off the western edge of Europe, and the Japanese archipelago, strung out across the eastern shores of Asia. Behind each is a great and variously peopled continent, beyond each is an immense stretch of ocean. Each was a pocket, in which immigrants driven by the pressure of hunger and fear, or perhaps by the plain desire for change, might assemble, and where, because they could not go farther, they must fuse or perish.[1]

The Stone Age in Japan is thought by most scholars to have persisted until about the beginning of the Christian era. Exact dates cannot of course be given, but there is evidence to show that neolithic culture was coming to an end in the west of Japan during the

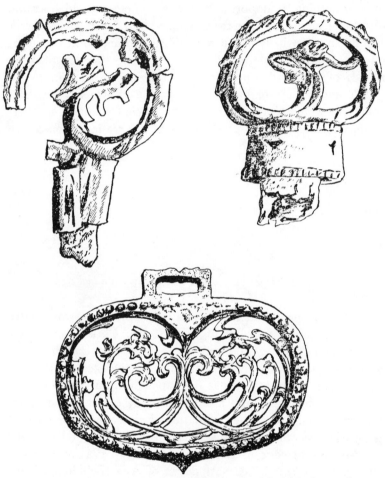

FIG. 11. *Bronze Sword Pommels from the age of Sepulchral Mounds.*

first century B.C., though it persisted in Central Japan for two or three centuries longer, and in remote places in the extreme north had not entirely vanished by the end of the first millennium of the

Christian era. The influence which brought the neolithic phase
to an end was the influence of the metal culture of China, exercised
first upon Korea and then by Korea upon Japan.

The bronze culture of China, at its zenith under the Chou
dynasty, is known to have spread to South Manchuria and along
the coasts of Korea to the extreme south of the peninsula, as is
proved by the appearance in neolithic sites in those regions of
coins (such as the metal tokens called "knife money") minted
towards the end of the Chou or the beginning of the Ch'in dynasty
—that is to say about 300 B.C. The bronze culture which first
spread in Korea was probably not exclusively Chinese, for there
is good evidence to relate a number of bronze articles found in
Korea to objects of Scythian type. It is likely that the bronze
culture of northern China contained Scytho-Siberian elements,
which were transmitted to Korea in the early phases of her bronze
period. This point is of special interest because it helps to account
for an important phenomenon in Far Eastern history—the
preservation by Korean culture of a strong individual character
despite the powerful influence and the propinquity of the
advanced civilisation of Han China. It is largely because Korea
was not merely a channel by which Han civilisation was passed
on to Japan, but a terrain in which cultural elements from various
sources were combined before they were transmitted, that from
its beginnings Japanese culture presents such a marked idiosyn-
crasy.

With the Han dynasty China entered upon the Iron Age, and
it is clear that this new influence also spread very soon to the same
regions, since coins minted in China in the first decade of the
Christian era have been found in neolithic sites in Southern
Manchuria and Korea together with implements of bronze, iron
and stone. So far no objects which can be ascribed to late Chou
times have been found in Japan, but coins of the Eastern Han
dynasty are not uncommon, and their presence shows what we
should on geographical grounds expect, namely that Chinese
bronze culture reached Japan by way of Korea after a delay of a
few decades or perhaps a century. Certainly by the beginning
of the Christian era Chinese bronze culture was beginning to
influence Japan, but before it had displaced neolithic culture

in Japan it was overtaken by an iron culture; and therefore it is generally held that there was no true bronze age in
Japan.

Following or perhaps overlapping the age of the shell mounds,
which are the chief repositories of neolithic remains in Japan,
comes the age of the sepulchral mounds. These are simple mounds
covering stone or earthenware coffins, but the characteristic
tumulus of this period is a great pile over a sepulchral stone
chamber. The tombs of the rulers, which are called *misasagi*, are
of almost stupendous dimensions, that of the emperor Nintoku
(died about A.D. 400) being some 1,200 feet in length and 90 feet
in height, covering with its moats a space of 80 acres. Such mounds
occur chiefly in western and central Japan. In these sepulchral
stone chambers are found vases almost identical in form and
decoration with Yayoi vases, but technically superior, harder and
nearly always moulded on the wheel, together with jewels, mirrors,
weapons and other objects of bronze or iron. Outside the mounds,
but associated with them, are found clay figures known as *haniwa*.
The clay figures of the Neolithic Age were misshapen and grimacing
objects, probably intended to ward off evil spirits. Those of the
later sepulchral mounds represent sometimes animals (in particular
horses and so far only in one instance an ox), but usually men and
women with oval faces and regular features, wearing sleeved
robes and ornaments such as necklets and ear-rings and having
the hair somewhat elaborately dressed, or covered with a coif or
other headgear. The faces were coloured, in definite patterns,
usually red. The *haniwa* are as a rule in the form of cylinders
surmounted by a bust, so that the complete costume is not often
represented; but the general impression they give is of the dress
of northern Asiatics, and not of peoples from tropical regions. The
weapons are for the most part of a continental type, Mongolian
or Chinese, and though certain knives are thought to resemble the
Malay kriss they can equally well be related to weapons found in
north-eastern Asia. The arrow known as the *nari-kaburaya*, or
humming-bulb, is a characteristic weapon of the period of the
sepulchral mounds, and is definitely not of Oceanic origin. The
armour, helmets, and horse-trappings, of iron and bronze, in-
dubitably show a debt either to China or to Mongolia, and not to

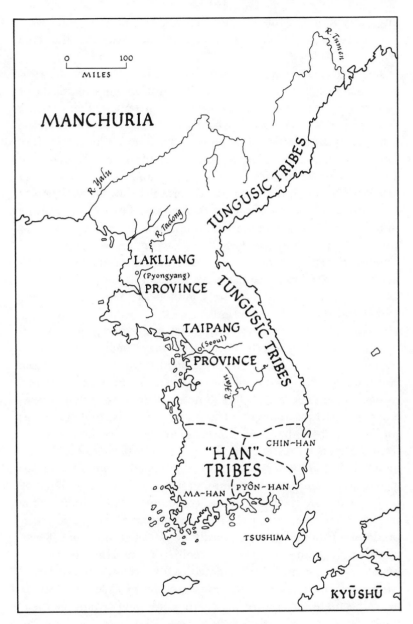

FIG. 12. *Early Korea.*

any southern culture. Many of the bronze mirrors were beyond question made in China, probably during the Han dynasty.

The articles of stone contained in the tumuli are not the tools and weapons proper to a neolithic culture, but ornaments or objects for ceremonial use. Most prominent among them are the "curved jewels" (*magatama*), which are evidently derived from the claws or tusks of animals. *Magatama* are found in neolithic sites, some of bone, some of horn, and some of stone. To these, no doubt, magic properties were ascribed, and indeed until very recent times in Korea and eastern Siberia the claw of the tiger was regarded as an amulet of the greatest power. The *magatama* of the tumuli are often of fine workmanship, and are made of a great variety of materials, such as agate, jasper, serpentine, quartz, glass, jade, nephrite and chrysoprase. It is important to note that neither of these last three materials is found in Japan, or even in China proper, though they are common in the region of Lake Baikal and the Ural mountains.

Such, in brief outline, is the story of prehistoric Japan as told by archæological research. From it we may conclude with some certainty that the country was inhabited towards the end of the Neolithic Age by peoples of the stock known to ethnologists, or rather to philologists, as Ural-Altaic, a stock including Finns, Samoyedes, Huns, Tungusic tribes and Mongols; that there was traffic between Japan and Korea, that successive immigrations from north-eastern Asia took place, probably through Korea and on a small scale; and that, as time progressed, among the immigrants were an increasing number who had, in their land of origin or during their migration, come under the influence of a bronze or an iron culture. That the influence in question was predominantly Chinese can hardly be doubted, and that it was increasingly Chinese from the zenith of the Han dynasty is certain. What cannot be estimated is the strength of the Ural-Altaic element in the racial characters of the Japanese, as distinct from the material culture which they adopted. Many of their qualities, much of their thought and behaviour, not only as revealed in their early legends but even as observed to-day, mark them off very distinctly from the Chinese, despite their great intellectual and even spiritual debt to successive dynasties of Han and T'ang and Sung and Ming. No student of Japanese history can fail to be impressed by this feature. The power and prestige of a foreign culture seem as if they would overwhelm and transform Japan, but always there is a hard, non-absorbent core of individual character, which resists and in its turn works upon the invading influence. It is interesting to speculate as to the source of this distinctive temperament. Doubtless it is to be sought in some special ingredient of the racial mixture. Nobody who has lived among the Japanese can resist the sensation that there is a warm, southern element in their composition. True, the archæological evidence points to northern affinities, but psychological impressions are not to be neglected. They are corroborated, too, by certain peculiarities of custom, notably in speech and dwelling and diet. These, together with the native mythology, if they furnish no positive proofs, offer data hard to reconcile with any theory which postulates an exclusively northern origin for the Japanese.

There is some evidence in legend, and a little in recorded history, to complete the picture of early Japanese civilisation which is furnished by archæological finds. Early Chinese records,[2] though they must be read with respectful doubts, give us some details of interest. The first authentic reference to Japan is probably a passage in the *Shanhaiching* which states that the Wa were subject to the Kingdom of Yen. The Wa are the Japanese, or at any rate some of the people inhabiting Japan, presumably not later than 265 B.C., when the Kingdom of Yen lost its independence. The ideograph used by the Chinese to represent Wa is related to the character for dwarf. It is possible therefore that there were relations of some kind (not necessarily of vassalage) between the Japanese and the Chinese in the third century B.C., and that the Japanese were known to the Chinese as a people of short stature. That there was some traffic between Yen and Korea is indicated not only by statements in the *Shanhaiching* but also by the occurrence in tombs in northern and southern Korea of coins minted by the rulers of Yen. Such coins have not been found in Japan proper, but they have been found in the Luchu Islands. The evidence for direct contact between Chinese and Japanese in the first half of the third century B.C. is therefore not negligible; but it is not very strong.

Even for the second half we have nothing but tradition to suggest that Chinese travelled as far as Japan. In the anarchy prevailing during that period the north of China was the scene of civil wars among the kingdoms of Ch'in, Chao and Yen which, having at the same time to protect themselves against the warlike nomads known to the Chinese as Hsiung-nu, built palisades and walls that were later (214 B.C.) combined to form the great wall of China. The king of Yen as part of his defensive measures entered country now constituting South Manchuria and North Korea, and it is known that in these troubled times refugees and groups of colonists began to leave China for those regions.

The first mention of Korea in Chinese records is in the *Shi Chih* where, on not very good authority, we are told that the Chou emperor Wu (1122 B.C.) gave Korea in fief to a statesman named Chitzu, who departed with some thousand followers and introduced the arts of civilisation into northern Korea. Centuries later, when the first Ch'in emperor, Shih Hwangti, had subdued his rivals he, wishing now to find the Elixir of Youth—so the legend has it—sent from the Shantung coast to an island in the East a Taoist sage named Sufu, with three thousand men and women, artisans of all kinds and a cargo of seeds. Not much faith is to be put in this tale, but it shows at least a tradition of early migration of culture-bearers in the direction of Japan. It is remarkable, too, as showing the persistence of that tradition, that in the earliest Japanese writings the word for a weaver is written with the Chinese character for Ch'in. This does not confirm the tradition but it does probably indicate that in the minds of the Japanese their first knowledge of the arts of Chinese civilisation was connected with the Ch'in dynasty. Certainly some of these arts were communicated to Japan, if only by Korean intermediaries, during or not long after the period of Ch'in rule, since in western Japan archæologists have found, in addition to bronze articles in Ch'in style, stone swords and arrowheads copied from bronze originals such as are common throughout Korea and belong to Ch'in or earlier times.

From the time (206 B.C.) when the Han dynasty replaced the

Ch'in the picture becomes gradually clearer. To speak of the flowering of the Han culture is to use too gentle a word. It was rather a gigantic explosion of energies slowly stored up since the dawn of Chinese civilisation. It thrust out and expanded and spilled over west to the Caspian, south towards India, north towards the lands of the Hsiung-nu and north-east towards the home of Tungusic tribes. In 108 B.C. Chao-hsien, a country corresponding roughly to the northern half of modern Korea, was conquered and divided into four Chinese provinces under Chinese governors, with a full system of administration on the Chinese model. The chief of the four provinces was called Lakliang (or Lolang—in modern Japanese, Rakurō), and the centre of the government was within a mile or so of the present town of Pyönyang on the Tadong river. The rise and fall of the fortunes of the Han dynasty produced changes in the size and importance of the colony, but at one time the Province of Lakliang included the whole of Korea down to the Han river and indeterminate territory south of that. On its southern and eastern confines the country was nominally under Chinese rule, and important points were occupied by military posts, so that, though the authority of the Lakliang government probably did not extend more than two hundred miles or so east and south of Pyönyang, Chinese cultural influence must have spread gradually over the peninsula, particu-larly southwards and along the coast.

From records of the early Han dynasty and from rich finds in a number of elaborate tombs excavated in recent years near Pyönyang, it is clear that Lakliang was one of the most prosperous Chinese colonies and an important outpost of Chinese culture. That its influence extended a long way southward is undoubted, since at various points in southern Korea there have been dis-interred bronze and iron implements and ornaments, coins, tokens and pottery which show that articles from Lakliang reached these parts approximately between 50 B.C. and A.D. 50. Further there is evidence that certain objects, such as bronze mirrors, swords, spears and personal ornaments, were made locally in imitation of Han work; and objects closely resembling these local products, as well as bronze mirrors made in China in early Han times, have been found in western Japan together with

Yayoi pottery at points within easy reach of the south coast of Korea. We may thus be sure that strong Chinese cultural influence from the Han colony reached Japan by the beginning of the Christian era and resulted presently in a regular traffic between Kyūshū and Lakliang. Moreover, though the political influence of the Han empire waned and the colony fell under the domination of the growing kingdom of Kōkuli (or Kōguryö), we know that Kōkuli succumbed in a large measure to the cultural influence of the Chinese in Lakliang. In this respect there was no break, and we may take it that such influence was continuous in northern Korea from about 100 B.C. and that it moved regularly south and towards Japan.

There is no doubt that, from this time onward, relations between Japan and China became increasingly close. We have no record of their beginnings, but we may be sure that travellers from the extreme west of Japan found their way to the Chinese colonies in Korea in the first century B.C. The first mention of such journeys occurs in the Han records, where, with an entry registering the arrival of a Japanese embassy at Loyang, the Han capital, in A.D. 57, the following passage occurs:—

"The country of the Wa lies south-east of South Korea in the middle of the ocean and is formed of a number of islands. It contains more than one hundred kingdoms. From the time when the emperor Wu-Ti conquered Chao-hsien (i.e. North Korea, in 108 B.C.) more than thirty of these kingdoms have held intercourse with China by envoys or by scribes . . . . They understand the art of weaving . . . . Their soldiers have spears and shields, wooden bows and bamboo arrows sometimes tipped with bone. The men all tattoo their faces, and adorn their bodies with designs. Differences of rank are indicated by the position and size of the pattern. They use pink and scarlet to smear their bodies with, as rice powder is used in China."

This chronicle gives further information as to Japan and Japanese customs, which with additional details is recorded in the Wei records also. These writings are not entirely reliable in their extant form. They were compiled, from materials not now surviving, a long while after the period which they describe—the

Hou Han Shu in A.D. 424, the *Wei Chih* and an earlier work, the *Wei Liao*, before A.D. 292—and they fall under suspicion of containing additions made by their writers in the light of contemporary knowledge. Certainly they display inconsistencies and their texts are in places corrupt. But the statements of the Wei records, though they cannot be fully accepted, are credible enough in general to furnish a fair picture of Japan as seen by Chinese observers in the first century of the Christian era.

Their information, combined with the archæological evidence from sepulchral mounds, reveals a country (perhaps only those parts of Japan nearest to Korea) settled by a number of independent tribes, each with its own ruler, all eager to increase their strength by the adoption of a superior culture, the strongest sending embassies in search of favours from the powerful Han, and anxious above all to obtain the products of Chinese skill and wealth, the swords, the mirrors, the jewels and golden ornaments, the silken stuffs. The envoy to the Chinese court in A.D. 57 was given an official seal and a ribbon; and it is a curious fact that, 1,700 years later, there was discovered buried in sand on the shores of the bay of Hakata (a most convenient port for embarking from Kyūshū on a voyage to Korea or China) a golden seal bearing the inscription "Han [? vassal] King of the Wa country Nu."

The Wei record gives names, many of which are identifiable, of districts, towns and officials, together with directions, distances and other particulars which, despite some obvious errors, give the impression of accounts by veracious eye-witnesses which have been mishandled by subsequent compilers. They state, for instance, that all males were tattooed, a fact for which there is no other evidence (except that tattooing is still practised by the Ainu); but what they say about smears of pink and scarlet is confirmed by the traces of colour found upon the clay images of the tumuli— the *haniwa*. Anyhow, what they tell us is sufficient to show that the people visited by Han and Wei travellers had reached a moderately high point of social organisation, were already emerging from neolithic culture at the beginning of the Christian era, and for their further cultural progress were indebted to Korea and China. On these points there is evidence in plenty, though there is no reason to suppose that the cultural movements in question were produced by movements of population from the mainland. Doubtless, during her transition from stone to bronze, Japan received small contingents from Korea; but by that time the Japanese were already formed in a process of ethnical fusion going back, as we have seen, to an antiquity of which we have no knowledge.

Apart from Chinese chronicles, our chief written sources of information about early Japanese history are two official records, the *Kojiki* ("Record of Ancient Things") and the *Nihongi*, or more correctly *Nihon-shoki* ("Chronicles of Japan"), compiled in 712 and 720 respectively. Both are somewhat tendentious works, in which myth and legend and history are so selected and set forth as to enhance the prestige of the reigning dynasty. Moreover, when they were compiled, the Chinese language and Chinese literature, both historical and philosophical, had been known to scholars in Japan in increasing measure for at least three centuries, so that it is difficult to say of any given statement that it is not under Chinese influence in some way or another. Both works are nevertheless invaluable sources of information as to the early beliefs and customs of Japan and, if used with caution, as to the main events of the first centuries of the Christian era. Before attempting a summary of their contents it will be best to anticipate a little and to describe briefly the circumstances in which they were written.

It seems that by the end of the first century certain clans in Kyūshū, having gained a position of supremacy over their neighbours, or having combined with them, began to extend their power towards the east, and pushing along the shores of the Inland Sea reached the province of Yamato, where they proceeded to establish a central state, and gradually to extend its authority as far as possible in all directions. It is true that there is not very good evidence for this eastward migration and some scholars are inclined to doubt it; but it is very likely that enterprising rulers in south-western Japan, making use of a superior equipment derived from contact with an advanced metal culture, should in their eastward progress have subdued without much difficulty tribes over which they had this advantage. In any case, by the beginning of the seventh century a central state had been established in Yamato and had gained some measure of control over western and central Japan and even as far north and east as Sendai. No other ruler or chieftain was in a position to break, but some might challenge, the supremacy of the Yamato sovereigns, so that it was thought essential to strengthen their dynastic claims; and it was chiefly with this object that the *Kojiki* and the *Nihon-shoki* were compiled. They therefore consist largely of a recital of early myths and legends pieced together in such a way as to glorify the reigning family and their ancestors. The following chapter will be devoted to a study of early history as related in these chronicles, but checked where possible by data from other sources. It must be repeated that both these chronicles were compiled at a date when Japan had been for centuries under the influence of Chinese culture, and that they are both written in Chinese script—since the Japanese had no writing of their own. The *Nihon-shoki* indeed is written in the Chinese language, and not in Japanese at all. Consequently, allowance must be made not only for purposed arrangement and selection of historical events, but also for the desire of the compilers to display their learning. At the time when they were written the prestige of Chinese studies was overwhelming. Subject to these criticisms, they deserve perhaps greater credence than it has been the custom of Western scholars to accord them, and for their time they are very remarkable cultural monuments.

NOTES TO CHAPTER I

[1] Since this chapter was first written Japanese archaelogy has made great advances, especially in the last ten years. There are still many points of controversy among scholars, and readers interested in this subject are referred to the following surveys in English: 1. Richard K. Beardsley, *Japan before History* in the Far Eastern Quarterly, May 1955. 2. J. E. Kidder, *Japan before Buddhism*, in volume 10 of the series "Ancient Peoples and Places", 1959. Both of these are published in the United States.

[2] Page 15 ff. It is not easy to assess the value of early Chinese writings as to conditions in proto-historic Japan. Travellers often bring back startling tales from countries visited, and later compilers are apt to misunderstand or embellish the materials which they use. It may well be, therefore, that the accounts of Japanese customs appearing in Chinese records are somewhat highly coloured and even in places invented. It is probably best to rely upon them for exact statements only when some corroboration can be found in archæological evidence, and to remember that what the travellers recorded may have been strictly local happenings and not necessarily representative of Japan as a whole.

Chapter II

EARLY MYTHS AND CHRONICLES

1. NATIVE TRADITION AND CHINESE NOTICES

THE chronicles begin with a cosmogonic myth, which is clearly of Chinese origin. There follows a theogonic myth, which bears a striking resemblance to Polynesian legends of the creation. After Heaven and Earth were formed from chaos, gods were produced, seven generations, ending with the god Izanagi and the goddess Izanami, who founded an island in the ocean and descended from Heaven to dwell thereon. They married, and Izanami gave birth to the islands of Japan, to the sea, to the rivers, mountains and trees. Then they consulted together, and produced Ama-terasu-ō-mi-Kami, the Heaven-Shining-Great-Deity, whose lustre was so great and far-reaching that they sent her up to Heaven. Then they produced the Moon God, and he also was sent to Heaven to share in the government with the Sun Goddess. Their next child was called Susa-no-wo, a fierce, cruel deity, for ever weeping and wailing. He brought many people to an untimely end, and laid waste green mountains. So his parents sent him to rule the Nether Land of Darkness. Then Izanami gave birth to the Fire God, who burned her so that she died, and as she died there were born from her excreta and from the tears of her husband many other gods. This legend sets the key of all native Japanese mythology. The manifestations of nature are deified, all animate and inanimate things are gods, the offspring of gods. Not only are the sun and moon divine, but so are the mountains and rivers and trees, and so is the storm, for clearly the weeping and wailing of Susa-no-wo are the flood and the tempest, and his violence is the damage done by storms. A great part of the legend therefore is concerned with relating the birth of gods to correspond with all objects and categories which the Japanese distinguished.

Unhappily, since the myths were, so far as we know, first committed to writing as late as the seventh century A.D., we cannot hope to distinguish exactly the earliest elements in these beliefs.

Much indeed of what was then recorded is clearly of very recent invention. Certain accounts of past happenings appear in a form which could scarcely have developed without a knowledge of writing, while the gods are described as possessing swords and mirrors, things unknown to the Japanese before they came under the influence of the metal culture of the Chinese; and in general the compilers of both *Nihon-shoki* and *Kojiki* conceive of events in the legendary past as if they had taken place in cultural conditions as advanced as those of their own times. There are many signs of the deliberate selection and arrangement of myth and legend for dynastic as well as religious ends, and it is not too much to say that these chronicles, in their early parts at least, are works compiled with a political aim, in which fact and fancy are combined in such a way as to justify retrospectively the supremacy of the leading clans over other families or tribes. Genealogies play an important part in these records, as indeed they do in all Japanese history. A suitably imposing pedigree is furnished for every house of importance, as when we are told of the birth of the god Ama-no-hohi, Heavenly-Burning-Sun, "who is the ancestor of the grandees of Omi and the governor of Idzumo and the chief of the Clayworkers' Corporation."

When Izanami died she went to the Land of Darkness, called Yomi; and Izanagi followed her. But it was too late, for she had begun to decay and putrefy, so that Izanagi was overcome with horror, and fled from the sight of death and corruption. Escaping after various adventures from the Land of Darkness, his first care was to purify himself by bathing in the sea. Here, abruptly, Izanagi vanishes from the myth. In one account he is said to have dwelt for ever after in silence and concealment, in another to have ascended to Heaven; but we hear no more of him, and the mythical narrative now takes up the tale of the Sun Goddess and the Storm God, Ama-terasu-ō-mi-Kami and her brother Susa-no-wo. Susa-no-wo had been sent to rule the Nether Region, but before departing he ascended to Heaven to take leave of his sister. His conduct was rough and unseemly. He insulted the Sun Goddess by breaking down the divisions between her rice fields, fouling the hall where she was celebrating the festival of first-fruits, and, most astonishing of all his misdeeds, flaying "a heavenly piebald colt

with a backward flaying"*he flung it through a hole which he made
in the roof of her palace, into a room where she was weaving garments for the gods. The outraged Sun Goddess entered the Rock-
Cave of Heaven, and darkness covered the world. The heavenly
deities, having in consternation debated how they should persuade
the Sun Goddess to come out, assembled outside the cave, where
they set up offerings and recited litanies. Then one of their number, the Dread Female of Heaven, having kindled a fire, chanted
inspired words and danced a rollicking indecent dance. Heaven
was shaken with the laughter of the gods, the Sun Goddess peeped
out in curiosity, so that one of the deities was able to grasp her
hand and drag her forth. Then the gods in council tried and punished Susa-no-wo, made him furnish, by way of fine, one thousand
tables of offerings, and banished him to the Land of Darkness.
Susa-no-wo did not at once descend to the shades, but, according
to one version, crossed over to Korea, where he dwelt for a time,
and then, dissatisfied, returned to the province of Idzumo. Eventually, after many adventures, he went down to the Land of Darkness, leaving on earth an immense progeny of gods and goddesses.

But his offspring were not thought fit to rule the earth and
the Sun Goddess sent down other deities, to prepare the way
for her grandson Ninigi-no-Mikoto. One of these divine messengers
thought he would like to rule himself, and stayed on earth without
reporting. He was killed by an arrow dropped from heaven, and
two other messengers were sent. They arrived in Idzumo, where
they went to Ōnamochi, the strongest and bravest of the sons of
Susa-no-wo, and asked him to deliver up the country to the grandson of the Sun Goddess. He refused, but at length an agreement
was reached, by which the august grandchild was to conduct public
matters, while Ōnamochi, to whom a great palace was promised,
should concern himself with divine affairs. This division of secular
and sacred sovereignty being made, the august grandchild, Ninigi-
no-Mikoto, left his heavenly seat and "thrusting apart the many-
piled clouds of Heaven, clove his way with an awful way-cleaving,"
and descended to earth. He alighted in the western island of
Kyūshū—a significant point, as we shall see—and he had with him

*Shamanistic ritual in certain parts of Siberia is said to include the flaying
of a horse.

as attendants the divine ancestors of a number of hereditary corporations, such as the ritualists, the exorcists, the jewel-makers, the shield-makers, the mirror-makers, and so on. He carried as tokens of his divine mission three treasures, a jewel, a sword, and a mirror, which he had received from the Sun Goddess when she declared that he should rule the fertile rice-ear land of Japan and his dynasty should prosper and endure for ever.

Whatever be the credibility of this mythical narrative which we have just outlined, there is no doubt as to its interest: for it does enable us, though vaguely, to form some picture of the early institutions of the Japanese and, making liberal allowance for late additions, of their primitive religion. Perhaps the first feature that attracts notice is the multitudinousness of the gods. The word usually translated "god" is *kami*, which has the primary meaning "upper." No doubt it would be a mistake to suppose that *kami* covered the same range of conceptions as "god"; but even if we take it to mean only something superior, something with special qualities of good or evil, its frequent use shows that to the early Japanese the visible and the invisible world were peopled with powerful influences. In its earliest forms the religion which, much later, came to be known as Shintō, the Way of the Gods, seems to have been a polytheism of a crude and exuberant type. The chronicles tell us of evil deities who swarmed and buzzed like flies, and of trees and herbs and rocks and streams that could all speak. To say that primitive Japanese conceived of all natural objects as harbouring a spirit, or that their religion was an animistic nature worship, is to apply exact terms to things which are too vague and various for simple definition. But certainly they felt that all perceptible objects were in some way living: and the history of Shintō is a history of the development of these inchoate ideas, through various stages, into an institutional religion. We shall return to this subject later, but first it is better to proceed with the political record, based on the two native chronicles and supplemented from Chinese and Korean sources.

It would be out of place to attempt here, with a view to setting forth a consecutive historical account, any critical study of the Yamato chronicles for the period up to the end of the 5th century. After that date their chronology is tolerably exact, and their statements seem to be on the whole credible; but for the preceding centuries their confusion of myth and history is such that accounts based upon them must vary with the taste and ideas of the interpreter. We had better therefore only give a brief outline of the main events, as some scholars describe them, warning the reader that the element of conjecture is very strong.

In several versions of the mythical narrative, the god Susa-no-wo goes to Silla (south-east Korea) where he says that gold and silver are to be found. He is also reported to have planted trees, because Japan needed "floating riches," by which he meant timber for shipbuilding. Silla as a kingdom arises in the first century B.C., but the name appears to be older. The Han records tell us that from an early date the peoples of northern Korea and of Japan went to southern Korea to purchase iron, and it seems almost certain that, several centuries before the Christian era, south-eastern Korea and the part of Japan which includes Idzumo were inhabited by people of the same stock; and that the story of Susa-no-wo is a transference to myth of a definite historical tradition of a chieftain under whose rule metals were found. This guess is borne out by the legend, celebrated in Japan, of his encounter with an "eight-forked" dragon in one of whose tails he finds a wonderful sword, which later becomes one of the three divine treasures that form the regalia of Japan. It has been suggested by some European scholars that the dragon represents a river with many tributaries; that its rapacious conduct is the destruction of life and property by a river in flood; and that the sword in its tail is a deposit of iron found at the head of one of the tributary streams.

Certainly the Idzumo people formed a separate group, with a culture of their own, shared with or derived from a kindred people in south Korea. This is clear, if only from the fact that the *Kojiki* and the *Nihon-shoki* both contain three legend-cycles, one recounting the ancestral history of the Idzumo clan, the second that of the Kyūshū people who settled and ruled in Yamato, and a third dealing with events in Yamato. There is an obvious effort to reconcile the conflicting mythologies of Kyūshū and Idzumo, of which perhaps the best illustration is the tale of the god Ōnamochi in Idzumo, surrendering the rule of the country to the august grandchild of the Sun Goddess. The august grandchild is represented as having descended in Kyūshū. Ōnamochi gives up to him secular dominion, and declares that he will henceforth direct "secret matters." The usually accepted interpretation of this myth is that the Kyūshū clans were able to assume the sovereign power, but that it was necessary to propitiate the Idzumo clans by leaving to them the control of religious affairs. There is little doubt that the Idzumo people were culturally further advanced than the Kyūshū clans. It is not known of what racial elements these latter were composed. Some writers have assumed that the clans which set forth from Kyūshū to conquer Central Japan were of Malay stock; but there is a good deal to be said for the hypothesis that the leaders of the expedition were, like the Idzumo people, of Mongolian origin, and had crossed over from Korea by the straits of Tsushima. Yayoi type pottery is certainly found in Kyūshū; and Hyūga, that part of Kyūshū from which the conquerors started, is rich in sepulchral mounds. These two points are evidence in favour of relationship with the mainland of China or Korea. These tombs contain, in addition to Yayoi type vases, iron swords and spears, and a variety of stone implements. Stone implements are not found in the Yamato tombs, which are richer in arms and armour; so that we may safely conclude that the Hyūga tombs belong to the beginning of the age of sepulchral mounds, and mark the transition from a late neolithic culture to an iron culture. The use of iron was not necessarily learned from the Chinese, for, if we may believe the Chinese annalists, certain Tungusic tribes worked in iron and gold from very early times, and were skilful makers of iron armour and helmets. Armour and helmets are found in the sepulchral mounds in Japan, and the clay figures (haniwa) associated with the mounds often represent warriors wearing armour and helmets. It is therefore probable that both Idzumo and Kyūshū clans were of Mongol extraction. It is, however, also probable that there were in Kyūshū at the same time large numbers of people of southern origin. Some scholars describe them vaguely as Malays; others bring to bear strong arguments to prove that they were of tribes akin to the Miao and other aboriginals of South China, whence they arrived direct, or by way of Formosa and the Lūchū Islands. It may well be that some of the fighting forces which took part in the expedition to Yamato were warlike people of this type, who had allied themselves with the Kyūshū leaders. All these questions are still in dispute, and we had better content ourselves with assuming that, in varying proportions, elements from several parts of the eastern coasts of Asia were present in the population of Japan at the opening of the Christian epoch.

To return now to the conquest of central Japan. The chronicles record a gradual progress, from Hyūga eastward by the shores of the Inland Sea, of the emperor Jimmu, who in the course of

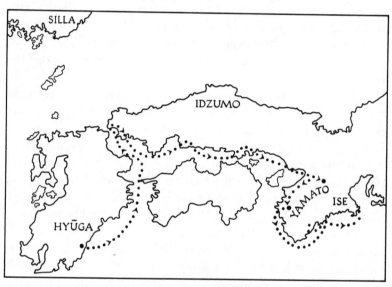

FIG. 13. *Map showing the Eastward movement of the Emperor Jimmu, as recorded in the ancient chronicles.*

several years defeated or pacified the tribes he found in his path, and made himself master of Yamato. In this region he built a palace, where, according to the chronicles, he celebrated his conquest by ceremonies in honour of the Sun Goddess on February 11th in the year 660 B.C. This is now officially considered to be the date of the foundation of the Empire of Japan and celebrated as such. But it is, of course, a purely traditional date, and even conservative Japanese historians do not all uphold this chronology. What was the real date of this expedition or whether it in fact took place it is impossible to say. Some scholars place it as late as the fourth century A.D., but it seems better to assign it to the beginning of the Christian era.

Leaving the native chronicles for a time, it is useful to turn to contemporary Chinese and Korean notices.[1] We have seen that the Han chronicles describe the country of the Wa as comprising more than a hundred kingdoms, over thirty of which were in relations with China by embassies or messengers after the establishment, in the first century B.C., of a Han colony in Korea. They mention missions from Japan in A.D. 57 and A.D. 107; and state that in the period A.D. 147-190 the country was in state of civil war and anarchy until a woman ruler arose, named Pimiku—a name in which it is easy to trace the archaic Japanese title Himeko, meaning "sun-daughter" or princess. This ruler "was old and unmarried, and had devoted herself to magic, by her skill in which she gained favour with the people, who made her their queen." The Korean (Silla) chronicles also speak of this princess as having sent envoys to Silla asking for assistance against her enemies, and the Chinese chronicles of the Wei dynasty (220-265) state that in the years 238-247 several missions came from her to the Chinese governors in north Korea, bringing tribute and asking for help against an enemy kingdom. The Japanese chronicles, recording expeditions of the Yamato rulers (in the third century A.D.) to subdue hostile chieftains in western Japan, refer frequently to female rulers in that region, while the Chinese chronicles generally speak of Japan as the "Queen Country." The resemblances between the Chinese notices of Pimiku and the Japanese versions of events at this period are so close as to justify us in concluding that the Chinese notices are in a general way correct. We may the more readily put faith in the descriptions left us by the Chinese historians of the conditions they found in Japan, though we must be careful to remember that the Chinese travellers whose reports they preserve probably got no further than the coasts of Kyūshū, and heard only by rumour of what was going on in other parts of Japan. The following are extracts from the Han and Wei writings, which even in the refashioned versions known to us may be regarded as tolerably faithful reproductions of contemporary descriptions of Japan in the third century of our era :—

". . . Father and mother, elder and younger brothers and sisters live separately, but at meetings there is no distinction on account of sex. They take their food with their hands, but have wooden trays and wooden trenchers to place it on. It is their general custom to go barefoot. Respect is shown by squatting down. They are much given to strong drink. They are a long-lived race, and persons who have reached 100 are very common, All men of high rank have four or five wives; others two or three. The women are faithful and not jealous. There is no robbery or theft, and litigation is infrequent. The wives and children of those who break the laws are confiscated, and for grave crimes the offender's family is extirpated. Mourning lasts for some ten days only, during which time the members of the family fast, weep and lament, whilst their friends come singing, dancing and making music. They practise divination by burning bones, and by that means they ascertain good and bad luck. When they undertake journeys and voyages they appoint a man whom they style the 'fortune-keeper.' He is not allowed to comb his hair, to wash, to eat meat, or to approach women. When they are fortunate and return safely, they make him valuable presents; but if they fall ill, or meet with disaster, they set it down to the fortune-keeper's failure to observe his vows, and together they put him to death."

.   .   .   .   .   .

"This is the limit of the Queen's dominions, south of which is the Kunu country, where a king holds rule. It is not subject to the Queen. From the capital to the Queen Country is over 2,000 li."

"The men, both small and great, tattoo their faces and work designs on their bodies. They have arrow-heads of iron as well as of bone. They use only an inner, and no outer coffin. When the funeral is over, the whole family go into the water and wash. They have distinctions of rank, and some are vassals to others. Taxes are collected. There are markets in each province where they exchange their superfluous produce for articles of which they are in want. They are under the supervision of Great Wa."

.   .   .   .   .   .

"When men of the lower class meet a man of rank, they leave the road, and retire to the grass. When they address him, they either squat or kneel with both hands to the ground. This is their way of showing respect. They express assent by the sound *A!*"

"In 247," the Wei records go on to state, "when the governor Wangch'i took office, a messenger was sent to him by Pimiku, Queen of the Wa, to explain the causes of the enmity which had always prevailed between her and Pimikuku, king of Kunu. A letter was sent admonishing them. At this time Queen Pimiku died. A great mound was raised over her, more than a hundred paces in diameter, and over a hundred of her male and female attendants followed her in death. Then a king was raised to the throne, but the people would not obey him, and civil war again broke out, not less than one thousand persons being slain. A girl of thirteen, relative of Pimiku, named Iyo (or Ichiyo), was then made queen and order was restored."

The first fact that emerges very clearly from these descriptions is that in the third century the eastward migration of clans from Kyūshū had not yet resulted in the formation of a central state with authority over the greater part of Japan. There were evidently independent rulers of greater or less importance throughout the country. As to the Japanese customs, we shall see that the Chinese observers bear out a good deal of what is written in the Japanese chronicles. But it is convenient first to recite very briefly the accounts given by those chronicles of the reigns succeeding that of the Emperor Jimmu, as follows:*

The names of eight emperors are given, reigning from 581 B.C. to 98 B.C. (*circa* A.D. 1 to A.D. 218) and nothing of great importance is recorded for this period. There follows the Emperor Sūjin, from 97 B.C. to 33 B.C. (A.D. 219 to 249) under whose reign, among a great deal of matter which was plainly fabricated after the introduction of Chinese learning into Japan in the fifth century, expeditions against rebellious tribes in the four quarters are described. It is pretty certain that the Pimiku of the Chinese records was the ruler of one of these powerful tribes or confedera-

---

*The first dates are the dates given by the native chronicles; those in brackets are conjectural dates based by Professor Kume on correspondences with events in Chinese and Korean history. But they are of course mere approximations, and the most recent researches tend to put them all a decade or more later.

tions. Her dominion extended over a large part of the island of Kyūshū. The King of Kunu was probably a neighbouring chieftain who acknowledged the Yamato sovereign as his overlord and on his behalf made war upon Pimiku.[2]

Under the Emperor Suinin, 29 B.C. to A.D. 70 (A.D. 249 to 280) there is mention of relations with Silla, such as the exchange of gifts, and a curious legend of the arrival from that kingdom by way of Idzumo of a prince, or, as in one version, a god bringing tribute in the shape of sacred swords, spear, jewels, and mirror. This legend is one of many indications that the early Shintō religion owed a great deal to Korea, and that the Korean elements were those contributed by the Idzumo people, who themselves were closely akin to some at least of the peoples of southern Korea. The Wei records remark on the similarity of customs in southern Korea and the country of the Wa, while as we have seen, one of the legend cycles of Japan reveals a definite tradition of common ancestry with Korea.

In the reign of the Emperor Keikō, A.D. 71 to 130 (A.D. 280 to 316), we learn of expeditions against barbarians in the southern part of Kyūshū, the Kumaso, who are thought to have been un-assimilated warlike tribes of southern origin, possibly of Malay stock. These were defeated by the bravery and cunning of Prince Yamato Daké, the Brave of Yamato, a son of the emperor. After subduing the southern barbarians, the young prince turned his attention to the eastern savages, passing into the mountainous country north and east of the present Tōkyō. Here he performed great feats, but died on his way back.

The next sovereign was Seimu, in whose reign, from A.D. 131 to 190 (A.D. 316 to 343), we are told further attempts were made to extend the imperial authority, by appointing governors and district officers in the provinces. In the next reign, that of the Emperor Chūai, from A.D. 190-200 (*circa* A.D. 340), further efforts were made to subdue the Kumaso, and an expedition set forth, in which both the emperor and empress took part. The emperor was advised to attack the kingdom of Silla, a land of dazzling treasure, rather than waste his efforts on the wretched Kumaso, but he would not listen, and attacked the barbarians, by whom he was repulsed, receiving a wound of which he died. His consort succeeded to the throne, and it is she who, under the name of the Empress Jingō, is said to have led a great army to the conquest of Silla in A.D. 200.

The Silla chronicles record an invasion by the Japanese in 249, and their story has a strong likeness in certain details to that of the Empress Jingō's expedition. They also mention the siege of a Silla fortress by Japanese in 346; and, according to them, a strong Japanese force was almost annihilated by Silla in 364. But the dating of all these chronicles is so dubious that it is idle to attempt to unravel the true sequence of events, and we must be satisfied with a general outline until the end of the fourth century, when it becomes possible to fix certain landmarks in this very misty region of history. We may however safely assume that Jingō was a powerful ruler in central Japan, who, somewhere about A.D. 360, held sway over the now subject kingdoms of Kyūshū and in whose reign the Japanese were united enough to contemplate continental expeditions on a larger scale than their accustomed raids on the Silla coast. It was she who first brought Japan as a more or less centralised state into contact with the Asiatic mainland, and thus prepared a way for the inflow of continental culture during the fifth century and onwards.

It is in the record of the reign of the Empress Jingō that mention is first made of other Korean kingdoms, Paikché (called by the Japanese Kudara), Kōkuli or, in the Korean reading, Koguryö (called by the Japanese Koma), and Imna (called by the Japanese Mimana or Kaya). These kingdoms correspond roughly with tribal divisions existing before the Christian era, but so long as the Chinese colony of Lakliang continued they were rather loosely-knit groups than political entities with definite territory. As the influence of Lakliang waned, it was eaten into and finally displaced by the kingdom of Kōkuli, which covered the northern half of the Korean peninsula. Its flourishing period was from the second to the fourth centuries A.D. In the fourth century Paikché and Silla come into prominence, weak states at the beginning, which gradually consolidate and challenge each other, as well as Kōkuli, for supremacy.

It is clear, therefore, that the varying fortunes of these Korean states were of great import to Japan, and we find the Japanese chronicles recording political and military relations with them in

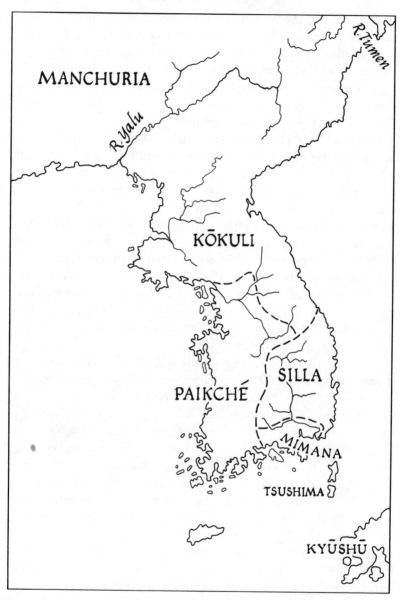

FIG. 14. *The kingdoms of Korea, circa A.D. 400-800.*

great detail from the reign of the Empress Jingō onwards. We can now afford to dispense with the chronology of the Japanese records, which has in any case been adduced here only as evidence of the manner and the motives of their compilation. A large memorial stone discovered near the site of an early Kōkuli stronghold on the upper waters of the Yalu river gives us an unexceptionable datum point for Korean history of the fourth century A.D. The inscription relates the exploits of a king of Kōkuli who came to the throne in A.D. 391, and states that in that year the Japanese crossed the sea and defeated Paikché and Silla and another country, of which the name is undecipherable. The Japanese chronicles tell us that, in the reign of the Emperor Ōjin, who succeeded the Empress Jingō, four generals proceeded to Paikché, dethroned the king, and despoiled him of some of his territory. There is no doubt that the two records refer to the same series of events. We have here the beginnings of a triangular strife between the kingdoms of Kōkuli, Paikché and Silla, which lasted until Silla overthrew both its rivals in the years between 660 and 670. In this rivalry each party attempted to combine with a second and crush the third, a situation by which Japan endeavoured to profit. She maintained a foothold in south Korea for a long period, but was in the end worsted by Silla diplomacy. We need not concern ourselves with details of these struggles, but it is important in any study of the cultural developments of Japan not to lose sight of the fact that her political relations with the mainland commenced at a very early date, and were continuous throughout several centuries during which there was frequent intermarriage between the ruling houses of Korea and Japan. The phenomenon of Japan's isolation is a comparatively late feature in her history. The small kingdom of Mimana, lying between Silla and Paikché, was under Japanese influence from about the end of the first century A.D. Later it seems to have served the Japanese as a base for their raids or their missions in neighbouring parts of Korea, and by the fourth century Japanese Residents or Governors were stationed there.

We now come to an event of outstanding importance in the foreign relations of Japan. The Yamato sovereigns in their endeavour to extend their influence in Korea chose to make friends with Paikché, no doubt in the hope of weakening Silla. Thus, after

the expedition of 391 we hear of the arrival of envoys from Paikché
bringing tribute and skilled workmen. Among them was one Achiki,
who was able to read the Chinese classics. He was asked whether he
could recommend a learned man as instructor to the heir apparent,
and on his advice officers were sent to bring over a scribe named
Wani, of whom it was said that there was no book which he did
not thoroughly understand. This was in A.D. 405.* The Chinese
language and the Chinese script were, of course, known in Japan
before this date. Rulers who wished to send messages to the Court
of China or to the Chinese colony in Korea must have used interpreters in the first century of the Christian era, for we know that
Chinese scribes and secretaries were employed by many tribes and
countries on the borders of China. But the arrival of Wani, and
his employment at court, meant the official adoption of the Chinese
written language, and its use for official purposes. It meant the
beginning of records, of registers, of edicts and written orders, and
so promoted the development of central authority. It created in
due course a class of literates competing with the military families
in prestige. It made possible the more rapid absorption of Chinese
culture, which was a culture bound up with the written word; and
it prepared the way for the introduction more than a century later
of a new religion and a new philosophy which could hardly have
been transferred by the medium of speech.

The adoption of a script by a people with no writing of their
own is of such interest and such importance in the history of oriental civilisation that it deserves the most careful study; but before
describing its effect, it is better to attempt some picture of the state
of society into which this new and insidious element was brought.

2. NATIVE INSTITUTIONS AND FOREIGN INTERCOURSE

MATERIALS are scanty for a description of social institutions in
Japan in the period preceding the formation of a centralised state
in Yamato, but it is possible, with the aid of Chinese notices and
of archæological remains, to eke out the information given in the
native chronicles, and so to reconstruct in outline the society of the

---

*This is the hitherto accepted date, but some scholars (e.g. Wedemayer) put
it at 378 or 379. It should be noted that there is no evidence of direct official
relations between Yamato and Chinese kingdoms before A.D. 400.

first centuries of the Christian era. The chronology of the native records is so defective that it is difficult to say what was the stage of development of a given institution at any given period prior to the sixth century. The following account must therefore be regarded as a general description, without particular reference to dates, of Japanese society before it began to be reorganised on Chinese lines. This society consisted of patriarchal units, called *uji*, which were communities formed of a number of households of the same ancestry, or which, for the purposes of solidarity, claimed the same ancestry. Each household was under the control of its master, and each community was under the leadership of a head, called the *uji no kami*. For convenience we may describe the *uji* as a clan and the leader as the chieftain of the clan. The members of a clan all worshipped a guardian god, the *uji-gami*, or clan-god, a term not to be confused with *uji no kami*, or clan-chieftain, for ancestor worship is not a specific character of this early culture.

Attached to each clan was another unit, called *be* or *tomo*, which was composed of households associated not by common ancestry but usually by a common occupation. The *be*, which may be translated "guild" and the *tomo*, which may be translated "corporation," were groups of individuals carrying out certain specialised functions of importance to the community, such as weaving, the making of tools, utensils, and weapons, military service or the performance of religious rites. Though the members of these groups had no common ancestor, their membership and their position in the group were hereditary, passing from father to son. Moreover, they could not leave their group but remained under the control of its leader, whose office also was hereditary. As a rule a guild or corporation was subordinate to the clan to which it was attached, and in the course of time tended to merge into the clan, claiming its name and its ancestry. In some cases, however, a corporation came to assume an independent existence, and to equal a clan in importance and influence, so that the leader of a corporation might be as powerful as a chieftain. Below the clan and the guild came a class of slaves, male and female. The *uji*, or clan, then, with its attendant guilds and its serfs, constituted a self-contained unit. Those parts of Japan which were settled by the Yamato race were ruled by a number of such clans, of which the most powerful

was the Imperial Clan. All the land held by this clan, that is by the
emperor and the members of the imperial family, was under the
direct rule of the emperor, as were all its inhabitants. But the imperial clan had no direct control over the land of other clans, nor
over its inhabitants. The imperial clan was regarded as the supreme clan, the emperor as the supreme chieftain, but he ruled
only indirectly, exercising his authority through the chieftains of
the other clans. The country was, in fact, occupied by a number
of clans—doubtless derived from those tribal groups which had
first conquered it—who agreed to accept the supremacy of a dominant clan, but did not hold their lands by service. As the head of
the imperial clan was the hereditary ruler of the group of clans,
so was the head of each other clan the hereditary holder of an
office of state, great or small according to the influence or lineage
of his clan. Thus we have the *ō-omi*, or great ministers, who were
appointed from among the heads of clans closely related to the
imperial family; the *ō-muraji*, territorial administrative officers of
high rank who traced their descent from gods other than the divine
ancestors of the emperor; the *omi* and *muraji*, of lesser standing;
the *kuni no miyatsuko*, local chieftains; and the *tomo no miyatsuko*,
at the head of certain corporations. In short, the social and the
political organisations were one, since the administrative hierarchy corresponded, at least ideally, with the gradations of nobility.

Among the most important clans were the Nakatomi (*Naka-tsu-
omi*,* "ministers of the middle"), and the Imibe ("guild of abstainers"). The Nakatomi family and the Imibe family traced their descent from gods who had respectively recited a liturgy and made
offerings before the cave of the Sun Goddess, thus being the chief
performers of the ritual which is the prototype of the religious
ceremonies practised by the Yamato people. At a time when religious worship and state ceremonial were merged one in the other
the standing of these families was very high. The Nakatomi indeed
reached a great influence, and were from early times almost equal
in strength to the imperial family. The Imibe, whose duties were
concerned with ritual purification, and who therefore played an
important part in government, gradually lost their power as that

---

*Omi is originally simply "great person" and "chieftain" is about as close as
one can get.

of the Nakatomi family grew. They lost their power at court; but they must have retained a good deal of local influence, since a "medicine man" would be needed for every community. So we find various "corporations of abstainers" (Imibe) established in the provinces, such as the Imibe of Awa, tracing their descent from the god Ama-no-hi-washi (Heavenly-Sun-Eagle), the Imibe of Idzumo, tracing their descent from the god Kushi-akaru-tama (Wondrous Bright Jewel), and several others, all claiming close kinship with the line of solar deities. Next in importance to these two priestly clans were the Ōtomo (Great Escort), and the Kumebe or Corporation of Soldiers, both military clans whose hereditary leaders claimed as ancestors gods who had assisted the first divine emperor in his pacification of the land. Another military group was the Mononobe or Corporation of Arms. It is easy to see that these important families were descendants of chieftains who, in combination with the imperial family, had in the past by conquest obtained supremacy over other groups in Japan. What exactly were these other groups we cannot tell. As well as the aboriginal inhabitants, there may have been—there probably were—less advanced tribes, some perhaps of the same stock as the conquerors, previous settlers who had to surrender to a more vigorous, or a better equipped people. There is good reason to suppose that these settlers were not exterminated, but were allowed to retain some territory. There is frequent mention in the semi-mythical parts of the chronicles of "country deities," as contrasted with "heavenly deities," and it is clear that these are references to strong local chieftains whom the invading clans found it wiser to conciliate than to attack. They remained as important landholders, and it is worth noting that a large number of them, for all their importance, were in succeeding centuries never given such high rank as the members of the invading clans. It was a part of the policy of the Yamato rulers jealously to guard the prestige of divine ancestry, and until the middle ages a sharp distinction was made between the home provinces and the "outside" provinces, whose notables were awarded only "outside" rank.

An integral part of the clan system, as would naturally be expected in a society so essentially aristocratic in structure, was the system of titles, or *kabane*. Originally there existed only clan names, such as Nakatomi and Ōtomo, and personal names such as Maro; but it became the custom to describe the more important members of a clan or a corporation by the name of their hereditary office or by some honorific title granted by the court. Thus we have *muraji*, which means "leader of a group," and might be translated by "duke," *agata-nushi*, "estate master" and, though of somewhat later origin, *fubito*, a scribe. As the clans grew in size, their different branches were distinguished by combining the clan name and the title of the hereditary office, and the latter persisted even when the office had been transferred or abolished. So Mononobe no Ōmuraji, though literally to be translated Grand Duke of the Corporation of Arms, is in effect a surname by which a certain member of the family of hereditary leaders of the corporation is distinguished from other members. As might be expected, these titles were held in high esteem, since they represented both pedigree and rank; and a time soon came when people took to forging pedigrees. The chief offenders were provincial notables, whether landowners or functionaries, who, not being under the eye of the court, could the more safely claim high lineage and thus justify extensions of their power and their lands. In the chronicles, under the date A.D. 415, we find an imperial decree on this subject which is worth quoting, because it shows how important in the eyes of the rulers was the maintenance of aristocratic privilege :—

"In the most ancient times good government consisted in the subjects having each his proper place, and in names being correct. Nowadays superiors and inferiors dispute with one another, and the hundred families are not at peace. Some by chance lose their true names, others purposely lay claim to high lineage. . . . The ministers, functionaries and chieftains of the various provinces all describe themselves either as the descendants of emperors or as issuing from a family of miraculous origin . . . . Single clans (*uji*) have multiplied and formed ten thousand titles of doubtful authenticity. Therefore let the people of the various clans and titles cleanse themselves and practise abstinence, and let them, calling upon the gods to witness, plunge their hands in boiling water."

An ordeal by boiling water was, it is reported, held shortly afterwards, and those who had not falsified their pedigrees came through unscathed, while the others were either harmed or ran away. The term rendered above by "the hundred families" is of interest. It is the word *hyakushō* (literally "hundred family names") which in later times came to mean simply the farmers, but in early Japan, as in China, stood for those families which had names, that is, for the provincial magnates (*miyatsuko*) and the small gentry. These were all free men, comprehensively described as *ryōmin*, or "good people," in contrast with *semmin*, or "base people," who possessed no family name. The "base people" included the members of the agricultural or industrial guilds (*be*) and the slaves (*yakko*). The members of the guilds were only semi-free, since their service or occupation was, as a rule, hereditary, and they lived by their labour for the governing classes. They were superior, however, to the *yakko*, who were slaves and nothing else. The slaves were probably for the most part captives taken in warfare. They do not appear to have been very numerous, for though particulars are wanting for early periods, registers of the seventh century, which were compiled with some accuracy, show, for example, in a township of fifty households in one of the home provinces, a population of 899, of whom fourteen were slaves. The guilds and corporations were without doubt the most numerous class. As we have seen, the Imibe and the Kumebe were of great antiquity, for they rendered services of the greatest importance to an early society, as priests and as soldiers. As the needs of society developed, more of these bodies were formed. So we have the Tanabe ("Rice-field guild"), of agricultural labourers; the Amabe, of fishermen; the Oribe, of weavers; the Ayabe, or "pattern guild," of skilled workers in brocade; the Hasebe, of potters; the Umakaibe, of grooms; the Fumibitobe, of scribes; the Osabe, of interpreters in Chinese or Korean; the Kataribe, of story-tellers, who appear to have recited legends at Court, before the adoption of Chinese writing; the Urabe, of diviners; and many others, of specialised functions, including even a *be* of wet nurses, another of rice-chewers, another of washerwomen, for the imperial babies. It will be seen that these guilds were bodies analogous to the *corporati* of the later Roman empire, particularly in that their members were bound to their callings, from generation to generation. In some cases, as of horse-keepers and bird-keepers, we hear of them being tattooed with a mark to prevent their desertion; but the treatment and standing of a guild and its members varied according to the nature of its functions. Members of the guilds that performed menial work were little better than slaves, but it is clear that the scribes, interpreters, reciters, and painters were persons of some consideration. Other guilds were influential for other reasons. The seamen and carters from the nature of the work and their mobility were powerful, and they could easily be used as military forces by their leaders. Much the same was true of the mountain wardens. Most important, however, to the community as a whole were evidently the *be* engaged in productive occupations, and chief of these was agriculture. Land was not a source of wealth without labour for its cultivation, and consequently we find very frequent mention of the formation of *be* to work the estates of members of the imperial family or great nobles. These were on a rather different footing from such guilds as the soldiers and priests, for they were special and local. Often a "namesake" guild would be established in the name of a princess, to provide her with an income. This meant that land would be allotted to her, and a number of peasants formed into a community for its cultivation, both land and peasants being made over, willingly or unwillingly, by a provincial magnate. Again the rulers of various provinces were ordered by the emperor Inkyō to establish Fujiwara-be, ostensibly to perpetuate the memory of his concubine Sotoori Hime, who lived in the palace of Fujiwara; later the emperor Seinei, who was childless, instituted three such *be* in each province, "so as to leave traces for posterity to see"; and many similar examples can be found scattered through the chronicles. This method of extending the imperial domains was much in favour during the fifth and sixth centuries; though it did not always profit the imperial family, for the supervisors of the crown-lands and cultivators in distant parts of the country as time went on appropriated them to their own uses, and developed into autonomous chieftains, sometimes claiming, as we have seen, imperial ancestry.

We have noticed already that relations between China and Korea and Japan began at a very early date, not later than—and probably before—the first century B.C. It is therefore not surprising to find that the Yamato population included a strong foreign element. By the time central Japan had been subdued and settled by clans from the west in the first century A.D., the country was peopled by a variety of ethnic elements, doubtless in different degrees of fusion; but we may suppose that a fairly stable and uniform composite type had already been evolved, particularly among those families which possessed clan names—the ruling families and the free men. The "base people"—the workers in the guilds, and the slaves—were probably of a variety of stocks, and their social position would prevent them from mingling with the dominant people, so that a distinct plebeian type would be evolved, to break up only as the strict caste system broke down. Similarly the unpacified tribes in the north-east and south-west, the Ainu and the Kumaso, would preserve their racial characters in the measure of their distance from the central power.

Into this heterogeneous population there were now introduced certain foreign elements whose cultural importance was out of all proportion to their numbers. It is tolerably certain that at latest from the beginning of the Christian era there was constant immigration of Koreans, and of Chinese who were as a rule refugees from dynastic wars in their own country, whence they had escaped to Korea in the first place. Early in the fourth century the population of whole villages was brought over to Japan from Korea and in the fifth and sixth centuries numbers of "men of Ts'in and Han" crossed over. They were mostly, it appears, skilled artisans, weavers, potters, painters, scribes, as well as farmers who were familiar with silkworm culture and other agricultural matters in which the Japanese were behindhand. Whether most of these were Chinese is doubtful. They were probably Koreans of Chinese origin, who claimed descent from great Chinese families. Under the date 540 we read in the chronicles that the men of Ts'in numbered over 7,000 households; which gives a total of over 100,000 individuals, if we take the average number of inmates in a household as fifteen, which is not an excessive figure, to judge from tax registers of the following century. To these must be added "the men of Han," who came almost certainly from the Han colonies of Lakliang and Taipang, which were now the prey of the Korean kings of Kōkuli and Paikché, and the "men of the frontier states," by which is probably meant Chinese from Manchuria, northern Korea and perhaps

Shantung. It is not possible to say what percentage of the total population was formed by these immigrants. Their leaders were persons of standing, and many of the workmen were in such important positions, because of their skill and knowledge, that they were accorded very favourable treatment. They were for the most part incorporated into *be*, under their own chiefs, to whom high rank was given. The Ayabe (brocade-makers' guild) was formed by "men of Han," and we hear of the head of their guild being granted a title of nobility. The aristocrats among these immigrants were, of course, the scribes and accountants, who in the beginning of the fifth century, when Chinese writing was officially adopted by the Japanese, naturally commanded respect among the unlettered nobles of Yamato. Indeed, by the end of the seventh century, according to the *Shōjiroku*, a peerage of that time, over one-third of the noble families of Japan claimed Chinese or Korean descent. The proportion of immigrants among the lower classes was obviously not so high, but that they left their mark is certain; and the influence of China and Korea, exercised through this assimilated alien population, should not be overlooked in any endeavour to trace the cultural development of Japan. It is a mistake to assume, as one is apt for convenience to do, that the influence of China upon Japan was of no great importance until the introduction of writing in the fifth century. It was persistent and increasing from the opening of the Christian era; and, if we accept the hypothesis that there is a strong southern Chinese element in the Japanese race, it began long before that. The adoption of the Chinese script was certainly a landmark in Japanese history, and shaped the subsequent development of nearly every Japanese institution; but the debt of Japan to Chinese culture is already apparent in the age of the sepulchral mounds.

NOTES TO CHAPTER II

[1] Page 29 ff. See note above as to the credibility of early Chinese notices of Japan.

[2] Page 32. According to Chinese historical records tribute ceased from "The Queen of Japan" after A.D. 266, and fiom the Chin-han and Pyön-han tribes of Southern Korea after A.D. 286 and 290 respectively. This is a very useful piece of evidence as to the date when the Yamato kingdom and the kingdoms of Paikché and Silla began to grow in organisation and power.

Chapter III

THE INDIGENOUS CULT

To judge from the native chronicles and from those Chinese notices which have just been cited, the indigenous material culture of the Japanese before the Christian era was not of a high level. The scanty population was distributed in small groups of dwelling houses along the coast or on the banks of streams; and since the descriptions of palaces which have come down to us show that the rulers lived in wooden, straw-thatched houses, of which the posts, beams, and ridge-pole were held in place by ropes made of twisted creepers, we may suppose that the homes of the ordinary folk were primitive indeed. Rice was cultivated, and rice spirit (*sake*) was made from very early times.* The Chinese observers of the third century after Christ mention that the natives of Japan were addicted to strong drink. Though fishing and hunting were important means of food supply, it seems that the population from an early date was formed into settled agricultural communities, for in the recital of the offences committed by Susa-no-wo we find the first place given to breaking down the divisions between rice fields, diverting water supply, sowing tares, and other misdeeds which are precisely those most abhorrent to an agricultural society.

If we may believe the Chinese annalists, spinning and weaving were known to the Japanese by the middle of the third century A.D. and the mulberry was cultivated for feeding silkworms. Though it is probable that silk was first brought from China at a comparatively late date, garments woven from hemp or paper mulberry bark were in use from very early times. Costumes appear to have been elaborate and specialised, with a free use of jewellery, in the form of necklaces, bracelets, belt buckles and other ornaments of semi-precious stones, such as agate and crystal. Pottery was of course known from neolithic times. Weapons and tools of iron were in fairly common use, and bronze articles are plentiful in the tombs, though it may be that the knowledge of

* By pressure and fermentation.

bronze in Japan was derived from China after the introduction of iron from Tungusic sources.

While the material culture of the Japanese of the mythical age was so poor that it was quickly overlaid by that of China as soon as contact could be established, their social and religious institutions show in some respects a rather higher development than is allowed by many writers. The native chronicles portray a society in which ritual observances played an important part, and though the earliest religion may be described as an untutored pantheism, it was by no means lacking in gracious elements. It was a religion founded upon a conception, a vague and unformulated conception, of the universe as composed of a myriad sentient parts. A nature worship of which the mainspring is appreciation rather than fear is not to be dismissed as base and fetishistic animism, and much that is kindly and gracious in the life of the Japanese to-day can be traced to those sentiments which caused their remote ancestors to ascribe divinity not only to the powerful and awe-inspiring, such as the sun and the moon and the tempest, or to the useful, such as the well and the cooking pot, but also to the lovely and pleasant. such as the rocks and streams, the trees and flowers. The worship of such objects has its counterpart in that delicate sensibility to the beauties of nature which is one of the most endearing characteristics of the modern Japanese. Beyond doubt it is a characteristic deeply rooted in the past. Their mythology includes much that is crude and primitive, but it is remarkable that, in a country so often riven by earthquakes and swept by storm and flood, there is no common myth of a terrible earthquake god, and the storm god himself appears chiefly in benign aspects. It may be that, to wayworn tribes from arid regions of Korea and northern China or inhospitable Siberian plains, the genial climate of Japan, with its profusion of trees and flowering shrubs, its fertile soil, and its wealth of running streams, was so pleasing as to make upon them a profound impression, stored up in the racial consciousness as a pervading sentiment of gratitude. Certainly their religion was, as Aston says, a religion of love and gratitude rather than of fear, and the purpose of their religious rites was to praise and thank as much as to placate and mollify their divinities. The very names given in their mythology to their country—the Land of Luxuriant Reed Plains, the Land of Fresh Rice Ears of a Thousand Autumns; and to their gods—the Princess Blossoming-like-the-Flowers-of-the-Trees, and Her Augustness Myriad-Looms-Luxuriant-Dragonfly-Island—testify to their strong sense of the beauty and richness of their environment. Even in these modern times a traveller on the beaten track can often see a tree or a rock by the wayside, adorned with the symbols of holiness, because it is of striking shape and therefore vaguely thought to harbour a divine presence. Such are the amiable features of the early religion. It is the expression of an awareness of the manifold forms of life. At the same time it is primitive in that it displays no great reaches of the mind, no faculty to combine or to correlate the impressions to which individually it is so sensitive. There is no definite idea of a soul, much less an immortal soul, no clear distinction between life and death, or body and spirit. Though the anthropomorphic conception of deities no doubt began to develop from early times, it must have been extremely vague and loose. The very word for god, the word *kami*, is evidence of this, for it means simply "superior," and is applied indiscriminately in the earliest legends to any animate or even inanimate object thought to have superior qualities. So at one end of the scale the Sun Goddess, that Heaven-Shining-Great-August Deity, is a *kami*, and at the other mud and sand and even vermin are *kami*. There is only the vaguest spiritual implication in all these ideas; and, though one should choose one's language very carefully in discussing the nature of ancient religious beliefs, it seems fair to say that the early Japanese religion was almost entirely lacking in speculative, philosophical elements. Such of these as can be discerned in its later forms are almost certainly due to the influence of Chinese or Buddhist thought. The imaginative faculty as revealed in Japanese mythology is, to quote Aston again, prolific but feeble. So we find lavish creation of deities, but their characters are confused and shadowy, their powers ill-defined, and their habitation either unknown or undistinguishable from that of ordinary beings. The fact that the deities were not represented by idols or pictures in early times, and only very sparingly later, is itself an indication of the nebulous quality of

the pantheon, and indeed it is less the gods of old Japan than the
ancestral beliefs and customs embodied in their worship which are
of abiding interest.

As might be expected in a religion so concerned with the powers
of nature, most of its observances had to do with growth and decay.
Growth is good, decay is evil, life is desirable, death is abominable.
So we find on the one hand prayers and thanksgivings for harvest,
on the other hand a severe ritual to guard against or to wash away
the pollution of sickness and mortality. Traditionally, it is true, the
religion of Yamato was a form of sun worship, and everywhere in
the legendary narrative can be found traces of a solar myth.
But, though the worship of the sun was at the core of all their
beliefs, there was a natural tendency for the Sun Goddess, splendid
and powerful, to grow remote, and for more familiar and ap-
proachable deities to replace her in popular adoration. The Sun
Goddess is the ancestress of the imperial line, the words, *hiko* and
hime, for prince and princess mean literally "sun child," and the
ancient term for imperial lineage is *ama-tsu-hi-tsugi,* "heavenly-
sun-succession," while the imperial regalia, the mirror, the
jewel and the sword, are thought to have represented the sun, the
moon, and the lightning flash.[1] But the solar quality of the
goddess tends to be obscured, and she becomes a supreme deity
of anthropomorphic character; so much that in later times the
sun is worshipped separately under other names and the goddess
herself is conceived of as the Empress of Heaven, with a court
and a council of gods who share in the celestial rule. A like
development is seen in other cases. The worship of the earth
god, of whom one name is Ō-kuni-dama, "Great land spirit,"
grows out of the worship of land, of the soil itself. As time goes
on this direct worship gives place to an anthropomorphic
conception, and the earth as a god becomes the Earth God,
or Master of the Earth, worshipped at the great shrine of
Idzumo, which is next in importance to those of Ise. It may be
thought that these early gropings of the mind have little bearing
upon the later development of the Japanese people, but the truth
is that, however deeply buried under layers of later culture, the
old conceptions have lived and operated until the present time.
Even to-day there are performed in great cities ceremonies to

propitiate a plot of land which is to be newly used for building; and when a new well is sunk offerings of wine and food are made and prayers recited to the spirit of the hidden water. In the early cult mountain gods were numerous, and at the present time there is hardly a summit without its little shrine. River-gods, rain-gods, well-gods, water-gods, wind-gods, all were abundant, and traces of their worship still persist. The food goddess, Ukemochi-no-kami, worshipped in Ise at a shrine not far from that of the Sun Goddess, appears to derive from an original worship of food, for there are traces of a deification of food itself. The rice-god, Inari, is probably the same as Ukemochi, and he is the most ubiquitous of all the gods, for his shrines are to be found in every town and village, and in many private houses and gardens.

Such is a brief description of the shadowy background of belief in the national religion. It now remains to describe in outline its institutions and observances. It appears that, in the earliest times, when the clans were virtually independent, it was the duty of the chieftain to worship the clan-god, from whom the clan claimed descent, and at one period no doubt there was no distinction between high priest and ruler. The Chinese notices of Pimiku show that she was at the same time queen and sorceress. But in due course some specialisation of religious function arose, and there is, as we have seen, an echo of this separation of secular and sacerdotal in the Idzumo legend of Ōnamochi, who gives up the direction of public affairs and takes charge of "secret matters." As the task of government grew in weight and complexity, the rulers tended to delegate priestly functions to special persons or families. This point is well illustrated by an edict of the Emperor Kwammu, as late as the end of the eighth century, in which it was decreed that the local nobles (*kuni no miyatsuko*) in Idzumo should not hold the office of civil governor, as experience showed that their administrative duties were neglected for their religious functions.

The earliest written account of the native religion of Japan is to be found in the Chinese chronicles from which we have already quoted the description of the "abstainers" or "fortune-keepers." These were evidently the forerunners of the Imibe, the hereditary corporation of abstainers, whose duty it was to ensure the ritual purity of all persons and things connected with religious observances. Of equal antiquity with the Imibe was the Nakatomi family, who may be described as the hereditary liturgists, communicating with the gods on the ruler's behalf, and conveying to him their oracles. A third hereditary religious corporation was that of the Urabe or diviners. It was their function to decide, by such methods of divination as were at the time in vogue, matters referred to them by the ruler, as for instance when he desired to explain or to avert some calamity.

Though these corporations existed from early times and though they each had specialised and delegated functions, it must not be understood that they were the exclusive means of communication with the gods, or that all religious acts were confined to them. The priestly caste was not numerous, and almost any official might, as part of his duties, have to discharge some religious function, no qualification being required other than the appropriate degree of ritual purity achieved by lustration, fasting and kindred practices. The priests of all but the most important shrines were (and still are) persons combining ordinary avocations with their priestly duties. It is an interesting fact that the earliest Japanese word for government is *matsurigoto*, which means religious observances. It should be noted that this word is never used of government by the sovereign, but of the work of his ministers, thus showing that their participation in acts of worship of the national deities was regarded as their chief function, and perhaps also that their work of administration was a form of worship.

Nothing is more difficult for the student of early Japanese history than to distinguish what are the earliest elements in their religion, and what are later additions, encouraged or even produced by the political ideas so clearly inspiring the compilers of the chronicles upon which we must rely for our information. Allowance must be made for this difficulty in reading the following account of Shintō observances before they came under the influence of Chinese thought. It must also be borne in mind that even the native religion in its earliest forms was certainly not homogeneous throughout the country, but comprised a number of different local cults, which tended to fuse as tribal units coalesced. The merging of the Yamato and Idzumo pantheons is doubtless an important example of such fusion.

The outstanding feature of Shintō observances is the attention paid to ritual purity. Things which are offensive to the gods were called by the early Japanese *tsumi*, a word which is now rendered by dictionaries as "guilt" or "sin." Avoidance of these things was called *imi*, a word meaning taboo. The Imibe, as we have seen, were a class of professional "abstainers," whose duty it was to keep free from pollution so that they might approach the gods without offence. Chief among the offences to be avoided was uncleanness. It might arise in many ways, none of which necessarily involved what in other religions would be moral guilt. Uncleanness of the person, from mere dirt, was scrupulously avoided, and it was a necessary preparation for religious observances to wash the body and to put on fresh garments. Sexual intercourse, menstruation and childbirth were regarded as causing ceremonial impurity, which must be removed by lustration, abstention, and prayer. In the earliest myth there is mention of "parturition huts," isolated sheds to which pregnant women withdrew so that the dwelling-house should not be defiled by childbirth, and we are told also of "nuptial huts," in which, for a like reason, marriages were consummated. Disease, wounds, and death were also sources of uncleanness. Death—or rather the contamination of death—as we have seen, was abhorrent to the early Japanese. The Han travellers from China noticed that the time of mourning was short, that after death friends came to dance and sing, and that after the funeral the whole family went into the water to wash. The house in which a death took place became unclean, and it was doubtless on this account that until the beginning of the eighth century the capital, or at least the palace, was removed to another site upon the death of a sovereign.*

Wounds were a source of pollution, and the word for a wound, *kega*, still in use, means defilement. Sickness and all the external signs of disease, such as sores, eruptions, and discharges, or con-

* The traditional accession ceremony, performed as lately as 1928, includes an impressive survival of this practice. The Emperor enters a ritual hall, containing a couch-throne, and goes through an elaborate communion meal with the national deities; then, during the same night, he proceeds to another ritual hall close by, identically furnished, and repeats the communion meal.

tact with sick persons, were also defilements. Eating flesh was not originally unclean, except perhaps for priests preparing themselves for worship, but it appears to have become taboo under Buddhist influence. Intoxicating liquors are not taboo. In fact they figure prominently among offerings to the gods at all times.

So far, it will be noticed, the list of offences does not reveal any distinction between ceremonial impurity and moral guilt. The consummation of a marriage is no less defiling than adulterous intercourse, a blow or a wound pollutes both parties to a conflict, and generally we find that the early religion is almost entirely deficient in abstract ideas of morality. Its code is not ethical but customary and ceremonial. It reprobates as sins only such acts or states as are visibly or immediately repulsive. It is worth while to examine more closely this question, for out of the early conception of morality grows the whole complex of religious and social organisation in later times, shaping and modifying even the powerful influences of Chinese philosophy and Buddhist doctrine.

In the great Purification Ritual, which is of uncertain date but which embodies matter of great antiquity, there is a list of offences (*tsumi*) from which the gods are asked to cleanse the people. These are divided into heavenly offences and earthly offences. The heavenly offences are so called because they are those committed by the god Susa-no-wo in heaven, and were given a prominent place in the myth because they were, as we have noticed, offences against a community whose principal occupation was agriculture. The earthly offences are wounding and killing; desecration of corpses; leprosy; tumours; incest (though, it appears, intercourse between children of one father by different mothers was not considered incestuous); bestiality (but not, it appears, sodomy); calamity from creeping things, from the gods on high, from birds and animals, and from witchcraft. The offences in this second category are, it will be observed, calamities affecting the welfare of individuals, and are not even necessarily the result of their own actions or their own fault.*

* It is hardly necessary to add that the ritual offences just named were not the only offences recognised by early Japanese society, and that there were virtues prized as well as ceremonial purity. The Han historians record with admiration the chastity and gentleness of Japanese women, state that theft is unknown, and that laws and customs are strict.

What is abhorrent, what must be washed away and expiated is not guilt but pollution. The conception of sin, as distinct from uncleanness, is wanting, or rudimentary, and throughout their history the Japanese seem to have retained in some measure this incapacity to discern, or this reluctance to grapple with a problem of Evil. Such a statement, once committed to writing, forthwith challenges contradiction in the writer's own mind, but it represents, if imperfectly, a truth; and much that is baffling in the study of their history, from ancient to modern times, becomes clearer when one remembers that they have never been tortured by the sense of sin.

At the core of all Shintō ceremonial is the idea of purity, and at the core of all Shintō beliefs is the idea of fertility. As "celestial offences" typify those misdeeds which interfere with the production of food, so the chief celestial blessings demanded are those most desirable to farmers and fishermen, such as, in the words recited at the Harvest Festival in honour of every deity in the pantheon, "crops in ears long and in ears abundant, things growing in the great moor-plain, sweet herbs and bitter herbs, things that dwell in the blue sea-plain, the broad of fin and the narrow of fin, seaweed from the offing, seaweed from the shore, clothing, bright stuffs and shining stuffs, coarse stuffs and fine stuffs." The most important ceremonies have, in one way or another, to do with food. The chief festivals of the year are the Tasting of the First Fruits (Nii-namé), the Divine Tasting (Kan-namé), celebrated in the imperial palace and at the Ise shrines, the Together-Tasting (Ainamé) in which the emperor joins with the gods in partaking of the new season's rice and *sake* of the new brew, and the most solemn festival of all, the Great Food Offering (Ōnie, later called Daijōe), an elaborate form of the festival of the First Fruits, celebrated after an emperor's succession to the throne, to give a sacramental authority to his sovereignty. There are, it is true, other elements in the accession ceremonies, but the essential characteristics of the Daijōe and its preparatory rites are that "they have preserved from ancient times a primitive technique for the production and preservation of food," and are "deeply stamped with an interest in safeguarding the growth and fertility of crops." Many other celebrations, national and local,

are wholly or in part thanksgivings or prayers for harvest. It is a
significant fact that at Yamada in Ise, the centre of the cult oi
the Sun Goddess and the resting place of the sacred mirror, there
is a shrine, only next in holiness to that of Ama-terasu, devoted
to the worship of the goddess of food, Toyo-uke-hime, the Rich-
Food-Princess; and there are some reasons for believing that the
Sun Goddess was enshrined in this place by the ruling house
because it was already in ancient times of great holiness through
its association with a popular cult. Further evidence that it was
the principle of growth and fertility which inspired, more than
anything else, the beliefs and observances of the early Japanese is
to be found in the prevalence of phallic worship and its strong
power of survival. Phallic emblems are found in neolithic sites,
and a phallic significance was seen in trees and stones of appropriate form, doubtless because they suggested procreation and
fruitfulness. Even to-day, in remote districts, there can be seen
sometimes stones of phallic shape, set up at the edge of fields, and
bearing rude inscriptions such as "God of the Rice." In the
earliest chronicles there are several references to phallic worship,
and there are numerous records of festivals and liturgies in honour
of "gods of the cross-ways," who were represented by phallic
emblems set up by the roadside.

It is hardly necessary to add that though the early Shintō was
in essence a nature worship, it developed in special directions
under official auspices. It is important to distinguish from the
traditional body of popular belief and observance the institutional
religion which was fostered by the ruling classes. The former is
a simple ritualism based on an animistic creed and tinctured
with magic, the latter an organised and elaborate cult closely
bound up with the political system. It is equally important to
realise that, although Shintō is often described as a form of ancestor worship, this is a loose and misleading statement. Ancestor
worship, as practised in Japan, is a cult imported from China.[2]
The objects of worship of the early Japanese were nature deities,
and not their own deified ancestors. It is true that the noble
families claimed descent from the gods whom they worshipped,
but making your god into an ancestor and making your ancestor
into a god are not the same thing. The worship of a clan god

(*ujigami*) by all the members of a clan (*uji*) at first sight seems to be a form of ancestor worship. The clan god, however, was not necessarily a family god, and might be even a tutelary local deity. There were even cases where the identity of the clan god was disputed. In no case do we find, before the introduction of the Chinese cult, instances of the worship of deified men by their descendants. The worship of deceased emperors, even supposing it to have been practised before the importation of Chinese

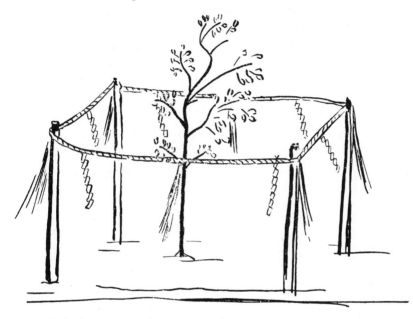

FIG. 15. *Himorogi. Sacred tree in its enclosure. A primitive form of consecrated site.*

theories of kingship—a supposition for which there is no evidence —is a special case, for the emperors were in their lifetime tinged with divinity.

To complete the foregoing account of early religious beliefs and observances, it is necessary to describe briefly how and in what places the gods were worshipped. In the earliest stages of the animistic creed, trees, rocks and springs were doubtless worshipped *in situ*, and obeisance made to the sun itself. Subsequently, it seems, ceremonies were conducted in an enclosure marked off by branches of evergreen trees thrust into the ground. Later, with the use of objects such as jewels and mirrors to symbolise the presence of a god, came the need for a dwelling in which to enshrine them. The word for a shrine (*miya: ya* "house," with an honorific prefix, *mi*) is the same as that used for the house of a chieftain, and it is clear that for centuries there was no distinction in type between a dwelling-house and a shrine. The special characteristic of Shintō shrines is the simplicity of their construction and ornament as contrasted with the great buildings of Buddhism. The shrines of Ise, which are pulled down and rebuilt in exact replica every twenty years, are thought to represent the

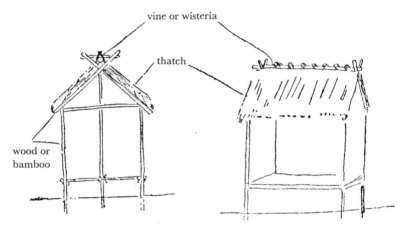

FIG. 16. *Conjectured style of primitive Japanese dwelling.*

purest and most ancient style of Japanese architecture, and they are essentially nothing more than thatched wooden huts, somewhat idealised. The Idzumo shrines, though larger and a little more elaborate, are still comparatively simple in design. There is no provision made for joint worship by a congregation, so that no more space is needed than will accommodate an altar and the priests or other attendants. The individual worshipper does not enter the shrine, but stands outside and makes his obeisance and his petition. It is not known how many shrines existed before the eighth century, but there were over 3,000 officially recognised shrines in A.D. 737, and of these about one-fourth were maintained at the expense of the government.

Worship consisted of obeisance, offerings and prayer. The offerings were primarily food and drink. Later, cloth was added, and eventually a symbolic offering came into use, by which strips of paper, representing strips of cloth, were attached to a wand and placed on the altar. Then, by a curious development, these symbolic offerings (known as *gohei*) themselves came to be regarded as sanctified, and even as representing the deity, who was

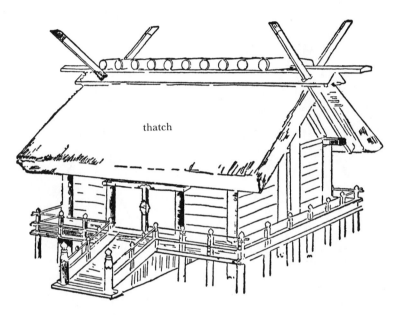

thatch

FIG. 17. *Sketch showing design of main shrine (shōden) at Yamada, province of Ise.*

sometimes mystically supposed to descend into them. Thus, in course of time, the *gohei* became objects of worship themselves, and were presented by priests to the devout, who set them up on their domestic altars; while strips of paper, cut in a prescribed way, and attached to a straw rope, to this day confer a special sanctity on places where they are suspended.

Purification was essential before worship and was achieved by various methods, exorcism (*harai*), cleansing (*misogi*) and abstention (*imi*). Exorcism was performed by a priest, and was intended to remove the pollution caused by an offence. It consists essentially of the presentation of offerings by way of fine, after which the priest brandishes before the person to be purified a wand in the form of a brush and pronounces a formula of purification. The exaction of fines gave to the *harai* a certain penal

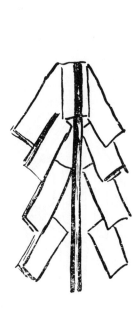

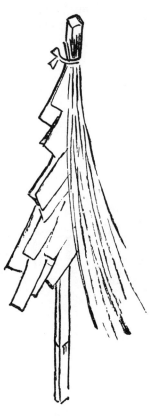

FIG. 18. *Gohei. Paper strips, symbolising offerings of clothing made from mulberry bark.*

FIG. 19. *Nusa. Wand for purification. Paper strips and hempen fibre.*

character. It is not clear how early this developed, but there are records under dates in the early part of the fifth century from which it would appear that at that time submission to the *harai* was a recognised punishment for civil as well as religious offences. Thus in 405 the head of the corporation of carters appropriated to his own service some peasants attached to the glebe of a shrine. He was commanded to perform expiatory rites, though his offence was as much civil as religious. In 469 a certain young nobleman debauched a court lady, and was made to purge his offence by the payment of eight horses and eight swords. He was unrepentant, and boasted in verse, saying that the adventure was well worth eight horses, whereupon the emperor confiscated all his property. We shall see that, with the growth of an administrative system on Chinese lines, there was later a clear division between secular and religious offences, the *harai* and its accompanying fines being confined to specified breaches of ecclesiastical law.

The *misogi* was a cleansing rite, intended to remove accidental defilement acquired by contact with unclean things, from simple dirt to the pollution of death and disease. It was effected by ablutions, or the mere sprinkling of water or salt. A number of practices common to-day are vestiges, or even complete survivals, of this ancient custom. In the courtyard of every temple and shrine is a font at which the worshippers wash their hands and rinse their mouths before worship. Outside the privy in the humblest house stands a basin of water and a ladle, used for rinsing the hands in a manner so perfunctory as to be merely symbolic. The indulgence of the Japanese in hot baths, though it is a habit which has survived because of its value in pleasure and health, doubtless owes something to the primitive belief in lustration. Salt is placed in little piles on the threshold of a house, at the edge of a well, or at the corners of a wrestling ring, and it is scattered about the floor after a funeral, with the object of purification. Offerings at a shrine invariably include a number of small dishes of salt.

The third, and perhaps the most interesting method of purification is *imi*, or abstention. Exorcism and lustration confer purity by removing uncleanness, whereas abstention is a method of acquiring a positive purity by avoidance of the sources of pollution. It was therefore the duty of priests rather than of laymen to practise the needful austerities, which consisted chiefly of the observance of certain prohibitions. They must avoid contact with sickness, death, mourning; they must eat only certain kinds of food and those only if cooked over a "pure" fire; they must wear only specially purified garments; and they must remain indoors, remote from noise, dancing and singing. Scrupulous care must be taken to avoid contamination of the sanctuary, the offerings and the utensils.

Private devotions seem from early times to have been confined to the deposit of offerings before a shrine accompanied by some reverent gesture, such as bowing, or clapping—not merely folding—the hands. It is curious that, in a country where kneeling and prostration are part of every-day social ceremony, kneeling before a shrine was not usual and prostration apparently not practised at all as a form of worship. Private, individual prayer seems to have been uncommon, and to have consisted at the most of some simple formula. Many examples of official liturgies are recorded in a book of Institutes compiled in the beginning of the tenth century. Some are inclined to regard them as preserving with a high degree of exactitude the form and content of very ancient addresses to the gods, but the probability is that they do not antedate the seventh century at earliest, and that when they were first committed to writing they underwent considerable change at the hands of scribes anxious to give them a certain literary elegance. In the present writer's view they smell too much of the lamp to be genuine survivals, by oral tradition, from a period much earlier than the spread of writing in Japan. They must contain, however, some ancient elements; and it is therefore worth quoting a few passages to show their style and purport. The following is an extract from Aston's translation of the Litany recited at the Ceremony of National Purification:

"Then shall no offences remain unpurged, from the court of the august child of the gods even to the remotest ends of the realm. As the many-piled clouds of heaven are scattered at the breath of the Wind Gods; as the morning breezes and the evening breezes disperse the morning vapours and the evening vapours; as a huge ship moored in a great harbour, casting off its stern moorings, casting off its bow moorings, drives forth into the vast ocean; as yonder thick brushwood is smitten and cleared away by the sharp sickle forged in the fire—so shall all offences be swept utterly away. To purge and purify them, let the goddess Seori-tsu-hime, who dwells

in the rapids of the swift stream whose cataracts tumble headlong from the high mountains and from the low mountains,
bear them out into the great sea plains. There let the goddess
Haya-akitsu-hime, who dwells in the myriad meeting places
of the tides of the myriad sea paths, swallow them up, and
let the god Ibukido Nushi (i.e. the master of the spurting-out
place), who dwells in Ibukido, spurt them out away to the
nether region. Then let the goddess Hayasasura-hime, who
dwells in the nether region, dissolve and destroy them."

The language is not without a certain elevation but the translation has a sweep and a finish which flatter the rather poorly
articulated original. The chief characteristic of its style is a
solemn pleonasm, as in the phrase "in the myriad ways of the
tides of the raging sea and the myriad meeting places of the tides
of the myriad sea paths." Some idea of the rhythm of the native
words can be gained from the original: *Ara-shio no shio no yaoji no
yashioji no shio no yaoai.*

The literary value of the remaining rituals is not great, but they
include picturesque and interesting passages, such as this declara-
tion to the Sun Goddess in the great prayer for Harvest:

". . . I do humbly declare in the mighty presence of
the Great Heaven-shining Deity who dwells in Ise. Because
the Great Deity has bestowed on him lands of the four
quarters over which her glance extends as far as where the
wall of Heaven rises, as far as where the bounds of Earth
stand up, as far as the blue clouds are diffused, as far as
where the white clouds settle down opposite; by the blue sea-
plain, as far as the prows of ships can go without letting dry
their poles and oars; by land, as far as the hoofs of horses
can go, with tightened baggage-cords, treading their way
among rock-roots and tree-roots where the long road extends,
continuously widening the narrow regions and making the
steep regions level, drawing together, as it were, the distant
regions by throwing over them (a net of) many ropes—
therefore will the first-fruits for the Sovran Great Deity be
piled up in her mighty presence like a range of hills, leaving
the remainder for him tranquilly to partake of."

And this, from a blessing of the Imperial Palace, after a recital of the circumstances in which the reigning dynasty received the celestial mandate:

> "And for the Sovran Grandchild who in Heavenly Sun-succession rules the Under-Heaven, to which he had descended, trees are now cut down with the sacred axes of the Imbe in the great valleys and the small valleys of the secluded mountains, and sacrifice having been made of their tops and bottoms to the God of the mountains, the middle parts are brought forth and set up as sacred pillars with sacred mattocks to form a fair Palace wherein the Sovran Grandchild finds shelter from the sky and shelter from the sun. To thee, therefore . . . I address these heavenly, wondrous, auspicious words of calm and blessing."

NOTES TO CHAPTER III

[1] Page 48. The Imperial Regalia have a curious history. Whatever symbolic qualities were later ascribed to the mirror, the sword and the jewel, it is clear that the tradition of their importance goes back to a period when neolithic Japan was coming under the influence of the metal culture of the Asiatic mainland, and when the possession of bronze weapons and precious ornaments by a Japanese tribal chieftain was a sign of superior power and wealth. The sepulchral mounds almost without exception contain bronze swords, bronze mirrors and "jewels" (magatama), because they were the most prized possessions of a great man in his lifetime. These are the objects which, in course of time, came to symbolise the Imperial authority as the Three Sacred Treasures and were enshrined in the holiest places of the land. Modern Japanese political writers have developed theories of the state in which these objects represent mystical, or at least unintelligible properties of the Japanese constitution, and one writer at least has gone so far as to proclaim that they are an embodiment of the Hegelian dialectic, in which presumably—though he does not explain—the contradiction of the mirror and the jewel is resolved by the sword.

[2] Page 54 ff. Ancestor worship. Some Japanese scholars have challenged my statement that ancestor worship is a cult imported from China. On such a point positive evidence is lacking, but it is perhaps significant that in the poems of the Manyōshū ancestor worship is scarcely referred to, while what we know of early burial customs indicates a horror of death and pollution which seems to be inconsistent with worship of the dead.

Chapter IV

THE INTRODUCTION OF CHINESE LEARNING

THOUGH, as we have said, the introduction of writing into Japan profoundly influenced her development, it was not until after a long period of incubation that its effects were clearly visible. It is a notable fact that the first Japanese book of which we have any record was not written for two centuries after the official adoption of the Chinese script.[1] Writing was, of course, used in the fifth and sixth centuries, but chiefly for such purposes as keeping accounts and registers, with an occasional despatch to some foreign court. In these uses it seems to have remained for a long time the special function of scribes of Chinese or Korean origin. The native chronicles state that recorders were appointed to the provinces "for the first time" in 403, but this chronology is dubious. Though we hear of letters from Japanese rulers to China at the beginning of the Christian era, the first of which the text has been preserved is a memorial from the Yamato sovereign to the Chinese court in 478. Certainly as late as 682, when the *Kojiki* was compiled, the services of reciters were of use, so that there cannot have existed any very considerable body of written records. We shall probably be not far wrong if we assume that writing was practically the monopoly of a small class of official scribes until the end of the sixth century. Some distinction should however be made between writing and reading. For reasons which require more elaborate explanation than can be given here, it is a much simpler task to learn to read a Chinese text than it is to write one, and it is therefore most likely that a number of Japanese students were able to spell out with a teacher's aid passages from Chinese books, without being able to compose themselves, or even to trace more than a few Chinese characters with the brush. Gradually, under their foreign tutors, they gained some idea of the contents of the canonical works brought to Japan, first the *Lunyü* or Confucian Analects, then the five major classics, the Odes, the Annals, the Rites, the Changes and the Spring and Autumn Chronicles. Perhaps the chief obstacle to the rapid spread of writing in Japan was the sheer technical difficulty of representing words in an agglutinated, polysyllabic

language like Japanese by signs standing for the monosyllabic
words of Chinese, a difficulty magnified by the dissimilarity between Chinese and Japanese sounds. Pending the development of a
suitable method—and this was, in effect, not evolved for centuries
—for a Japanese to benefit fully by the Chinese script he must learn
the Chinese language, a language differing as widely as possible
from Japanese in vocabulary, syntax and idiom. It must be remembered that for the greater part of the sixth century Japan had little
or no direct intercourse with China and was therefore dependent
upon Korea for instruction. It was precisely during this period that
she was fully occupied with Korea, and this no doubt contributed
to delay in the spread of writing. The government was intent
upon schemes of conquest, the material benefits of literature were
not so obvious as those of warfare, and the nobles perhaps felt
that, as they could purchase the service of specialists, there was
no reason why they should suffer the drudgery of learning to
read and write Chinese. So long as writing appeared as a mere
mechanical accomplishment, a craft not much different from, say,
weaving or painting, it might be left to clerks. It was when it
was seen to be the vehicle for a new religion and a new political
philosophy that it first became essential to the ruling classes.
A desire to go to the sources of Confucian doctrine was an important motive, but it is probable that it was the emotional
stimulus of Buddhism that gave the strongest and most widespread
impulse to learning in Japan.

A close study of the intercourse between Japan and Korea in
the fifth and sixth centuries is not necessary for our purpose, but a
knowledge of its main features is important if one is to understand
how, and when, and in what measure, Japan adopted Chinese
civilisation. The Japanese, we have seen, were at the beginning
of the fifth century on friendly terms with Paikché, and generally
hostile to Silla. Japan's policy was to extend her influence in the
Korean peninsula, by supporting one of the three warring states
against the other two. During the whole of this century there
were constant Japanese raids upon Silla, some of which appear
to have been undertaken by large forces. In the memorial presented in 478 to the Wei Emperor by the Emperor of Japan the
latter describes himself as Supreme Director of Military Affairs in

Japan, Paikché, Silla, and other Korean kingdoms, so that, even allowing for boastful language, it is clear that the Japanese, through their military prowess, exercised an important influence in Korea at this time. By the beginning of the sixth century the position had changed. Paikché was under the influence of Chinese civilisation, richer than Silla, and perhaps less vigorous or, at any rate, more peacefully inclined. The Silla men were as warlike as the Japanese, to whom they were doubtless racially akin, and to whom they never submitted in the same way as those of Paikché, who paid tribute regularly to Japan as the price of military help. In 516 a strong Japanese fleet was repulsed off the south coast of Korea. By 527 the Japanese were in danger of losing their foothold in Korea, in the enclave between Paikché and Silla. They hurriedly got together an expedition, which was intercepted by a powerful provincial chieftain in western Japan—probably bribed by Silla —and it was some years before they could resume their efforts. Meanwhile, as Kōkuli in the north and Silla in the south-east grew in strength, the position of Paikché became weaker, and its dependence upon Japanese help greater. Year after year the king of Paikché implored the court of Yamato to despatch troops, and he sent with each appeal valuable presents. It was all of no avail, for Silla and Kōkuli combined to crush Paikché notwithstanding the desperate resistance of the Japanese auxiliaries, and by 562 the Japanese had lost to Silla their little colony of Mimana. They made attempts to retake it from time to time, but by the beginning of the seventh century Silla was paramount in Korea, and Japan had nothing to say, though for long afterwards she endeavoured at intervals to regain her foothold.

Paikché, which had sent in 404 and 405 the learned scholars Achiki and Wani, in 552* sent an image of the Buddha, with a number of volumes of the sutras, and in 554 a number of men learned in, respectively, the Chinese classics, medicine, divination, calendar-making and music, as well as certain Buddhist monks. Paikché, it should be stated, appointed Chinese professors and officially adopted Chinese writing in 374, and Buddhism appears to have been introduced ten years later (384). Knowledge of Buddhism had doubtless reached Silla in the fourth century, but

* This date is by some scholars rejected in favour of 538.

its official adoption was in the reign of Pep-Heung, 514-539, probably from Kōkuli. We may therefore suppose that the knowledge of Buddhism obtained by the Japanese from Korea was not very extensive at first. Nor were conditions in China favourable to the steady spread of the religion beyond her frontiers, for there was confusion and division in North China from the downfall of the Han almost uninterruptedly till the rise of the Sui. The fortunes of Buddhism in this long period ebbed and flowed, but in the first part of the sixth century the Liang emperor Wu-ti (502-537) and the Wei empress dowager (516-528) were both champions of Buddhism. As the end of dynastic struggles neared in China, so the prospects of the spread of Buddhism increased with more settled relations between the Chinese courts and the Korean states.

The progress made by Buddhism in Japan can be inferred from scattered references in the chronicles. The image of Buddha was accompanied by a message from the King of Paikché, recommending the adoption of this new religion, which he said, though hard to explain and hard to comprehend, was of all doctrines the most excellent, and brought the realisation of all desires. The emperor of Japan felt unable to decide upon the merits of the new faith, and submitted the problem to his ministers. The choice followed the line of cleavage between powerful factions at court. On the one side were the Nakatomi clan, hereditary liturgists, as we have seen, and the Mononobe clan, who were charged with the protection of the palace and were the leading military family. The combination of sacerdotal and military functions made the alliance between these two families a powerful one; and that they combined at all is evidence of the strength of their common rivals, the Soga family. The Soga, though they claimed ancient and noble descent, did not come into prominence until about this period and they owed their rise in fortune largely to their services in administering crown estates. In 536 Soga Iname was made Ō-omi, Chief of Chieftains, a position which may be described roughly as equivalent in authority to that of Chancellor of the Empire. He consolidated his position as far as possible by marrying his daughter into the imperial house, but the most serious obstacles to his family's progress were clearly the other great clans, who derived their power very largely from their connection with the state religion. Therefore Soga, when the question was put to him, came down on the side of Buddhism, while the Nakatomi and the Mononobe both objected that to worship foreign gods would only invite the anger of the national gods, worshipped since the foundation of Japan. The emperor therefore presented the image to Soga, who set it up in his own house. For a time the fortunes of the new religion hung in the balance, as an epidemic of sickness which began to rage shortly after this was ascribed by the Nakatomi and the Mononobe to the anger of the native gods. The emperor thought they might be right, and the image was thrown into the canal at Naniwa. The emperor who succeeded in 572 (Bidatsu) was not a believer in Buddhism, but was devoted to Chinese literature, while about the throne the rivalry between Soga and Mononobe persisted, so that the prospects of the new religion continued poor. Indeed there is no reason to suppose that Soga himself had any but political reasons for promoting it. Certainly we find him, not long after the image was thrown away, advising the Paikché envoys, if they wanted their country to prosper, to worship the "founder of the land," by which he meant Ō-na-mochi, the creator-deity of Idzumo myth (who was possibly a deity of Korean origin). Under Bidatsu the Great Omi was Soga no Umako, son of Iname, and he followed his father as a patron of Buddhism.

The story of the first steps is a curious one. One might almost suppose, from his business-like procedure, that Umako made up his mind that the new religion was a necessary feature in an up-to-date country which had already imported other advantages of civilisation such as literature and geomancy. For its proper introduction he required evangelists and disciples, images, a holy relic, and a temple to contain them. These he set about procuring. He got his images and a holy relic, and he sent in all directions for a practising Buddhist. Only one could be found, a former Korean monk who had settled in Japan and become a layman again. Umako ordered him to resume his holy character and caused him to receive into the faith three maidens of tender age. These three nuns—one was eleven years old—were instructed to fast and worship; the images were enshrined in a temple annexed to

Umako's own dwelling; a pagoda was built to contain the relic;
and Umako himself with a few others unremittingly practised the
faith. "From this," says the Nihon-shoki, "arose the beginning of
Buddhism." Naturally the beginnings were not so clear-cut as
this, but we may take it that, with the patronage of a powerful
statesman, it gained a permanent footing from this time—say
A.D. 575. But some knowledge of Buddhism must have reached
Japan long before this, through refugees and other immigrants
from the continent. It is significant that, apart from Soga himself,
the first recorded Buddhists in Japan were almost all of alien
descent. The three nuns were of Korean or Chinese origin, one
being the daughter of Shiba Tattō, Soga's chief helper in his
religious task. Shiba is the Japanese version of the family name
Ssu-ma, celebrated in Chinese history. In 577 monks and
ascetics, a temple architect and a maker of images came over from
Paikché, bringing religious books; and in 579 Silla also sent an
image. All these were signs of the permanent establishment of the
new faith. But it had difficulties to contend with, for shortly after
these events another pestilence broke out and again the factions
opposed to the Soga made capital out of disaster, and persuaded
the emperor to proscribe the new cult. The emperor agreed, and
the Mononobe and Nakatomi had (says one version) the pleasure
of destroying Umako's holy edifices. The poor little nuns were
stripped of their vestments and publicly whipped in a market
place. Umako, however, obtained from the emperor permission
to worship the Buddha privately, and he took the nuns back into
his charge, and built a new shrine wherein they should practise
their devotions. This, briefly and with such truth as the chronicles
permit, is how the Three Precious Things came to Japan—
Buddha, Dharma, Saṅgha—the Buddha, the Law, and the Priesthood. There is a somewhat ironical interest in the fact that this
gospel of gentleness was recommended to the Japanese by a hard-
pressed monarch begging for the loan of troops, and owed its
adoption by them in a great measure to the bitter jealousy of
political rivals.

The next emperor (Yōmei) "believed in the law of Buddha and
reverenced the way of the gods." He was, in fact, what most of
his countrymen have since been, a Buddhist and a Shintoist at

once. It is in this passage that the native religion is, for the first time, referred to as Shintō, the Way of the Gods. It was a new term, because no distinguishing name had been necessary before the introduction of a new religion. From the succession of Yōmei, under the protection of the throne and the Soga family, the fortunes of Buddhism advanced rapidly. When the emperor was taken ill, he told his ministers that he wished to be received into the new religion. The Nakatomi and the Mononobe were strongly opposed to what they called "turning their backs upon their country's gods," and the Soga, of course, were on the side of Buddhism. The breach gradually widened, and after some sordid succession quarrels and a short but bloody civil war (587) the Soga gained the upper hand and Umako was paramount in Japan. Temples were built, more holy relics were brought from Korea (A.D. 587), with priests, monks, and temple carpenters, painters, artists in bronze and clay, all clearly men of some standing, since their names are recorded. More daughters of noblemen became nuns, and a number of men of Chinese descent renounced the world and became priests or ascetics. Umako sent the nuns who had been whipped in the market place to Korea for study, and in general promoted the new faith. Promoted it in its external manifestations, we must hastily add; for his personal conduct was ruthless and cruel. To gain his political ends he would stop at nothing. In the course of his career he was responsible for the murder of many of his enemies, including two imperial princes, and finally (593) of the emperor Sujun himself.

The murdered emperor was succeeded by the Empress Suiko at the age of 39, and the control of affairs was vested in the Prince Umayado*—a son of the Emperor Yōmei—better known by his posthumous title as Shōtoku Taishi, the Crown Prince "Sage-Virtue." It was he who was the real founder of Buddhism in Japan, and its further growth, after the introduction of its outward forms under the patronage of the Soga, can best be described by briefly relating his career.

* Umayado means "a stable," and there was a legend that the Prince was born in a stable. There is nothing to support this in the chronicles, though it is the sort of thing they are fond of recording. It is therefore suggested by some Japanese scholars that the legend was invented after the Prince's death, when some faint echo of the story of the birth of Christ had reached Japan.

Naturally gifted, he devoted himself to study from an early age, and he is said to have become proficient in both the doctrines of Buddhism and the learning embodied in the Chinese classics. The great Soga appears to have exercised his power with moderation, and not to have interfered with the Prince's plans, partly, no doubt, because he was satisfied with the ascendancy he had gained for his clan, and also because he recognised the Prince's great gifts. The chief concern of Shōtoku Taishi was to propagate the moral and intellectual benefits of Buddhism, but he did not neglect the outward aspects, the temples, pagodas, vestments and ceremonies, which must constitute its first appeal to the unenlightened. The building of temples proceeded apace.[2] The heads of great families, from the beginning of his regency, "vied with one another in erecting Buddhist shrines for the benefit of their lords and parents." The great temple called Shitennō-ji (Temple of the Four Deva Raja or Heavenly Kings), precursor of the building which gives its name to a busy quarter of present-day Ōsaka, was commenced in 593, and also the temple called Hōkōji or Asukadera. The latter was completed at the end of 596, and some idea of the importance attached to this event may be gathered from the fact that the name of the era was then unofficially changed to Hōkō in its honour. By the end of 624 there were 46 temples, 816 priests and monks and 569 nuns. The debt of Japan to Korea at this period must not be overlooked. Shōtoku Taishi's teachers were Koreans, and two of them in particular (the first abbots of the Hōkōji) are described in the records as together "the mainstay of the Three Precious Things." From this time on there was a stream of priests, monks, scholars and artists from Kōkuli and Paikché. They settled in Japan and engaged in teaching or the exercise of their arts, often intermarrying with Japanese, and so creating a nucleus of imported culture, and a fusion of racial elements which must have been of great advantage to Japan. We have no exact knowledge of their origins, but it is known that while Paikché was sending teachers to Japan she was obtaining teachers from China, and it is highly probable, on these and other grounds, that many immigrants to Japan at this period —the latter half of the sixth century—were Chinese from the Liang or Wei courts, arriving by way of Korea.

In A.D. 604 the Prince issued a code which has been mistakenly described by some writers as a Constitution.[3] It is rather a collection of moral injunctions addressed to the ruling classes, and their interest lies in the fact that they represent not a new system of administration but a turning point in the ideals of government, inspired by the new learning, both religious and secular, from abroad. The native religion, whatever its merits as a pagan creed, had tended, under the influence of the developing clan system, to become at its best a complex of ceremonial divorced from the inspiration of its primitive beliefs, and at its worst a means of oppression, devoted to maintaining caste privilege. Apart from a certain customary code, exemplified in the proscriptions of the liturgies, it had but a small ethical element, and it was bound therefore to develop on its ritual and superstitious side, unless it received some strong stimulus from without. Many instances might be quoted to illustrate this development, but it is sufficient perhaps to refer to the way in which the early rites of purgation, by a not uncommon transition, assumed a punitive character. Offerings to the gods degenerated into fines or even blackmail, levied by priest and layman alike, and ritual offences were thus often punished more severely than crimes. Buddhism, too, in its earliest days in Japan, was clearly regarded as another means of obtaining material benefit or warding off calamity. This is a natural development. The sutras were recited before they were understood. They were thought to be magical formulæ, and indeed among the first priests to arrive from Korea were reciters of *mantra*, or incantations. Soga no Umako worshipped a Buddhist image in the hope of recovery from disease, the Emperor Yōmei wished to enter religion when he found himself sickening, and for many years after this the greatest and most lavish Buddhist rites were held when a monarch was ill, or when the crops needed rain, or when some other very concrete advantage was sought for the country. Amongst the finest early temples are those devoted to the worship of Yakushi ("The King of Medicine").

It was Shōtoku's chief title to celebrity that he was attracted by and endeavoured to propagate the moral and philosophical content of Buddhism. It is interesting to study from this point of view the Prince's injunctions. They provide at the same time a useful key to contemporary sentiment.

Article I insists upon the value of harmony in the community, and gives a warning against the evils of class feeling. Those above must be harmonious, those below must be well disposed. This is Confucian doctrine.

Article II enjoins reverence of the Three Precious Things.

Article III sketches the Chinese theory of sovereignty. "When the Lord speaks the Vassal listens." A hierarchy, dependent upon obedience.

Article IV states the complementary proposition that, if the duty of the inferior is obedience, the duty of the superior is decorum. Decorum here is "ceremony," the code of behaviour laid down in the Book of Rites. This again is a Chinese conception of government.

Article V warns against gluttony and covetousness, and is addressed primarily to those who have to judge suits. It is an appeal for justice to inferiors.

Article VI is against flatterers and sycophants.

Article VII is against patronage in public office, and includes an instruction to fill posts by merit.

Article VIII enjoins hard work upon officials.

Article IX enjoins good faith between inferior and superior.

Article X is against anger. If we disagree with others "we are not unquestionably wise, and they are not unquestionably foolish."

Article XI urges upon high functionaries the importance of rewarding merits and punishing faults.

Article XII says "let not the provincial governors or the local chieftains levy exactions upon the people. In a country there are not two lords, the people have not two masters. The sovereign is the master of the people of the whole country, the officials to whom he gives control are his vassals. How can they, as well as the government, presume to tax the people?"

Article XIII is against neglect of official duties.

Article XIV is against envy.

Article XV is a restatement of Article I.

Article XVI is an instruction as to the seasons of forced labour.

Article XVII enjoins consultation between officials on important matters.

At first sight these appear to be nothing but vague exhortations and pious hopes, but it must be remembered that (so far as we know) there existed under the prevailing system no considered theory of government, no body of instructions for officials and no moral code beyond the ceremonial injunctions and prohibitions of the national religion and certain customary rules of conduct. The mere formulation of a set of moral laws was therefore almost revolutionary, and we see here the first results, in the abstract field, of the importation of Indian religion and Chinese philosophy, for the seventeen articles are a compound of Buddhist and Confucian principles. Hidden in these apparently harmless exhortations to governors and governed is a new view of the state, for while they exact obedience from inferiors to superiors they insist equally upon the duties of superiors to inferiors, and, what is most significant of all, they enunciate very clearly the theory of a centralised state, in which the ultimate power resides in the emperor and is exercised through his functionaries. "The sovereign is master of the people of the whole country, the officials to whom he gives charge are all his vassals." This is a pregnant sentence, of which the importance can be realised only by considering the political conditions of the day.

At the time of Shōtoku Taishi's Injunctions, Japan was still far from being a single political unit. Rather it was a loosely connected group of clans, in which the imperial clan had the first place. The clans (*uji*) were divided into three sorts, according to their origin—the Imperial Clan, whose members claimed descent from the Sun Goddess; the Divine Clans, whose members traced their ancestry either to the Heavenly gods, through the divine companions of the first Emperor Jimmu, or the Earthly gods, by which is to be understood those territorial rulers who were already established in Yamato when Jimmu arrived; and the Stranger Clans, who were immigrants from China and Korea at various dates. The Imperial Clan comprised several divisions, for it included not only the reigning house but a number of great

families, whose heads were called *omi*, "great men." The senior
of these was the Ō-omi, or "Great Omi," who was the leader and
representative of all the *omi*. Next in importance to the *omi* were
the chieftains of the divine clans, who were called *muraji* (group
chiefs), and at whose head there stood a leader, analogous to the
Great Omi, known as the Ō-muraji, or Great Muraji. The clans
recognised the supremacy of the imperial house, but it was a
supremacy that allowed the emperor a very limited authority.
Each head of a branch of a clan was the master of the people and
the property of that branch, and control over him could be exercised only by the leader of his clan, the Great Omi or the Great
Muraji, as the case might be.

The state therefore consisted of groups in unstable equilibrium.
The equilibrium was maintained through the prestige rather
than through the strength of the imperial house, and in such
conditions there is a natural tendency for one group to seek to
obtain power at the expense of other groups. The political history
of Japan for many centuries, from the earliest times of which we
have some exact knowledge, consists of a series of events arising
out of the struggle of the great clans for mastery, whether by
control or by overthrow of the imperial house. In this struggle the
imperial house had certain advantages. First, being the descendant and heir of the Sun Goddess, the head of the imperial house
represented, as high priest in her worship, not only the powerful
clans described above as Imperial Clans, but also all other clans,
since the Sun Goddess was the supreme divinity of the whole
people. To what extent the cult of the Sun Goddess as the supreme
divinity was deliberately fostered by the reigning house it is
difficult to say. There are some reasons for supposing that, as a
national deity, the Food Goddess had stronger and more ancient
claims; but, be that as it may, the worship of the Sun Goddess
was at an early date transferred from the palace to a special
shrine in Ise served by imperial princesses, and became thus a
national rather than a family cult. By the sixth century it was
firmly established as a state religion, and thenceforward its
development is as much political as religious. A second advantage
was the position of the emperor as representative of all the clans
in relations with foreign states, particularly the rival kingdoms of

Korea, and as these relations involved warfare, he possessed at least in theory the supreme command of fighting forces sent overseas. The autonomy of the clans was so complete that only for such a purpose as a military expedition could the imperial house hope to levy taxes upon them. A third advantage was the position of the emperor as arbiter between clans, or between members of clans, in disputes as to succession and similar matters. It will be seen that these advantages rested not upon superior strength but rather upon prestige and habit. Government, so far as it went, was government by consent, and consent might easily be withheld by powerful clans if they felt their own interests were at stake or if their leaders were ambitious enough to challenge imperial authority. Several instances are on record, in the historical period, of attempts to seize the throne, generally by Great Omi, since they were kinsmen of the imperial family. Thus, in 498, according to the *Nihongi*, "Heguri no Matori no Omi usurped the government of the country and tried to reign over Japan." He was crushed by the Crown Prince, with the military aid of the leader of a rival clan, the Muraji Ōtomo no Kanamura. This appears to have been a typical example, showing that the emperor, however supreme and inviolable in theory, was in practice dependent upon the support of one or other of the great families. The removal, even the murder, of an emperor or an heir to the throne is a common incident, and it is just to say that the continuance of the imperial house depended not upon its own strength but upon the fact that no single one of the rival factions could be suffered by the remainder to usurp imperial functions. When in course of time one great clan did in fact achieve a paramount position, it was expedient for them to control rather than to overthrow the reigning family, and to strengthen their influence by giving their daughters as consorts to imperial princes. This, indeed, is a characteristic phenomenon in Japanese history until recent times—the persistence of a *de jure* sovereignty long after all but its external forms have been taken over by a *de facto* government.

It was the Soga family who first established such domination in its fullest measure, although it had been exercised to some extent by other families before them, as for example the Ōtomo clan just mentioned. Paradoxically enough, it was the rise of the

Soga clan that contributed most to the growth of a firm and far-reaching central government in Japan, in place of the loose grouping of practically autonomous units which persisted until the seventh century. *De facto* rulers like the Soga want more than the exercise, through a *de jure* sovereign, of an empty authority. They want the concrete benefits of overlordship, the wealth and the power to bend men to their wills. These the Soga chieftains could secure only in such measure as the other clans could be deprived of their autonomy, the right to enjoy and dispose of the product of their land and their people. This autonomy was very considerable. Apart from the domains of the leaders of the great clans, the whole of the settled country in Japan was held by landowners of various degrees of importance. The names of a number of classes of these landowners have come down to us. Comprehensively described as *Kunitsuko* or *Kuni no Miyatsuko* (country rulers), there were *Ō Kunitsuko* (great country rulers), *Agatanushi* (estate masters), *Inagi* (rice custodians), and several other categories,* which constituted a small territorial gentry. Below them were the slaves, and above them were the members of the noble clans, the *muraji* and the *omi*. Some were little more than small farmers, others were territorial magnates of considerable strength in land and in men, others were offshoots of or had affiliations with the noble clans, which could exercise influence over them only if they were not far distant. An idea of the strength of some of these provincial chieftains may be gathered from the instance referred to above, of the "country ruler" Iwai, who in 527 was paramount over a large area in the island of Kyūshū, and was able to bar the way to an army of 60,000 imperial troops on an expedition to Korea. It was only after more than a year and with the greatest difficulty that the central authorities were able, in a fierce battle, to subdue him. Iwai's, no doubt, was an extreme case; but such, in varying degrees, was the position throughout Japan. The central government strove constantly to

---

* The etymology and exact significance of these terms is uncertain, but they have approximately the meanings here given. The *agatanushi* were in theory tenants of Crown estates, and the *inagi* wardens of granaries where tax-rice was stored. It is impossible to say what degree of political or fiscal allegiance they in fact yielded.

foster the conception that the provincial magnates held and ruled their territory as delegates or even as officials of the crown. As early as 534 we learn of a minister in a speech quoting the Chinese doctrine, "of the entire surface of the soil there is no place that is not the king's grant. Under the wide heavens there is no place which is not the king's land." Although the record of this speech may be an invention, and although the doctrine was certainly not at that time accepted in japan, the conception itself was growing, and whenever possible was acted upon by the ruling house. Naturally the spread of Chinese learning contributed a great deal to its growth, and it is perhaps here that we have the first concrete manifestation, on an important scale, of the effects of the introduction of writing. Writing made it possible not only to keep accounts and registers but to give definite shape to ideas. The very words for the offices and acts of a centralised bureaucratic state were missing from the vocabulary of Japanese, as is clear from the fact that though the Great Omi and the Great Muraji were not only leaders of their clans but also became, as an administrative system gradually developed, holders of the greatest offices of state, they continued to be called merely the Great Omi and the Great Muraji. While the rank developed into an office, the name of the office was not distinguished from the name of the rank. Other high officials were known comprehensively as *taifu*, a Chinese term meaning merely "great man." The later Han chronicles refer to an envoy from southern Japan to the court of China in A.D. 57, who styled himself *daibu*, and even if this notice is anachronistic in regard to Japanese usage at that period, it is certain that from an early date the Japanese were indebted to the Chinese for the nomenclature as well as the idea of their official hierarchy, and that the knowledge of writing sped the growth of the thing as well as the name. Perhaps too little weight is given to mere language as an essential factor in the growth of political ideas. Under a highly developed system of government there are occasions when the limitations of language may hinder the correct treatment of a problem, because many situations are falsified by the mere attempt to describe them; but for the settlement of forms of administration in its early stages the precision of a written instrument is probably essential, and in this sense the Japanese were indebted in the first place to the Chinese script for such success as they gained in substituting official for tribal institutions.

It need not be supposed that any notable change in the forms or the essence of government was brought about forthwith by the issue of Shōtoku Taishi's Injunctions. They were merely the enunciations of principles which he desired, with the goodwill of the Soga, to apply. The actual circumstances, at the time of his edict, were almost exactly contrary to these which he describes as desirable. All subjects did not render implicit obedience to the throne, all officials were not chosen for merit, the ruling classes did not set an example by their observance of the Confucian rules of conduct, the nobility and gentry certainly did not regard the taxes and forced labour of their peasants as belonging to the crown. Nor as yet did the whole people eagerly cherish the Three Jewels of Buddhism. Indeed for the most part the great clung to the worship of their ancestral deities, the small to the ubiquitous gods; and it is not without significance that Shōtoku, while he does not condemn the native beliefs, nowhere in his injunctions mentions them. They did not need his support, and he dare not, if he would, condemn them. Indeed, an edict of 607 of which he must have been cognisant, enjoins unremitting worship of the gods of Heaven and Earth, and speaks reverently of nature deities.

But the ground was prepared for change, by many circumstances in conjunction. It was prepared by the simple lapse of time, for the clan system was of its nature unstable; by the need for solidarity, if treasure and territory were to be gained in Korea; by the slow spread of learning; and by the ferment of new ideas, embodied in the politics and ethics of Confucianism and the religion and philosophy of Buddhism, two systems which, though strongly contrasted, were not to eclectic minds mutually exclusive. So the exhortations of Shōtoku Taishi found a not entirely unreceptive audience and, since they bespoke reform implicitly rather than explicitly, they aroused no open opposition, and he could proceed, though only gradually, to put his ideas into further execution.

To consolidate the imperial power, the first essential was to increase the wealth, in goods and land and men, of the imperial house. For centuries past mere human greed had seen to that, so far as the competing greed of others would allow. One important source of wealth was the tribute from Korea. The word tribute is regularly used, on grounds of national pride, to describe commodities furnished by Korean kingdoms, but these were frequently brought in exchange for goods or services furnished by Japan, and it is likely that we have here the beginnings of foreign trade, by which the reigning house profited, though not without leaving an important share to the leading clans. Another source of strength, derived also from continental relations, was the fact that the corporations and other groups of immigrants, whether composed of scholars or artists or artisans or even slaves, were regularly attached to the reigning house, which thus had the first claim upon their products or their labour. This accretion of property of the kind which they produced was of special importance because of its scarcity value, since it gave to the imperial family control over the supply of objects, such as books, paintings and buildings, fine silks, precious metals and ornaments, that are most coveted in an expanding culture. All possible devices were resorted to by the reigning house in order to extend their holdings of land, and though they met here with strong competition from other land-hungry clans, they were in some respects in a favourable position. For one thing, as *primus inter pares* of the great clans, it was as we have seen their prerogative to settle disputes among clans or branches of clans and this sometimes involved degrading or even suppressing a unit which was not strong enough to resist, or could not obtain protection against the imperial mandate. In such cases the emperor would confiscate for himself or his family part or all of the property, in land and slaves, of the offending unit, and a whole family might, if not put to death, be made into slaves. Further, succession disputes, particularly where succession failed, might be solved by the appointment to the headship of a house of an imperial nominee, who was very likely to be one of the imperial offspring. Another, and perhaps the most effective means of increasing the imperial domains was the creation of new units, whether families or corporations, and the allocation to them of lands and the labour for their cultivation. This was achieved by means of one of the most curious and interesting institutions of old Japan, the *minashiro* (namesake) or *mikoshiro* (succession) groups, which have already been mentioned but deserve some further description.

In Japan as elsewhere the idea of property in land was slow to develop. In an almost exclusively agricultural community, land without labour for its cultivation is not wealth, and we therefore find that the acquisition of land is nearly always bound up with the formation of a group to work upon it. Conversely even where a corporation (*be* or *tomo*) is primarily an industrial group, as of jewellers, mirror-makers, sword-makers and so on, the allocation of land is an essential of its formation, in order to furnish food for the specialist workers. Such groups were in fact self-supporting productive units, artificially created but continuing upon an hereditary basis. It must therefore be understood that the name of such a corporation as a Potters' Guild (*Hashibe*) or an Attendants' Guild (*Toneribe*) indicates not the occupation of all its members but the nature of the service which the corporation as a whole rendered to the clan, or other body to which it belonged.

Consequently the formation of a "namesake" or a "succession" group was little more than a convenient method of increasing the revenues of the crown without corresponding outlay. Therefore when the Emperor Seinei (Shiraga), "vexed that he had no children," established, in the provinces, *be* of archers, stewards and attendants named *Shiraga-be* after him, he was appropriating for the use of the reigning family not only their services but also the labour necessary for their maintenance. These were "succession groups." When the Emperor Yūryaku established an *Anaho-be* in memory of a deceased sovereign of that name, he was by this formation of a "namesake" group in effect raising funds for the crown by levying a local tax. It is an interesting commentary on the importance of family sentiment in Japanese life that such levies were made in the name of family tradition.

NOTES TO CHAPTER IV

[1] Page 63 ff. Early writings in Japan. The date given on page 63 for the compilation of the Kojiki, 682, is not strictly accurate, since it is the date when the Emperor Temmu ordered the compilation of records, but these certainly formed the basis of the Kojiki.

Perhaps I exaggerated the scarcity of written records and the slow progress of learning before 700. There is no doubt that the introduction of Buddhism greatly stimulated the use of writing in the seventh century, when the copying of sutras was undertaken with enthusiasm, and perhaps there was more recording of history than we suppose; but apart from the rather doubtful provincial records of 403 we know of very few important works produced before 700. There are Shōtoku Taishi's "Constitution" (604), certain commentaries upon the Buddhist scriptures of about the same date, and the Omi code of laws, promulgated in 666. These, together with a few brief documents and inscriptions on stone or bronze, are all that is known to have existed in the seventh century. Apart from them all the great literary monuments of early Japan are subsequent to 700—e.g., the *Kojiki* (712); the *Nihon-shoki* (720); the provincial gazetteers called *Fūdoki* of which the earliest is probably the *Harima Fūdoki* (? 708): the *Semmyō* or Imperial Edicts (recorded in the *Shoku Nihongi*, 794, though the first was probably compiled about 700); and the Shintō liturgies called *Norito* which one would expect to find in writing at a very early date but which are first recorded in the *Engishiki* in a form which can scarcely date back as far as 700. Some clue to this rather puzzling delay in the progress of learning is furnished by a study of the references to education appearing in the chronicles. Before the Taikwa reform there were private seminaries for young nobles, but there was no tuition on a large scale until the foundation of the University, which was part of the system of ministries and bureaux set up after the Taikwa reform. The first appointment as head of the University was that of a Korean priest in 647 and there may have been a few score of students in residence in the following decades but the institution evidently did not prosper since we are told in the chronicles of the Fujiwara family that during Temmu's reign (672-686) the country was so disturbed by civil strife and the "hundred families" were so occupied with political matters that they had no taste for study, and the lecture rooms were empty. It was not until the Taihō period, i.e. after 700, that the University began to flourish moderately and the treatment of professors and students was gradually improved.

[2] Page 70. Some idea of the progress of Buddhism can be gained from the fact that the 46 temples and monasteries of the year 624 had increased to 545 by the year 692.

[3] Page 71. Shōtoku Taishi's Constitution. Although this document is in its inspiration primarily Buddhist and Confucianist, it also shows evidence of other Chinese influences. The number of its articles, 17, is based upon certain mystical properties ascribed to the numbers 9 and 8 in Chinese magical lore, while the date chosen for its issue was selected for its auspicious position in the sexagenary cycle. In these and other

respects the form and content of the document seem to indicate that the Japanese of the period had not yet reached a discriminating knowledge of Chinese literature. It is interesting to note that in this short document there is evidence of acquaintance with the Odes, the Rites, the book of Filial Piety, the Analects, the Tso-chüan, the Han Chronicles, the anthology called Wên-hsüan, besides the works of Chwang-tzŭ and other classical Chinese writers.

Chapter V

CULTURAL RELATIONS WITH CHINA AND THE POLITICAL REFORM OF TAIKWA

THE Prince Shōtoku continued to encourage the spread of Buddhism by his personal activities. He lectured on the scriptures, in particular the Lotus (the *Saddharma-pandarika* sutra), encouraged the building of temples, the painting of holy pictures, the carving of holy images. Nor did he and his ministers neglect to promote secular learning. A stream of teachers of art and letters flowed from the continent to Japan, year after year envoys and students sailed to China to acquire knowledge at the T'ang capital or to sit at the feet of holy men in remote monasteries. The latter part of the reign of the Empress Suiko coincided with the opening years of the T'ang rule in China, and now once more Japan was to feel the influence of a culture superior to her own in power and depth and beauty. But this time it was not the indirect influence of an energetic, sprawling culture—such as characterised the Han—working at a distance across Korea, hesitatingly, through the almost furtive traffic of little chieftains, who could prize the material wealth of China but could only vaguely understand the strength that had produced her system of government, her bronzes, her pictures and her books, and what magic resided in them. At the opening of the seventh century China was in a better position to teach, and Japan to learn, than at the beginning of the Christian era. The Han culture in its abundant vitality might be envied and feared, but it could not be imitated. The civilisation that centred in the T'ang court was, for all its vigour, more regulated and systematised; it had an external form, manifested in its laws and its ceremonies and its arts, of which the elegances could be copied; it was itself in process of absorbing and digesting new elements, notably Buddhist faith and learning; and it had therefore a communicable touch of modernity. It is worth remembering, at the same time, that the T'ang period was a renaissance period. It was a spiritual return to the great days of the Han empire and it had the vigorous optimism of a renaissance, with all its creative energy and spread. From the point of view of the Japanese, contact with

China was easier than it had been for many centuries. Communications were better; they had now for over two hundred years been slowly acquiring knowledge of the indispensable medium, the Chinese language; and China itself, after protracted strife and confusion, entered after the Sui dynasty (589-617) upon a period of brilliance and luxury, described by one historian as the time of "la Chine joyeuse"—the T'ang dynasty (618-906).

So much of the later growth of Japan is to be traced to her borrowings from China under the T'ang dynasty that it is necessary to describe, as briefly as can be, conditions in China and Japan at this time. Politically China was at this moment perhaps the most powerful, the most advanced, and the best administered country in the world. Certainly in every material aspect of the life of a state she was overwhelmingly superior to Japan. The frontiers of her empire stretched to the borders of Persia, to the Caspian Sea, to the Altai mountains. She was in relations with the peoples of Annam, Cochin China, Tibet, the Tarim basin, and India; with the Turks, the Persians, and the Arabs. Men of many nations appeared at the court of China, bringing tribute and merchandise and new ideas that influenced her thought and her art. Persian and, more remotely, Greek influence is apparent in much of the sculpture and painting of the T'ang period. There had since the days of the Wei emperors been friendly intercourse between China and Persia, a Zoroastrian temple was erected in Ch'ang-an in 621, and not many years later a Persian king—a throneless king, it is true, the heir of the last of the Sassanids—died there as a refugee from the Arab conquerors of his kingdom. We need not discuss the extent of these various alien influences, we need only notice that their presence must have been a stimulus to invention and creation in many provinces of life, and at the same time remark that the bulk of China was so great, her strength so formidable, that they could easily be absorbed without disturbing the balance or the individuality of her own culture. Along the streets of Ch'ang-an there passed in those days Buddhist monks from India, envoys from Kashgar, Samarkand, Persia, Annam, Tonkin, Constantinople, chieftains of nomadic tribes from Siberian plains, officials and students from Korea and, in now increasing numbers, from Japan. It is easy to imagine the effect upon the eyes and

the minds of these last of a capital so rich in interest and excitement, their despair at the sight of such profusion, their proud
resolve to rival it, if industry and courage and restless ambition
could eke out their country's material shortcomings. No doubt
with that tireless curiosity and patient attention to detail which
characterised their study of other alien civilisations with which
they later came into contact—those of Portugal, of Holland, and
later of the industrialised Occident of the nineteenth century—the
Japanese set themselves to observe and report on every aspect of
Chinese life, and to consider what features they might profitably
adopt in their own country. First, in the political field, they
would notice that the T'ang sovereign was an absolute monarch
surrounded by able ministers, who were both scholars and statesmen, from whom he exacted and obtained obedience and loyal
service. The country was divided into administrative districts
under governors who were carefully selected for their capacity,
and constantly supervised by inspecting commissions. Officials
were selected and promoted for merit. Appointments were usually
limited to those who had passed examinations in the classics, and
this test, though it might exclude certain useful types of vigour
and ability, had the inestimable advantage that it set learning
above warfare and gifts above family. The career was open to the
talents; circumscribed talents no doubt, but none the less society
was established on an intellectual basis, and to have even attempted to form an aristocracy of brains is a stupendous achievement.
So the Japanese travellers saw, and perhaps understood in some
measure, a centralised, organised state, a vast but united empire,
with a great regular army, victorious against all its enemies
except—and this must have afforded them some hope and consolation—the Koreans, who more than once repulsed Chinese
invasions on a grand scale, notably in 646. The Japanese, then,
could not fail to be impressed by the sheer power of China, and
they must have been soon convinced that it was due principally
to her system of government, which was in almost all essentials
the exact opposite to their own aristocratic, caste-ridden tribal
institutions.

Less apparent, but equally impressive to the seekers of knowledge, was the prodigious activity of China in the intellectual

sphere. Not only were there important developments of Buddhism under the Sui and the T'ang, but other faiths became known in China through her contact with surrounding peoples. Converts were made to Tantrism, Manichæism, Nestorianism, and amidst the Chinese, if not by them, there were practised Islam and Zoroastrianism. These new religions, moreover, stimulated a revival of the ancient national cult, which is known as Confucianism, though Confucius himself was rather its annalist and codifier than its founder. A new edition of the canonical works was compiled early in the seventh century, with the standard commentaries but a new gloss which was a reinterpretation of the traditional cult in the light of competing modern doctrines. The first T'ang emperor, announcing that the teaching of the sages was what air is to birds and water to fish, surrounded himself with scholars, remodelled and enlarged the imperial academy, increased its students to 3,000, and reformed the provincial seats of learning. Much might be said of the vanity, the jealousies and the squabbles of the *literati* of this time; but for all that it was an age of intellectual ferment, of spiritual fervour, and of artistic excitement. Already there existed a long tradition of architecture and carving, of tombs and palaces and memorial avenues dating from the Han; of Buddhist temples, dating from the Wei and Ts'in. Now to this was added the delicate skill of T'ang sculpture and drawing, with which there was compounded a new emotional element furnished by the tender and refining influences of Buddhist thought as it had by then developed. The offspring of this marriage between craftsmanship in its prime and inspiration in the freshness of youth could not fail to be of surpassing beauty. So the carvings on the great T'ang emperor's mausoleum excel in grace the Han reliefs, though perhaps lacking their vitality; the lovely clay figures of horses and riders, dancers and singers, deposited in tombs with the dead, have a lyrical charm which is of their very essence; the Buddhist images, in metal or stone or wood, have moving qualities of dignity and truth as great as those of any Greek masterpieces, for though they speak another language they say perfectly the same things. It would be too much of a digression to go on to speak of the paintings, the bronzes, the pottery, the coloured silks, the poems and the fine calligraphies. It is enough to say that all these arts were blossoming in profusion when the first Japanese missions found themselves in the T'ang capital. And what perhaps impressed them more than the quality of Chinese culture was its heroic dimensions. Nothing but was on a grand, a stupendous scale. When the Sui emperor builds a capital, two million men are set to work. His fleet of pleasure boats on the Yellow River is towed by eighty thousand men. His caravan when he makes an Imperial Progress is three hundred miles long. His concubines number three thousand. And when he orders the compilation of an anthology, it must have seventeen thousand chapters. Even making allowance for the courtly arithmetic of official historians, these are enormous undertakings; and though the first T'ang emperors were rather less immoderate, they did nothing that was not huge or magnificent. To the Japanese it must have been staggering.

The first official envoy to the Chinese court representing the whole of Japan appears to have been one Ono no Imoko. He left Japan in 607, with an interpreter named Kuratsukuri (probably of Chinese descent), passed along the coast of Paikché, and in the autumn reached the then capital of China, Lo-yang, where he presented a letter from his sovereign. The opening words were "The Emperor of the sunrise country writes to the Emperor of the sunset country." The Sui emperor was annoyed at being thus addressed as an equal, and is said to have refused to accept the letter, observing that the barbarian memorial was insulting and could not be listened to. However, the trouble was somehow got over, for Ono returned in the following year, accompanying two envoys from the Sui court, who were received in Japan with great ceremony. The letters which they brought were couched in the language usually held by the Chinese towards foreign states. Japan was treated as a vassal. But on the whole Ono's mission was successful, for he had brought the two countries into official relations, amd had obtained a number of books, thus achieving the main objects for which Shōtoku Taishi had despatched him. Unfortunately, on his return he was, he said, robbed of his letters at Paikché; but as his Chinese companions brought their letters through in safety, it is probable that Ono himself destroyed the haughty message, which he thought would cause trouble at home.

Late in 608 the Chinese envoys left, again accompanied by Ono,
who carried a letter said to have been written by Shōtoku Taishi
in his own hand. With Ono there travelled a number of scholars
chosen by the prince for study abroad. It is interesting to record
their names, for they were pioneers in an important task, and
some of them played an important part in Japan upon their
return. They were, Fukuin, probably a priest; Emyō, Nara no
Wosa, an official interpreter; Kuromaro, Takamuku no Ayabito;
Okuni Imaki no Ayabito; and Nichibun, Shōan, Eon and Kōsai,
four student priests. To judge from these names and titles they
were all naturalised Koreans or Chinese, or of Korean or Chinese
descent.

Shōtoku Taishi died in 621, his task of reform uncompleted.
After the Sui dynasty fell in 618, to be replaced by the T'ang,
Japanese envoys and students reported that the government under
the new monarchy was highly organised, and that much more
was to be learned from China than the rudiments which they had
so far acquired. There is no record of a new mission until 630,
but students were regularly returning to Japan in the intervening
period, and there were no doubt constant goings and comings
which are not noticed in the chronicles because they had no
official character. Official embassies, indeed, seem to have been
rather infrequent, for no more than twelve are recorded in the
period from 630 to 837. These, however, were carried out on an
imposing scale. The envoys and their staffs were selected with
great care for their rank or their learning, and the *Shoku Nihongi*
(an official chronicle covering the years 700-790) records with
satisfaction that the T'ang officials were favourably impressed by
the dignity and sincerity of Awata no Mabito, leader of one of
the early missions, and were encouraged to think well of the
country which he represented. The missions were composed of a
leader; two or three subordinate envoys; secretaries; specialists,
such as interpreters, doctors, diviners; artists and craftsmen, such
as carpenters, smiths, founders; and of course seamen and pilots.
Their numbers all told varied from one hundred to two hundred
and tended to increase as time went on. In the early part of the
eighth century as many as four ships used to sail together, each
carrying about one hundred and fifty, so that at least five hundred

persons must have been despatched on such occasions. Various routes were taken. The ships started from Naniwa, the present Ōsaka; went through the Inland Sea; and then either passed along the Korean coast and entered harbours in the Shantung peninsula, or, as knowledge of navigation increased, boldly sailed westward to the mouth of the Yangtse. The voyage was no light undertaking. The travellers might be driven on to the then hostile shores of Silla, or their little ships swallowed up by the China Sea in one of the typhoons that sweep over it in summer and autumn. Not one party that took the southern route escaped some damage, and they were lucky if not more than one of their ships was driven ashore and wrecked. There are records of many of these hazardous journeys, one of which may be recounted here as an example. A mission returning from China, bringing with them Chinese envoys, set sail in four ships from the mouth of the Yangtse. In a storm the Chinese leader and some twenty-five of his party were washed overboard from one ship and drowned, as were one of the Japanese envoys and some forty of his followers. A day or two later the mast snapped and the ship broke into two pieces, both of which fortunately floated and were washed ashore at different points on the coasts of Kyūshū, with about fifty survivors on each. The second ship reached the shores of Satsuma in a battered condition nine days after sailing. The third ran aground in the Yangtse estuary, but was hauled off, and found a haven in Kyūshū after a voyage that lasted over forty days. The fourth was wrecked on Quelpart Island and her company made captives by the islanders, but a few of them managed to escape and got back to Japan after further and protracted maritime perils. All this was as late as 778, when shipbuilding had made some progress, so that sea travel in the early part of the seventh century, when the first missionaries crossed over, must have been a perilous adventure. There are many traces in contemporary literature of the anxiety with which the travellers and their friends regarded these enterprises. Young men were selected who must practise asceticism and, thus purified, pray constantly for the safety of the envoys during their voyage; and in temples throughout the country appropriate sutras were recited, to placate the anger of the sea gods; and sometimes special messengers were sent by the court to plead with the deities of the great national shrines and urge them to protect the travellers. If they returned safely, there were great banquets and services of thanksgiving.

Though the formal purpose of the missions was to exchange compliments between the two courts, their most important object was to obtain new knowledge; and therefore each party included a number of scholars who remained in China to pursue their special studies. Some stayed for long periods, and some indeed never returned. The pioneers were Takamuku and Bin, who went with the mission of 607; but perhaps the most celebrated was Kibi no Mabi, who left Japan in 717, at the age of twenty-two, and came back after a sojourn of seventeen years, with a great store of knowledge and books on many subjects. He was made head of the University at Nara on his return, and lectured to the Court on the Book of Rites and in general upon the Chinese classics. He was later sent to China as an envoy, and at his death was an important minister of state. To him and his hardly less distinguished colleagues is due the credit of spreading in Japan a knowledge of the Chinese system of government and the fundamentals of Chinese philosophy and art. Not less important than the lay scholars were the student priests vho were sent to study under celebrated teachers in China. The records give the names of over seventy of them, from Eon in 608 to Kwan-Kan in 877. Some stayed one year, some ten, some twenty, some thirty; some died in China; some lost their lives at sea on the way home. There must have of course been many more than those of whom we have a record, for there was frequent communication with China by merchant vessels as well as by the ships which carried official envoys and students.

These scholars, then, these priests, artists and craftsmen, brought back to Japan the knowledge and the material objects by which their country was to take over, and fashion to her own requirements, a superior culture. The process was obviously a defective one, because it operated at a distance, with little personal contact. Not very far in miles, China was separated from Japan by great differences of race, language and custom. For most Japanese, a knowledge of China, Chinese institutions and Chinese thought was to be obtained only at second or third hand, passing at one stage through the medium of an alien language. It is therefore to be expected that in its transit it would be diluted, if not distorted, and that what would reach Japan would be the forms rather than the essence. In studying the history of the seventh century in particular, one is constantly struck by this feature, as one is at the same time struck by the artistic development of Japan, which was as rapid and real as the political and social changes were slow and superficial. Not that this difference is to be wondered at, for the Japanese could see before their eyes the ravishing loveliness of statues and paintings brought from the continent or created in their midst by Chinese and Korean masters. The other gifts which China had to offer were intangible or invisible, and tainted with human fallibility. You might be breathless with adoration before a serene and faultless golden Buddha, but you could dislike or criticise the Chinese way of thought and the Chinese principles of government, the more so if they ran counter to your vested interests. Splendour and beauty are easier to accept than the austerities of reform, and the consolations of philosophy are more welcome than its discipline.

Let us, in order to understand this aspect of the adoption of a new culture, trace the successive steps by which the Japanese modified their administrative system on Chinese lines. It is significant that one of the first measures was the formation of a court hierarchy based on official ranks, distinguished by titles and costumes according to Chinese practice. In 605, under the regency of Shōtoku Taishi, twelve grades of rank were established, named after six virtues, subdivided into greater and smaller, each "virtue" being distinguished by a cap of a prescribed colour. Thus a man might be given the rank of Lesser Benevolence, and would on official occasions wear a cap of the appropriate colour, in this case blue. Junior to him would be the wearer of the red cap of Greater Righteousness, because the virtues were arranged in an arbitrary order of merit. The importance attached to these ranks and insignia can be gauged from the frequency with which they were revised by solemn edicts. In 647 and again in 649 the numbers and names of the ranks were altered, and the colours of the caps changed. In 664 the number of grades was increased to twenty-six and further changes made in the colours of the caps.

In 685 cap grades were abolished, forty-eight new grades were fixed, distinguished now by the colours of the robes. Minor changes were introduced in 691, and in 702 the cap grades restored, with new appellations. Finally in the period Yōrō (717-723) a new system was introduced, which, as it has persisted until to-day with little change, had better be described. The ranks were in numerical order, the first being the highest; and each rank was divided into two classes, senior and junior. The highest rank was therefore the senior class of the first rank, and the lowest (apart from certain special categories for minor officials) was the junior class of the eighth rank. At times some of the middle classes were further subdivided so that you might have, say, both upper and lower grades of the senior class of the fifth rank. The Yōrō institutes provided for twenty-eight grades in all; and, further, the ranks below the fifth were of two sorts, inner and outer, the former being reserved for people domiciled in or near the capital, the latter for provincial notables.

These details may appear to be insignificant, but they deserve attention because they show how much rank was esteemed, how great was the distinction between the society of the court and the rural communities outside. Here is the little crack, the beginning of the line of cleavage, which later grew into a great fissure dividing the capital from the country at large and resulting in the collapse of the imperial power and the rise of great territorial magnates. It must be remembered, too, that the cap grades and court ranks were not empty honours. They carried with them emoluments in the form of grants from the court, whether of land or produce. They had an economic significance.

In the year 640 there returned to Japan, after a sojourn of over thirty years in China, the lay student Kuromaro Takamuku no Ayabito; and with him, or shortly before, there had returned the Buddhist priest Bin. When they had set forth from Japan the Crown Prince Shōtoku had just begun his programme of reform, but during their absence the strife of great families had shelved all other occupations. The Great Omi, Soga no Umako, had not during the Prince's life-time attempted to interfere with administration, and had even joined with him in studying Buddhist sutras and Chinese classics and compiling historical records.

Perhaps Umako was satisfied with the power which he could exercise indirectly, for he was the chief of chieftains and the uncle of the empress, so that his interests, if not identical, were parallel with those of the imperial house. It is pretty certain that his predatory tendencies were restrained by the commanding character of the Prince, who was a man of great gifts and noble nature. Freed from restraint by the Prince's death in 621, Umako began to show his teeth, in efforts to add to his wealth and power at the expense of the throne. He died in 626, however, and was succeeded as Great Omi by his son, Soga Yemishi, whose conduct was even more turbulent. He, and later his son Iruka, decided questions of succession to the throne, arbitrarily made and deposed rulers, and did not stop at murder to gain their ends. In 642 Yemishi showed clearly that he was aiming at imperial power. He set up his own ancestral temple; levied forced labour from the guilds and corporations to build for himself and his son great tombs such as were reserved for members of the reigning family; and gave a purple cap to his son, thus usurping the imperial prerogative of bestowing rank and office. His sons and daughters were called princes and princesses, and lived in palaces which were fortified, moated and guarded by soldiers. He made it his policy to conciliate and use the alien groups in the population, both the Chinese and Korean settlers, who could help him with their knowledge and their craftsmanship, and the half-tamed bellicose tribesmen, Ainu from the north-east, Kumaso from the south-west, whose ferocity made them an admirable bodyguard. Clearly there was at this period in Japan no settled administration and no racial homogeneity. The times were apt for rebellious disorder; the central government's power extended very few days' journey from the capital, and even there it was flouted and challenged by greedy and ambitious nobles. Chaos was near; and only a new principle, enforced by a strong hand, could reconcile all these warring elements.

In the quarrel over the introduction of Buddhism, more than half a century before, the Soga had overthrown both the Mononobe and the Nakatomi clans. The Mononobe were virtually extirpated, but the Nakatomi merely withdrew into the background. Their chieftains were the hereditary chief priests of the

Shintō religion, but with Buddhism growing in favour, this office had lost its prestige; and when under the Soga ascendancy the head of the Nakatomi house was pressed to take up his duties, he refused, and went to live in retirement. This was Nakatomi no Kamatari, one of the greatest figures in Japanese history. In his leisure he "took in his hands yellow rolls," which means that he devoted himself to the study of the doctrines of the Chinese sages. After a careful estimate of the character of various imperial princes, he made friends with Prince Naka no Ōye, with whom he plotted the downfall of the Soga. Iruka was assassinated by a mean stratagem, in the presence of the empress; and within a few days Yemishi and a number of Soga leaders were killed. The Soga had gone too far and too fast, so that, when the moment came, the families which had hitherto rendered them unwilling obedience now ranged themselves on the side of Kamatari and the Prince Naka no Ōye. The Soga fortresses were burnt, and the empress—a Soga nominee—was made to abdicate, and was suc-ceeded (645) by her younger brother, the Emperor Kōtoku, who was a devout Buddhist and "despised the way of the gods." Prince Naka no Ōye was nominated heir-apparent. Two fathers of im-perial consorts, a Soga and an Abé, were appointed to high office, but they served under Kamatari, who was now the supreme power in the state and was granted great wealth and honours.

In this bald narrative of the overthrow of the Soga are com-pressed a number of features characteristic of Japan in those days, and prophetic of much that is peculiar in her later political development. Kamatari's study of the doctrine of Confucius and his paragon the Duke of Chou typifies the influence upon Japanese thought of Chinese conceptions of monarchy. His bloody dispute with the Soga shows how far removed were actual conditions in Japan from the Chinese ideal of a sovereign ruling by virtue and served by a loyal hierarchy of officials. The new emperor's con-tempt for the native religion shows how firm a hold had been obtained by Buddhism over the minds of the ruling classes, for to despise the gods of Japan was to reject the theory upon which their own prestige was founded. The abdication of the empress was the first of a long series of surrenders of the throne, more or less voluntary. The choice as her successor of an easy-going

devotee, advised by great ministers with only the outward semb-
lance of authority, is an excellent example of the practice, from
which during the next thousand years there was hardly any
departure, of government from behind the scenes. All honour,
all reverence, were given to the empress; all initiative, all power,
was in the hands of Kamatari. So it continued, until the restoration of 1868. Always behind the nominal ruler was a regent or a
counsellor or a prompter, who ruled in fact, but never claimed
the titles of supremacy. It is true that in all countries and in
most careers there is one who wears the honours and another who
carries the burden, but the history of Japanese institutions—not
only the institution of monarchy—presents this feature in its
extremest degree. The mere usurpation by Kamatari of the power
of the Soga was clearly not sufficient, since, without some radical
change in the system of government, it could only end in further
strife for supremacy among the clans. It would be Soga yesterday, Nakatomi to-day, and another great house to-morrow.
It had by now become quite clear that the only safe policy was to
break the power of the clans, and the best method was to con-
centrate authority in the throne, to convert the political system of
Japan from an uneasy confederation of tribes into a centralised
bureaucratic state on the Chinese model.

In 645 the returned students Takamuku Kuromaro and the
priest Bin were given the rank of Kunihakasé, "national doctor,"
and it was no doubt these two who advised and instructed
Kamatari as to Chinese methods. Apart from some minor inno-
vations, the first positive step of an important nature was the
nomination of governors of the eastern provinces. They were
appointed to rule those provinces in the name of the emperor; to
examine the titles of the territorial magnates to the lands and
powers which they claimed; and they were to disarm all individuals and store their weapons in government armouries. Somewhat distant provinces were, on the whole, a suitable ground for
this experiment, for there it could be tried without arousing the
opposition of the great families nearer home. After some further
preparatory measures of this nature, in the first month of 646,
before the pleasant excitement of the new year's festivities had
died down, the emperor issued an edict of four short articles

which, if it were enforced, would completely change the political and economic fabric of Japan. We shall see that, in the result, the reform was not so radical as the text required, nor so beneficial as the underlying theory presupposed. But it did produce new and important results. The terms of this edict (which gave to the period 645-650 the name of Taikwa, or Great Reform) may be summarised as follows:—

I. The "namesake" and "succession" groups (*minashiro* and *mikoshiro*) are abolished, and the various local magnates are deprived of the manors and serfs which they had appropriated to themselves.

II. Governors are appointed to the home provinces and to the "outer" provinces. A regular arrangement of roads, ferries, barriers, and post-horses is to be developed; travel is to be made safe by guards and watchmen; and the capital is to be "regulated" with a full system of municipal government.

The home provinces are to be divided into rural districts, of so many townships, and each district is to be under the authority of a district governor, chosen from among the local gentry ("country rulers") and assisted by clerks with a good knowledge of writing and arithmetic.

III. Registers of population are to be drawn up, account books to be kept, and the allotment of land to be regularised. Rural government is to be on a basis of townships of 50 houses, under the superintendence of a headman responsible for the cultivation of crops, the maintenance of order, and the levy of taxes in kind and in labour. The units of area of allotment of land and the rates of land tax are specified.

IV. The old taxes and forced labour are abolished and a new system of commuted taxes introduced, by which silk and other textiles, or other commodities locally produced, are payable in fixed amounts in lieu of labour. Contributions are to be made, in a fixed ratio to the number of houses, of post horses, weapons, and manual labour on behalf of officials, with permission in certain cases to supply rice instead of labour.

It will be seen at a glance that the enforcement of these articles meant the introduction of a new system of land tenure, a new system of local government, and a new system of taxation. Each several item involved, in theory, the transfer to a central power of rights of ownership and jurisdiction which had been held by the territorial gentry. It was an application to Japan of the system then in operation in the T'ang empire. Obviously if such a paper scheme were to be applied to Japan, where social and even topographical conditions were so different from those of China, it would need great modification, or it would collapse. And collapse it did, as we shall see, despite frequent revisions.

Before describing the results of the Taikwa reform edict, it will be as well to comment upon it briefly so as to make clear its import. With regard to land tenure, it was naturally too dangerous for the reformers to deprive influential people of their land or their power without offering them a substitute. The more powerful heads of families and groups were therefore given official posts or official rank, and emoluments to suit their standing. In most cases it is clear, though the records do not specifically say so, that important chieftains and landowners were confirmed in their possessions, but they now held them in theory as grants from the throne. These grants were known as "sustenance fiefs," a term which will be explained presently. An additional sop to those who might feel themselves injured by the new system was the grant of court ranks, which, if we may judge from subsequent Japanese history, were highly prized.

The second article of the edict, by providing for the appointment of governors in all provinces, deprived many territorial magnates of their autonomy; but here again the reformers took care to leave undisturbed as far as possible the most influential chieftains and group leaders. The difference was that they now derived their authority in theory from the imperial government. The provision of roads and ferries and a post service was essential if the central authority was to keep in touch with its provincial representatives. Communications at this period in Japan were extremely inadequate. The country is mountainous, yet there were no good public roads, no canals, hardly any bridges. Travel between the capital and distant provinces was difficult and dangerous, for, quite apart from the lack of facilities, the remoter districts were infested with bandits and pirates, or at best inhabited by settlers who were so hard to reach that they could defy tax collectors and other officials. Consequently, unless the roads were improved and policed, to convey messages from the capital to local officials was a long and risky business, and—even more important to the growing urban population—the transport of produce to the government granaries and storehouses was slow, laborious, and expensive. It must be remembered that, until the introduction of metallic currency, all taxes had to be delivered in kind. The third and fourth articles of the edict both deal with taxes. Their main object was to introduce a uniform system of taxation, and at the same time, by means of detailed registers of population and land, to assess the capacity of each district and to ensure, as far as possible, that the local magnates did not divert to their own uses the imperial share of its produce. In short, the prime purpose of all four edicts was a redistribution of economic, rather than of political power, in favour of the central government. It is, of course, difficult to dissociate the two; but there are very strong indications that the court party as a whole was more concerned with drawing wealth from the provinces than with diminishing the autonomy of great landowners in districts to it remote and barbarous.

It is necessary now to describe in outline the system of land tenure and taxation in Japan in the period following the Taikwa reform. Their earlier history, which is chaotic and obscure, need not detain us, but without some knowledge of economic conditions from the seventh century onwards it is difficult to gain an idea of social conditions in general.

The official chronicles repeatedly cite the Chinese doctrine, "Under the heavens there is no land which is not the king's land. Among holders of land there is none who is not the king's vassal.' Even in China this theory of eminent domain was not always followed, and in Japan its practical application was strictly limited. It was of course a doctrine which the reigning house did their best to inculcate, but they were only one among many land-hungry clans. We have just noticed that, when in 646 the system of territorial rulers was replaced by a system of provincial governors, it was of course necessary, if the reform was not to come to grief, to conciliate the magnates by giving them court ranks and titles in compensation for their dignity as local chieftains. It was partly for this reason that the court paid so much attention to apparently trivial matters like the nomenclature of grades and the colours of ceremonial robes. They had to do all they could to bring the new honours into esteem. Nor would the landowners object to the theory of eminent domain so long as their property did not effectively pass to the throne; and as we have seen, though there was a change in their title to the land, they were as a rule confirmed in their tenure. The chief object of the reform must therefore be to systematise the holding of land by the actual cultivators, and to leave the apportionment of its produce to be dealt with gradually. As the central government increased in power, it hoped to find ways to obtain an increasing share. So, one of the first measures of the Taikwa reform was the promulgation of a system of land allotment, by which arable fields—chiefly wet rice-fields—were distributed among cultivators, their extent being based upon the number of members of a household. These fields were called *ku-bun-den*, which means literally "mouth-share fields." Since the number of "mouths" would vary from time to time, some method of census was entailed. The system of registration was developed to a high pitch of accuracy and detail, for the very good reason that it was the only check upon the taxes derived from the peasantry. Without these records—and even with them, as later events proved—it was impossible to prevent not only evasion by the taxpayers but embezzlement by the provincial and district officials.

The taxes payable by the cultivators were of three main types, as follows:—

1. The land tax (*so*), which was paid in rice, and may be regarded as land rent levied by the state upon the allotment holder, since it was assessed upon the normal yield of a unit of area.

2. The labour tax, which was levied by the state upon individuals, irrespective of their land, and was payable either in actual labour (*yō-eki*, corvée) or in produce (*yō*) at a fixed rate of commutation.

3. The produce tax (*chō*), which was a levy on the output of the individual in respect of commodities other than rice.

It was payable in silk or other articles, according to the locality.

For the assessment and levy of these taxes, it was necessary to keep registers both of land and of population: the land registers to show what land had been allotted and what land rent was due, the population registers to show which persons were taxable and which were exempt. Fragments of such registers in use not long after the Taikwa reform have been preserved in the imperial repository known as the Shōsōin, and the reproduction of parts of these will give a better idea of the working of the systems of land tenure and taxation than a long description. The following is an extract from a register dated 702, and refers to a village in Kyūshū which was probably part of the glebe lands of the great Tōdaiji temple at Nara. The head of the house, to judge from his name, was descended from a member of the ancient corporation of diviners:

	Name.	*Age.*	*Category.*	*Remarks.*
Head of the House	Urabe Nomoso	49	Able-bodied male, full age	Taxable household.
Mother	Kayabe Ishi-me	74	Female, over age	
Wife	Urabe Hoshito-me	47	Female, full age	
Son	Urabe Kuromaro	19	Able-bodied male, under age	Eldest son, by wife
Son	Urabe Wakashi	6	Male child	Younger son by wife
Daughter	Urabe Kagora-me	16	Female child	Daughter by wife
Daughter	Urabe Kokagora-me	13	Ditto	Ditto
Brother	Urabe Katana	46	Able-bodied male, full age	
Wife	Nakatomibe Hitame-me	37	Female, full age	
Son	Urabe Kuro	17	Able-bodied male, under age	Son, by wife
Son	Urabe Akai	16	Male child	
Son	Urabe Okoji	2	Infant	
Daughter	Urabe Hisudzu-me	18	Female, under age	
Daughter	Urabe Aka-me	13	Female child	
Daughter	Urabe Hitsuji-me	9	Ditto	
Daughter	Urabe Maro-me	1	Infant	
	In all 16 mouths of which		Exempt .. 12 Taxable .. 4	

Here we have a household of 16 persons, counted as "mouths"

for the purpose of allotting land. The details of age and sex are necessary for assessment purposes, since the amount of land allotted is greater for men than for women, while women and minors are not liable to the labour tax or the produce tax.

Both land tax and allotment varied from time to time and from place to place, but at the period of the register from which we have quoted the area was two *tan* (1 *tan* is 1,000 square yards) for a male and two-thirds of that amount for a female. The allotment, once made, held good for five years, and was in theory revised in the sixth. The land tax alone was not a heavy burden. It ranged from fifteen sheaves of rice per *chō* (10 *tan*) in the "outer" provinces to twenty-two sheaves per *chō* in the home provinces, the lower rate being in compensation for the higher cost of transport. The average land tax was thus from 3 to 5 per cent of the total crop in a normal year. Further, considerable abatements were allowed on various scores, such as poverty of the soil or a diminished yield. Certain ricefields were entirely exempt from land tax, in particular those in the possession of shrines and temples, those granted to officials by way of salary, and those cultivated by serfs on government account. It was the increase, legitimate and illegitimate, of these exempt fields which in the succeeding centuries broke down the whole system of land tenure, and, in combination with other tendencies, brought about a feudal régime.

The remaining taxes differed from the land tax in that they were pure exactions, for which the tax-payer obtained no benefit in the form of land, goods, or services. They were payable in textiles, which served as the currency of the time, though certain districts were allowed to substitute their own special products, such as fish from coastal provinces or timber from mountain lands. The labour tax and the produce tax were in principle levied in respect of all able-bodied males, and were graded according to their capacity. Thus the maximum tax was required from males of between 21 and 60 years of age; half the amount from males between 60 and 65; and one quarter from males between 17 and 21. There was partial exemption for those partially incapacitated by disease or infirmity, and total exemption for total incapacity or age over 65. In addition there was partial or com-

plete exemption for persons of many categories, such as members of
the imperial family; men holding rank of the eighth class and
above; members of certain professions and trades like doctors and
scribes, or smiths and carpenters; and those whose occupations
were in the nature of conscripted labour, like soldiers, postboys,
office servants, or porters. The categories and numbers of exempted persons tended constantly to increase, as did the types of land
exempted from land tax, so that the burden upon the remainder
grew more and more oppressive. Moreover, the erection of government buildings in the capital, and to a less extent in the provinces,
the making of roads, and public works in general, augmented the
call upon able-bodied men for the corvée, and thus lessened their
agricultural output. Further, certain supplementary imposts were
levied from time to time, to the distress of the smallholders. There
was a levy of millet, to be stored in local granaries as a provision
against famine, and there were forced loans of seed rice by the
government to farmers, which had to be repaid at harvest with
interest at 30 and even 50 per cent. Military service was one of the
forms of forced labour, but it was particularly onerous, and much
dreaded by the small families. In contemporary memorials there
appear such phrases as "The wretchedness of a soldier is not different from that of a slave. When one man is called up one household
perishes," and "of all forms of forced labour that of a soldier is
most bitter." Where a man could commute his labour by the payment of the labour tax in kind, he could remain at home and
cultivate his fields, leaving his women to reel and weave the silk;
but a soldier had to serve one year as a frontier guard, and three
years as a guard of some palace or official mansion, supplying his
own food, his own weapons, and travelling to his post at his own
expense. The richer households made every effort to avoid con-
scription, by commutation or by paid substitution, and the natural
result was that the soldiers were recruited from the lowest and most
poverty-stricken class. Often boys of 16 were sent as soldiers, so
that their families might obtain the abatement of tax for a full-
grown man whom he replaced and who remained at work on the
land.

It will be clear from the above description that taxation and
the corvée bore with the greatest severity on those who were

least able to endure them. Poverty was heavily taxed, wealth got off lightly, and the disparity was naturally emphasised by the progress of time. It is not to be wondered at, therefore, that the people made every effort to evade taxation. Contemporary documents show that false information was given to registrars, the number of male adults concealed, and claims for exemption multiplied on all possible grounds. Men absconded to distant frontiers to avoid the levies, and those who were left presented as taxes articles of the worst possible quality. One official despatch from a provincial official to the court complains that "the silk brought as tax is not like silk, but resembles a spider's web in autumn." It is true that this refers to a period considerably later than the Taikwa reform, but there is no doubt that abuses of the new system crept in very soon after its inception.

Despite constant efforts to enforce it, and frequent revisions, it proved a failure, chiefly because it was too close a copy of the Chinese system. The Chinese system was based on what may be roughly described as a theory of agricultural communism. Its aim was to distribute land equally among the population, so as to get the maximum returns from the productive capacity of each cultivator while ensuring his own sustenance, and though it probably was schematic rather than practical, it seems to have worked in some fashion. It had its origin in a very ancient rule by which communal fields were divided into nine squares, and the produce of one square was reserved for the state.[1] After successive revisions and additions through the centuries, it was embodied in codified land laws under the Sui and T'ang emperors. It was these laws which formed the basis of the system of landownership and taxation instituted by the Taikwa reformers. The Japanese evidently in this instance copied the Chinese too closely, for conditions in the two countries were so dissimilar that what applied in China was inappropriate to Japan. In China there were great level tracts of dry fields, in Japan tracts of wet rice-fields, interspersed with dry fields and broken by hilly country. Society in China was acquisitive, but it had an equalitarian trend and a feeling for uniformity and schematic arrangement, while the prevailing sentiment of Japan was aristocratic. She had not yet outgrown the slave economy, there was not complete homogeneity in the racial and cultural elements in her population, nor had she, like China, a long tradition of bureaucratic government. It is not surprising, therefore, that her experiment of borrowing a foreign system of land tenure and taxation was a failure, despite constant struggles to modify and adapt it as its defects emerged in the succeeding centuries. Since she was, and for more than a thousand years remained, an agricultural state, this means that the application of the Chinese system hastened, if it did not cause, a complete economic collapse. In that respect the imitation of a foreign model was disastrous to Japan.

Having surveyed the economic basis of Japan in the seventh and early eighth centuries, we may now turn to the political aspects of the reform. The first steps had been taken by the institution of cap ranks, and the appointment of provincial and district officials. It was now necessary to reorganise the central government. We have no account of the stages of this work, though we know that schemes were drawn up by Takumuku and Bin in the light of their knowledge of Chinese practice. In 702, however, there was promulgated a code, called the Code of Taihō, or Great Treasure (this being the name given to the era 701-704), by which the machinery of administration was set up. The supreme organ of government was the Dajō-kwan, or Great Council of State. Of equal rank was the Jingi-kwan, or Department of Religion, a kind of ecclesiastical commission which controlled affairs pertaining to the national cult, such as its festivals and ceremonies, the treatment and discipline of the wardens and other attendants of shrines. Under the great Council of State, which was presided over by the Chancellor, supported by two ministers of state, the Minister of the Left and the Minister of the Right, were placed eight boards or ministries as follows:

The Ministry of the Central Office (Nakatsukasa).
The Ministry of Ceremonies (Shikibushō).
The Ministry of Civil Affairs (Jibushō).
The Ministry of Popular Affairs (Minbushō).
The Ministry of War (Hyōbushō).
The Ministry of Justice (Gyōbushō).
The National Treasury (Ōkurashō).
The Ministry of the Imperial Household (Kunaishō).

We need not stop to describe their separate functions in detail, but it is as well to remark that the most important ministries, those with the highest prestige, were those which dealt with the affairs of the emperor and his courtiers, namely the Ministry of the Imperial Household, the Ministry of Ceremonies, the Ministry of Civil Affairs, and the Treasury of the Imperial Household. The remaining four departments, dealing with public finance, public works, agriculture, commerce and defence, were inferior in importance. In other words, the strong departments were those which looked after the affairs of the court aristocracy, the weak departments were those which were charged with the interests of the people. It would have been better for Japan if the reformers had copied the Chinese administrative system as closely as they copied her land tenure and her taxation. Unfortunately, they neglected to take over—perhaps they failed to perceive—the one feature which gave the Chinese system its strength and stability. There was in China a rigid class division, composed, in ascending order, of merchants, craftsmen, farmers and gentlemen. It was the business of the first three classes to keep to their vocations, and to produce goods for the consumption of their rulers. But the ruling caste was not an aristocracy of birth, it was an aristocracy of learning. Every official must have proved his worth in the examination cells, and all posts in the administrative career were open to the scholar, irrespective of his lineage.[2] The curriculum of the schools was severely classical, to our modern view cold and arid; but it provided an intense if narrow mental discipline, and it raised knowledge to the zenith of esteem. When the Japanese adopted Chinese administrative methods, which by the time of the T'ang rulers had developed to a high pitch of efficiency, they borrowed the forms and the terminology, but not the underlying principles. The constitution of society in Japan was now perhaps even more aristocratic than it had ever been, for the creation of new offices merely gave to the privileged classes new powers and more prestige. It is hardly too much to say that the new system merely perpetuated under other names, and often emphasised, the abuses of the old.

We have seen that, when in 646 the territorial nobility were deprived of their autonomy, they were given rank or office in compensation. Both court rank and official functions carried with them emoluments, in the higher grades revenues from land, in the lower grades payments in produce. All were immune from taxation, and the position of many gave them welcome opportunities for making illicit profits. There was therefore hot rivalry for posts at court, where promotion might come quickly, through your family connections or, in the dilettante society that soon developed, your skill with the brush, your memory for an apt citation, or indeed your amorous prowess. It followed that provincial appointments were not at first relished, and those who took them were often courtiers in disgrace or men who meant to profit financially by their term of exile. This they could not do—for they were poorly paid—unless they practised extortion upon the peasantry by embezzling taxes, or cheated the throne by incorporating public land in their estates. Here we have the most vital weakness of the system of provincial administration, and consequently of the whole system of government, for its stability depended upon a just apportionment of wealth between the producers and the state. What actually happened was that, with a growing non-productive population, the claims upon the producers increased, the share of the throne became relatively less, and a number of landholders, great and small, throve at the expense of the oppressed peasantry. Despite all the efforts of the central authority to check the expansion of tax-free estates, there grew up once more a class of hereditary chieftains whose power rivalled that of the throne and in the course of some centuries finally overtopped it.

At the beginning of the eighth century, of course, matters had not advanced to this stage. The reform was in full swing, and new ideas in all spheres of life were being imported, spread, and assimilated in varying degrees. One of the essentials of a stable culture is, presumably, a permanent centre of government and learning. Until the Taikwa period, the capital of Japan had been migratory, the imperial palace having been rebuilt on some new site in one of the various imperial manors in the home provinces at the beginning of each new reign. This constituted a transfer of the capital, but it must not be supposed that prior to the seventh century there existed in Japan any such towns or cities as were then the pride of China. Tales of the magnificence of Lo-yang and Ch'ang-an brought to Japan by returned travellers inspired their countrymen, and the Reform Edict of 646 provided for the "regulation" of a capital which was not yet built. It was not until 710 that the first permanent capital was erected, with a full apparatus of palaces, government offices, mansions of high functionaries, storehouses, granaries, and—most beautiful and most enduring—the great tile-roofed temples and the tall pagodas. This was the city of Nara, which typifies the blossom time of Japanese civilisation, the few bright decades of political ardour, æsthetic awakening and religious exaltation, that were followed, in the seemingly inevitable cycle of events, by the sophistication, and then the decadence, and then the collapse, of the next, the Hei-an period.

NOTES TO CHAPTER V

[1] Page 103 ff. It is doubtful whether Chinese administration in practice followed closely the schematic arrangements set forth in early Chinese works. For instance, some modern scholars contend that the division of communal fields into nine squares, which is referred to by Mencius, was never a general usage. If the Chinese models which the Japanese copied were more theoretical than actual, the failure of the borrowed system in Japan is the easier to understand.

[2] Page 105. Examination system in China. It is probably true, as research into Chinese biographical records suggests, that the examination system tended to build up an hereditary official class, since the sons of officials had the advantage of influential and wealthy parents; but the Chinese system was nevertheless equalitarian in principle, and the Japanese system was not.

PART TWO—NARA

Chapter VI—CONFUCIANISM AND BUDDHISM

THE city of Nara was laid out in 710, on the model of the Chinese capital at Hsian. Designed on a grand scale, in the form of a rectangle intersected by wide, straight avenues, its construction was an expressive symbol of the transfer to Japan of foreign institutions. The Chinese liked to have things symmetrically disposed and nicely classified. They were fond of regular shapes and balanced arrangements. They had a passion for neat divisions and numbered categories, of ideas as well as objects. So in their earliest political theory you find everywhere such groupings as the Two Principles, the Three Rules, the Five Forces, and the Eight Aims; in their philosophy, a reading of the universe in terms of trigrams and hexagrams; and in their literature, a strong taste for the parallel and the antithesis. This schematic habit of mind was by no means the whole of Chinese genius, but rather the brimming vessel in which it was confined and whence on occasion it escaped in violent overflow. But the Japanese were naturally better aware of the vessel than of the secret springs which filled it. Certainly, in the earlier phases of their contact with Chinese culture we find them sometimes taking over systems with an attractive look of simplicity, regardless of the complex reality beneath. It must always be remembered that, though we speak of their contact with Chinese culture, the Japanese, owing to their insular position, had but scanty direct knowledge of China. For the most part they had as their patterns not things, but only descriptions of things; and, more than that, descriptions in writing, in a language not their own. But the plan of a great city could be borrowed even if the life that filled it could not be reproduced; and though Nara was a copy, it was more splendid than anything that had ever before been known in Japan. Even to-day a visitor to its ancient site can with but little effort of imagination reconstruct its vanished glories from the remains of its great temples and their treasures, peopling its palaces with courtiers in ceremonial robes, its holy edifices with priests who chanted litanies in a strange tongue, its workshops with artists from China and Korea and their eager Japanese pupils, who wrought the exquisite shapes of gods in bronze and wood and lacquer.

A settled home was necessary for the growth on native soil of all those alien arts and sciences which were then being studied with such ardour, and it is for this reason that their development, in the relatively short period of seventy-five years during which Nara remained the seat of government and the centre of learning, was more rapid and intense than it had ever been before. It is difficult to realise how complete a revolution was effected in all departments of life in the capital. Life in the country went on as before. Peasants grew their rice, fed their silkworms, grudged their taxes, and worshipped their native gods. But in the city all was new, all was foreign. The very architecture of the palaces and the temples was Chinese; the sutras were read in Chinese translations if not in Sanskrit; laws, ordinances, public documents, official despatches, chronicles, and even poems were in Chinese; the costume of the courtiers, their etiquette, their ranks and appellations were borrowed from China. The political doctrines of the statesmen of Japan, the philosophical ideas of her scholars, the religious beliefs of her priests could be expressed and expounded only in an alien tongue and an imported script; and even their native speech was now being enriched with words of foreign origin. It is hard to find a parallel for this curious phenomenon of a small society, busily digesting and assimilating a superior foreign culture not imposed from without by conquest or proximity, but voluntarily, even enthusiastically adopted. It numbered probably not more than twenty thousand in a city of perhaps two hundred thousand inhabitants, and the total population of Japan at this period is estimated at six million. Where should one start in describing the activities of this microcosm? Perhaps it is best to turn first to the question of language, for the Chinese language was not only the vehicle by which knowledge was imported, it was the very foundation of the new learning and the new institutions. It was, indeed, an institution in itself, and one of the most important.

The affinities of the native Japanese language are not yet known. One school doggedly relates it to the Ural-Altaic group, on the score of resemblance to Korean, Mongol, Manchu, Finnish and Turkish. Another with a great wealth of illustration urges kinship with Polynesian tongues. Probably both are right, and the language, like the race, results from a fusion of elements drawn from many parts of Asia. One thing, however, is certain: that in vocabulary, in the structure of words and the structure of sentences, there could hardly be a language more strongly contrasted to Chinese than the Japanese of the first centuries of the Christian era, the earliest form of which we have any knowledge, whether exact or presumptive. Japanese was polysyllabic, composed of simple sounds, either vowels alone, or vowels preceded by a single consonant—such sounds as *a, ka, sa, ta, na, ma, mi, mu, me, mo*. No double consonants, no true diphthongs. It was a highly agglutinative tongue, its long sentences articulated by means of particles, and the order of words was from the particular to the general: adjective preceding noun, subject and object preceding verb. It was almost without accentuation, its vocabulary was poor, its sentences were long and diffuse, and it was a language without a script. Chinese, on the other hand, was monosyllabic, with a wide range of tones, a number of sounds unpronounceable by Japanese, and an immense vocabulary, both abstract and concrete. Its sentences were short and concise, articulated partly by special vocables, but chiefly by variations in the order of words. An ideographic script had been used in China two thousand years before the Christian era, and was developed and transformed from about 200 B.C. into a scientific system, logographic rather than ideographic, by which words could be figured with reference to both sense and sound, but without uniform representation of either.* Under the influence of this complicated method, the Chinese written language developed in a way which is difficult to understand for those who are familiar only with languages represented by writing on a phonetic basis. A language written by means of an alphabet never escapes entirely from the boundaries of speech. The most stilted literary English, though its vocabulary be recondite and its construction tortuous, can be understood when read aloud, but the written language of China appeals to the eye and not the ear. The diver-

* For a full explanation of these points of difference see the introduction to the writer's *Historical Grammar of Japanese*, Clarendon Press, 1928.

gence between speech and writing is so great that the spoken language and the written language are practically two different, though related, modes of expression. Imagine therefore the situation when the Japanese were confronted with the need of utilising Chinese as a means of acquiring knowledge from China. Such contact as there was between the two peoples was not enough to allow spoken Chinese to become a familiar speech in Japan, and anyhow what the Japanese wanted to learn from China was written by Chinese brushes rather than spoken by Chinese tongues. Since the Japanese had no script, it was impossible to translate Chinese words into Japanese, even apart from the shortcomings of the native vocabulary, lacking in names for so many things and ideas that were foreign to them.   The only way out of such difficulties was an unfortunate compromise. It is too involved a subject to be treated here in detail, but we may summarise by saying that at first the Chinese texts had to be studied in the original; then schemes were worked out by which, with the aid of diacritic markings, a Chinese sentence could be turned into a Japanese sentence by changing the word order and supplying the necessary joints and inflections, very much as our schoolboys, by jumping backwards and forwards, construe a piece of Latin prose and produce a translation which is not English but a specialised hybrid. There could hardly be anything more unsatisfactory than this system, and its effects upon the development of the native tongue were deplorable. It need hardly be added that the vocabulary of Japanese soon came to contain a great number of Chinese words, principally those for which there was no Japanese equivalent, but often adopted for reasons of pedantry or fashion rather than convenience. It is an interesting fact that the same Chinese words were borrowed and reborrowed at different periods of Chinese history, so that the same Chinese character will often have two or three different pronunciations in Japanese, according to the date when, or the place whence, the word (not the character) was imported. Thus the character which stands for the Chinese word meaning "bright," is read in Japan either *myō* or *mei* or *min*, sounds approximating to the Chinese pronunciations of successive periods.

It will be clear that the prestige of the language, the script, and the literature of China was overwhelming, and that the native language for all but everyday colloquial purposes must be driven into disuse. That is what happened. No scholar, no priest, no courtier, and indeed no ordinary clerk or accountant, could get on without being able to read a Chinese text and to write a Chinese sentence. It may be imagined that the standard of accomplishment varied enormously. There were probably very few Japanese who could compose Chinese that would pass muster at Chang-an or Lo-yang, and no doubt all important communications with the Chinese court were drafted by scribes of Chinese origin. But everyone who valued his standing must have a smattering; must be able to cite appropriately a tag from the canonical works; to quote or embroider upon a Chinese poetical theme; and, maybe the most desirable accomplishment of all, to write an elegant and well-proportioned hand. It is important to understand that, at the period of which we are writing, and for many centuries afterwards, calligraphy was not only the means of education, it was an end in itself, an art like painting and a discipline as well.

The study of the Chinese language and Chinese literature was, then, the chief intellectual employment of the aristocracy of Nara. It does not appear that there was any movement to spread knowledge beyond Court circles. A university was founded some twenty years after the Taikwa reform edict, and reorganised during the Nara period; but entrance was confined, with few exceptions, to the sons of nobles and officials of high rank, and even the small schools in the provinces were reserved for the instruction of the children of officials. The Japanese failed, in borrowing the greatest of all Chinese institutions, to take over its essence, which was a respect for learning coupled with a desire for its spread. They seem to have refrained very deliberately from tampering with the aristocratic structure of their own society, and we may here fitly anticipate by stating that in the long run they paid a heavy price for this neglect. Learning that was a mere ornament of the privileged, divorced from reality and common needs, could not but be unsound and unfruitful. It produced a certain futile elegance, some charming frivolities, some picturesque, if barren accomplishments.[1] It was the special property of a little group, interesting in the world's æsthetic history, but destined to collapse, because it rested upon shaky economic foundations, and because its inspiration was so thin and arid. Far more profound and lasting in its effects was the vital impulse of Buddhism, to which we must presently turn. But first we ought to sketch rapidly the chief features of Chinese culture, other than its Buddhist elements, which influenced life and thought in Japan at this time.

The early Japanese records refer again and again to the acquisition of Chinese books. Chief among them, apart from the Chinese versions of Buddhist sutras and their commentaries, were the Chinese canonical writings, consisting of the Book of Changes, the Annals, the Odes, the Book of Rites, the Spring and Autumn Chronicles, the Treatise on Filial Piety, the Great Learning, the Doctrine of the Mean, the Analects of Confucius, the Teachings of Mencius, and a considerable literature of treatises, dissertations and commentaries based upon them. To these must be added a number of works upon astronomy, geography, geomancy, divination, music and medicine.

The Chinese canon, while it includes many and various doctrines, consists largely of the classical works which embody the moral and political philosophy of Confucius and his school. Though modern research denies that Confucius was, as he claimed in the *Analects*, "a transmitter and not a creator," it was to antiquity that he appealed, however fictitiously, for wise precept and virtuous example; so that in effect his teaching was conservative. It is indeed of a conservatism and a formalism almost beyond belief to those unfamiliar with Far Eastern modes of thought. It has other qualities, however, and it seems to have suited or expressed the Chinese character well enough, for it has shown great powers of survival. Despite the hostility and contempt which it provoked in other schools, it moulded Chinese institutions for more than two thousand years, and had a profound influence on those of neighbouring countries, particularly Korea and Japan. Korea may even be said to have suffered from a Confucian malady, since in later centuries her growth seems to have been arrested by excessive devotion to its forms. But the Japanese were saved by some happy strain in their temperament which resisted its mortal dangers and allowed them, while respecting its tradition, to conform its teaching to their needs.

It is not easy to compress into a few paragraphs the essentials of Confucian doctrine, but we must make the attempt, because it colours so many aspects of Japanese life. In the first place, the Confucianist recognises a supreme entity, which is called T'ien, Heaven. Originally T'ien may have been an anthropomorphic concept, but in general it is thought of as an impersonal first cause or governing principle. The distinction is of some importance in the religious history of the Japanese, because it means that in their borrowed notions of philosophy there was nothing to give their speculations a monotheistic trend. Heaven is mute but omnipotent, and in concert with Earth produces and controls all life. All ordinary phenomena result from the interaction of two principles: the male, bright or progressive principle, *yang;* the female, dark or regressive principle, *yin.* Phenomena that cannot be explained by the fusion or alteration of *yang* and *yin* are the actions of spirits, and spirits are the powerful *manes* of the great dead. Confucius himself, for instance, claimed to have been constantly aware of the presence of the Duke of Chou, a ruler of antiquity, whose laws and rites were the source of his teaching. We are not told that the spirits are immortal. On the contrary, their disembodied life seems to be terminable sooner or later, according to their importance to the survivors. As time progresses they become more and more tenuous, till finally they cease to be. It is all very vague and inexplicable, as such beliefs had better be if they are to survive. Since the dead exist, their wants must be attended to. Offerings must be made to them, of food and drink, and their wishes must be ascertained and followed. Thus a posthumous child must be announced to the bier, or to the memorial tablets of its father, a bride must be presented to the bridegroom's ancestors. Here we have the fundamentals of ancestor worship. For the purposes of the family, the dead are not dead: they must be consulted, comforted and revered.

The family is the unit of the social organism, of the very political system, and the central point of Confucian doctrine is the cult of the family. As worship is due to departed ancestors, so is obedience due to living parents. The highest, almost the only duty of a man, is his duty to his parents, and if Confucianism can be called a religion, it is the religion of filial piety. Let us quote from the treatise on Filial Piety—one of the canonical works attributed to Confucius himself—some passages which will throw light upon its nature:

> "The law of filial piety is that one should serve one's parents as one serves Heaven."—"At every step he takes, the pious son should remember what precautions filial piety requires of him."—"So long as one's parents are living, no enterprise must be undertaken without their counsel and approbation."—"Parents must be obeyed during their lifetime, and after their death their son must do as they did. Living, they must be served as the Rites exact. Dead, they must be buried as the Rites exact. After death they must be given the offerings which the Rites exact."

The literal observance of these rules must affect every department of life, and they were indeed literally observed, and governed the conduct of millions from the days of Confucius down to recent times. One of the earliest works to be widely studied in Japan, the classic of Filial Piety was by the end of the eighth century part of the curriculum of every school, and its commandments were known by heart to every child that had learned its letters. Whatever may be said as to the place of ancestor worship in the aboriginal Shintō cult, there can be no doubt that as an important factor in Japanese life it grew out of Confucian doctrine. In the present writer's opinion the Shintō religion in its early forms had very little to do with ancestor worship, except in so far as all men tend to revere their own forbears and to claim descent from heroes.

If the basis of society in China was the family, its apex was the emperor, the Son of Heaven, who holds the mandate of the supreme T'ien. It is to be noted that this mandate depends not as in early Japan upon divine ancestry, but upon virtue. If he is deficient in virtue, his deposition is not an offence against Heaven. He is to shine as an example to his people, to guide and instruct them. Thus the state reproduces on a grand scale the family, and as the chief duty of the subject is filial piety, so is the chief duty of the sovereign the worship of Heaven, the supreme Parent, and the accomplishment of the rites due to his imperial ancestors. The Confucian theory of the state is based upon, or at least it is made to square with, the Confucian ethical principles, of which the basis is the assumption of native rectitude in men. Man is naturally inclined to good, and he requires only instruction and example, not commands and punishments, to induce him to keep in the right road, and to avoid evil, which is caused by ignorance. The sovereign must be a model to his people, just as a parent must be a model to his children, but since his lofty position does not allow him personally to instruct his subjects, he is assisted by wise officers, who must convey his light to all parts of his dominions. These are the Superior Men, sage altruists, devoted to the common good. Their qualifications are learning and cold, impersonal judgment. The sage must adhere to the middle way, must not be deflected either by sympathy or antipathy, enthusiasm or despair. The *Chung-yung*, or Doctrine of the Mean, ranks with the Great Learning, the Analects of Confucius and the Discourses of Mencius among the chief canonical works, and its influence upon China has been profound. The sovereign being equipped with virtue, and his counsellors with wisdom, it remains only for the common people to learn their duties and fulfil them. Since they are not capable of understanding the abstract morality of the sages, of determining for themselves what is correct conduct, they must be instructed by means of concrete and positive precepts. It is these precepts which are embodied in the Rites. The good citizen is one who fulfils regularly and completely his ritual obligations. Instead of a code of morals he has a code of manners.

It will be seen that both the political and the ethical ideas outlined above were likely to have an appeal to the Japanese reformers. They appeared to fit with but little alteration the structure of society in Japan, a patriarchal society ruled by divine mandate, and supported at the base by an obedient people. There could, indeed, hardly be a more convenient model. Everything pertaining to public and private life was, in the Chinese system, nicely regulated, classified and labelled, and all that was needed was to take it over as it stood and issue a few edits to enforce it. But the Confucian system envisaged a static society, in which all change was undesirable. Once fixed, it must endure for ever. This might do for the Chinese, who in the course of centuries had worked it out to suit their own needs, but clearly it was of no permanent use to the Japanese. Neither by tradition nor by temperament were they suited for its chilly conservatism; and, it is important to remember, they were now a young people in an early stage of rapid development, so that they were likely to borrow more than they could assimilate, to take over outward form rather than inward significance. Consequently the history of Japan, for a long period after the Taikwa reform, is the history of a conflict between native habits and alien principles.[2]

The adoption of the Chinese political system alone would probably have made no fundamental difference to Japan, but it was accompanied by other and more powerful influences. First, in point of date, was the introduction of writing, which, as we have seen, opened to the Japanese a new world of thought; and second was the gradual spread of Buddhism, which in time wrought essential changes in Japanese life and enriched it in almost all directions.

The beginnings of Buddhism in Japan we have already traced. It was natural that its first appeal should be to simple desire for material benefits, and that its prayers and ceremonies should be looked upon as rituals of incantation rather than spiritual exercises. So, in its early days, the sutras and the images seem to have been conceived of by the Japanese as containing a magic more powerful than their own native liturgies and symbols, but akin to them in nature. Prior to the Nara period they knew of the Lotus, the Diamond Cutter, and many other sutras, but these were recited without understanding, as formulæ by which to secure good health and long life, or to avert disaster. Several instances are recorded in the sixth century where priests are ordered by the Court to pray for an emperor's recovery from illness, or for rain in times of drought. But the spiritual element in Buddhism could not for long remain without appreciation, the more so because the native religion was lacking in all but the crudest moral and philosophical conceptions; and it is significant that, after its first appeal to the ordinary material hopes and fears of the Japanese, Buddhism found a quick response in their strong natural affection. Family sentiment was powerful. It was strengthened by the Chinese doctrine of filial piety, which in Japan lost a great deal of its dry formalism; and among the first Buddhist images made in Japan many were dedicated to parents, living or dead, as a token of their children's gratitude. Thus an image of the Buddha made in 654, an Amida of 658, a Kwannon of 690, bear inscriptions showing that they were thank-offerings on behalf of father and mother. On the halo of the Buddha of 690 is written "we pray that our father and mother may so profit by this virtue (that is, the virtuous act of erecting a holy image) as to live happily in this life, and in their future existences may not pass through the three evil states, and may not suffer the eight calamities, but may forthwith be born again in Paradise, seeing the Buddha and hearing the Law."

By now, it will be seen, ideas foreign to the native religion were already gaining ground. Virtue and its rewards, life after death, reincarnations, paradise—these are religious conceptions, still vague, but far in advance of those appearing in the literature of early Shintō, which are shadowy in the extreme, even though they may be already under Buddhist influence. The fusion of Chinese notions of filial piety with religious sentiment is perhaps characteristic of the Japan of those days, engaged in an effort to assimilate new thoughts from all quarters with ardour, but as yet without complete understanding. Already, for instance, in the records of the early part of the seventh century there are traces of Taoism, imperfectly appreciated, it is true, and relished chiefly because of its magical claims.

As the early ideas of life after death disappeared, as it seemed less and less probable that the dead lived in the tomb a thinner sort of life, in which they still needed food, weapons, ornaments and servants, the custom of mound burial died out, and by A.D. 700 cremation had begun to take its place. Now, in memory of the dead, or to secure their well-being in future lives, temples and monasteries were erected, and filled with images or other sacred objects. It is these buildings, and their treasures, which characterise the civilisation of the Nara period and a few preceding decades.

As knowledge of the new religion increased, and as the Japanese monks and priests passed from a study of its general principles to a closer enquiry into finer points of doctrine, certain sectarian divisions arose, and by the end of the Nara period six sects were distinguished. These depended for the most part upon developments of exegetical study in China, where a long tradition of scholarship and a closer contact with India naturally favoured a more critical examination of texts than could be expected in Japan. But, though the Japanese sat at the feet of great Chinese ecclesiastics and ascetics, they had their national pride, and were anxious from an early date to arrive at independence. So we find notes by the Prince Shōtoku on standard Chinese commentaries, such as "My own interpretation differs slightly," or "This view is no longer accepted." At the beginning of a commentary upon the Lotus sutra, thought to be in the Prince's own hand and now in the possession of the Imperial family, there is written "This is compiled by the Crown Prince of the country of Yamato. It is not a foreign book." It seems that the scholarship of the prince was respected even on the continent, for at a later period Japanese monks studying in China found one of his commentaries, with notes by a Chinese scholar, in use in a great monastery.

Naturally, however, the Japanese as a people could not rival the Chinese in weight of learning and tradition, and throughout the Nara period they can hardly be said to have made any original contributions to the development of Buddhism. The six sects of the Nara period derive from so many continental schools, and represent not so much antagonistic doctrines as variations upon a common theme. The first sect in point of time was the Sanron sect, or school of the Three Treatises, introduced in 625 by a Korean monk (Hyé-kwan or Ei-kwan) who had studied in China, and was sent to Japan by the King of Kōkuli. It is not known how far his teaching spread beyond purely ecclesiastical circles, but one of his disciples, a Chinese domiciled in Japan, reached eminence by 645, holding a rank equivalent to that of bishop, and heading an important group of priests established in the temple called Gangōji. In a general way, therefore, it may be said that, in so far as the philosophical side of Buddhism was developed in Japan in the pre-Nara period, it was through the teachings of the Sanron school. Neither in those days, nor since, have the Japanese as a people taken very eagerly to the elaboration or critical study of imported philosophies. They have, in regard to Buddhism, always shown more enthusiasm for organisation and ritual than for abstruse speculation; but they have nevertheless studied with

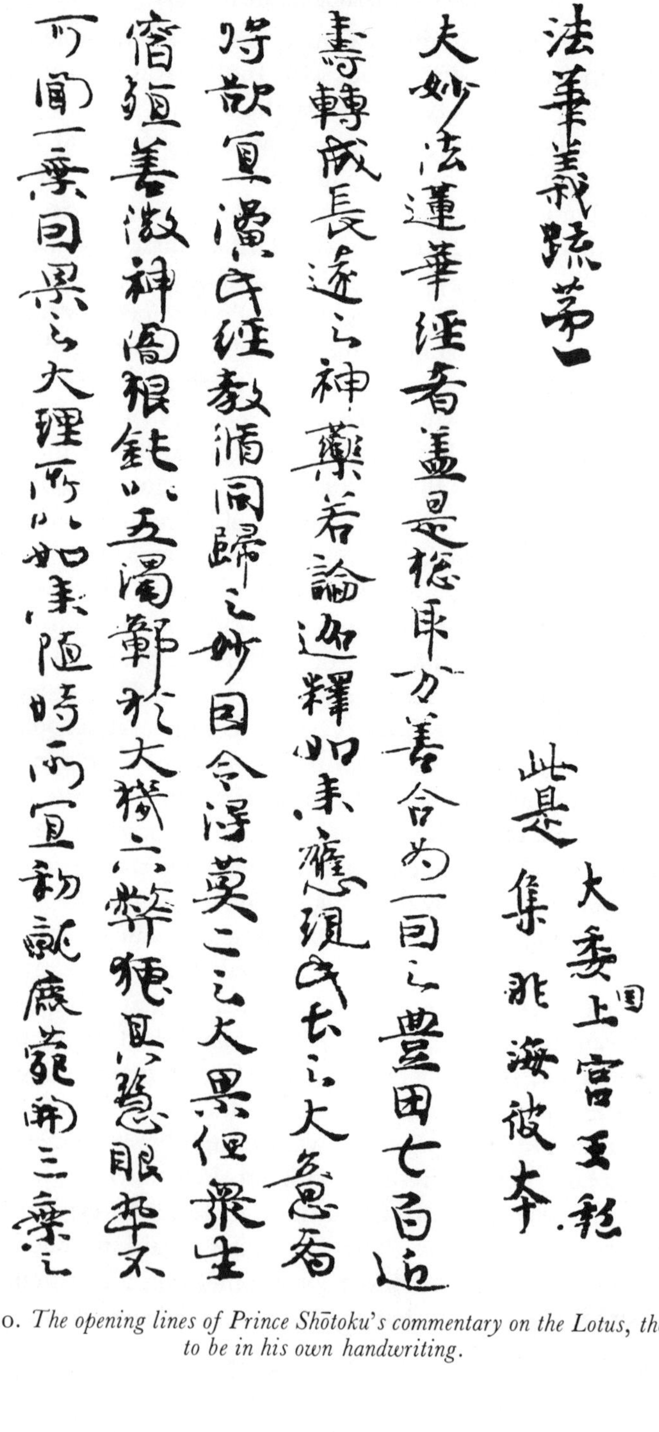

法華義疏第一

夫妙法蓮華經者蓋是統林万善合為一因之豐田七百遍

壽轉成長遠之神藥若論迦釋如來應現氏長之大意看

時獻眞當彌氏經教渭同歸之妙因令浮莫之之大黑但眾生

宿殖善微神唱根鈍以五濁鄲於大樹六弊猶且慈眼邪不

可聞一乘目果之大理所以如未隨時而宜勃就庶寵開三業之

此是

集 大委上宮王私

非海彼本

FIG. 20. *The opening lines of Prince Shōtoku's commentary on the Lotus, thought to be in his own handwriting.*

respect every new school that was brought to their notice and, whether they have accepted or discarded it, have scrupulously preserved its traditions, with the result that there exists in Japan today a greater mass of material for the study of the growth of Buddhist doctrine than in any other country. It is here that lies the chief interest of the Sanron and other early sects in Japan. They represent the first attempts of the Japanese to comprehend the philosophical systems which are the foundation of the Buddhist faith; and, since the native religion was deficient if not entirely wanting in ethical and metaphysical elements, they represent the first serious attempts of the Japanese to study the nature of the universe—their first steps in ontology.

The teaching of the Sanron sect is embodied in three treatises, of which the most celebrated is the *Chūron*, the Chinese version of a work by the famous Nágârjuna, whose views as to the relationship between appearance and reality inspired an important body of Mahayanist literature. This treatise was first translated in China in A.D. 409. It is the work of a subtle dialectician who preaches an extreme idealistic philosophy, asserting that all phenomena are unreal and do not exist separately but only relatively to one another. Such a conception of the nature of the Absolute must have been very difficult of comprehension for Japanese students; but the Sanron sect, no doubt because of its prestige as the first philosophical school of its kind in Japan, survived well into the Nara period, when its influence began to decay. Shortly after the formation of the Sanron sect in Japan came the Jōjitsu sect introduced from Paikché. Its teachings appear to have been freely studied in the Nara period, but it was soon merged in the Sanron school, and there is now very little trace of its separate existence beyond a few references in Shōsōin documents. The next sect in Japan was the Hossō or Yuishiki sect, introduced from China by a Japanese student-monk named Dōshō about A.D. 650. The treatise upon which it is based is a work, called in the Japanese the *Jōyuishiki-ron*, which consists of a digest of commentaries upon a short poetical statement of idealist philosophy by Vasubandhu, with other matter, arranged in 648 by the famous Chinese monk and pilgrim, Hsüan-Tsang, and further expounded by his disciples. The whole work sets forth the doctrine that the only reality is consciousness, and the word *yuishiki*, meaning "only consciousness," is used as a name for the sect as well as for the canon on which it relies. Hsüan-Tsang had commenced a new era in Buddhist studies in China by his accurate versions of Sanskrit texts. His teaching was the most recent and complete in China, and it is interesting to observe that it was brought so quickly to Japan. Disciples of Dōshō continued to propagate the tenets of the sect after his death, and several of them attained high rank in the priesthood, such rank being at that time in the gift of the court. It is to be remarked that Dōshō's immediate successors were sent by the court to China for further study, and that they were not Japanese, but men of Silla. Following them, however, comes a line of distinguished Japanese priests, whose names figure prominently in the records of the period. The best known of them is Gyōgi, of whom we shall presently hear more. He lived from 670-749, and became the patriarch of the Hossō sect towards the end of his career. It was this sect which took the lead in Buddhist studies during the Nara period, displacing the two schools above mentioned. It not only controlled its own temples, the Gangōji and the Kōfukuji, but had influence, at least so far as doctrinal questions were concerned, in the Tōdaiji, the Yakushiji and the Saidaiji, which were rich and powerful temples closely connected with the imperial family, and associated with other sects. The Hōryūji, too, which had formerly professed the Sanron doctrine, soon became the centre of study for the Hossō school, and is to-day the headquarters of the Hossō sect, though its adherents are but few in numbers.

The beginnings of the Kusha sect are not clear, and it is doubtful whether it ever existed as a separate sect in Japan.[3] Its tenets appear to have been studied at the time of the first introduction of the Hossō doctrines. They are based on an encyclopædic treatise of Vasubandhu, called the *Abidharma-kośa-śāstra*, written before his conversion to the theory of "only consciousness." This treatise gives its name to the sect (*Kośa* becoming *Kusha* in Japanese) and is accepted by most Chinese and Japanese sects as an authoritative exposition of the metaphysical thought of the earlier Buddhist schools, which, though they might hold that individual phenomena were illusions, did not deny reality to what they called *dharmâḥ*, the ultimate elements of existence. In other words, the Kusha sect stands for a realist philosophy of the Hinayana type of Buddhism, the Hossō sect for an idealist philosophy of the Mahayana type.

It will be seen that the sects above described were not formed in Japan in the order in which they developed in India, but rather as their teachings became known to the Japanese through contact with different Chinese schools, and as a direct result of the stimulus given to Buddhistic studies by the researches and translations of Hsüan-Tsang. What they all had in common was a desire to apprehend the nature of the universe, because it is only by ridding the mind of sensory illusions and perceiving the transcendental reality behind them that man can attain salvation. The difference between the sects was a difference only in their ways of solving the metaphysical problem of being. Whether their approach was rationalistic or mystical, all had the same goal, and in essence their creeds were not mutually opposed. Their disagreements were largely academic, concerning only an initiated few. They involved no serious differences in dogma or in ritual for the ordinary believer, nor is there anything to show that one sect regarded another as damned by heresy. Often in the same monastery the doctrines of several sects were studied and expounded.* It would perhaps be better to call them not sects but philosophical schools, whose theories must be studied as an initiation to profounder knowledge. Thus, according to an old saying in Japan, a novice is supposed to prepare himself by devoting three years to the Yuishiki and eight to the Kusha doctrines. It is worth insisting upon this feature, because history shows that, although bitter religious quarrels did at a later period break out, the Japanese as a people have been spared the pains of *odium theologicum*. Whether or not this was the result of a certain intellectual torpidity we need not enquire here; but it does seem to be fairly well established that they have not as a rule been disturbed by a fervid interest in transcendental problems. Their genius on the whole has been empiric and practical, their sentiment romantic rather than passionate.

* Thus the full name of the Hōryūji was Hōryū Gakumonji or Learning Temple, and it was as much a seminary as a monastery.

One sect, however, must be contrasted with those whose doctrines have been just outlined, on account not of its metaphysical
teaching but of its special institutional character. This was the
Ritsu sect, a knowledge of which can be traced as far back as the
time when the first Japanese nuns were sent to Korea to study
monastic "discipline," but which began to take firm hold in
Japan from the end of the seventh century. *Ritsu* is the Japanese
equivalent of the Chinese *lü*, rendering the Sanskrit word *vinaya*
(discipline). The Ritsu sect did not trouble much about doctrinal
questions, but paid special attention to discipline and correct
spiritual succession. In fact, its various branches developed as a
reaction against the metaphysical subtleties of the other schools,
and as a protest against the laxity of behaviour current in the
priesthood. They therefore attached great importance to ceremonies of ordination and held that admission to the order could
be properly granted only by a chapter of monks who had themselves been properly admitted. A postulant or a novice must
submit to searching enquiries into his character and convictions
and, further, the ceremony of ordination was not valid unless it
took place on a special platform called *kaidan* in Japanese, *simâ*
in Sanskrit. The full development of this system in Japan was
due to a Chinese monk named Ganjin who crossed over at the
invitation of Japanese ecclesiastics to found a true *kaidan* in
Japan. The circumstances of his visit, though perhaps rather
irrelevant to our theme, are worth describing, for they illustrate
the spiritual fervour and the missionary zeal of the Buddhists of
those days. In 733 two Japanese monks travelled to China and
pressed Ganjin to come to Japan. He promised to make the
journey as soon as possible, but he could not start until 742.
Setting forth in that year he was stopped by pirates and his vessel
confiscated. Two more attempts were frustrated by storms, a
fourth by the Chinese authorities, who forbade the departure of
so bright a luminary. On a fifth attempt one of his Japanese
disciples was drowned, others died of exposure and the ship was
wrecked. Ganjin by this time had gone blind. But he persevered
and on his sixth attempt, in 753, now sixty-six years of age, he
landed on the coast of Kyūshū. In the following year he reached
Nara, with a number of books and images, and was lodged in

the Tōdaiji. There he was visited by Kibi no Mabi, who brought him a message from the emperor (Shōmu), authorising him and no other to perform the rites of ordination. Shortly afterwards a seat of ordination (*kaidan*) was set up before the great Buddha in the Tōdaiji, and over four hundred persons, led by the empress-dowager, were received into the order, while forty more were re-ordained, their previous ordination being deemed irregular. This institution of an order, under a fixed rule, with a prescribed ceremony and in a prescribed place approved by the sovereign, was akin to the foundation of a state church, and marks therefore an important phase in the history of Japan. The number of *kaidan* was limited to three, one in Nara, one in western Japan and one in eastern Japan. It was only in one of these that, after vowing to observe the precepts (*kai*) and submit to the rule (*ritsu*) a monk or priest of whatever sect could be ordained; and until the early ninth century the Nara priesthood successfully opposed all attempts to set up new seats of ordination. Ganjin remained in Japan until his death at the age of seventy-seven in the year 763, spending the last years of his life at the temple called Tōshō-daiji, where the central *kaidan* was now established. Some seven-teen of his disciples remained permanently in Japan, as abbots of the Tōshōdaiji and other temples.

One more sect of the Nara period remains to be mentioned. This is the Kegon sect. The Kegon (*Avatamsaka*) sutra is an im-portant work, or rather group of works, commentaries on which were first brought to Japan from China in 736, though the sutra itself had been known for some time. A few years later a Silla priest expounded these scriptures at Nara in a course of sermons which lasted three years and was attended by most of the Nara priests. As a philosophical school the Kegon sect could not rival the other sects, but in Japan it outstripped them in its develop-ment on the ritual side, partly, it appears, thanks to certain picturesque features of its doctrine which were attractive and convenient to the monarchy. Crudely stated, this doctrine, which claims to be an interpretation of the Kegon sutra and the sutra known as the Net of Brahmâ, holds that the Buddha Śâkya (in Japanese, Shaka) is a manifestation of the supreme, universal and omnipresent Buddha, Locana (in Japanese, Roshana). The object of worship of adherents of the Kegon sect is therefore the Roshana Buddha, who in their scriptures is portrayed as dwelling upon a lotus flower of a thousand petals. Each petal represents a universe, and in each universe there are a myriad worlds. On each petal is a Shaka, who is a manifestation of Roshana, and in each of the myriad worlds is a small Buddha, who is, in turn, a manifestation of Shaka. The Court or the priesthood seem to have perceived some analogy between this hierarchy and the hierarchy of the State, comparing Roshana to the emperor, the great Shakas to his high officers, the small Buddhas to the people. How deliberate and conscious was this effort to identify government with religion it is hard to say; but there is no doubt that the Court looked with special favour on the cult of Roshana. The Emperor Shōmu decreed in 749 that the Kegon sutra was to be the authoritative scripture and, in circumstances which we shall presently study, he erected to the worship of Roshana the greatest temple in Japan, the Tōdaiji, which was also known as the Dai-Kegonji, or Great Kegon Temple.

Apart from the special patronage of the Kegon sect by the Court, and from the specially devout conduct of the Emperor Shōmu, there was in general a close connection between government and religion. From early in the seventh century there were held in all temples annual celebrations of Buddha's birthday and the Feast of All Souls (*Avalambana*), at which maigre fare was bestowed by the Court upon priests and laity. Before long these festivals were regularly celebrated in the palace, to say nothing of services on special occasions; and by the end of the Nara period Buddhist ritual formed an important part of Court ceremonial. A further step towards the adoption of Buddhism as a national religion was the establishment of provincial temples (*koku-bun-ji*) by order of the government. As far back as 684 provincial governors had been ordered to install Buddhist shrines in their official houses, and in 741 an imperial edict commanded the foundation in each province of a temple and a seven-storeyed pagoda. Copies of certain sutras then in vogue were made for distribution among these temples and the emperor himself copied in gold letters holy texts which were to be enshrined in the pagodas. Forming part of each temple were a monastery for twenty monks and a nunnery for ten nuns. Each temple was provided with a sustenance-fief of fifty households, and sixty acres of rice land. The duties of the incumbents were to read publicly on fixed dates the sutra called *Saishō-ō-gyō*, to say masses regularly and to fast on six days in each month. On those days hunting and fishing were forbidden to the laity. The reading of the sutras was performed by the method called *tendoku* ("skipping"), which consists of intoning a few words at the beginning and end of each volume, the intervening portions being turned over rapidly in one movement. This was regarded as equivalent in point of religious merit to the recitation of the whole work. The masses appear to have been in the form of a public profession of repentance coupled with prayers for freedom from pestilence and disorder. Indeed it seems clear that the immediate motive for the official encouragement of Buddhism was the fear of disease, for we know that in this period plague or smallpox was rife, causing great consternation at Court. There was moreover a precedent for the establishment of provincial temples in the practice of the Sui and T'ang emperors, who had similarly ordered to be set up in each provincial capital a Buddhist temple and a shrine for Taoist rites. There are clear indications that the promotion of official religious observances was part of a definite policy, which aimed at ranging on the side of the monarchy a new and powerful influence. Important from this point of view was the relationship between the great Nara temple, the Tōdaiji, and the provincial temples. The Tōdaiji may be regarded as the headquarters of Buddhism in so far as Buddhism was the state religion; and the various provincial temples as its branches in the chief centres of local government. This relationship followed naturally from the circumstances in which the Tōdaiji was founded and developed. They were as follows:

In 735 the Emperor Shōmu (probably stimulated by the smallpox epidemic which had now reached Nara and carried off a number of patricians) planned to set up a large image of Roshana. A revolt in western Japan and other hindrances delayed the undertaking for some years, and an image commenced in 744 had to be abandoned for lack of technical skill. Finally in 747 a new image was begun at Nara, and after several failures the casting was completed under the supervision of an expert of Korean descent, in the year 749. Meanwhile work on the great hall which was to contain the image was commenced in 747. The construction and decoration of this edifice, together with a great number of subordinate buildings, all within one immense enclosure approached through splendid gates, continued for some decades. The whole was on a grand scale, without parallel in Japan for size and magnificence. The Great Hall in particular was of imposing dimensions, being 284 feet long, 166 feet wide and 152 feet high. It was burned down in the twelfth century but the present building, though only about two-thirds the size of the original, is still the largest wooden building under one roof in the world. The great Buddha which it enshrines, though negligible as a work of art,* represents in wealth and in labour a stupendous effort for the Japan of those days, and its construction was a technical feat of no mean order. The seated figure is 53 feet high, and contains over one million pounds of metal—copper, tin, and lead. It was built up to the shoulder in some forty separate segments, the mould being added to foot by foot as the segments cooled, and finally surmounted by the head and neck, cast in a single shell some 12 feet high. Mercury and a great deal of gold were needed for gilding the image, and as gold was scarce in Japan there was anxiety over its supply. Luckily a provincial governor in the north-east made the timely discovery of a gold mine in his territory in 749, and sent several hundred pounds to the capital. This was looked upon as an event of such importance that rejoicings were held on a national scale. Imperial messengers were despatched to announce the good news to shrines throughout the country and a great ceremony was held, of which we have a contemporary record in the official chronicle called the *Shoku-nihongi*. In "the fourth month of summer" of the year 749 the Emperor proceeded in state to the Tōdaiji, entered the front part of the Hall of the Image of Roshana and took up his position facing north towards the image, the position of a subject in audience with his sovereign. The Empress, the Princess Imperial,

---

* It has been frequently restored, and there remain of the original shape only a part of the trunk and legs and a few petals of the lotus on which the figure was seated.

the great Ministers of State, the court nobles, the civil and military functionaries, all were present, the latter drawn up in ranks at the end of the hall. The Minister of the Left advanced to address the Buddha in the sovereign's name, in language so remarkable that it is best given in exact translation :

"This is the Word of the Sovereign who is the Servant of the Three Treasures, that he humbly speaks before the Image of Roshana.

"In this land of Yamato since the beginning of Heaven and Earth, Gold, though it has been brought as an offering from other countries, was thought not to exist. But in the East of the land which We rule, the Lord of Michinoku, Kudara no Kyōfuku of the Junior Fifth Rank, has reported that in his territory, in the district of Ōda, Gold has been found.

"Hearing this We were astonished and rejoiced, and feeling that this is a Gift bestowed upon Us by the love and blessing of Roshana Buddha, We have received it with reverence and humbly accepted it, and have brought with Us all Our officials to worship and give thanks.

"This We say reverently, reverently, in the Great Presence of the Three Treasures, whose name is to be spoken with awe."

It will be noticed that the Emperor abstains from all reference to his own divine ancestry, and styles himself the servant—indeed the word used, *yakko*, can be translated "slave"—of the Buddha. Yet in other rescripts of the time he consistently styles himself "the Sovereign that is a manifest God," because he is of divine descent, and, though the gods that dwell in heaven are hidden, those who descend to rule on earth are visible to men. This and many similar phrases show that the doctrine of divine ancestry had by no means been abandoned. But it was clearly necessary to reconcile it in some way with the worship by the emperor of other deities, and the solution of this problem was reached in an extremely interesting way. It will help to explain what happened if we first quote and comment upon some extracts from an imperial rescript addressed, after the above ceremony, to the court and the officers of state. Speaking in the sovereign's name, the Minister of the Imperial Household said :—

"Hearken ye all to the Word, of the Sovereign Prince of Yamato that is a Manifest God, saying :

"A report has been made to Us that in the East of this land which We rule from the throne of Heavenly Sun Succession, Gold has been found.

"Now We, considering that of all the various Laws the Great Word of Buddha is the most excellent for protecting the State, did desire to place the Great Scripture called *Saishō-kyō* and images of Roshana Buddha in all the various countries under Our rule, so that by praying to the Gods that dwell in Heaven and the Gods that dwell on Earth, and by worshipping the reigns (sic) of Our Distant Sovereign Ancestors, whose names are to be spoken with awe, We might guide and lead the people and serve with such a heart that Evil would cease and Good arise, and Peril would change and become Peace indeed. But people doubted and thought this could not be, and We Ourself grieved because We thought there would not be enough Gold. Yet now the Three Treasures have vouchsafed this excellent and divine Great Sign of the Word, and We think that this is a thing manifested by the guidance and grace of the Gods that dwell in Heaven and the Gods that dwell on Earth and by the love and kindness of the August Sovereign likewise Spirits.

"Therefore We have joyfully received it and reverently received it, and not knowing whether to go forward or backward, night and day We have humbly reflected, thinking that whereas such a thing might come to pass in the reign of a King wise in the cherishing and soothing of the people, We are indeed ashamed and overcome with thankfulness because it has been manifested in Our time, who are unworthy and unskilled.

"Shall We alone, therefore, receive this Great and Precious Sign? Nay, it is right that We should humbly receive it and accept it in rejoicing together with Our people. And inasmuch as We, even as a God, do so consider, We will cherish and reward them All and We will add words to the name of this August Era.

"To all the Gods, beginning with the Shrine(s) of the Great God(s) We will present rice-lands and to all their Wardens We make gifts. To the temples We will allow land to cultivate and to all monks and nuns We pay homage and make gifts. Newly-built temples which can become public temples We make into public temples. To some among the Keepers of the August Tombs We will make gifts. Further, in those places where are (the tombs of) subjects who have excelled in serving the Realm and guarding the State, We will set up monuments which as long as Heaven and Earth endure shall not be dishonoured or defiled by men."

*   *   *   *   *   *   *

"And as to the children of those of Our subjects who have served us as Ministers, according to the manner of their service their sons have been rewarded but their daughters are not rewarded. But are men alone to bear their fathers' names, and women not to be called thereby? We consider that it is right for them to serve together side by side. We reward you therefore, so that, neither mistaking nor neglecting the teachings imparted by your fathers—that you might become as they desired—nor letting their house decay, you may serve the Sovereign Court."

*   *   *   *   *   *   *

"We will reward aged persons, and We will grant favour to poor persons. In the case of persons of filial piety We will grant exemptions and bestow rice-lands.

"We will pardon criminals and We will reward (scribes?) and learned men.

"We will reward also those who found the Gold, and the Governor of the province of Michinoku and the officials of the District, and (all) down to the peasants. All the peasants of the Realm We will cherish and love."

This rescript, besides vividly suggesting the court atmosphere of those days, illustrates conveniently several aspects of the political situation created by the impact of Buddhist ideas upon the native tradition. In the first place, it definitely treats the new religion as an instrument of government, "excellent for protecting the State." The *Saishōkyō* is the *Suvarnaprabhasa-sutra*, one of the scriptures most revered in the Nara period and indeed for some succeeding centuries. It was this sutra above all others which was copied and distributed to the provincial temples. It is frequently mentioned in the chronicles, first under the date 676, and it was regularly recited at certain official functions in the Palace down to the 10th century. Though first brought to Japan in a Chinese translation of about A.D. 400, it was better known in the retranslation by I-Tsing, of about A.D. 700. Both this and the *Ninnō Hannya* sutra treat in certain chapters of the duties of kings and the protection of states. Both are comparatively late compositions which do not rank so high as, say, the great Lotus sutra, from the purely religious standpoint; but, perhaps because the Japanese have always been more interested in government than in pure religion, they assumed a special importance in Japan, and certainly in the records of the Nara period they are mentioned as often as the Lotus, and in one imperial edict at least, in 767, are quoted in support of the dynasty and against treasonable plots.[4]

The passages in the Rescript which follow upon the reference to the sutra are a curious medley of Buddhism, Shintō and Confucianism, a little syncretic masterpiece. The word is vouchsafed by the Three Treasures, that is, by Buddhism; this is a manifestation of the grace of the gods that dwell in Heaven and the gods that dwell on Earth, that is, the Shintō deities ; and the discovery of gold is such a thing as comes to pass in the reign of a king wise in the cherishing and soothing of his people, that is, a monarch endowed with virtue as postulated by Confucian theory. Grants are to be made not only to Buddhist monks and nuns, but to the wardens of Shintō shrines, and, so that no interests shall be neglected, ranks and rewards are to be bestowed upon women as well as men. It is all very tolerant, and probably, in the circumstances, very wise; for though Buddhism was powerful in and around the court, the native cult was by no means moribund and had better be conciliated than neglected. The policy adopted illustrates so well the assimilative powers of Buddhism, and displays on such a grand scale the eclectic genius of the Japanese, that it is worth describing in some detail.

To erect a great Buddha in the middle of the capital, and to make it, linked up with its counterparts in the provincial temples, an object of national worship was, on the face of it, a serious blow to the native divinities, unless some means could be found of reconciling the two faiths. A solution of this problem was found by the monk Gyōgi, already mentioned as a leader of the Hossō sect. He was an extremely able and energetic man, who, as was not uncommon with the great ecclesiastics of the period, interested himself in the promotion of material as well as spiritual welfare in Japan. He travelled widely, encouraged arts and industries, and made efforts to improve communications by building bridges and dykes and opening up new routes in difficult country. To him, so tradition has it, occurred the idea of reconciling Buddhism and Shintō by saying that the two religions were different forms of one faith. Carrying a holy Buddhist relic, he journeyed as an imperial envoy to the great shrine of the Sun Goddess in Ise, to take her opinion as to the erection and worship of the great Buddha proposed by the emperor, who, it should not be forgotten, was according to the native creed her descendant and her vice-regent upon earth. Gyōgi, then an aged man, after seven days and seven nights spent in prayer at the threshold of her shrine, received an oracle from her divine lips. Using (if we may believe the records) the astonishing medium of Chinese verse, she proclaimed in a loud voice that the sun of truth illumined the long night of life and death and the moon of reality dispersed the clouds of sin and ignorance; that the news of the emperor's project was as welcome to her as a boat at a ferry, and the offering of the relic as grateful to her as a torch in the darkness. There is nothing of the native cult about this phraseology. The "sun of truth" and the "moon of reality" are purely Buddhist imagery. However, the oracle was duly interpreted as favourable, and it was confirmed shortly afterwards by a dream in which the Sun Goddess appeared to the emperor as a radiant disc, and proclaimed that the Sun and the Buddha were the same. This was in 742, and in the following year an edict was issued, announcing that the image would be made. It contains the following interesting passage: "The wealth of the empire is Ours. The power of the empire is Ours. With this wealth and this power it is easy to

complete the form; but it is hard to achieve the spirit." Work
was commenced soon afterwards, but, as we have seen, the casting
was not completed until 749, and the final dedication ceremony,
at which the eyes of an image are touched to symbolise bringing
it to life, did not take place until 752. At that ceremony there
was great rejoicing, and it was followed by music and dancing,
and a maigre feast provided by the court for ten thousand monks.
The leading part in the rite was taken by an Indian ascetic named
Bodhisena, known in Japan, whither he had come some time
before, as Baramon Sōjō, or the Brahman High Priest.

The great Roshana, it should be added, was seated upon a
great bronze lotus, formed of a central core surrounded by curved
bronze sheets which are its petals. On the few petals which
remain from those days there can still be seen beautifully incised
figures of great and small Buddhas, in appropriate settings,
symbolising the hierarchy of the Kegon doctrine which has been
explained above. The erection of this immense image was probably, like so many undertakings of this time, inspired by a Chinese
precedent, for a stone image of Roshana some 85 feet high was
commenced in Lo-yang in 672 and completed in 675 by the
T'ang emperor. Though the erection of the Nara image raised
in an acute form the problem of assimilating Buddhism and
Shintō, it was a problem which had naturally been thought about
for some time beforehand, and the picturesque legend of the
oracle is only the representation in a palatable form of a syncretic
doctrine which the Buddhist priesthood had been gradually
evolving. They argued that the native gods were avatars, phases
of being, of Buddhist deities; and identifications like that of the
Sun Goddess with Locana were multiplied, so that in time many
native shrines were taken over by Buddhist priests and lost more
or less of their original character.

Buddhist priests now regularly took part in Shintō rites. There
is an interesting edict of the year 765, concerning the Great
Festival of the First Fruits, celebrated at the commencement of
each reign. No ceremony could be more exclusively Shintōist in
origin and intention, none more steeped in the indigenous beliefs
of nature worship and theocracy. Yet we find the empress publicly
proclaiming that this is an exceptional occasion, because she her-

self is a disciple of Buddha and as such has received the commandments; and considers that her duties, now that she has returned to the throne, are "first to serve the Three Treasures (Buddhism), then to worship the Gods (Shintō) and next to cherish the people." She goes on to say that there are some who think that the Shintō Gods should be kept distinct from the Three Treasures; but if they examine the Buddhist scriptures it will be seen that it is proper for the Gods to protect and revere the doctrine of Buddha. Therefore, because there is no reason why Buddhist and non-Buddhist should not mix together, she considers that there is no objection to what has hitherto been thought wrong, namely, the participation of priests and nuns in this distinctively Shintō worship.

The economic strength of the Buddhist priesthood in Japan rivalled that of all other classes, for their holdings of tax-free land were large and widely spread, and they attracted from the devout wealth of every description. As a religion Shintō could not challenge the new faith, which was profounder in doctrine, higher in ideals and vastly more efficient in organisation. Apart from these superiorities, Buddhism owed something of its triumph to its missionary zeal, which was fervid without being militant; and it certainly owed a great deal to the fact that the priests held, especially beyond the narrow court circle, almost a monopoly of liberal learning. Each monastery or temple in the province was a nucleus of culture, and many priests and monks regarded it as part of their vocation to spread material as well as spiritual benefits other than knowledge, which we may suppose to partake of both characters. The first infirmaries, orphanages, and similar charitable institutions in Japan were founded by Buddhist priests.

In one respect Buddhism in Japan was in a stronger position than in China or India. In both these countries there had existed, long before the birth of Buddhism, highly developed schools of religion and philosophy, and a powerful class of learned men. Buddhism in India had to compete with rival doctrines of great age and power; in China it aroused bitter opposition from Taoists and Confucianists. In all three countries the same principle was adopted of recognising native deities as manifestations of the Buddha, and it is more than likely that the idea of identifying the

Sun Goddess with Locana was suggested to the Japanese by application of that principle in China to both Confucius and Lao-tzŭ. It is related that a celebrated Chinese sage, known as "the noble-minded Fu," when asked whether he was a Buddhist priest pointed to his Taoist cap; when asked whether he was a Taoist, pointed to his Confucianist shoes; and finally, being asked whether he was a Confucianist, pointed to his Buddhist scarf. The practice illustrated by this tale was gradually developed to such a point in Japan that by the twelfth century a new type of Shintō had been formed, called Ryōbu, or Dual, Shintō, which was a compound of both religions, though Buddhism predominated in all its essential features.

Though the Buddhist religion brought to Japan great spiritual and even material benefits, the institutional growth of the Buddhist church, in its rapid rise to wealth and power, was accompanied by grave evils. These became more apparent in the following century, but already by the end of the Nara period certain abuses had become manifest. The intimate connection of the clergy with the court encouraged unscrupulous priests to interfere in politics. The prospect of enjoying such privileges as immunity from taxation and the lavish gifts of the faithful attracted to the priesthood a crowd of men quite unfitted for the religious life, who used their holy office merely for gain. There was at the same time, and partly for the same reason, an undue increase in the numbers both of temples and of clergy, resulting in an undue drain upon the resources of the laity, by whom they must needs be supported. So easy was life in holy orders that, as we learn from an official memorial of 779, most of the monks and nuns belonging to the provincial temples actually lived in comfort at Nara, and performed no duties at all. And not only was the religious order to a great extent parasitic; but also it comprised a large element of the ignorant and the dissolute.

NOTES TO CHAPTER VI

[1] Page 112, last five lines. Perhaps it is rather hard on the elegants to say that their accomplishments were barren and futile. An historian of Japanese æsthetics might well argue that their "futility" has left a more enduring mark than more sober and worthy activities.

Indeed the whole of this passage is far too moralistic; and on reflection I would prefer to say that the elegant society formed at Nara and developed in the Heian period bequeathed to subsequent Japanese life its high æsthetic tradition, its strong sense of form, its feeling for simplicity—in a word some of its most admirable qualities. Nor is it quite fair to say that the Japanese of the Nara period were deficient in respect for learning. These were their apprentice days, and it was not long before they developed a feeling for scholarship and a fraternity of scholars.

2 Page 117. It is worth noting, with regard to Japanese borrowings from China, that most Chinese philosophy is the study of human relationships from the point of view of government. Even doctrines of a mystical nature are often expressed in terms of the Ruler and the State. Chinese quietism, as typified by Taoism, is certainly as much a theory of government as a theory of individual conduct.

3 Page 122. Kusha teachings. The *Abhidharma-Kośa-śāstra* had an important influence upon intellectual life in T'ang China and in mediæval Japan. It has been described as occupying a position something like that of the *Summa Theologiae* in the Catholic Church. Since it deals with ultimate problems of ontology, with the nature of mind and matter, it probably was the foundation in Japan of organised studies in this field —at any rate in conjunction with the *Yuishikiron*. Such studies, however, as will have appeared from the note just above, were always highly specialised and exotic. They did not flourish in the philosophical climate of Japan.

4 Page 132. The full titles of these sutras are in translation "The sutra on the Benevolent King who protects his Country" (Ninnō) and "The Golden Radiance Excellent King Sutra" (Saishō).

Chapter VII

ART AND LETTERS

1. THE NATIVE LITERATURE

If there is one feature that time after time impresses a student
of the cultural history of the Japanese, it is the malign influence
of the linguistic handicap under which they have always suffered.
We have already noticed that, in taking over the elements of
Chinese learning, they were at once faced with difficulties arising
from the inadequacy of their own language and the lack of a
native script. These difficulties were overcome in part by various
makeshift devices too complicated to describe here. They were
ingenious, almost heroic devices; but it followed from their very
complexity that, sooner or later, some easier method had to be
worked out for representing Japanese sounds. Those sounds,
simple and few in number, are very well suited to notation by an
alphabet, and it is perhaps one of the tragedies of oriental history
that the Japanese genius did not a thousand years ago rise to its
invention. Certainly when one considers the truly appalling
system which in the course of centuries they did evolve, that
immense and intricate apparatus of signs for recording a few
dozen little syllables, one is inclined to think that the western
alphabet is perhaps the greatest triumph of the human mind.

Having no script of their own, the Japanese, if they wished to
write down a word of their mother language, must have recourse
to the Chinese characters. If they wished merely to record its
meaning, there was as a rule no difficulty; for, to take a simple
example, the symbol which stands for "mountain" will serve
as well for the Japanese word *yama* as the Chinese word *shan*,
since both have the same meaning—just as the symbol 5 stands
equally for "five," "cinq" or "fünf," according to the language of
the context. But when they wished to record the sound of a native
Japanese word, they were obliged to employ the Chinese character
as a phonetic sign, without reference to its meaning. This necessity
arose at an early date, since one of the first domestic uses to which
they put the Chinese script was the recording of Japanese personal
and place-names. Thus the place-name Nara could be written by

means of any two Chinese characters of which the reading approximated to *na* and *ra* respectively. At first the choice of characters to represent Japanese syllables was a matter of individual fancy, and it may be imagined that in the beginning there was great confusion. The subsequent history of their phonetic script is a gradual progress towards uniformity, but even to-day the ideal of one symbol for one sound and one sound for one symbol, though it has been approached, has not been reached.

The first book in Japanese of which we have knowledge is a chronicle compiled in A.D. 620, but this was lost and the oldest extant work is the *Kojiki*, or Record of Ancient Matters, completed in 712. It was written in a composite style, partly semantic, partly phonetic. The method was long and cumbrous, and therefore it had little chance of competing with the normal use of the Chinese script unless it were simplified. Simplification could at best be only relative, and it was delayed by the superior prestige of Chinese studies, which was, as we have noticed, overwhelming. It is however pleasing to record that the chief impetus to the development of a phonetic script was the Japanese love of poetry. Already in the two great national chronicles there had been preserved some two hundred early poems, which testify to an ancient impulse to verse. These have a certain appealing artlessness, but except to a highly patriotic taste they are crude things, and their interest is more historic than literary. They can hardly date further back than about A.D. 400, and they may be even later. Then, with an abrupt transition, we come upon an anthology of verse which is clearly the product of a refined and polished culture. This is the *Manyōshū*, or collection of a Myriad Leaves. It was compiled towards the close of the Nara period, and the more than four thousand poems which it contains, except for a few which may belong to the fourth century, were all written during the hundred years before 760. There can be little doubt that this poetic flow was stimulated by the example of Chinese literature, as it was given artistic form by the medium of the Chinese script. The poems are written by means of Chinese characters used phonetically in the way just outlined, and not as the names of things. The characters are borrowed, so to speak, for a special purpose, and when so employed are called by the

Japanese *kana*, or "borrowed names."[1] Those used as in this anthology are known as *Manyō kana*, and they are the parents of the modern Japanese syllabary. They are so numerous and were used in so irregular a fashion that (to translate from the preface of the most recent Japanese edition) "the difficulty of giving them the correct reading is indescribable . . . and though they have been studied incessantly from ancient times there are still many obscure passages."

These poems, except for a few which seem to echo ancient folk songs, are the product of a small, cultivated, aristocratic society. They are composed according to a strict and fastidious canon, and they have a somewhat narrow emotional range. Most of them display a delicate sensibility, and many a fresh inspiration, a light and charming impressionistic touch. It is noticeable that to our western judgment the longer poems are the least successful. They seem to be ill-sustained, to lack in sweep and vitality, while the short poems of thirty-one syllables are sure, rapid pictures of things seen, felt and remembered. But it is vain to hope to penetrate to the heart of a stranger's poetry, and we had better content ourselves with suggesting that the Japanese language, without foreign admixture, is a graceful but not a noble instrument; for, its sounds being few in number and wanting in variety, it can scarcely compass strong or delicate rhythms or subtle harmonies.

The *Manyōshū* is practically the only contribution to pure literature produced in the Nara period, but there was throughout the eighth century considerable literary activity of other kinds. The *Kojiki* and the *Nihon-Shoki* (in Japanese and Chinese respectively) belong to its first decades, and there were other important compilations of a similar nature. Chief among these were the *Fūdoki*, surveys of the natural resources and local traditions of the various provinces; and a continuation of the official histories, the *Shoku-Nihongi* or Further Chronicles of Japan, which carries the record on from 700 to 791. It is a valuable source-book, written in Chinese except for a number of imperial edicts, which are recorded phonetically and so provide us with probably the most ancient specimens extant of prose writing in pure Japanese. But even these documents reveal traces of Chinese influence, and thus furnish one more example of the penetration of Chinese thought and the Chinese language, subjects which had first claim upon the interest and the energy of any educated person and were indispensable for a career at court or in the Buddhist church. The foundation of all this learning was a knowledge of reading and writing. One is apt to overlook the simple fact that these were still new and rare accomplishments, confined to a special class, in which men from China and Korea or their descendants predominated. Consequently most of the literary labour of the Nara period was spent on transcribing or imitating foreign models, and there was little time or talent for original activities. The mere copying of manuscripts brought over from the continent was a tremendous task, and one of national importance. It was the function of a department of state, in which there was a special bureau, charged with copying, mounting and binding, and the provision of requisites therefor. This bureau had a numerous staff of clerks, binders, paper makers, pen makers, and ink makers. It supervised the work of copyists, who were supplied with materials and hired by the day for a ration of food and drink and clean garments to be worn at their task. At its head was an official of high rank, such as Kishida Yoroshi, a prominent scholar of Korean origin, who held the post in 733.

On a still larger scale was the copying of sacred Buddhist writings. The records state that scribes were assembled in a temple in Yamato in 673, and set to copying the whole canon, the voluminous *Tripitaka*; but the oldest extant Japanese copy of a complete sutra seems to be one dating from 686. By the middle of the Nara period the enthusiasm for sutra copying had grown to a fever. The holy writings were transcribed not only for use but to acquire merit, and pious persons would lavish great wealth on the production of beautifully illuminated scrolls and costly cases to contain them. There was an official copying bureau in the imperial palace, presided over by a prince of the blood, another in the empress's household; in the provinces official funds were allotted to copying sutras and commentaries, while all the great temples and monasteries had scribes at work upon the same task. It is said that nearly half the documents in the Shōsōin deal with payments to scribes, the cost of paper and ink, and other related matters. Fragments have been preserved showing how the work was arranged, how the scribes practised characters before finally writing on the scrolls, how they scribbled poems and notes on the backs of bills. The following is a typical extract from the accounts:

FIG. 21. *A scribe in the Sutra Copying Bureau. Taken from a caricature on a piece of waste copying paper dated 745 and preserved in the Shōsōin.*

Jinki, fourth year (727), twelfth month, fourth day. Received, paper for copying *Dai Hannya sutra*, 10,000 pieces.

Jinki, fifth year, fourth month, first day. Returned, 2,600 pieces, left over from *Dai Hannya*.

All this labour, though much of it was mechanical, helped to spread at least the rudiments of learning, since it brought into being a new class of clerical workers. It promoted calligraphy, and developed the crafts of making paper and ink and brushes and colours, to the general benefit of art.

There is little more to say about literature or learning in this age. A collection of Chinese poems composed by Japanese scholars was made—the first of its kind.[2] Much work went to the compilation of laws and regulations, the framing of codes, and such-like efforts. But all this was derivative, for Japan was still at school; and, if we except the purest native verse in the *Manyōshū*, the first expression of an original spirit is to be seen in art rather than in letters.

2. ART

IF the Japanese mastered somewhat painfully and slowly the learned and literary elements of Chinese culture, their hearts leaped to welcome all its beauty. The progressive influence of Chinese taste and technique is visible in objects found in their early tombs, but it was not until the introduction of Buddhism that their latent artistic impulse attained full scope and vigour. The year 552 may be taken as marking the disappearance of their primitive indigenous art and the beginning of a stage of unalloyed borrowing. But when the Japanese began in their religious art to copy Chinese models, they were, though they did not always know it, drawing inspiration from most distant occidental sources, for Chinese art itself had for centuries past been subjected to diverse foreign influences. Recent researches seem to have established Hellenic influence, working through an Iranian medium upon the art of China even before the Han dynasty, while it is known that the westward expansion of the Han empire in the direction of Kashgar led to traffic with the West, so that the Han Chinese knew about the Roman empire and the Romans knew of the Chinese as *Seres* and China as *Serica*, the country of silk. But it was the spread of Buddhism which brought about a closer intercourse between East and West. Buddhist monks began to visit China in the first century of our era. During the second and third centuries missionaries from India laboured in Lo-yang or Ch'ang-an, while from the fourth century many teachers and students made the long journey between India and China, along a regular route which passed through Gandhara and Khotan. Among the earliest of these were several of Iranian origin. The Tatars who overran Northern China in the fourth century favoured Buddhism, and some of the Tatar kingdoms, notably Wei, adopted it as their state religion. This patronage brought from India many holy men, and encouraged Chinese pilgrims to journey to the home of the faith. Before long a chain of holy places was strung along their road, monasteries and settlements where sutras were copied or translated, pictures painted and sacred figures carved. Then, as unity was restored to China under the Sui and the T'ang dynasties, her secular power spread westward once more. Soon after 600 she was suzerain of Turfan, Kucha and Khotan. Early in the next century there was a Chinese garrison in Bokhara, Samarkand was captured by Chinese troops, and Iranian princelings of Transoxus and the ancient Bactria put themselves under Chinese protection. Before 750 the Chinese had sent troops across the high passes of the Pamir, and their governor in Kucha, who was a Korean, was thus able to overlook India (Gandhara and Kashmir), Persia and Sogdiana, as well as Tibet and Kashgaria, the country later known as Turkestan.

It may be imagined, therefore, that wave after wave of occidental influence, mounting in volume, passed towards China, chiefly through Kashgaria, a region as Buddhist as India in its faith, but revealing in its art the imprint not only of India but of Gandhara, which was Hellenic, of Persia, and of Byzantium. Thus, in the Turfan desert there have been found tombs of the first half of the seventh century containing silks of various manufacture and design, some Chinese, some Sasanian; and in those tombs, between the lips of the dead, sixth century coins, Byzantine and Sasanian. Such objects passed along the caravan route, in the baggage of monks and traders, to Lo-yang, to Ch'ang-an, and thence to Korea and to Japan as gifts from the Chinese court or treasures purchased by returning travellers. Knowledge of alien arts was thus conveyed eastward. Sometimes a style or a method was transmitted without change, sometimes it would undergo a transformation and, because the Chinese genius was too individual

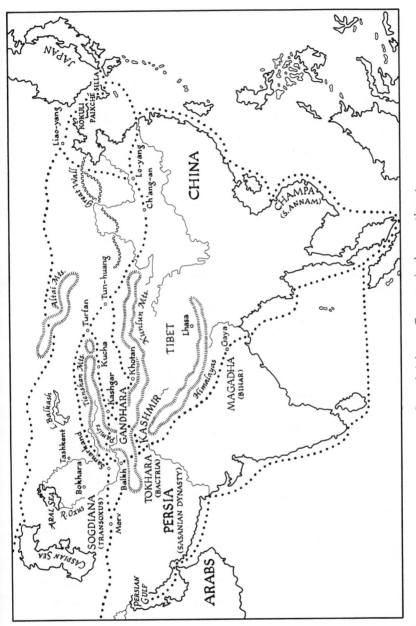

FIG. 22. *Central Asian traffic routes in the seventh century.*

to be merely receptive, composite types would be evolved in which sometimes the western element is almost submerged by the eastern.[3] So, in sites ranging from Khotan to the Pacific coast, archæologists have found paintings and statues that might have been copied from Graeco-Roman originals; frescoes recalling Persian miniatures; figures that present "the happiest mixture of Indian suppleness, Greek elegance and Chinese loveliness"; images of divinities in whose countenance Chinese eyes are combined with Hellenic features, or again of angels and demons so Chinese in aspect, costume and surroundings that little Indian is discernible beyond their origin in Buddhist legend. It seems that a definite, separate continental art was created of all these foreign elements, a standard type which spread over central and eastern Asia, so that an image or a picture found in some buried site of, say, Turfan may have its very counterpart in the ruins of the ancient capital of Silla or among the treasures of a Nara monastery. In a very general way, the early developments of Japanese art may be said to repeat the history of this continental art, and to reveal traces of all the various ingredients of which it was compounded. But, because of her situation on the far-eastern edge of the continent, Japan as a rule received only what had been absorbed by China and given a certain Chinese flavour before transmission. She was generally some decades behind China, so that she was not so open to ephemeral influences. Though from time to time objects from distant western places reached her shores, they remained for the most part exotic; and in the arts, as in learning and government, China was her chief pattern and instructor.

It is as well, in outlining these developments, to follow the practice of art historians by distinguishing quite arbitrary but convenient periods.* The first of these is the Asuka Period (552-645), so called because the court was during those years at or near a place of that name, not far from the present Nara. In this age Buddhism in Japan began to gain in strength. Images were brought over from Korea, and as religious fervour grew men desired to acquire merit by worshipping images and building

---

* There is no uniformity in this practice. Different scholars prefer different dates for the beginning and end of each period. See the Preface for an account of the divisions now recommended by eminent Japanese scholars.

temples to contain them. In the first decades of this period many artists and craftsmen came to Japan from Korea or China, so that it is difficult to assert of any early work that it was made by Japanese hands. Probably most of the masterpieces of the Asuka period were wrought by foreign artists, and certainly they were under wholly foreign influence. As to what was made on Japanese soil, we cannot tell. The buildings, of course; but in statuary, large pieces of wooden sculpture could be carried over in sections, and even extremely heavy metal images are known to have been brought from South China to Japan at a somewhat later date. Yet, generally speaking, the difficulties of transport were so great that it must have been better to bring over skilled men than to risk loss and breakage of such precious cargo on a sea-journey. Of such skilled men there was no lack, for a temporary proscription of Buddhism in North China from about 574 had driven many monks, artists, and craftsmen across from Shantung to settle in the various kingdoms of Korea, and it was common for one ruler to send another a painter or a sculptor by way of gift or tribute.

From the records we know that 46 temples were built in Japan by 640, but nearly all of these have perished completely, being wooden structures that could not easily survive the stress of weather and the always imminent danger of fire. By remarkable good fortune there have, however, been preserved certain splendid monuments of which the most celebrated are the Golden Hall (*Kondō*), the pagoda, a roofed gallery and a gate, of the Hōryūji, a monastery founded in 607 by the Empress Suiko.* Their architecture is of a style current in China in the sixth century and introduced into Japan from Korea. The Golden Hall is a double-roofed structure with sturdy pillars showing entasis and surmounted by somewhat heavy brackets; but its proportions are so just and the curves of its great tiled roof so pleasing that it gives an impression not of weight but of soaring boldness. It is probably the oldest wooden building in the world, and one of the most beautiful. It is the product of a fine taste and an architectural

---

* Documentary evidence seems to prove that the whole fabric was destroyed by fire in 670 and rebuilt in the same style soon after 708. But the most important treasures of statuary, &c., were probably saved.

technique which, though slightly crude in detail, is surprisingly advanced and free in style. This is true also of the graceful pagoda and the other surviving relics. It is an interesting feature of Buddhist architecture of this period in Japan that extensive sites on level ground were chosen, and the buildings, besides being well-proportioned in themselves, were generously spaced and harmoniously grouped.

In these buildings were enshrined statues, paintings, and other treasures, some of which have been preserved. Like the temples themselves, they were inspired by Chinese models or by Korean copies of Chinese work. While the buildings are not exact imitations but show signs of adaptation to Japanese materials and habits, the Buddhist images are either imported or bear a very close resemblance to Chinese originals. They exhibit in the treatment of drapery, the modelling of faces, and the use of certain ornamental motives, close correspondences with stone images in the cave temples of Yun-kang and Lung-men, which belong to the Wei dynasty (420-534); and there is reason to suppose that they owe some of their character to the fact that their makers endeavoured to transfer to bronze or wood features which are proper to a stone technique. Two styles can be discerned. One is a stiff archaic style, displaying a tendency to bilateral symmetry and a neglect to observe the natural proportions of head, limbs and trunk. Inscriptions and other evidence show that images in this style were for the most part the work of Kuratsukuribe no Tori and his pupils. Tori, as we have seen, was of Chinese descent. He is known to have made certainly a large gilt bronze Shaka trinity in 623 and probably the central figure of a Yakushi trinity in 607,* both fine pieces still in the Hōryūji. Since we know that image makers came over from Paikché as early as 577 and frequently after that date, it is likely that they formed one or more schools in addition to that of Tori. It is clear that there was another master working in another tradition, for there are certain images which, though undoubtedly of the same period, and inspired by Chinese originals, are the products of a more advanced technique and show a much greater command by the

---

* See Plate II. The inscription on the halo of this image is the oldest existing example of Chinese script as used in Japan.

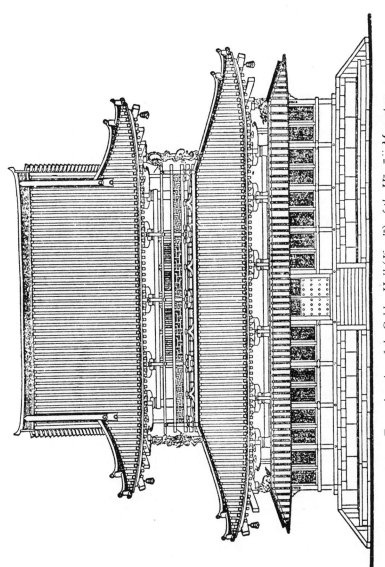

FIG. 23. *Front elevation of the Golden Hall (Kondō) of the Hōryūji Monastery.*

artist of his material. Three at least of these are so remarkable that it is hard to choose among them and impossible to resist superlatives in their description. There is the Kudara Kwannon, a wooden figure, graceful, tall and slender, which, as its name shows, is thought to have come from Korea, and has all the marks of Wei influence. There is the Maitreya (?Kwannon) of the Kōryūji, known as the Kudara Miroku, which is a gilt image of dry lacquer over wood, a sweet-faced pensive figure, exquisitely poised. And lastly there is the wooden image of Kwannon—now dark and shining from incense smoke and over twelve centuries of pious rubbing—which sits in the Chūgūji nunnery, where once was the home of Prince Shōtoku's mother. It is a profoundly moving work, of such perfection that it seems to belong to no time or place. Its exact date is unknown, but it is thought to have been made shortly after the Prince's death, and to represent him as the Goddess of Mercy of whom he was an incarnation. All these are far more appealing than the bronze images of the school of Tori, which have nobility as well as a simple archaic charm but are wanting in sheer loveliness. No doubt there were technical reasons for this difference, since bronze is a difficult medium; but the wooden images are the work of master hands and could stand proudly by the side of any other sculpture in the world.

The relics of the Asuka age do not show such progress in painting as in sculpture. The formation of guilds of painters in 605 is recorded and in 610 there was sent to Japan by the king of Kōkuli a monk named Donchō, skilled in making paper, ink and painters' colours. It seems that so far painting in Japan was confined to decorating temples and images and the illumination of sutras. Certainly the works of importance that remain from this period are examples of applied rather than pure art: objects such as the "Tamamushi" portable shrine, the panels of which display an interesting technique called *mitsuda-e*, a method of lacquer-painting with lead colours mixed in oil. Considerable advance was made also in metal work, if we may judge from certain specimens of casting, chiselling, inlay and repoussé in the form of banners, crowns, aureoles and the ornamentation of

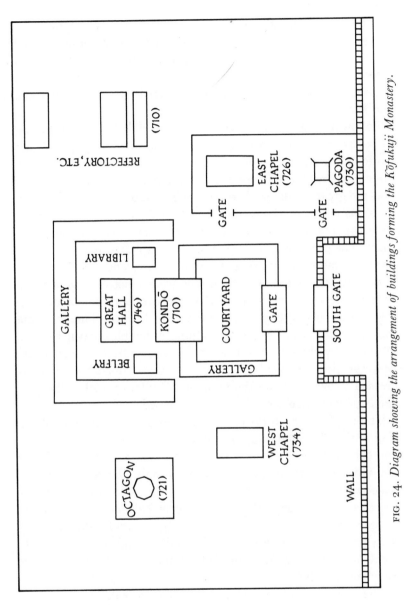

FIG. 24. *Diagram showing the arrangement of buildings forming the Kōfukuji Monastery.*

woodwork. These all show high skill and a strong feeling for design. The arabesques and other patterns in frequent use as well as the general treatment of figures and drapery indicate in most cases direct Korean influence, transmitting Chinese motives and methods which in their turn were affected by the arts of India and Western Asia.

Following the Asuka period comes the Hakuhō period, lasting from 645 to 724. It is a transitional period in which Japanese art made rapid strides, being now subjected to Chinese influence directly, as well as by way of Korea. The Sui dynasty had fallen and the great T'ang era had begun. The Japanese were in direct relations with the T'ang court and, as we have seen, were feverishly copying T'ang models in religion, law, ceremony and costume. The projected building of the new capital at Nara naturally gave an important stimulus to architecture, and we know that a number of palaces and mansions were erected; but of these hardly any traces remain, so that we can only conjecture the appearance of the city which sprang up by 710. The Japanese took so enthusiastically to the building of temples that it became an abuse by the end of the seventh century. By the time of the Empress Jitō (687-697) the number of sacred edifices had increased to over 500 and the number of buildings within the precincts of each monastery had also increased.

The chief architectural relic of the period is the pagoda of the Yakushiji. This monastery was founded in 680, but removed to another site near the centre of the new city of Nara in 718. Of the fabric of 718 there remains now only the three-storeyed pagoda, a beautifully proportioned tower, which gives an impression of lightness and grace. In technical details, such as its compound brackets and the design of eaves and balustrades, it shows an advance on the Hōryūji building, and in artistic treatment an increasing freedom and originality, well displayed by the charming finial.

The sculpture of the Hakuhō period reveals strong direct Chinese influence, coupled with an increasing technical mastery. It consists for the most part of images of divine personages, but there is some secular or quasi-religious art in the form of carved masks (to which no parallel can be found in China or Korea)

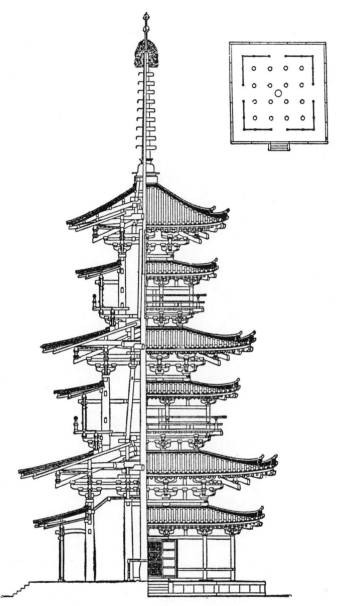

FIG. 25. *The pagoda of the Yakushiji Monastery at Nara.*

used in ceremonial posturings called *gigaku* at festivals held in the great Nara monasteries. In the Buddhist images there is visible not only the inspiration of T'ang models, but the complex of influences which formed T'ang art—the development of the Sui tradition together with the motives and treatment of the con-

FIG. 26. *Finial of Yakushiji pagoda, circa 720.*

tinental style which we have already noticed. It is deeply interesting to study the masterpieces of this time, which have been preserved in Japan more numerously than in war-ridden China, in a search for parallels and affinities to throw light on the spread of artistic impulses, echoing and re-echoing over the vast Asiatic

continent. But this is work for experts, and here we can only
glance at some of the chief examples in passing. Thus the remarkable bronze in the Yakushiji known as the Shō-Kwannon, an
imposing figure seven feet high, in clinging and flowing draperies
that contrast sharply with the stiff swathes of Asuka images,
shows a strong sense of form which evidently combines Indian
grace with Chinese strength. It is suggested by some that it is the
image presented to Japan by the king of Paikché in 720, and this
doubtless is its approximate date, though other authorities identify
it with an image made in memory of the Empress Kōgyoku soon
after her death in 644. In the same monastery is also enshrined
a great bronze image of Yakushi which in inspiration unmistakably belongs to the early T'ang school and is not a development
of the older Korean tradition. It is a majestic work, perfect in
the flow of its curved surfaces and the justness of its proportions.
It is mature in conception and, though in detail not entirely flaw-
less, shows an astonishing triumph over technical difficulties. Set
on a white marble pediment, its massive bronze dais, over which
the draperies fall in boldly asymmetrical folds, bears carvings of
queer dwarf-like naked creatures, conjectured to portray members
of some backward Indian tribe receiving the benefits of religion.

Most of the sculpture of this period is in bronze, wood or dry
lacquer,[4] and it is noticeable that the Japanese do not seem to
have taken to stone, although in China and Korea much of the
finest carving, whether of statues or reliefs, is in stone or marble.
This is the more curious since certain beautiful stone images still
preserved in a cave chapel (the Sekkutsu-an or Sok-kul-an) near
the old capital of Silla closely resemble both Japanese statuary of
the Nara period and early T'ang clay figures in the Tun Huang
grottoes in western China. The Japanese genius seems to have
expressed itself best in a more plastic medium. Clay was at first
relatively little used, no doubt because of its fragility, but there
are certain unbaked clay works of this period which, though not
of surpassing beauty, show most plainly the debt of early Japanese
art to China. They are the surviving members of four groups of
statuettes in the base of the Hōryūji pagoda, portraying in suitable
surroundings such incidents from Buddhist scripture as the Entry

into Nirvana and the Partition of the Relics. The setting in miniature grottoes must surely have been suggested by cave chapels in
China, and the figures are so Chinese in aspect that one might
almost suppose they were imported from China or at least made
by Chinese craftsmen.

In pictorial art the most important relic of this period is the
mural painting, representing scenes of Paradise, in the Golden
Hall of the Hōryūji. These frescoes, which date from about 710,
clearly owe their original inspiration to Indian models and have
even been somewhat rashly ascribed to Indian artists. They are
grand compositions, and their bold, free outlines are typical of
early T'ang painting as influenced by Buddhist themes and
Central Asiatic treatment. Their technique is similar to that of
mural paintings in Khotan and of the Ajanta frescoes.[5] It is best
therefore to assume that they were executed by or under the direction of a Chinese or Korean artist familiar with continental styles.

A painting, often reproduced, of Prince Shōtoku and his two sons
is sometimes ascribed to this period, but some authorities consider
that it is a copy, made a good deal later, of a seventh century
original.

The third and final Nara art period (725-794) is known as
Tempyō, after the official name of an era covering most of those
years. It was the golden age of Buddhist art in Japan. The
Japanese had passed out of their apprenticeship, and were now
masters in their own right. They did not, it is true, cut loose from
Chinese tradition. On the contrary, in nearly all their work of
the Nara period T'ang influence is clearly visible; and since the
art of those days was almost exclusively religious art, they could
not have developed a purely native style without being false to
the Buddhist ideals by which they were inspired. There were
certain fixed canons, both of subject and of treatment, from
which they could not depart, and therefore they must in general
follow Chinese leaders, whose work was in any case of such
quality as to command their high respect. But though they used
T'ang models, they did not slavishly imitate. There is a slight
but quite recognisable Japanese flavour about the sculpture of
the seventh century, and it is increasingly plain as the eighth century grows older. Previously the energies of the Japanese had been

absorbed in the effort to keep up with rapidly developing Chinese styles, and they had at first lagged far behind, as can be seen from the Hōryūji bronzes, which though made in T'ang times are in the Wei manner. But after Nara had been built for over a generation, let us say from about 750, when stable conditions fostered the arts and promoted regular intercourse with China, the Japanese were not more than a decade or so behind, and could afford to be self-reliant, within the limits imposed by their natural desire to be entirely up-to-date. Tempyō art, then, and particularly Tempyō sculpture, may be described briefly as a slightly conservative reflection of mature T'ang, but revealing an unmistakable native character.

In output the Tempyō period was so prodigal that here we can do no more than indicate its principal features. In architecture there was rapid advance, and a more and more national style was evolved, in keeping with national habits. Many great monasteries were erected in the new capital, or moved thither from other sites, not only for the embellishment of the imperial city but because such sacred edifices were deemed necessary for its protection. Among those that were transferred was the Kōfukuji (710), a spacious group of buildings under the special patronage of the Fujiwara family. But most symbolic of the age was the Tōdaiji, or Eastern Great Monastery, so called from its position in the eastern quarter of the capital. It was conceived on a grand scale, its enclosure being over two miles square and containing numerous buildings, of which the largest and most splendid was the Hall of the Great Buddha. The growth of the Tōdaiji summarises much of the social and political history of the time, and it also provides an epitome of artistic progress. It was founded in 745, but work was not commenced in earnest until 747; and though the Great Hall was completed as a structure in 751, more than a decade passed before it was fully decorated within and without, and the monastery equipped with the various chapels, oratories and offices which were regarded as essential. Hardly anything is left of all this imposing fabric, but many of the treasures which were lavished upon the Tōdaiji have been preserved, and enable us to picture its great wealth of precious and beautiful things. Of Tempyō statuary there is so much that is

important that it is difficult to single out any one work, but perhaps the large clay image of Bonten (Brahma) in the Lotus Hall
(Hokkedō) of the Tōdaiji is among the most characteristic pieces
of Tempyō sculpture. Its modelling is superb in grace and
smatery, and it shows an almost secular naturalism as compared
with such imagined, supernal forms as the Kwannon of the
Chūgūji nunnery. Yet it is not a mere triumph of visual observation. Realism is there, but with it is harmoniously combined an
idealism that could not have flourished in a tired, incredulous age.
The same is true of the statues of the Four Guardian Kings now
belonging to the ordination chapel of the Tōdaiji. Their threatening postures and terrifying countenances are marvels of representation, and yet the artist has managed to convey the impression of an underlying benevolence, which they share with
divine persons of more apparent benignity. It is, indeed, characteristic of the Buddhist art of this period in Japan that its pure taste
rejects the monstrous and the ungracious. It does not overflow
into the extravagances and excesses of which the Chinese genius
is so prolific. It tends to the delicate and the restrained, it is instinctive rather than intellectual, gentle rather than vigorous.
As Japanese art passed out of Chinese tutelage, it seems to have
lost the benefit of a certain brutal energy and imaginative luxuriance. Perhaps it has suffered from this want of power; but
nobody who is familiar with its early masterpieces can fail to be
grateful for its other abundant charms.

The realistic trend of the Tempyō period manifested itself in
a number of fine portrait statues, principally of famous ecclesiastics. Notable among these are images of the monks Ganjin and
Rōben, who were great figures in their day at Nara. There seems
also to have been a school of painters of religious portraits, but
little is known of painting in general in this era beyond the fact
that it was assiduously practised and, if we may judge from the
few surviving examples, reached a high standard in purity of
line and brilliance of colour. Among these relics is a six-fold
screen of peculiar historical interest. It is decorated with paintings
which represent female figures standing under trees, and bears a
startling resemblance, even in such details as the treatment of

foliage, to a picture discovered in a tomb at Astana, in Central Asia. Here we have almost conclusive proof that one style at least of T'ang art was spread widely over Asia, from west to the farthest east. There is no mistaking the type of T'ang beauty, then doubtless in vogue in China. The tall, slender, gently drooping Botticellian figures of the previous era have given place to well-poised ladies of ampler curves, whose full throats are lightly creased and whose costume is of a befitting richness. The charming 'Sri, a Hindu goddess, as portrayed in a painting of about 770 belonging to the Yakushiji might be a Japanese princess following the T'ang mode. Nor is this strong continental influence surprising when one considers the exotic contents of the repository known as the Shōsōin. This storehouse contains personal belongings of the Emperor Shōmu, which were in 756 dedicated to the Buddha of the Tōdaiji by his widow, and have remained there, intact, until this day. They include manuscripts, pictures, ornaments, weapons, musical instruments, utensils, and various articles which had been used in the dedication ceremonies of the Great Buddha, so that together they provide a picture of life at the court in the eighth century. Remarkable among them are objects of foreign origin or betraying strong foreign influence. There are vessels of glass and pottery, metal work, lacquer and textiles, several of which were either brought from Central Asia or Persia or Greece or are reproductions of things from those regions. Such are a marble relief in the Byzantine manner, and a painting of a lady in Persian dress. At the same time there are many beautiful objects which were undoubtedly produced in Japan, and these all go to prove that by the eighth century the Japanese had arrived at a mature craftsmanship, and could henceforward in the arts progress upon lines of their own, as in the ensuing period they plainly did.

NOTES TO CHAPTER VII

[1] Page 140. "Borrowed names." This is the usual etymology but the word *Kana* may perhaps be derived from the first two letters of the Korean syllabary, which began with *Ka na ta ra*. Korea had a syllabary as early as A.D. 690, which no doubt influenced the development of the Japanese syllabary. It is interesting to note that—much later—another

syllabary (called *Un-mun*) was devised in Korea and introduced by royal proclamation in 1446. This is really an alphabet, since the syllabic signs are built up of elements representing vowels and consonants. One asks why the Japanese did not light upon a similar method. The reason perhaps is that, their native words being composed entirely of open syllables, they did not think of analysing sounds. Korean has both open and closed syllables, and the distinction between vowel and consonant is therefore more apparent. When the Japanese took over a Chinese word consisting of a closed syllable, they turned it into two open syllables. Archaic Chinese *mok*, for instance, became in Japanese *moku*.

[2] Page 143. The first collection of Chinese poems composed by Japanese was the anthology called *Kwaifusō* compiled in A.D. 751.

[3] Page 146. Perhaps the most striking example of the transmission of an iconographic motif is the appearance, on the head dress of Bodhisattvas figured on the Tachibana shrine in the Hōryuji, of discs and crescents proper to the diadem of a Kusano-Sassanid prince.

[4] Page 155. The first dry lacquer is probably post-Hakuhō.

[5] Page 156. The use of shading for relief in the Ajanta and Hōryuji frescoes is not a Chinese technique. Perhaps it would be better to say of the Hōryuji murals that they are typical of early T'ang painting as applied to Buddhist themes brought to China through Central Asia. They form part of a continental tradition of mural painting of which examples remain in Ceylon, Ajanta, Khotan and Tunhuang.

Chapter VIII

LAW AND ADMINISTRATION

THOUGH the Japanese had some knowledge of Chinese administrative and judicial methods from an early date in their intercourse with the continent, they could not apply it, except in a
tentative way, so long as the clan system lasted; for the heads of
clans exercised full administrative and judicial powers over their
own units, while the essence of the Chinese system was a centralised bureaucratic authority. It was not therefore until, following
upon the Taikwa reform edict, some progress had been made in
breaking down the clans' autonomy, that the Japanese began in
earnest to compile laws. From that time they never stopped.
Their first models were chiefly the Sui and T'ang codes, which
had already been copied by the kingdoms of Korea; and they
followed Chinese practice by dividing laws into four categories,
named *ritsu*, *ryō*, *kyaku* and *shiki*, which correspond roughly to
prohibitions, injunctions, institutes and forms, and may be regarded as a penal code (*ritsu*), a civil and administrative code
(*ryō*), and a miscellaneous body of regulations (*kyaku* and *shiki*)
for the enforcement of the codes in points of detail and, as time
went on, for their amendment. These analogies would perhaps
offend a legal historian, but the distinction between the groups
was never a very clear one, even in China; and the correspondence is therefore close enough for our purpose. The first
code of which we hear is that of the Emperor Tenchi, dating from
662, but though it is often referred to in the chronicles and appears
to have been revised and enlarged on several occasions, it has
not survived. The earliest extant code is the Taihō code, completed in 701 by Fujiwara no Fubito, Awata no Mabito and
others. It was promulgated that year, and Doctors of Law were
despatched to the various provincial governments to explain it
and see to its enforcement. Its exact contents are not known, for
it has come down to us only in a commentary dated 833, an
important work called *Ryō no Gige*, and a similar but larger work,
the *Ryō no Shūge*, of 920. These embody successive revisions and
commentaries of the intervening period, in such a form that the
early elements cannot easily be distinguished from the late.

The Taihō code was revised in 718, but the new code, known as the Yōrō code, was not enforced until 757. These various dates are significant, because they show how much attention was paid to legislation in those days, and how the unsuitability of parts of Chinese law was revealed by practical experience in Japan. The later codes, though similar in form, differ very considerably in content from their Chinese models. The Japanese penal code was less drastic, while the administrative code underwent considerable modifications so as to suit it to conditions in Japan. Thus the chapters dealing with religious matters, though they correspond to certain T'ang models in terminology and arrangement, are in substance almost entirely original.

We cannot here trace in detail the development during the Nara period of the various administrative and judicial institutions which grew out of these codes. It is, however, as well to describe them in broad outline, premising that the description cannot be taken to represent accurately the sum of conditions at a given moment, but rather an average of conditions through the eighth century. It is obviously impossible in a short space to follow exactly the changes which, as one might expect, took place so continuously in that age of reform and experiment.

Taking first the administrative system, we have already noticed the formation of a council of state, controlling eight boards or ministries, and the division of the country into provinces administered by provincial governors appointed by the central authority. Outside the four (after 716, five) home provinces, which were on a special footing owing to their proximity to the capital, the country was divided into provinces, which were subsequently divided into districts, further subdivided into townships, these three constituting the units of provincial, district and local government, respectively. There was a major division of the country into groups of provinces, styled *dō* or circuits, of which there were seven. This was a topographical rather than administrative division, though, it is true, the circuits corresponded to territories under the jurisdiction of certain inspecting officers. Their chief interest, however, is that they have survived until to-day as geographical names, such as the familiar Tōkaidō, or Eastern Sea Circuit. The number of provinces and districts at the time of the Reform is not known, but their boundaries shifted and their numbers increased as the influence of the central authority spread, until by the beginning of the ninth century there were altogether 66 provinces, comprising 592 districts.

Such being the framework of the administration, we may now deal briefly with the functions of the officials by whom it was worked. The administrative hierarchy was in the main modelled on the T'ang system, but certain concessions were, from the beginning, made to native sentiment and local conditions, and we shall see that in the century or so following the Taikwa reform many changes became or appeared to become necessary, as institutions adopted from China proved unworkable or irksome in Japan. This was to be expected, since the first reformers took over the Chinese system more or less as it existed on paper, and, even if we make the bold assumption that Chinese practice squared with Chinese theory, it was unlikely that the highly organized T'ang framework would fit at every point the Japanese background to which it was applied. Perhaps the most interesting point of difference between the T'ang model and the Japanese copy is the formation of the Department of Religion (*Jingikwan*), which was not only higher in rank than any single ministry, but was of the same standing as the supreme administrative body, the Council of State itself. The importance attached to this department shows that, whatever temporary eclipse may have been suffered by the native cult as a religious and social institution, the ruling class did not lose sight of its value as an instrument to uphold and strengthen the prestige of the dominant clans. It must not be supposed, therefore, that Buddhism swept the field clear. The performance of certain Shintō rites in the palace seems to have lapsed, or to have become perfunctory, for a short time during the Nara period, especially in the reigns of such devout Buddhists as the Emperor Shōmu; but it was soon resumed, and the proper observance of the great traditional fasts and festivals has continued until the present day to be an essential part of government and perhaps the most serious duty of the sovereign.

The functions of the various ministers of state have already been mentioned, and we need only add that, though they corresponded pretty closely with the Chinese model, there were some interesting differences. In the first place under the T'ang sovereign the supreme organ was a Council of State composed of six high officers, supported by three bureaux and assisted by two vice-chancellors, but in Japan all these powers were combined in the person of the Chancellor, supported by the Ministers of the Right and Left. This simplification was more in keeping with the autocratic tradition of Japan, and was, no doubt, designed to perpetuate the monopoly of authority enjoyed before the reform by the Great Omi or the Great Muraji. Under the T'ang system the council of state controlled the six ministries, which may be looked upon as roughly equivalent to departments of Internal Affairs, Taxation, Rites, War, Justice and Works. The Japanese followed this division on broad lines, but they added two departments, the Nakatsukasa, literally the Central Office, and the Kunaishō, literally the Department of the Palace Interior. These differences, too, are significant. The Nakatsukasa corresponded to one of the bureaux under the T'ang Council of State, but whereas in the Chinese arrangement it was rather in the nature of a cabinet secretariat, in Japan it was raised to the rank of a ministry, and one of the most important. It was responsible for the drafting of imperial decrees and proclamations, and dealt with memorials to the throne, besides having to do with the compilation of state records and the affairs of court officers. The Kunaishō was concerned chiefly with the provision of supplies for the emperor and his household. In other words, these two additional ministries served primarily to maintain the imperial dignity.

Turning now to the provincial administration, we find that the duties of a provincial governor were extremely comprehensive, because he represented in his person all departments of state. He was, in theory at least, responsible for the supervision of the shrines in his territory, and in a sense acted as a deputy of the sovereign in religious ceremonial pertaining to the national cult: he had to control the compilation of registers of land and population, the levy for military service, the collection of taxes, the apportionment of forced labour, the judgment of suits: he combined, in short, all civil, military, judicial and religious functions, as mouthpiece and agent of the central authority. Such wide and various powers were naturally in most cases delegated to subordinates, but the ultimate responsibility was supposed to lie with the governor himself, although in practice it was often neglected or abused. The provinces were graded according to their importance; by what criterion it is not quite clear, but probably that of the revenue which they yielded. The selection of provincial governors was a delicate matter, from the earliest times when it was necessary for the central authority to walk warily for fear of the opposition of powerful local chieftains, down to a later stage when the governors themselves became a danger, owing to their arbitrary and grasping conduct. The beginnings of the system are not very clear, for, though there is mention of "provincial authorities" in Shōtoku Taishi's injunctions, this refers doubtless to a transition stage between the autonomy of local chieftains and the administration of fully accredited officials on behalf of the sovereign. Struggles for land and armed encounters among territorial nobles, great and small, seem to have continued for another half century after the Taikwa reform; but by the first years of the eighth century mutual seizures of territory stopped or diminished, and a relatively stable division, for administrative purposes, was reached. Though it is a slight digression from our immediate topic we may here point out that one of the conditions favouring the introduction of the new régime was, apart from the exhaustion following upon prolonged fighting, the custom which prevailed, at any rate with the small and middling chieftains, of dividing their land and property among their sons. There was no law of primogeniture, and clans or septs were therefore constantly breaking up into smaller units, each bearing the clan name; so that while the groups multiplied, their individual holdings decreased, and the weaker units were bound to scatter in search of land elsewhere. This loss of cohesion between the members of a clan counteracted the natural acquisitive tendency of the landholders, and so furthered the policy of the central government. Thus, in registers of 702 we find mention of a great number of small households specifically recorded as offshoots, now independent, of greater families, not only of the small nobility (*miyatsuko*), but also, though less frequently, of *omi* and *muraji*. This was no doubt a natural tendency, for the slaves and other unfree classes were not numerous enough to support a rapidly increasing free class upon a cultivated area which could be extended only very slowly. This is borne out by the register just mentioned, where we have such entries as:

(a) Household of Kawashima, Kuni no miyatsuko (i.e. local chieftain), 26 "mouths," of which 3 slaves ;
and

(b) Household of Toyoshima, of Kuni no miyatsuko family, 26 "mouths," of which 3 slaves ;
and

(c) Household of Ōba, Kuni no miyatsuko, 96 "mouths," of which 59 slaves.

It will be seen that in (a) the rank is retained with but little property; in (b) though the family connection is recorded, the rank is lost, and the property is small; and in (c) both rank and property are retained. It need not, however, be supposed that this break-up of families produced a condition permanently favourable to the policy of the central government. Land hunger soon grew again, though there was a change in the classes which could satisfy their appetites; and the multiplication of small groups, having insufficient property for their needs, led in due course to further struggles, and to the formation of a class of bellicose settlers, half bandit and half farmer, forerunners of the fighting men of later feudal days.

The early holders of the post of provincial governor do not appear to have been persons of much consequence, and it is not until about 700 that we begin to find mention of their names in the chronicles. Thenceforward men of good standing were appointed, nobles of the fifth grade, which was at that time relatively high, since grades above the fifth were held only by princes and the heads of great clans. So we have among the governors in the first decades of the eighth century such names and titles as Ōtomo no Sukune, Kibumi no Muraji, Abe no Asomi, Tajihi no Mabito, whose holders belonged, doubtless, to cadet branches of the leading families. Indeed some of them were of such importance that there is ground for suspecting that they were only titular holders of the post, absentees who enjoyed its dignity and emoluments while deputies did the work. There is, however, not much to show how the duties of provincial governors were performed. The staff allotted to them by law was small, not more than three or four high officials and three or four clerks even in the largest provinces, though they were of course assisted by subordinates recruited locally. It is therefore not surprising that most provincial governors exercised only vague administrative control or even neglected their duties altogether, while the real influence and the executive work fell to the district governors under them. That the government soon began to feel dissatisfied with the services of its provincial governors is shown by its frequent despatch of inspecting officials to inquire into reported abuses. From the beginning of the eighth century an annual inspection was the rule. Further, when a provincial governor was replaced at the end of his term he was not allowed to leave his post until he had received from his successor a certificate showing that there was no outstanding deficit in taxes or other property of the government, and in time a special office was created, which alone could, after inquiry, give a retiring governor a clean discharge. Without this his private property might be confiscated to make up for any losses the government might have sustained. The salary of a provincial governor was moderate, but his opportunities for illicit gains were plentiful. His official income would be the amount derived from his rank-land, twenty-four acres for persons of the fifth rank, and from his office-land, an average of six acres, and this corresponded fairly closely with the value of an equivalent post at the capital. But the provincial governor and his staff were also entitled to a percentage of certain taxes in grain which they collected, so that actually they were much better off than their colleagues in the departments at home. So, in an imperial edict of 775 we find such phrases as: "It has come to our ears that, while the functionaries at the capital are poorly paid and cannot escape the hardships of cold and hunger, provincial governors make great profits. In consequence all officials openly covet posts in the provinces." A little later a memorial to the throne says: "Those who govern a province are excessively prosperous. Their storehouses are full of gold and cloth, their tables piled with wine and meat." Occasionally the records mention governors rewarded for integrity and loyal service, but for the most part they seem to have grown fat on bribes and commissions and perquisites, thriving, as may be imagined, at the expense of the taxpayers.

The district governors (*gunshi*) were recruited from a class other than that which supplied the provincial governors. The *gun* or rural district superseded the overlapping administrations of the various types of minor territorial gentry (*kuni no miyatsuko, tomo no miyatsuko, agatanushi,* and so on). The district governors were appointed by the court on the recommendation of the provincial governors, who almost without exception selected for these posts influential local notables, generally members of the territorial gentry in question. Their appointments were in theory life appointments, but in practice the office became hereditary. It was local as well as hereditary, and there were few cases of transfer from one district to another. The *gun* were classified according to the number of townships they comprised, ranging from three to forty. Naturally, as the settled areas were extended and the population increased there were changes in the number and area of these districts. As there were sixty-six provinces and 592 districts, the average number of districts forming a province was nine, and we shall have a fair idea of the size of a district by the end of the Nara period if we regard it as covering about one hundred square miles, though in remote and sparsely populated provinces the area might be much larger. The real work of local administration was performed by the district governors, who had the necessary local knowledge and influence over their clansmen. The duties of the provincial governors were supervisory and administrative, those of the district governors executive and to a certain extent judicial. Contemporary documents laying down the necessary qualifications for a district governor state that he must be a man of high character, and capable of hard work; and though this does not prove that the hereditary principle was abandoned and district governors chosen for their capacity, it shows that their office was exacting and important. In the measure that it was important it was also, of course, influential, and one of the problems which confronted the central authorities, in their attempt to evolve an efficient system of local government, was the due balance of power as between the provincial and the district officials. If too much was allowed to the provincial governor, he would tend to

acquire just that local autonomy which the reformers had wished
to cut down, while there was a danger of the same kind in permitting the district governors virtually to control large tracts of
territory in which their clansmen were the leading people. In
fact, it was found necessary to limit the size of a district to forty,
and later even to twenty townships; and by 730 provincial
governors were being told that, in recommending candidates for
such posts, they might, other things being equal, give preference
to chieftains of local clans, but that, though family connections
were important, they did not justify the appointment of stupid
men! In 744 an edict forbade the succession of close relatives to
important posts in the district governments. None of these prohibitions was strictly observed, but that they existed shows that
the system had begun to betray defects which caused anxiety to
the central power. A study of the relevant documents of the period,
however, makes it plain that the real fault lay not so much in
the system—which was workable enough granted a moderate
number of dependable officials and a moderately contented populace—but in the spirit in which it was administered. It emerges
very clearly from the tone of the edicts and memorials of the
time that the Court regarded the organs of provincial and district
government chiefly as tax-collecting machinery. There is a great
deal of high-flown language, on the best Chinese models, concerning the duty of the rulers towards the people, who are to be
cherished and soothed, nursed and guided. But only the most
innocent and unwary student of early texts will be taken in by
such protestations. It may be that, then as now, in the East as
in the West, there were advanced thinkers who held the doctrine
that the aim of government was to produce agreeable states of
mind in the governed; but all the evidence goes to show that the
prime object of the Nara statesmen was to obtain revenues to
meet the growing needs of metropolitan life, and that the welfare
of the people was not their first care. There is a term of frequent
recurrence in the edicts, *Ō-mi-takara*, literally "great august
treasure," which is used figuratively to stand for "the people."
Some writers have adduced this word as proof that the rulers
looked upon their subjects as jewels, to be carefully guarded and
preserved by the sovereign. But a less romantic, if more plausible

interpretation, which fits the contexts much better, is that the term referred originally to the peasants working the imperial estates, who were in truth the "august treasure," because they produced the personal revenues of the emperor. Be that as it may, the chief function of the district governor was to keep registers and collect taxes, and though he had other duties, such as punishing criminal offences and settling civil suits, these too were chiefly connected with tax evasion and disputes about land and property. A more detailed picture of the functions of these officers can be got by studying some of the facts as to taxation which will be presently given, but it will be clearer if we first complete this account of the system of local government. The district, we have seen, was composed of a certain number of "townships." The word is a makeshift translation of the Japanese term (which varied from time to time), and stands for a group of houses, with the arable and forest land pertaining to them. Perhaps "village" would be more accurate, but it has to be understood to represent a number of scattered dwellings, often spread over a considerable space. An extract from the tax registers of the beginning of the eighth century will show the typical constitution of these divisions:

Household Register of the District (*gun*) of Yamagata.
Province of Mino.
Township of Mita. 50 Households.

Class I households	11
II households	21
III households	18
Number of "mouths"	899
Males	422
Persons holding rank (of whom 3 able-bodied adults, 3 minors, 1 infirm, 1 aged person)	8
Able-bodied adults	153
of whom soldiers	32
which leaves	121 (taxable)
	(one smith)
Males not of full capacity	10
Able-bodied minors	41
of whom soldiers	3
which leaves	38 (taxable)
Children	144
Infants	52
Males partly infirm	5
Males totally infirm	2
Aged males	7

Females	..	..	..	..	..	463
Persons holding rank		..	..	..	..	1
Adult females	..	..	..	..	..	212
Minors	..	..	..	..	..	15
Children	..	..	..	..	..	168
Infants	..	..	..	..	..	45
Aged women	..	..	..	..	..	22
Slaves:						
Male	..	..	..	..	..	7
Female	..	..	..	..	..	7

This "township" may be taken as a typical example. It will be seen that the households are divided into three classes. There were, in fact, three further subdivisions of each class, exactly as provided in the T'ang code, under which households were graded according to their property, in other words, their taxable capacity. The division of men into categories, such as able-bodied, infirm, and so on, is similarly a classification by capacity to work, that is, to pay tax in labour or the produce thereof. If we take this settlement of some 900 people as an average specimen, and allow twenty such settlements to a district (*gun*), we see that in a populous province the district governor has jurisdiction over about 20,000 people. In the smallest districts there might be as few as two townships, comprising only two or three hundred people in all.

In addition to the civil officials, military officers under the orders of the provincial governors were responsible for the training of men conscripted for military service, and the custody of military supplies. An average command included four districts, and the number of soldiers in each command ranged from 500 to 1,000. It will be seen that in the township of which the register (which may be taken as typical) is quoted above, out of one hundred and fifty-three able-bodied men, only thirty-two were liable for military service; and all these were not necessarily called up. Many of those conscripted were in practice not engaged on military duties, but spent their time doing manual labour for the officials. The forces were therefore not numerous, and they seem to have constituted a kind of gendarmerie rather than a standing army. They were reduced in numbers very soon, and by the end of the Nara period had been altogether abolished, except for detachments on the northern frontiers and on the Kyūshū coast.

They were replaced in the provinces by a militia composed of young men from the families of district governors. It is well to realise that, in Japan as in China at this period, the profession of arms was not highly respected, and the growth of a dominant fighting caste was a later development arising out of anarchical conditions which followed the collapse of the borrowed system of land tenure and taxation. There were certain military forces needed to push forward the frontiers east and west against un-pacified tribes, or to cope with bandits and pirates in remote mountain regions or coastal waters. Such turbulent elements served to keep the military spirit alive, but at the Nara court the position of the soldiers was not a lofty one. There were only a few appointments which brought them any prestige, and these were mostly posts as officers in the guards, which had for generations belonged to families like the Ōtomo. They conferred some stand-ing, but they required neither military knowledge nor military prowess. That they were ornamental rather than martial is clear from edicts, issued soon after the foundation of Nara, in which they were described as weaklings unskilled in arms, soldiers in name alone, and useless in emergency. Both officers and men were chosen on social grounds, without reference to their military capacity. They wore elaborate and costly uniforms, and were really only a decorative kind of servant, very expensive to main-tain. Guards were allotted to princes and nobles of high rank, in whose households they performed domestic tasks.

What we have called the township was administered, under the orders of the district governor, by a mayor or headman, chosen from among its inhabitants. There was a still further sub-division of authority, by which the population of a township was grouped into units of five households. This grouping was com-pulsory, and the members of each group were responsible for the maintenance of order within the group, and, what is more, for the tax due by a defaulting or absconding member. This curious institution, which was of Chinese origin, persisted until late Tokugawa times in a slightly modified form.

We have said that what the Nara statesmen chiefly required from their provincial officials was a high yield of taxation to meet the growing needs of metropolitan life. The institutions adopted from China were expensive to keep up. Money, or rather wealth in the form of grain and textiles and tools, was wanted for the support of the aristocracy, to clothe them in fine silks, to keep their servants, to build their houses, to buy them ornaments, pictures and books; and it must be remembered that in a polygamous society the aristocratic population increases fast. Moreover the standard of living rose among the lesser folk also, particularly those who lived in the home provinces. An equal drain upon the resources of the country was perhaps the building of Buddhist temples, their equipment with precious objects, and the maintenance of a numerous priesthood. There were two obvious ways of increasing the wealth of the upper classes. One was to bring more land under cultivation, the other was to squeeze more out of the farmers. Both methods were practised. In 711 an imperial ordinance refers in disapproving language to the conduct of princes, nobles and territorial gentry, who were appropriating great tracts of new land to the detriment of the small farmers. The practice is strictly forbidden, and it is decreed that henceforth unreclaimed land suitable for cultivation is to be disposed of only by the provincial governors acting on behalf of the state. In 713 a similar prohibition is aimed at the Buddhist monasteries, which are accused of taking possession of "unlimited numbers" of fields. From land thus appropriated the state could obtain little or no revenue, for the holders were as a rule men of rank, and therefore themselves untaxable; and they managed to ensure immunity, at least partial, for most of their estates. The government therefore in 722 ordered 1,000,000 *chō*, say three million acres, of new land to be brought into cultivation. The task was to be carried out under the supervision of the provincial and district governors, and the workmen were to be supplied with rations and tools at official expense. The farmers in each district were to be encouraged to take part in the scheme, and any who could produce from the new fields one thousand *koku* of rice were promised lifelong immunity from tax, while those who could produce as much as three thousand *koku* were to be given a merit rank of the sixth class. It is quite certain that this plan was not carried out in full, for it meant more than doubling the area of land under cultivation; but, particularly in Northern and Western

Japan, a great deal of reclamation took place at this time under the pressure of growing population and stimulated by the privileges granted to those who improved the land. The progress of the scheme created an ironical situation, for though its object was to provide more land for allotments, in practice its result was to destroy the allotment system. The government, in furtherance of its policy, went so far as to promise uninterrupted tenure for three generations to households that developed new fields. This was a surrender of the principle upon which the current system of land tenure was based—the Chinese principle of equal partition—and, as the system of land tenure was an essential part of the whole economic fabric, its disintegration must be accompanied by changes in the social structure. For a long time already the regulation by which allotment lands were redistributed every sixth year had tended to become a dead letter, and indeed it is doubtful whether the allotment system was ever strictly applied in most parts of Japan; but a critical point was reached when the state gave positive sanction to rights in land practically unlimited in scope and duration. This was to legalise abuses, which is a very different thing from winking at them. No doubt the government were conscious that they were destroying their own system, but they were driven by economic necessity. They later tried to put matters right by remedial laws and edicts, but without avail. The damage was done, and the longer a landholder had been in possession of his land the harder was it to wrest it from him. This was to be expected, on simple grounds of human nature; but there was also a very cogent reason why farmers should hold tight to any land which they could acquire beyond their allotment fields. The Japanese land system differed from the Chinese in that taxation, in kind and in labour, was largely assessed upon persons and not upon land. Therefore land held in addition to the allotment fields did not necessarily impose any further obligation upon the holder, and it was sometimes even profitable to neglect the allotment fields and pay attention to the new ones, which were by one device or another kept off the registers. A further reason for preferring unregistered land was the high rate of interest charged by the government on their advances of seed rice. This was sometimes as high as 35 per cent.

per annum, and there were cases, when payment was delayed, in which the interest exceeded the capital, and small farmers were ruined, their families dispersed and landless. From time to time the central authorities, influenced by memorials from comprehending officials, remitted the peasants' debts, but the provincial and district officers appear to have shown less clemency, and to have insisted upon payment in many instances, because they stood to profit by taking, often illicitly, a proportion for themselves. The registers of the middle of the Nara period show that great numbers of "free" people, finding the burden of taxation and forced labour more than they could bear, absconded from their homes, and either fled to remote parts where they could settle and farm on their own account, or put themselves under the protection of more powerful persons, such as nobles or the heads of great monasteries. The building of the new capital at Nara was a great strain upon the people in the neighbouring country, for it was they who were handiest and had to contribute most in forced labour. It was hard to get men from distant provinces, and when they did come for the corvée or on transport service, they were most harshly treated. Many died of starvation and exposure on the way back, until the government established stores of food on the main routes from which to supply them. Altogether there was every reason for taxable people to evade the corvée or other levies by escaping to some region where they were not too closely observed by officials and where they might take undeveloped land and cultivate it on their own account or, if not industriously-minded, could engage in banditry. An extract from a register of 726 will illustrate this state of affairs:

Female. Idzumo no Omi Shimame. Age 19. Scar on left cheek. Escaped 722.

Younger brother (of head of house). Idzumo no Omi Otasu. Age 40. Escaped to Prov. of Musashi, 709.

The original of this register, which refers to a family of good standing (omi), is not complete, but the fragment which has been preserved gives the names of some thirty members of a household, of whom seven have moved to other provinces, taking with them four slaves. Some of these are entered as having transferred to another domicile with official sanction, others are, as the extract shows, regarded as absconders. Against most names identifying marks, such as moles and scars, are recorded. Local officials were instructed to force absconders to return, or to tax them as if they belonged to the district in which they now resided, but these instructions were certainly not always complied with, and a large class of vagrants was gradually formed, always tending to move away from populous centres.

It will be clear from what has been set forth above that in the Nara period pure cultural development in art and letters and religion outran economic and political growth. The æsthetic advance was almost miraculous, and bears witness to the power of the artistic impulse in the Japanese people. Their economic and political progress was limited by a number of adverse conditions. It was too much to expect that a rich and varied culture could be, without difficulties and breakdowns, borrowed from abroad and erected upon a social basis in which tradition was so strong, and an economic basis which was inadequate to support it. The new culture not only brought a new and rapidly rising standard of living; it created a numerous class of leisured or at least unproductive people. The privileged nobles, the monks, the nuns, the priests, the ornamental officials and soldiers, with all their servants, had to be supported in increasing luxury by a farming population which, though it also was doubtless increasing in numbers, was constantly drained of able-bodied men for unproductive work and crippled by taxation. The measures taken to cope with this situation were doomed to fail. The development of new land merely emphasised the disparity between the rich proprietor and the small cultivator. The appointment of inspectors to supervise, in the interest of the peasants, the conduct of local officials merely gave more scope for patronage, already a grave abuse. The financial expedients of the statesmen were ineffective if they were not dishonest. The records of the short Tempyō period, known to students as a glorious age in Japanese art history, show that at the height of Nara's magnificence its economic collapse was already inevitable. The particular example of Fujiwara Oshikatsu (Nakamaro) aptly illustrates the situation in general. In 761, on the occasion of one of those temporary transfers of the imperial residence which were so burdensome to the people at that time, Nakamaro was granted one million sheaves of rice to meet his expenses. This is equivalent to the crop of 6,000 acres of rice-field. He received in addition a fief of 3,000 households and 300 acres of rice-land. At about the same time he was promoted to the highest possible rank, carrying the highest possible emoluments, and was given privileges which in practice amounted to the right to mint coins and to collect interest on rice-loans. He issued silver and copper coins, in exchange for a currency already debased and nearly half of which was counterfeit, at such rates that the money cost of commodities must have been raised at least fivefold. Other courtiers and officials received grants and privileges on a lavish scale, so that it is not surprising to learn, from memorials of the following period, that the national treasure was diminished by half through the extravagant expenditure of the court on buildings and gifts in the last decade or so of the Tempyō era, which ended in 767.

Chapter IX

A SUMMARY OF POLITICAL EVENTS IN THE NARA PERIOD

HAVING sketched the cultural background of the Nara period, we may now return and relate, as briefly as may be, the political or rather the dynastic events which took place on the stage set by the Taikwa reformers. For convenience we had better open with a tabular statement of important names and dates commencing, for clearer perspective, at the end of the 6th century:

A.D. 593 Accession of SUIKO (Empress).
         Prince Shōtoku named Regent.
    604 Injunctions of Prince Shōtoku.
    621 Death of Prince Shōtoku.
    629 Accession of JOMEI.
    642 Accession of KŌGYOKU (Empress).
    645 Accession of KŌTOKU, on abdication of Kōgyoku.
    646 The Taikwa Reform Edict. Kamatari in power.
    655 Second accession of Kōgyoku, as Empress SAIMEI.
    658 Attempt on the throne by Prince Arima.
    662 Accession of TENCHI (assumed title only in 668)
    668 Silla becomes paramount in Korea.
    669 Kamatari dies.
    672 Accession of TEMMU after brief reign of Kōbun and civil war. Fujiwara Fubito in power.
    681 Historical commission organised by Temmu.
    687 Accession of JITŌ (Empress) after succession.
    697 Accession of MOMMU after Jitō's abdication. Quarrel ended by execution of one of Temmu's sons.
    701 Confucian festival first officially celebrated.
    702 Code of Taihō promulgated.
    708 Accession of GEMMYŌ (Empress). Copper found in Japan. Coins minted.

---

    710 NARA FOUNDED.
    712 Official chronicle called *Kojiki* completed.
    713 Topographical records (*Fūdoki*) commenced.
    715 Accession of GENSHŌ (Empress) on abdication of Gemmyō.
    720 Official chronicle called *Nihon-shoki* completed. Death of Fujiwara Fubito.
    724 Accession of SHŌMU.
    740 Rebellion of Fujiwara Oshikatsu (Nakamaro).
    749 Accession of KŌKEN (Empress) on abdication of Shōmu.
    752 Dedication of Great Buddha at Nara.
    758 Accession of JONIN on abdication of Kōken.

765 Deposition and murder of Jōnin by Empress Kōken, who resumes throne as Empress SHŌTOKU.
769 Plot of priest Dōkyo to upset throne.
770 Accession of KŌNIN.
782 Accession of KWAMMU.

A glance at this table will show that, while obvious cultural progress was being made, the century was marred by bloody succession quarrels and dynastic intrigues. We need not, fortunately, relate their sordid details, but it is as well to gain some general notion of the attitude in those days of the people, or at least the governing classes, towards the dynasty. It is usually stated that veneration of the emperors, amounting almost to religious worship, is a national characteristic of the Japanese, going back to the dawn of their history, and this belief is supported by the dogma that the succession has been and shall be "unbroken for ages eternal." It is only in a very broad sense that this theory will bear examination in the light of early Japanese history. If we neglect the very dubious record of the first four or five centuries, and start with the well-authenticated times of Shōtoku Taishi, we find even that benevolent and high-minded prince heavily engaged in a succession quarrel which culminated in civil war in 587. The murder, or the death in battle, of imperial princes with dynastic rights was common at this period, and in 592 a reigning emperor (Sūjun) was killed by a subject. During Shōtoku Taishi's regency there was an interval of peace. After his death the Soga were not content with nominating as heir-apparent a prince of their own choice, but endeavoured to establish themselves as a new dynasty. They failed because of the strength of Kamatari, the founder of the great Fujiwara family, but very soon after the Taikwa reforms succession quarrels broke out again and, although the Fujiwara did not aim at occupying the throne themselves, they contrived by constant intermarriages with the imperial family to gain all but the outward titles of sovereignty. The succession quarrels usually took the form of disputes between rival factions as to the claims to the throne of various imperial princes, and their frequency is not surprising since the emperors usually had several wives and many children, and there was no fixed succession law. A characteristic quarrel was that which broke out on the death of the emperor Tenchi in 671. Tenchi

had five consorts, who gave him eight children, and he had six
more children by palace ladies. His younger brother had nine
wives, four of whom were daughters of Tenchi and therefore his
own nieces. One faction supported Tenchi's brother against his
son, and the son succeeded for a short time as the Emperor Kōbun,
but he lost his life in the ensuing civil war, and the brother came
to the throne as the Emperor Temmu.

It was in Temmu's reign that was set up an historical commission which subsequently produced the official chronicle called
Nihon-shoki, and no doubt at this time some attempt was made
to formulate a definite succession law. But, though the succession
did for a century remain roughly speaking in Temmu's family,
disputes continued. When Temmu died in 686, he was succeeded
not by one of his numerous sons, but by his widow, the Empress
Jitō. That lady abdicated in 697, and was succeeded by the
Emperor Mommu, her grandson, who was then only a minor.
This was the second recorded instance of abdication, and the
first of the accession of a minor. The preamble of the edict pro-
nounced by the Emperor Mommu on his succession is worth
reproducing in exact translation, for it serves as a useful text for
commenting on the current treatment of dynastic problems. It
reads as follows:—

"He says:—Hearken all ye assembled August Children,
Princes, Nobles, Officials and People of the Realm-under-
Heaven to the Word which He speaks even as the Word of
the Sovereign that is a Manifest God ruling over the Great
Land of Many Islands.

"He says:—Hearken ye all to the Word of the Sovereign
who proclaims thus: We have listened with reverence to the
noble, high, broad, warm words of the charge vouchsafed to
Us by the Sovereign Prince of Yamato.

"Who is a Manifest God ruling over the Great Land of
Many Islands in performance of the Task of this High Throne
of Heavenly Sun Succession, in the same wise as the August
Child of the God of Heaven, as it was decreed by the God
which is in Heaven, that from the beginning of the High
Plain of Heaven, through the reigns of our Distant Ancestors
down to these days and onwards, Sovereign August Children

should be born in succession for ever to succeed to the rule
of the Great Land of Many Islands."

The introductory words, "He says," show that the edict was
read aloud at Court in a ceremonial manner by some high
functionary, usually the Minister of the Household. The "charge
vouchsafed to Us by the sovereign Prince of Yamato" is the
throne surrendered by the empress to the new emperor, on her
abdication. The edict uses language we have already noticed, in
its reference to the sovereigns as manifest gods, ruling in unbroken
succession from the days of the divine ancestors. There is in this,
and in similar edicts, no reference to the Chinese doctrine that a
sovereign rules by "virtue" rather than by hereditary right; or, if
it is mentioned, the doctrine of divine ancestry is not thereby displaced. Thus, there is an edict of 729 of the Emperor Shōmu,
which contains the words "the Sovereign, being a Sage, and
being served by wise Ministers." This use of the word "sage" is
tribute to the Chinese doctrine, but the same edict opens with
the usual assertion that the dynasty goes back in unbroken line
to the gods. It seems therefore to be well established that, although
the Japanese adopted, as part of their political apparatus, the
Chinese theory of kingship, they used it only when it was convenient and so long as it did not conflict with their own doctrine.
The claim of divine ancestry and of unbroken succession was
never abandoned; and this fact is of considerable interest as
showing that even the prestige of Chinese institutions was unable
to break down the aristocratic habit of mind of the Japanese.
With regard to the practice of abdication, it is to be noted that
it was promoted by the growth of Buddhism, which afforded a
plausible and often a welcome excuse for laying down the burdens
of sovereignty and for escaping its perils. Both were very real.
The perils arose from the ambition of contending factions, and
the burdens, though perhaps more physical than mental, were
extremely heavy from the time when Chinese ceremonial began
to oppress the Court. In an edict of 743 it is stated that, to ensure
tranquillity in the state, it is necessary to have "everywhere and
always these two things, Rites and Music." There is ample
evidence that the time of a ruler in those days was, unless he
were of unusual strength of character and so able to break his

bonds, consumed in ritual, and his movements hampered by the restraints of etiquette. It was the exactions of the ceremonial code which forced many men in high positions ostensibly to retire from the direction of affairs and, with time and energy thus freed, to exercise a real if hidden power. This habit persisted in almost all classes of society until recent times, and indeed some traces of it are still visible in modern life in Japan.

During the reigns of six sovereigns, from Tenchi to Gemmyō, the chief power in the land was Fujiwara Fubito (659–720), son of the great Kamatari, and founder of a family which was destined to play a great part in subsequent Japanese history. His influence was derived not only from his ability but from the policy, developed by Kamatari, of attaching the Fujiwara house to the imperial family by bonds of kinship; by marriage, remarriage and inter-marriage on every possible occasion. Fubito himself was the father-in-law of two sovereigns and the grandfather of another. But despite the real power which he wielded, his name appears rarely in the official chronicles. An imperial edict records the gift to him of a fief in perpetuity of 5,000 households, in 708. Other references to him are brief, and though we know that he had a good deal to do with administration, and is thought to have compiled a code of law, he did not reach the highest office during his lifetime, but was made Chancellor posthumously. It is probable that he, like many before and after him who ruled Japan, preferred to remain in the background.

After Mommu's death, the throne was occupied by his mother, the Empress Gemmyō, who soon abdicated in favour of Genshō, her daughter. She in turn abdicated, in view of the instructions of her two predecessors, who had nominated Mommu's son, then a small child. The practice of abdication was now in full swing. It will be noticed that, though there was no rule prescribing succession in the male line, it was evidently thought desirable, since the Empress Jitō abdicated in favour of Mommu as soon as he was fourteen, and two empresses in succession abdicated in favour of Mommu's son, Shōmu. If there was any rule, it seems to have been that the throne should be occupied by the prince nominated by a dying or an abdicating sovereign, but the rule was broken almost as often as it was observed.

Shōmu, we have seen, devoted himself wholeheartedly to the promotion of Buddhism, and after a reign of twenty-four years abdicated and entered religion. He described himself as a *shami*, which is the Japanese equivalent of *śrâmanera*, a novice. He was succeeded in 749 by his daughter, the Empress Kōken, in whose reign remarkable things happened. From the official chronicles we learn that in the opening year of her reign the god Hachiman, a Shintō deity of extremely uncertain origin, whose shrine was at Usa, in western Japan, had declared his wish to proceed from Usa to the capital. A retinue of high officials was sent to escort him, and a guard of soldiers to clear the road. Upon his arrival —by which is to be understood the arrival of a sacred car containing the symbol of his presence—he was installed in a specially constructed shrine in one of the palaces, where forty Buddhist priests recited masses for seven days. Then a priestess of his shrine, who it should be remembered was at the same time a Buddhist nun, worshipped in the Tōdaiji, and on this occasion the abdicated Emperor Shōmu, the Empress Kōken, and all the court were present. Five thousand monks prayed and recited from the sutras, dances were performed, and a cap of the first grade was conferred upon the god. One can hardly imagine a more perfect display of the spirit of compromise than a religious ceremony for the bestowal of civil rank upon one deity in the shrine of another. The priestess in question was evidently a lady of high birth, and it was she, it seems, who conveyed the oracle to the empress. As a reward she and a Shintō priest named Tamaro were promoted in court rank, while a fief of 4,000 households, together with 200 slaves, was conferred upon the Tōdaiji. The exact significance of all these curious incidents cannot be determined, though it is clear that they formed part of the policy of amalgamating Shintō with Buddhism. But they seem also to have been connected with some plot against the throne, for a few years later we learn that the priestess and Tamaro were found to be involved in a conspiracy and banished, while successive edicts of 757 deal with "bad and mutinous men," who "inciting and leading a band of rebels, planned to surround the Household Minister's house and kill him; then to surround the palace and drive out the Heir Apparent; next to strike down the Empress

Dowager, to seize the Bell Seal and Token, to summon the
Minister of the Right and force him to make a proclamation to
the people. Thereafter they schemed to overthrow the Emperor
and set up one of the four princes in his stead. So on the night
of the 29th day they entered the garden of the Chancellor where,
drinking salt water, they swore an oath to the Four Quarters of
Heaven and Earth, agreeing to begin fighting on the second day
of the seventh month." The intrigue was unmasked and the ringleaders punished. In 758 the Empress Kōken abdicated in favour
of the Emperor Jonin, a grandson of Temmu. She remained in
the background, but continued to exercise her power. The young
emperor was supported by Fujiwara Nakamaro, also known as
Oshikatsu, while the ex-Empress Kōken was advised by a monk
named Dōkyo, who, if we may eke out the official records with
popular legend, had seduced his imperial mistress by his abundant
physical attractions, and shared her couch as well as directing her
conscience. This double office brought him to a situation of
great power in the state, and aroused the jealousy of Fujiwara
Oshikatsu, who revolted but after some sharp fighting was defeated and slain with most of his chief followers in 765. The
empress had already in 762 superseded the young emperor,
having proclaimed that henceforth he would deal only with ceremonial routine, while she herself would attend to great affairs of
state. After Oshikatsu's revolt she gave up all pretence of abdication, and sent troops to arrest the emperor. They found him un-
dressed, and with difficulty persuaded him to put his clothes on.
His own guards had deserted him. He was at last marched out
with only a few companions, including his mother, was halted on
the way, and made to stand in the cold while an edict of banishment was read to him.   He was deprived of the title of emperor,
granted the rank of prince, and sent to the distant island of Awaji,
where he was strangled not long after. Meanwhile the ex-Empress
Kōken, having reassumed the throne as the Empress Shōtoku,
announces that, although on her abdication she shaved her head
and donned the robes of a nun, she is obliged to carry on the
government, and it is fitting in the circumstances to have a monk
as Minister of State. She therefore confers upon Dōkyo the new
rank of Minister-Priest. In 769 he went to live in the Palace, and

was now made Chancellor-Priest, thus filling the highest office under the throne, and given the title of Hō-ō, a word to-day used to translate "Pope," and similar to the appellation at that time assumed by abdicated emperors on joining the priesthood.

At this point Dōkyo, like many other favourites, appears to have lost his head and misjudged the extent of his mistress's infatuation. Remembering the oracle of Hachiman, twenty years back, he trumped up a tale that the same deity had now appeared to a medium in a trance, and had declared that Japan would enjoy perpetual tranquillity if Dōkyo were made emperor. Dōkyo announced this to the empress, who decided, or was induced, to consult the god herself. She sent one Wake no Kiyomaro to Usa, and he came back with the god's reply, which was to the effect that Dōkyo, not being of imperial lineage, was not eligible for the imperial throne. Dōkyo was of course furious. He inspired, if he did not actually write, an edict by which Kiyomaro was degraded and exiled for having brought back a false reply from Usa, but his influence began to wane, the empress fell ill, and on her death in the following year he left the court and was banished. It is a testimony to his force of character that he got so far and survived so long; though he probably escaped assassination thanks only to his sacred office, since it was one of the gravest sins to take the life of a priest, and at this time the fear of the vengeful spirits of the dead was a powerful deterrent. It is appropriate to mention here that the Buddhist prohibition of life-taking was the chief reason for the frequency of sentences of banishment where execution might have been expected. Thus after Oshikatsu's revolt in 757, several hundred of the rebels were condemned to death, but the punishment was reduced to banishment at the prayer of a Buddhist nun named Hiromushi, a sister of that Kiyomaro who, as we have just seen, was banished by Dōkyo, but escaped the death penalty.

It is customary for occidental writers, when describing such incidents as the intrigues of Dōkyo, to take a very patronising line, and express either righteous horror or refined amusement at the credulity of those days. One learned historian treats his readers to such phrases as "air heavy with enervating superstition," "the brood of the brazen-faced charlatan," and similar flowers of the downright rhetoric of his school. But the plain student of early Oriental history had better avoid assuming the superiority of other countries and other times. He had better, for instance, remember that oracles now issue daily from the printing press, and are not without credence; that imposture and bloodshed, both on a stupendous scale, are features not absent from modern life. The Nara period had its share of human fallibility, but was on the whole a creative, ardent epoch; and it is a mistake to emphasise its superstition while overlooking its faith.

On the death of the wayward Empress Shōtoku, the Japanese seem to have made up their minds that female rulers were dangerous to the state, and with good reason, for there had been four empresses in the last few generations and all had been under priestly influence. After this the influential laity saw to it that the throne was occupied by a man, and it was many centuries before another empress reigned. The growing political power of the priesthood, combined with their economic strength, caused grave fears to the statesmen and nobles, so that a good deal of the administrative policy of this period aimed at curbing the ambitions of the Buddhist church. There was from the close of the seventh century a certain reaction in favour of Shintō, probably due in part to this feeling; and though, as we have said, it could not compete with Buddhism, a number of observances and festivals which seem to have been neglected for some time were now revived. Both the great national chronicles, the *Kojiki* and the *Nihon-shoki*, which were compiled in the first decades of the eighth century, are occupied largely with the mythology of the national religion, and there are in the records of the Nara period frequent notices of the celebration of such ceremonies as the National Purification and the various rituals connected with harvest. Shintō tended more and more to become the vehicle of official ritual, emphasising the functions of the emperor as the intermediary between the people and the ancestral gods.[1] It therefore developed as an official cult, gradually divorced from the popular nature worship out of which it sprang; and, borrowing some organisation and a little philosophy from Chinese sources, it became part of the political machinery, leaving Buddhism and Confucianism to satisfy the emotional and intellectual appetites of those who were not content with the simple indigenous beliefs.

The Empress Shōtoku was succeeded by an elderly monarch, Kōnin, who was under the influence of a capable Fujiwara minister. He was followed, on his death in 782, by the Emperor Kwammu, who soon after his accession decided to move the capital. With the opening of his reign the Nara period comes to a close.

NOTE TO CHAPTER IX

[1] Page 186. In considering the rivalry between Buddhism and Shintō, it should be remembered that it was principally confined to the official field. The unorganised Shintō, which is little more than the expression of traditional Japanese ways of thinking about life, did not come into conflict with Buddhist doctrine, and its simple beliefs persisted with little change. It is important to distinguish, even at this early stage, between Shintō as a popular creed and Shintō as an official cult.

PART THREE—THE HEIAN PERIOD

Chapter X—THE NEW CAPITAL AND THE PROVINCES

THE Heian period commences with the removal of the capital from Nara to Nagaoka. The removal of the capital meant primarily the transfer of the imperial palace, and this was no new thing in Japan when the transfer was made from Nara. It had its origin in the taboo by which a house was regarded as defiled by death. A number of cases in early Japanese history are recorded where the capital is said to have been changed, but it is clear that most often there was nothing but a removal to another palace. During the first forty-three reigns recorded in the chronicles the capital was generally in the province of Yamato, and, though there was at the beginning of each reign a change of palace or of capital, the distance moved was often only a few miles and sometimes, it would seem, not many hundred yards. The buildings of those days were of simple construction, and probably at the end of a reign it was anyhow easier to rebuild than to repair. By the Nara period, when architecture had developed under Buddhist influence, larger and more permanent buildings were erected, and there was therefore a strong financial objection to moving the capital. Ceremonial defilement could be got over by a change of palaces, but to transfer a city was a large and costly enterprise. Nara remained the capital during seven reigns (710-784), except for a period when Shōmu moved to Kuni and Naniwa under the pressure of feuds between the two dominant clans, the Fujiwara and the Tachibana. The removal to Nagaoka is then the more surprising, particularly in view of the number of great buildings—temples as well as palaces—at Nara. It is a mystery which historians have not solved. It is known that the imperial finances were at a low ebb at the end of the Nara period, largely because of the very costliness of those buildings, and there must accordingly have been very strong reasons for the move. Clearly one of the deciding factors was the growing power of Buddhism, from which it was difficult to escape if the court remained in the midst of temples and monasteries presided over by rich and influential ecclesiastics. The emperor Kwammu succeeded to the throne after a period when priestly ascendancy over female sovereigns had continued for several generations, and grown to an excessive point. He himself, as Prince Yamabe, had been in charge of the University, and this was a secular institution in which Buddhism was not part of the curriculum. It was, if anything, a Confucianist establishment, and indeed the annual Confucian festival was held there. Without assuming that Kwammu was positively hostile to Buddhist influence, we may certainly suppose that he was aware of its dangers, and it is even more certain that his advisers wished to remove him from it. Other reasons for the transfer are alleged, of which the most interesting is perhaps that Fujiwara Tanetsugu, an influential noble who was related to the rich Hata family, obtained money from them in return for a promise that he would secure their advancement in rank. Something of the sort no doubt happened, and though we cannot be sure of details, the history of this transfer of the capital illustrates three important features of the life—at least the metropolitan life—of those days, namely, the influence of the priesthood, the incessant intrigues of the Fujiwara and other great houses, and the wealth of some of the landholders.

The removal appears to have been a costly business. It was hurried. In 784 (fifth month) a commission under Tanetsugu was sent to commence building, on the site which had already been selected after approval by the diviners and announcements to the gods. They started on the Palace at once, and five months afterwards the Emperor took up residence. There were at one time over 300,000 men on the work, which proceeded day and night, and it appears that the arrangements for clothing and feeding these great numbers were so inadequate that their sufferings were intense. As to the cost we have no full information, but it is recorded that all the provinces were ordered to send to Nagaoka all their taxes for the year, together with material needed for the workmen. Of the taxes, 680,000 sheaves (of rice) were allotted to princes and nobles above a certain rank as funds for building their private houses in the new capital, while 43,000 sheaves were paid to landowners in compensation for the incorporation in the new capital of land and peasants forming part of their estates.

The removal of the emperor to Nagaoka meant only that his palace was ready for occupation. The government did not move from Nara for some years. The building of the new city, the making

of roads and bridges, continued in fact for ten years, until the
beginning of 793. Then, suddenly, an edict was issued, commanding the removal of the capital from Nagaoka to a site only a few
miles distant, the present Kyōto. The reasons for moving the
capital from Nagaoka, at a moment when the work was nearing
completion, have not been discovered. No doubt the motives were
many. All we can do is to recount the main incidents which
preceded the removal, and guess their bearing upon it.

While Tanetsugu, who was a great favourite with the emperor,
by whom he was allowed " to decide all matters, within and
without," was pushing on the work at Nagaoka, he was assassinated in 785 by the emperor's younger brother, Prince Sawara, who
was plotting to succeed to the throne but was thwarted by Tanetsugu, who supported the emperor's eldest son. We need not
concern ourselves with the details of this quarrel, which is one
of many sordid disputes and intrigues regarding the succession.
It is enough to notice that almost every major political event of
this period arose from the rivalry of powerful families grouped
around the throne, complicated by astrology, by omens and the
fear of vengeful spirits. Thus, when Tanetsugu was murdered, the
conspirators were punished by death or by exile, Prince Sawara
himself being banished to Awaji and allowed to die of starvation,
if not actually murdered, on the way; but soon after his death ill-
fortune seemed to overtake the emperor. His son, the heir-apparent, then a child of twelve, fell ill. Messengers were sent with gifts
to the great shrine at Ise to pray for his recovery, but the Prince
grew no better. Next year offerings were made and prayers recited
at all shrines in the home provinces and diviners were called upon
to discover the reasons for his prolonged sickness. They announced
that it was due to the vengeful spirit of the dead Prince Sawara.
A recital of the steps then taken shows how great and widespread
in those days was the fear of the dead. Imperial envoys of the
highest rank were sent to Awaji to make humble excuses to the
offended spirit; and it is interesting to note that the chronicles
which record this incident speak only of the grave of "a certain
Prince," because it was inauspicious to mention the name of a
great personage commanding awe and reverence. A tomb was
made and enclosed, which the local officers were commanded to

keep under strict and respectful guard. Later, in 794, the Crown Prince's consort, a Fujiwara lady, fell ill and died suddenly. This misfortune was ascribed to the same influence, and further efforts were made to pacify the spirit of the Prince Sawara by paying him still greater honours.

In the palaces of the Emperor and the Crown Prince the Diamond Cutter Sutra was recited, while priests were sent to Awaji to say masses and to express repentance at the grave. In 799 Prince Sawara was posthumously made Emperor, under the name of Sūdō Tenno, he was reinterred in a grave in Yamato, his tomb was promoted to an Imperial Mausoleum, and a temple was erected in his honour. Subsequently this mausoleum was treated like that of a dead emperor, in regard to ritual and offerings and in every other way. Thus, when a mission returned from the T'ang court bearing gifts, some were sent as offerings to his tomb, as well as to those of the two previous emperors, Tenchi and Kwōnin. Further, when the reigning emperor Kwammu fell ill in 806, he issued an edict proclaiming that all those who had been banished for taking part in the conspiracy of 785 should, "whether alive or dead," be released and restored to their former ranks; and that the priests of all provincial temples throughout the country should recite the Diamond Sutra twice a year, in Spring and Autumn, on behalf of the Emperor Sūdō.

This story, pieced together from scattered references in the chronicles, serves to show how great a part was played by religious belief in those days. It portrays an orthodox development of the Shintō cult of the dead, owing something to Buddhism and something to the Chinese system of divination, but testifying to the vitality of the native animistic creed.

Abuses among sorcerers and diviners and priests claiming magic powers were so flagrant that in 807 an edict was issued in the following terms: "Priests, diviners and the like take advantage of the common people by wantonly interpreting good and evil omens. The people in their ignorance put faith in their predictions, so that gradually false cults come to flourish and evil magic to prosper. Such customs gather strength and impair simple habits. They are henceforth strictly forbidden and all persons studying these arts, or continuing to practise them, will be banished." As might be expected, the ruling classes were not free from the vices which they found so dangerous in the common people, but they practised them in a more elegant and costly form. Extravagant expenditure upon religious rites, particularly on Buddhist masses for the dead, reached such a point that, in the same year as the above proclamation against necromancers, an imperial edict set limits to the amount of offerings which might be made to temples in payment for such masses. Princes of the blood and ministers of the first rank were restricted to 500 *tan** of cloth (for this was the form which payment took): those of the second rank to 300 *tan*, and so on down to officials of below the sixth rank, who might not expend more than 30 *tan*. The edict mentions that in all classes people vied with one another in the lavishness of these rites, and that the poor would sometimes sell their land and their houses for such purposes, and, far from doing credit to their families, would so bring them to ruin. There are records of the engagement of a hundred, and even a thousand priests, to recite prayers for the dead.

Prayers for good weather for the crops, prayers to avert or to stop pestilence, are recorded in the chronicles almost as part of the business of government. So, in 818, after a succession of bad harvests, we find the Emperor and his court fasting and praying for three days. All officials are put on short rations and reduced pay, but the priests, whenever they are called upon to pray for rain or for sunshine, receive rich gifts; so rich that taking only the amounts mentioned in the official histories of this period, their total in about three years amounted to over 100,000 bolts of cotton cloth, exclusive of other offerings. With sickness it is the same. Disease is regarded as due to the influence of the spirit of another person, living or dead, and the first essential is to drive out or pacify that spirit, by the help of priests or exorcists.

As to omens, we have already seen that they were of such importance that to record them was one of the main functions of official chronicles. The legendary history of the early sovereigns is full of tales of signs and portents, nor do they diminish in the later works, though the influence of Chinese astrology is more perceptible. Thus in 723 a white tortoise was found, and decided to be a good omen of the highest class. The name of the era was changed to

* One *tan* is about 10 yards.

Jinki which means Divine Tortoise. As time progressed it became the habit, if not the duty, of provincial officials to report to the throne anything in the nature of an omen, so that the court diviners could be summoned to interpret and advise. Uncommon birds flying over a house, curious noises, clouds of unusual shape or colour, animals with strange markings, any of these might demand serious study and, according to the verdict of the diviners, prayers and litanies, offerings to temples, messengers to distant shrines. Happy the provincial official who could report from his post a happy omen, such as that cloud of five colours which once appeared and was regarded as so auspicious that presents were made to "the hundred functionaries" and an amnesty granted to all criminals.

We may now return to the transfer of the capital from Nagaoka, which, unreasonable and extravagant as it appears to have been, is perhaps easier to understand in view of the conditions that we have just described. Not only did it seem likely that Tanetsugu's enemies would after his death be averse to the completion of a task which he had commenced, but also, since ill-fortune seemed to have pursued the emperor since his favourite's death, and the work had dragged on for ten years amidst constant difficulties, perhaps His Majesty was anxious to make a fresh start, in a better-fated spot. Be that as it may, in March of 793 the new site was selected, after the advice of geomancers had been taken, and building was commenced without delay. The removal was notified to the tutelary deity of the district at the Kamo shrine and to the Sun Goddess at Ise, as well as to the tombs of the Emperor's ascendants for three generations. Some use was made of the buildings at Nagaoka, for we learn that the emperor was obliged to shift to temporary quarters, as his palace was pulled down, together with other pavilions and halls, doubtless for trans-fer to the new site. The new palace was ready in 795, and in the tenth month the Emperor moved. The transfer of the capital was announced to shrines throughout the land. The new capital, which was not more than five miles distant from Nagaoka, was styled Heian-kyō, "the capital of peace and tranquillity," in an edict issued at the close of this year. Much building remained to be done, and it was not until ten years later that the Commission of Works was dissolved.

We know so little of life in other parts of Japan at this date that there is a danger of giving too much importance to events in the capital. But, after all, it is chiefly with the life of the court that the records deal, and we must make the best of this material, searching it for hints and conjectures from which we may piece together some account of conditions elsewhere. For this purpose a description of the capital city is not without value.

This Capital of Peace and Tranquillity was laid out, as had been Nara, on the plan of the capital of the Sui dynasty of China at Ch'ang-an. It was a rectangle measuring about three and a half miles from north to south and three miles from east to west, surrounded by a moat, and symmetrically divided by broad roads into squares, in their turn subdivided by narrow roads. Alongside each road was a moat and, as the city was on a gentle slope, all was running water. In the north centre of the city was an enclosure, about one mile by three-quarters, which contained the imperial residence, various residential apartments, ceremonial halls, and the great departments of state. It had fourteen gates. Outside the enclosure, but mostly near it, were palaces used for various reasons by the emperors in preference to that within the enclosure; palaces where abdicated emperors resided; mansions belonging to great families; and certain government offices and institutions. Chief among the latter was the University, which adjoined the great southern gate. It comprised a number of buildings, small and large, including three great faculty halls, devoted respectively to Chinese studies, to mathematics, and to law. There was also a small temple devoted to Confucius.

When the capital was commenced there were already a number of shrines on or near the site, chief among them being the Kamo shrines; the Yasaka or Gion shrine of the god Susa-no-wo; and the Udzumasa temple or Kōryūji. The celebrated temple called Kiyomidzu was constructed from the materials of a great hall moved from the abandoned city of Nagaoka; and the first temple on Mount Hiei, the Komponchūdō, was built to guard the city against evil influences coming from the north-east, the malignant quarter. The emperor Kwammu had soon after his succession issued an edict setting limits to the building of temples and the admission of priests to holy orders. All over the country temples were springing up and priests were swarming; but what seems like a sign of religious fervour was in fact only a scramble to acquire tax-free estates, since the clergy and church property were immune. "If this continues, in a few years there will be no land which is not temple property," says the edict, and forbids the gift or sale of land to religious institutions. But despite these prohibitions, from the foundation of Heian temples and shrines were multiplied throughout the city and in all its environs, till in a century or two the flanks of the hills were covered with sacred buildings, and warlike monks were a greater danger to the capital than ever was anticipated by those who moved from Nara to escape the ecclesiastical power.

If we may judge from modern Kyōto, the city of Heian did not present as a whole an imposing spectacle. It must have lacked in grandeur, for apart from a few great palaces an observer looking down from an eminence would see only a flat expanse of shingled roofs, in monotonous rectangular patterns, broken rarely by some tall pavilion. But on more intimate examination he would no doubt have found, as one finds in many modern Japanese towns that give a first impression of drab ugliness, charming details revealed only to more intimate knowledge—handsome gates, pleasant courtyards, glimpses of neat gardens; here the noble tiled roof of a temple, there the red pillars of a shrine; in the streets a diversity of coloured costume and the grave movement of oxen drawing the carriages of nobles or carts from the farms. The capital was, it seems, not crowded, for curiously enough the western half was never prosperous, despite efforts made by the government to encourage residence there; and it is an interesting fact that the tendency to spread eastward was so strong that the modern city of Kyōto lies almost entirely east of the old central avenue of Heian. There is no means of knowing the population of Heian in its beginnings, but one authority estimates the number of houses at the opening of the ninth century as 100,000 and the inhabitants as 500,000. This is probably excessive, since the population of the present city, which has a much greater area, is less than 700,000; but there is no doubt that Heian in those days was one of the largest cities in the world. It was, of course, a city of wooden structures, great and small. Of the buildings in the great enclosure

the most magnificent was the Daigoku-den, or Great Hall of
State. It stood on a stone platform, guarded by red lacquered balustrades, and consisted of a hall about 170 feet long and 50 feet
wide, under a roof supported by 52 pillars. The whole was painted
red, and the roof was of emerald blue tiles. In the centre of the hall
stood, on a raised platform under a canopy surmounted by golden
phœnixes, the Imperial Throne. Other important buildings were
the Hōgaku-den, or Hall of Rich Pleasures, where ceremonial
banquets were held; and the Butoku-den, or Hall of Military
Virtue (similar to Daigoku-den), near which were a parade
ground and enclosures for equestrian games and archery. Within
the great enclosure stood a group of buildings, surrounded by a
wall thirteen feet high, of double red wooden pillars set in plaster
and roofed with tiles. A further enclosure, within this wall, contained a block of connected buildings which formed the imperial
residence. This smaller enclosure was bounded by a wall in the
form of a double corridor, with a roof supported by pillars. The
principal buildings within were the Shishin-den, or Purple Dragon
Hall, a ceremonial pavilion, and the Seiryō-den, or Pure Cool
Hall, which contained the emperor's living apartments and rooms
for the use of his consort and concubines. Near the Seiryō-den was
the Naishidokoro, a small apartment in which was enshrined the
Sacred Mirror. At the north of the inner enclosure lay the "Forbidden Interior," where lived the empress and the imperial
concubines, and close by their residences were apartments of ladies-
in-waiting, styled, after the trees in their courtyards, the Pear
Chamber, the Wistaria Chamber, the Plum Chamber, and so on.

Some modern writers describe the buildings in the second enclosure as making up a palace of unparalleled splendour.[1] The red
pillars, the blue tiles, the white plaster, the green lattices, the gold
characters on black tablets, the tubs of flowering trees, were doubtless given full value by the restrained simplicity of spacious halls
and bare courtyards; but architecturally the total effect must have
been one of cold and severe beauty rather than of magnificence.
Remembering the aspect of ancient palaces that have been preserved in China, Japan, and Korea, and making full allowance for
their present desolation, even peopling them in the imagination
with richly-dressed courtiers and officials, one cannot help feeling

that, though they satisfied rigid æsthetic standards, they must have lacked the warm qualities of exuberance and splendour.

The life of the court seems to have accorded in tone with its surroundings. Just as the buildings were of strictly prescribed dimensions and arrangement, so were the behaviour and costume of their inhabitants regulated to the minutest point. The code of ceremonial of the T'ang court was adopted and rigorously applied. The legislation of the early Heian period is concerned to an amazing extent with matters of ritual and etiquette, and it is easy to see that the seclusion of the sovereign and his constant preoccupation with details of dress and deportment made it difficult, if not impossible, for even the strongest-minded ruler to comprehend, much less to cope with, the urgent problems of government. So, in 810, we find solemn edicts fixing the colour of officials' robes, the length of their swords, the nature of their salutations. Ministers of state of the second rank may wear dark purple, and not medium purple, princes and high officers of certain ranks may wear medium purple and not light purple. In 818 new regulations are introduced, for ordinary dress as well as court dress, and exact rules are laid down for the behaviour of inferiors towards superiors. Chinese etiquette is to be universally observed. When greeting a Prince of the Blood, or the Great Councillor of State, the Ministers of the Right and Left shall move forward in their seat and bow, but all others shall stand up in front of their seats and salute, except that those of the sixth rank and under shall stand up and make a deep obeisance, bending the body from the loins. Busy with such matters, occupied for many days of the year with elaborate rites, the emperor and his ministers could not, if they would, pay attention to the serious questions, both political and economic, which had begun to arise as soon as the centralised state had begun to develop in early Yamato days. They could not fail to be aware of those questions, for they struck too closely at the imperial finances and the imperial authority. The breakdown of the system of taxation, as administered by greedy provincial officials, was plain from the emptiness of the imperial chest. The weakness of the military authority was plain from the incursions of the Ainu and the ravages of pirates. The quarrels and rivalries of the great families were only too apparent from the plots and counterplots

which centred round the throne and the succession. But, obvious
as were these abuses, there is little sign of constructive policy to
remove them. All students of the chronicles of this period must be
impressed by the failure of the central authority to cope with
events, its almost pathetic reliance upon government by exhortation. This method, Chinese in fashion, seems to have taken fast
hold of the mind of the ruling classes in Japan, despite its repeated
failure, year after year, century after century. Even to-day, when
the administration is completely organised and backed by powerful sanctions, one is sometimes surprised to find the highest authorities resorting to magniloquent rescripts, expounding to the people
the benefits of, let us say, frugality, or unremitting toil. One seems
to hear ancestral voices, as of remote patriarchs admonishing their
clans. In the early Heian period the system was at its height. It
consists of a stream of edicts indifferently enforced, or despairingly
withdrawn, and it is well described by a phrase, commonly quoted
in Japan from the later Han chronicles, *chōrei bokai*, which means
"to issue orders in the morning and revise them in the evening."

Such being the background at the capital, it is easy to see that
the effective power of the sovereign must continuously diminish,
and that the significant events of the period are, unfortunately,
not those recorded in the official histories, where we find such
entries as: "The Emperor gave a winding water banquet and
caused scholars to compose verses," or "A great wind broke down
two trees in the Southern Park. They turned into pheasants," or
"Red sparrows collected on the roof of a palace building and did
not leave for ten days." We should not lightly scorn the graceful,
elegant society which these records faintly picture, for it was a
centre from which spread a culture and refinement of importance
in the world's æsthetic history; but it is important to realise how
strongly it contrasted with the life of the people outside the court
circle. The contrast is perhaps best emphasised by describing
briefly some events which were taking place in other parts of
Japan while the capital at Nagaoka was under construction.

In the early part of the century incursions of the Emishi, or
barbarians, by which name the Ainu were known, had made it
necessary to send strong forces against them to the north of Japan.
Frontier posts were established at various points in the province of

Mutsu, notably at a placed called Taga, a few miles north of the present town of Sendai, but the Ainu, though generally held in check, were not subdued, and made frequent raids towards the south. The constant fighting was a great drain upon the treasury, so that in a memorial to the throne in 805 a Fujiwara minister said: "At present the state is suffering from two things, building and warfare." He referred to the cost of the new palaces and the campaigns against the Ainu. During the reign of the emperor Kōnin, Kwammu's predecessor, the government had ordered various measures to be taken on the frontier, but nothing had been done. From an indignant edict of 783 we learn the reason why. For years past, we are told, the military commanders and the civil officials in the eight eastern provinces—that is, roughly speaking, territory including the modern Tokyo and stretching as far north as authority could reach—had cheated the government by diverting military supplies and taxes to their own use, and by employing the soldiers on their own farms, so that the frontier troops had no training in the use of arms and were quite unfit for war. Meanwhile Dewa and Mutsu were in a most unsettled state. Districts corresponding to the present Akita prefecture were laid waste by the Ainu, and though the government helped the farmers to rebuild their homes, there was no security, for the Ainu "gathered together like ants, but dispersed like birds"—a pleasant simile for mobility—and the frontier troops were no match for them. The government therefore endeavoured to reform the system of recruiting. They ordered the formation of provincial defence forces, to be composed of the able-bodied young men in the families of district chiefs, and to number from 500 to 1,000, according to the size of the province. This was, of course, the peace strength, and the object of these units was to provide, in the first place, a nucleus of fully-trained soldiers who were exempted from taxation in kind or in labour, and could devote themselves exclusively to policing the unsettled regions. The formation of this small permanent territorial force, which did not exceed 4,000 combatants, is of great interest from several points of view. It shows that the central authorities could not depend upon the honesty of the provincial governors or the efficiency of the garrison levies, and so decided to throw the burden of defence upon the propertied classes, whose

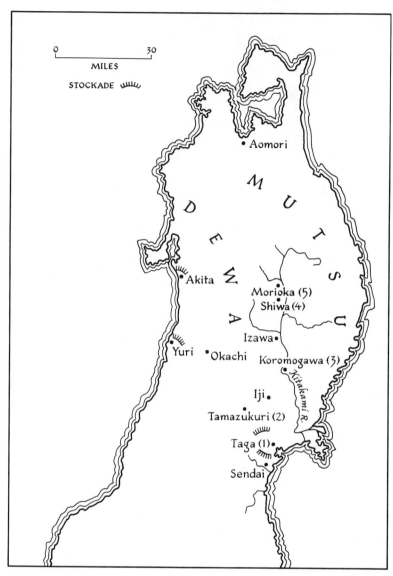

FIG. 27. *Area of Kosami's campaign in 789. (1) Permanent base. (2) Fortified post used as base. (3) Encampment. (4) Advanced post. (5) Scene of Kosami's defeat. Place names are given for geographical reference.*

direct interests were at stake. They thus brought into existence a
kind of yeomanry, recruited on a hereditary basis, since its members were drawn from the households of hereditary local chiefs;
and we have here the beginnings of the privileged class of soldiers
which later characterised the feudal period in Japan.

In the following year (784), Ōtomo Yakamochi was given a
commission as Seitō Shōgun, or "General for Subduing the East,"
and went east, or rather north-east, with two other commanders.
Later we hear of him establishing defensive posts, but no offensive
campaign was undertaken; and no successor was appointed when
he died in 786. Early in 788 orders were sent to the eastern provinces to convey to Mutsu, by August of that year, 23,000 bushels
of dried rice and a supply of salt, and to assemble at the fortress
of Taga by spring of the following year 52,000 horse and foot
soldiers. A new commander was appointed, one Ki no Kosami,
and by the appointed date in the spring of 789 he reported to the
capital that the imperial forces were concentrated at Taga, whereupon imperial messengers were despatched to the great shrine of
Ise to announce that the campaign would now commence. It was
a miserable failure. Kosami's despatches explain in the spring that
it is too cold to move, in the summer that it is too hot; but, stimulated by an imperial edict, he advanced in July and was thoroughly beaten by the Ainu, his casualties in one engagement being,
according to his own reports, "25 killed, 245 wounded by arrows,
1,316 thrown into the river and drowned," while over 1,200
"reached the bank naked," which evidently means that they had
been stripped of their armour by the Ainu and pushed into the
water. The imperial troops had less than 100 Ainu heads to show
as trophies of this fight. Kosami and his colleagues were evidently
men of the pen rather than the sword, for their despatches were
much more cunning than their strategy. Soon after arrival at the
frontier they wrote to Kyōto, in elegant Chinese, that they would
shortly attack in great force, and that the barbarous enemy, who
lived in holes in the mountains and caves by the sea, would be
brushed away by the heavenly (i.e. the emperor's) troops like
morning dew. Such a matter of rejoicing was this prospect, they
said, that they hastened to report it to His Majesty. The emperor
was furious, and issued an edict, in which he said "What is there to

rejoice about? From subsequent memorials, we find that our generals have been beaten with great losses. They make all sorts of excuses, complain of the difficulties of transport, but the truth is that they are incompetent cowards." There is a good deal more in the same strain, and the generals were recalled. An inquiry was held on their return to the capital where they were found guilty on all the charges. What follows has a familiar ring. The emperor proclaims that, although Kosami ought by law to be severely punished, he will be pardoned in view of his previous services to the state, while his subordinate generals, though they have incurred the penalty of death or banishment, will only be deprived of official and court rank. The fact is that Kosami was a person of high social standing, and his appointment to the supreme command was merely a piece of patronage. It was this kind of abuse of aristocratic privilege which, combined with other factors, led gradually but surely to the breakdown of the central authority and the dominance in the succeeding centuries of a class more competent and vigorous, if less refined, than the court nobility.

After Kosami's failure, the government realised that the subjugation of the Ainu was a serious matter, and it was seen that for the next expedition more thorough preparation and a more careful choice of commanders was necessary. In the spring of 790 the provinces were ordered to furnish within a specified time 140,000 bushels (*koku*) of dried rice. This time the inhabitants of the capital and the home provinces did not escape the levy. Princes, ministers and officials down to the fifth rank were ordered to make contributions. Mention is made of requisitions of 20,000 suits of leather armour, 3,000 suits of iron armour and 34,500 special arrows, and later of a further supply of 120,000 bushels of dried rice. It is interesting to note that the Council of State ordered lists to be made in Kyōto and in all the provinces, of people of all ranks and classes who had sufficient property to permit of their being called upon to furnish supplies, giving as a reason the fact that hitherto a great number of able-bodied and well-to-do people had evaded both military service and the requisitions. In 791 the commanders of the new expedition were selected, but the preparations for the campaign took so long that it was not until the beginning of 794 that Ōtomo Otomaro was received in audience and handed the sword (*settō*) which was the symbol of his commission as Sei-i-Tai-Shōgun, or Barbarian-Subduing-Generalissimo. This was the first use of the title which later adorned the *de facto* rulers of Japan. Its first holder was not appointed for his military capacity, but as representative of a great family, who had for centuries past been hereditary guards—Ōtomo means Great Escort—of the emperor. The real work was to be done by his subordinate, Sakanouye no Tamura Maro, a heroic figure in Japanese history. We have no details of this campaign, but it appears to have been successful, for in 795 the Generalissimo was received in audience, and honours were bestowed upon him and his commanders. A number of the enemy were captured, brought back to the capital, and thence banished to the extreme south of Japan. From the fact that some of them are recorded as having Japanese names and holding court rank, it would appear that they were persons of importance and it may be that they were not Ainu, but Japanese settlers who had obtained influential positions among the Ainu. A few years later the chronicles mention a Japanese land-holder and his wife, living among the Ainu and speaking their language, who were arrested and banished to southern Japan because they encouraged the Ainu to resist. It is to be expected that the pioneer Japanese settlers in the north would be of an independent nature, and would not welcome the extension of the imperial rule and imperial taxation to their domains; but the point is worth remembering because it shows that, as the distance from the capital increased, the respect for the authority of the court diminished; and this goes a long way to explain why, as the prestige of the court nobles declined, the centre of real power shifted to the East.

Further measures were necessary before the Ainu were completely subjugated. A number of imperial soldiers, some 300, who had run away during battles in this campaign, were rounded up and instead of being executed were sent to live at frontier posts. A year or so later 9,000 people from various eastern provinces were transferred to the neighbourhood of Iji in Mutsu. It is possible that many of these emigrants were cultivators who had abandoned their farms to escape from oppressive taxation in the central provinces. In the seventh and eighth centuries we hear frequently of bands of men roaming about the more distant provinces, sometimes marauding, sometimes settling peacefully. A line of frontier posts was established, and these settlers were to form a permanent frontier guard. The frontier was gradually pushed northward, and for this purpose several military expeditions were required. Early in 802 Tamura Maro was despatched to Mutsu, where he constructed a fortress at Izawa, which was garrisoned by 4,000 men* from various provinces east of and including Suruga. At the same time the fortress at Okachi was strengthened, and its annual ration was fixed at 10,600 *koku* of rice and 120 *koku* of salt. Many Ainu chieftains began to see that they could no longer resist the pressure of the Japanese, and 500 of them gave themselves up to the garrison of Izawa. Their leaders, who described themselves as Princes, were taken to the capital by Tamura Maro and there, after some argument among the authorities, were put to death. In 806 a fort was built at Shiwa, and the fort at Akita abandoned. The sketch-map will give some idea of the progress of the work of pacification. In twenty years the effective frontier was pushed forward, roughly speaking, from the neighbourhood of Sendai to the neighbourhood of Morioka.

There is no doubt that the task was a very severe one. The Ainu were in difficult terrain † which they knew well, and there is good reason to believe that between the stronger Ainu chieftains and the Japanese settlers there was not much difference. There was a good deal of intercourse and doubtless some inter-marriage, and consequently the imperial troops were not fighting against a completely inferior people.

* *Rōnin*, "wave-men": men who had no official occupation, or who owed no duty of service or employment to anyone. Note the early use of this term.

† Moreover, the difficulties of transport for the imperial troops were great. We need not believe Kosami's despatches, but it is significant that in reporting his failure in 789 he states that the transport of his supplies from Tamatsukuri to Koromogawa took four days, from Koromogawa to Shiwa six days, in good weather and if they were not attacked on the way. Adding the time required for loading and unloading at each point, he calculated that a minimum of twenty-four days was required by the coolies to get supplies up to the front and return to the base for a fresh load. The maximum which they could carry was 6,215 *koku* of rice, requiring 12,440 men. The number of fighting troops was 27,470 men, consuming 549 *koku* a day, so that it took, according to his calculation, over 12,000 men twenty-four days to keep 27,000 men fed for eleven days. It was therefore necessary, he urged, to reduce the number of fighting troops and to bring them back nearer to the base, transferring the men thus made available to the transport service.

The building of the two capitals, and the successive campaigns against the Ainu were of themselves enough to exhaust the imperial treasury, and to throw desperate burdens in the shape of taxation and forced labour upon the peasants, who, of course, being the only producers, were the ultimate sufferers. But, quite apart from these emergency demands upon them, their position was extremely unhappy. That the officials at the capital were incompetent and corrupt and the officials in the provinces oppressive and greedy is clear from the stream of admonitory rescripts which were issued at this period; and that the rescripts were quite ineffective is equally clear from subsequent events.

The Kyōto government, after Tamura Maro's work of pacification, seems to have taken some measures to encourage settlers in the new territory. The provincial officials were instructed to refrain from including in their registers of taxable fields land newly brought under cultivation by settlers. It appears that many farmers, discouraged by the interference of these officials, had run away. Perhaps because of the oppression of the governors and district chiefs, there were sporadic Ainu revolts, followed by punitive expeditions. The commander, Watamaro, is commended and awarded promotion in a rescript of 811 for "destroying the lairs of the barbarians and exterminating their tribes."

It seems that the Kyōto authorities did, at this period, genuinely endeavour to promote the interests of the farmers settled in the eastern provinces. It was, of course, to their advantage to do so, since more land under cultivation meant more taxable capacity. But the local authorities were too far away to be effectively supervised, and it was they and not the court who profited by the increased yield. A study of the following chapter will show how this came about.

NOTE TO CHAPTER X

[1] Page 196 ff. When considering the elegance of the Heian court one should not think of it only in terms of extravagance and luxury. There has been in Japanese life a persistent strain of simplicity and frugality which has tended to prevent gross excesses. Interesting evidence on this point is to be found in the literature of the period, notably in the admonitions to his descendants of a nobleman named Kujō-den, who recommends standards of behaviour of a most Spartan kind, with great emphasis on personal cleanliness and modest living.

Chapter XI

THE DEVELOPMENT OF CHINESE INSTITUTIONS
ON JAPANESE SOIL

WHEN the new government was installed in Kyōto, it had a number of extremely difficult questions to tackle, most of which were variations of a fundamental theme—the relation between land tenure and taxation. We have already dealt with these questions, perhaps at excessive length, in previous chapters, but we must refer to them again, for they have an important bearing upon the development of nearly every social and political institution in later Japanese history.

The leading economic feature of the Heian period is the rapid growth in size and in numbers of tax-free estates, the manors known as *shō* (or *shōen*). The grounds for exemption from tax were numerous. In the Nara period the chief owners of tax-free estates were Buddhist temples and monasteries, which in the first years of religious fervour received both from the state and from pious individuals large gifts of land. Such land, as church property, became immune from national and local levies. The government subsequently forbade the private transfer of land to Buddhist temples, but the prohibition was a dead letter from the beginning and the holdings of the temples grew steadily throughout the eighth century, not only by gifts from private persons, but also by grants from the government itself. In the ninth century, while the expansion of temple lands continued, still further additions to tax-free lands resulted from two processes which now became common. One was the relatively legitimate process by which tracts of land, cultivated or uncultivated, were granted (with immunity from tax) by the emperor to members of the very prolific imperial family or to imperial favourites or to high officers of state. The other was the arbitrary appropriation by private persons of unreclaimed arable land or pasture or forest, none of which was taxable. The amount of land at the disposal of the throne for grants was of course limited, but it was not long before powerful territorial families began to claim immunity by alleging that their lands were originally untaxable imperial lands, and if they were powerful enough they did not even trouble to secure charters but obliged the local officials to endorse their claims. Alongside of these two processes there grew up the two customs of commendation and benefice, which resulted in the further increase in numbers and extent of estates either completely or partly immune. The subject is an extremely complex one, but it is sufficient to explain here that, as we have seen in the study of administration in the Nara period, the growing burden of taxation drove small or middling cultivators either to abandon their allotments and become vagrants or to put themselves under the protection of influential tax-free landowners. There were various forms of commendation, but in typical instances the taxable owner of a piece of land surrendered it to the owner of a tax-free estate, with which it was then incorporated. This surrender was nominal inasmuch as the commendor retained the possession and use of the land, and paid as fee for the protection or the immunity which commendation brought him an agreed proportion of the income obtained from the commended area. The commendee himself for further security might commend his own manors to some more powerful immune person, and this process might be repeated until the final commendation was to some institution or person of unchallengeable immunity, such as a great temple like the Tōdaiji or an official of the highest rank or even a prince of the blood. The converse practice of benefice consisted of the grant by the owner of a tax-free estate, to a person employed in its management or cultivation, of certain rights or privileges appertaining to it, as for instance a share of its produce or of the labour of men attached to it, or the full use by the beneficiary of a portion of his holding. It was therefore a form of lease and, though the lessee's tenure was at first precarious, it tended to assume an hereditary character. In any case most small cultivators would rather take the risk of working beneficed land than spend their labour on allotment land which left them little after they had satisfied the tax-collector. It may easily be imagined that, with commendation and benefice in a great variety of forms and resting upon agreements sometimes verbal, sometimes written, with privileges and obligations of every description attaching often to the same piece of land and passing through a long scale of lessees and sub-lessees, the system of land tenure in the Heian period had become so chaotic that there was every inducement for those with a strong arm to sweep aside all legal hindrances and to establish themselves in plain ownership by force or threats. The government did its best to resist these disruptive tendencies, but it was powerless, partly because there were too many people in high places who themselves depended on tax-free manors, and partly because the allotment land was never more than a small proportion of the total cultivated or cultivable area. It is probable that the allotment land at the time of the Taikwa reform was only rice-land, and moreover only such rice-land as was cultivated and registered. But in addition to the allotment land there was certainly a great deal of unregistered rice-land under cultivation, and very considerable tracts of tilled land of other kinds, to say nothing of unappropriated arable and non-arable land in its vicinity. Since the system of state organisation was based on the equal division of land, and yet only an increasingly small proportion of available land was thus divided, the collapse of the system of land tenure must bring about a collapse, or at least a readjustment, of the system of state organisation.

This readjustment is the characteristic political feature of the Heian period. The T'ang administrative cadres, already simplified to some extent when they were first borrowed, were found to be still too elaborate and none too well suited to their purpose. To govern such a small and sparsely-populated state as Japan by a great and complicated apparatus of councils and boards and officials was, to use a Chinese proverb, "like carving a chicken with a butcher's cleaver"; and it was not long before the official hierarchy laid down in the administrative code (*ryō*) lost most of its real functions, and was replaced by organs of irregular growth. The power of the Council of State waned, and the various ministers and councillors lost their authority, though they increased in numbers as their offices became merely nominal and their titles honorary. The new organs of government grew almost accidentally in a fashion familiar to students of English constitutional history. The most important of them were the *Kwampaku* or Regent, the *Kuraudo* or Archivists, the *Kebiishi* or Police Commissioners, and the *Kageyushi* or Audit Officers. An account of each of these authorities will serve to bring out several features of political and social life of the times.

The word *kwampaku* first appears in writings of the Han

dynasty, and it denotes an officer of state who acts as the mouth-piece of a sovereign, reporting to him and taking his commands. The office of *Kwampaku* in Japan developed from that of the regents who controlled state affairs during the minority of an emperor. The first to bear the title was Fujiwara Mototsune, who became regent at the opening of the reign of the child emperor Yōzei (877-884) and continued as *Kwampaku* after he had deposed that monarch and set up the elderly emperor Kōkō in his stead. Before long the office of *Kwampaku* became the highest office in the state, ranking above that of the chancellor. Sometimes the *Kwampaku* held both posts, but his titular position, his cabinet rank so to speak, might be only that of Minister of the Right, or Minister of the Left, and still he would take precedence over the chancellor, having direct access to the emperor, whose policy he ostensibly carried out but in reality dictated. He was in fact a dictator, and the dictatorship was, from the beginning of the tenth century, exercised by successive leaders of the Fujiwara clan, thus setting the seal upon their dominance, which began with Kamatari at the time of the Taikwa reform, was interrupted in the eighth century by rivalry within and without the clan, was gradually resumed in the ninth century, and lasted until well into the twelfth. This ascendancy of a powerful family illustrates features which seem to have been inseparable from government in Japan until the Restoration of 1868. The nominal head of the state, while receiving deference amounting to worship, exercises no authority, but is replaced in the actual conduct of affairs by a powerful minister. We have seen the beginnings of this practice in the attempts of the Soga family to outstrip rival clans and to secure for themselves a paramount position in the state. The dual system of government was brought to a high stage of completeness by the Fujiwara family, and it was continued until modern times by successive dynasties or regents or military dictators. Analogies in the history of other countries—mayors of the palace, king-makers and so on—are easy to find, but there was one way in which the Japanese custom was peculiar. It was the expression, in terms of government, of the family system; for, though the Fujiwara clan threw up a number of great men, its dominance came from family solidarity rather than from the merit of individuals. Family affection, family pride, family cohesion, were always strong among the Japanese, and they were reinforced by the Chinese doctrines of ancestor worship and filial piety. It was by family connections rather than by any other means that the Fujiwara achieved and maintained their power. Fujiwara ladies were married to successive emperors and to imperial princes, and none but the offspring of a Fujiwara consort had any prospect of coming to the throne. Fujiwara filled all the important offices of state, and Fujiwara took great pains to acquire the leading rights to tax-free manors, without assuming the burden of working them, so much so that a Fujiwara in the twelfth century boasts that his family have never managed an estate, which means that they were always the final commendees, who drew revenues from land but did not stoop to work it. It is an interesting commentary on the strength of the family system in Japan that this powerful clan hardly ever found it necessary to use violence against their rivals. Those who seemed likely to thwart them were quietly if ruthlessly banished to some distant province or persuaded to take the tonsure and withdraw to a monastery. Silent, steady family pressure was more effective than bloodshed. The career of one of their greatest rivals, Sugawara no Michizane, aptly illustrates this point, beside throwing some light on contemporary affairs in general.

Michizane was born of an ancient but not powerful family, well reputed for scholarship. He grew up at a time when Chinese studies stood in high esteem. Excelling in composition, verse and calligraphy, he was a popular teacher at the University, where he came under the notice of the families of young nobles who were preparing for their examinations. He was taken into favour at court, became the tutor of the heir apparent and gave his daughter as an imperial consort, thereafter rising rapidly to high office. In 894 it was decided to send an embassy to the T'ang court, and Michizane was chosen as ambassador. But he was loth to go, no doubt because he did not wish to lose chances at home. He petitioned the throne to stop sending embassies to China, quoting reports from Japanese monks studying there, which said that conditions were very bad and the journey very dangerous. His petition was granted and from that time official relations with the Chinese court ceased. It was true that the T'ang dynasty was tottering; and moreover the Japanese were, or felt they were, at a stage where they might best be left to themselves to assimilate and adapt to their own needs and tastes the Chinese culture which they had imported. The lapse of official relations did not, of course, mean that all contact with China ceased. There was still a going and coming of priests, students and traders; but generally speaking the first enthusiasm for T'ang institutions had waned, and the Japanese had begun to stand on their own feet, and to work out their own methods, by the end of the ninth century. There was even a slight reaction at this period in favour of purely Japanese studies. Michizane himself, for that matter, could compose deftly in the native style. But he was now in high repute for his administrative talents as well as for his learning, and in 899 he was the second official in the state. The man above him was, of course, a Fujiwara. So high was he in the imperial favour that the Fujiwara, and other great families, resented his rapid rise and forced the sovereign to appoint him supernumerary Viceroy of Kyūshū. This was equivalent to banishment; and Michizane never came back, nor did the Emperor ever dare to recall him. Such was the Fujiwara method of dealing with a strong imperial favourite. It can therefore be easily imagined that less powerful political rivals stood little chance against them; and when the Fujiwara downfall came, as come it must, it was to be caused not by political rivals at the capital, but by a family which had been steadily accumulating material strength in the distant eastern provinces. This was the great Taira house; and it is to be remarked that, although they owed much to their military prowess, they were of the imperial blood, and their family prestige and family cohesion were important factors of their success.

Just as the strength of aristocratic feeling in Japan, by giving to the highest office of state a virtually hereditary character, broke down the bureaucratic structure of the borrowed Chinese system of government, or, at least, gave it a decidedly Japanese quality, so is the imprint of the national temperament visible in many of the administrative expedients which were worked out in practice during the Heian period. The development of the special organs of government named above is an illustration of this feature, and may be recommended to the attention of those who are inclined to think that the Japanese have excelled only as copyists of foreign institutions. That they had the courage and wisdom to copy in the first place is greatly to their credit; and their later history shows that they have never rested content with an uncritical acceptance of imported models.

The *Kuraudo-dokoro* or Bureau of Archivists was a small office, dating from 810, which originally had custody of confidential papers in the Palace. Gradually, owing to the close contact of its officers with the sovereign, its powers expanded until, under Fujiwara influence, it became the supreme organ for the conduct of palace affairs and the channel through which imperial decrees were issued, or suits and memorials brought to the notice of the throne. In 897 Tokihira, then head of the Fujiwara clan, became Commissioner of the Bureau of Archivists. This appointment, while adding to the prestige of the Bureau, gave Tokihira an opportunity to use it as a convenient executive machine. The early procedure as laid down in the Codes for the issue of imperial edicts had been extremely cumbrous. They were drafted in one office, presented for the august inspection by another, passed to the Chancellor's office for countersignature by various counsellors, then returned to the Emperor for his approval and seal, and finally issued, after many more formalities, to the metropolitan and provincial authorities. The Archivists took short cuts, and issued ordinances which, though less formal than the full-dress edicts, were quite as effective. Naturally, with a powerful Fujiwara at its head, the Bureau did not confine its ordinances to routine matters, and by the end of the 9th century it had acquired administrative, and even legislative powers, the exercise of which left to the Council of State (*Dajō-kwan*) and the Central Office (*Nakatsukasa*) very little real authority.

The Police Commission (*Kebiishichō*) was as adventitious in its rise as the Bureau of Archivists. Its beginnings, indeed, are obscure, for all we know is that, by about A.D. 817, certain officers of the palace guards were commissioned to see to the execution of imperial warrants, under the title of *Kebiishi*, which means literally "officers to prosecute offences." Originally, it seems, the arrest of offenders by these officers was merely an occasional extension of their proper military functions, but it soon became in practice their constant duty, because the procedure laid down in the codes was so elaborate; and before long the Commissioners had established a separate office of their own, which usurped the prerogatives of arrest, examination, sentence and appeal belonging respectively to the Guards, the Board of Censors, the Department of Justice and the Metropolitan Council. By 870 the Police Commissioners took cognizance of practically all crimes of violence, which they dealt with from arrest to punishment. Such was their power that their orders had the same validity as an imperial command, and those who disobeyed them were treated as guilty of treasonable conduct. In the 10th century they even took to arresting and punishing taxpayers who were in arrears. Strictly speaking their jurisdiction did not extend beyond the capital, or at least its vicinity, but as their powers grew in scope they tended to exercise them a distance, while bodies modelled on the *Kebiishichō* were formed in provincial areas, so that there was a great increase in the number of subordinate police officers. For such work as theirs, strong and determined men were needed, and the Commissioners naturally drew upon the warlike classes for recruits. We have already remarked that most of the military posts at the capital were held by young men of good family, the gilded youth who were rather ornamental than pugnacious. Consequently it was the real fighting men who were employed by the Police Commission, which thus gradually came to exercise a measure of control over them, thereby developing authority as a military as well as a judicial organ.

The *Kebiishi*, as their authority grew, began to neglect the penal codes, and built up a body of case law of their own. There are records of a number of works compiled by the Police Commission for the use of its officers, bearing such titles as "Summary of *Kebiishi* Edicts," "Private Instructions," "Formulary for Police Commissioners," "Manual of Interrogation," and so on. These are no longer extant, but it is evident from quotations preserved in other books that, taken together, they constituted a guide to the exercise of summary jurisdiction, replacing and supplementing the codes. The *Kebiishichō* administered a kind of customary law, developed by them as they went along. Its nature is not exactly known; but its punishments seem to have been less severe than

是モ中サ将ノ粧衣束ナリ
平胡籙ナリ是ハ時ニヨリ
カワルヘシ

FIG. 28. *Court uniform of a General of the Guards in the Heian period.*
(From an early MS. book.)

those laid down in the codes, though much more rigorously and promptly enforced. As a concession to Buddhism the death penalty was abolished, but there were other cruel punishments, such as cutting off the arm of a robber. It was partly to the prevalence of armed robbery in the capital that the *Kebiishi* owed their powers, for it could be checked only by prompt and drastic methods.

The Audit Officers (*Kageyushi*) were functionaries who examined the accounts of governors of provinces at the end of their term of office. They were first established in about A.D. 800, by which time the malpractices of the governors had made it essential to look closely into their dealings with official funds and property. The Board of Audit gradually grew in importance, and by the end of the century it had usurped the functions of the regular audit and revenue authorities at the capital, and was staffed by officials of high standing under the control of a member of the Council of State.

The foregoing changes in the central administrative system were accompanied by corresponding changes in local government. Perhaps the most astonishing was the change which took place in the character of the provincial governorships. These carried certain privileges which, despite the scrutiny of the auditors, were extremely lucrative and therefore very tempting to the free-spending nobles at the capital. But service in the provinces was distasteful to such elegant persons, and they gradually managed to secure the advantages of the office without the hardships of exile. At first a needy favourite would secure an appointment as provincial governor with special permission to remain at home and, ostensibly at least, to adminster his province by written instructions to his staff. Soon even this pretence was dropped, and nomination to the highest posts in the provincial governments became merely a method of granting an annual stipend to courtiers. Later an even more surprising development took place, when a court favourite would be granted the privilege of nominating one or more provincial governors each year. The appointment then became entirely titular, for the nominee never went to his post; nor did he receive any of its emoluments, for these were paid direct to the nominator. At first country magnates were glad to purchase the title of provincial governor, however empty; but as it grew common

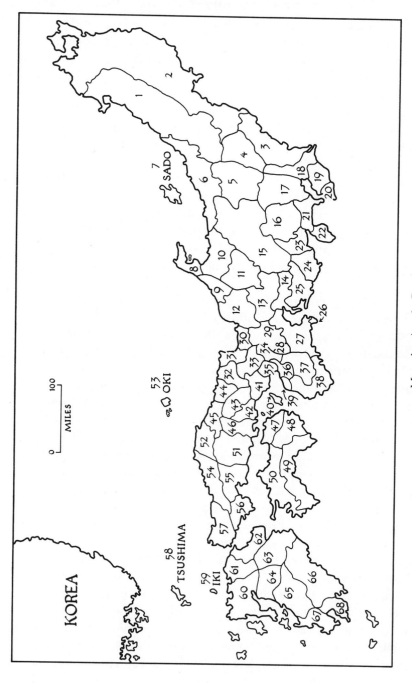

FIG. 29. *Map showing the Provinces.*

it was less esteemed, and a final point of absurdity was reached when those who had the appointments in gift could find nobody to accept them and nominated imaginary persons with fanciful names, such as Lakeside Zephyr or Ridgetop Pinewind.

While absentee officials were living at ease in the capital on emoluments which they did not earn, the work of provincial administration was performed by subordinates in government service or by local notables anxious to promote their own interests. It may therefore be easily imagined that, by the middle of the Heian period, both provincial and district administrations were in a chaotic state, and from top to bottom corrupt. The machinery set up by the Taikwa reformers proving thus inadequate, and official prestige having fallen so low, the rise of a new class, flouting the central government and exercising more and more autonomy, was bound to follow. There was a return to pre-Reform conditions, and family influence began to reassert itself at the expense of the crumbling bureaucracy. It is to be noted, moreover, that even those bureaucratic institutions which survived tended to become the hereditary preserves of certain families. The most powerful and lucrative places fell to the Fujiwara, but other offices and professions were monopolised in a similar way by such families as the Abe, the Miyoshi, the Wake, the Shirakawa, and so on. Indeed it cannot be too strongly emphasised that the hereditary principle defeated the Chinese doctrine of merit. Where family continuity could not be assured by direct succession the powerful machinery of adoption was brought into use, and, as we shall see, developed to a high point of complexity in later periods.

If we turn now from the forms of government to the constitution of the governed we shall find that here also the native tendencies proved too strong to be confined within the bounds of an alien system. The Chinese idea, as applied to Japan, meant the abolition of clan privileges, and the division of the people into two classes, the "good," that is, the free, and the "base," that is, the unfree, all under a supreme monarch. In theory all the free people had equal rights, and all the base people, though unfree, were direct subjects of the ruler. It was far otherwise in practice. There were minute gradations of rank and privilege among both free and unfree. The highest of the free people were the leaders of the clans, the lowest were the members of the guilds and corporations attached to the imperial house. All these, and the numerous intermediate classes, might be distinguished by court ranks and titles, but the hierarchy was essentially based upon family origin, and there was hardly any inter-marriage between different classes of free people. The highest ranks and titles became the privilege of the former clan leaders; the middle ranks fell to members of the minor nobility, the *miyatsuko* class, who in practice rarely rose to the fifth rank, and were thus debarred from the highest offices in the state. They therefore tended to enter learned professions, or to devote themselves to art; and often, in the disorder of the later Heian period, the career of arms furnished an outlet for their energies as well as a protection for their interests. It is this middle class which in the subsequent history of Japan brought forth most of her great warriors, administrators, scholars and artists. This was the branch on which blossomed the flower of Japanese culture.

The lower ranks of free people comprised the pre-Reform clansmen, who may be looked upon as a peasant class of small-holders; and the members of guilds and corporations who were freed by the first article of the Reform Edict. These were the people who held allotment land, and supported the state by their taxes in kind and in labour. It was possible, but unusual, for them to emerge from their class, to receive a family name and through service in official posts to rise in the social scale. There were numerous subdivisions of this large plebeian class. The free clansmen were regarded as superior to the freed guildsmen, and among the guildsmen there were many degrees, in greater or less consideration according to the nature of their work. The guildsmen were, in fact, the industrial workers, skilled and unskilled, and naturally a smith, an armourer, or a lacquer-worker was held in higher consideration than a groom or a scavenger. Though technically free men, both peasant cultivators and industrial workers were subjected to a form of servitude, for the peasants were in reality attached to the land, and the guildsmen were attached to various government offices which disposed of their labour or its product. The distinctions among these groups, however, tended to disappear and the guildsmen to merge with the other free people, so that by the beginning of the tenth century only a few specialised groups were retained.

The unfree people were of five classes, but for our purpose it is sufficient to say that they comprised public and private slaves, the public slaves for the most part being workers either on the land or in base occupations such as scavenging and grave-digging, the private slaves being menial workers in the houses or on the land of

FIG. 30. *The Plebs in the Heian period.* (*After the Ban Dainagon scroll, circa 1170.*)

their owners. The public slaves engaged in agriculture received allotment land on the same scale as free people, but all its produce went to the state and they received only a food ration. The private slaves, with some exceptions, were the absolute property of their masters, and could be disposed of by gift, sale or testament. The great temples owned a number of slaves, and in registers of temple property slaves and their children are found inscribed alongside of cattle and horses. Thus in a document of 750 by which the Province of Tango presented two male and two female slaves to the Tōdaiji under the orders of the central government, their value is assessed at 1,000 sheaves of rice each. In another document we find a borrower mortgaging his daughters as part security for a loan. Slaves were not however entirely without civil rights, since killing or wounding a slave was punishable like killing or wounding an ordinary person. Materials are wanting for a precise estimate of the total number of slaves, but to judge from typical household registers and similar documents they formed about one-tenth, and certainly less than one-fifth, of the total population in settled areas at the end of the Nara period.

The slave class of the early Heian period was composed of several elements. Many of its members were descendants of captives taken in warfare centuries before, during the settlement of the country by the dominant tribes. There were a number of Korean slaves, either captured or received as gifts, and a number of "barbarians," mostly Ainu taken in more recent campaigns. There were also criminals whose punishment had been degradation to slavery. This last category included some who had committed political offences, and, by the eighth century, a number of persons convicted of counterfeiting coin, an offence which was savagely punished, since not only the offender and his accomplices but also his family were enslaved. Children were frequently sold as slaves by their parents, and insolvent debtors occasionally were taken by their creditors as slaves. The numbers of the slave class were maintained and increased by such means and also, of course, by the birth of children to parents of whom one was a slave. But the collapse of the allotment system brought about, very early in the Heian period, the collapse of the slave economy which was bound up with it. Economic change was, as always, accompanied by social change. As the condition of the free peasants came to resemble slavery because of the growing burden of taxation, the distinction between free and unfree lost its meaning; and documents of the Engi period show that by that time—the beginning of the tenth century—it was in practice hardly observed. Thus we see that at both ends of the social scale there was a merging of classes, for as the lower

layers of free people absorbed the slaves and made one more or
less uniform plebeian class, so the upper end was composed almost
entirely of Fujiwara, by whom the other great families were so
completely overborne as to fall into comparative unimportance.
Both extremes could hardly escape the devitalising influence of
their position, the upper being weakened by idle luxury and
corruption, the lower by grinding labour and poor living. It was
therefore to be expected that the middle class should come to the
fore and, as we have said, constitute the vital elements in the
state from the tenth century onwards.

There was one element of the population about which we have
unfortunately but little exact knowledge, and that is the people
of alien origin. They seem to have been numerous and important,
for there is frequent mention of a class of unnaturalised aliens, who
were perhaps Koreans or Chinese only temporarily domiciled in
Japan, as contrasted with families of foreign origin settled for a
generation or more on Japanese soil. It is remarkable that special
provision is made for this class in the codes, which prescribe that
offences in which only aliens of the same origin are concerned
shall be dealt with according to the laws of their own country, but
that where aliens of different origin are concerned Japanese law
shall be applied. Aliens were freely allowed, if not encouraged, to
become Japanese subjects, and aliens who in their own country
had been slaves became free upon settling in Japan. This liberal
treatment of foreigners seems very creditable to the Japanese of
those days. It tends to show that racial feeling was not strong, and
there is a good deal of other evidence to support the view that
Korean and Chinese settlers of all classes were as a rule welcomed,
and indeed invited, no doubt because most of them could contribute something to Japan in learning, or in arts and crafts.

From time to time in the foregoing chapters we have mentioned
legislation, in the form of edicts, ordinances, or codes, bearing
upon most departments of life. But it must not be supposed that a
law was enforced because it was promulgated; and it would be
extremely dangerous to draw any precise inferences as to conditions in Japan up to the end of the ninth century from the
official texts of enactments that have come down to us. The mere
fact that peremptory edicts were repeated sometimes year after

year is evidence that they were not enforced, and the development of the special administrative organs that we have just traced is in itself almost enough to show that the most important institutions of the eighth and ninth centuries were illegal or at least extra-legal growths, none of which had been contemplated by the Taikwa reformers. It is hardly an unfair summary of events to say that during the first half of the Heian period the monarchy became a dyarchy; bureaucratic control gave way to hereditary privilege; land ownership evolved from individual small-holding to feudal tenure; the revenue system utterly collapsed; and the administration of justice depended no longer upon codes but upon summary rules and precedents. Half-way through the eleventh century the imperial government had lost most of its power and much of its prestige; the whole country was ravaged by family feuds and civil war; and such law as prevailed was the house law of the clans. Daylight robbery was rife in the capital and bandits flourished on the main highways by land and by sea. It is not a pretty picture; but it is redeemed by the rise of a vigorous, self-reliant class of rural magnates, and by the growth of an independent national culture, freed to some extent—though not entirely, for that would be impossible—from the almost overwhelming influence of Chinese models. In art and letters and religion the Japanese began to evolve on their own lines, and it is to these developments that we now turn.

Chapter XII

RELIGION AND THE ARTS

1. EARLY HEIAN BUDDHISM

FOR a proper understanding of the growth of Buddhism in Japan from the Heian period onwards, it is best to have some general idea of the development of the parent religion in India, since the conceptions of later Buddhism play an important part in the history of Japan.

Buddhism in India showed almost from its beginnings a strong tendency to create and multiply divinities, and it is in this respect that the difference between early (Hinayana) and late (Mahayana) Buddhism is most apparent. The Hinayanists regarded the Buddha Śākya-muni as a transcendent and miraculous personage, but not as a god. The Mahayanists, while not proclaiming him a god, looked upon him as possessing all the attributes of divinity, as being an embodied phase of wisdom eternal, infinite and all-pervading. He then came to be conceived of as one figure in an endless, cosmic procession of supernatural beings, and so, while "theoretically the metaphysical heaven remained always empty, the buddhological (we dare not say theological) heaven was peopled with innumerable figures."* In such a countless host of Buddhas and Bodhisattvas it is easy and indeed natural to emphasise the importance of one divine personage, to make him the centre of adoration or the symbol of some philosophical concept. It is the exercise of this power to multiply and select which gave to later Buddhism its bewildering pantheon, its varied cosmology, its numerous rituals, its immense canon and its vast metaphysical range. All these came in due course to China, and were thence transmitted to Japan; but from their birth-place in India to their destination in the farthest East they gained many accretions and suffered many changes, until in their final form they bear traces, more or less plain, of Brahmanism, of Iranian Mazdaism, of Chinese Confucianism and Taoism, and finally of Japanese Shinto-ism. Though these wide variations between the earliest and latest forms of Buddhism did not necessarily involve violent disagree-

* Grousset.

ment between the adherents of different cults, there were many sectarian divisions, each revering in particular one group of divinities, or relying in particular upon one group of canonical works. Thus by some sects Śākya (Shaka) is honoured as the central figure of the myriads of Buddhas described in the Lotus Sutra. In others we find him overshadowed or displaced by such divinities as Vairocana (Dainichi), the Great Illuminator; or Amitâbha (Amida), the Lord of Boundless Light; or Maitreya (Miroku), the Messiah; or Avalokiteśvara (Kwannon), the Merciful One who surveys the World with Pity. Sometimes a Buddha is conceived of as having three forms,[1] human, celestial, and metaphysical, or as being the revealed counterpart of a hidden reality, or as forming one of a composite group, a triad, tetrad or pentad, of divine beings. To these we must add such humbler deities as the Four Heavenly Kings (*shi-tennō*), a number of saints (*rakan*), and many popular personages, from Indian, Chinese and Japanese mythology, who are welcomed in this hospitable pantheon and find themselves often the object of a more ardent worship than is devoted to sublimer figures. All these beliefs, all these conceptions of divinity, as they became known to the Japanese, enlarged the scope of their knowledge and entered into many departments of their life. They have left a deep imprint upon art and literature and social institutions; and much of the terminology of Buddhist thought, many of the names of Buddhist legend, now form part of the everyday vocabulary.

Buddhism in the Nara period in Japan, though in its external forms under Mahayana influence, had on its philosophical side been most preoccupied with Hinayana doctrine. Here it had developed within a narrow, almost professional circle, and its popular appeal had been limited to its ritual and magic aspects. The influence of the Nara clergy, apart from a small number of devout ascetics and studious monks, was not an elevating influence and consequently, with the removal of the capital, the ground was now prepared for a new stage in the development of religion in Japan. There was a clear space for some comprehensive doctrine which would satisfy growing spiritual needs, something which would, without going either to metaphysical or to ritual extremes, summarise for ordinary men essentials of the Buddha's teaching.

Buddhism in Japan had hitherto been in process of digestion and henceforward there must follow a variety of attempts to assimilate it, to adapt it to the circumstances and the temperament of the Japanese people. In China such successive stages had already been passed through, and it is therefore not surprising that the first steps taken by the Japanese towards a specifically national type of Buddhism followed the path of Chinese precursors. In 575 a Chinese monk, Chih-k'ai,[2] who had propagated in China the doctrines of the Lotus Sutra, founded on Mount T'ien-t'ai (in Japanese, Tendai) a celebrated monastery, and formed there a school of Buddhism which, though based on those doctrines, has certain ideas in common with Taoism and may be regarded as a Chinese product. We must be excused from an endeavour to explain the metaphysical creed of this school. It was a sort of monistic pantheism of which the central feature is the notion that the absolute is inherent in all phenomena, and that each separate phenomenon is but one manifestation of an unchanging reality. But this reality can be comprehended not by study of the scriptures alone, not by religious practices alone, and not by ecstatic contemplation alone. Enlightenment comes neither from wisdom nor works nor intuition, but from a combination of these three.

Knowledge of these doctrines had spread to Japan at an earlier date, for the T'ien-t'ai monastery was famous, and the Chinese monk Ganjin, who established the first seat of ordination in Japan (754), had brought with him T'ien-t'ai writings. It remained, however, for a Japanese priest to found a new sect, based on the teaching of Chih-k'ai. This was a man named Saichō who, having by his talents attracted the attention of the Emperor, was sent to T'ien-t'ai for study and on his return in 805, after a year's absence, applied to the court for licence to form a "Tendai Lotus Sect," in addition to the six Nara sects which were officially recognised and whose leaders were maintained at official expense. This was granted, and a yearly income allotted to the heads of the new sect. In 807 Saichō instituted its chapter of monks by ordaining over one hundred aspirants at the monastery on Mount Hiei which he had previously built. From that time until the end of his life much of his energy was spent in combating the opposition of the Nara clergy. On the doctrinal side there was hot dispute as to the merits of the Three Vehicles and the One Vehicle, that is as between specific bodies of doctrine and one doctrine which includes and transcends them all. This battle had already been fought in China, and was now repeated in Japan with a vigorous interchange of polemical tracts and treatises. Most of them are now lost, though we can judge of their nature from titles still on record, such as *A True Argument Pointing Out False Views*, a work by a Tōdaiji monk in which the Tendai sect was charged with 28 errors and to which Saichō retorted by pointing out 28 errors of his adversaries. But it was as a rival institution that the older sects most resented the rise of the Tendai, and their enmity was focused against Saichō's claim to set up an ordination platform on Mount Hiei. They contended that the rite of ordination could be performed only at one of the established *kaidan*, and only by priests of their own chapter. Their opposition was so strong that the court did not grant Saichō's petition until 827, five years after his death, though they bestowed great honours upon him during his lifetime. He was the first priest in Japan to be granted the holy title of *Daishi*, "Great Teacher," and he is generally known by his posthumous style of Dengyō Daishi. He holds an important place in the religious history of Japan. Not only was he the first to break away from the traditions of Nara, but he was the forerunner of a line of distinguished ecclesiasts who developed in Japan forms of Buddhism of a progressively national character. Though he brought the T'ien-t'ai system bodily from China, he did not treat it as sacrosanct and self-contained. Though it is based upon the Lotus, he studied and employed in his system material from many other sources, so that the Tendai sect in Japan is sometimes described as compounded of four elements, meditative, disciplinary and esoteric as well as T'ien-t'ai proper. Yet it is doubtful whether Saichō can be fairly regarded as an original and powerful thinker who was able to weld these parts into a coherent whole. It seems more likely that he was an ardent rather than a profound spirit, whose energies were given scope by lucky circumstance. His little temple on Mount Hiei chanced, when the new capital was built, to stand at one of the points of danger, the "demon-entrance" where a holy edifice was needed to ward off evil influences. It was nearer than the Nara monasteries, whose monks were troublesome, and he himself was in close touch with the palace, where he was respected as a scholar lately returned from the fountain of learning in China. It was he, for instance, who brought back the rite of baptism (*kwanchō*) and first baptised an emperor. Moreover, so all-embracing a school as his was at an advantage at this time in so far as it could by its very comprehensiveness gain ground at the expense of more rigid single sects. But a loose grouping of irreconcilables tends always to break up into its separate parts. Therefore, though the Tendai sect grew to considerable influence during the Heian period, its great temple, the Enryakuji, which arose from small beginnings on the flanks of Mount Hiyei, in time became the home of many schisms. It was the Tendai sect which gave birth to most of the later forms of Japanese Buddhism, and so it may be said that it was the eclecticism of Saichō which first engendered religious animosity in his own country.

Contemporary with Saichō was another and a greater ecclesiast, Kūkai, better known by his canonical title of Kōbō Daishi. His career both as an individual and as a churchman is of first-rate importance in the history of Japan. As a youth he read deeply in the Chinese classics, and then turned to Buddhistic studies. He went to China at the same time as Saichō and returned in 807 after a three years' sojourn, during which he travelled and studied under various masters, including priests from Kashmir and Southern India, who are said to have instructed him in Sanskrit. The teaching that most impressed him was a new form of Buddhism, recently brought to China from Southern India. It was one of those later developments to which we have just alluded, the cult of Maha-Vairocana (in Japanese, Dainichi Nyorai). Here Dainichi is regarded as the primordial and eternal Buddha, from whom emanate all other Buddhas, and he is conceived of as surrounded by four such emanations, at the four points of the compass. On the West, we may note in passing, is Amida, the Lord of Boundless Light, and it is this divinity who, by that transfer of emphasis which we have already noted, assumes a supreme position in other cults.

The body of doctrine surrounding the worship of Dainichi was brought back to Japan by Kūkai, who called it (after its Chinese name Chên-yen) Shingon, or True Word, and this is the name of the sect which he in due course established. On his return he found the religious world upset by dissensions due to the rise of the Tendai sect, and he kept in the background for some time, devoting himself to study and travel and ascetic practices. He wrote a great many works, of which most are still extant, developing and expounding his system. But the Shingon doctrines are mystical, and not to be explained in words. The believer is, however, helped to enlightenment by talismanic devices. Not that the Shingon sect is deficient in ethical elements, for Kūkai throughout his life and on his death-bed enjoined upon priest and layman alike the observance of cardinal Buddhist commandments and moral precepts. But the Shingon (and to a less extent the Tendai) is marked off from other sects by its liking for magic and symbolism, its free use of incantations, spells and ritual gestures. It therefore attaches great importance to recitation of the formulæ known as *mantra* (i.e. *shingon*), such as the syllables A—BI—RA—UN—KEN, representing the components of the universe. "The universe," says a commentary, "being nothing but the absolute spiritual presence of Dainichi, one can realise this conception by repeating the formula." Baptism, too, though not essential as in Christianity, is an important rite in the mysteries of Shingon.

In these respects Shingon is of Tantric origin and character. On its philosophical side it gave an impetus to that movement, already started in the Nara period, by which the native gods were reconciled with the Buddhist divinities. For the Shingon believer regards the universe as a manifestation of one truth under two categories (in Japanese *ryōbu*, two divisions), noumenal and phenomenal. It was tempting and easy, therefore, to identify the Great Illuminator Dainichi with the Sun Goddess Amaterasu, and to apply a similar dualism wherever else it seemed desirable. Both the Tendai and Shingon sects fostered such ideas; but it should not be inferred that Shintō was reluctant to adopt them, since there is good evidence that in many instances the Shintō priesthood themselves came forward and proposed identifications.* They also took care to copy features of Buddhism which

---

* The first recorded instance of a Shintō deity being styled a *bosatsu* (i.e. *bodhisattva*) is that of the Usa Hachiman, in 783. The Yakushi temple at Nara possesses an image of Hachiman, of the Kōnin period (810-824), which represents him as a Buddhist priest. Hachiman is the god of war.

they thought attractive. Thus, though the worship of images was unknown to the indigenous religion, the *Engi-shiki* records that after 900 several thousand images were carved and distributed to Shintō shrines. And Shintō architecture took many hints from Buddhist temples. It would, however, be a mistake to suppose that complete fusion of the two religions was ever reached. What may be called Pure Shintō always retained a territory of its own, however shrunken. Nor was the process of compromise so rapid as is sometimes suggested.* Its growth can be clearly traced through many successive phases, commencing with the idea that the gods were favourably disposed to Buddhism and were gratified by Buddhist prayers. It was not until the close of the Heian period (say 1100) that the fully syncretic Dual Shintō (Ryōbu Shintō) was evolved. Saichō and Kūkai are sometimes spoken of as the originators of Dual Shintō, but there is nothing in their writings to prove that they went further than to look on the Shintō gods as guardian deities or spirits, sometimes perhaps as bodhisattvas. They saw nothing irregular in the common practice of combining both forms of worship in the same building or the same precincts, but the more specific theory (expressed in the formula *honji suijaku*, "traces of descent from true home") which regards the gods as manifestations of the Buddhas, was elaborated in later times. Kūkai died in 836, after having founded on Mount Kōya a monastery which is now the largest and perhaps the most flourishing in Japan. His memory lives all over the country, his name is a household word in the remotest places, not only as a saint, but as a preacher, a scholar, a poet, a sculptor, a painter, an inventor, an explorer, and—sure passport to fame—a great calligrapher. Many miraculous legends cluster about his name. A great light shone when he was born, a bright star entered his mouth in his youth,

---

* Thus the Sun Goddess is said to have sent a curse upon the land in 780 because a Buddhist temple was to be erected near her shrine. And on her account worship of the Pole Star, a Chinese practice, was officially forbidden in 811. Buddhist priests could not enter within her precincts, and many curious taboos were observed in Ise, such as calling the Buddha "the child of the centre"; Buddhist scriptures, "coloured paper"; and Buddhist nuns, who were shaven, "long-haired women." A Buddhist priest who wished to make a pilgrimage to Ise had to wear a wig, and in the middle ages, if not earlier, these could be purchased on the outskirts of the town.

by his prayers he could cause wells of pure water to spring up from foul places, could make rain fall in times of drought, and conjure away the pains of an ailing emperor. When he passed out of this life on Kōya he did not die, for he lies uncorrupted in his sepulchre, awaiting the coming of Maitreya, the Buddhist Messiah. More authentic, if less wonderful, merits ascribed to him are the introduction of tea into Japan, much useful work like bridge-building and path making, and the invention of the *kana* syllabary. Such traditions of excellence cling only to the memory of truly exceptional men, and we may be sure that in him Japan nourished a genius, probably one of the greatest in her history. It is hard to assess his real qualities. Despite his travels, he does not appear to have been a true missionary, striving to carry the benefits of religion to the people. In his day Buddhism was still an aristocratic faith, and it was evidently his chief concern to convert the nobility to his doctrines. He owed his success in part to their love of fashion, their interest in the newest thought from China. He frequented the palace, where he was admired as much for his accomplishments as for his piety, and he was evidently a better courtier, a more tactful bishop, than Saichō, for though an innovator he contrived to keep on good terms with everyone, including the Shintō priesthood and the Nara clergy.

Without departing far from the theme of religious compromise we may allude to certain correspondence of Kūkai which has happily been preserved. It shows that Saichō respected him greatly, asked him for instruction in the Shingon doctrines, and was with several followers baptised by him. Kūkai on his side wrote to Saichō, begging him to come and discuss how best they could promote the faith. They exchanged books, and were clearly on friendly terms; but they seem to have been estranged through the desertion of so me of Saichō's most cherished disciples, who left him and went over to the Shingon sect. There is a touching letter from Saichō to one of these converts, in which occur words like these: "We were baptised together. In company we have sought the Truth, in unison we have hoped for Grace. Why now have you turned your back upon the Original Vow and left me for so long? It is the way of the world to reject the worse and take the better, but how can there be worse and better as between the doctrine of the Tendai and the doctrine of the Shingon? For good friends, Truth is one and Love is one . . . Let us live together and die together. Let us travel in company all over Japan, sowing the seeds of virtue, and then retire to Mount Hiei and await fulfilment of our purpose, careless of fame. This is my deep desire." But the disciple replied, in a letter written for him by Kūkai, that there was a difference between the two doctrines. He begged his old master's forbearance, but he must now remain an adherent of the Shingon sect.

The spread of Buddhism did not destroy, though it may have transformed, the ancient beliefs of the Japanese; nor did it prevent them from practising other forms of religion. The ancient Chinese cult of Heaven Worship was not neglected, as is clear from the official chronicles. The *Shoku Nihongi*, under the date 787, records that an envoy was sent by the Court to a place called Katano, to worship the Sovereign of Heaven before the tomb of a deceased emperor. The text of his prayer is given in full, and it is couched in language like that employed by the Chinese emperors on such occasions. Similar notices are frequent after this date, and some of them describe how the emperor himself performed the rite of adoration, and how sacrifices were offered. At the beginning of the Heian period this celestial worship seems to have been common among the farmers in many parts of Japan, for an edict was sent to several provinces at this time forbidding them to sacrifice oxen to Heaven; and there is a story, in a contemporary Buddhist collection of miraculous legends, which tells how a certain rich man sacrificed to Heaven one ox each year for seven years, and was punished by severe illness, after which he fell down into Hell. This moral tale, it should be added, shows not that Buddhism was intolerant of other faiths, but that it could not condone a breach of the injunction not to take life. So long as there was no conflict with its few positive precepts, Buddhism could live happily with any other faiths and practices. Therefore Confucian studies made progress in Japan side by side with inquiries into Buddhist doctrine, although in essence the two are profoundly different.

2. CHINESE LEARNING

IN general, as we have seen, it was the magical aspect of Buddhism which first appealed to the Japanese, its spells and incantations, the mysterious power of its prayers and images. In the same way they were attracted by the occult side of Chinese thought, its concern with omens and divination. Consequently, apart from the severer type of Confucian study, there grew up in Japan a heterogeneous body of Chinese learning, an incoherent mixture of the magical elements of Buddhism with the superstitious lore of astrology, geomancy, demonology, and many other kindred sciences in which the Chinese imagination has shown itself so fertile. Most characteristic and most popular among them was the study called *On-yō-dō*, the Way of Yin and Yang, those two principles, the active and the regressive, which by their operation upon the five elements (fire, water, wood, metal and earth) produce all phenomena. This very ancient conception of the universe was at the basis of Chinese thought, and it was not without merit as a working hypothesis for serious studies in natural philosophy, such as astronomy or calendar-making. But it easily degenerated into a kind of pseudo-science like fortune-telling or astrology. To the Japanese, however, such practices seemed much more advanced than their own crude method of reading portents from cracks in a deer's shoulder blade, a relic from ancestral hunting days; and they soon adopted the Chinese system of divination. In the Heian period the study of *On-yō-dō* grew to great importance. There was a bureau (the *On-yō-ryō*) devoted to it in one of the departments of state, and official practitioners were appointed at the capital and in the larger provincial centres. They dealt with many matters which, strictly speaking, were outside the scope of *On-yō-dō*. Apart from reading events in terms of Yin and Yang and the Five Elements, they were called upon by the government to give advice about evil spirits, to say how demons and vengeful ghosts should be placated, to decide auspicious days for journeys and ceremonies or auspicious sites for buildings, and in general to act as official soothsayers. Until about 950 there was no division between astronomy and divination, but after that date the bureau was separated into two branches, and the professors of *On-yō-dō* devoted themselves to divination alone. Their influence was very strong, and it was often abused. Traces of their teaching can be seen in many popular beliefs to-day, particularly in regard to lucky and unlucky days and directions.

Though these curious studies were held in what seems to us un-merited high esteem, they were not entirely barren, for in their way they promoted scholarship; and apart from them there took place during the Heian period an advance in purer learning. In China, Confucianism had tended to become formal and traditional, and the official commentary issued under the T'ang dynasty in 640 (?) is described by some authorities as being an evasive compromise with modern thought. In Japan, in the Heian period, however, classical Confucian studies had not reached this point of fatigue. They were still regarded as of great importance, and held the chief place in the University curriculum. Great store was set on orthodoxy, and the commentaries to be used were fixed by law. They were for the most part commentaries of the Han dynasty, and not those lately produced in China; for Japan, though always striving to keep up, was generally a little behind in such matters. Perhaps the most interesting feature of Confucian studies in Japan at this time was the specialisation of Japanese scholars. Certain families devoted themselves especially to certain works and became hereditary authorities in their own branches. Such were Mifune on the Three Books of Rites, and Yamaguchi on the Spring and Autumn Chronicles. Another significant point, which seems to bear out the common verdict that the Japanese were not given to abstract speculation, is the preference shown by their scholars for the historical and political side of Confucianism. The ethical and the somewhat meagre philosophical elements were neglected, except in their most practical aspects. Consequently we find that great attention was paid to maxims of government and to such questions of morality as seemed to have a bearing upon govern-ment; so that, for instance, the classic of Filial Piety was widely read but the study of the Analects was almost abandoned. Most of the men who rose to high positions in the administration, if they were not members of great families, were Confucian scholars of the type of Shigeno Sadanushi (785-852), a minister, a jurist, and a prolific writer, who took the leading part in the compilation of a prose anthology of 1,000 volumes.

In matters of knowledge it may be said that the Nara period was acquisitive, the early Heian period assimilative and the later Heian period selective. Therefore in the ninth century there is

evident a desire to survey and ponder the learning already acquired, to arrange the imported ideas. This, no doubt, is why we find at this time a great activity in compiling anthologies and collections of poetry and prose, chronicles, laws and commentaries. The literary output of this kind during the years from say 800 to 930 was immense—greater, perhaps, in proportion to the numbers of the instructed public, than at any later time. Many of these works were compiled by imperial command and at official expense. Such were the *Shoku Nihongi* and four other national chronicles carrying on the national record from 700 to 887; a very important and compendious body of laws and rules with many commentaries and supplements dealing not only with civil and criminal offences but also with administration, ceremonial and ecclesiastical affairs; treatises on medicine; three great anthologies of Chinese poetry; an official book of genealogies; and the work above cited, in 1,000 volumes, containing selections from ancient and modern Chinese authorities, chiefly on politics and history.*
In addition to these there was a mass of literature produced by individuals, dealing with the same subjects, but including also encyclopædias, treatises on language, lexicons and aids to the study of Sanskrit. Perhaps the most numerous single class was that of Buddhist literature, ranging in great variety from learned disquisitions to miraculous tales. Nearly all these works were produced in the ninth century or the opening years of the tenth. During this period Chinese studies were paramount, and all learned writings, all official documents, were in the Chinese language. A native literature had not yet developed, partly because of the superior prestige of Chinese scholarship, which implied a certain contempt for the native tongue, and partly because the Chinese script was as yet imperfectly adapted for representing Japanese words. In the domain of *belles lettres*, Chinese prose and poetry were supreme, and the increasing respect in which classical learning was held may be judged from the fact that in 821 all Doctors of Literature were raised to the

---

* It will give some idea of the voluminous nature of these works to mention that, in a modern printed edition of early historical documents, these five national chronicles, without commentary, occupy 2,100 octavo pages of smallish type, and an incomplete collection of the legal texts, 2,600 pages.

fifth rank from the seventh rank which they had formerly held. There was a particular reason why Chinese poetry should at this time have influenced the Japanese so powerfully, for the T'ang epoch between 750 and 780 was the golden age of literature, when there flourished such brilliant figures as Li Po, Po Chü-i and Liu Tsung-yüan. The taste for Chinese poetry at Court was a craze, almost a madness. Everybody sought distinction as a poet, from the sovereign (notably the Emperor Saga) to his minor courtiers, and an official languishing at a provincial post might hope for preferment from a well-turned stanza. The Emperor Saga, it is said, was always accompanied by poets on his excursions, official festivals were not complete without some poetical exercises, and the curious entertainment known as the Winding Water Banquet was in high favour in those days. The guests sat by the edge of a stream, or an artificial rivulet in the palace courtyard. As a wine cup floated by them on the water, they took it up and drank, recited a poem or capped a verse, and let the cup pass on. But though the works of T'ang celebrities were known at the court of Saga, the models which the Japanese imitated were for the most part those of an earlier stage. In prose what they admired was an extremely ornamental style (of the Six Dynasties) in which the chief feature was a monotonous arrangement of syllables, or rather of characters, in groups of six and four, and an antithetical balance of phrases. This fashion of writing became so popular that it was used even in official edicts and is common in the chronicles and legal compilations. It persisted for a long time, and the language of the lyric dramas (nō) shows signs of its regrettable influence; though it must be admitted that, like unpromising material in other arts, it could be shaped to beauty in the hands of a master. In poetry the Japanese were rather more modern. The anthologies of the early Heian period, of which the chief is the *Ryōun-shū* or Cloud Topping Collection, show that they had studied early T'ang models, and there are signs that they knew and admired the work of Po Chü-i. But they were after all composing in a foreign language. They could never, so fettered, emerge beyond a facile mimicry. Far less could they achieve the spontaneous and pregnant simplicity of genius expressing itself in its natural medium. Perhaps in this failure we have a more striking example of the misfortunes of their early cultural history than in the distortion or collapse of so many of their borrowed social institutions. Predisposed to learning, alive to impressions, sensitive to beauty, restless and ambitious, strive as they would they could not overcome an insuperable difficulty, they could not naturalise a stubbornly alien speech. What throws this unhappy situation into relief is their startling success in the field of art, for here they could employ a universal instrument, the painter's brush or the carver's knife, that transcends the bounds of language.

3. THE NATIVE LITERATURE

From the beginning of the tenth century several tendencies combined to diminish the supremacy of Chinese and to give to native literature a place in the national life. There was a linguistic, a political and a social trend, and these three worked, as is usual, through the genius of individuals who gave direction to the groping movement of the times. Firstly, as the phonetic style of writing (the *Manyō kana*) came into more common use, the need for some less cumbrous method was plainer; and during the ninth century a syllabary, composed of abbreviated Chinese characters selected to represent one Japanese sound each, was invented or evolved. Tradition ascribes this service to Kōbō Daishi, and it is quite likely that he made the choice, for he was a renowned calligrapher, and his Sanskrit studies must have convinced him of the advantages of a simple phonetic script. In any case, these brief cursive signs (called *hiragana*)* proved extremely convenient, and therefore encouraged the writing of Japanese in many cases where previously Chinese had been customary. A man could now write a Japanese poem in a few graceful flourishes, where hitherto he had been obliged to trace a character of many strokes for each of his native syllables. He could set down on paper the sound of any Japanese word, and he could write the Japanese name of a thing for which he did not know the Chinese symbol. Second comes the political tendency which favoured the native language.

* The invention of another syllabary, the *Katakana*, is ascribed to Kibi no Mabi in the eighth century, but this is extremely doubtful. It is true that the Sanskrit alphabet was studied at this time, and may have suggested the idea of phonetic writing by simplified characters.

In 894, as we have seen, it was decided to send no more embassies to the T'ang court. The Japanese had begun to feel independent. There was, in fact, from about this time, a certain reaction in favour of native institutions, or at least the native versions of Chinese institutions. Chinese remained the vehicle for the learned

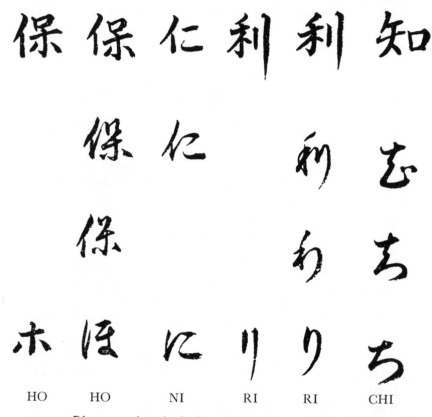

HO   HO   NI   RI   RI   CHI

FIG. 31. *Diagram to show the development of the Kana syllabary. At the top of each vertical column is a Chinese character. Below it come successive stages of abbreviation, the lowest being simple Kana or phonetic symbols.*

work of historians, jurists and theologians; but since the Heian society was both sentimental and frivolous, it needed a lighter literature also, and for this the native language was supremely well-suited. It is the very thing for rambling romances, little love-songs and elegant praise of flowers. And this brings us to the third reason for its increasing use. It is usually supposed that the men in the Heian period, absorbed in graver studies, looked down upon poetry and romances and regarded the native language in which they were written as an inferior medium. This view is not unfounded, but it does not go far enough to explain why most of the best literature of the day was the work of women, and the men wrote little but tiresome and pompous treatises. The true reason, in the present writer's opinion, is that the wits of the men were fuddled with Chinese books and second-hand Chinese ideas. The women, on the other hand, particularly in aristocratic circles, held a position where they were neither subordinate nor repressed nor weighed down by barren learning. In their little world where almost any one of them might become the favourite of an emperor and the mother of a prince, they were courted and respected, and within the limits of a formal etiquette they could give free play to their emotions, their instincts and their fancy. They could express what they saw and felt, in a living tongue which they had spoken from childhood. But when the Japanese wrote Chinese they were using, in effect, a dead language. In prose their model was a style fashionable in China five hundred years before. Not only this, China was distant and hard of access. Only a selected few could cross the sea and come into direct contact with Chinese minds and Chinese things. Therefore most of the men, unlike the women, wrote about what others had seen and felt. It was not that they despised light literature. Heian society was by no means made up of sober male philosophers and gay female diarists. Profound study of the Confucian classics needs a dry and lugubrious temperament, luckily scarce among the Japanese, who in sketches and tales of the period often treated the learned doctors of law and ethics as figures of fun. Most of the nobility had a grounding in the canon, and they might have looked into the writings of Lao-tzŭ and Chwang-tzŭ. But by far the most popular works, the most studied, were the poems of Po Chü-i and volumes of Elegant Extracts from Chinese literature; while a mildly improper little romance called the Cavern of Disporting Fairies had a great vogue and, we are told in the T'ang records, both Japanese and Korean envoys always made a point of buying copies, at great expense, when they got to China. What gave a social cachet in those days was not learning but poetical dexterity. The men rather prided themselves on their Chinese verse, but to be admired it need not be original, it must be very like some celebrated model. Nothing more delighted these Japanese writers than to be compared with a Chinese master. They tried to envelop themselves in a Chinese atmosphere, and this was not impossible at the Heian court. Distinguished scholars and statesmen, like Miyoshi Kiyoyuki (847-918), called themselves by Chinese names, and were happy, we are told, if they could commune with a Chinese poet in their dreams. But Miyoshi's famous memorial urging reforms upon the emperor, which is regarded by the Japanese as a prose monument, to the foreign student has not the flavour of a masterpiece and is merely a competent state paper. As for the poems in Chinese of his generation, they seem to an alien judgment little more than mechanical exercises upon well-worn themes.

If many of the activities of this age were artificial to the point of silliness, they did, we must remember, express a culture remarkable, probably unique, in that it was almost entirely æsthetic. Into the remoter origins of this phenomenon we will not inquire, but its immediate reasons are plain. For some centuries past Japan had been peaceful and undisturbed, except by a little frontier fighting and brief factional quarrels that did not check the smooth flow of metropolitan life. She had been supplied with a religion, a philosophy, a theory of the state, all ready-made; and since she had no criterion by which to judge these gifts she accepted them on the whole without reserve. She might have been more critical or more uncertain had she known other civilisations, but she was isolated, and her communication with the outside world was scanty and irregular. Though her rulers were dominated by foreign ideas, as a country she never suffered a violent cultural invasion and the first hostile descent upon her shores of any consequence was the Mongol attack of 1274. The Chinese did not force their customs on her, and she was never stimulated by close contact with other peoples, whereas the history of the rest of Asia and Europe is one long record of the marching and mingling of tribes and nations.

Therefore—and this is true in greater or less degree of sub-

sequent times—the Japanese of the Heian epoch tended to treat
each element of their imported culture as if it were something
integral and perfected. Yet, while they did not question the
perfection of the whole, for they were acute observers rather than
restless critics, their temper and their circumstances modified its
parts and changed its very essence. This is why much of the
Heian culture seems to us thin and unreal. It was a product of
literature rather than of life. So the terms of Indian metaphysics
became a kind of fashionable jargon, Buddhist rites a spectacle,
Chinese poetry an intellectual game. We might almost summarise
by saying that religion became an art and art a religion. Certainly what most occupied the thoughts of the Heian courtiers
were ceremonies, costumes, elegant pastimes like verse-making
and amorous intrigue conducted according to rules. Perhaps most
important of all, because it entered into all, was the art of pen-
manship. These were the subjects of their literature and in these
they attained a prodigious virtuosity. Let it be added that, if
they transformed whatever they borrowed and sometimes refined
away its essence, they and their descendants also rejected what
was gross and cruel. Under the kindly Japanese touch the terrifying deities and demons of Chinese mythology become merely
amiable grotesques, the harsh Confucian code is softened, the
grim Indian ascetic mortifying the flesh is transmuted on Japanese
soil into an abstemious recluse enjoying books and flowers. An
extreme but suggestive example of this humanising gift is the
evolution of Maitreya, the Messiah of Indian Buddhism, who by
some strange process came to be figured in both Chinese and
Japanese iconography as Hotei, one of the Seven Gods of Luck,
a fat-bellied, smiling divinity.

Japanese poetry, then, having suffered after the *Manyōshū* a
temporary eclipse by the vogue of Chinese verse, came into
fashion again at the end of the ninth century, and was given a
strong impetus by the various causes which we have enumerated.
In 905 there was commenced under imperial auspices a collection
of the best poems since the *Manyōshū*, and this was completed in
922 in the form of an anthology known as the *Kokinshū*, or Ancient
and Modern Collection. It contains over 1,100 short poems and
practically no long ones. We shall avoid the task of assessing their

merits and observe merely that in form they display an exquisite finish always hovering on the edge of artifice, and in content they reveal an emotion usually more delicate than powerful. To say more is only to provoke endless argument as to the nature of poetry, the subject—could anything be more apposite?—of the first masterpiece of Japanese prose. This is the preface to the Ancient and Modern Collection, written (*circa* 922) by one of its compilers, Ki no Tsurayuki, himself a great poet and a stylist of repute. It is a short piece, evidently written by a man used to composing in Chinese, for though its sentiment is indigenous enough it is betrayed by the trick of antithesis so dear to Chinese authors. Indeed it is said to be a translation of an original preface in Chinese, which prevailing taste demanded in any work of importance. For some time yet a scholar might write in Japanese only the lightest trifles, and then with a gesture of apology. Thus Tsurayuki himself prefaces his best work, the *Tosa Niki*, a pleasant limpid diary of travel (935), with a statement that he is writing as a woman writes, to wit using Japanese words and the Japanese syllabary. From about this time date a number of short romances and fairy tales plentifully sprinkled with poems. Works of this type were produced at intervals throughout the tenth century, and so helped to forge the native language into an instrument which was given edge and temper by skilful hands in the opening of the eleventh.

The *Genji Monogatari*, written by a court lady-in-waiting named Murasaki Shikibu some time in the years between 1008 and 1020, is a remarkable romance which it is difficult to describe without superlatives. Certainly it is one of the world's great books; and apart from its almost epic literary quality, it is of special interest in the cultural history of Japan. While it marks a critical stage in the development of language it also exhibits, illumined by the play of an exquisitely sensitive mind, that Heian society which we have called unique. The difference in point of language between the early romancers and Murasaki is astonishing. They are almost childish in comparison with her sophistication. She moves without faltering through long, intricate sentences, and is the mistress not the slave of a most complex grammatical apparatus. She extracts the fullest value from a vocabulary which is in the nature of things restricted, and the Chinese words that she uses are not pedantic intruders but seem to be at home in their surroundings. In some ways, of course, she profited by improvements which time had made before her day, but no classical Japanese work gives so strong an impression of individual style as hers, and there is no doubt that it was largely her sure taste and skill which made of the contemporary language a fit medium for sustained artistic effort. But even her genius could not overcome its inherent defects, and though the style of the *Genji* was much copied by later writers it was never attained and far less was it surpassed. The Chinese language, perhaps inevitably, continued to exercise a baleful influence, and Japanese developed as a hybrid of two conflicting strains.

One other work of this period in pure Japanese should be mentioned. This is the charming and vivacious "Pillow Book" or Miscellany of Sei Shōnagon (*circa* 1000). Together with the *Genji* it gives a full picture of life at court, and only the very faintest hint of life outside. It shows us a little society preoccupied with art and letters, quick to criticise a weak stroke of the brush, a faulty line of verse, a discordant colour or an ungraceful movement; great connoisseurs in emotion and judges of ceremonies and etiquette; sentimentally aware of the sadness of this dew-like fleeting world, but intellectually unconcerned with all its problems; prone to a gentle melancholy but apt to enjoy each transitory moment; and quite without interest in any outlook but their own.

4. LATE HEIAN BUDDHISM

IN both sacred and secular writings of the Heian epoch there occurs very frequently the word *mappō*, meaning "the latter end of the Law." It is derived from Buddhist scriptures which predicted that, some 2,000 years after the Buddha's death, his teaching would lose its power and, owing to man's depravity, fall upon degenerate days. The word was a technical religious term, but it seems to have seized the imagination of the Japanese and to have gained a wide currency by the eleventh century. The number of years that had elapsed since the Buddha's death accorded with the prophecy, and there were reasons enough for regarding the times as degenerate. At the capital and in the country there was strife, disorder and suffering. The sovereigns were weak, the nobles were despotic and extravagant, the clergy were greedy and quarrelsome, the military families were beginning to show their teeth, and unsound economic conditions were causing widespread distress among the people. The characteristic unmorality of the age had been tempered by its æsthetic standards, but these tended to break down as luxury dethroned refinement. To judge from contemporary literature, conduct was thought to have become both lax and gross to the point of social danger, especially in the matter of sexual relations. Intercourse between court officers and maids-of-honour was extremely unrestrained, and in such matters the clergy were not behindhand on the many occasions when those ladies made pilgrimages to fashionable monasteries. Altogether society presented a distressing spectacle to any pious priest, and there were many who retired in despair to solitary hermitages. Others attempted to revive and disseminate the faith by popular methods, because they felt that the old religious institutions were either feeble or degraded. In this judgment they were correct, for the Nara schools, though retaining prestige, were obsolescent, while the great Tendai and Shingon sects were either out of touch with current religious feeling or were busily engaged in acquiring wealth and power by very dubious methods. The times were evidently ripe for a new movement in religion. A monk named Kūya, who had preached in the streets of Kyōto during an epidemic in 951, spent most of his life travelling about Japan, teaching the people to invoke the name of Buddha, so that he was known as the Saint of the Market Place. These open-air meetings were clearly of a revivalist nature, and seem to indicate that there was now room for some popular evangel which would afford an easy outlet for religious emotion, some satisfying but not exacting faith. It was a marked characteristic of the Japanese of this period (a characteristic which shows itself in their earliest native beliefs and which, some think, time has not altogether eliminated) that they were not tortured by a sense of sin, not racked by a desire to solve the problem of Good and Evil. There was little of the cruel puritanical strain in them and little of that restless spirit of doubt and inquiry which has driven other peoples either to seek refuge in quietism or to escape from their thoughts by incessant activity. They were impressionable and lively, but without metaphysical bent. Being impressionable, they were quick to feel the sorrows and delusions of earthly life, readily believing those Buddhist preachers who taught its emptiness and dwelt on the terrors of hell and the glories of paradise. Being lively, they could live happily in the moment, and pass with an easy reaction from fear of suffering to hope of bliss. To a society of this temperament, or in this mood, the teaching of Genshin (942-1017) was especially welcome. He belonged to the Tendai sect, and was a very learned man, but he is best known as the author of a popular religious work called *Ōjō Yōshū*, the Essentials of Salvation. In doctrine he was a precursor of the Japanese sect called Jōdo or Pure Land, which teaches the worship of Amida (Amitâbha), the Lord of Boundless Light. This worship is one of the most widespread and powerful influences in the Buddhism of China and Japan, and is of great interest in the history of religions in general. Its origins are obscure but in India it can be traced back at least to the second century after Christ, while in China it began from about 400 to take a sectarian form in the hands of a succession of teachers who are looked upon as the patriarchs of the Ching-tu (Jōdo) school. In Japan there are traces of Amidism in Shōtoku Taishi's day, but in its fullest form it was derived from China after it had reached great prevalence there in the time of the patriarch Shan-tao (Zendō, d. 681), who is regarded by its Japanese teachers as an incarnation of Amida and the chief source of their doctrine.

Amidism is distinguished from preceding types of Buddhism by its eclipse of Shaka and its insistence upon faith as a means of salvation. Early Buddhism maintains that man's future depends upon his own deeds, that he can find salvation only by his own efforts. This contrast is expressed in Japanese by the two terms *jiriki*, one's own strength, and *tariki*, the strength of another; and it is clear that the passage from salvation by works to salvation by faith radically altered the character of Buddhism. Its cardinal feature had hitherto been the attainment of enlightenment by arduous spiritual and metaphysical exercises and holy living. For this lofty ideal the cult of Amida substitutes a much easier and more comforting conception. In the latter degenerate days of the

Law, say its exponents, common mortals cannot hope to follow the Holy Path pointed out by Shaka, and therefore Amida made his "Original Vow," declaring that he would not accept enlightenment for himself unless he could be sure that all sentient beings would be saved by faith in him. This Original Vow sets forth all the essentials of the Amidist creed. Relying upon the strength of another (*tariki*), the believer who desires salvation has only to invoke the name of Amida Buddha in simple faith, and then he will be born again (*ōjō*) in that Western Paradise, the Pure Land (Jōdo), there to attain that enlightenment which by his own efforts (*jiriki*) he could not reach. This was the theme of Genshin's book, and one can well understand its attraction for a people living in troubled times, easily moved to anxiety by omens and portents, and thirsty for consolation. The writer, having described the corruption of earthly life, paints vivid pictures of hell and heaven, for which he has been widely read ever since his day.* He uses vivid colours and portrays punishments so awful and pleasures so tempting that his easy rule for salvation was bound to find many followers. The rule is that the believer shall put all his trust in the power of Amida and invoke repeatedly the sacred name. This is the practice of *nembutsu*, which strictly rendered is "meditation upon the Buddha"; but the Jōdo doctors insisted that it meant only the repetition of his name, in the formula *Namu Amida Butsu*, "Homage to Amida Buddha."

The practice of *nembutsu* by monks in their own holy edifices was of much earlier date than Kūya or Genshin. In most monasteries there was a chapel or a hall where worshippers endeavoured, singly or in congregation, to reach a condition of religious ecstasy (known as *sammai*, Skt. *samādhi*) by fixing the mind upon one thought; and a common aid to concentration was the continuous repetition of one formula. In the Tendai monasteries on Mount Hiei there were many such chapels, but the *nembutsu* was adopted

---

* He sent a copy to China, where it is said to have been enthusiastically received. His work had an immediate influence upon literature, painting and sculpture, and it was probably among the first books to be printed in Japan. It certainly is among the oldest extant printed books, the earliest copy that has been preserved dating from 1217. There were six printed editions at least in the Kamakura period, and in the Tokugawa period it was freely issued in the *kana* script, with illustrations.

by Nara sects also, and a hall of invocation, the Nembutsu-in, was erected in the Tōdaiji precincts in 939. The truth is that the doctrine of salvation by faith and a belief in the paradise of Amida were so simple and so attractive that all sects* felt obliged to incorporate them in their creeds, and it was not until the twelfth century that there arose a distinct Amidist sect marked off from other schools and exciting their enmity as a serious rival. What Kūya and Genshin did, therefore, was not to introduce Amida worship into Japan, but to spread it among the people; and it is interesting to observe how several technical terms associated with the Pure Land doctrine have become part of everyday speech. Thus *sammai* is used to mean simply whole-hearted effort, and *ōjō*, rebirth in paradise, stands in common parlance for death, so that a man run over on a railway line is said to have suffered *kisha-ōjō*, which might be translated "train salvation."

From the days of Genshin the cry of *Namu Amida Butsu* was increasingly on the lips of the faithful, bringing comfort to many troubled souls; and from the following century down to recent times there must have been very few Japanese indeed to whom those powerful syllables were unfamiliar. The invocation of Amida was further spread by a Tendai monk named Ryōnin (1072-1132), who favoured a particular type called the *yūdzū* or "circulating" *nembutsu*. His idea† was that the merit gained by an invocation of Amida was circulated and transferred to all sentient beings, so that the *nembutsu* of one believer procured salvation for all others. He preached this doctrine widely, both at court and among the people. He was followed by further apostles of Amidism, and by the end of the Fujiwara period (say 1150) temples were thronged with worshippers of Amida or of those great national gods, such as Hachiman and the deity of Kumano, who were by now identified with Amida. The way was prepared

---

* Thus Tendai believers, while relying upon the Lotus, often prayed to be born in Amida's paradise; images of Kwannon sometimes bore the inscription *Namu Amida Butsu* as well as an invocation to the Lotus scripture; and in general during the Fujiwara period laymen from the highest to the lowest were extremely impartial in their devotions.

† It is at first sight somewhat queer; but it is in reality based quite logically upon certain metaphysical conceptions of Tendai.

for a new evangelist, the monk Genkū (1133-1212), better known
as Hōnen Shōnin, who founded in Japan the Pure Land (Jōdo)
Sect. He belongs rather to the Kamakura than to the Heian
period, and we shall therefore leave to a later chapter a sketch of
his life and work.

5. HEIAN ART

THE Heian era may be suitably divided, for purposes of cultural
history, into the Kōnin period lasting from 794 to 894, and the
Fujiwara period lasting from 894 to the establishment of a
military dictatorship at Kamakura in 1185. The divisions are of
course arbitrary. There are Tempyō works which anticipate
Kōnin as well as Kōnin works which conserve the Tempyō style;
and the æsthetic standards of the Fujiwara prevailed long after
their political power had waned. But 894 is the date when official
relations with the T'ang court were suspended and it is therefore
an appropriate terminus for the Kōnin period, which forms a
bridge between the derivative Tempyō and the more independent, national art which flourished under Fujiwara patronage.
In the Kōnin period there can already be discerned signs of the
expansion of secular art, but Buddhism remained the chief inspiration in architecture, painting and sculpture. These, however,
followed a new trend, parallel with the development of the new
sects, the Tendai and the Shingon, which had broken away from
Nara traditions. Marked changes are to be seen in ecclesiastical
buildings. The Nara monasteries were groups of edifices symmetrically disposed on flat ground, and as institutions they had been
in close contact with the Court. But, partly from topographical
reasons and partly because of a growing fashion among religious
teachers to seek distant retreats for meditation and ascetic practices, the new monasteries were built on the summits or the flanks
of mountains, and their construction and arrangement were made
to accord with the irregularity of the ground and with their
natural surroundings. Further, because the new sects were
esoteric, their oratories were often divided into two portions, an
outer, beyond which the ordinary worshippers could not proceed,
and an inner, where the sacred image was enshrined but screened
from their gaze by doors or hangings. In these and other respects,
such as the nature of the internal decoration, the new monasteries

differed from those of Nara and they tended gradually to somewhat greater elaboration. The syncretic tendency of the new
sects had moreover an increasing effect upon Shintō architecture.
Already in Nara the latest Shintō shrines had shown traces of
assimilation to Buddhist temple architecture, for the Kasuga
shrine (768) was in a compromised style, being painted red and
showing a slight curve in the roof. But after the removal to Kyōto
the process of fusion went still further, and such types as the
Hachiman-dzukuri and the Hiyoshi-dzukuri replaced the simpler
Kasuga style.

In religious sculpture and painting certain interesting changes
may be observed in the Kōnin period. The divinities mostly
worshipped were of a different nature or at least were different
conceptions of the same divinities. There was a new iconography.
In the Nara monasteries the Shaka and the Yakushi, the Maitreya
and the Kwannon had been objects of open and familiar worship,
figures radiating grace and benignity. To them were now added
somewhat remoter and sterner presences, such as the grim Fudō
(Acala, a form of the Hindu god Siva) regarded by the mystic
sects of Buddhism as a manifestation of the Great Illuminator,
Dainichi. He wears a forbidding expression, and holds a rope and
a sword for the binding and chastisement of the powers of evil.
There are several celebrated pictures of Fudō belonging to this
epoch. One of them, attributed to Kōbō Daishi, and now kept at
Kōya-san, is of such sanctity that it is revealed only very rarely
and then with a ritual of the deepest veneration. Generally
speaking, the images most worshipped by the mystic sects took
rigidly prescribed forms, since their expressions and gestures,
their attire and their emblems were held to represent special
attributes or even to symbolise cosmic truths. Owing to these
limitations of subject and treatment the statuary of the ninth
century suffers from a lack of spontaneous feeling, which is the
more marked on occasion because bronze, dry lacquer and clay,
materials which bespeak a fluid modelling, tended to be replaced
by wood, which demands masterly handling if harshness is to be
avoided. It must be admitted that the challenge was often bravely
met, as in certain statues of the many-armed Kwannon. The
problem of representing such a symbolic figure without sacrificing

natural grace seems insoluble, and yet more than one sculptor overcame the difficulty and carved an image of great beauty, such as the lovely Kwannon of the Murō-ji. But taken altogether the statuary of this period, despite its technical excellence, seems uneasy. One feels that the artists, for all their scrupulous effort to combine symbolic motives and realistic execution, were irked by their themes and would have been happier in new and freer modes. The same is true of painting. The religious impulse is no longer fresh and simple, but sophisticated and a little fatigued. Under the influence of the mystical doctrines of Shingon, artists strove to express difficult cosmological ideas in painting. They undertook the hopeless task of representing graphically the spiritual universe by means of pictures called *mandara* (Skt. *mandala*, a circle). The *mandara* of the Nara period are comparatively simple compositions, showing realms of bliss and their inhabitants; but those produced under Shingon influence are attempts to portray extremely complex systems or cycles in which are hierarchically arranged the various manifestations of one central spiritual reality. These, and the representation of individual figures from the cycles, were the chief types of religious art in the Kōnin era; and though they no doubt contributed to technical progress by providing a kind of discipline and by encouraging delicate colouring and careful design, they were the enemies of imagination and boldness. They therefore provoked a reaction in secular and even, to a less degree, in religious painting. Two great lay artists are recorded as having worked at this time, Kawanari of Kudara and Kose Kanaoka. None of their work has survived, and though there are various ancient tales illustrating their marvellous prowess, they are perhaps only legendary persons. But it is certain that a small group of gifted men, who were not priests, came into prominence during the ninth century, by painting figures and landscapes for the ornamentation of the imperial palace and mansions of the nobility. They were the precursors of schools of profane art which flourished during the Fujiwara period.

The Fujiwara period was an age of luxury and profusion, in so far as a small aristocratic society developed a standard of living much in advance of that of the rest of their fellow-countrymen. The Heian culture was not widespread. It was (but for a late and exceptional flowering in the provinces which will be noticed presently) distinctly metropolitan, and its surviving monuments are to be found chiefly in or near the capital city. In domestic architecture there was evolved a type of dwelling called *shinden-dzukuri*, composed of spacious apartments connected by galleries; and for the embellishment of their floors, ceilings and sliding partitions a new class of secular artists was called into being. The keynote to this decoration is usually supposed to have been an elegant simplicity, but there is evidence that some of the mansions of the nobility aped the imperial palace in design and were not without elaborate ornament. So long as religious inspiration was paramount neither architecture nor sculpture nor painting could escape from foreign influence, but now the artists could give play to their native fancy. The characteristic Japanese love of nature asserted itself. Great care was given to the design of gardens, and landscape painting came rapidly into vogue, so much so that even in Buddhist pictures celestial beings were often painted against a natural background of rocks, trees and flowers. Current taste seems to have rebelled a little against depicting a monotonous succession of divine personages in rigidly prescribed surroundings, and the arts tended to throw off their alien styles and take on a native character. Moreover, by the year 900 the T'ang dynasty was tottering and Chinese influence was on the wane. There is no doubt that the growth of a native literature also had much to do with bringing about this change, for the use of the native speech must have encouraged artists to look nearer home for themes, by giving native sentiment strength to compete with foreign ideas.

Not of course that Buddhist art languished. In its own field it prospered exceedingly, since the great monasteries, ever growing in power and riches, spent much of their wealth on fine buildings and treasures for their adornment. And the rise of the Pure Land sect stimulated a new style, contrasting with the severity of Shingon art. It is best seen in images of Amida, whose compassionate qualities are suggested by mildness of expression and the smooth flowing treatment of surfaces, which in early Fujiwara carvings results in a happy elegance but later degenerates into mere facility and elaboration. Everywhere there is a strong touch of femininity. Even such fierce embodiments of divine wrath as Fudō, the Destroyer, are given a sweet benign appearance. Perhaps the most interesting feature of Fujiwara art in general is the growth of hereditary schools of sculpture and painting. A sculptor named Jōchō carved many important images, was much in favour at court, and was given in 1022 a high ecclesiastical title, though himself a layman. He was the forerunner of a long line of sculptors, but it need not be supposed that their talent was inherited from him, for it has always been the practice to perpetuate a family tradition by adopting a promising pupil. Similarly a number of lines or schools of painters sprang from masters of this period, whose names and careers are somewhat uncertain. We know however that there were court artists of the Kose school, who served in turn as heads of the official Bureau of Painting, and followed in their work the T'ang tradition. Many artists of this day were members of noble families. Art, or at any rate æsthetic enjoyment, was the chief business of Heian society. In that business all were engaged, from the Emperor downwards, and therefore, though there must have been dilettantes without number, the standard of achievement was remarkably high. Several members of the Fujiwara clan are recorded as painters of distinction, among them one who is looked on as the originator of the peculiarly Japanese style called Tosa. Not only did aristocratic laymen devote themselves to painting, but many distinguished priests are said to have painted secular as well as religious pictures; and though we may suspect that great skill was often attributed to them with more piety than truth, there is no doubt that the monasteries were homes of æsthetic culture, where men could serenely exercise their gifts. The monk Eshin, the author of the Essentials of Salvation, and leader of the revivalist movement which proclaimed the virtues of *nembutsu*, used pictures to propagate his beliefs. To him is ascribed a great picture showing Amida, with Kwannon and Seishi, welcoming a believer to Paradise. Members of the celestial host with gay countenances sit making music among bright clouds, and in the foreground is a glimpse of pleasant landscape.

In general, religious painting tended to resemble secular painting in its attitude. The lofty and the severe gave way to the tender and the graceful, just as the majestic but difficult conceptions of the early Heian Buddhism were outmoded by the more popular doctrine of salvation by faith. Of this tendency there could hardly be a more striking example than the drawings usually but wrongly ascribed by tradition to the monk Kakuyū, more generally known by the ecclesiastical title of Toba Sōjō (1053-1114). The work belongs to the decline of the Fujiwara, but it expresses in one of its best aspects the artistic spirit of their age. The artist is a delightful draughtsman. His pictures of animals disporting in the garb of monks are alive with satirical fun. They are a true fruit of the native wit; they owe nothing to China beyond a vague debt to her older artistic tradition; and they bear witness to that reaction against the solemnities of Buddhist art which we have noticed. Another embodiment of the contemporary æsthetic is the monastery called the Byōdō-in of Uji. It stands on a site originally occupied by a Minamoto villa which came into the hands of the Fujiwara. Here, in 1052 when he entered religion, the Regent Yorimichi erected a group of sacred edifices to the worship of Amida and the glory of his clan. Most beautiful among them is the central pavilion, the Phœnix Hall, a structure of such exquisite balance that it looks almost as if it were some great bird poised for flight. With its attendant buildings it was placed skilfully in relation to its natural environment; the lines of its façade are diversified but harmonious; it was lavishly decorated within and it enshrined Buddhist images by well-known sculptors of the day, including an imposing Amida by Jōchō. It is a happy blend, in architecture of temple and palace, in ornament of sacred and profane. In this successful compromise and in its careful landscape setting it is a triumphant example of the untrammelled native taste. It may be looked upon as a typical expression of the Heian culture, being of a most deliberate elegance and splendour. If it falls short of perfection, it is for lack of certain heroic qualities.

During the second half of the eleventh century, in the twilight of the Fujiwara, some lassitude is visible in the arts.[3] In sculpture especially technique outstrips inspiration, and under the influence of Pure Land teachings sacred images achieve an elaborate nullity. Fat, complacent figures abound, probably modelled on

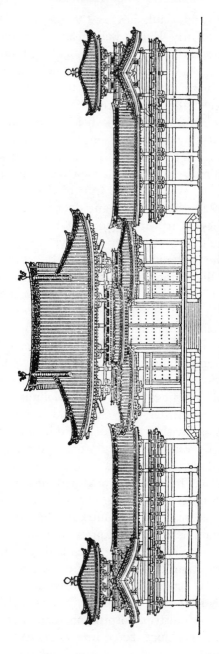

FIG. 32. *The Phœnix Hall of the Byōdō-in.* (*Front Elevation.*)

Sung standards of beauty, for with the rise of the new dynasty there was a renewal of Chinese influence in the arts. In the applied arts, such as lacquering and metal-working, there is great progress to meet the demands of a luxurious age. Everywhere there is profusion of ornament and wealth of design. Taste and workmanship veer towards the florid and the extravagant.

But there was one powerful influence which tended always to restrain and purify, and which, though its working is most apparent in pictorial art, has made itself felt in many branches of Japanese life. This was the practice of calligraphy. No full understanding of Japanese æsthetics can be reached by those who do not appreciate the written characters. They are symbols of ideas, but they are not pictures of things; and therefore a man who takes up his brush to trace them is not distracted by any desire to represent or even to suggest a concrete reality, but aims at making shapes whose beauty is their very own and does not depend upon their significance. He moves, as it were, in a world of pure form, and he is concerned only with abstract design. For him, to write beautifully is to solve fundamental problems of art. The line must be unerringly placed, it must be in just relation to its fellows, and though it may pass from strength to softness it may never falter, but must be alive throughout its length. The ink must merge with the soft paper, neither lying inert upon its surface nor spreading aimlessly beneath. The brush, suitably charged, and directed, not as is the pen by a niggling motion of the fingers but by a bold impulse of the whole body transmitted from the shoulder to the wrist, will produce a subtle range of tones between the faintest grey and the deepest black. To a discerning eye such modulations, under the sure touch of a master, can give as profound satisfaction as the most harmonious blend of colour. In Japan, therefore, calligraphy was not a mere convenient handicraft but an art, the sister and not the handmaid of painting. A skilled calligrapher is already an artist equipped in most essentials, for in learning to write he has undergone a rigorous training in brushwork, in composition, in design, and lastly in speed and certainty of execution, for the nature of his materials will permit of no fumbling hesitation. No wonder, then, that in a society whose outlook on life was almost entirely æsthetic, an art governed by such severe and yet elegant canons should be pre-eminent. For a Heian courtier to be unable to write well was to be hardly respectable; to have a good hand was to have breeding and taste. Learning in an official, piety in a priest, beauty in a lady of fashion, these scarcely mattered without that indispensable accomplishment. Handwriting was the companion of poetry, and the beauty of a stanza might depend as much upon its script as upon its turn of phrase. Often a verse would be accompanied by a picture suggesting its theme. So far such decorations were slight and fanciful, and the finished expressionism of line and wash drawings in Chinese ink had yet to be developed. But it was under the inspiration and the discipline of calligraphy that it later grew to maturity.

Another important branch of pictorial art had its beginnings in late Fujiwara times.[4] This is the *e-makimono*, or coloured picture-scroll. As a form it was not originated by the Japanese, but in their hands it gained a distinctive character. We depend on not very reliable traditions for the names of the painters of the earliest scrolls that survive; but there are a few examples which undoubtedly belong to the end of the Fujiwara period and are the work of court painters and calligraphers of distinction. Among them are the *Genji Monogatari* scroll, illustrating the great romance of that name; the *Shigi-san Engi*, illustrating the foundation of a monastery; and the *Ban Dainagon Monogatari*, illustrating a popular narrative of the day. They represent different sentiments—poetical, religious or realistic—and different technical methods; but they have one important character in common, and that is a strong native quality. They may be looked upon as the nucleus around which grew the purely Japanese style of painting, called *Yamato-e* in contrast to the various schools of Chinese derivation.

The *Genji* scroll is the oldest,* and of its kind the most beautiful. Its curious perspective is at first baffling, for you are given a bird's-eye view of interiors in which walls, screens and elaborately costumed figures seem dangerously aslant. But once the convention is accepted its oddity becomes a charm, and you feel that this is not a mere fantasy, but a most fitting and indeed

* The oldest extant: except for certain illustrated sutras of the Nara period. It is uneven, for it is the work of several court painters.

inevitable way of representing such figures in such a life as theirs; for no realism could so adequately depict the personages of that insulated and transient society with which the *Genji* deals. Far from being immature, the method is original and immensely sophisticated. It may be said to anticipate certain modern European paintings, just as Murasaki's romance anticipates modern novels of the psychological school.

A curious attempt was made, at the end of the eleventh century, to imitate the Heian culture in the provinces. Fujiwara Kiyohira, the Lord of Mutsu, in 1095 erected a stronghold at a place called Hiraidzumi in northern Japan. He built a monastery, the Chūson-ji, and founded a city which he hoped would rival the metropolis as a centre of art and learning. His descendants, including that Hidehira who sheltered Yoshitsune, and Yasuhira who betrayed him, carried on the work and kept a kingly state. But the family was crushed by Yoritomo in 1189, and little remains of their splendour but a small mortuary chapel built by Kiyohira in 1124 to receive his own remains. There is, however, enough to show that gorgeous decoration and a lavish use of gold was the keynote during the brief life of this northern capital.

NOTES TO CHAPTER XII

1 Page 225. Three forms of the Buddha. This concept of Mahayana Buddhism, though it belongs to an abstruse realm, has had a considerable influence upon Far Eastern thought and therefore deserves some special consideration. The doctrine of the three forms or bodies (*Trikâya*) distinguishes:

> The body of transformation (*Nirmânakâya*)—the historical Buddha.
> The body of bliss (*Sambogakâya*)—the Buddha as he appears in Paradise.
> The body of truth (*Dharmakâya*)—the Cosmic Buddha.

Both of the first two are only temporary or partial manifestations of the true Buddha, because the true Buddha is ultimate reality. The universe is merely the phenomenal expression of reality, and therefore the universe and the Buddha are the same. This difficult idea in course of time tended to be interpreted in simple and familiar terms, and to communicate its flavour to contemporary feeling as expressed not only in religion, but also in literature and art. The belief that the true Buddha can take diverse forms naturally made it easy to accept the identity of Buddhist and Shintō divinities by supposing that all were manifestations of one reality. In another field this doctrine of the Three

Bodies gave a kind of metaphysical sanction, gave shape and coherence to traditional native animistic beliefs. To describe the Buddha as identical or coextensive with all nature was to give expression to the feeling that all nature is of one essence. It is obvious that such an idea must be a powerful force in art, because it means that there is no subject that the artist can treat where he is not expressing a religious truth. It also must tend to divert the artist's mind from those anthropocentric habits which dominate Western thought. Man figures in the Far East not as the supreme masterpiece of creation, but as one of many forms of ultimate reality.

I do not want to press this argument too far. It can easily be overworked. But I think that it may help to explain, for instance, why the human likeness and the portrayal of dramatic events in human life are not common in Far Eastern art. A favourite theme of the painter in the Far East is a landscape suggesting space and distance, in which human figures are only incidental. He is apt to depict a large mountain and a small philosopher, not as in the West a bulky statesman or general dwarfing a modest background of Nature.

All this seems very remote from the Trikâya, but there can be no doubt that Japanese life has been profoundly influenced by certain philosophical concepts of Buddhism which have encouraged the sentiment of transience, of the illusory nature of all observed phenomena, and the sentiment of immanence, of the identity between all forms of existence.

[2] Page 226. Chih-k'ai, also known as Chih-I in Chinese, in Japanese is styled Chisha Daishi or Tendai Daishi. It is not strictly correct to say that he introduced the doctrine of the Lotus sutra into China, since the earliest Chinese translation is previous to A.D. 316, but he regarded it as the quintessence of truth and gave it the principal place in his system, which is "more than any other school an independent attempt of the Far East to deal with literary and metaphysical problems which confront the student of Buddhism, It is marked by its catholic, many-sided and almost encyclopædic character." (Eliot.) The importance of the T'ien-t'ai school in the history of Far Eastern thought lies in the fact that it exhibits on a grand scale the characteristic Chinese and Japanese reaction to a conflict of philosophies. In India the general run of the faithful are not irked by apparent inconsistencies in doctrine. In China, where the critical study of classical works was more advanced and scholars were addicted to collating sources, students of Buddhism found it hard to accept the contradictions manifest in the various discourses ascribed to the Buddha. In the West in such circumstances there usually arise earnest, even bitter, sectarian disputes, but in the Far East a more tolerant or a less dogmatic spirit is prevalent, and men seek to compose rather than to assert their disagreements. It is this trait which accounts for the growth of such a sect

as the T'ien-t'ai. Chih-k'ai accounted for divergences in Buddhist doctrine by showing that the Buddha taught in different ways at different
times, adjusting his teaching to the comprehension of his hearers. No
form of Buddhism is rejected, all are incorporated in one eclectic school.

³ Page 253 ff. It has been suggested to me that this passage is an
unfair summary of artistic trends in the late Fujiwara period, and I con-
fess that it is misleading in so far as it gives the impression that there
was an all-round decline from the middle of the eleventh century.
Indeed, towards the end of that century a new impulse is discernible
in both sculpture and painting, especially as the Kamakura era is approached. But I think it is true to say that from the middle of the
eleventh century the inspiration of Fujiwara art began to fail. It is
generally agreed that a certain lassitude is visible in much of the sculpture and some of the painting which continued unchanged in the early
Fujiwara tradition. Contemporary sentiment was under the influence
of the pessimistic Mappō doctrines (v. under Late Heian Buddhism,
page 243), and in the arts this lack of a constructive emotion, though it
may sometimes have produced a pleasing effect of melancholy repose,
in less happy instances was responsible for what seems to me only a
complacent emptiness. It is a question of taste, which the student had
better solve for himself by looking at originals. From the historical
point of view, it is sufficient to understand that the main trends of art
in the late Fujiwara period reflect pretty clearly its social and religious
changes—the decline of a metropolitan aristocracy preoccupied with
æsthetics and the rise of a vigorous military class; the growth of Amidist
beliefs, and the reaction of more positive doctrines.

While it is true that in late Fujiwara times, as intercourse with China
was restored, Japanese art came under Sung influence, that influence is
visible in technique rather than in themes and treatment. The fat,
complacent figures are not modelled on Sung styles, but are a repetition of the Nara period versions of T'ang.

⁴ Page 256. It is not correct to say that the e-makimono had its beginnings in late Fujiwara times. The celebrated In-gwa-kyō scroll of the
Tempyō period, though it is an illustrated sutra rather than a picture-
scroll, is obviously a precursor; and there were doubtless other examples.

Nor is it exactly true that the e-makimono was the nucleus around
which the Yamato-e style grew. It would be better to say that it was
an early and important stage in the development of the mature
Yamato-e style.

Chapter XIII

A SUMMARY OF POLITICAL EVENTS IN THE HEIAN PERIOD

1. THE FUJIWARA DOMINANCE

THE following are the dates of the outstanding political events in the Heian period, during the Fujiwara domination :

A.D. 782 Accession of KWAMMU.

784 The capital moved to Nagaoka.

794 Foundation of the new capital, Heiankyō (the modern Kyōto).

797 Completion of chronicle called *Shoku-Nihongi.*

802 Successful campaign against the Ainu.

806 Accession of HEIJŌ. 809 Abdication of Heijō and accession of SAGA

812 The Ainu finally subdued.

823 Abdication of Saga, accession of JUNNA. 833 Abdication of Junna, accession of NIMMYŌ.

850 Accession of MONTOKU.

858 Accession of SEIWA. Fujiwara Yoshifusa becomes Regent.

876-877 Accession of YŌZEI on abdication of Seiwa. Fujiwara Mototsune becomes Regent and, later, Kwampaku.

884 Accession of KŌKŌ on deposition of Yōzei. 887 Accession of UDA. 891 Abdication of Uda, accession of DAIGO.

901 Downfall of Sugawara Michizane. Fujiwara Tokihira in power. Completion of chronicle called *Sandai Jitsuroku.*

907 Compilation of official anthology of verse called *Kokinshū.*

914-949 Fujiwara Tadahira in power.

927 Completion of *Engishiki* (Institutes of Engi period).

930 Accession of SUJAKU.

937 Revolt of Masakado, being the beginning of the rise of the Taira clan.

946 Abdication of Sujaku, accession of MURAKAMI.

961 Beginning of Seiwa Minamoto clan.

967 Accession of REIZEI. 969 ENYŪ. 984 KWAZAN. 986 ICHIJŌ.

999 Taira feuds in western Japan.

1011 Accession of SANJŌ. 1016 ICHIJŌ II. 1036 SUJAKU II. 1045 REIZEI II.

1028 Revolt of Taira Tadatsune.

1050 Revolt of Abe family in northern Japan, ending in their defeat by a Minamoto general in 1062.

1068 Accession of SANJŌ II, under whom the power of the Fujiwara receives a check.

The first striking feature in this list of events is the frequency of abdication by an emperor after a comparatively short reign. The practice of abdication was not confined to the imperial family. It grew up, under the influence of Buddhism, at a time when increasing power brought increasing burdens and increasing perils to leaders in all careers. To abdicate and enter religion did not necessarily mean to lead a holy life and practise monastic austerities, but rather to escape from the demands of a public career and to devote yourself at ease to your favourite pursuits. You might prefer a meditative sojourn, soothed by poetry or painting, in the calm atmosphere of some rustic monastery, just as in other lands a fatigued statesman retires to his country seat and writes a learned book. Or you might like to keep in touch with the world, and give advice to your successors. They, whatever your choice, would encourage you, if indeed they did not oblige you, to remain in your retreat. In many cases abdication was compulsory. It was a habit that the Fujiwara regents sedulously fostered, and as a rule emperors who abdicated were too frightened, or at least too prudent, to interfere in administration once they had retired. There were exceptions, such as the ex-emperor Uda, who came into conflict with the Fujiwara through his support of their rival Sugawara Michizane and thereafter found it wiser to live a truly devotional life; but of most of the sovereigns in the early Heian period, whether they died on the throne or abdicated, there is nothing in the way of administrative success or failure to record, not because they were incapable, but simply because they were not allowed to govern. The emperor Kwammu appears to have been a gifted and industrious ruler, but of most of his successors for many centuries we know very little. All were poets, several were fine scholars, some were great calligraphers, some were genuinely devout Buddhists, a few were vicious. Many may have had a talent for administration, but if so it was atrophied for want of use, and all were forced by circumstances into the life of a dilettante or a recluse, or a compound of both.

As for the Fujiwara regents, though they were not in effect successful administrators, they were often extremely clever politicians, whose failure was due not so much to their lack of talent as to the inevitable pressure of events. The development of Japan under their rule might well be taken as a proof of the theory of economic determinism by those addicted to such doctrine. Tokihira, so far as we can gather, endeavoured during his brief regency to check the growth of tax-free manors, to prevent the peasants from leaving their allotments and entering the service of immune landlords or in other ways evading the corvée; to enforce sumptuary laws and reduce corruption among officials; and in general to arrest the tendencies which, as he clearly perceived, were impoverishing the central government and depriving it of real authority. He revised and enlarged the codes of law to meet changing conditions, and the results of his labours are to be seen in the collection known as the *Engi-kyaku-shiki*, the Forms and Institutes of the Engi period, completed in 927, after his death. But the economic forces now at work were far too powerful to be resisted by mere legislation, and Tokihira himself was part of a system already doomed. It says a great deal for the political dexterity of Tokihira and subsequent Fujiwara regents that they were able to maintain their supremacy when the real power had shifted from the capital to other parts of Japan. Their survival was due to a certain inertia by which prestige remained with the court after its authority had vanished, and to the skill with which, making use of that prestige, they manipulated the jealousies and ambitions of their rivals, great families now growing rapidly in strength but contending among themselves, and as yet mere beginners in the political craft. Such breathless feats of balance could not, however, be repeated without end; while the Fujiwara clan itself had so multiplied that it began to lose cohesion, and some of its subordinate members began to behave as independent units. One Fujiwara, Sumitomo by name, successfully defying the court and the Regent (Tadahira), was paramount in western Japan for several years, until in 941 he was captured and killed. In eastern Japan too there were a number of almost independent Fujiwara landowners, and certain other magnates, preparing to challenge the imperial authority. Some of these other magnates were of noble, even imperial origin. Quite early in the Heian period, as we have noticed, the court began to nominate absentee governors of provinces, and the most lucrative of such appointments fell as a rule to princes of the imperial blood. One of these, a younger son of the emperor Kwammu, was made governor of the rich province of Hitachi, in eastern Japan. His descendants were so numerous that they could not all find posts at the capital, and a group of them settled in the eastern provinces where they devoted themselves to increasing their wealth in land and dependants, while not neglecting warlike training to protect them. This offshoot of the ruling house became soon an independent family, with the surname of Taira. In the same way other emperors, at a loss to provide for their numerous sons, reduced them to the rank of subjects, gave them lands or office, and left them to fend for themselves as the heads of new families, under a new name, Minamoto. There were several clans thus styled, each distinguished by the name of the emperor whose son was its founder. Thus there were the Saga-Genji (Genji being the Sinico-Japanese form of Minamoto-uji, the Minamoto clan), the Uda-Genji, the Seiwa-Genji and several others. All the great clans, as time progressed and their numbers increased, split up into smaller groups, at first merely subdivisions of the main clan, but tending, as they acquired land and adherents in different localities, to form independent families, sometimes even at enmity with other branches but in a general way linked with them by a community of interest in opposition to one or both of the remaining great clans. The political history of the Heian period is in fact a tale of ebb and flow in the fortunes of the great clans, the Fujiwara, the Taira and the Minamoto, and subsequent history is largely concerned with the doings of families which issued from those three houses. Thus a member of the Minamoto clan who settled at a place in the province of Shimotsuke called Ashikaga took that place-name as a family name. In a like way there arose, from the Minamoto clan such families as the Nitta, and the Satake and the Tokugawa; from the Taira clan the Miura and the Hōjō; from the Fujiwara clan the Kikuchi and the Utsunomiya. These are all prominent names. They are, in fact, the *daimyō* (literally "great names") of Japan and most of them were originally the names of localities in which the ancestors of their holders had acquired tax-free manors. It may therefore be judged what an important part these manors, the *shōen*, played in Japanese history.

During the tenth century, though the holdings of such territorial magnates, especially in the east, were steadily growing in size, none was yet powerful enough seriously to challenge the central authority except in his immediate domain. There were, it is true, occa-

sional revolts on a comparatively large scale, such as that of a
Taira chieftain named Masakado, who was for a brief space the
virtual ruler of the eight eastern provinces. His success, like that of
Sumitomo, was due not so much to his own strength as to the
slackness of the government, who when they saw that the threat
was serious were able to crush him without much difficulty, in 940.
The feudal system was only in its early stage of growth, and the
picture this period presents is of a great number of small chieftains
warring amongst themselves, endeavouring to acquire supremacy in
land and men. Masakado started his revolt with only 1,000 men,
not all of whom were his own retainers. By 998 we learn of a powerful Taira in northern Japan attacking a Fujiwara neighbour with
a force of 3,000 men, though this number was perhaps exception-
ally large. The governor of a province, especially if he himself was
a local magnate and had armed retainers of his own, was generally
able to hold the balance between contending chieftains and thus
to prevent one from absorbing the other. Moreover, the Fujiwara
had in their gift court honours and appointments and there were
many Minamoto and Taira chieftains to whom these things were
attractive; for, though provincials by domicile, they were aristocrats by origin. The later Fujiwara regents were acute enough to
make use of this attraction, and their policy was to range on their
side at the capital and in the country influential members of the
contending clans, generally Minamoto. But there was a price to
pay for the services of these supporters, for whom court honours,
though welcome, were not enough. They wanted land, they wanted
immunity from tax; and it followed that, when they confiscated an
estate, or declared one of their own manors immune, their Fujiwara patrons must see to it that complaints against them did not
succeed. This is how the great estates grew up: and they were soon
to become still greater when the Taira and the Minamoto, realis-
ing their strength, added to their own manors those of the Fujiwara which, in the beginning, they had managed on behalf of the
dominant clan. But the Fujiwara contrived to retain their supremacy until well into the eleventh century. In 995 Fujiwara Michinaga became *Kwampaku*, and he, followed by his son Yorimichi,
who was *Kwampaku* from 1018 to 1069, held high estate at the
capital. Now was the zenith of the Fujiwara prosperity, and of an

ostentatious luxury so great that a contemporary historical work, devoted chiefly to the rule of Michinaga and his sons, is entitled "Tales of Glory and Splendour." Michinaga carried his ostentation with him into retirement; for in 1019, falling ill, he took the tonsure and entered religion after an ordination ceremony in the Tōdaiji on a scale of magnificence like that of the first great ordination in which the emperor and all the court had taken part in 754. When he lay at the point of death ten thousand priests were ordered to pray for his recovery, a general amnesty was declared, and arrears of taxes were remitted throughout the country. The Fujiwara clan claimed and secured for their leader honours which would scarcely have been accorded to the sovereign in those days.

Meanwhile, both at the capital and in the provinces, disorder and crime and misery grew fast. The great temples were at odds with the government, which had from time to time attempted to check their acquisition of tax-free lands. The abbots, seeing that other landowners, when backed by force, could do pretty much as they liked in this respect, trained a number of priests and men from their estates in the use of weapons, and formed small standing armies of their own. Not only did the temples fight among themselves, but they often raided the capital; and during Yorimichi's regency (1027-74) they swooped down from Hieizan and threatened the regent's house with some 3,000 men. The imperial guards were by now almost useless, and the Fujiwara when they reluctantly appealed to force had to rely upon members of the military families, whether Minamoto or Taira. Time after time, towards the end of the tenth century and throughout the eleventh, bands of armed priests and their troops of mercenaries brawled, rioted and fought in the streets of the city of Peace and Tranquillity. They would besiege and blackmail the Fujiwara statesmen and even the emperor himself. Once, early in the twelfth century, two great monasteries came near to fighting a pitched battle in Kyōto, with forces numbering, it is said, as many as 20,000 a side. So great was the danger to the Fujiwara on such occasions that, one might say, it was the turbulence of the priesthood rather than the rise of the clans which precipitated, if it did not cause, their downfall. For, though they were comparatively secure so long as provincial magnates struggled among themselves at a distance from the capital

and got a buffet now and then at the hands of a Taira or a Minamoto general, their position became extremely unsafe once they
themselves had to depend for protection upon those military
families. There is some irony in this situation, for it was the Fujiwara statesmen who had been the most munificent patrons of
Buddhism, building great temples, filling them with costly things,
and richly endowing them with land and serfs.

Every successful warlike enterprise by a Taira or a Minamoto
general added to the prestige of those families, and usually increased their wealth, although their holdings of land could not yet
rival those of the Fujiwara in value and extent. What staved off the
decline of the Fujiwara clan was strife between other clans and
dissension within them. From the time of Masakado through the
eleventh century there were constant feuds, raids and forays, varied
with campaigns on a grander scale, in both eastern and western
Japan, in which Taira and Minamoto and smaller but no less
bellicose clans such as the Abe and the Kiyowara were engaged
in a confusion of partnership almost impossible to disentangle; and
though it cannot be said that any one group had gained a firm
supremacy by, say, 1100, a great and significant change had now
taken place in the constitution of society. A new military class had
come into being and had assumed an important position in the
state. Though the court remained the fountain of honour and the
civil officers controlled the court and inspired its edicts, now everywhere but in the capital land mattered more than honours, and
force was more effective than law. In 1050 an Abe was master of
great tracts in northern Japan, and defied the central government
for many years, till he was broken after desperate campaigns in
1062, by Yoriyoshi, a Minamoto warrior. Yoriyoshi's forebears
were distinguished fighters, but he may be taken as the first of a
line of great captains who, after displacing the civilian power and
overthrowing their military rivals, were for centuries to dominate
Japan. With him began a definite cult of the war-god Hachiman,
and from his day there began to develop a distinct military caste,
with its own traditions, its own code of morals and indeed of
law.

Yet the first check to the civilian authority did not come
from the soldiers, but from the sovereign, for when the emperor

Sanjō II came to the throne in 1068 he at once endeavoured to cope with urgent problems of government himself and to thrust the Fujiwara aside.

2. THE RISE AND FALL OF THE TAIRA

THE outstanding dates are as follows:—

A.D. 1068   Accession of SANJŌ II. Abdicated 1072, died 1073.
     1072   Accession of SHIRAKAWA. Abdicated 1086.
     1087   Accession of HORIKAWA.
     1107   Accession of TOBA. Abdicated 1123.
     1124   Accession of SŪTOKU.
1087-1129   Shirakawa, though retired and in holy orders, holds a court and governs. (*Insei*, "Cloister Government.")
1130-1156   Toba succeeds Shirakawa and continues Cloister Government.
     1141   Accession of KONOE.
     1155   Accession of SHIRAKAWA II. Abdicated 1158.
     1156   Beginning of the Taira family's dominance.
1156-1185   Rise and fall of the Taira.
           Emperors NIJŌ, ROKUJŌ, TAKAKURA, ANTOKU, TOBA II.
     1185   Final defeat of Taira by Minamoto.
           Minamoto Yoritomo supreme in Japan.

The emperor Sanjō II attended to state affairs in person, and without reference to the *Kwampaku*. At once after his accession he decreed the confiscation of all *shōen* formed since 1045 and of any *shōen* of earlier creation for which valid charters could not be produced. The decree was specially communicated to the retired *Kwampaku* Yorimichi, who merely replied that if there was anything wrong with his title deeds, he would put it right. The emperor gave way at this veiled threat, and made an exception in favour of Yorimichi's estates. He was therefore helpless, since the Fujiwara clan held land all over Japan and none but the weakest landowners of other families would surrender their manors on the strength of a decree which could not be enforced if the Fujiwara were against it. This and other measures of reform which the emperor tried to carry out were resisted by the Fujiwara; but such little power as the court could exercise was now exercised by the sovereign himself, and though the Fujiwara continued to hold high office it was more titular than real. With the death of Sanjō II after a brief reign, we come to a truly astonishing development in the history of government in Japan. From 1073, for more than half a century, there sat on the throne titular emperors, with titular regents, chancellors and ministers; while during each reign not far away, in a palace of his own, keeping imperial state and assisted by his own officers, was an abdicated emperor in holy orders who, in name a monk, was in fact a ruler. It was his edicts and not those of the titular emperor which were valid, in so far as any order of the court in those days was obeyed. The government, therefore, appeared to consist of an emperor, delegating his authority to a regent who controlled a council of state and the ministerial boards; and of an ex-emperor whose commands overrode those of the occupant of the throne. But it is obvious that such a complicated machine could exist only so long as it did not have to function effectively, and the truth is, of course, that outside the court itself there was no government at all, except self-government in the clans. The usual stream of imperial edicts poured forth, aimed chiefly at the manorial system; but they were ineffective because the only people who could enforce them were busily acquiring manorial rights themselves. The codes were no longer operative, the summary jurisdiction of the Police Commission (*Kebiishi*) could be exercised only by, and at the discretion of, Minamoto or Taira generals with a strong force behind them; and order was kept within the domains of the clan chieftains not by enforcing the common law, but by applying the laws of their respective houses.

It will be clear that, under such conditions, as soon as there should emerge from the confused strife of the military families one strong group with a single purpose, the imperial house would lose even the vestiges of power which it still possessed, while the Fujiwara, since they relied on prestige and wealth and not on armed forces, would follow the emperors in the decline of their fortunes. What delayed the change was no power of resistance on the imperial side, but, as we have observed, dissension among the clans. Though the Fujiwara themselves were not free from this internal weakness, their central position and their preference for intrigue rather than violence gave them a certain solidarity. The military families, on the other hand, of their nature depended for success upon conflict. Their various branches were scattered all over Japan, and though a Minamoto might be the neighbour of a Taira, he might equally hold domains next to those of an Abe or a Kiyowara, or he might find himself, as a general in the employ of the court, called upon to chastise some rebellious kinsman of his own. Feuds arising out of such conflicts were closer to the heart of these soldiers than distant prospects of empire, and they brought more immediate gain and satisfaction. It must be remembered that many of the branches of the great clans were closely attached to the soil. Their interests were territorial, and, while of patrician origin, through marriage and property they were closely connected with local gentry, such as the families of district governors, themselves mostly descended from hereditary local chiefs. It is altogether doubtful whether they had, as a rule, any clear conception of national unity. The growth of the manor system had, in fact, produced not only an economic and a political change, but also a change in social organisation. Loyalty to the clan, and such national feeling as was represented by loyalty to the imperial house, was displaced, or at least modified, by strong ties binding men to their land. They owed their chief duty not to the state, or even to the leader of their clan as such, but to their superior in the scale of commendation and benefice, or to a military protector upon whose strength their tenure depended. In other words, the Taikwa reform had only arrested, but had not been able to prevent the natural development of a feudal system.

It would be wearisome to recount in detail the confused political history of the remainder of the Heian period. It can be easily summarised by stating that the rivalry between Taira and Minamoto, now widespread and intense, came to a head in a series of bloody battles fought in 1156 and 1160.

The immediate cause of such conflicts was usually a question of the imperial succession, and the apparent protagonists were leaders of court factions: but essentially these were struggles for supremacy between the military clans. After 1160 the Fujiwara were no longer dangerous, the Minamoto had been overborne, and their great captains killed. Now for the first time a military family was in unquestioned power. Both the emperor and the empire were under the domination of the Taira house. Their supremacy was not to endure, for the Minamoto gathered strength again and, fortunate in producing a great leader, Yoritomo, they finally overthrew the Taira, after protracted warfare. This terrific struggle to the death between rival houses established beyond question the dominance of the military families and created a definite warrior class which, under the stress of danger and conflict, developed a special code of behaviour, a special morality. The events of those years have left deep marks upon the imagination of the Japanese, and the rise and fall of the two clans is perhaps their true epic. Its history abounds in heroic legends of loyalty and courage and sacrifice, which have inspired their art and their literature and shaped their sentiment. This was the period of the formation of the *samurai* caste, cultivating as supreme virtues fidelity and contempt of death. A *samurai* is "one who serves," and the idea of utter faithfulness to an overlord can be traced far back. Of the old clans that were hereditary escorts of the sovereign it was written in the earliest Japanese books that their forbears had said, "We will not die peacefully, but will die by the side of our king. If we go to the sea, our bodies shall steep in the water. If we go to the hills, over our corpses the grass shall grow." This tradition of loyalty gave cohesion to the separate clans as indeed it embittered the conflict between them. Up and down Japan war was waged, bravely and ruthlessly, with romantic turmoil and savage cruelty. The whole country was convulsed from North to South by battle, famine and pestilence, culminating in the defeat of the Taira forces and the death of the child-emperor, whom they had carried off, at the great sea-fight of Dannoura in 1185. From that time, until the restoration of 1868, Japan was governed by successive dynasties of military dictators, nearly all of whom sprang from Minamoto stock.

It must not be supposed that these dictators usurped the imperial dignity. They wielded imperial power, and some of them kept imperial state; but the throne was always occupied by a descendant of the Sun Goddess, by a sovereign to whom, however weak and impoverished, the real ruler paid the outward forms of homage, and from whom in theory he derived his authority. Life at the court went on very much as before, a round of religious observances, of official ceremonies, banquets, poetical tournaments, excursions to view the flowers or the moon, the whole diversified by quarrels about precedence, intrigues for title and office and, if we may judge from contemporary romances, a good deal of elegant debauchery. This refined but somewhat thin and bloodless society continued to survive despite the transfer of power to a more vital stock, partly because it remained the fountain of honours and partly because it carried on a definite social and æsthetic tradition which the military classes secretly respected. They, meanwhile, were rapidly developing a culture of their own, based naturally upon warfare, by which they had achieved their dominance. There is much to admire in this culture, for it was virile and adventurous; but one need be only the mildest of cynics to remark that the ideals which it fostered were such as tended to keep privileges in the hands that had lately grasped them. The virtues most prized were military virtues—bravery and obedience; since they were the qualities which a feudal lord most required in his adherents, for protection against his rivals. The code of honour of the military class tended therefore to emphasise these merits at the expense of others. A great deal of the literature of the period following that which we have just described consists of historical romances recounting in dramatic style, with great elaboration of detail, heroic feats of arms, tragic deaths in battle, marvels of generalship, chivalrous encounters, examples of loyal service, heraldic splendours, fine armour, conquering weapons, all the pomp and glory and excitement of war. In the background, unregarded, is the dull peasant, patiently tilling his ravaged fields. In the forefront is the bright sword.

The sword is not merely a romantic symbol of those times, it is a concrete manifestation of their material culture. The swords of the Heian courtiers were ceremonial weapons, in jewelled scabbards of rich design. But those of the feudal chiefs were the deadly product of an advanced technique, that had grown up to meet the demands of men whose trade was war. We do not know very much about the early developments of mining and metallurgy in Japan, but it seems clear that they were stimulated by the growth of the manorial system as well as by the rise of a military class, for the opening up of new land and the more intensive culture of old land meant an increased requirement of tools. In the seventh century iron implements were so scarce that they served as a kind of currency, and in the chronicles we read, for instance, of the grant to a minister in A.D. 701 of 10,000 iron spades and 50,000 lbs. of iron. But such entries grow gradually rarer, and by the beginning of the Heian period iron ore deposits were worked and iron tools made locally in many parts of Japan, for the use of peasants working on the *shōen*. We know that one of the earliest Minamoto generals to come into prominence, Mitsunaka by name, developed mining on one of his manors in western Japan; and it is recorded of him that he took great pains to promote the swordsmith's art. After many experiments, he found an artificer who, prepared by seven days' prayer and abstinence, at length forged two surpassing blades, which became heirlooms in the Minamoto house and figure in many an heroic tale. It is a sign of the importance of this art that the great historical romance called the *Heike Monogatari*, which was written about A.D. 1240 and describes the rise and fall of the Taira, opens with a chapter on swords. Here are to be found praises of famous swords and accounts of their miraculous qualities. Here, and in subsequent Japanese history, the sword is conceived of as a living, sacred thing. So, when Minamoto Yoshitomo, defeated in battle, prays all night at the shrine of Hachiman, he asks why he has been abandoned by the war god, and why his sword has lost its spirit. From those days there developed a definite cult of the sword. It is invested with mystical properties, is almost an object of worship. It stands for the honour of the soldier; is indeed his honour itself, for to part with or defile his sword is to lose or stain his honour. To this day—such is the power of survival of a strong tradition—before a sword of the old type is forged and tempered the smiths undergo a ritual purification, and while at work they wear white garments of a priestly cut.

Technical progress in sword-making was such that, for strength and edge, the Japanese sword of the thirteenth century, if not even earlier, excels the work of all other makers in whatever country, before or since. It was a definitely original contribution by Japan to the applied arts. At the same time the related military arts made rapid advances. Armour combining great strength and lightness was evolved at an early date, to meet the growing efficiency of weapons. Fortification seems only to have developed under European influence in the sixteenth century, but strategy and tactics were studied by the Minamoto and the Taira in the Chinese military classics, of which the best known is the treatise of Suntzŭ, who flourished about 500 B.C. One might almost say that, just as the

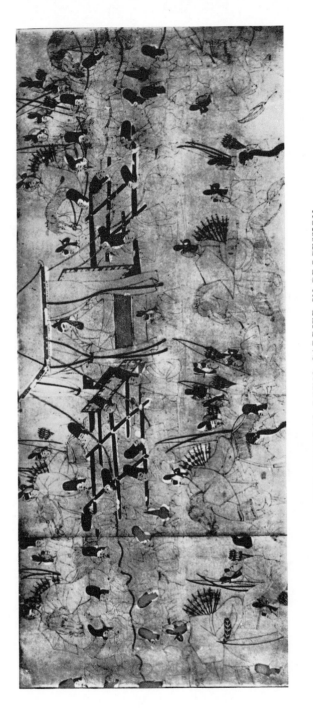

THE EMPEROR BEING CARRIED IN PROCESSION

PART OF THE *Genji Monogatari* SCROLL

sword had ousted the pen, so had these treatises taken the place of the canonical works as the text-books of the ruling class. It is an interesting, if melancholy, reflection, that it was under the pressure of militarism that the Japanese cut loose from the ethical dogmas of their teachers and developed along lines of their own. The laws of filial piety were not rejected, but duty to an overlord must now come before family ties. The gentle doctrines of Buddhism were not abandoned, but they must be made to square with current practice. So one war-worn general, taking monastic vows at the end of his campaigns, feigns deafness when they read to him the commandment against taking life. Another soldier, a Taira retainer, arrested by palace officers for breaches of a devout sovereign's edict against hunting, observes that he has furnished game for his chieftain's table on his chieftain's orders, and since by the law of his house to disobey his chieftain means death, he prefers to disobey the imperial command, for thereby he incurs no graver penalty than banishment.

PART FOUR—KAMAKURA

Chapter XIV—THE GROWTH OF FEUDALISM

WITH an engaging disregard for truth, the official soothsayers and astrologers had, upon a new emperor's accession in 1159, given to the opening era, in which there ensued a most desperate civil war, the name of Peaceful Rule. Hardly less unsuitable was the name of Literary Government, which they gave to the period commencing in 1185, for from that date the supreme power in Japan was held, as it had been gained, by military men: so much so that Yoritomo, the leader of the Minamoto clan, established himself at Kamakura, in eastern Japan, and set up there an administration styled the Baku-fu, which means something like Army Head-quarters.

The description of a feudal régime is apt to be dull reading for all but specialists, but there is an unusual interest in the study of Kamakura politics, for in them we can trace the early growth of institutions which endured in Japan for seven hundred years, and perished only within living memory, leaving a mark, not yet effaced, upon a modern people.

There is nothing to show that Yoritomo consciously shaped his policy so as to become the ruler of all Japan. Even in the first flush of victory over the Taira he (according to one account) treated their leader with great deference, because he held high rank at court; and generally, it seems, although the military dictators did in effect deprive the emperors of almost all but the bare title of sovereignty, they did not conceive of themselves as replacing the ruling dynasty. Their main object was to acquire as much land and as many adherents as possible. It is true that by securing economic and military dominance they in fact became politically supreme, but it is very doubtful whether Yoritomo and his immediate successors ever had any precise conception of national unity. This is not to say that they were without clear ideas of state and sovereign; for the Japanese, having now for five hundred years accepted the Chinese doctrine of monarchy, were in this respect farther advanced than most of their European contemporaries. But the Chinese theory provided also for the delegation

of a ruler's power, so that to Yoritomo his own dictatorship would
present no anomaly. Moreover he thought in terms of fiefs and
manors, not of people and government. He established himself at
Kamakura, three hundred miles from the capital city, because
that was a convenient centre from which to oversee his vassals.
The chief Minamoto manors were in eastern Japan, and here also
were great estates of allied families, held in fief from him as leader
of the Minamoto clan. Yoritomo did not derive his power from the
court, nor had he taken it from the court, since the emperors had
never held full sway in those regions. They had exercised authority
there only in so far as the territorial magnates had chosen to
recognise it. Now Yoritomo, strong as he was, depended on the
support of feudal chieftains, and it was his business to keep them in
order, to check any movement likely to weaken his own position;
in short, to establish himself firmly as their overlord rather than
to displace the dynasty reigning at Kyōto. Indeed he judged it
expedient to make use of the imperial prestige on many occasions,
and for a long time after his accession to power we find him quite
humbly, so far as forms go, praying the Kyōto government to
sanction this or that item of his policy. He sought and obtained
high court rank, and was appointed a Minister of State and a
General of the Guards, but it was some years before the emperor
—or rather, the cloistered ex-emperor—would grant him what he
greatly coveted, the commission as Seii-Tai-Shōgun, or Barbarian-
Subduing Generalissimo, which gave him supreme and unlimited
control over all military forces in the country. It is worth remembering these details if we are to understand subsequent history,
even down to very recent times. The tradition of reverence for the
imperial house was so strong that, through checkered centuries,
though it smouldered and died down, it was never extinct, and
before the restoration of 1868 it was ablaze once more.

The court, then, retained at this time a certain social prestige
and a certain negative authority. But for any capable man with a
sense of reality it offered no career. Under the Fujiwara there had
always been room for a number of competent officials, members of
a sort of hereditary civil service, who were experts in the interpretation of the codes, the drafting of public documents, account-
ancy, and such-like matters. They were the working members of

the administration, but their position, always subordinate to the heads of departments, whose posts went by birth and not by competence, had with the gradual corruption and decline of the court become intolerable. Some of them, disgusted with the emptiness of court life, or even frightened by its dangers in such times of intrigue and disorder, retired to country hermitages and lived in frugal comfort. Some became real recluses or wandering monks. Others, more ambitious, were attracted by the prospects of advancement under the military chiefs, to whom they offered their services. The Kamakura government, not too rich in administrative and literary talent, welcomed such experienced men, who, besides knowing from the inside palace affairs and the technique of official business, had some general ideas about politics and law. Eastern Japan therefore tended to draw from the capital some of its ablest civilians; and this movement was of considerable importance in promoting the transfer of power to Kamakura, and making it a centre of learning of a special type.

Among the scholars who took a share in the organisation of the Shōgun's government was one Ōe Hiromoto, of an ancient family of *literati* which had served the imperial house for several centuries. To him and to his colleagues of similar antecedents is due probably most of the credit for the administrative successes of the thirteenth century. To make clear the nature of their task, it is necessary to sketch the condition of Japan at the end of Yoritomo's successful campaign against the Taira. Now, as ever, at the root of all problems was the system of land tenure, and to describe this is to describe the sum of economic and political conditions. During the period of disorder culminating in 1185, private warriors in all parts of Japan had seized rights in land, and had reached a position of dominance in their own localities. This was the logical outcome of the growth of immense estates (the *shōen*), which has been outlined in a previous chapter; but it was a process accelerated and magnified by the weakness of the central authority. In eastern Japan, as the military strength of the Minamoto grew, many landholders had, from the end of the eleventh century, for the sake of protection commended their estates to the leaders of that clan. Indeed the practice was so common that in 1091 it was forbidden by imperial edict, though, of course, without effect. After the downfall of the Taira, Yoritomo granted to his own supporters lands seized from the enemy, who had been overlords of thirty-three provinces out of sixty-six and held besides five hundred immune domains. He also invited a number of their former allies to transfer their allegiance to him. To the many who complied he made new grants, or he confirmed them in the rights which they already held, while they on their side became his immediate vassals, his *ke-nin* or "house men." Thus, scattered over all parts of Japan, thickly in the east, more thinly elsewhere, were land and armed forces which the Minamoto overlord controlled either directly or through his lieges. It should be noted that the lands held by his vassals were often situated in the domains of other lords,* such as princes, or court nobles, or powerful abbots, or in the districts of provincial governors, for these officials continued to function in some places, if not as public servants, at least in some form of authority or possession. In such domains, the power exercised by

---

* Such domains varied greatly in extent and in character of tenure. Thus the Tōdaiji had, by about 900, received from the court alone fiefs amounting to 8,000 households scattered in blocks of from 50 to 250 over nearly all the provinces of Japan; and according to an inventory of 998 it then held in addition manors donated or commended, ranging in area from a few rods to several hundred acres, in about one hundred different districts. Even as early as 850 it was officially estimated to have in all nearly 30,000 acres of rice-land. Under a pastoral system this is not an immoderate holding, but in terms of small plots of arable land it is enormous. These figures take no account of the possessions of subsidiary temples of the Tōdaiji, which were considerable.

As to the domains of court nobles, the celebrated Shimadzu *shōen* in southern Kyūshū may be taken as a good, though somewhat extreme example. Beginning in about 1030 as a piece of unoccupied land cultivated by a Taira official and commended by him to the then Fujiwara regent, it became an hereditary immune domain of the Konoe branch of the Fujiwara family. By accretions of various sorts it grew, by the end of the 12th century, into an immense *shōen*, covering more than 40,000 acres—more than half the arable area of the three provinces over which it spread—and exhibiting in its various components almost every kind of tenure and every degree of fiscal immunity.

The Tōdaiji and Shimadzu manors, though extreme cases in regard to extent, were otherwise typical. From a cadastral survey made by the Kamakura government in about 1280 we learn that out of a total arable area of some 9,000 acres in the province of Ōsumi only 750 acres was public, taxable land; out of 120,000 acres in Hitachi, only 27,000; and out of 4,800 acres in Tamba, only some 600. In this last province, nearly 300 acres belonged to Shintō shrines, 1,000 acres to Buddhist monasteries, and nearly 3,000 acres consisted of *shōen*.

the Shōgun varied, according to circumstances, from an almost nominal suzerainty to complete effective control. But the confusion did not stop here, for, though we have for brevity's sake loosely used the words "manor" and "ownership," it must be understood that the manor in Japan differed in several essentials from the European feudal manor, and that plain ownership of land was a rare phenomenon. The private domain called *shōen* consisted of a group of small units of individual cultivation, very loosely bound together. The size of these units was governed by the customary method of agriculture, which required the division of land into small dyked wet rice-fields or small terraced upland fields. Pasture plays no part in this system, of which the basis is an intensive culture of rice by individuals, and not communal husbandry. Consequently the strongest and, as Japanese history shows, the most tenacious sense of ownership resided in the peasant. Yet he, in reality, enjoyed only the right of cultivating the soil, and drawing from it often but a meagre sustenance; for he had to satisfy many claims upon his labour. Attaching to each parcel of land were numerous and various rights, known as *shiki*. Each *shōen* was a complex of *shiki*, and it is the *shōen* and the *shiki*, the manor and the rights, which in their division and ramification give to the feudal institutions of Japan their special character.

The word *shiki* properly means an office or function, but it came to be applied to the rights rather than the duties of a holder in respect of land. It is sometimes loosely used for income, and in later feudal documents for the land itself. A broad classification of these rights shows us, in ascending order, the rights of the cultivator of a plot or plots; the rights of a manager or bailiff of such plots as part of a *shōen*; the rights of the proprietor of the *shōen*; and finally the rights of the patron who, standing at the apex, ensures by his high position the immunity of the estate, whether from tax or aggression. All such rights were of very diverse origin and nature. The rights of a cultivator might derive from the use of land under the early allotment (*ku-bun-den*) system; from the occupation of waste land brought under cultivation by his predecessors either on their own account or through the enterprise of some local notable; or again his plot may at first have been worked by his ancestors as serfs upon a sustenance-fief. But the cultivator's rights, as a general rule, were not much more than the rights to live on the land, to till it, and to consume such residue of its fruits as was left after the satisfaction of rights higher in the scale; though he might have some special privileges, as for example in respect of irrigation, fishing, woodcutting or taking game. The rights of the bailiff varied. In a typical case a prince or a nobleman or a religious body, having acquired or enlarged an estate in a distant province, where they could not oversee it themselves, would entrust its supervision to a third party, whose rights would depend upon his duties, and whose duties would be governed by such conditions as the size and position of the estate, the nature of its immunity and so on. The bailiff of a small *shōen* might be not much more than a small farmer himself, supervising the peasants and remitting to the proprietor an agreed share of its produce. He might be a land-holder receiving from the proprietor a fixed fee, or a percentage of the yield of the estate, in return for its supervision and, if he were a person of local importance, its protection against neighbouring landholders. In some regions, where the provincial or local government was either powerful or corrupt, it was expedient for the holder of a *shōen* to commit it to the charge of some local offi-cial, who would for a fee oversee it, keep its accounts and remit funds to the absentee landlord. Conversely the local importance of the bailiff of a large estate sometimes gave him a prescriptive right to a post as clerk or accountant in the district or provincial govern-ment office. We therefore find such public appointments treated as *shiki* pertaining to private estates, and though this seems at first sight surprising, it must be remembered that men with a good knowledge of writing and accounts were rare in country districts.*

As the *shōen* grew in size and immunity, they tended to become autonomous units, and their administration involved, as well as

---

* Moreover, by the end of the twelfth century, the governors of provinces and districts were no longer, as a rule, able to exercise administrative functions, except to a very limited extent. They were now rather the bearers of hereditary titles, owning or controlling hereditary estates, and the titular public servants under them were small landowners. The district governor class (the former *gunshi*) in particular, since they had formerly acted as magistrates, tax collec-tors, and police commissioners, and had been appointed because of their local influence, developed into a class of hereditary landowners with adherents skilled in the use of arms. They were perhaps the most important element in the formation of the warrior class.

managing and accounting, keeping order within their boundaries and protecting them against aggressors from without. Thus there came into being various classes of wardens, constables, inspectors, and foremen, all deriving sustenance from the land. These posts also were sometimes held by officers of the local government. All were *shiki* and a charge upon the estate.

It will be seen that the rights comprehensively described as managers' *shiki* were of many varieties. In an inventory of the estates of a great temple in 1214, eighteen different styles of estate officers are mentioned, and though some of these may represent only differences in name, one *shōen* of 150 acres has a supervisory staff of twenty-three persons, in eleven categories, holding *shiki* worth from about one acre in the lowest grade to eighteen acres in the highest. The produce of these areas formed their incomes, which in this particular case amounted to seven-tenths of the total yield of the estate.

The highest in the ascending scale of rights was that of the patron. It might arise in several ways. He might be a high personage who had received a grant from the court, or a local magnate who had brought land under cultivation or acquired by confiscation the land of others; but in all typical cases he is the landholder, as contrasted with the manager and the cultivator. His is the leading right, though by no means necessarily the most valuable. Before the right profits him it may have passed through many stages of commendation, each creating one or more *shiki* which, when they are all satisfied, may leave him little more than a nominal share. Moreover, in times of disorder and insecurity, even he, as well as the holders of rights lower in the scale, may be dependent upon the protection of some other powerful patron, such as a great general, and so new rights or interests may come into existence.

The *shiki* were not only numerous and diverse. They could also be divided and transferred for consideration or by testament; and since primogeniture was of slow growth in Japan there was a tendency for *shiki* to be split up among the children of a holder. A *shiki* or even a part of a *shiki* might on the death of its owner pass to one of his daughters, and thus become hereditary in her husband's family. Thus these rights continuously separated and combined, growing, as families ramified, in numbers and complexity.

Intricate as was this tangle of rights and duties in respect of land, it was not without a certain flexibility. In one aspect the *shiki* appears almost as a medium of exchange. Its fluid nature and the fact that its value could be exactly computed in terms of units of the staple crop, gave it something of the character of a currency in an age when money economy was far distant in the future. Further, because the *shiki* could be divided and transferred, and could in many cases be enjoyed at a distance, effective changes of ownership could be made without disturbing the productive balance of an estate, and without disturbing the tenure of actual cultivators. It is, indeed, a special feature of the system that the rights grew from below rather than descended from above. The typical private warrior was a man attached to the soil, in the same way as the peasants, and the lower grade of warrior was hardly differentiated from the higher grade of cultivator, whose origins he shared. He did not receive, as a return for service, lands carved out of his military overlord's domain, but was confirmed and protected in his existing rights by the lord, as the price of his vassalage. His tenure was not specifically military, and though he was his lord's vassal he was often at the same time a tenant under obligations to another person, or even to the civil government as landlord-in-chief.

It followed from the diversity of the interests at stake that Yoritomo must, to make his own position stable, find some way of controlling them, to his own advantage but without too great offence to their holders. The establishment of his government at Kamakura is comparable to the Great Reform of 645 in that it heralded a change in the administrative system. But the Great Reform was based on a theory and carried out as a scheme, whereas Yoritomo's methods were largely empiric. He did not attempt to replace or overhaul the existing machinery, but added to it apparatus of his own devising, to meet his needs as he discerned them. Counselled by Ōe Hiromoto he appointed, in provinces where it was expedient, a military governor known as the Constable (*sō-tsuibu-shi*) or Protector (*shu-go*) and in a great number of private and public domains he nominated officials called Stewards (*ji-tō*). It was characteristic of his methods that these titles were not

FIG. 33. *A feudal warrior in the field. Helmet with gold crest: armour with heraldic pattern: under-dress of silver cloth. (After a scroll of the Kamakura period.)*

new ones, though the functions of their bearers had a new significance. He himself was made Constable-General and Steward-General, thus standing at the head of all constables and stewards, who were, moreover, all his immediate vassals. The creation of their posts was an improvisation, aimed at strengthening his influence in territory over which he had no direct control. Such territory was considerable, for feudal institutions were still immature. All over the country there resided warriors firmly entrenched in their own localities and enjoying private rights, while there lingered in many districts remnants of the civil authority. It was necessary to conciliate or suppress those interests when they competed with his own. The Protectors, therefore, consistently with the high office of their master, the Commander-in-Chief, were put in supreme control of military and police affairs in each province, and their authority in their respective spheres extended over all direct vassals of the Minamoto. Their duties were: to call up men on the roster for the Imperial Guard; to suppress uprisings; and to arrest violent criminals. But in practice they assumed many other prerogatives, with the connivance and sometimes the encouragement of Kamakura.

As for the stewards, permission to appoint them was given very grudgingly by the court, and that only after one of Yoritomo's generals had appeared at Kyōto with a thousand cavalry to underline his request. The reason given for the creation of these posts was that, in order to protect the throne from rebels and to keep order in the provinces, the Commander-in-Chief must have efficient troops at his disposal. The stewards therefore were to levy on the areas to which they were posted a tax for military purposes. This tax was called "commissariat rice" (*hyōrō-mai*) and was fixed at five measures of rice per *tan* of land, approximately one-fiftieth of the yield. It was levied not upon the cultivator but upon the landlord. On the ground that the proceeds of the tax were to be used in the general interest, it was assessed upon all cultivated land, whether public or private. This was a revolutionary step, for it meant that there were to be no longer any completely immune estates. There was great consternation among the holders of *shōen* who were not allied with the Minamoto. The court nobles in particular were so dismayed at the thought that their cherished fiscal immunity was to be violated by the stewards, and their domains threatened by the intrusion of the constables, that a severe earthquake which took place early in 1186 was regarded at the capital as an omen, signifying that the Kamakura government was about to swallow up their lands. In the beginning, at least, Yoritomo took some notice of this opposition, and appointments of stewards were not made, or were cancelled, in several districts. But the system, though modified at different times and in different places, was in general applied. The constables and the stewards took up their posts and carried out their duties.

The creation of these new offices was the first phase in a long process by which the bureaucratic institutions of Japan were replaced by an organised feudalism. It was a long process because, in the days of Yoritomo, though the old bureaucracy was decrepit, the new system was feeble, and it needed the trials and discipline of civil war to bring it to maturity. Private rights which had grown up at the expense of public authority were in the aggregate as strong as either the civil or the military power; and if it came to open conflict they might emerge supreme from the disorder that would ensue. Yoritomo's learned advisers saw that he must walk warily, and their policy was not to attack opposing interests directly but to diminish them relatively by strengthening their own. The gradual increment in the powers of the stewards illustrates this process, which may be described as the use of the wedge rather than the axe. They collected the taxes or other dues of the *shōen* under their charge and (after deducting their own incomes, in a proportion which tended always to increase) remitted the proceeds to the officials of the district or, in so far as the estates were immune, to the landholders. In these respects they replaced the officials of the civil government, and at the same time, in return for their incomes, they were under an obligation of military service to the Bakufu. This capacity to render military service was what made them both useful to the Minamoto and dangerous to other interests. Each steward disposed of a number of armed men, members of his family, or his local adherents, so that in each *shōen* where a steward resided the Minamoto had, so to speak, a loyal garrison. The steward's power to collect taxes, coupled with his military strength, gave him a commanding position in his district;

so commanding, in fact, that at a later date some of them, in places remote from Kamakura, acquired such wealth in land and men that they became serious rivals of the military dictators themselves. As time went on and their local influence grew, the stewards were charged with still more functions. The chronicle known as the *Adzuma Kagami*, "The Mirror of the East," and other records, show that by 1200 they were, whether under instructions or of their own accord, carrying out the reclamation of waste lands, supervising roads and post stations, arresting criminals and judging suits, while those in estates which included a harbour engaged in coasting trade, and probably in traffic with China and Korea. All these extensions of their activity ate into the authority of the civil government and lessened the influence of great landholders who were not Minamoto vassals. In some cases the rights of a steward clashed with the powers of a constable, and in general there was rivalry between the two offices, which were meant to be complementary. Both came to be regarded as *shiki*, and as such divisible and transferable. They thus assumed an hereditary character, but as the rights of a steward were specific and local they were more easily split up than the wider and less definite powers of a constable. A steward's office might even be inherited by a woman. For these and other reasons in the long run the constables outstripped the stewards, and during the following centuries they developed into the greater feudal barons, while the stewards became the lesser local gentry, the middling landowners and the small squires. In exceptional cases the stewards had influence equal to that of a constable, for though many of them controlled only a dozen acres or so, there were a few whose jurisdiction was almost as extensive as a province. So, in the provinces of Tamba and Tango, the cadastral surveys of about 1200 record *shōen* ranging from 10 to about 500 acres, while in Satsuma, Ōsumi and Hyūga there were *shōen* of over 1,000 acres and stewards who controlled an amalgamation of several such estates. Thus, to make a short digest from the registers: In the province of Satsuma alone the steward (*jitō*) Uemon Hyōe no Jō controlled in 1197 eighteen *shōen* of a total area of 4,300 acres, including tracts classified as—

Public domains—i.e. land which in theory belonged to the state, but was so burdened with *shiki* as to be in effect a private *shōen*.

Confiscated domains—e.g. land which had formerly belonged
to the Taira or other opponents of the Minamoto.

Temple and shrine domains—i.e. lands managed on behalf of
the churches by the Steward.

Name fields (*myōden*)—generally lands, bearing the name of some
original cultivator, commended to a *shōen* and then absorbed
by it.

Hyōe no Jō was the court title of Tadahisa, founder of the fortunes
of the famous Shimadzu, lords of Satsuma, who in later feudal
times were a danger to the strongest Shōguns. He was not only
steward of this great manor, but also a private official, managing it
on behalf of the patron, a Fujiwara noble. He was further a Police
Commissioner, and at the same time he was constable of the three
provinces in which the Shimadzu estates lay. It is typical of the
institutional medley of this period that Tadahisa as Police Commissioner (*ōryōshi*) was subordinate to the Commissioner-General
of Kyūshū, but as constable of the three provinces he could override the Commissioner-General's authority and prevent the intrusion of his officers into the *shōen*. His court rank gave him a nominal
command in the Imperial Guard but he could not present himself at the palace, even under the sovereign's orders, without sanction from the Kamakura government. Situations equally anoma-
lous in kind if not in degree everywhere arose. But we need not
stop to examine them, for we have already seen enough to show
that the system of rights and duties in respect of land, military service and fiscal obligations was so complex that it required constant
adjustment to preserve its delicate balance. This was the function
of the Bakufu, and there grew up in the thirteenth century at
Kamakura a full organisation of government offices in which policy
was framed and directed and of courts in which disputes were
judged. We need not describe it at length, but it is important
to notice that it contrasted strongly with the bureaucratic machine
which it replaced. The Taikwa reformers had tried to fit facts to
their scheme, but Yoritomo's counsellors fitted their schemes to
facts, as they perceived them. Consequently the Kamakura central
administration, though in many ways variable and inconsistent,
functioned efficiently for several generations. There were three
chief organs, the military, the administrative and the judicial. The

first of these, the *Samurai-dokoro*, was a kind of disciplinary tribunal which, beside the pursuit of criminals, dealt with the affairs of the military class. It decided matters of promotion and degradation, reward and punishment, allocated military duties and in general supervised the conduct of the Minamoto vassals, so that its decisions embodied and helped to form the ethical code of the warrior caste. The *Man-dokoro* was an administrative board, consisting of a president and several counsellors, among whom were men of the type of Ōe, capable members of what we have described as an hereditary civil service. The *Monchū-jo* was a judicial body, a court of appeal for the final decision of suits which could not be settled locally by the stewards and constables or other representatives of the Shōgun. The need for such an institution arose naturally from the confusion of jurisdiction, the diversity of rights and obligations, that the *shōen* system brought forth.

These three organs, in common with most of the machinery of the Bakufu, were not newly devised *ad hoc* by Yoritomo, but were extensions of existing practice. The *Samurai-dokoro* was modelled on a similar council instituted by the Fujiwara regents for the control of their military adherents. The *Man-dokoro* was, both in name and in kind, a replica of the offices which the regents and other great landowners set up for the administration of their domains. The *Monchū-jo* was in nature akin to the Police Commission (*Kebiishi-chō*) in its later judicial development, and to the private manorial courts which settled disputes arising out of the interplay of rights of tax and tenure in the immune estates. All three were thus in origin unofficial bodies, and they gained their public character because of the vast extent of the Minamoto interests. They waxed and waned in importance during the thirteenth century, and other institutions of adventitious growth succeeded them; but essentially they survived and, as they developed and their influence spread, the central authority of the monarchy was displaced by the feudal authority of Kamakura, the provincial and local executive power was concentrated in the hands of the constables and stewards, and there remained only vestiges and survivals of the bureaucratic régime.

Perhaps the outstanding feature of the Kamakura government, particularly in its early days, was the prompt and impartial administration of justice by the highest courts. No doubt Yoritomo, aware that a prevalent sense of grievance among his vassals would be against his own interests, was anxious that they should learn to count on his fairness; but this was not his only motive. The military caste as a whole had, in the give and take of civil warfare, evolved a strong ethical feeling of mutual obligation, which found expression in their house laws; and the Kamakura code was in essence a feudal house law on the grand scale, dealing with the rights as well as the duties of vassals among themselves and towards their overlord. Consequently we find, in studying the decisions of the Bakufu tribunals, that they rarely sacrificed to the suzerain's own interest the just claims of litigants who were his house-men. They dispensed a stern, practical justice, and though their conceptions, being shaped by their caste feeling, were narrow and one-sided, they displayed in many respects a surprising liberality. Evidence was carefully examined, precedents were scrupulously observed and recorded, and the greatest importance was attached to documentary proof. The importance of the pen in this culture of the sword was truly remarkable. Oral arguments played only a small part in judicial procedure. Pleadings were submitted in writing, while agreements as to property and service were regularly drawn up in the form of charters, deeds and bonds. Symbolic ceremonies of homage and investiture were rare, their place being taken by written oaths and warrants. To keep the records and accounts of a large estate required a fairly high standard of literacy, so that the growth of the *shōen* promoted the spread of learning in the provinces. Many of the feudal gentry were themselves almost unlettered, but in their households were skilled clerkly men, as is evident from the fine calligraphy of a number of extant feudal documents dating from the thirteenth century.*

These characteristics of early feudal justice in Japan no doubt

---

* Thus when Hōjō Yasutoki, after defeating the imperial troops in 1221, received a messenger bearing a letter of submission from the Emperor, he said (according to the *Adzuma Kagami*): "Is there anybody here who can read the Imperial Message?" He had with him at that moment five thousand men. One of his captains came forward and said that Fujita of Musashi was a great scholar. And Fujita was told to read the message. In fairness to the captains it should be added that imperial missives were written in extremely difficult, almost esoteric language.

owed a good deal to the influence of the borrowed Chinese codes, which, decayed and transformed as they were by five centuries of use in Japan, had left a legacy of respect for written authorities and dependence upon specialists. This tradition was carefully guarded by a long line of official scholars, from the Illuminators of the Law (*myōhō-hakase*), who lectured in the University of Nara, to learned assessors like Ōe, Miyoshi or Nakahara, who sat on the bench sometimes with Yoritomo himself and always with his highest deputies.

The House Laws of the great families had much to do with shaping the development of Japanese institutions, and a study of them reveals the interesting fact that some of the distinguishing features of the feudalism evolved in Japan can be traced back to the early patriarchal system, while others show the influence of Chinese political theory. We have seen that, in spite of efforts to change the structure of society, clan feeling again and again asserted itself, and found expression in the rise, one after another, of powerful families tending to act as self-contained units. Even the imported codes, as adapted in Japan, allowed a considerable independence to nobles of high rank, providing for a regular hierarchy in their households of functionaries, guards and menials. As their lands grew they acquired an almost complete control over the persons and property of those inhabiting their estates, including the power to inflict punishment. Some forms of tenure even conferred freedom from the entry of public officers. As these autonomous units expanded, each developed customary rules governing the relations between its members. Such rules dealt with the duties of members of the clan, matters of marriage, succession and ancestral rites, and in general they formed and preserved a family tradition of conduct. It was under the influence of this habit that were built up the house laws of the military families; and thus the code which regulated, for example, the behaviour of a Minamoto warrior towards his clan leader was of the same type as the body of instructions which were observed by the Fujiwara and their dependents. Consequently the early feudal relation between lord and vassal in Japan can be said to owe something to the patriarchal system of pre-feudal and even of pre-historic times. The warfare which brought the fighting classes to the fore naturally emphasised

FIG. 34. *Bannerman (hatasashi) of a feudal warrior. (After a scroll of the Kamakura period.)*

the military aspect of the bond between the leader and his man, but it remained true for a long time after the establishment of the Bakufu that the relation between lord and vassal partook more of the nature of family loyalty than of a contractual obligation. As the Minamoto extended their powers and acquired supporters outside their own clan, they were, of course, obliged to offer their new vassals some material return; but even Yoritomo's former enemies were invited to become his "house-men," and so to establish with him a connection approaching kinship.

Though it would be foolish to suppose that the feudal régime subsisted upon abstract loyalty, without nourishment in the shape of concrete benefits, it can be said that, ideally, loyalty came first. In theory the vassal owed service to his lord simply because he was his lord, and he did not claim, though he might reasonably hope for, protection and reward. Thus Sasaki Sadatsuna, a partisan of the Minamoto, for whom he and his forebears had wrought valiantly and suffered, in his injunctions to his son spoke as follows: "It is the duty of a warrior to be like a monk observing a rule. It is his business to preserve the state by protecting the sovereign. Whether he holds but a pin's point of land or rules a thousand acres, his loyalty must be the same. He must not think of his life as his own, but as offered by him to his lord." The lord may grant favours to a vassal who has done him no service, or he may deny gifts to one who has given him aid; for the personal relationship exists, independently of reward, on a basis of mutual reliance and trust. This conception of a vassal's duty, ethical rather than practical, was naturally fostered by the feudal chieftains, who found in Confucian doctrine a very convenient warrant for promoting their own interest. True, the Chinese teaching was in origin and growth designed to stabilise a peaceful, bureaucratic order and, though it insisted in general terms upon the importance of loyalty, it had in view chiefly such civic virtues as filial piety and obedience to officials. But it was easy to naturalise this morality in a warlike society by giving special eminence to one type of loyalty, that of a warrior to his overlord. So we find Tameyoshi, the grandfather of Yoritomo, when summoned to the court of a cloistered emperor, saying: "I come because I have been told to come by the head of my house. Otherwise not even an imperial edict could bring me to the palace, for we Minamoto do not serve two masters." Not only does the warrior serve only one master, but he owes him a loyalty which transcends all other loyalties. They are evanescent relations, but the bond of service belongs to past, present and future. The saying was, "Parent and child one generation, husband and wife two generations, lord and retainer three generations"; and the catharsis in classical Japanese tragedy is usually provided by the clash between duty to a superior and the natural affections. A mother substitutes her child for the infant of the chieftain, and reveals no emotion when her own offspring is slain before her eyes by the enemy whom she has tricked. A son sacrifices his parents on his war-lord's behalf, a husband sells his wife into harlotry to get funds for the defence of his own honour as a soldier.

Of such a kind was the ethical code of the military caste, described in early works not as *Bushido* (which is a word of recent currency) but as "the way of the horse and the bow," a term analogous to our word "chivalry."[1] Yet the likeness is largely philological. The code of European knighthood grew up in an atmosphere of religious fervour, and centred round the duty of the strong towards the weak, which was expressed in the cult of deference to women. The Japanese feudal warrior, though he might worship the god of war and pray devoutly to Buddhist deities, was not inspired by crusading zeal. He did not go into battle wearing a holy relic, invoking the angels and the saints, but cried out in a loud voice his name and his pedigree. A Taira soldier, in a great sea-fight, boards a ship proclaiming, "I am he, known to the very children in the streets in these days as an ally of the Heike, the second son of Etchū Zenshi, Shimōsa Akushichihyōe Kagekiyo!" In the lyric drama called "Benkei-in-the-Boat" even a wraith announces his ancestry, in these words: "This is I, offspring of the emperor Kwammu in the ninth generation, Taira no Tomomori, his ghost." In the life of intrigue and ceremony at the imperial court, feminine influence was strong, while women seem to have had a good deal to do with the practical management of feudal estates; but in Japan the knight of mediæval romance did not ride abroad to succour damsels in distress, and he would have been deeply shocked at the thought of tilting for some lady's favour. Though there are many tales, sad and heroic, of noble Japanese women of this age, they figure not as queenly beauties compelling homage and inspiring passion, but as devoted servants and companions.

Both the European and the Japanese codes subserved the interest of a special class, and both had grave shortcomings. The Japanese ideals, in their way and within their limited scope, helped to create a fine tradition of duty and self-sacrifice. Conduct, of course, fell far short of ideals, and even in the early feudal period, when military aspirations were fresh and before the code had been subjected to the strain of greed and the wear of time, there were many revolting examples of treachery. Yoritomo himself, the keystone of the arch of loyalty, was guilty of cruel and cowardly acts, and often a knight, who would go to fantastic lengths to keep his plighted word, would commit the basest and most unnatural crimes if they were not expressly forbidden by the unwritten law of his caste. Yet, for all that, the code fostered a certain power of resistance to moral and material hardship, and a high sense of obligation, which have been of much value to the nation.

Though these virtues, it is interesting to observe, are based upon a philosophy rather than a religious faith, it must not be supposed that the thoughts and the deeds of the military class were free from the influence of religion. The spread of the doctrines of the meditative Zen sect—perhaps the most remarkable development of Buddhism in Japan—had its beginnings in this age. Throughout the feudal period both lords and vassals frequently founded religious institutions, and attached to most great manors were Buddhist temples and Shintō shrines supported by the landholders and devoted to the worship of some patron deity or the performance of rites on behalf of the dead. A warrior past his active campaigning days would shave his head and enter religion, taking a Buddhist name; though this did not as a rule mean that he forsook the world and secular affairs. In oaths of fealty and in legal bonds the gods were called upon to punish a breach of faith. In times of peril all the Buddhist and Shintō deities were invoked, with prayer for strength or victory in battle. Sometimes a great soldier's spirit was deified and worshipped in a shrine erected by his posterity. In general the military class were liberal in their expenditure on ecclesiastical buildings and ceremonies, but—if a distinction can be made between their creed and European chivalry—the ideals which they cherished were not religious ideals, and religion was a subsidiary and not a primary motive of their conduct. Here we cannot speculate as to whether this difference arose from deep springs of racial instinct, or was caused by external conditions. But it is worth remembering that, in the middle ages, it fell to feudal warriors to protect Western Europe against the encroachment of heathen peoples, and it was as the defender of Christian territory that feudalism fought for the Christian church. In Japan there arose no such circumstances to identify feudal and religious interests. Buddhism had spread over the whole Far Eastern world, and even Khubilai Khan's Mongols had come under its influence when they invaded Japan; so that it would have been difficult for a Japanese Peter the Hermit to rouse the Minamoto vassals by crying that dangers assailed the faith.

The foregoing account of the early feudal age, perforce consisting largely of drab extracts from chronicles and registers, makes a dull picture. For the sake of truth as well as interest it should be enlivened, and this may best be done by adding pigment from contemporary romance. The canvas should show a background of rice-fields, where peasants bend at their toil. On a hillside stands, in a pleasant grove, a temple in whose dim interior chanting priests kneel before an image of Amida. Not far away is a village of thatched houses, of which some, hardly more imposing than the rest, are the homes of the steward of the estate and his subordinates. Across the foreground move laden carts hauled by oxen or by straining men in loin-cloths; a messenger bringing documents from the governor's mansion; a wandering monk soliciting alms or maybe a gift towards the rebuilding of the Tōdaiji Monastery of Nara; and a group of warriors on horseback, brightly dressed, on their way from hawking or from archery. Such is the scene in the intervals of peace. For the colour and movement of war, we can turn to the Tales of the House of Taira. Dating from the first half of the thirteenth century, they recount in elevated language feats of arms and the lives and deaths of warriors and princes. Their priestly writers present the history of the struggle between the factions as a tragic witness to the evanescence of all things that men prize, as a great spectacle revealing the inevitable sequence of events throughout time, the chain of causation of Buddhist teaching. So the great military romances open with words like these: "The temple bell echoes the impermanence of all things. The colours of the flowers testify to the truth that those who flourish must decay. Pride lasts but a little while like a dream on a spring night. Before long the mighty are cast down, and they are as dust before the wind." But, though this philosophy strongly coloured the Japanese view of life at that time, there was always room for cheerfulness to break in; and these romances show us, alongside of melancholy and resignation, joy in battle, the humour of camps, pride in rich garments, an engaging braggadocio and, as always, a fine sensitiveness to beauty.

Kiso no Yoshinaka, a Minamoto but a rebel against his clan, approaches his end. "Last year he rode forth with fifty thousand horse. Now he passes along the river bed with only six followers. Sad!—and sadder still to think that he is travelling in the dim space between two worlds." He meets a retainer, Imai, with a handful of men, and they gather together a small force of three hundred, to meet the attack of six thousand enemy troops. "Well-matched," says Yoshinaka, and rides into the fight. "That day my lord Kiso was arrayed in a silk underdress of brocade on a red ground, and armour with cords of Chinese silk. He had girded on a long sword, richly mounted, and fastened tight a helmet with a horned crest of gold. . . . Rising high in his stirrups, he cried in a loud voice, 'You have often heard of me, the Knight of Kiso. Now you can see me! This is I, Master of the Horse, Lord of Iyo, General of the Rising Sun, Yoshinaka of the Minamoto. Come, take my head if you can, and show it to Yoritomo!'" The fight, of course, is desperate. Yoshinaka's beautiful mistress, a girl named Tomoe, takes a hand and kills a man. But before long the small band is almost wiped out and Imai persuades Yoshinaka to flee. He rides off. "Darkness was at hand, and everything was coated with thin ice, so that he could not see where the deep rice-fields lay, and his horse soon plunged into the thick mud up to its neck. He whipped and spurred, but could not stir it. Yet even in this plight he was concerned for Imai, and turned to see how he fared, when a man of the province of Sagami, Miura no Ishida-no-Jirō Tamehisa, rode up and shot an arrow which pierced his helmet. He was stricken, and fell forward with his crest bowed over his horse's mane. Thereupon two of Ishida's men fell upon him and struck off his head. Holding the head high on the point of his sword, Ishida proclaimed in a loud voice: 'Kiso no Yoshinaka, known throughout the land as the Demon, has been slain by me, Miura Ishida-no-Jirō Tamehisa!' Imai was still fighting when he heard this, but then he said: 'Now who is left for me to follow in battle? See, you men of the East country, learn from this example how the stoutest fighter in Japan ends his own life!' and he held the point of his sword in his mouth and flung himself headlong from his mount, so that he was pierced through and died.''

The above story illustrates well the fighting spirit of the age, and the view of loyal duty which led a warrior to follow his master in death. The custom of suicide no doubt arose in days when self-inflicted death was preferable to capture and mutilation by a merciless enemy, whose triumph was measured by the number of heads he could display. But it was fostered by the knightly code which taught that death was better than disgrace. One more extract will help to suggest the atmosphere of those days, for though the tales are legendary rather than historical they had a basis in fact, and they preserved, if they exaggerated, the flavour of reality. Their popularity was such that, in depicting the manners of one age, they formed the ideals of the next. Perhaps the story of Yoshitsune, though well-worn, is the most compendious illustration of military life in early feudal times. His career is one of the most romantic in Japanese history. The youngest brother of Yoritomo, he was as a child spared by the Taira after their defeat of the Minamoto, and sent to live in a monastery to prepare for the priesthood. But he, preferring military adventure, escaped, and roamed about, always in danger, until he found shelter with a friendly noble in the North. In the final struggle between the two great clans he won battle after battle for Yoritomo, and it was his generalship and his courage which secured the final triumph and the downfall of the Taira in 1185. The tales of his prowess are endless, and he was immensely popular among soldiers and at court, where he was regarded as the pattern of chivalry, slim, handsome, accomplished and brave. A great fencer, he had easily overcome as a mere boy, in an encounter on the Gojō bridge at Kyōto, a sturdy militant monk who had waylaid him. This was Benkei, who thereafter figures in the legend as his inseparable companion and loyal henchman. These two, with Shidzuka, a dancing-girl who was the faithful mistress of Yoshitsune, are the heroic personages in many stage plays, and a number of the lyrical dramas (*nō*) depict incidents in their lives. But Yoshitsune's success only served to arouse the jealousy of his brother who, settled at Kamakura, was now prepared to sacrifice both friends and kinsmen to his ambitions, when he thought he could do it without danger. It was indeed on the plea that it was necessary to chastise this rebel that he later obtained special powers, which have been described above, from the court. Fresh from victory Yoshitsune came to Kamakura, but Yoritomo would not see him, though he lay for three weeks at a village not a mile away. At last he wrote this letter to his unrelenting brother: "Here am I, weeping crimson tears in vain at thy displeasure. . . . These many days I have lain here and could not gaze upon thy face. The bond of our blood-brotherhood is sundered. . . . But a short season after I was born, my honoured sire passed to another world. Clasped in my mother's bosom I was carried down to Yamato, and since that day I have not known a moment free from care or danger. Though it was but to drag out a useless life, we wandered round the capital, suffering hardship, hid in all manner of rustic spots, dwelt in remote and distant provinces whose rough inhabitants did treat us with contumely. But at last I was summoned to help in overthrowing the Taira house, and in this conflict I first laid Kiso Yoshinaka low. Then, so that I might demolish the Taira men, I spurred my horse on frowning precipices, careless of death in the face of the foe. I braved the dangers of wind and wave, not recking that my body might sink to the bottom of the sea, and be devoured by monsters of the deep. My pillow was my harness, arms my trade . . . "

At last he turned away from Kamakura and made his way to the capital. There he tried to assemble forces against his brother, from which we may judge that his loyalty had a breaking point. He failed, and as Yoritomo was hard on his track he hid himself in the hills. At last, accompanied by Shidzuka and Benkei, with a few men he set off northwards, the whole party disguised as mendicant friars collecting funds for the rebuilding of the Tōdaiji, the Nara

FIG. 35. *The encounter between Yoshitsune and Benkei on Gojō Bridge. From a theatrical poster.*

temple which, with its great bronze Buddha, had lately been destroyed in the civil war. Now Yoritomo's spies are searching for them, guards wait on all mountain passes to question travellers, and it is only by a ready stratagem that they pass the barrier of Ataka. The warden has marked the delicate features and the proud bearing of Yoshitsune, when Benkei, to avert suspicion, feigns anger with him, scolds him as a lazy coolie and belabours him with his staff. There is a breathless moment, but the warden cannot believe that a retainer would lay hands on the sacred person of his lord. Then "the barrier guards dismiss them and they, feeling as men who've trod scatheless upon a tiger's tail or escaped a serpent's poisoned fangs, shoulder their chests and cry Farewell, and down to Mutsu make their way." There they were given a place of refuge by the chieftain who had sheltered Yoshitsune in his boyhood; but soon afterwards the old man died and his son feared Yoritomo's power. So, in the following year (1189) he betrayed his father's guests, and Yoshitsune was attacked by a great force in his small stronghold. Rather than surrender he killed his wife and family and took his own life, which, full as it was, had lasted only thirty years.

It is difficult to tell how large were the armies which Yoshitsune and other feudal generals of his day commanded. Arithmetic has not usually been a strong point with oriental historians, and their systems of notation make for error. But chronicles which are in other respects reliable mention armies of fifty and a hundred thousand men, while in the final campaign of Yoritomo (1189) for the subjugation of the fighting Fujiwara who swayed northern Japan, three great forces converged upon Mutsu which, it is said, numbered at their junction over 280,000 men. Pitched battles on a grand scale seem, however, to have been uncommon, and the fighting to have consisted chiefly not of the impact of large masses of troops, but of collisions between small bands, sallies, skirmishes and a medley of hand-to-hand encounters, in which single combat played a spectacular if not a principal part.

NOTE TO CHAPTER XIV

[1] Page 292. The term *Bushido* comes into use in the seventeenth century with a specific connotation. Prior to that there were several terms used to denote the code of military honour in a general way.

Chapter XV

THE HŌJŌ REGENTS

YORITOMO died in the last year of the twelfth century. He was succeeded as titular head of the Kamakura government by his two
sons in turn, but neither was the man their father had been and
power passed into other hands than theirs. Their mother, Masa-ko,
was a lady of great strength of character, who as a girl had eloped
with Yoritomo in spirited fashion on the day set for her wedding
with another; and her later career was in harmony with this dash-
ing overture. She was the daughter of an influential chieftain of
Taira stock settled in eastern Japan, one Hōjō Tokimasa, who
must have been a person of great parts, for he discerned the
genius of Yoritomo at a very early stage and threw in his lot with
the Minamoto against his own clan. It was Tokimasa who stood
behind Yoritomo with counsel when the Kamakura government
was being formed, and it was he who, with the scholars from
Kyōto, worked out the details of its administration. After Yoritomo's death a council of regency was formed, over which he presided. But its members wrangled, so that before long, when Yoritomo's second son succeeded as Shōgun, Tokimasa became sole regent, and from that time for more than a hundred years the Hōjō
regents controlled the Shōguns just as the Fujiwara regents had
controlled the Emperors. We have thus, in Japan of the thirteenth
century, the astonishing spectacle of a state at the head of which
stands a titular emperor whose vestigial functions are usurped
by an abdicated emperor, and whose real power is nominally delegated to an hereditary military dictator but actually wielded by an
hereditary adviser of that dictator. By qualifying and elaborating
this statement it can be shown that the situation was not so irrational as it appears, but it was none the less remarkable. One
would suppose that such a system of multiple rule was too anoma-
lous to endure; and it did, in fact, break down in the long run because those who saw authority thus passing from deputy to deputy
began to feel that the process of delegation might profitably go
further, until it brought a share to them. But the regency was well
organised and in capable hands, and the first attacks upon it from
without merely evoked its strength, leaving the Kamakura govern-

ment more firmly seated than before. There were several attempts
to overthrow the Shogunate by disaffected feudal lords, sometimes
in concert with the court party at Kyōto, where there was always
an element ready to plot against Kamakura. In 1221 the ex-
emperor Toba II, who was a particularly able and accomplished
man, had by patient and skilful preparation got together a considerable following. He had some trained troops of his own. He had
also cleverly managed to enlist on his side the great monasteries of
the home provinces, and that was no trifling help, for the church
was rich and militant and the ecclesiastical troops were certainly
practised fighters, since they spent their whole lives in brawls and
raids. He sent out broadcast appeals for support in suppressing the
Hōjō regent, whom he proclaimed a rebel and an outlaw. He
came very near to success, but the Easterners were too prompt for
him. The regent mobilised a large force, marched from Kamakura, and in less than a month from his setting out was master of
the capital. The emperor, the ex-emperor, and several members of
their families, were banished to remote islands, while the princes,
court nobles and other leaders in the rising were either executed on
the spot or sent to exile or imprisonment. Most of these were put to
death on the way. The emperor's plot really turned to the profit of
the Kamakura government. It gave them a chance to clean out a
dangerous nest of disaffection and—what was even more urgent—
an excuse to seize great domains which had belonged to rich
Kyōto families. This increment of land was badly needed by the
military rulers, for the struggle between the clans had brought
into being a large class of warriors who were neither inclined nor
fitted to work their own farms. They were essentially unproductive
but they were extremely prolific; and in the generation which had
elapsed since 1185 their numbers had increased to such a point
that there was not enough land to go round among them. An
economic condition had been reached in which a large number of
the Shōgun's vassals were in such distress that they might well say
to themselves, "If we rebelled our situation could not be worse, and
it might be better." That is a dangerous position for any society,
and it was the more dangerous here in that most of the dissatisfied
class were men who took pleasure in their only trade of war. The
regent's advisers saw these perils clearly, and they liberally shared

out the confiscated manors among adherents whom they wished to placate or reward. Before the rising of 1221 the Kamakura government had refrained from placing their own stewards over manors belonging to the court in half the provinces, or at least from levying the military tax upon them. These manors are said to have numbered over 3,000, so that they provided a rich windfall for the hungry retainers of the Shōgun. The land was not wholly made over to them, but they were appointed stewards (*jitō*) and their emoluments were on a much more generous scale than heretofore. The new class of stewards received one acre of land out of every eleven acres which they administered, and were allowed to levy a tax on the remaining ten acres. The emperor approved of this scheme, of course under duress, in an edict of 1223. From that time, although the Kamakura government treated liberally the sovereign and certain noble houses, the total wealth and strength of the court nobility and even of the imperial house were seriously reduced, and the military rulers now had, in parts of Japan which had been under the influence of Kyōto, vassals unlikely to be disloyal to masters who had installed them in such lucrative posts. An anecdote in one of the earliest historical accounts of the rising of 1221 throws an interesting light on the value of a stewardship. The cloistered emperor (Toba II) on a pilgrimage to the Kumano shrine fell in with a samurai named Nishina, travelling with his two sons of 14 and 15. His Majesty was attracted by the good looks of these boys, and took them into his service. The father, out of gratitude, also went to court, and when this came to the ears of the Shogunate they confiscated two manors which he possessed, since it was an offence for one of their vassals to have dealings with the court without their permission. Meanwhile a favourite of the cloistered emperor, a dancing girl named Kamegiku, to whom he had given two manors in Settsu, complained that the steward appointed by Kamakura was cheating her. His Majesty therefore sent a message ordering the regent at once to restore his manors to Nishina and to dismiss the offending steward. The regent, as was usual when it was desired to make an emphatic communication to the court, appeared in Kyōto with a thousand horsemen and stated in reply that a former emperor had made Yoritomo Steward-General of all Japan, that Yoritomo had given stewardships to men who had helped him to crush the enemies of the throne, and that these posts, being rewards of merit, could not be taken from their holders. This story, while illustrating the opportunities of a steward, shows how well the Minamoto looked after their vassals.

FIG. 36. *Kyōto ladies in outdoor dress. After a Kamakura period scroll representing the life of Hōnen Shonin.*

Its writer goes on to relate that the emperor was so infuriated by the regent's reply that he thenceforward began to plot the overthrow of the Shogunate. His Majesty might have succeeded had the men around him been as capable and, we might add, as honest as those who were now running the machine at Kamakura. But

the life at Kyōto was not of a kind to bring good organising men to
the top, whereas the leaders in Eastern Japan had been trained
in a hard school which encouraged practical wisdom, and for such
book learning as they needed they could rely upon scholars drawn
from the capital itself. The Shōguns themselves were now of less
importance at Kamakura than were the emperors at Kyōto. When
the Minamoto succession failed, a Fujiwara baby was brought from
the capital and invested with the rank of Shōgun. From that time
(1226) for over a hundred years the office of Shōgun was held by
puppets; so that the supreme command of all military forces in the
empire and the leadership of the Minamoto clan was nominally
exercised by an aristocrat who was neither a soldier nor a Minamoto, but a Fujiwara or, later, an imperial prince. The anomaly
did not end here, for the actual power of the Shogunate was
wielded by successive regents of the Hōjō family, and they were of
Taira and not of Minamoto stock; but it should be remembered
that this situation was not to Japanese eyes so strange as it appears
to ours, for by their custom adoption creates a family bond differing
in kind but not in strength from the tie of kinship.

Though usurpers in theory, the Hōjō regents were in practice,
by the standards of their time, extremely competent administrators. The first of them, Tokimasa, was forced to resign by his
daughter, the strong-minded Masa-ko, and his son Yoshitoki, who
succeeded him as regent, a post which was held by nine members
of the family in succession, down to 1333. It will be enough if we
describe their rule in general terms, without reference to individuals, but it is worth mentioning that this family seems to have
been gifted with a dominant and transmissible strain of ability, of
which Masa-ko inherited her full share. On the death of her second
son she entered religion, but this did not prevent her from taking a
hand in public affairs, and she was known from that time as the
Ama Shōgun or Nun General. She died in 1225 at the age of over
seventy after a very active life. Hers was a supreme example of a
woman's rise to eminence, but it was by no means without parallel
in early feudal Japan. At that time, both in the elegant circles of
the capital and the sterner military society, feminine influence was
strong and there is nothing to show that the position of women was
definitely subordinate, as it later became.

PORTRAIT OF YORITOMO (detail)

PART OF THE HELL SCROLL

The chief title to praise of the Hōjō regents was their earnest and on the whole honest administration of justice, in the tradition of Yoritomo. In 1232 the Council of State at Kamakura adopted a code of law known, from the name of the era in which it was compiled, as the *Jōei Shikimoku* or Formulary of Jōei. This was the work of the regent Yasutoki and the scholar Miyoshi. It was not, like the code of Taihō, a systematic body of laws, nor was it based upon any comprehensive jurisprudence. It was rather a collection of maxims and rules brought together for the guidance of judges and administrators, which embodied the results of half a century's experience of the working of the feudal system. In this respect it was typical of Kamakura methods, being practical, direct, based upon actual conditions and unfettered by theory. Yasutoki, writing to his Kyōto officers, said of this formulary, "It does not follow closely any particular original . . . but has been drawn up as just principles demand." It did, in point of fact, owe something to previous codes, but it covered rather different ground, for its chief intention was to regulate the affairs and the conduct of the military class. It contains brief statements of the leading features of their ethical code, such as loyalty and filial piety, and is as much a handbook of morals as a legal compendium. No attempt was made to apply it outside feudal domains. The landed proprietors who were not Kamakura vassals, the civilian officials and the great monasteries were still subject to the Taihō code in so far as it was operative, and to the laws, edicts and ordinances which had grown up like a jungle over it; or else they exercised in their own domains their own customaries. But, since the Taihō code was based upon conditions which had long ago vanished, the feudal code was much more suitable to their needs, and it was therefore gradually extended to a number of private and public domains, not at the instance of the Bakufu, but because of its practical advantages. Before long, then, a law which was in substance and in essence the house law of the Minamoto family became the common law of Japan, in particular as to questions of land tenure and rights arising therefrom—questions which, in an agricultural economy, are fundamental. That the Jōei Formulary should have exercised such a widespread influence in later days is remarkable in view of its modest beginnings. Yasutoki, when circulating it to his vassals, wrote: "I am afraid that people at the Capital will laugh at such ordinances, put together by ignorant barbarians."

This code, with its subsequent amendments, tended naturally to favour the interests of feudal magnates rather than minor tenants and officers. But those who compiled it and, what was more important, those who administered it, saw that a harsh law impartially applied would give them better results than a gentle one that could be abused and evaded. The peasants, though heavily taxed, knew at least that they would be protected against unauthorised extortions, and they were allowed to sell their holdings and migrate, if they desired. These were rights which had previously been denied to them, and which they later lost, under a less enlightened régime. It cannot be said that their position was a happy one, for slavery was not yet abolished, either as an institution or an actual condition. But the Kamakura rulers have it to their credit that they perceived in the cultivator the basis of the country's economy, and saw the importance of justice in their dealings with him as with others higher in the scale. Much might be written on this subject, but here we can only point out that in mediæval Japan the idea of justice does not appear to have developed as an abstract conception, compounded of the right of a litigant and the duty of a judge. It was rather looked upon as something expedient but not incumbent, something granted by the ruler as a favour. This view colours all subsequent feudal administration, to such a degree that later we find codes of law which, far from being widely promulgated, are in part guarded as official secrets.

In addition to perfecting its judicial methods, the Kamakura government paid careful attention to local administration, so as to enforce in its own domains policies which it had centrally decided. The constables and stewards were strictly supervised by inspecting officials, and any irregularity discovered was severely punished. A keen watch was kept on boundaries, water rights and harvests, and a sincere effort made to adjust taxation to the varying yield. This was a most important consideration, in particular because the rice crop sharply fluctuates according to rainfall and sunshine. For that reason rice culture has always been the weakness as well as the strength of the agricultural economy of Japan. Rice is the staple foodstuff and rice is the standard crop, other grains being grown in relatively small quantities. Since, until recent times, no such foodstuffs as meat, milk and eggs were available in sufficient bulk to supplement rice when the harvest failed, famines have been frequent. This danger was perceived as far back as the Nara period, when on more than one occasion the authorities tried to make the peasants grow as a reserve grains which would withstand conditions unfavourable to rice. But they did not succeed, because they could not enforce their edicts; and the Japanese peasants have for many centuries continued to prefer wet-field rice culture, which in normal seasons yields a richer crop and a more welcome diet. Under such conditions, where fields are small and dyked and carefully irrigated, questions of boundaries and water supply are of vital importance to the cultivators, and can arouse their deepest passions. The military caste, therefore, displayed a wisdom unusual in those times when they made it their policy to protect the peasants against private oppression. In this respect they compare most favourably with earlier rulers, who were professedly patriarchal and benign, and with later feudal autocrats, who aimed at strict efficiency.

Another strong feature of the Kamakura régime was its simplicity and even its austerity. A refined but effeminate luxury, social rivalries, the drain of expenditure on dwellings, costumes and feasts, had ruined one proud Kyōto family after another; and it was partly for this reason that Yoritomo and his successors kept at a distance from the cultural metropolis and strictly controlled their vassals in matters of court rank and office. There was a glamour about the polished society of the capital which attracted the simple soldiers whom the patricians despised as "Eastern Barbarians." Yoritomo doubtless knew his own people and feared the results of that deep respect for titles, that hierarchical sentiment which the Japanese seem to share with the English. Certainly it was when the simple life of Kamakura was invaded by the insidious social standards of Kyōto that the strength of the Regency began to wane. For a generation or so it kept its early freedom from taint, and continued inelegant but earnest and industrious.

Although there were frequent changes in the detail of its organisation, this was due not to vacillation but to constancy in a desire to find the right solution of problems as they arose. It was

FIG. 37. *Attendant (probably a Falconer) of a Kyōto noble. (From a scroll of about 1270.)*

characteristic of the Kamakura leaders that they followed no
theory, but used the method of trial and error. They would develop one organ and allow another to decline, but their guiding
principle was continuous and they aimed always at corporate
success rather than private achievement. Thus the Council of
State, presided over by the regent, preserved solidarity in a remarkable degree. Its deliberations on important questions were
secret, and its decrees were announced as unanimous. Responsibility was collective and this had two advantages.* It discouraged
factions and intrigue within and without the chamber, and it prevented individual members from claiming personal credit while
sheltering them against the ill-will of parties aggrieved by the
council's decisions. The councillors, in short, could safely act
without fear or favour. This interesting experiment in government
by committee might have given valuable results had it not broken
down from external causes. The puppet Shōguns who followed
Yoritomo's sons were not allowed to exercise administrative
power, but they kept great state and they had a numerous retinue of Kyōto nobles with metropolitan tastes and manners.
Presently there grew up a court society, encouraging ideas and
pastimes not consonant with the preservation of those severe
military virtues on which the success of the regency depended.
It seems that an austere and frugal society, such as moralists
admire, always harbours the germ of its own decay. The very fact
that its manners and behaviour are rigidly prescribed means that
it is imperilled by change. But an unchanging culture is not a
living culture; and change is of itself attractive and desirable. To
most men, after all, the satisfactions of food, dress, pictures, poetry,
and even social rivalry are, we have to admit, more agreeable than
unrelieved hard discipline and plain living. So it was found by
many provincial warriors under the stern rule of Kamakura. The
regent Tokiyori himself was celebrated for his simple habits. A
story current in his lifetime relates how, to entertain a guest one

---

* This is true also of the ecclesiastical law of the period. The abbot of a monastery could not decide policy or settle cases of his own authority. He must
submit all but routine matters to the judgment of all the monks in council. It is
therefore perhaps significant that a monk, named Enzen, took part in framing
the Jōei formulary.

night, he could find nothing in his bare cupboard but some sauce at the bottom of a bowl and a little wine. There were many such tales, in which high personages figured as patterns of thrift. But for them life was filled by the exercise of power, while the ordinary warrior had nothing to occupy him, now that he was denied the excitement of fighting. So the younger men sought posts in the Shōgun's household, and were inclined to neglect military exercises for politer accomplishments, such as music, dancing and versification. Academic historians, both Japanese and European, are given to deploring this lapse from simple standards, but the movement was not entirely retrograde. The culture of the feudal society was narrow and it was well that it should be enlarged by the interest in art and letters, and even by the social graces, which the Kyōto nobles fostered.

The standard of living continued to rise among the eastern gentry, while the Kamakura rulers did their best to stem what seemed to them a rising tide of luxury, by sumptuary legislation of various kinds. This is a phenomenon which occurs at frequent intervals throughout Japanese history. A given group or class ascend to power, and their demand for commodities rises, as indeed do their own numbers, since their economic situation is favourable to increase. But, while their consumption grows, production remains stationary or makes no proportionate advance, because it is limited by a factor which is nearly constant—the amount of available rice-land. A point is therefore reached when the rulers endeavour to reduce consumption by artificial means, but these are ineffective. Then follows a struggle among consumers, which in feudal times takes the form of a civil war and a redistribution of power. In the second half of the thirteenth century this was the course that events were following, but it was interrupted by troubles which had been long brewing within and without the borders of Japan. Internal conditions were bad, despite the merits of the Hōjō administration. There had been a destructive earthquake in the Kamakura district in 1257. In 1259 there was a severe famine and a plague of sickness so deadly that, it is said, the streets of Kyōto were choked with dead and dying, while in the country the stewards were ordered to remit taxes and to give relief to the sufferers, who were living on grass and roots. In the following year the pestilence still raged, and the Bakufu, at a loss for practical measures, ordered the constables to have prayers and sutras recited in the shrines and temples of all provinces. The shortage of able-bodied men seems to have been so serious that they even released criminals under sentence for murder. In the capital itself, to make matters worse, fierce quarrels broke out between great monasteries and the militant monks intimidated the whole populace, from the emperor downwards. Not that this was a new or a rare thing, for the Enryakuji monastery had threatened the court with violence as early as 969, and during the thirteenth century its armed forces descended upon the city more than twenty times. There had been very serious affrays in 1235 and 1236, and again in 1256, 1257 and 1264. The Kamakura rulers usually kept aloof, but at times they were bound to intervene. In 1259, for instance, when a dispute between the monks and the emperor threatened to become serious, several hundred Bakufu warriors entered the capital. There was danger of a clash till the monks thought better of it, retired and shut themselves within their gates. But the Bakufu soldiers had to keep a very strict guard against sorties and incendiarism. One may judge, therefore, how near to anarchy was the situation at the capital, and in the home provinces where the great temples stood. At this time, we learn, lampoons were scribbled on the palace wall, such as "At the new year, ill omens," "In the land, disasters," "In the capital, soldiers," "In government, unfairness," "In the palace, favouritism," "In the provinces, famine," "In the river bed, skeletons," "In the shrines, conflagrations," and so on.

If we turn from domestic affairs to foreign intercourse at this period, we find a set of unstable and dangerous conditions. Since the time of Sugawara Michizane (894) there had been no official exchange of missions between the courts of Japan and China, though, as China remained the fountain of culture, merchant vessels still carried Japanese monks and students to Chinese seats of learning. The Chinese were at this time well ahead of the Japanese in matters of shipbuilding and navigation, and the traffic between the two countries seems to have been largely in the hands of Chinese ship-owners. But Japanese vessels did cross the sea, though not always as peaceful merchantmen. We hear, for instance, of a protest against their depredations on the Korean coast, made in 1263 by the king of Kōrai (or Kōryö: a state which, from the fall of the T'ang dynasty, comprised the whole of the peninsula now called, after it, Korea). He complained that, whereas it had been

FIG. 38. *Serving-man (Hakuchō) of a Kyōto noble.*
(After a scroll of the Kamakura period.)

agreed between the two countries that only two Japanese ships should visit Korea each year, more than this number had come and they had plundered towns and villages on the coast. It is interesting to notice that, though the Japanese were extremely touchy in their relations with foreign courts and easily took offence at language which they thought disrespectful, the Kamakura government recognised that their own people were at fault. The raids were private excursions of their vassals in western Japan, who were rebuked and told to make restitution of their plunder, consisting chiefly of grain and hides. This sort of thing had been going on intermittently for a century or more and there had always been some danger of a war between Japan and Kōrai. It had been averted chiefly because the Bakufu was too deeply concerned with domestic problems, and too financially embarrassed, to risk an overseas campaign. And now there was another very good reason on the Japanese side against quarrelling with Korea, for by 1263 Khubilai, the great Khan of the Mongols, had become emperor of all China, and suzerain of many bordering states. These "circumjacent kingdoms," as Gibbon describes them, "were reduced in different degrees of tribute and obedience by the effort or terror of his arms." Korea became a docile vassal of the Mongols, and her king was given one of Khubilai's daughters to wife. Then, to continue in the words of Gibbon, "the boundless ambition of Khubilai aspired to the conquest of Japan; his fleets were twice shipwrecked; and the lives of 100,000 Mongols and Chinese were sacrificed in the fruitless expedition." The story of these invasions, though in part obscure, is full of interest and excitement, but we must content ourselves here with the briefest summary of events. In 1268 Khubilai sent an envoy to Japan, carrying a letter from "the Emperor of Great Mongolia" to the "King of Japan." The letter was handed to the Bakufu representative at Dazaifu in Kyūshū, and thence forwarded post-haste to Kamakura. It suggested that Japan should open friendly intercourse with China, and ended by pointing out that, where relations were not harmonious, war was bound to ensue. This threat was followed by other menacing despatches in five succeeding years. Kyōto was frightened, but Kamakura, though aware of the peril, refused to answer Khubilai's envoys, and sent them back to their master. Finally, in November, 1274, after more than a year's preparation, a Mongol army sailed from Korea, in Korean ships manned by Korean sailors. Japanese authorities differ as to the size of this fleet and the number of men it carried, but a probable figure is

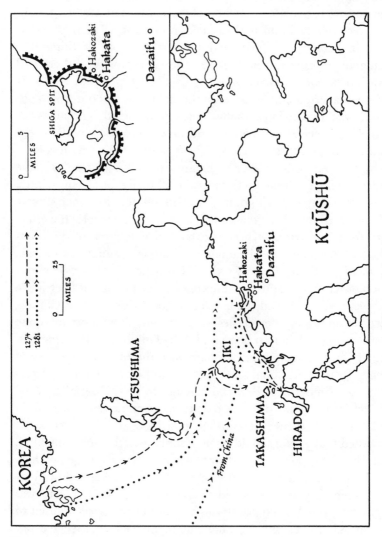

FIG. 39. *Routes of the Mongol attacks.*

450 ships and 15,000 Mongol troops, besides 15,000 Korean seamen and auxiliaries. They captured without difficulty the islands of Tsushima and Iki, which the small Japanese garrisons defended with great bravery to the last man. The inhabitants were treated with revolting cruelty. The ships then sailed over to Kyūshū, and troops were landed at points on the shores of Hakozaki Bay. The Japanese at first made the mistake of despising their enemy. They thought very little of the Koreans, usually an easy prey to their keen blades; but the Mongols were fierce and skilled in warfare, their leaders had long experience of handling large bodies of men, and they were equipped not only with powerful bows that shot a deadly bolt at 240 yards, but with machines flinging heavy missiles.* The Japanese, on the other hand, were at a disadvantage, for they were used to fighting in loose formation, or no formation at all. They were, moreover, taken aback by the Chinese firearms, which seem to have consisted of some device for discharging a combustible projectile. Yet in sheer courage they were a match for any troops in the world, and when they got to close quarters it wanted the deftest adversary to withstand their terrible swords. Those who first met the Mongols were the local chieftains, owners or stewards of estates in Kyūshū. They knew that large armies were on their way, from Kamakura and western Japan, every man that could be mustered. Yet they had not waited. They had attacked at once. They suffered heavy losses, but they fought on until dusk, and withdrew behind their earthworks to await the reinforcements. These were not needed, for before dark the invaders decided to get back to their ships. They may have intended to attack again next day, but a tempest was brewing, and they had suffered severe losses, so that they felt safer on board. That night a great storm burst, and by dawn the whole fleet had been driven or was running for safety out to sea. In this flight they lost many of their ships, and when they got back to Korea they found that the expedition had cost them over 13,500 men. Meanwhile the Kamakura government had issued to the constables of all the western circuits orders to collect troops against the invaders. Their

---

* These were perhaps the machines which Marco Polo mentions as having been made by his father and uncle.

despatch to the hereditary constable of Bungo in central Kyūshū was in the following terms :

> To the Lord Ōtomo Hyōgo no Kami Nyūdō.
>
> The Mongols have attacked Iki and Tsushima and a battle will ensue. Therefore an army will be sent. Further, you are to proclaim to all landholders of the Nine Provinces, even if they are not house-men of the Shōgun, that such as do good war service will be rewarded in accordance with merit. 11 Bunyei 11th month, 1st day [November 30th 1274].
>
> As above, by order [of the Shōgun].
>
> (Seal) The Lord of Musashi [i.e. Hōjō Yoshimasa].
> (Seal) The Lord of Sagami [i.e. Hōjō Tokimune].

Even before this despatch was written the Mongols were retreating across the straits to Korea; but the Bakufu knew enough of Khubilai's ambitions to guess that he would make another attempt. Sure enough, a few months later he sent envoys summoning the Japanese ruler to do him homage at his new court at Peking. Nothing could have been more infuriating to the Japanese than such insolent language, and six unlucky members of this embassy, who had been escorted up to Kamakura without touching at the capital, had their heads cut off and exposed in public as a gesture of defiance. It even seems, though it is not quite certain, that the Bakufu contemplated at one time an expedition overseas "to punish the foreign pirates." They instructed their officers in the coastal provinces of western Japan to get together steersmen and sailors in preparation for an attack on "a foreign country" in the following spring (1276), and to be ready to despatch them to Hakata when word was given. Probably their plan was to forestall an invasion by raids on Korean harbours, as soon as they should learn of the formation of a fleet by the King of Kōrai, for they knew that Khubilai would depend upon him for transport. Japanese ships did, in fact, according to Kōrai records, attack their coasts in 1280 and they may have done so in 1276, but this we cannot tell. Meanwhile the Bakufu pressed on defensive measures. They ordered the Kyūshū landholders to construct a stone rampart on the shores of the bay of Hakozaki. The work was to be completed in six months, each chieftain undertaking one inch of wall for every *tan* (say $\frac{1}{3}$ acre) of his holding. It actually

took five years. During this period Khubilai had been busy round-
ing off his overthrow of the Sung dynasty by a campaign in
southern China. It was not until 1280 that he could again turn
his attention to Japan. He sent one more mission, inviting or
rather commanding Japan to enter into relations with the Mongol
empire, in other words to submit to him as a vassal state. The
Bakufu cut off his envoys' heads, and pressed on their preparations. They were pretty well informed of affairs on the continent,
for merchant ships continued to ply between Japan and China,
and priests went to and fro on learned errands; and for that
matter Khubilai had made his intentions quite clear, for his last
despatch had been an ultimatum.

The feudal vassals responded on the whole with alacrity to the
call of the Bakufu. Many stewards and other "house-men" had
before this on their own account come forward with offers. It is
related of one of them that he was so chagrined at having missed
the first attack that he swore an oath to cross over and seek the
Mongols himself if they did not come again within ten years.
Others made more sober but not less earnest proposals, in written
oaths to their overlords. In 1276 the great Kyūshū chieftains
(Shōni, Ōtomo and Shimadzu) had been ordered to obtain from
their adherents lists of the men and materials they could supply.
Some of these documents are extant, and extracts from them will
suggest the atmosphere of the times better than a laboured
catalogue of events. Thus:—

"Izeri Yajirō Fujiwara Hideshige, a vassal, of the province of Higo, in
holy orders (religious name SAIKŌ), respectfully states as follows:
Land, men, horses, bows and arrows and arms.

Item. Rice lands.   (Here follows a detailed inventory of land in
specified *shōen* showing his rights and obligations,
which leave him a balance of about 40 acres
unencumbered.)

Item. Men, bows and   Saikō, aged 85, cannot walk. Nagahide, his son,
arrows, weapons   aged 65. Has bow and arrows and weapons.
and horses.   Tsunehide, his son, aged 38. Has bow and arrows,
weapons, corselet, 1 horse.
Matsujirō, kinsman, aged 19. Has bow and arrows,
arms, and 2 followers.
Takahide, grandson, aged 40. Has bow and
arrows, weapons, corselet, 1 horse and 1 follower.

FIG. 40. *The Mongol Invasions, 1274-1281. Mongol soldiers behind a wall of shields. (After a contemporary Japanese scroll.)*

These are at His Lordship's orders and will serve faithfully. Humbly presented as above.

    April, 1276.   The Shami [i.e. *śramanera*].
                        SAIKŌ. (Seal.) "

This gives a picture of the household of a middle class warrior now retired from active life and subsisting with his family, of three generations, upon the income from some forty acres of rice land. An even more modest household is revealed in this next example:

"The written command of the 25th day of the third month (1276) arrived yesterday and has been reverently perused.

The order calls for a list of men, horses, weapons, etc., for an expedition to punish a foreign country. These are as follows:

My son Saburō Mitsushige and my son-in-law Kubojirō will hasten to present themselves, joining night on to day. They await commands. Fearfully and respectfully stated.

              The Nun Shina, Steward of Kitayama Mura."

This document (which, incidentally, illustrates the tenure of a stewardship by a woman) has a slightly romantic tinge, leading one to suspect its authenticity; but there is no doubt that in the years just following the first Mongol invasion a brave spirit was abroad, especially among the men of Kyūshū, who bore the brunt of these attacks and have in general throughout Japanese history been distinguished for their martial virtues and their Spartan way of life. Not all the Bakufu vassals, however, displayed such patriotic zeal, and it must be admitted that, even among those who fought the hardest, there were some who displayed an unseemly eagerness for reward. When the Bakufu came to examine the record of the first invasion they discovered that a number of important warriors had proceeded to the front, but had not joined in the fighting, while some had stayed at home on the plea that they were defending their own districts. Great difficulty was found in dealing out just rewards and rebukes, and the delay so exasperated certain of the more independent vassals that they set off to Kamakura to press their claims in person. Japanese historians often assert that the Mongol invasions, by causing a feeling of national peril, created a sense of national unity. In a general way this is perhaps true, but it is doubtful whether the idea of nationality, in its modern meaning, was one that had occurred to the mind of a people who lived on an island and had no political relations with neighbouring states.

However, the military class within their lights showed a proper spirit and when danger was close at hand they threw themselves into the struggle with ardent courage. They did not lose sight of their own interests, but their behaviour compared well with the reckless egotism of other elements in the population. The priesthood, we have already seen, was turbulent almost beyond belief, and throughout the decade when the Mongol menace was most grave the great monasteries quarrelled and fought almost incessantly. Scarcely had the news of the Mongol defeat reached Kyōto in November, 1274, when the Kōfukuji monastery of Nara, intervening in a land dispute between two Shintō shrines, sent an armed force to demonstrate in the capital. They remained for more than a month, and so terrorised the court that the emperor dare not appear in public and the usual New Year festivals and ceremonies were suspended. These Nara priests were at last bought off, but no sooner were they pacified than other disturbances arose. There was a fierce dispute between the Enryakuji of Hieizan and the court about the succession to the leadership of the Tendai sect in 1276, in which the Bakufu had to intervene, after it had dragged on for two years. In 1278 the Enryakuji, on the plea that another monastery was stealing its prerogatives, began a riot in Kyōto, which was at last quelled by Bakufu soldiers. In 1279 there was a breach between the Shintō priests of Iwashimidzu and those of Hiyoshi. If the ecclesiastics were unruly, the laymen were not impeccable, though their disputes often took a less violent form. There was a line of Fujiwara whose members had all been celebrated, each in his generation, as great poets. Sadaie took part in compiling a new anthology of Ancient and Modern Verse. His son Tameie was also a great poet in his day, and he had four sons who all were poets. One of them, Tameuji, was appointed by the emperor to make a collection of verse, which was completed in 1279. He appropriated to his own use the stewardship of a certain manor which belonged to his youngest step-brother, then a minor. This boy's mother was a poetess herself. She much resented Tameuji's arrogant behaviour, in regard to poetry as well as to property, and she made a journey to Kamakura, to put her case before the courts there. Her journey is described in a short travel diary (*Izayoi Nikki*) containing a

number of short poems, which has come down to us. The suit
dragged on until 1313, when a final decision was given in favour
of Tameuji's son, both the principals having meanwhile died at
Kamakura. So serious a matter was poetry in the life of Kyōto
that the enmity which this dispute engendered infected the world
of letters and from it there arose two rival schools of verse makers,
in bitter opposition.

By the end of 1280 the Bakufu learned that the Mongols would
attack in the spring of the following year. The regent (Tokimune)
issued through his constables a proclamation calling upon his
vassals to prepare to resist the invaders. He promised rewards to
those who should acquit themselves well, and threatened severe
and lasting punishment for disloyal conduct. One passage in this
document is of particular interest. It says :

> "It has come to our knowledge that many constables and
> vassals, either through disputes arising out of their functions
> or through dissatisfaction with verdicts of the courts, have of
> late years been at odds. To harbour private grievances in
> disregard of the national peril is highly treasonable conduct.
> Let all warriors, from the (Shōgun's) house-men downwards,
> obey the orders of the constables."

Similar orders were issued by the emperor, at the instance of
the regent, to those land-holders who were not vassals of the
Bakufu, including the officers of the manors belonging to the great
temples. The revenue due to the crown from estates in a number of
western provinces was placed at the disposal of the armies. The
court had at last realised how grave was the danger. They did not
stop at these material contributions to the forthcoming campaign.
The emperor took the lead in invoking the aid of all the unseen
powers. He ordered prayers to be said and religious exercises to
be performed at temples and shrines throughout the country.
Services were continued day and night. All the princes and nobles
kept prayerful vigil. In the monasteries of the great sects the chief
abbots and the monks intoned continuously their most revered
sutras and recited the incantations called *darani*, while the shrines
of Hachiman, the War God, were thronged with worshippers of
all conditions and all beliefs. The emperor sent letters in his own
hand to the tombs of his great ancestors. The abdicated emperor

did the same, and also made a vow that 300,000 scrolls of a certain sutra should be read.* A thousand scrolls each were distributed to nobles and courtiers in his suite, and these were shared out among their relatives and friends, who undertook to recite them. Special messengers were sent to the Ise shrines and to the homes of other great Shintō deities, and Imperial Progresses were made to holy places to plead for victory. The regent Tokimune, though busy with warlike preparations, did not neglect his devotions, and he is said to have copied out sacred writings in his own blood.

The blow fell in June, 1281. Two formidable hosts sailed for Japan, one of about 50,000 Mongols and Koreans from Korea and one of about 100,000 Chinese from southern China. The Korean fleet landed troops in Kyūshū on June 23rd. The southern fleet arrived later in separate divisions, one after another. They put strong forces ashore at points near Hakata Bay. We do not know exactly what course the fighting took, but we do know that the wall proved an effective defence, that on shore the Japanese fought bravely and on the water with their small craft played havoc with the less handy Mongol ships. Whether they could have achieved a final victory unaided we cannot tell. Probably they could, for given time they could outnumber the Mongols, and they could certainly outfight the unwilling Chinese. The struggle seems to have lasted, from the time of the first landing, for more than fifty days. Then a great storm arose and blew for two days. It was of such a force that it uprooted large trees. A great number of the enemy's vessels were driven in confusion by wind and tide into the narrows. Here many were jammed and wrecked, their crews becoming an easy prey to the Japanese. One record says that of 4,000 ships only 200 escaped, and of the invading army of 150,000 not one-fifth survived. This is probably an exaggeration, but there is little doubt that the army from Korea, consisting largely of Mongols, lost nearly half its men, and that the losses of the southern fleet were even heavier.

A recital of events following immediately upon the defeat of the Mongols brings out strikingly the characters of the three main divisions of the people, namely the Kyōto aristocracy, the warriors

*The *Prajñāpāramitā-hridaya* sutra.

and the priesthood, for here we may exclude the peasants, who though numerically the strongest merely did what they were told. The Bakufu sent instructions to all Kyūshū vassals that they must

FIG. 41. *The Mongol Invasions, 1274-1281. A Mongol Bowman.*
(*After a contemporary Japanese scroll.*)

repair defensive works and continue with unrelaxed precaution on a war footing. They were not to leave their districts. The menace of a further invasion lasted for twenty years, and it was not until 1300, after the death of Khubilai, that the Mongols appeared to have given up the idea of subduing Japan. This constant anxiety was a grave embarrassment to the Bakufu, faced as it was with many difficult problems in dealing not only with the intriguing court and the militant church but also with its own hungry vassals. The priests who had, during the hostilities, ceased their quarrels and devoted themselves to prayers for victory, soon broke out again in tumult. They fought over questions of landed property, and they threatened the persons of members of the imperial family in their endeavours to gain advantages in wealth or influence. The court party was torn between fear of their violence and hope for their success in harassing the military party. The church, moreover, was in high esteem just after the defeat of the Mongols, for all classes, not excluding the soldiers themselves, attributed the astonishing success of the Japanese arms to divine succour, granted, as they believed, in response to the prayers of the clergy. The priests were quick to take advantage of this sentiment, and urged that they had a better right to rewards than the mere fighting men.

The military rulers after 1281 were in a position of unstable equilibrium. On the one hand their finances were weakened by the drain of war, on the other hand they had increasing claims upon them. The Kamakura government, in the century that had passed since its establishment, had survived one crisis after another because after a civil war it had always been able to reward its supporters with property wrested from its enemies. But the Mongol war, far from bringing an increment of wealth, had impoverished the whole country. There had been considerable destruction of life and property in Kyūshū, and great expenditure on the maintenance of troops. Even more serious was the fall in production, for, in the words of a contemporary memorial, "During the last few years, owing to the Mongol attacks, in both east and west, while warlike arts have not been neglected, agriculture has been practically abandoned by the peasants and the land holders." Out of these diminished resources the Bakufu was called upon to satisfy the demands of vassals who considered themselves entitled to payment for their war services or to compensation for their disbursements. The almost inevitable result was that the Kamakura government antagonised more people than they pleased, for whatever they gave to one they had to take from another, and neither was content. They could not, like the early Minamoto overlords, rely upon clan loyalty, for the Hōjō regents were not members of the Minamoto family, and though they were nominal deputies of the Shōgun, in the feudal hierarchy they stood no higher than other great vassals. They made efforts to shelve the question of rewards, or to shift the burden and the odium of decision to high provincial officers, but they only succeeded in rousing widespread dissatisfaction. They incurred the opposition or the positive enmity of many influential barons, and they undermined the loyalty of smaller warriors who had suffered in the war. The following extract from a petition dated 1296, that is, fifteen years after the invasion, will show what feeling prevailed.

"Respectfully stated by Kuroo Fujiwara Sukekado, Houseman, of the province of Hizen.

During the Mongol attack, I, the above-named, at Chigasaki, boarded an enemy vessel and, though wounded, took one prisoner. Later, in the attack on Takashima I took two prisoners. These facts were duly reported to the court of inquiry and witnesses were examined. Yet, though a reward was recommended, I have been left out of the general recognition of merit, and my grief is extreme. What is the reason of this? Mere bystanders have put in claims and been rewarded. The fact that I was wounded was proved to the authorities, why therefore am I omitted from the rewards? I have been told that all the men in defence posts and on watch duty have already been recompensed. Why should I, who was wounded, have to wait empty for months and years and get nothing for my loyal service? . . ."

From all sides difficulties pressed upon the Hōjō regents. Their collapse was near. The Kamakura machine, thanks to the virtues of its designers, ran by its own momentum for another twenty-five years or so, but its doom was already fixed by the time of the Mongol invasion. Kyōto nobles began to plot against Kamakura, and they found allies among disaffected feudal magnates. The regency, by the end of the thirteenth century, had lost nearly all the qualities which had hitherto preserved it. The old frugal simplicity

FIG. 42. *Part of the Daijōe or Accession Ceremonies. The Emperor in procession.*

had vanished, and the integrity was no more. The Kamakura law courts no longer administered prompt and practical justice, but were vacillating and corrupt. No doubt this change was due in part to an unhealthy influence from Kyōto, but its true and ultimate causes are to be found in the economic weakness of the military dictators. They had not enough wealth to meet the demands of their vassals and in efforts to stave them off were driven to desperate expedients. Among such devices was the fatal practice in the courts of postponing settlement of claims which they knew they could not satisfy or of giving inconclusive judgments in disputes submitted to them. These were blunders which merely drove the contending parties to use force or fraud, and so brought about a cumulative laxity of feudal discipline. Perhaps the best illustration of the helplessness of the Bakufu in the face of inevitable economic pressure is the legislation which they introduced at this time. Many vassals had got into financial difficulties, either through expenditure on war service against the Mongols or simply through keeping up with the rising standard of living. They had sold or mortgaged their estates and could not pay their dues to the Bakufu. The Bakufu therefore promulgated an Act of Grace, which not only forbade the sale or mortgage of vassals' estates but also declined to take cognisance of suits for the recovery of principal or interest arising out of past transactions of that nature. The result of course was to antagonise the creditor class, which of its nature included wealthy feudal landowners, and to worsen the situation of the debtors, because such a law was quite easy to evade.* This and other legislation of the period was revoked almost as soon as it was enacted, but that very fact is eloquent, and absolves us from further description of the hopeless situation in which the Hōjō regents found themselves.

Meanwhile at Kyōto the practice of abdication had reached such a point that there were in the year 1300 five ex-emperors living, all of whom exercised in greater or less degree authority which belonged to the reigning emperor, and hoped to see him succeeded by members of their respective families. It may be imagined what

---

* This law was styled *Tokusei*, or "Virtuous Administration." Deeds of sale or mortgage of this and later periods often contain a "*Tokusei* clause" providing that their validity shall not be affected by any such enactment.

rivalries centred round the throne, what factions arose. By 1330 the disputes had been narrowed down to a conflict between two lines, a junior and a senior. The emperor Daigo II, of the junior line, desired to overthrow the Bakufu, which supported the candidate of the senior line. He succeeded by 1333 in finding armed support not only in central and western Japan but also in the north and east, and even among direct Kamakura vassals. By the summer of 1333 Kamakura had been captured and destroyed by fire, the regent Takotoki and more than two hundred of his kinsmen and loyal retainers had killed themselves rather than surrender. The regency was now at an end, and Kyōto became once more the seat of government. The emperor Daigo II occupied the throne and was surrounded by his own ministers, drawn from the court nobility. But in the background, holding posts of no apparent importance, were a number of feudal warriors who had given him support. Among them was one Ashikaga Takauji, a powerful Minamoto vassal, who, though despatched by Kamakura against Daigo II, had crossed over to the emperor's side. With him and certain other feudal lords lay the real power. But this truth the court party did not or would not perceive, and for a few years they strove to revive the institutions of the pre-feudal days, when the emperors ruled through their great ministers and their provincial officials. The real issue in Japan, however, was no longer the conflict between bureaucratic government and feudalism, but the conflict between rival feudal interests; and for more than fifty years after the fall of the Kamakura government the country was torn by the rivalry of great barons, usually under the mask of wars to decide the imperial succession. In these struggles the Ashikaga family generally had the upper hand, though they met frequent checks, and it was not until 1392 that, with the settlement of the dynastic quarrel, they could feel secure in their position as Shōgun.

Chapter XVI

RELIGION, ART AND LETTERS

1. BUDDHISM

PERHAPS the most striking feature of the Buddhism of the Kama-kura period is its growth as a popular religion. We have already hinted at the reasons for this change. They are to be found in the decline of the patrician society which had fostered Buddhism largely as an æsthetic cult; the pride and corruption of the bene-ficed clergy; the rise of a military class; and in general the disorder of the times, when death and misery were rife and soothing doctrine was welcome to men's minds. No doubt, as time pro-gressed, some elements of learning had filtered down from the aristocratic classes to the people, and it seems that the gradual adoption of a simple native script was helpful in spreading among them such easy teachings as those of Genshin and Ryōnin. Most of the great evangelists of the twelfth and thirteenth centuries wrote learned treatises in Chinese, but also popular works in Japanese, employing the "mixed *kana*" script. Shinran, for instance, justi-fies the use of this script in one of his books, by saying, "Country people do not know the meaning of characters and are extremely slow-witted. Therefore, in order to make them understand easily, I have written the same thing over and over again. Refined per-sons will think it strange, and will no doubt laugh me to scorn. But I do not care for their abuse, for I have written with the one idea of making my meaning clear to stupid people."

As Buddhism became popular it tended to become national, to assume a Japanese complexion. This movement is visible as one studies the lives of the great teachers of the Kamakura period, each of whom in his own way expressed the current feeling of reaction against the formal Buddhism of the Fujiwara. The re-action took three distinct forms: a revival of the old Nara sects, particularly the Kegon and the Ritsu; the birth of important new protestant sects, Jōdo, Shin and Nichiren, which broke away from the Heian sects; and the rise of the Zen sect as intercourse with China grew closer under the Sung dynasty.

The revival of the Nara sects, though of great interest, hardly succeeded in bringing them back into the main stream of religious development and must therefore be passed over, but not without mentioning that the Tōdaiji, which had been burned to ashes in 1180, was rebuilt in 1190 under the auspices of Yoritomo, with funds subscribed from all parts of Japan. The first of the new sects to be formed was the Pure Land (Jōdo). Its doctrines had been preached for some time past, but it remained for the celebrated Hōnen Shōnin (1133-1212), inspired largely by Genshin's "Essentials of Salvation," to build them into a consistent whole. His conviction, expressed in words that he wrote on his deathbed, was as follows. "The method of final salvation that I have taught is neither a sort of meditation such as that practised by many scholars in China and Japan in the past, nor is it a repetition of the Buddha's name by those who have studied and understood the deep meaning of it. It is nothing but the mere repetition of the name of the Buddha Amida without a doubt of his mercy, whereby one may be born into the Land of Perfect Bliss." He believed, then, in the absolute efficacy of the *nembutsu*, not the relative efficacy which was claimed for it by other schools. Salvation was therefore open to the common man, for faith is the sole essential, and learning or good works are almost a hindrance in so far as they induce men to yield to pride and depend upon their own efforts rather than upon the compassion of Amida. Hōnen thought that Amida chose the *nembutsu* as the way of salvation because it could be practised anywhere and at any time by all classes of people. Such doctrines were as unorthodox as they were popular, and therefore he decided that he must found a new sect, the Jōdo, which may be regarded as dating from the year 1175. His influence increased daily and his converts grew in numbers "like the clouds in the sky." They included men and women of all degrees. He had the confidence of several emperors, and the cloistered Go-Shirakawa is said to have repeated the *nembutsu* several million times and to have died uttering the potent formula. Among his lay followers were many nobles, including the regent Kanezane, while many ecclesiastics, high and low, especially from the Tendai and Shingon sects, went over to him. The authoritative biography contains several anecdotes to show that his influence extended to distant parts of Japan, and there are records of correspondence on points of doctrine between him and members of the warrior class at Kamakura and elsewhere. Most celebrated among these soldiers is that Kumagai no Jirō Naozane who, according to the legend, took the tonsure out of remorse because he had killed a young boy in battle. Alas for romance! Authentic records show that his motive was chagrin at the loss of a law suit. It is none the less significant of Hōnen's influence that a soldier of high standing should have been converted to his faith. In general the military class were on a flood tide of fortune, and did not stand in need of the consolations of religion; but it was a stern, bleak life in early Kamakura, and not all Yoritomo's warriors can have been of the same hard-bitten breed as their master. It seems to be established that a number of world-weary samurai, under the spell of Hōnen's teaching, sought to hasten their entry into Paradise by suicide, though there is nothing in his tenets to justify such a step. As to the spread of his doctrines among the common people, we have his recorded death-bed saying, "Wherever among high or low the *nembutsu* is practised, there is my monument, be it only the thatched hut of a fisherman."

The growth of a free church which was dependent upon neither priests nor ceremonies or buildings was certain to arouse the enmity of the older sects, who at this time were so jealous of their privileges that they resorted to force among themselves or against the court on the most trivial grounds. They petitioned for the prohibition of the *nembutsu*, and though Hōnen stemmed their attack for a while with the help of friends in high places, he was at last unable to stand up against the slander of his enemies and, what seems to have been almost as dangerous, the zeal of his followers. This was the first instance of bitter religious animosity and persecution in Japan, and it must be noticed that it came not so much from doctrinal bigots as from corrupt and licentious monks. It is true that among Hōnen's opponents were a number of learned clerics who believed that his teaching was subversive of morality, but on the whole it is fair to say that the attack upon him was a fight for privilege rather than a battle for truth. The emperor (Toba II) took sides against Hōnen. Several of his most ardent disciples were beheaded, others were banished, and he himself was exiled early in 1207. He was pardoned at the end of the year but was not allowed to enter the capital until 1211. There he found a great popular welcome; but he was now old and ill, and in the first month of the following year he died. As he lay on his death-bed his disciples brought an image of Amida, and according to the custom of the Amidists fastened a coloured cord to its hand, and wished the dying man to hold the other end, so that the Buddha could draw him into Paradise. But Hōnen refused, saying that he needed no such help, for he could already see in the sky a host of Buddhas awaiting him amidst the glories of the Pure Land.

The death of Hōnen only served to quicken people's faith in his teaching, and to excite still further the anger of the Nara and Kyōto priesthood. The court actually prohibited the *nembutsu* at their instance on more than one occasion, there was further persecution, and the saint's tomb was desecrated. Such hostile sentiment lasted for a generation, but the vitality of Jōdo beliefs was too great for them to be suppressed by mere force, and Hōnen was followed by indomitable evangelists, chief among them being Shinran (1173-1262), who during the founder's lifetime had been spreading the gospel of *nembutsu* while exiled in northern Japan, but now returned to work in the eastern provinces. In one sense Jōdo did not yet really exist as a sect, partly because of the persecution which it underwent, partly because of the growth of competing religious movements, and finally because it was, so to speak, parasitic, and could be practised consistently with other doctrines. This last feature was in fact a source of strength, for it was able to secure adherents without detaching them from other sects, until in the early 17th century it was organised as an independent body. Originally it had had few temples and little property, and was therefore weak as an institutional religion. Probably on this account it had great powers of survival as a creed, with the result that the Jōdo sect is influential to this day, and is said to have over sixteen million believers. Of these, two million belong to the Jōdo proper, the remainder being adherents of sects which sprang from it soon after Hōnen's death as a result of separatist movements.

The most important of these was the Jōdo Shinshū, or True Sect of Jōdo, founded by Shinran. He modified the doctrines of Hōnen in an extremely interesting and effective way, which merits notice as the expression of a characteristic Japanese attitude towards religious problems. He pushed to a logical extreme the theory of the *nembutsu*, arguing that one sincere invocation of Amida was sufficient to ensure salvation, and that all further repetitions of the formula were merely praise of the Buddha, desirable but unnecessary. Once certain of Paradise there was no reason why a man should devote himself to religious practices or bother his head with abstruse teachings. He should not worship other Buddhas than Amida. He had better live an ordinary life, as a parent and a member of society, following the ordinary lay rules of good behaviour. Shinran himself set an example to his followers, for he was neither monk nor layman, but what was already called in the Heian period a *shami* (*śrāmaṇera*), a person who leads a religious life but does not follow the Rule in its entirety. He had six children by a lady (said to have been the daughter of the Regent Kanezane) styled Eshin the Nun, who was in fact his wife. Since his time not only have the priests of the Shin sect been allowed to marry, but celibacy has been positively discouraged and the incumbency of Shin temples is often hereditary. He held that priests are not men who should strive alone after perfection, but teachers, who need not, in their dress or their way of living, be marked off from others. He even went so far as to disapprove of the distinction between teacher and disciple, regarding all believers in the *nembutsu* as equal members of a fellowship. The words used to describe these groups show that the Jōdo sects were at first congregational ni type,* and it is clear that one important reason for their popularity was that they welcomed converts of the lowly classes. Shinran himself in one of his works says that he wishes "to be the same as the rudest peasant from farm or field." It will be seen that Shinran reduced religion, so far as conduct is concerned, to the extremest simplicity, but it must not be supposed that either he or Hōnen had only elementary notions of religious philosophy. They were both very learned and subtle theologians. They could express them-

* The memorial chapel built after Shinran's death, which later grew into the great Hongwanji, the Temple of the Original Vow, was jointly managed by its congregation.

selves in easy language for the ignorant, but their more erudite writings are voluminous and difficult to understand without considerable special knowledge.

There were several other offshoots of the Jōdo sect, of varying importance, but they may all be comprehensively described as relying upon the invocation to Amida, in contrast with the other great popular sect of the day, the Hokke or Lotus Sect. Its founder was Nichiren (1222-1282), one of the greatest figures in the history of Japan. His life and work display in an intenser degree those characteristics of the Buddhism of the Kamakura period which had already begun to appear in the Amidist sects, for his teaching was a protest against established forms of faith, it was popular in its appeal, and it was strongly national in its aims. Nichiren may be said to complete the long process by which Buddhism was assimilated and made Japanese. Like all the great teachers of the age, he first studied Tendai doctrines. But these are too comprehensive to suit men of an ardent and decisive temperament, and he was soon dissatisfied. When about thirty years old he began to declaim against Shingon mysticism as practised by the fraternities on Mount Kōya; against Amidism as practised by the believers in the *nembutsu*; against the monastic discipline (*ritsu*) of the Nara sects; and against the now rising school of Zen or Meditative Buddhism. It will be seen that his denunciation was all-embracing, and it is important to notice that the chief reason which he gave for attacking these different forms of religion was that they were sapping the vitality of the people and corrupting the state.

He was a political as well as a religious reformer, inspired by a strong sense of nationality, as can be seen from the title of his great tract, *Risshō Ankoku Ron*, a Treatise on the Establishment of Righteousness and the Safety of the Country. In his writings he constantly uses such phrases as "the prosperity of the nation," and in an essay called the Eye-opener he says, "I will be the pillar of Japan. I will be the eyes of Japan. I will be the great vessel of Japan." This was a new thing, for though the Buddhist priesthood had often influenced the secular power, no previous teacher had thus related the spiritual welfare of the people to the temporal fortunes of the state. But Nichiren was of an ambitious and vehement nature, likely not to fear, and rather to enjoy, a clash with authority. His life is an example of the militant reforming spirit, not of the gentle and saintly. He broke the tradition of religious tolerance in Japan, for hitherto sectarian differences had aroused little or no animosity, but Nichiren, regarding all other doctrines as heretical and damned, burned to have them suppressed. He was at the same time a constructive teacher, and a man of great learning. After protracted studies he decided that the Lotus Scripture was the sole depository of eternal truth, and the only way to salvation. He preached therefore a return to the early purity of Tendai Buddhism as expounded by the patriarch Dengyō. But being strongly under the influence of the current idea that the Latter Degenerate Days had come, he argued that man needed some simple method of gaining truth, and though he arrived at his conclusions by an arduous philosophical route his popular teaching reduces the essentials of religion to the simple utterance of the name of the revered canon, in the formula *Namu Myōhō-Renge-Kyō*, "Homage to the Scripture of the Lotus of the Good Law."

In practice, therefore, there would seem to be little to distinguish the follower of Hōnen, saved by invoking Amida, from the follower of Nichiren, saved by invoking the Lotus. Yet each was inspired by a different kind of faith, the one passive and pessimistic, the other lively and defiant. The Lotus Sect has always partaken of the nature of its founder, whose career has therefore more than a biographical interest. When he had decided upon the truth, he commenced an active propaganda. Hunted from his native village by the local steward, who was incensed by his violent language, he settled in Kamakura, where he preached to crowds in the streets and open places, boldly attacking the Amidist sects and admonishing the rulers of Japan. This was in 1260, when conditions all over the country certainly justified the deepest pessimism. In 1257 there had been a great earthquake, followed in a year or so by storms, floods, famine and plague. The Hōjō administration was showing signs of collapse, the military class were restive, the priests of the occult sects were profiting by the panic of the people. Nichiren ascribed all these calamities to the corrupt religions of the day, and foretold that, if the nation did not turn to the Truth and their rulers suppress false teachings, further disasters would overtake them, especially a foreign invasion. This remarkable

statement, based perhaps on prophetic insight, only annoyed the
Bakufu, to whom he presented a stiff memorial. He was exiled,
and did not return to Kamakura until 1263. Again he preached,
more vehemently than ever, always in danger, but always
making converts. His field was in eastern Japan, the stronghold of feudalism, and his militant doctrine won him many
adherents among the samurai and their masters. He was un-
sparing of invective, and it is a pleasure to read such unstinted
abuse in a language which is as a rule elaborately honorific. He
called Kōbō Daishi "the greatest liar in Japan," the Shingon
doctors were "traitors," Zen was "a doctrine of fiends and devils,"
the members of the Ritsu sect were "brigands" and the *nembutsu*
"a hellish practice." Writing to a friend after hearing the news
that the Mongol envoys had been executed, he said: "It is a great
pity that they should have cut off the heads of the innocent Mongols and left unharmed the priests of Nembutsu, Shingon, Zen
and Ritsu, who are the enemies of Japan."

From his correspondence it seems that although his natural
impulse was to challenge authority he was tender in his dealings
with the weak and humble. Charming, kindly letters have been
preserved, which he wrote to members of his congregations—both
male and female, for unlike the older sects he, as well as Hōnen
and Shinran, regarded women as capable of ultimately becoming
Buddhas, though he doubtless thought that they would first have
to be reborn in Paradise as men. But he was by his own confession
the "most intractable man in Japan," and such are doomed to
persecution. When Khubilai Khan's mission arrived in Japan in
1268 Nichiren renewed his remonstrances to the government and
to great ecclesiastics; but it is rare for high officials to enjoy criti-
cism if it is well-founded, and before long he was tried for high
treason and, after a miraculous escape from execution, was once
more sent into exile. His confidence in himself and his mission
remained unshaken. Indeed during this term of banishment he
reached the conviction that he in his own person realised a
prophecy of the Buddha and was the Messenger destined to reveal
the truth in the Latter Days of the Law. He even saw himself as
the chosen instrument for the foundation of a Universal Church
with its Holy See in Japan.

While Nichiren was in banishment he had influential friends at work in Kamakura, for there were men in the government who admired his character, and there were others who superstitiously feared that persecution of such a holy man might call down upon them the anger of the Buddhas. In the spring of 1274 it was known that the Mongols meant to attack Japan, and this confirmation of his prophecy brought him still higher in their esteem, so that they went so far as to recall him to Kamakura. There they asked his advice, and he replied that the only safeguard against disaster was for the whole nation to adopt his religion, while all other religions must be suppressed and their leaders punished. The authorities offered to meet him half-way, but he would accept no compromise. The soldiers decided to rely upon their own swords and the incantations of the mystic sects, and Nichiren left Kamakura for ever, to retire into a mountain hermitage. It seems a curious anti-climax to so militant a career, but he was impelled by a strong mystic belief in his own destiny. He lived until the winter of 1282, and twice before his death the Mongols fell upon Japan. They were repulsed, but he was neither elated by the victory nor cast down by the failure of his prediction of disaster. Mystic though he was, he had a realist's outlook on events, and he saw that the defeat of the Mongols was due to chance, and that the social disintegration which he had foretold was postponed but not prevented by the defeat of the enemy armada. The military claimed that success was due to their valour, the Shingon priests that it was due to their prayers, but Nichiren, writing to an old soldier friend a few months later, said, "Ask them if they took the head of the Mongol king?" Events proved that he had truly diagnosed the malady of the times, though he may have been wrong about its treatment. The evils against which he had thundered grew and spread, government collapsed, and Japan knew no true peace for centuries. The Nichiren sect survived much oppression, and prospered, always assertive, and full of missionary zeal*. It has to-day three million adherents. They are addicted to persistent drumming and chanting, which are said to produce apocalyptic ecstasies, and they thus bear some likeness to the

* Most of Nichiren's successors displayed this spirit, and one of them (Nichiji) is said to have gone to Siberia as a missionary, in 1295.

Salvationists of Europe. Until quite recent times at least Nichiren priests claimed power to cure persons possessed by evil spirits, an ironic development in view of the founder's hatred of the sorcery of the occult sects.

To a reader of the foregoing account of the growth of creeds and the lives of saints, there will probably occur many close parallels in other countries. He will recognise, perhaps with melancholy interest, all that embellishes or blots our western chronicles—the saints, the martyrs, the zealots and the bigots, sublime visions and the contamination of truth. But he will perhaps conclude that the Japanese as a people have displayed in matters of belief a tolerance, amounting almost to indifferentism, which has been rare in Europe. And there is one respect in which their religious history is probably unique, namely the development of the Zen sect. The influence of this school upon Japan has been so subtle and pervading that it has become the essence of her finest culture. To follow its ramifications in thought and sentiment, in art, letters and behaviour, would be to write exhaustively the most difficult and the most fascinating chapter of her spiritual history, which here we dare only sketch in hesitating outline.[1]

The word *Zen* is derived, through Chinese, from the Sanskrit *dhyana*, meaning meditation, and the Zen school differs from other sects in holding that enlightenment can come only by direct intuitive perception. It does not rely upon the efficacy of a sacred formula or the power of a merciful saviour, but upon the effort of the individual to grasp the meaning of the universe. Logically Zen Buddhism can be traced back to India, but the historical line of transmission is not clear. It probably owes a great deal to early Buddhist thought, in so far as its central idea is the spiritual experience known as Enlightenment (*sambodhi*); but even its reputed history begins only with the arrival in China in A.D. 520 of an Indian monk named Bodhidharma, and is a record of the development of an Indian doctrine under the influence of Chinese thought. It is clearly a manifestation of that habit of the Chinese mind which found another and not very different expression in the mysticism of Lao-tzu; and whatever its origins it ought to be regarded as a peculiarly Far Eastern product. Zen doctrines were known in Japan in the Nara period, and the idea that certain religious truths cannot be explained in words but are to be grasped only by intuition was common to most sects, particularly those of a mystic tendency such as the Tendai and Shingon. But Zen as a separate school in Japan arose in the Kamakura period, and it prospered especially among the warrior class. It may be said to have commenced with the foundation of the Rinzai sect by the monk Eisai, soon after 1200.

It is at first sight surprising that the vigorous society of Kamakura should have patronised a sect usually described as contemplative. But Zen has other than contemplative qualities. Its princlpies were at an early date in China summed up in the following lines:

> A special transmission outside the scriptures,
> No dependence upon the written word,
> Direct pointing at the soul of man,
> Seeing one's nature and attaining Buddhahood.

It will be seen that even on simple, practical grounds there was much in Zen to appeal to a soldier, particularly one of a self-reliant character. Zen does not depend upon scriptures, it has no elaborate philosophy; it is indeed almost anti-philosophical in that it stresses the importance of a realisation of truth which comes as a vision due to introspection and not to the study of other men's words. To feudal warriors of the sternest type, the emotionalism of the Pure Land sects must have been distasteful, and they were no doubt impatient of the metaphysical subtleties of other schools. Most of them, for that matter, were not learned enough to comprehend their difficult terminology. But the sudden enlightenment, called *satori*, at which a Zen practitioner aims, is an intimate personal experience. A Zen teacher reads no sutras, he performs no ceremonies, worships no images, and he conveys instruction to his pupil not by long sermons but by hints and indications. The pupil must examine himself, master himself and find his own place in the spiritual universe by his own efforts. So incommunicable is Zen that it has no canon, and its earlier literature, though voluminous, consists chiefly of biographical anecdotes of the masters and collections of test problems. The masters taught *obscurum per obscurius*, using paradoxical sayings, or blows and kicks or deafening shouts which were intended to jolt the learner into sudden awareness.

Naturally a system so empty of dogma and theory could accommodate the most diverse types of adherents. Enemies of Zen are not always without excuse when they allege that it is a sham and pretentious mysticism. Since it is, on the whole, opposed to ritual and convention, it is apt to encourage eccentricity in its practitioners, and in extreme cases a certain charlatanry. It is not unduly sceptical to suppose that some of the Zen worthies, when they tweaked the nose of a seeker after truth, or treated contemptuously an inquiring potentate, were so to speak "playing to the gallery"; and there is something to be said for the argument that what cannot be expressed clearly may perhaps not be worth expressing at all. Zen was bitterly opposed in the beginning by the Tendai, Shingon and Nara sects, and that was the chief reason why Eisai moved to Kamakura, where vested religious interests were less powerful. On one or two occasions at least hostile parties attacked and burned down Zen monasteries. What especially annoyed the older sects was the Zen claim to "a special transmission outside the scriptures." There is on record a slashing attack, written about 1295, by a high court dignitary, who says that Zen believers depend upon the sayings of their masters, "but however wonderful their teachers may be, how can they presume to improve upon the words of Shaka?" As for their so-called meditation, he continues, they just "doze in their seats and think depraved, wanton thoughts." Since that day it has often been suggested that Zen professors deal in hocus-pocus, and certainly their calm assumption of superiority can be rather exasperating. But it is foolish to suppose that a cult which has been so assiduously practised and has had such far-reaching effects upon the intellectual life of two great peoples is a mere farcical imposture. It is easier and more rational to conclude that in its genuine forms it is a display of the characteristic reaction of matter-of-fact Chinese and Japanese minds to the transcendental flights of Indian philosophy. It was by means of Zen that Buddhism was able to compromise with native Chinese thought, as expressed in Confucianism and Taoism; and that was principally because Zen left room for a simple, practical code of social ethics, while in Indian Buddhism ideas of everyday morality tend to be obscured in a glorious cloud of metaphysics. No doubt it was the ethical element

in Zen which helped it to find favour among the samurai. It is
interesting to note that, of the various Chinese schools, it was the
southern, particularly that known as the Sōtō, which had the
greatest success in provincial Japan. This school teaches that
enlightenment is sudden, not gradual, it insists upon rigorous self-
discipline and introspection. Such teachings accorded well with
the temper and ideals of the feudal warrior. They are, after all,
practical and immediate. They do not recommend abstractions,
for they tell a man to deal with himself, to "look into his own
nature." They inculcate calm and self-reliance; and the bare Zen
monastery where the monks clean and cook, the plain garden
where they sweep and dig, were in harmony with the frugal
standards of early Kamakura.

Since Enlightenment is a mystic personal experience it would
be idle for us to inquire closely into its nature. But we may assume
that it leads to a conviction that the universe is pervaded by one
spirit. This sentiment of Immanence, of the unity of the individual
with all nature, permeates the national thought and finds expression in the arts. Always sensitive to natural beauty, the Japanese found in Zen an outlook upon life which not only justified but
gave purity and strength to their appreciation. Zen may be said
to have brought them æsthetic as well as spiritual illumination.

2. ART AND LETTERS

In a society dominated by feudal warriors, the arts might have
fallen upon hard times had there been, as some writers suggest,
a clear division between degenerate aristocracy at Kyōto and
simple feudal standards at Kamakura. In practice such convenient
categories do not exist. The late Fujiwara civilisation had in some
respects reached a sterile phase of decadence, and the rise of the
fighting clans no doubt threw the elegants of the metropolis into
despondency while it gave confidence to a class more energetic, if
less refined, than themselves. But the influence of Kyōto was strong
and persistent. The capital remained for centuries the fountain
of culture, the true home of æsthetic accomplishment; for in the
long run unrelieved virility has to capitulate. The culture of the
Kamakura period is, save for its specifically feudal aspects, not
the culture of Kamakura but the spread of Heian culture in the

wake of feudal power. After the first years of struggle the new rulers were anxious to cultivate the arts of peace. Yoritomo and the Hōjō regents were interested in government and religion. They respected learning even if they had no taste for it themselves. As we have seen, many of the best Heian scholars took service in Kamakura, and Kamakura became a centre of important religious activities, which had all originated in the western capital. There were two influences at work—the soldier's reaction against the effeminacy of city life and a countervailing envy of its ease and polish. So two currents can be perceived in ways of living. At first opposed, they gradually blended, for the Kamakura warriors adopted more and more the fashions of Kyōto and the aristocrats began to turn their attention to warlike measures.

These varied tendencies are well displayed in architecture. The simple standards of the Bakufu had their effect upon building and decoration, but it is easy to show that life in Kamakura was not so uniformly severe and parsimonious as is generally suggested. Temple architecture continued without much change from the Heian period, with one notable exception, which was the introduction of a style called *kara-yō*, from China, under the influence of Zen Buddhism. Zen monasteries of this period were usually of plain construction and bare of ornament, but their simplicity was based on æsthetic principles and not on mere frugality. It is recorded that the regent Tokimune sent architects to China to study the correct design, and it seems that the buildings were often extensive and the foundations richly endowed. Even the severe Yoritomo after his expedition against the Fujiwara in northern Japan, impressed by the magnificence of such monasteries as the Chūsonji of Hiraidzumi, interested himself in the decoration with frescoes and carvings of the Kamakura temples which he founded. Moreover he by no means confined himself to Kamakura. He spent large sums on the restoration of shrines and temples throughout Japan, and contributed handsomely to the repairs of the imperial palace. It was under his encouragement that great monasteries destroyed in the wars, such as the Tōdaiji of Nara, were rebuilt, and in general ecclesiastical architecture profited by the rise of feudalism. As for dwelling-houses, a new type was evolved, called *buke-dzukuri*, or "military style," in which provision was made for defence by means of an encircling wall, solid gates, and quarters for guards. Within one enclosure a large number of retainers were sheltered, so that the whole was extensive. Gradually these residences approximated in style to the Kyōto type called *shindendzukuri*, and became more luxurious, but the tendency to elaboration was checked by the simplicity of Zen taste.

In sculpture the vigorous sentiment of Kamakura prevailed over the fatigue of the late Fujiwara period, and a new era was commenced. Artists came over from Sung China, and perhaps a new stimulus was given by the rebuilding of the Nara temples, when sculptors of the line of Jōchō (Kyōto men, it should be noted) could study the masterpieces of Tempyō. Unkei, in the fifth generation from Jōchō, is known to have restored some of these, and he is the greatest sculptor of the period, worthy to rank with his greatest predecessors. Though there were some plastic styles which pursued the late Fujiwara tradition and, with thick pigments and metal inlay, carried ornamental detail to the point of absurdity, the finest Kamakura sculpture is distinguished for its lifelike energy. It is extremely vigorous and withal simple, leaning to the use of plain wood and not relying upon colour or other forms of decoration. Some of the best work is portrait statuary of a vivid realism; and it is a long way from the sublime, ideal beings of Asuka and Tempyō sculpture to the very human figures by Unkei, saints and patriarchs though they be. The great bronze image of Amida, known as the Kamakura Daibutsu (1252), ought to be mentioned here. It has been much admired by travellers, but as a work of art it does not deserve the highest praise. Though its sheer bulk and its slightly forward-leaning pose are impressive, as sculpture it is weakly executed.

In painting the Kamakura period shows further progress in the direction of realism already taken by several schools which had developed in late Fujiwara times. The tendency appears in both religious and secular art. It is true that there are many Kamakura Buddhist paintings, of the conventional iconographic type, which under the influence of the mild Amidist sects represent, skilfully enough though without spirit, bland and uninteresting divinities. But there were other and more beautiful pictures, not necessarily of religious subjects yet painted with religious intent. Pre-eminent

among these is the famous Nachi Waterfall, the work of a monk in
the thirteenth century. It is one of the finest landscape paintings
in the world and it illustrates aptly the intimate bond between
religious sentiment and a love of nature. The great cascade, in its
perpetual rhythmic movement, seemed to symbolise, or rather to
express, some cosmic truth, and it was worshipped by pilgrims as if
it were divinity itself. The painting also seems to have been hung
in a temple as an object of adoration and prayer, and even to-day
its owner, when he shows it to a guest, will follow with his finger
the line of the falling water, intoning a fragment of a Buddhist
prayer in harmony with its course down from the edge of a high
cliff to rocks and trees beneath. Many other landscape paintings of
this and the following age aim not merely at furnishing a sensuous
enjoyment of scenery but at portraying natural beauty as a manifestation of one spirit that pervades the universe. It is easy to
overestimate the importance of this mystic element in eastern
art; but there can be no doubt that a conception of the visible
world as an expression of ultimate spiritual realities has urged
great artists to seek the essence of forms which they perceive rather
than to labour for a dull topographic faithfulness.

The Kamakura period is especially notable for the great number
and variety of its *emakimono* or picture scrolls. Of these several
hundred are still extant. They deal with many kinds of subjects,
and together provide us with a vivid representation of life in the
Middle Ages. Some record the history of famous shrines and temples
or the lives of holy men such as Hōnen; some illustrate military
romances like the *Heiji Monogatari* and contain remarkable
miniature battle pieces; some portray scenes from popular works
of fiction and are delightful studies of manners and costume, others
are lavishly decorated sutras; and others again are of a didactic
religious type, graphically handling such Buddhist themes as the
Chain of Causation in Past and Present. Interesting rather than
beautiful specimens of this last category are a group of scrolls of
the Six Migratory Stages of Existence, such as hells, burning and
cold, the world of Hungry Ghosts, the world of False Kings, and
so on to the various worlds of Bliss. These pictures are clearly the
reflection in art of Eshin's tract and bear witness to a current

belief in damnation; but it need not be supposed that it was a belief earnestly and persistently maintained, for very soon Hell becomes the subject of popular jokes and light-hearted aphorisms. Even in the scrolls themselves a certain grim humour can be detected, and the infernal flames leap up in enjoyable patterns.

By the latter half of the Kamakura period nearly every important temple or shrine possessed a picture scroll recording its miraculous origin or the life of its founder. These *emakimono* gained a special sanctity from their themes, and were jealously preserved. Many were kept secret, and some were worshipped as the embodiment (*shintai*) of the deity of the place.

Portrait painting was very much in vogue. Pictures called *nise-e* ("likenesses") took various forms. Some were scrolls showing court dignitaries, others were a single sheet on which was drawn the likeness, real or imagined, of some famous poet, with a verse of his composing. These are examples of that kinship of draughtsmanship and calligraphy to which we have already alluded. It was common also to commission a court artist to paint pictures of horses or oxen. These were much prized, and one which represented the favourite carriage-ox of an Empress Dowager was, we learn, hung in the main oratory of her family temple. Some large portraits in colours on silk were painted in this period. A fine likeness (about four feet high) of Yoritomo is extant, which is ascribed to a contemporary artist. It may be a later work, but there is no doubt that a tradition of large-scale portraits was well established by the thirteenth century.

Progress in the applied arts was not interrupted, but stimulated rather by the social upheavals of the time. Warfare promoted metal-working, because the soldiers needed fine swords and armour. Religion promoted carving and lacquer-making because the devout and despairing felt that they must please the gods with rich gifts. Philosophy may be said to have promoted ceramics, for tea-drinking came into fashion among Zen adepts as an aid to their meditative vigils. Eisai made of it a kind of ritual, from which the later "tea-ceremony" sprang. Ornamental glazed tea-jars, teacups, incense-burners and such-like utensils were made by one Tōshiro, who went to China to study pottery early in the

FIG. 43. *The poet Narihira and one of his verses. Drawing and calligraphy by the Emperor Toba II (reigned 1183-1197).*

thirteenth century and on his return set up a kiln at Seto. He may be regarded as the father of the art in Japan, and the modern word for porcelain is *seto-mono*, the ware of Seto.

Despite their Spartan creed many members of the military class, newly risen to prosperity as landed proprietors, demanded luxuries, and in general the Kamakura period exhibits a remarkable artistic activity which superficial study of its political features would not lead one to expect. Literature, however, cannot be said to have kept pace with the arts. Some academic writers are in-

clined to dismiss the thirteenth century as an unfertile age, but a
cursory examination of the works of the leading religious reformers suggests that this view is perhaps unfounded. Though both
Hōnen and Nichiren, for instance, wrote well and vigorously,
their correspondence and their polemical essays are not usually
regarded as classics. Yet they are probably to modern taste
superior to the rather sentimental and high-flown war tales
whose authors, it is quite likely, modelled their language on that
of the great churchmen. But it is true that secular learning was at
a low ebb, for the Kyōto schools suffered from the poverty of the
imperial treasury and in eastern Japan there were only two
centres of instruction, the Ashikaga College and the Kanazawa
Library, the former founded by the Ashikaga family in about
1190 and the latter by the Hōjō regents towards 1270. The
military class were in general unlearned and few of them could
write either correct Chinese or, what probably required greater
skill if less knowledge, good, fluent Japanese. Yet they depended
a great deal upon writing for their laws and regulations and the
recording of transactions in land. It is a peculiar feature of early
feudal institutions in Japan that they were based upon a profusion
of documents, such as charters, oaths, registers and the notes of
judicial proceedings. To meet this need there was evolved a
peculiar linguistic compromise, in which a somewhat stilted
Japanese colloquial masqueraded in Chinese dress. It would have
pained the classical scholars of former generations, being analogous to dog-Latin; but it was on the whole fairly concise and
intelligible and seems to have served its purpose well enough. In
time it became the common form for official despatches, chronicles
and laws. It was a mating of incompatibles, but it grew out of
necessity, and from it there arose in course of time and after
strange vicissitudes the written language of the nineteenth century.
The spread of Buddhism as a popular faith introduced into the
spoken language a large number of religious terms which are now
familiar locutions. It also influenced the character of popular
literature and popular sentiment by describing events in terms of
Buddhist conceptions, and words and phrases which entered the
vocabulary through this channel have left their mark upon every-

day speech. Thus the word *en*, meaning affinity, was adopted to signify *karma*-relation, and now is used where we should say fate or destiny.

The great war romances such as the *Hōgen Monogatari*, the *Heike Monogatari* (cited in a previous chapter) and the *Gempei Seisuiki* belong to this period and are all fundamentally of the same style, more flowing and ornamental than that of the serious historical works, for example the *Ima Kagami* which, despite its name, meaning the Mirror of the Times, is far from bright and reflective. The *Heike Monogatari* is written in poetical prose and, it is said, was intended to be chanted to the accompaniment of a lute. In themes and in language it is the source of many popular ballads and also of a number of the lyric dramas of the following centuries. All these romances have the power to move a Japanese hearer to tears or to martial ardour and we must therefore conclude that their renown has a solid basis, though it is difficult to comprehend for a foreigner whose blood is stirred by trumpet calls of different ancestry. It seems that only the wars could at this time inspire sustained flights in literature. The *belles lettres* of the period, apart from poems, consist largely of a kind of writing called *zuihitsu*, "following the pen," which are random reflections, frequently on religious themes. The best known of these is the note book, the *Hōjōki*, written by a recluse in his rural retreat, not very far from the capital. It is a slight thing and perhaps scarcely deserves the attention that has been given it by critics and translators; but it is a good specimen of the skilful use of the written language of the day. Kamo Chōmei, its reputed author, was an educated man with a taste for poetry who lost his small fortune and his prospects in the disorder which marked the close of the twelfth century. He was not a true ascetic, but a disappointed man who very sensibly made the best of his failure by living quietly in the country and consoling himself for his poverty by suitable Buddhistic reflections on Evanescence and the Hereafter.

In the early part of the Kamakura period Japanese poetry still flourished under the patronage of the court. A number of poets of this time are still celebrated in Japan. Important anthologies were made, including the *Shin Kokinshū*, or New Ancient and Modern Collection, and the *Hyakunin Isshu*, which contains one poem by each of a hundred reputed masters. In succeeding ages this, or a similar collection, was put into the hands of all young persons, especially of girls, since some knowledge of the native verse was held to be an essential part of their education. There is a traditional card-game in which the poems are matched with their composers' names. But though the production was immense, most of the later Kamakura verse is undistinguished, being little more than dexterous variation upon well-worn themes in forms prescribed by the leaders of various quarrelsome schools of pedantry. It had become a pastime rather than an art. This is deplorable no doubt; but versifying at its worst is an amiable weakness and perhaps it helped to keep the spirit of poetry alive.

Kamakura literature is of interest chiefly in that it displays the formation of a truly national written language, blended of foreign and native elements. The language of the *Genji Monogatari* was, so far as one can judge, not very different from contemporary speech, except of course that it was stylised and handled with supreme competence; but from the beginning of the feudal period there is a divergence between prose and colloquial, so marked that, in extreme cases, documents in a certain type of Sinico-Japanese are barely intelligible when read aloud.

SUMMARY OF POLITICAL EVENTS IN THE KAMAKURA PERIOD

A.D. 1185 The Minamoto family, under Yoritomo, supreme in Japan.
1192 Yoritomo made Seii-Tai-Shōgun.
1199 Death of Yoritomo.
1205 The Hōjō regency commences.
1226 A Fujiwara puppet Shōgun set up in Kamakura.
1232 The code of law called *Jōei Shikimoku* promulgated.
1274-1281 The Mongol invasions.
1332 Imperial succession dispute, between "Northern" and "Southern" dynasties.
1333 End of Hōjō Regency, and destruction of Kamakura.
1336 Ashikaga Takauji sets up Emperor KŌMYŌ in Kyōto, and Emperor DAIGO II establishes "Southern" Court in Yoshino.
1338 Ashikaga Takauji nominated Shōgun. Civil war continues.

NOTE TO CHAPTER XVI

[1] Page 338 ff. Zen Buddhism. Seeing that Zen cannot be explained in words and can be grasped only by intuition, it is a rash thing for any writer on Japanese thought to commit himself to precise statements about this topic. Yet most historical students cannot help wishing

to formulate the undefinable. I am afraid that here and later (in Chapter XVIII, page 395), I have been guilty of this rashness and have been severely contradicted by Zen scholars. Professor Suzuki says that what I have described as Zen "is not at all Zen," and that Western modes of thinking "can never do away with the eternal dilemma of this and that, reason or faith, man or God, etc." With Zen, he says, all these are swept away as something veiling our insight into the nature of life and reality. In the face of such statements from such an authority I have nothing to say except that here is some evidence that the Japanese approach to philosophical problems seems to alternate between the matter-of-fact and the mystical, and tends to reject what seems to us a rational dependence upon analytic methods.

The intending student of Zen ought perhaps to be warned, in the words of William James, that "the incommunicableness of the transport is the keynote to all mysticism."

PART FIVE—MUROMACHI

Chapter XVII—THE ASHIKAGA SHŌGUNS

In 1336 the Emperor Kōmyō was set up in Kyōto by Ashikaga Takauji, and the Emperor Go-Daigo fled south to Yoshino to establish there a rival court. The period from 1336 to 1392, when the succession dispute terminated, is known to Japanese historians as Namboku-chō, the age of the Northern and Southern Courts. From 1392 to 1573 is styled the Muromachi period, after the name of a quarter of Kyōto in which the Ashikaga Shōguns established themselves.

We will pass rapidly over the political history of the first period, which is a desperate prelude to the uneasy rule of the Ashikaga Shōguns too intricate in its warfare and its intrigue to be described here in detail. Ostensibly a contest between rival courts, essentially it was a phase of redistribution of feudal privilege in the form of lands and adherents. For more than sixty years the whole country was wasted by struggles between feudal barons of all degrees, espousing one cause or another, but always, save for a few conspicuous models of chivalry, striving to satisfy their personal ambitions and their hunger for domains. A champion of the creed called Bushidō would be hard put to it to justify the breaches of faith which are revealed so clearly and so frequently by feudal documents of the fourteenth century. The code of feudal ethics did not entirely break down, but the sense of obligation was restricted to the narrow confines of the family, or some correspondingly small group. To promote the fortunes of his own unit, the warrior would freely sacrifice a wider loyalty. The fact is that feudal discipline depended on the power of the overlord to reward and punish, and it could not withstand the strain of anarchy. The Ashikaga family were fighting for supremacy and, far from being able to exercise the rigorous control of the Minamoto Shōguns over their "house-men," they had to bargain with strong warlords for support. There was no just feudal court to which injured parties might appeal, and the imperial authority was not only weak but disputed by two factions. Consequently the constables, the stewards, the holders of name-fields (*myōden*), tended each up to the limit of his power to become autonomous within his holding and to absorb into it the lands of neighbours who could not resist. Though many of the old titles and offices remained, their character changed or they were empty fictions. The complex system of *shiki*, the distribution of powers and income among overlords, stewards and provincial officers, all this began to break down and to be re-integrated in another form. It was "superseded by a new relation-ship frankly based upon vassalage; . . . all domains tended to become fiefs held by lords above and divided among vassals below. . . . Civil and religious lords having all but vanished and the Shōguns' authority having been almost forgotten, the old Con-stable (*shugo*) had become the overlord under whom the other lords and warriors were vassals and rear-vassals holding fiefs in a descending gradation in a scheme of hierarchical feudal relation-ships."* In other words the remnant of that centralised rule which the Kamakura government had—in a diminishing degree, it is true—wielded over the great feudal landholders was now gradually swept away, and power in Japan was divided among a number of great barons, over whom the Ashikaga Shōgun exercised a shadowy authority. As for the Imperial Court, it had lost much of its prestige, most of its wealth, and nearly all its strength. The Kyōto nobles who had hitherto managed to derive some revenue from their provincial manors were now often reduced to poverty, because the former stewards had appropriated all the rights in their lands. To apply for redress to the Shōgun's tribunals was useless, for the Shōgun dare not press his followers and could not force them.

The first Shōgun, Takauji, spent his life campaigning up and down Japan. The second, Yoshiakira, was constantly at odds with his great vassals, and some of them went over to the southern side. The record of the Yamana family illustrates succinctly the features of the times, such as the constant warfare, the shifting allegiances, the failure of central authority and the growth of great baronies. The Yamana were of Minamoto stock, senior collaterals of the Ashikaga. They had been only moderately influential vassals of the Kamakura government in the provinces of Hōki and Inaba and after the downfall of the Hōjō regents they fought on the side of

---

* Asakawa, describing the Shibuya and Shimadzu Shōen.

the Ashikaga. But feeling that their rewards were inadequate they negotiated with the Southern Court and prepared to attack Kyōto. In 1353 the capital was taken by a Southern army and the Shōgun decamped with the Northern Emperor in his keeping. Then the Ashikaga got fresh forces together, and occupied the capital once more. The Yamana, dissatisfied with their treatment by the Southern Court, drew off. But other factions took up the struggle, and the Ashikaga were in 1355 again driven from Kyōto for a short time. The Southern Court now began to weaken, but the power of the great vassals grew. The Yamana, still ostensibly on the Southern side, consolidated their own position while the Ashikaga fought. Then, secure in their own strength, they patched up a peace with Yoshiakira who, to keep them quiet, made the head of their clan constable of half a dozen provinces in which they were now paramount. And to be constable at that time was to be almost an independent ruler. The *Taiheiki*, a chronicle of those days, says of the constables: "Now all matters great and small were determined by the Shugo, who was master of the fortunes of his province, treated the (Bakufu) stewards and vassals like servants, and forcibly took over the manors of shrines and monasteries, using them as a source of military supplies." By 1390 members of the Yamana family were in control of eleven provinces, one-sixth in number of the provinces of Japan, and in 1392, having previously submitted a written oath of fealty to the Ashikaga, they rose against them and attacked Kyōto at the head of a large army. They were eventually defeated, and deprived of their control of all but the two provinces (Hōki and Inaba) of which they had first been made constables. This family, it will be seen, were engaged in almost constant warfare from 1336 to 1392. In that period they changed their allegiance at least twice; and they rose from a moderate position to great power by absorbing the land and the rights of others, including even imperial estates. Theirs was a characteristic record, repeated by one great family or another all over Japan, except perhaps in the eight eastern provinces which were under the jurisdiction of an Ashikaga at Kamakura and where the Shōguns had a useful nucleus of strength.

The almost incessant warfare which filled the era of the rival courts was yet sporadic enough to allow of, and even to promote,

a very distinct and interesting cultural development. So long as
the centre of military power was at Kamakura there was only an
imperfect contact between feudal society, which was provincial,
and civilian society, which was metropolitan. But when the Ashikaga moved to Kyōto and the home provinces became the main
theatre of events, the two societies tended to merge in many
respects. The fourteenth century therefore may properly be described as an age of fusion between the two elements, or rather,
because they were in many ways irreconcilable, of compromise.
In this difficult and often violent process the military caste seemed
to be dominant, for most of the material gain was on their side;
but in fact they were themselves strongly influenced by the more
ancient culture of the Heian court. Kyōto, after the downfall of
Kamakura, was thronged with soldiers from all parts of Japan,
who came to claim their reward for helping to overthrow the
enemies of the throne. The courts were so crowded with claimants
that, according to a celebrated lampoon of 1335, among the common sights of Kyōto were "petitioners up from the country" with
"baskets full of documents." But there was much law and little
justice. Bribery and violence carried the day. It was, says the same
lampoon, "a world of licence and disorder," in which "upstarts
aped their betters." Here were the usual fruits of war, the "sudden
lords" (*niwaka daimyō*) uneasy in their court dress, the penniless
soldiers pawning their armour, the hectic search for pleasure, the
extremes of profusion and want. The successful warriors, while
treating the court nobles with contempt, aspired to their breeding
and their elegance. Yoritomo's vassals had been strictly and of set
purpose segregated from the aristocrats, but now many great
feudal families from eastern and western Japan had their residences
in Kyōto. There was the Shōgun's palace in Muromachi, and near
by it the mansions of the Hosokawa, the Shiba, the Yamana and
suchlike chieftains, where they revelled in the intervals of their
campaigns. Thus the *Taiheiki* in one chapter treats of a battle
fought in 1348 by Kō Moronao, one of the ablest supporters of the
Ashikaga, and then turns to describe his luxurious mode of living,
his fine palace and gardens and his short way with high-born ladies
on whom he had cast his amorous eye. Even the august person of
the sovereign was not safe from the truculence of the Eastern war-

riors. A band of retainers of one Sasaki, swaggering through the streets, began tearing down maple branches from the cloistered emperor's garden. They were reproved, a brawl ensued, and next day Sasaki sent men to set fire to the palace. There was a great uproar in Kyōto, and the Shōgun was obliged to punish him. He was exiled from Kyōto, but was so little abashed that he set off with a gay procession of his followers, all on horseback fancifully attired and carrying each a caged nightingale. They stopped frequently on the way, to enjoy banquets and dancing girls. This conduct, says the *Taiheiki*, was meant to show their contempt for the nobles and the priests of the capital.

The succession dispute was somehow settled in 1392, by which time the country had settled into unstable equilibrium. The Ashikaga government, whether because the feudal barons were exhausted or because they were sated, was able to function with moderate efficiency. It never was able to exercise the same stern discipline over its vassals as did the governing body developed by the Hōjō, and there were sporadic revolts in all parts of the country for several years more; but on the whole there was peace for two or three generations, and then a gradual break-up of society culminating in further armed strife and disorder which brought the Muromachi period to a close. A survey of political events in this period shows us a succession of Ashikaga Shōguns established in Kyōto and living a life of elegance and profusion, in which the arts flourished and government was neglected, until they, like the monarchs and the regents of the Heian age, were displaced by men of a coarser but more vigorous type. Very soon after the first years of Muromachi the Ashikaga Shōguns, like the Minamoto Shōguns before them, became only nominal rulers, and their great feudatories exercised the real authority in the state. The third Shōgun, Yoshimitsu, carried to an extreme point the parvenu ostentation which marked the behaviour of the military class when they found themselves the masters of Kyōto. The Kamakura dictators had been satisfied with comparatively modest court ranks, but Yoshimitsu took the highest offices open to a subject, and exacted almost imperial honours. When he abdicated in 1395 he continued to govern from his Golden Pavilion, as if he were a cloistered emperor. The feudal warriors, each in his degree, followed this ex-

ample, and one of the few sources of income of court nobles was
the slender commission which they drew for assisting soldiers to
obtain honorary court offices. But the new aristocracy, or rather
the *nouveaux riches*, though they had a weakness for titles, were
not content with the frugal elegance which was all the courtiers of
the old style could permit themselves. Later, it is true, they fell
under the subtle influence of traditional Kyōto æsthetics and
surrendered to a deeper-rooted culture than their own, but in the
beginning of the Muromachi period they regarded most of the
ideals and pastimes of the true Kyōto people as effete and preferred more full-blooded pleasures. One great baron said of the
Imperial Accession Ceremony, "This is a useless business, unsuited to the times," and generally he and his kind were eager for
new things and inclined to be iconoclastic in the flush of their new
strength. That was one reason why they turned their eyes towards
China again and why they welcomed all that seemed up-to-date,
such as the paintings of Sung artists now in fashion, or the latest
developments of Zen Buddhism.

The Japanese of all classes and at all times seem to have had
a strong taste for novelty, from the Nara period when they
adopted most ardently the T'ang fashions, through the Heian
period when the last word of praise was *ima meku*, "to have a
modern air." It was natural, therefore, that in the Muromachi
period, when most old institutions and standards were being
challenged, the liking for modernity should grow into a craze.
There was another good reason why Japan should look towards
China at this time. Yoshimitsu and his followers had a mania
for building and decorating, and they needed money badly.
Trade with China was a lucrative source of income. It had been
carried on intermittently for long past, and even in Taira days the
harbour at Hyōgo (near the present Kobe) had been improved in
order to encourage the visits of Chinese merchant ships; but now
it was officially promoted. The Shōgunate, after the fall of the
Mongol dynasty, sent envoys to the Ming Court to arrange trade
between the two countries and to give undertakings that they
would suppress Japanese sea rovers who, whether as corsairs or as
"free traders," were the scourge of all the coasts of eastern Asia.
The Chinese do not appear to have been particularly anxious for

traffic with Japan, but they were so embarrassed by these pirates that they agreed to a fixed number of voyages each year, although with their traditional haughtiness they looked upon the Japanese cargoes as tribute from a vassal state. The Shōgun Yoshimitsu did not let national pride interfere with business, but accepted the Chinese terms, except that the Chinese limitation of the number of vessels was not observed in practice. It is a curious feature of this trade that the actual enterprises, the despatch and receipt of cargoes, were in the hands of Zen priests, though of course the Shōguns and the great feudatories took a large share of the proceeds and also profited by levying or farming out customs and harbour dues. Under the Ashikaga Zen was practically an official religion, and Zen priests acted as advisers to the Shōguns in other than spiritual matters. They are known to have drafted despatches in Chinese to the Ming Court, and to have supervised the commercial intercourse with China.

This close connection between trade and religion may have prepared the minds of the Japanese for the arrival about a century later of friars and merchants from the West.[1] While the Jesuits were only the forerunners of the traders, Japanese monks themselves took part in the trading ventures. The voyages of the Japanese ships were usually undertaken in the name of some great temple which took a share of their earnings. The first voyage of this kind was that of a vessel known as the Tenryūji-bune (1342), because it was to bring back treasure for the building of a temple of that name in which the Shōgun Takauji was interested. Subsequently the practice grew, and by 1451 there was a fleet of ten such ships, some named after various temples and shrines, such as the Tenryūji, the Shōfukuji and Hase-dera, others after feudal lords such as Ōuchi and Ōtomo, who were now prominent as merchant venturers. The cargo from Japan consisted usually of copper, sulphur, fans and lacquer ware, with a large number of swords, halberds and other weapons, in making which the Japanese were supreme.* It is interesting to note that gifts to the Ming Court were sent by important feudal lords, such as Yamana

---

* Thus in 1483 as many as 37,000 swords were sent. It is pleasant to think that the Sung masterpieces now preserved in Japan were bought with weapons sent to China, where they probably did very little harm.

and Hosokawa, in their own names; but they usually received
presents of at least the same value in return. The chief imports
from China were copper coins, iron, textiles and embroideries, pictures, books and drugs; but the Japanese generally received money
in exchange for their goods. The chief circulating medium in
Ashikaga times was Chinese copper coinage, and in 1432 the
Chinese complained that they were losing too much of their currency and sent an envoy to insist on reducing the number of
Japanese ships trading to China. Records show that the vessels
trading to China were of about 1,000 *koku* capacity. There were
larger vessels, but they kept to the coast, being unmanageable on
the high seas. The crew numbered about 100 men, and passengers
were carried. These passengers were as a rule merchants, both
priests and laymen, who had chartered space in the ship. It was a
profitable business, for it seems that Japanese goods sold in China
at four or five and sometimes even ten times their value in the
domestic market.

This lucrative traffic gave a great impetus to the growth
of a number of seaports, which were already assuming importance in domestic trade. The constant warfare of the fourteenth
century had forced the feudal commanders to improve transport
facilities, since they had to move about large bodies of men
and quantities of supplies. In the early Kamakura period the
landholders of the western mainland and Kyūshū, though far
from pacific, had not usually been involved in campaigns on a
national scale; but later their troops fought in distant localities and
they themselves moved freely between their fiefs and Kyōto. Consequently there sprang up a number of relatively important provincial towns, and those which were most favourably situated became thriving cities. Thus the town of Sakai (the port of the modern
Ōsaka), originally a centre of salt production in an imperial manor,
became during the age of the rival courts a doorway to Kyōto and
the home provinces for warriors coming up from the west and
from Shikoku, and was thus an important strategical point and
also a commissariat centre. Its position encouraged the growth of
a class of army contractor and moneylender, and its prosperity
was vastly increased when it became, in competition with Hyōgo,
a port of departure for vessels trading overseas. As the Ashikaga

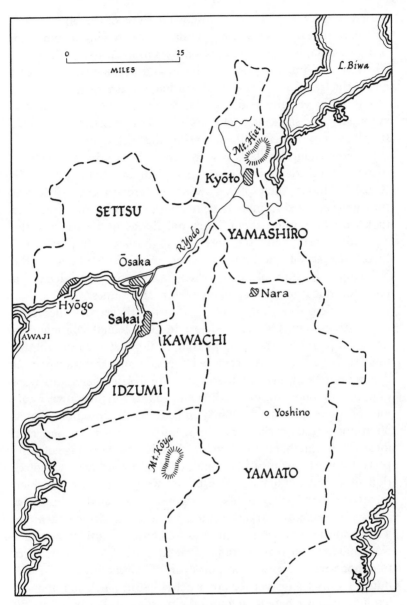

FIG. 44. *Map of the Home Provinces and important cities.*

period progressed its fortunes rose while those of the Shōguns declined, so that by 1543 we find the Bakufu borrowing money from
Sakai merchants on the security of taxes from Ashikaga domains.
The city was granted many privileges and in some ways was like
one of the free cities of mediæval Europe. Its citizens were to some
extent self-governing and enjoyed a certain degree of judicial
autonomy; and since many of them were *rōnin* (masterless warriors),
they knew how to defend themselves against aggressors.

Other harbours similarly rose to importance during these times,
such as Yamaguchi in Suwo, Onomichi in Higo, Hakata in
Kyūshū. Most of these places owed their growth to the fact that
they were situated in manors belonging to influential people who
took care to develop them. Thus Sakai was in a manor of the
Sumiyoshi shrine, and the port of Hyōgō, originally part of the
Fukuwara *shōen* of the Fujiwara, later came into the hands of the
Kōfukuji monastery of Nara, which from about 1470 derived a
large revenue from the monopoly of its customs dues.

The widespread warfare of the fourteenth century furthered
rather than hindered domestic trade. The feudal commanders
needed supplies for their troops and, if they were successful, for
their domains. All this promoted the sale and the transport of
commodities and, because the times were unsafe, merchants were
obliged to co-operate in devising safeguards for their own interests. So there arose trade guilds and similar organisations, based
often upon much earlier groupings, but now in a more perfected
form. They usually placed themselves under the patronage of some
powerful person or institution and, of course, paid for the protection they thus obtained. These bodies were known as *za*, which
means a "seat," and perhaps originally indicated a "pitch"*
allotted to them at markets in the precincts of a shrine or temple.
The connection between them and religious institutions was very
close and very ancient in origin. Traders would attach themselves
to a monastery, ostensibly as purveyors of commodities for its use,
but in reality as a cover for other activities, in particular money-
lending, because here they found the prestige of the church useful
in enforcing payment of debts. Usury was a special feature of the

* But other bodies attached to shrines were also known as *za*, e.g. companies
of dancers and musicians; and the modern word for a theatre is still *za*.

FIG. 45. *The Harbour of Onomichi. (From an eighteenth century guide-book.)*

early Muromachi period, when so many of the court nobles had
lost their offices and their estates in the civil wars. But those
engaged in more legitimate trades also tended to form themselves
into monopolistic groups under a patron. Thus in Kyōto the cotton
clothiers' guild was composed of parishioners of the Gion shrine,
the yeast-brewers belonged to the Kitano shrine, and they relied
upon those shrines to support them when they complained to the
court or the Bakufu of any infringement of their privilege. The
Tendai monastery on Mount Hiei was patron of the warehouse-
keepers, the Iwashimidzu Hachiman of the oil merchants, and
some of the threatening descents of armed priests upon the capital
were demonstrations in support of these clients of theirs. Certain
trades, again, were protected by great families. The Kyōto paper
makers depended upon the Bōjō, the gold-leaf makers on the
Konoe family, and even the courtesans had a guild which was protected by the noble house of Kuga. There were guilds of all descriptions in the country as well as at the capital, and it appears that
there was some liaison between guilds of the same trade in different
localities. Indeed the *za* in Japan and the *hansa* in Europe show a
parallel growth, and the relationships subsisting between *za* have
been described as a kind of Hanseatic league. No doubt a close
study would reveal contrasts as well as likenesses, but it is clear that
a privileged urban mercantile class developed under the decen-
tralised feudalism of Ashikaga times. It might have become a very
powerful element in the state, but the centralised feudal bureaucracy which (as later chapters will show) ruled Japan from about
the year 1600 would tolerate no rival autonomies, and therefore the
trade guilds, like the ecclesiastical corporations, were gradually
deprived of their liberties.

The monopolies held by these various bodies of merchants and
artisans, while no doubt a necessary phase in the development of
trade during a period of disorder, were liable to abuse of many
kinds. The patrons took exorbitant fees, and the guildsmen under
the shelter of their exclusive rights exacted high prices to recoup
themselves. A serious obstacle to traffic was the system, or rather
the reckless multiplication, of customs levies and tolls of all
descriptions. Barriers were arbitrarily set up by the Bakufu, by
constables, by stewards and civil, military and religious lords of

manors, who thus were able to derive an income from taxes they imposed upon passengers and goods in transit. In the archives of the Kōtukuji monastery there is an account showing the cost of transporting two baldachins to one of its chapels in Mino, a distance of under 100 miles. The freight charges were 1466 *mon*, while the tolls, levied at no less than 28 different barriers, amounted to 1496 *mon*. The total cost of transport (calculated on the basis of the price of rice) was therefore about £30, of which over one-half was paid in tax. Towards the end of the Muromachi period the merchants were able, sometimes by negotiation, sometimes by force, to withstand such impositions, though they did not succeed in abolishing the tolls altogether.

If the merchants were on the whole strong enough to look after their own interests, this was not usually true of the peasants, who had no means of resisting the extortions of public officials and private landlords. Yet even this long-suffering class were more than once during the Muromachi period goaded into revolt by the misery of debt and by hatred of the rich. These agrarian risings invariably followed close upon a famine or an epidemic of sickness, and the object of attack was usually a warehouse or a brewery, because the warehouse-keepers were pawnbrokers and the brewers were offensively wealthy and had stocks of a desirable commodity. The first of such riots on a large scale took place in 1428, and they were frequent after that date. They were sometimes suppressed by force by the constables, but more than once the military were overpowered, toll-barriers smashed, monasteries looted, and merchants plundered. In 1502 the constable of Iwasa, with his family, was murdered by angry farmers. Sometimes the mob was so threatening that the Bakufu, urged by the great temples, which feared incendiarism, gave way and proclaimed a general cancellation of debts.* This was called *tokusei*, but it was an entirely different thing from the acts of "Virtuous Administration" during the Hōjō regency. They were intended to conserve the property of the

---

* The *tokusei* edicts of this time abound in picturesque details. Thus in 1457 the Bakufu proclaimed that pledged articles could be redeemed by a payment of one-tenth of the sum advanced, and to prevent brawls at the pawnbrokers' shops they decreed that goods were to be taken out of pawn only by women, and during the daylight hours. If there was any quarrel, both parties would be punished.

Shōgun's vassals, whereas this was a concession to popular feeling and dictated by fear. There were at least 13 *tokusei* edicts under the Shōgun Yoshimasa, to say nothing of *tokusei* proclaimed by local magnates. That the military dictators should have thus surrendered to demonstrations by hungry peasants shows how weak was the central government, and how chaotic the local administration. It also indicates, as is confirmed by other evidence, that the rioters included a number of poor samurai, half soldier, half peasant, who were ready to join in any form of conflict or uprising. These were now a numerous class, and several war-lords turned it to their advantage by taking its members into their service.

Such risings were characteristic of the times, in that there was now an almost complete breakdown of allegiance, of the habit of submission to authority. It is visible throughout all grades of society, down to the lowest. The clan system collapses and is replaced by the family system, loyalty to the head of a clan is superseded by obedience to the head of a household and may even involve active hostility towards other members of the clan. There is a general feeling that the social order is disintegrating, a general scramble for power; and it is common to find in books of the period such phrases as "nowadays the low chasten the high," or "the rulers are weak and their vassals are strong," or "there is no loyalty as between master and man, the ruler cannot control the subject." These are, of course, the perennial laments of conservatism and may therefore be discounted; but it is true that the Ashikaga period was an age of violent re-arrangement of classes. "Even an outcast," mournfully observes an abbot of the Kōfukuji when he learns that a common soldier is seeking to obtain the post of constable of Idzumi, "can aspire to the rule of a province."

The foregoing account will have conveyed, perhaps the better for being disjointed, some idea of the confusion and turmoil of the Muromachi period. It was an age of ferment, but not of decay, for during the whole of the fourteenth and fifteenth centuries new institutions were developing out of the old and moving towards a maturer feudalism than that of Kamakura. One of its most important features, of which modern Japan shows traces, was the growth in importance of the family as the social unit. The old system of *shiki*, under which rights and offices were divisible and transmis-

sible, broke down because in times of insecurity it was essential to
consolidate the strength of a family and to entrust the control of its
fortunes to the strongest and ablest member. So long as the
Bakufu could protect its vassals against aggression, there was no
reason why a father should not split up his wealth among his
children, putting his trust in the cohesion of kinship and the
power of the overlord. But when anarchy and warfare prevailed
he could not, for instance, afford to let his property go to
daughters who could not fight to protect it. Nor could he allow
even part of a *shiki* pertaining to his holding to pass into another
family. Accordingly there grew up the privilege of masculinity and
the custom of primogeniture, and it is from this period that begins
the subordination of women, in striking contrast to their high
position under the Fujiwara régime and in the earlier stages of
feudalism. The word primogeniture only loosely describes the
system of succession which obtained in Japan, for the heir was not
necessarily the first-born male, but the son who showed most
promise; and if there was no boy who seemed likely to be a credit
and a bulwark to the household, then the head of the family might
adopt a suitable person, generally a kinsman, as his prospective
heir. It was not unknown for this son to be as old as, or even older
than his adoptive parent, and sometimes the property and the
headship of the house would be made over during the lifetime of
the parent, if he felt too old for active life. The following extract
from a collection of pious anecdotes (written about 1300) throws
light on current sentiment in these matters:

"In the province of Tango there was a certain man, who
though a small landholder (*shōmyō*) was not badly off. When
he died he left a will which was to be opened after the mourning. He had many sons and daughters and when they opened
it they found that he had left a large share to the eldest son, a
little less to the next, and so on down to the last. The eldest
son said: 'Since the late lord has bequeathed in this fashion we
cannot object . . . but if this estate is divided up into so
many parts and each of us is confirmed (by the Bakufu) in his
share, then, when we take service we shall find ourselves in
difficulties, all in reduced circumstances and unable to make a
proper showing in the world. Therefore it is better that one of

us should carry on the family, and the others should build a hermitage in some suitable place, enter religion, and pass their lives in prayer, thus assuring their peace in this world and the next. I myself, though the eldest son, am without talents, and conscious of this I wish that you would choose one of your number to succeed.'"

Finally, the tale runs, they selected the fifth son as the heir, and the others settled down to a quasi-monastic life, cultivating the land on behalf of the head of the family. This edifying story is perhaps untrue, but it shows very clearly that the ideal of the time was the maintenance of the family, the preservation of its property and the enhancement of its prestige; and by family is here meant not the proliferating clan but the small household. The clan, in other words, had grown too unwieldy and had split up into smaller units. It is a development which follows naturally from the growth and movement of population, together with the diversity of interests brought about by increased numbers and a more complex social structure. Conditions in the Ashikaga period merely accelerated and emphasised a process that had begun centuries before, but had been slowed down by the bureaucratic reforms of 645. These changes were at the same time a cause and an effect of the partition of Japan into a number of self-governing territories, whose occupants were bound together no longer primarily by the blood-tie but by community of interests and also by proximity. Supreme over each such group was a powerful warrior, usually the constable of a province, and attached to him for protection were less powerful families holding land within the territory which he ruled, but not necessarily related to him or to one another. The business of the overlord was to consolidate his power for offence and defence against other overlords, by conserving the strength of each family unit in his domain while preventing its use in any combination unfavourable to himself. The business of the lesser warrior was to secure the prosperity and the continuance of his own family. So we find on the one hand constant interference by the overlord in the family affairs of his vassals, on the other hand a sacrifice of the individual to the interests of the family. The lord's approval had to be obtained before the vassal could nominate a successor to the headship of his family, and before any property could be devised. The codes of some great feudal houses contained most stringent instructions to their vassals on this and similar points. Particular care was taken to ensure that land or rights should not, through adoption or marriage, fall into the hands of a vassal of another lord. A watchful eye was kept upon the marriages not only of knights and their sons and daughters, but also of the better class of peasants and craftsmen, so that the lord should not lose their land or their service to another fief. The members of a family depended even for sustenance upon the head of the house and must obey him, whether he was their father or their brother or even an adopted stranger.

This development of the family as an economic and social unit so profoundly influenced Japanese life that the civil code now in force embodies certain survivals of mediæval notions as to property and succession. The new constitution of society made it the chief duty of a man to consider first not his own individual interests, but those of his house. It thus placed high in the scale of virtues obedience, patience and sacrifice; it encouraged a habit of respect for age and authority, of courtesy in speech and demeanour; and it stimulated the holder of a name to keep it unsullied. These ideals of conduct were not, of course, new, for they grew naturally out of ancient beliefs and customs; but feudalism tended always to single out for emphasis those conceptions of morality which seemed to contribute to its own survival, and to neglect, if not to discourage, all others. Its code, though strict, was therefore narrow. Since it aimed at preserving an economic unit, its basis was in essence material rather than ethical.* Through the heraldic battle cries and the lofty speeches of feudal warriors there can be heard the persistent murmur of Property! Property! The temper of the leaders of the feudal class was acquisitive and conservative.

* A curious sidelight is thrown on this aspect of feudal thought by the history of certain common words. *Katoku*, literally "house-leadership," for instance, originally meant the control of the head of a family over its members, but from mediæval times it began to signify his control over its goods as well, until finally it was used primarily in the sense of the inheritance of property, just as *familia* in Roman law came to stand for the family estate. Similarly the term *sōryō*, "the whole domain," became the style of the heir-presumptive, and in to-day's common parlance means simply the eldest son or even daughter. *Shiki*, as we have seen, though originally meaning an office, was later used to designate the holder of rights in land, and then the land itself.

Being acquisitive, it easily condoned offences against the persons
and the property of those outside the group, and being conservative it fostered a hierarchical sentiment but gave little encouragement to initiative. Since the interests of the family are paramount,
the movement of its individual members is fettered, and the most
trivial decision can be reached only after prolonged consultation
and discussion. A pitiless social pressure strangles independence of
thought and behaviour, makes servants of younger sons and
chattels of women. Only the stimulus of warfare, which needs quick
judgment and bold action, could keep such a system from decay.

Warfare there was in abundance after the unstable peace which
lasted from the days of Yoshimitsu until half way through the
fifteenth century, and even during that period there were feuds
and conflicts here and there throughout Japan. Great houses rose
and fell in struggles sometimes with their peers, sometimes with
their own vassals. These dissensions spread and at length took the
form of a succession war between two rival Ashikaga houses, just
as the Ashikaga themselves had divided the country into two
camps fighting for the rival courts. By 1467 there had broken out
a great civil war (called, from the era-name, the War of Ōnin)
which, centring chiefly in or near the capital, lasted until 1477
and then was transferred to the provinces, where it continued
until the close of the fifteenth century. In this period many of the
ancient feudal families succumbed, or struggled on with diminished power. The Yamana, who with their allies had mustered
nearly 100,000 troops in the Ōnin war, were reduced to insignificance. Their enemies the Hosokawa were in the same case. The
Shōni and Kikuchi, who had grown to high estate in Kyūshū after
the Mongol invasion, almost disappeared, as did Shiba, one time
deputy of the Shōgun at Kamakura and ruler of six northern provinces as well as overlord of great vassals in central Japan. No
wonder that the poet Bashō, visiting in a later and more peaceful
day the scene of a famous battle, said:

> *The summer grasses!*
> *All that is left of the warriors' dream!*

The fluctuating fortunes of the feudal houses often deprived
samurai of their holdings, and thus produced a number of landless
soldiers. Those who were willing to take service with another lord

PART OF THE SO-CALLED TOBA SŌJŌ SCROLL

PORTRAIT OF THE SHŌGUN ASHIKAGA YOSHIMOCHI

had usually no difficulty in finding good employment. Others drifted into the towns, or joined the troops of the monasteries, and some dropped into the category of *ashigaru* or light foot-soldier, thus helping to form a new class of fighting men, a kind of mercenary ranking below the samurai proper. There is mention of the *ashigaru* in Kamakura books, but as an important phenomenon they date from the latter half of the Muromachi period. Most of them appear to have been peasants and serfs who had deserted farms burdened with debt and ravaged by war. In the codes of some feudal houses their position was defined as just above that of peasants, whose dress they had to wear. They were an unruly class, joining in all popular riots for the sake of loot, and in war-time plundering both friend and enemy. Their rise was significant for it went along with a complete change in the character of feudal campaigns. In Yoritomo's day the small landholder had ridden to the wars on his own horse, accompanied by a follower or two. Now battles were decided not by cavalry skirmishes and hand-to-hand encounters on a small scale, but by the movement of large bodies of men, both horse and foot. These and related changes helped to abolish the already faint distinction between "free" and "base" people, and to establish two main divisions of society, the soldier and the farmer. Beneath these in the scale came first the artisan and last the merchant. But in general during the civil wars of this period such divisions were uncertain, and for a time men could pass more freely than before from one class to another.

During all this period both the Imperial House and the Ashikaga Shōgunate continued free from attack, not because they were feared but because they were impotent. The difference between them was that the emperors were poverty-stricken and the Shōguns led a life of luxury. Perhaps the lowest ebb of the imperial fortunes was reached in 1500, when because there was no money in the Treasury the body of the emperor (Go-Tsuchimikado) remained unburied for six weeks. For the same reason his successor's enthronement ceremony was postponed for 20 years. The Ashikaga family had rich domains, but the Shōguns spent their wealth freely and were often hard pressed for funds since, with a few exceptions, they devoted themselves rather to pleasure than to the duties of a ruler. Theirs was an age when the delegation of authority was carried to extremities remarkable even in Japan. There was now hardly ever a cloistered or abdicated emperor, largely because the court could not bear the expense of the rites of abdication and succession. But the Shōgun, who bore the title of *kwampaku* and was thus the emperor's deputy, exercised his proper functions as military dictator through constables (*shugo*) who became practically autonomous. Even these constables in many cases ceased to reside in their territories, leaving them to be administered by deputy constables who, though their vassals, often became more powerful than the constables themselves. The Ashikaga continued to hold the title of Shōgun until 1597, when the fifteenth and last of them, who had abdicated his office in 1573, died in exile, as had done several of his line just before him.

NOTE TO CHAPTER XVII

[1] Page 357. Strictly speaking the traders were the forerunners of the missionaries, their first arrival being in 1542 whereas the first Jesuits landed in 1549. The Jesuits participated in trade to the extent that they had a share in the silk trade between Nagasaki and Macao, the profits going to mission funds.

Chapter XVIII

RELIGION AND THE ARTS

IT is only a seeming paradox that in this destructive, subversive age the arts should have flourished in Japan as never before. The reasons are plain. In the first place, the Japanese, whether by instinct or by tradition, have always had a thirst for beauty of colour and form, a taste which even great disaster could not suppress. Secondly, social conditions were such as fostered rather than discouraged the creation of fine things, since they were the symbols of success, the means of ostentation needed to satisfy the pride of men newly risen to power and riches. Lastly, and perhaps this was most important, the church was strong enough to provide a refuge for artists and men of letters. Monks, therefore, and laymen who took care to keep clear of war and politics, could devote themselves to painting or writing in monasteries where they were tolerably safe, or they could attach themselves to some great baron who chose to act as a patron of learning. We have seen that the feudal gentry were anxious not to be mistaken for country boors. The exquisites of Kyōto had for long despised them, and now when they were masters of the capital they wanted to cut a fine figure. There is an interesting passage in the *Gempei-Seisuiki* which relates that although Yoshitsune, when he appeared at court, with his white skin and his graceful movements looked quite at home in Kyōto, the courtiers thought he was "less than the refuse of the Taira." But now there was a change and it was the soldiers who led the fashion. After Nawa, constable of Hōki, escorted the emperor into the capital in 1333, his style was all the rage, and was known as the "Hōki manner." The military class were no longer content with distinction in the field, and so, from the Shōgun downwards, they set themselves to enjoy the benefits of culture as they conceived it; and in fact they did succeed in stimulating the arts of peace.

But it was in reality the monks, with the artists nourished by the old régime, who carried the torch, and therefore it is better, in describing this culture, to treat first of the religious institutions to which it owed its existence. Chief among these, without any doubt, was Zen Buddhism, which, taken up with enthusiasm by the military class in the Kamakura period, profited by their complete dominance in the next, and flourished under the patronage of the Shōguns and the great barons to such an extent that it might well be described as the official if not the state religion.

Not that the comfort of other doctrines was abandoned for the self-discipline of Zen. While it must be granted that the ethical code of the samurai set before them high, if circumscribed, ideals, when we come to the comparatively well-documented Ashikaga period we find little trace, except in heroic legend, of that stoic temperament, that impressive sternness which many writers like to ascribe to feudal warriors. They seem to have combined fortitude and sentimentality, strength of mind and credulity, in the proportions usual among professional soldiers, and they mostly displayed a characteristic military inability to grasp the rudiments of civil administration. They were therefore very much in the hands of astute and learned clerics. The relations of Ashikaga Takauji with the Church reveal this aspect of feudal manners in an interesting way. His chief mentor was a monk known as Musō Kokushi, who lived from 1275 to 1351, and was an important figure in the Muromachi age. Though Eisai may be fairly regarded as the patriarch of Japanese Zen Buddhism, yet there was in his teaching an admixture of mystic Shingōn elements, and it was Chinese monks who brought over from its source, in particular between the years 1214 and 1280, the unadulterated Zen doctrine. This was handed on to two great Japanese divines, who were the first to receive the title of *Kokushi* or National Teacher. One of these was Daitō and the other was Musō. It is clear that Musō by his personality and his learning greatly influenced many prominent feudal warriors, notably Ashikaga Takauji and his brother Tadayoshi. It was he who persuaded them to set up in each province a temple and a pagoda, in imitation of the provincial monasteries (*kokubunji*) of the Nara period. These temples were styled *Ankoku-ji* (*Ankoku* means Peaceful Country) and Takauji's motive in founding them was in part political. He wanted to have in every province an emblem of the spread of his influence over all Japan. But also he hoped to create good feeling by this pious enterprise, which was meant to comfort the spirits of those who had perished in his campaigns, both friends and foes. A similar motive animates in modern times the butchers of large cities, when they have Buddhist masses said for the animals which the needs of their calling have obliged them to slaughter. No doubt Musō worked upon Takauji's feelings, for he seems to have been moved by genuine remorse. A surprising number of documents are extant, some in his own hand, which show that he was extremely anxious about his salvation. There is his vow to the Kwannon of Kiyomidzu, in which he prays for grace and protests that he would like to live in retirement so as to improve his prospects in the next world. There is another vow, to the Gion shrine, in which he says that he has practised Zen but is very ignorant, and pleads for a few more years of life in which to arrive at enlightenment. He felt, or he professed to feel, that he had been guilty of a great crime in deposing the emperor Go-Daigo, and he undertook various pious works for the consolation of the soul of the departed monarch, as well as the souls of all those who had died in battle. Such was the object of the building of the Tenryūji, and also of the transcription of the whole Buddhist canon, commenced in the first month of 1354 and finished, it is said, in the third. Several hundred priests from temples of all sects took part in this latter task and at the end of each volume is a block-printed epigraph, signed by Takauji. These instances will have served to illustrate the very comprehensive religious ardour of the Ashikaga and their kind. It can hardly be said that they had mastered Zen, for they did not dispense with the written word. Still Musō Kokushi is reported to have said of Takauji that even after a heavy drinking bout he would always go through a long session of Zen before sleeping; and it is true that Zen masters, if not Zen doctrines, had great power over their minds.

The growing power of Zen is shown by the desperate struggles which the Tendai monasteries made to retain their old supremacy. Their position was a difficult one since Zen, as well as being the favourite sect of the military class, was taken up by the Court, doubtless under pressure exercised by Zen priests through the Shōguns. One curious piece of evidence in favour of this supposition is the fact that Musō received the title of National Teacher from seven emperors in succession, three times during his life and four after his death.* The Zen sects had lost their early simplicity and were no longer content with plain hermitages. They now possessed great buildings both in Kamakura and in Kyōto. In each place were the Five Monasteries and the Ten Chapels headed in Kamakura by the Kenchōji which had been built under the Hōjō and in Kyōto by the Tenryūji. Over all these was the Nanzenji, or Southern Zen Monastery, the headquarters of the Rinzai sect, which was now pre-eminent except in the northern and western provinces, where the Sōtō sect was most favoured. Zen monks were familiar guests at the palace and the mansions of civil and military nobles, where they were welcome for their learning, their wisdom and often for their skill in capping verses, the favourite pastime of the day. Altogether there were few quarters in which they could not make their influence felt. It is somewhat surprising, therefore, to find that in their quarrels with the Tendai monasteries they did not always carry the day. There was a bitter dispute in 1344, when it was suggested that the emperor should take part in the dedication of the now completed Tenryūji. The facts are hard to disentangle, but it is clear that the Tendai opposition was so strong that the ritual was performed in the absence of the emperor, who went to a service next day, secretly, so as not to offend the Hieizan monks. The sects exchanged terrific abuse in which the Hieizan monks from long practice easily excelled the Zen priests. Mass meetings were held in the Hiei monasteries, and resolutions passed reproving the court for dealing with heretics. These documents are liberally sprinkled with such phrases as "demons masquerading as churchmen," "false views," "evil practices," "enemies of the state," and so on. Feeling ran so high that on this occasion the Bakufu, although they were entirely on the side of Zen, preferred to compromise. In 1368 there was another serious quarrel, in which the Bakufu took up the cause of the Zen and the Tendai monks threatened to bring down their sacred emblems to the capital. This was their usual form of intimidation, which was as a rule successful because nobody dare incur the anger of the gods whose

---

* His full canonical name thus consists of fourteen characters prefixed to "Kokushi."

presence these emblems symbolised. On this occasion they did
not at first succeed in frightening the military party and were
forced to carry out their threat. They descended upon Kyōto
with their sacred cars, to find the palace guarded by soldiers
under the command of Hosokawa, Yamana, Akamatsu and other
prominent leaders. Yet the Bakufu did not wish to use force, and
the emperor gave way to the extent that he exiled the monk
Sosen who was a friend of Yoshimitsu and held an important
office in the Zen chapter. Their success encouraged the monasteries to further threats but at this point the Bakufu lost patience.
When the armed monks again entered the capital on their way to
the palace they were attacked by the soldiers, and, after losing one
or two men, ran away, leaving their cars behind. Even then they
did not entirely lose the day, for they gained some points against
the Nanzenji, partly, it seems, because the Bakufu did not take
these quarrels seriously and anyhow did not mind if the court was
embarrassed, but also, there is no doubt, because the military
leaders were bungling amateurs in the tactics of controversy by
comparison with the clerical parties. The great Enryakuji monastery had a long tradition of prestige, and was regarded as a guardian not only of the capital city but of the whole state. The monks
well knew how to make the best use of these powerful attributes
in their dealings with the credulous war-lords. And, it must be
remembered, they were rich and extremely numerous. At one
time Mount Hiei was covered with temples, seminaries and other
buildings to the number of 3,000, which collectively formed the
Enryakuji.

But these were almost the last flickers of the militancy of the
Tendai monasteries, though they continued to terrorise Kyōto when
they could, until in the sixteenth century they were submerged
in a civil war, their buildings burned to the ground and their
monks put to the sword. Zen, on the other hand, increased its
power by peaceful means. We have already seen how close was
its connection with diplomacy and trade. It was a Zen monk
who made a collection of diplomatic documents called a Treasury
of Friendly Neighbours and it was in the Zen monastery called
Myōshinji that there was perfected a new method of accounting
and the systematic investment of church funds. Zen in its best

manifestations seems to have encouraged a useful type of practical wisdom, and thus no doubt made it easy for clever Zen teachers to deal with military men who like simple answers to difficult questions. It is significant of their position that, in an age when learning though respected was not in the ascendant, the most important academies were in their hands. The celebrated Ashi-kaga College grew in importance during the Muromachi period, under the patronage of the Uesugi family and the presidency of Zen monks, especially after the year 1400. For a great part of the disturbed century that followed it was the greatest and practically the only centre of Chinese classical learning. It specialised in philosophical studies, was visited by scholars from China, and had in one of its rooms an image of Lao-tzŭ. By 1550 it had as many as 3,000 students, most of whom came from distant parts of Japan. The Five Monasteries of Kyōto were devoted at first to less serious studies such as Chinese poetry, and later to historical research. In short there were very few departments of life into which Zen monks did not penetrate and their influence was the greater be-cause their favoured position, their somewhat pragmatic outlook, and the almost laïcal way of living which their tenets permitted, made it convenient for artists and men of letters to join their fraternity. It is also much to the credit of Zen monks that, in an age of ambitious prelates and grasping sects, they devoted them-selves to popular education. If we may judge from contemporary comedies, many country priests were stupid and unlettered, but the little church schools known as *terakoya* increased in numbers during the Muromachi period, and they were generally conducted by Zen monks, who taught young people (even up to the age of 20, it seems) reading and writing. They also gave them simple moral lessons, and the text books which they used remained in use until recent times, the best-known, perhaps, being the *Teikin-ōrai* or Correspondence Manual of Home Teaching.*

The history of the other great religious bodies must be passed over briefly. The breakdown of centralised government and the fluid state of society favoured the growth of the popular sects, which reached the zenith of their influence in the period of dis-

---

* Its morality is not entirely admirable. It contains for instance advice as to the bribery of officials by those going up to the capital for lawsuits.

order following the Ōnin civil war. Their behaviour shows traces
of a rising democratic sentiment which under more favourable
conditions might have modified the whole national structure. But
this sentiment grew out of confusion and was in the end suppressed
by force. The followers of Nichiren, as might be expected from so
pugnacious a tradition, soon got into trouble in this quarrelsome
age. Nichiren had instructed his disciples to spread the Lotus
(Hokke) Sect in western Japan and for a time they had some
success in Kyōto, one of their leaders (Nissei) even being invited
thither by Takauji, and others being patronised by great families
like the Hosokawa. But when one of his successors, Nisshin, began
in 1440 to admonish the Shōgun in the sharp manner of his
master Nichiren he was thrown into gaol and cruelly tortured. In
the provinces, however, they had gained many followers. They
established numerous centres where they lived in self-governing
communities which were strong enough to withstand attacks from
their rivals, and in general their influence among the poorer
classes was very strong. Nisshin took several months to make a
journey to Kyōto from one of the Nichiren strongholds in Bizen
because, as he explained, the people on his road were so ardent
that they would not let him pass. Most of these believers were
humble folk, peasants, tradesmen, or small samurai, but it is
interesting to note that the great artist Kano Motonobu was an
adherent of the Lotus sect.

The Pure Land (Jōdo) doctrines continued to flourish under
leaders of the Shin sect who followed in the line of its founder
Shinran. Most notable among these was Rennyo (1415-1499).
He raised the sect to great eminence, and the Hongwanji, the
temple of the Original Vow, at Kyōto, flourished exceedingly.
But it was inevitable that he should incur the enmity of the
Tendai monks on Mount Hiei, and in 1465 they attacked the
Hongwanji and burned it to the ground. Rennyo, barely escaping
with his life, made for the eastern and northern provinces. His
teaching seems to have spread like wildfire in those regions, for
by 1473 we find him established at a place called Yoshizaki in
Echizen, deliberately chosen because of the advantages of its
position as a defensive stronghold. Here and in other fortified
places his followers (consisting largely, to quote his own words,

of tradesmen, servants, hunters and fishermen) formed autonomous communities which preserved their independence by offensive as well as defensive methods, fighting with their sectarian
enemies and also challenging the authority of feudal lords in their
own territories. Their whole-hearted militant belief in the *nembutsu* and the mercy of Amida gained them the name of Ikkō or
Single-Minded,* and their revolts and attacks which were so frequent during the sixteenth century are known as the Ikkō Ikki,
which might be translated as the Fanatic Risings. The first of importance took place in 1487, when they besieged and defeated
Togashi, the feudal lord of the province of Kaga. Thenceforward
they became paramount in many parts of Japan, even eating into
the power and the lands of the great barons, and it was not until
the following century that they were finally overcome.

More than once the feudal leaders went so far as to ally themselves with these religious bodies, sometimes in order to suppress
agrarian risings, sometimes to play off one sect against another.
Thus in 1532 the Hosokawa in league with the Nichiren party
stormed the Ikkō stronghold of Yamashina, and in the following
year they attacked the Hongwanji of Ishiyama (Ōsaka); but this
temple having been built in a good defensive position, the Ikkō
people held their ground. On the other hand the followers of
Nichiren finally made themselves so detested all round that they
were driven out of Kyōto by a combination of their enemies. The
incident which led to this result was characteristic of the Nichiren
manner, for it arose out of the behaviour of a member of the
Hokke (Nichiren) sect who heckled a Tendai preacher during
his sermon. This was in 1535. The quarrel spread, and in 1537
the Bakufu joined with all the other sects but particularly the
Ikkō to suppress the followers of Nichiren, and shortly afterwards
a great battle took place in the streets of Kyōto, which ended in
the destruction of all the Hokke temples in the city, 21 in number,
and the slaughter of many Hokke believers, who as they fought
shouted for a war-cry the syllables *Namu-myōhō-renge-kyō*. Both
sides appear to have fought in disregard of death, because both
were certain that they would be reborn in paradise. The Nichiren
sects never regained their former importance, doubtless because

---

* *Ikkō-Isshin* is a phrase often used by Rennyo—"One direction, one heart."

their quarrelsome habits prevented cohesion among their members. On the other hand it is significant of the power of loyalty in Japan that the Pure Land sects, especially the branches which derived from Shinran, were bound together by a common allegiance to their founder. Devotion to the persons or the memory of their patriarchs was a strong link in their communities. They owe their survival not only to the nature of their beliefs but also to this conformity with the feudal pattern; and to-day the great Hongwanji sects, which had their origin in the early congregations founded by Shinran, are the most numerous and the most wealthy in Japan.*

Something should be said about the fortunes of Shintō during this period. As an institutional religion it continued to be overshadowed by Buddhism but it survived and in some respects even prospered thanks to its capacity to compromise with Buddhist tenets, particularly in its Dual (Ryōbu) form. It had a greater vitality than is admitted by certain critics, who are inclined to ascribe its revival in the nineteenth century almost entirely to deliberate political motives. Even in its darkest days the ancient cult was preserved at the great shrines of Ise and Idzumo, while the nature worship upon which Shintō was based was too deeply rooted to allow of its complete decay. Shintō ceremonies were neglected by the Court, at first in their enthusiasm for Buddhism and later out of sheer poverty, but many Shintō shrines, it is true by assuming an extremely Buddhist complexion, retained great influence throughout the Middle Ages. Such names as Hiyoshi, Kumano, Kasuga, Kitano, recur constantly in history, and we know that the national deities were given a share of the credit for the victory over the Mongols. In the fourteenth and fifteenth centuries there was a certain philosophical revival of Shintō which seems to have been called forth by the decline in the fortunes of the Imperial House. Kitabatake Chikafusa, a supporter of the Southern Dynasty, wrote (*circa* 1340) a history of Japan and other works based on the national theology. Later the court noble and state

* According to official returns in 1928, they had 19,701 temples as against 12,108 of the Shingon sect, and 5,019 of the Nichiren sect. Their priests number 16,000, and their believers are estimated at about 12,000,000 out of a total of 41,000,000 Buddhists in Japan.

minister Ichijō Kanera, the most eminent classical scholar of his day, based upon the symbolism of the Divine Imperial Regalia a treatise (*circa* 1470) harmonising the fundamental principles of Shintoism, Confucianism and Buddhism. At about the same time there was formed by the Urabe, the ancient family of court diviners, a new school of Shintō, called Yuiitsu or Unique, ostensibly fundamentalist but in reality highly syncretic. There is no doubt that the eclectic habit manifested in these movements helped Shintō to endure; but it should be added that the ancestral deities, though they may have been neglected, were never forgotten. Their names appear frequently in the chronicles and romances, warriors prayed to them for victory, and innumerable ancient legends combined to preserve their memory. Moreover the disorder of the times helped in a curious way to preserve the cult of the Sun Goddess. The misery of the reigning family naturally grieved members of the old court aristocracy, and caused them to lament its lost dignity, to look backward rather than forward. Men like Ichijō Kanera began to study the ancient chronicles, and in particular that section of the *Nihon Shoki* which describes the age of the Gods and traces from them the Imperial descent. A small body of reactionary opinion was thus formed which, though not influential, at least helped to preserve continuity of the tradition of divine lineage. In an even stranger way the poverty of the throne contributed to the cult of the Sun Goddess. The great shrines of Ise were essentially the family shrines of the emperors, reserved for their worship and maintained at their expense; but when the imperial chest was empty their priests had to look elsewhere for support, and they borrowed from the Buddhists the system of religious associations (called *kō*), by which bodies of worshippers in the provinces were, so to speak, affiliated to the shrine of the Sun Goddess and helped to maintain it by their small offerings.* The members of these associations were encouraged to make pilgrimages to Ise, and given facilities to that end, so that ultimately the cult lost its exclusive character and became popular and widespread, until in subsequent cen-

---

* So valuable was this source of income that one shrine would "sell" so many worshippers to another. Deeds thus conveying a given number of members of a specified association are still extant.

turies most Japanese felt that they ought to journey to worship at the shrines of the Sun Goddess and the Food Goddess at least once in their lifetime. Another source of income for the priests of Ise was the sale of calendars, which had hitherto been prepared especially for the court, but were now written in a simple script for popular use.

Turning now from religious to literary and artistic movements under the Ashikaga Shōguns, it is best to premise that certain fairly well marked cultural periods can be distinguished. First is the period of the Rival Courts, lasting until 1392. Then comes the period of the third Shōgun Yoshimitsu and his successors down to the seventh, Yoshikatsu (1442), rulers who led a life of luxurious elegance centering round their villa called the Golden Pavilion; and finally the period of the Shōgun Yoshimasa, known as the Higashiyama (East Hill) period, because it was there that he built his Silver Pavilion and there that the Muromachi æsthetic reached and passed its fullest bloom, dropping its full-blown petals one by one as the fifteenth century drew to a close and the country was once more plunged into disastrous civil war. We cannot stop to examine the special characters of each of these periods, but it is important to understand that in the brief interval of about seventy years (say between 1395, when Yoshimitsu abdicated and went to his Golden Pavilion, and the Ōnin war which broke out in 1467 and left Kyōto in ashes) there was compressed a most important and of its kind a most original and energetic phase of culture. It was as if the arts hurried to take advantage of a short breathing space between two deadly periods of strife, and indeed this phase does display in some of its aspects that feverish, spendthrift character which marks a society threatened with destruction.

We have noticed that it was the Buddhist Church which kept the arts alive during the years of turmoil, but it must be said that religion was now their nurse and not their mother. Architecture, painting, literature, all took a secular turn. This movement is perhaps best exhibited in the record of the school of writing known as the Literature of the Five Monasteries, the Zen institutions to which we have already alluded. Their activities can be traced back to Chinese scholars naturalised in Japan in the thirteenth cen-

tury, but their true Japanese patriarch was a Zen monk named
Sesson Yūbai, who after twenty years' study in China returned to
Japan in 1329, a year which may fairly be regarded as the date
of the foundation of this important school. It is significant of the
nature of their works that Yūbai while abroad lived like a Chinese
in every respect, was offered by the Chinese emperor the incumbency of a large monastery, and was praised by Chinese men of
letters for his verse, which (they said) excelled that of their own
poets. He had many successors and imitators, of whom the most
celebrated are Zekkai and Gidō, both pupils of Musō Kokushi.
They flourished exceedingly, and were in high esteem in literary
circles. Gidō's discourses attracted great crowds to his monastery,
and Zekkai, who spent a long time in China, was much esteemed
there as a poet. All these men occupied themselves almost exclusively with pure Chinese literature, and in particular poetry.
Their ambition was to compose verses which could be mistaken
for the work of Chinese poets, and though we should discount
the flattery of their Chinese friends they did, if we may believe
competent judges, turn out better Chinese than the nobles of the
Fujiwara period. Though the chief masters of this school were
monks, who gave lessons to their rich patrons in Kyōto, modern
Japanese specialists say that its verse "has not a monkish smell,"
but is in the best lay tradition. Chinese models were in favour all
round. The great feudal lords prized highly Chinese goods. Yoshimitsu liked to wear Chinese dress and had himself carried about
in a Chinese palanquin.

   This passion for Chinese things was a marked characteristic
of the intellectual circles of Muromachi. It was favoured, of
course, by the then frequent communication with China, by
appreciation of the fruits of the Sung renaissance in art and
literature, and by the dependence of Zen monks upon their
Chinese leaders; but it was in part a passing mode of elegance
due to the current restlessness and the desire for exotic things.
Learned and talented scholars and poets followed Zekkai and
Gidō in the Zen priesthood, but the taste for Chinese verse declined
in Japan with the decay of poetry in China under the Ming
dynasty; and by about 1400 the Five Monasteries school began to
transfer its attention to philosophy and historical research. Among

its leading scholars were those monks who wrote for the Shōguns despatches to the Ming Court; others who wrote learned theological works; and others, perhaps the most important, who revived the study of the Confucian canon which had been lately neglected owing to the downfall of the old Kyōto schools. In this last class a prominent figure was the Zen monk Keian who, on his return from studies in China in 1473, settled in Western Japan. At this time it was the habit of great families like Shimadzu, Ōuchi and Kikuchi to invite to their domains scholars from Kyōto and Kamakura, who came the more readily because the capital was in ruins and life was unsafe in central Japan. Thus there were formed small nuclei of culture in the provinces, which aided the spread of knowledge as in earlier days the provincial monasteries (*kokubunji*) had done. But now learning was no longer dependent upon the Church. Keian, though he was a monk, lectured in Satsuma upon Chinese philosophy of the Sung school. It was he who introduced into Japan and had printed at his patrons' expense the commentaries of Chu Hsi upon the Great Learning and other works in the canon. These were new expositions of Chinese moral philosophy which were to have a powerful effect upon Japanese thought in the seventeenth century. Another service rendered to learning by the Five Monasteries was their promotion of historical studies. The early official histories were bare annals of the monarchy, the mediæval chronicles were romantic rather than exact, and the work called *Gukwanshō*, written (in *kana*, by the way) by the Tendai abbot Jichin about 1223, was the first attempt to survey and interpret, not merely to record the past.* Thenceforward Japanese scholars, many of whom were Zen monks, began to study history from a philosophical stand-

---

*Other important works of this type are:—

Kokonchōmonshū, 1254, a somewhat encyclopædic treatise dealing with the Heian period; and *Genkō-shakusho*, 1322, a work on the history of Buddhism in Japan, with biographical notices. There was also an immense literary output in the shape of exegetical work, temple records, etc., which are now becoming available. Some monks were almost incredibly prolific writers. Gyonen, of the Tōdaiji, died in 1321 at the age of 82, having to his credit 127 works in over 1,200 fasciculi covering a wide field of learning from music to commentaries on the sutras.

Yet the literary remains of the period show disappointing gaps, the result of war and conflagrations.

point, to record events without romantic embroidery. The work of Kitabatake Chikafusa was composed to support dynastic claims, and is therefore highly tendentious, but it is characteristic of the day in so far as it displays an effort to expound events in the light of general principles. There is an important class of book belonging to this period, called *shō-mochi* or "extracts." These are usually the work of Zen monks, and consist of notes and commentaries upon a wide range of subjects, from Confucian philosophy to native history and literature. Some of them seem to have been prepared as lectures, and are written in *kana* in colloquial style, so that they are important documents for philologists.

This new treatment of history is the expression of a new outlook in keeping with the changing times. It portends the close of the Middle Ages, for men awake to the interest of the old only when it is vanishing under the pressure of the new. To the Heian courtiers Japan had no past but only a barbarous infancy. Their concern was with the present, and if history meant anything to them it meant the records of ancient China, immutable doctrines, established precedents. To the Buddhist priesthood it meant the acts and words of the saints, to the feudal warriors of Kamakura legends of strife between the clans. But in the Muromachi period the Japanese seem to have developed a new sense of the past. One sees traces of an antiquarian sentiment, which was no doubt strengthened by a feeling that old institutions were tottering and that their memory must be preserved. Even the intricacies of the Heian court etiquette seemed to the feudal newcomers to have the charm of ancient, venerable things; and the intruders who had in the early fourteenth century imposed their parvenu standards upon the capital were by the Higashiyama period taking lessons in deportment from needy aristocrats. Yoshimitsu was instructed in Court precedents by the Chancellor Nijō, and Yoshimasa's captains no longer studied the warlike records in the Mirror of the East but heard lectures on the *Genji Monogatari* from a Fujiwara poet.

To the dispossessed, the Court nobles and officials and such like members of the former Kyōto society, the vanishing of the old order was a matter of more than sentimental regret, and in their writings is expressed a deep pessimism. They are well represented by one Kenkō (1283-1350), a court officer of middling rank who lived during the transition from patrician to feudal culture. His work, *Tsure-dzure-gusa* (i.e. Grasses of Idleness), consists of stray notes written in the hermitage where he had taken refuge from the dangers and difficulties of residence in Kyōto. It contains reflections upon life, death, morality and religion, interspersed with anecdotes, reminiscences and antiquarian jottings. It betrays a discontented man, uncomfortably stranded between two phases of society. Through it there runs a thread of melancholy and disapproval of modern ways. "In all things," he says, "one looks back with longing to the past. Modern fashions are growing from bad to worse . . . and as for the style of letters, even a scrap of waste paper from olden times is admirable." Some passages give a brief vision of the elaborate formalism and the æsthetic sensibility of the now faded world which he used to frequent; for he writes fluently and with relish of nice problems in etiquette, and in a few sentences he can call up sights, sounds and perfumes that have stirred him in former days. The Imperial Falconer tells how a pheasant should be presented to a person of distinction:

> "Branches of plum-tree should be used, either in bud or from which the blossom has fallen. They should be seven feet long, and cut to a point with two equal cuts, and the bird tied in the middle. There must be two branches, one for the feet to rest on, the other to attach the bird to. This should be done in two places, with unsplit tendrils of creeping vine, the end being cut short, so as to reach as far as the long tail feather, and bent into the shape of a bull's horns. Then on the First Morning of Snow in the year the messenger, bearing the branches on his shoulder, should ceremoniously take the bird in at the middle gate, following the stone pavement under the eaves so as not to spoil the snow with tracks."

And so on to the minutest detail. This habit of regulating behaviour according to precedent was very strong: and though the feudal warriors may at first have been impatient they succumbed to it in the end, and ancient rules continued to govern simple acts. These persistent notions of taste and propriety would provide a fruitful study, for they have entered into Japanese life at all points, profoundly influencing both speech and thought.* In the æsthetic field they have had far-reaching results. Their effect upon conduct has been of debatable value, for they have checked what is spontaneous while they have served to eliminate the grosser blunders.

Kenkō's work may thus be read with profit as a mirror of native sentiment formed by a fine if somewhat narrow canon which guides the weak but need not fetter the strong. The sights by which he was pleased, the thoughts by which he was saddened, are those which since have moved many generations of his countrymen. Yet as a man of letters he is not representative of his times, but is rather a chance survivor from a former age. The typical literature of the Muromachi period broke away from the tradition of the *Genji Monogatari*, which was the flower of a culture doomed to perish, and developed as a natural expression of the changing temper of society. Most characteristic, but not most admirable, among all its forms is the *renga* or linked verse, which is a social rather than a literary phenomenon. The normal Japanese poem of 31 syllables falls into two hemistichs, and it had been a common pastime since Fujiwara days for one poet to supply a first hemistich to which others would attempt to fit a suitable second. This habit spread until in the Muromachi period it had become not merely a popular game, but a craze and a serious business to boot, with most elaborate rules and a complicated system of marking embodied in a tremendous literature of codes and commentaries. There grew up a class of professional teachers and judges (*tensha*, markers) who were in great demand at social gatherings, of which a contemporary satirist said: "Everywhere a jumble of Kyōto and Kamakura, ill-assorted parties of mock poets and self-appointed judges." Diaries and other records of the time show that almost all classes indulge in these contests. There are extant manuscripts containing collections of initial verses made by emperors and nobles of all degrees, and suitable hemistichs were so prized that copies were bought from professional poets and presented as offerings at shrines by soldiers going off to the wars or women

---

* To take a simple instance, honorific words and phrases grow out of social habits, and in their turn influence social conceptions.

praying for easy childbirth. So great a part did poetry play, even
in its debased forms, in Japanese life.

A liking for popular entertainments was clearly in the air, and
to it we owe perhaps the most original contribution that Japan
has made to the arts, the so-called Lyric Drama, or Nō, which has
its remote origin in a very early form of rhythmic posturing to

FIG. 46. *A performance of dancing (sangaku?) at the dedication of the Great
Buddha of the Todaiji at Nara, A.D. 752.*

the beat of drums and other instruments. This was styled *sangaku*,
which means "scattered" or irregular music as contrasted with
solemn ritual performances. At the dedication of the Great Buddha
in 752 there were various kinds of dancing and music described
as Chinese and Korean, and we know that during the Nara and

Heian periods such performances were frequent at great religious festivals. Perhaps the *sangaku* itself was imported from China; but early documents and pictures show that it consisted in part of humorous antics, acrobatics and even some kind of juggling, and therefore it is reasonable to assume that fragments of indigenous folk-dancing were soon incorporated. The comic element at one time predominated, as can be guessed from the corruption of the name, which from *sangaku* becomes *sarugaku*, "monkey music." This and similar mimetic dances became exceedingly popular, and the names of several other types are known, among which *dengaku*, or "rustic music" seems to have flourished particularly in the Kamakura period. At first little more than posturings in the costumes of legendary characters, they gradually took on a dramatic form. The details of this intermediate development are obscure, but we know that whereas, for instance, in the years 1100-1150 the dancers gave representations of demons and dragons or of divine personages like Bishamon, by the beginning of the Muromachi period there were frequent performances styled Nō, which were dramatic interludes in or variations of *dengaku* and *sangaku*. The word *nō*, which means "ability," was used at that time to signify a finished, expert performance, something that had been arranged and rehearsed by specialists, no doubt in contrast with more or less impromptu words and gestures.

There is a celebrated passage in the *Taiheiki* describing a grand open-air performance of *dengaku-nō* in the summer of 1349, which was attended by thousands of spectators. It was given in aid of building a bridge, and took place in the dry river-bed. There were present not only crowds of humble citizens but also high civil and military dignitaries from the Shōgun (Takauji) and the Regent downwards, as well as clergy of all degrees. The entertainment was in the form, not uncommon at that time, of a competition between two companies of actors. The scene is described in detail and appears to have been of considerable magnificence. The stage was spread with cloth of green and crimson and decorated with tiger and panther skins. The smell of incense filled the air. Hangings of gold brocade waved in the breeze like leaping flames. All hearts were uplifted as the music played, cool and sweet. Then two troops of performers filed on to the stage, keeping time to flute and drum, beautiful young boys from the east greenroom, handsome priests from the west. The boys were in bright silken robes; the priests, lightly powdered and painted and with blackened teeth,* wore rich dresses dyed and woven in fantastic patterns. A new piece was performed, a *sarugaku* representing the legend of the Sannō shrine, and little boys of eight and nine in monkey-masks danced up and down and across the stage, turning somersaults and climbing balustrades. The excitement was intense. The spectators rose in their seats and stamped and shouted so vigorously that part of the staging gave way and there ensued a panic of which robbers took advantage to plunder the dead and dying. Swords were drawn and the day ended in bloodshed.

From this and other accounts it is clear that there were already several competing schools of actors under leaders of established reputation whose names are on record, and the Nō had already gone a long way towards becoming a stage play in which music, dancing and speech were all used to elaborate a theme or recount a story. But it remained for certain men of genius to perfect it. There were Kwanami (1333-1384) and his son Zeami (1363-1444). They profited by the popularity of stage performances of the type which the foregoing story illustrates, and Zeami himself relates that his father always gave credit to former masters of other styles, such as Itchū, who was a *dengaku* actor of some repute. Kwanami was a Shintō priest (*negi*) of not very high rank attached to the Kasuga shrine at Nara, who was taken into favour by the Shōgun Yoshimitsu. The Shōgun was an æsthete, and he was doubtless enchanted by Kwanami's acting; but he also had a weakness for beautiful young boys, and there is very strong evidence to show that he was smitten by the charms of Zeami, then in his early 'teens. Favoured by the protection of the great and by the growing public taste for spectacles, the *sangaku* actors, who had hitherto been poor hangers-on of shrines and temples, regarded as little better than outcasts, suddenly rose in the social scale, and the ablest among them began to associate on easy terms with people of high standing. Kwanami himself seems to have been a man of not very extensive learning, but he was an undoubted artist. Both he and his son clearly profited by their intimacy with cultivated members of a superior class,

* This was a fashion among the Kyōto nobility.

to meet whose æsthetic demands they worked out a new dramatic entertainment. Their achievement lay in the harmonious blending of materials ready at hand in poetry, music and dancing, for these separate elements of the Nō were traditional to the verge of commonplace, and yet out of them there was created, by Kwanami, an actor with a high sense of dramatic values, and Seami, a gifted producer, a new and integral form of beauty.

The text of the plays contains very little original writing but is largely composed of fragments of more or less familiar verse woven together into narrative or lyrical passages. The Japanese poetical genius is often described as incapable of sustained flights, and perhaps this is true enough as a general view. Yet there are in Japanese literature signs of an effort to escape from the limitations of the short stanza. The long narrative poems of the *Manyōshū* do seem to have had no direct successors. But romances like the *Heike Monogatari* are in essence poems of an epic quality chanted to musical accompaniment, and it is possible that the "books" of the Nō plays, which drew freely both for incident and language upon those works, were a response to some desire for a more capacious poetic medium. Even the popularity of linked verses at this period may be looked upon as evidence of dissatisfaction with the brief isolated stanza. Buddhist hymns (called *wasan*) in simple Japanese were much in favour among the Amidist sects. Some of these were of considerable length.

As to the orchestral music of the Nō, produced by drums and flutes, all we can profitably observe here is that its most important feature is the beat, in its intricate relation with the chanted word and in particular the movements of the actors. It is the dance which is the dominant element in these plays, and all else is ancillary. Those familiar with the more popular drama, the *kabuki*, will recognise that here also the supreme moment of a dramatic performance is generally not a telling speech but a tableau. The movement of a play proceeds until it culminates in an elaborate pose, taken and held by the actor, who thus creates by posture rather than by words the emotional tension. The Nō betrays even more clearly its origin in the dance, because it became stereotyped at an early stage in its development, whereas the *kabuki* is of later, freer and more popular growth.

There is a great disagreement among Japanese as well as foreign writers concerning the artistic merits of the Nō. Its importance in cultural history is, however, undeniable. Though it is a compound of traditional elements, sacred or profane, as a coherent dramatic form it was definitely the creation of Kwanami and his school. In this sense it is original and unique. It owes nothing to China, except perhaps that it profited indirectly by the popularity of stage plays in Yüan or early Ming times. Where it borrows from Chinese poetry and legend its source is never the literature current in Ming China, but the anthologies which had already been familiar to the Japanese for centuries and were now part of their national literary heritage. It is sometimes suggested that the plays were introduced by Zen priests who had seen performances in the Chinese theatre, but there is no trace whatever of direct Zen influence upon the language or the sentiment of the Nō texts, whereas they abound in ideas and terminology from the popular Amidism of the day, and they retain, doubtless from their ancient connection with the great shrines, an important Shintō element. The indirect influence of Zen, however, cannot be exaggerated. The producers and the actors worked primarily for an audience whose æsthetic standards were those of Zen, and whatever may be said of the literary content of the plays, their structure, the method and the atmosphere of their presentation, were in full accordance with Zen canons of taste. Everywhere there is a careful avoidance of the trite, the obvious and the emphatic. The most powerful effects are those which are obtained by allusion, suggestion and restraint, and in this respect the Nō is a counterpart of the contemporary painting which was governed by Zen principles. Seami in his works lays it down that realism (*mono-mane*, imitating things) should be an actor's chief aim, yet it is clear that he did not contemplate the grosser forms of mimicry, but had in mind more subtle indications of truth. The modern Nō actor stigmatises as *keren*, trickery, any gesture which closely reproduces such an act, for instance, as weeping. This is the spirit, both in the detail and the ensemble of their construction, which gives to these plays their special significance. They are a remarkable testimony to the æsthetic importance of form, showing how unpromising materials can be forced into a mould of beauty.

The rigid convention, the hieratic mode, the deliberate avoidance of excess, all these guard against lapses from pure taste; but in another aspect they are the expression of a timid orthodoxy and if they refine they also attenuate. Perhaps this is why the Western student of Japanese art has at times a sensation that he is dealing with something a trifle undervitalised, and at the risk of æsthetic heresy would prefer a more impulsive squandering of effort, an heroic if unregulated luxuriance. But, if he is on occasion impatient of a deliberate and rather self-conscious æstheticism which results in so much nervous dread of overstatement, he must be grateful for the superb ink paintings of this period. He may regard the mannered restraints of the tea-ceremony and incense-parties and formal flower-arrangement as so many types of painful inhibition, but he must surrender to the conquering simplicity of Sesshū and his school.

These masters depend, historically, upon Chinese forerunners of the Sung dynasty.* The first of their line were (apart from certain obscure Buddhist painters who worked also in black and white) Mokuan and Kaō, Japanese monks who derived their inspiration from the great Chinese painter Mu Ch'i (or Mu-hsi; in Japanese, Mokkei) and were even, until lately, sometimes thought to be themselves Chinese. Mokuan worked and died in China under the Yüan dynasty. Entering the fifteenth century we find two painters, Minchō, known also as Chō Densu (d. 1431) and Reisai (op. 1435), most of whose work was religious painting, but who have left a legacy of ink drawings in the Zen spirit. Their fame is scanty compared with that of their slightly younger contemporaries and successors Josetsu (*circa* 1410), Shūbun (op. 1414-1465) and Sesshū (1420-1506). Of Josetsu's work there is left only one fully authenticated piece, which he painted for Yoshimitsu; but he was highly esteemed in his day and his pseudonym (which means "as if unskilful") is derived from an encomium by the scholar Zekkai who, in a characteristic Zen paradox, said of one of his pictures, "Great mastery is as if unskilful." Sesshū

* For the data which follow I am indebted to the brilliant researches of my kind friend Professor R. Fukui of the Imperial University at Sendai. He is not, however, to blame for the opinions.

states that he learned painting from Shūbun, who was the disciple of Josetsu. There are many pictures attributed to Shūbun but few if any which can be ascribed to him with absolute certainty. Praise of his work, however, is to be found in the literature of the Five Monasteries, from which we learn also that he was a plain, almost foolish looking man of modest and gentle nature, and that his appearance belied his gifts, since he was amazingly versatile, a talented sculptor as well as a magician with the brush. It is interesting to note that he visited Korea in 1423 and that he was official painter of the Shōgun, from whom he received an allowance. Though other names are better known, Shūbun is the true patriarch and, some think, the supreme painter of this school. His reputation was so high that within a few years of his death his pictures were being hung in the Shōgun's apartments, an honour hitherto reserved for the work of Chinese masters. Of his talented followers we can mention here only the most celebrated, such as Jasoku (op. 1452 to after 1483), Kei Shoki or Secretary Kei (op. 1478 to after 1523), Nōami (1397-1476), Geiami (1431-1485), Sōami (1472-1523). The three "Amis," father, son and grandson, are important figures in the history of Japanese æsthetics. Nōami was a monk, a favourite of the Shōgun Yoshimasa who, when he abdicated in 1474, betook himself to the Silver Pavilion on Higashi-yama to enjoy a life of voluptuous elegance. Here he and his circle appraised and savoured the Sung paintings and porcelains, the precious adjuncts of the tea ceremony, discussed the merits of calligraphies, or looked out in the moonlight over the landscape garden, composing suitable verse. In all these pastimes Nōami was the arbiter of taste. Not only was he, through familiar handling of his master's treasures, a connoisseur of high authority, but he was also himself a skilled executant in the difficult arts of the tea-ceremony, incense judging, verse-linking and landscape-gardening, as well as being a competent painter in the manner of his master Shūbun, and of Mu Ch'i whom he adored. No picture by him is known for certain to have been preserved, but his æsthetic influence was deep and wide. He set up severe standards of critical appreciation, which were fixed and perpetuated by Geiami and Sōami. He created a rarified atmosphere of fine taste in which only supreme artists like Sesshū could thrive.

Sesshū's work might well be taken as a fine and clear exposition of Zen principles of taste, and indeed of the Zen outlook upon the world. But it would be wrong to suppose, conversely, that Ashikaga painting flowed out of Zen theory, or indeed that its quality was due to some rare and exclusive discovery of an æsthetic secret. We must beware, in discussing the arts as well as the manners of a foreign country, lest we stress their fortuitous strangeness and forget their essential identity with our own. Current metaphysical ideas and even local habits may direct an artist's activities this way rather than that; but it is the blessing and salvation of art that it is not pinioned by philosophy. The artist is impelled not by theory but by a desire to create, and those who propagate a belief that Oriental art is for ever alien and incomprehensible are doing a disservice to truth. Anything that is said here as to schools, influences and tendencies must be taken as mere detail of an historical framework. It is easy and pleasant, for instance, to enlarge upon the spiritual element in the arts of Muromachi and to overlook the, let us say, temporal, the almost purely technical side of their development. The subtle simplicity of Zen landscapes and figures is certainly in harmony with the mood in which the artists looked at nature, but it owes much to their tools and materials, the brush, the ink and the absorbent paper which were miraculously suited to the bold stroke and the graded washes and which, thanks to the practice of handwriting, they could use with amazing mastery. In the same way the linear archaism of Asuka sculpture is the result not so much of simple idealism as of the translation into bronze of the stone technique of its models.

Granted all this, the æsthetic coterie of the Higashiyama period is an extremely important phenomenon in cultural history, out of all proportion to its size. This small society of aristocrats, monks and artists—it is regrettable that we do not know more intimately the details of their life—not only preserved but promoted the arts while all else was falling in ruins about them. To the refinement and delicate perceptions of the Heian elegants, which were adventitious and partial, they added a rationalised and more universal sense of beauty, and thus if their heads were

in the clouds their feet were firmly planted on earth. They
were moved by a belief that all nature is permeated by one
spirit,* and it was the aim of the Zen practitioner in particular, by
purging his mind of egotistic commotions, to reach a tranquil,
intuitive realisation of his identity with the universe. Such vague
and transcendental notions must always be under suspicion, and no
doubt they can shelter much that is eccentric and insincere; but
certainly this belief has been a genuine inspiration and has conditioned the subjects and the treatment of a great part of Oriental
painting.

Such a sentiment of kinship with nature is of course abundantly
expressed in Western literature, where however it is always of a
somewhat anthropocentric cast. Wordsworth in youth felt dizzy
raptures in the presence of beauty, and in his maturer age he heard
"the still, sad music of humanity." But the Zen artists and the Zen
poets—and it is often hard to say where their poetry ends and
their painting begins—feel no antithesis between man and nature,
and are conscious even of an identity rather than a kinship. What
interests them is not the restless movement on the surface of life,
but (as Professor Anezaki puts it) the eternal tranquillity seen
through and behind change. So Nōami, a fine judge, approved
highly of a critic who said in esteem of a Chinese painter's work:
"It is a quiet picture." The landscapes of Sesshū, despite his energetic brush, have this precious and lovely quality of peace. It is as
if the artist had been able to seize the very core and essence of
beauty, to reduce it to terms of the uttermost simplicity. These are
lavish praises of a few strokes and washes of ink on a small sheet of
paper. But it is as well to emphasise the importance of this school
in the history of art; and it may be that before long the names of
Sesshū and his peers will be better known than those of the somewhat melodramatic figures which now represent Japan to the
West. A mystic love of nature appears in Japanese poetry long
before it can, by rare exception, be discerned in Europe. When
Blake saw "a world in a grain of sand, and a heaven in a wild

* The germ of the idea is present in primitive nature worship, but it is given a
philosophical form by the Buddhist conception of Dharmakâya, the "True
Body" of the Buddha, which is not his manifestation in human form, nor his
manifestation in paradise, but his permeation of all nature as one spirit.

flower" he was feeling what Chinese and Japanese poets had expressed many centuries before him, and what was almost a commonplace of Zen attainment. Similarly when the great Chinese and Japanese masters of ink drawing suggested shape and texture, light and distance, by a technique of unerring economy, they were anticipating the impressionistic idealism of much later European painting.

It will be asked what was the share of Japan in this contribution made to the arts by the Orient. The question is difficult; but it can be said that, if its inspiration was remotely Chinese, it was most thoroughly naturalised. Sesshū himself, returning to Japan after a sojourn in China (1467-1469), said that he had seen famous mountains and great rivers, and had sought for a master in four hundred provinces, but he had journeyed in vain, for he had found that there was none to match Shūbun and Josetsu. Sesshū perhaps stands alone, above time and country. But from Shūbun there derives a school which is peculiarly Japanese.

Painting in the Ashikaga period shows the same kind of development as has been displayed by the arts in Japan throughout their history. A foreign mode is adopted and faithfully pursued until in due course it receives an impress of the native temperament and from it there arises a school whose work is distinctly Japanese in quality. The prestige of the great Chinese masters of black and white of the Sung and Yüan dynasties was at first unassailable. The careful colouring and the delicate line drawing of the Fujiwara artists and the Kamakura scroll painters were superseded by the virtuosity of the ink painters, partly no doubt under the influence of Zen and Taoist ideas (which were at one in favouring simple forms of expression), but surely for the most part because no artist of spirit could resist the desire to explore the fascinating possibilities of this new technique, by which subtle effects could be obtained through the mastery of simple materials. Artists all over the world are an instinctive tribe, and are apt to work first and philosophise afterwards. Art historians are given to reversing this process, and of course it is agreeably simple to attribute movements in Japanese art at this time to Zen "influence." But a more rational explanation of the eclipse of the Yamato schools is that the greatest and most vigorous artists were attracted by the new method, while the old styles were left in the hands of less competent, mechanical painters. There is a temptation to describe all *suiboku* ("water-ink"—this is the Japanese name for black and white drawings of wash and line) as "simple ink sketches of a few bold lines," and it is true that, judged by mere size, many of the greatest Ashikaga paintings are slight affairs. But a work such as one of the famous landscape scrolls by Sesshū is a considerable effort of sustained composition. It is not a mere haphazard collocation of sketches, but has a rhythm, an architecture of its own, and might be compared with a musical symphony of interwoven motives. From such pictures rather than from the little Zen parables in the method called *haboku* ("broken ink") arises the distinctly Japanese school called Kanō, after its founders, Kanō Masanobu and Motonobu, his son. These painters gave new life to the Tosa school, by applying to its traditional subjects and manner the *suiboku* principles, with suitable modifications.

Great importance has always been attached in Japan to the inheritance of occupations, not only among traders and artisans, but also among painters, poets, historians, doctors, lawyers and even philosophers: and where there was no suitable successor in the family recourse was had to adoption. It is therefore interesting to observe that the alliance between these two schools was, so to speak, ratified by the marriage of Kanō Motonobu with the daughter of Tosa Mitsunobu (1434-1525), then the leading exponent of the older manner. The Tosa alone of the earlier schools had managed to retain vitality. Artists brought up in other conventions had, like Minchō (who belonged to the Takuma school), gone over to the Chinese method; but the Tosa besides having a certain official standing was lucky in producing a number of talented artists, mostly scroll painters, whose subjects were taken from the national history, sacred or secular, and would have been difficult to treat in an expressionistic style. Mitsunobu (1434-1525), moreover, was a fine colourist and designer, who also worked in black and white; so that the Tosa school by no means came empty-handed into the union. Indeed it long survived as an independent school while the pure Chinese style, though it left its mark on all subsequent painting, gradually fell out of favour as the æsthetic society of Higashiyama suffered the erosion of war and anarchy.

It was, however, the school founded by the Kanō family which remained supreme in Japan for centuries. Masanobu and in particular Motonobu were skilled black-and-white men, who had deeply studied the Chinese masters, but the style that they evolved has an unmistakably native character.

A brief glance at other art will complete this survey of culture under the Ashikaga Shōguns. Architecture reveals its character in an interesting way. Among the scarce remains of this period the

FIG. 47. *Side elevation. Upper storey of the Golden Pavilion (Kinkaku).*

Kinkaku or Golden Pavilion is the most important, ranking as an historical monument with the Hōryūji Monastery and the Phœnix Hall (Byōdō-in). It stands overlooking and slightly overhanging a pond in a garden which originally contained the country villa of a Kyōto noble in Kamakura times, and it is characteristic of Muromachi culture in that it is a work of deliberate æstheticism. It is so designed and placed as to harmonise with a landscape garden itself the product of most conscious, one might say literary, artifice. Indeed the structure and the garden together formed an integral whole in the minds of those who planned them, and the shape of the building was of no greater importance than the distribution of the rocks and trees, which were selected with the utmost care and given, after the Ming manner, recondite and symbolic names. A detailed study of the Pavilion and its setting would illuminate many points of contemporary æsthetic theory; but here we must confine ourselves to its principal features. Of its three storeys, the lowest, containing living rooms, is an example of the type of domestic architecture called *shinden-dzukuri*. The middle storey is in a mixed style, with a decorated ceiling. It was probably used by Yoshimitsu for his musical and poetical parties and other entertainments. The upper storey is in the Zen style and consists of one apartment only, which was used as an oratory, where a sacred image was doubtless installed. Its interior was entirely covered with pure gold leaf and it is this decoration which gives the building its name. To the uninitiated tourist this Golden Pavilion is a disappointing affair, for it is neither imposing in size nor rich in ornament, but it is none the less both a technical and an artistic triumph. Its technical merits, according to specialists, lie in its successful blending of styles and in a lightness of construction obtained by what in those days must have been a daring sacrifice of the accepted margin of safety. As for its beauty, it relies upon a harmony and a delicacy of proportion so just that because of its very rightness it leaves no impression upon a careless observer.

The Kinkaku, and the Ginkaku or Silver Pavilion built some 50 years later by Yoshimasa, are the expression in architecture of that sophisticated simplicity which we have seen in the painting and in the dramatic forms of the period. Beauty must not be displayed and underlined, but must lie modestly beneath the surface of things, to be summoned forth by the trained taste of the connoisseur. There are mysteries of enjoyment as well as of creation.

It is difficult to say whence these canons of taste arose. They are not the expression of a mere transient cult, but correspond to an age-long habit. Of this there are signs in early Japanese poetry, and especially in the preface to the *Kokinshū*. Here already occurs the word *yūgen*, later so freely used by such artists as Seami to express the special quality of beauty at which they aimed in their work. The æsthetic code of the Heian period, particularly where it is free from direct Buddhist influence, depends largely upon the efficacy of suggestion and allusion. In the Kamakura period Zen gives purity and strength to the rather wanton delicacy of Heian culture. Early in the Muromachi period Zen ideals are even more widespread, and Chinese cultural influence pervades the arts. Later these various elements are assimilated and combined to form that characteristic Japanese taste, which seems to have no exact national counterpart elsewhere and which, in however thin a form, persists to-day through all classes, though it must be admitted that it has to struggle hard against the pressure of mechanical civilisation.

This, of course, is a crude summary of an æsthetic evolution and needs to be qualified at every point; but it does seem to be true that from the Higashiyama period a unique and definitely Japanese standard was formed. The moral and intellectual influence of all but Zen Buddhism had waned. Art and letters had broken away from the religious tradition, and were feeling for new forms of expression. Perhaps it was natural that, in such warlike times, men should turn for refuge to the purposed simplicity and peace of the Tea Ceremony.[1] This is a subject upon which Japanese and foreign authors alike have written a great deal that is partial or exaggerated or merely foolish. There are enthusiasts who would have one believe that the Tea Masters hold the key to all problems of taste and conduct, and this is absurd, for no student of the history of this curious phenomenon can fail to see that it is a cult which lapses with dangerous ease into empty and arbitrary forms or, if it takes another turn, into a mock simplicity. But its underlying sentiment is admirable, and its traces are to be found in the most unexpected corners of Japanese life, so that no student can afford to neglect its history. Essentially a Tea Ceremony is a gathering, conducted according to a prescribed etiquette and in simple, quiet surroundings, of friends who have artistic tastes in common. In a small room bare of all but a few beautiful things tea is prepared and drunk according to a strict rule, and the guests discuss gravely the merits of some object of art, perhaps one of the utensils they are using, a bowl of which the glaze harbours rich lights, or an effortless-seeming picture on the wall, or a poem or an arrangement of flowers. Such meetings, especially under the early in-

PORTRAIT OF DAITŌ KOKUSHI

PORTRAIT OF SHŌITSU KOKUSHI

fluence of Zen principles of frugality and restraint, made for a calm withdrawal from worldly cares and a serene enjoyment of beauty. The slight touch of ritual encouraged grace in deportment and discipline in taste. But very soon the cult lost its simple character and at least among its wealthy practitioners tended to become extravagant and elaborate. Under the Ashikaga Shōgun Yoshimasa it was a costly aristocratic pastime. The Zen monk Jukō (who is regarded as the founder of the cult in its regulated form) laid down rules of which the keynote is restraint and simplicity; but he was himself a connoisseur of unrivalled judgment and, along with Nōami and other experts, assisted Yoshimasa to make a costly collection of porcelain and pictures, which they discussed and savoured in Yoshimasa's tea room by the Silver Pavilion.

The Silver Pavilion (Ginkaku) is an insignificant structure which belies its name; yet it is a landmark in cultural history. It is a three-storeyed building, less graceful and less ornate than the Kinkaku, and displaying far less technical competence. It is indeed simple to the verge of insipidity, but in this respect it is an expression of the taste of Yoshimasa's circle. Architecturally its chief interest lies in the compromise which it exhibits between religious and domestic types, and in a new style of living apartments (called *shoin-dzukuri*), which specialists regard as the true forerunner of the modern Japanese dwelling. The same style is followed in an adjacent building (the *Tōgūdō*), used by Yoshimasa for his devotions. It contains a small chamber which is the prototype of the classic "tea room" of $4\frac{1}{2}$ "mats" (about 9 feet square). There is no doubt that the tea-ceremony had an important influence upon the arrangement of the Japanese house in later times. The familiar *tokonoma* (alcove), for instance, though of earlier origin owes its decorative use largely to the habit of Zen priests and tea-masters who placed in it, rather than a shrine, a picture or a vase of flowers.

The Silver Pavilion stood on a hill called Higashiyama, and most of the treasures which Yoshimasa assembled there survive still, under the name of "Higashiyama pieces." They were jealously guarded, sent into safety in times of disturbance, and at every change of hands their history was vouched for by solemn certifi-

cates. Perhaps the most celebrated piece of all is the small tea jar
(about 4 inches high) known as the Koga jar, brought back from
China in 1227 by the Zen patriarch Dōgen. This, at first owned by
the Koga family, after many vicissitudes, during which it passed
through the hands of Shōguns and powerful barons and rich
citizens, is now owned by a well-known collector, and regarded as
of incalculable worth. Jukō himself was the purchaser of several
famous pieces, among them a small jar, known from its shape as
the Tsukumo Eggplant (*Tsukumo Nasubi*), which was at one time
highly prized by Yoshimitsu, was badly damaged in the siege of
Ōsaka in 1615, repaired, passed from hand to hand, and finally
came to rest in the collection of a modern merchant prince.
Another piece, also bought by Jukō, formed part of the collection
of a rich man of Nara (Matsuya Genzaburō) famous as the owner of
three superb things, a tray, a picture, and a tiny tea-jar. This last
was the jar which Jukō bought, and later it came into the possession of the lords of Satsuma, the Shimadzu family, by whom it was
sold in 1928 for £13,000.

So much for the frugality, the almost rustic simplicity which the
great tea-masters enjoined upon their pupils. But we need not
complain if they fell short of their stern ideals. The Ashikaga
Shōguns are generally treated by historians as bad, selfish rulers
who did nothing for the State, and certainly as administrators
there is not much to be said for them. Yet if we compare their
record with that of more respectable characters in the national
story, it seems that they did as good service to posterity as most
great captains and statesmen. Feudal policies have left little more
trace than feudal battles; but Yoshimitsu and Yoshimasa, through
their reprehended indulgence in pleasure, have left however in-
voluntarily a most valuable legacy. It is thanks to their eager and
quite selfish promotion of foreign trade that Japan is now so rich
in treasures of Chinese art, notably Sung, Yüan and Ming
paintings and porcelain. It was under their patronage that the
fine arts still flourished, in an oasis of taste and learning around
which was a desert of war and barbarity. Nearly all of the applied
arts, but especially ceramics, owe a great deal to their practice of
the tea-ceremony, whose adepts were liberal if exacting patrons.
And if their own particular culture faded quickly away, it was not

until it had given shape and substance to an æsthetic tradition which, though it has suffered transformations, in essence still survives.

TABLE OF MAIN POLITICAL EVENTS IN ASHIKAGA PERIOD

A.D. 1338 Ashikaga Takauji becomes Shōgun, and resides in Kyōto; but civil war continues until 1392.

1358 Ashikaga Yoshiakira succeeds on Takauji's death.

1367 Ashikaga Yoshimitsu succeeds. Diplomatic intercourse and trade with China.

1392 Succession dispute ends. GO-KOMATSU emperor.

1395 Yoshimitsu abdicates and governs from the Golden Pavilion (died 1408). Yoshimochi succeeds as Shōgun.

1400 Feudal warfare in various parts of Japan, and continuous economic disturbances in the shape of epidemics and famines, culminating in

1467 The Ōnin Civil war, during the rule of Yoshimasa (1449-1474), the eighth Ashikaga Shōgun. Redistribution of feudal power.

1477 Ōnin war ends, but fighting continues in most provinces. Ashikaga Shōguns powerless, and Imperial house almost penniless. Central government collapses, and anarchy prevails in most provinces, until by about

1500 The whole of Japan is at war.

NOTE TO CHAPTER XVIII

¹ Page 400. Tea Ceremony. The Shōgun Yoshimasa took it up on the recommendation of Nōami, who wrote to him "there is a thing called Tea Ceremony," and explained that the monk Jukō had devoted 30 years to its study. This shows that it was a comparatively new æsthetic development in the early fifteenth century.

PART SIX—THE SENGOKU PERIOD

Chapter XIX—THE COUNTRY AT WAR

1. THE POLITICAL SCENE

THE period from the close of the fifteenth century to the close of the sixteenth century is known to Japanese historians as *Sengoku Jidai*, the age of the country at war. Warfare indeed, in one region or another, had continued with very little pause throughout the fifteenth century, but from the outbreak of the Ōnin war (1467) it had become, as it were, endemic and within a few years there was not a province in Japan free from the armed rivalry of territorial barons or lords of the church. Once more, as at the close of the Kamakura period, the country was plunged into a struggle for the redistribution of feudal power; but this time it was to be decisive and final.

Under the early Ashikaga Shōguns, thanks to the weakness of the central governments both civil and military, a number of powerful families had carved out for themselves great domains where they were practically independent rulers. By the close of the 15th century Japan exhibited what may be described as a truncated feudalism. The regional hierarchies were complete but the national hierarchy was without an apex, since neither the Emperor nor the Shōgun was able to enforce his will against the regional lords, who, though they might profess loyalty to the throne and even to the Shōgunate, were in effect autonomous princes, holding their own land, ruling their own vassals, maintaining their own armies and enforcing their own laws. We have already noticed the power of some of these great families, such as the Yamana, who rose to eminence in early Muromachi times and then collapsed. Many others might be mentioned, whose names bulk large in mediæval annals, such as the Takeda and the Uesugi, the Ōuchi and the Amako, the Date and the Imagawa. All these rulers, land-hungry and ambitious, were constantly alert to increase their domains by attacks or by alliances, and such peace as there was depended therefore on a precarious balance of power. Obviously this was a state of affairs that could not endure, and there must be a further struggle to bring the feudal system to maturity, through the emergence of one group which, alone or in combination, was more powerful than the remainder. This struggle was so widespread and protracted that volumes would be needed for its full description, but its main features can be rapidly summarised in simple terms. Previous to the Ōnin war (1467) there were in Japan some 260 feudal houses (*daimyō*). By the year 1600 all but a dozen or so of these had disappeared or sunk into insignificance, while other families, rather less in number, had risen to power in their stead, often from small beginnings as vassals or rear-vassals and sometimes from complete obscurity. The houses that survived were for the most part those entrenched in the western or north-eastern extremities of Japan where they were beyond the easy reach of central authority. Such were the Shimadzu family in Satsuma, the Nambu in Mutsu, the Uesugi in Echigo or later in Dewa. Apart from these the feudal aristocracy which emerged from the hundred years of war was a new aristocracy, and it is not an exaggeration to say that, so far as concerns the personnel of her dominant classes, Japan was entirely refashioned by the year 1600. One authority goes so far as to say that a modern Japanese wishing to study his civilisation in the light of national history need go back no further than the Ōnin war, for all previous to that might as well be the history of a foreign country. This is an extreme view but it indicates how far-reaching were the political and social changes brought about in this distressed age. One example will suffice to illustrate its violent fluctuations. The Ōuchi family which rose to importance in the province of Suwo in the twelfth century became extremely powerful under the Ashikaga. They played a great part in the dispute between the rival courts and in other important political questions of the day; their military strength was such that neighbouring magnates dared not attack them; and they ruled over extensive domains comprising at least six provinces. In their territory was the castle town of Yamaguchi, which had an important harbour and whither as we have seen there came to settle scholars and court nobles driven from the ruined capital. In the early sixteenth century Yamaguchi was a flourishing centre of culture, even of elegance, and St. Francis Xavier, who stayed for some months in Ōuchi's fief in 1551, described him as a king, and the most powerful lord in Japan. Yet hardly a decade elapsed before the Ōuchi family was practically extinct, and its place was taken by the house of Mōri. The Mōri were descended from Ōe Hiromoto, the Kyōto jurist who advised Yoritomo's government at Kamakura. In 1550 they were small vassals of Ōuchi, with only a thousand retainers or so. Before 1600 they not only ruled all the domains of their former lord but had absorbed those of his great rivals, the Amako, so that they were supreme in thirteen provinces; and they remained until the restoration of 1868 one of the five most powerful families in Japan.

A similar process was going on all over Japan. For the first half of the sixteenth century it was a process of destruction. Former groupings were broken down, their units rearranged if they were not destroyed. Then, as the weaker elements were eliminated from the struggle, a certain reintegration took place, and in the latter half of the century, say towards 1560, the conflict resolved itself into a rivalry between some half dozen groups, and terminated by about 1600 in the supremacy of one.

In one sense a progress towards order and unity was an inevitable sequel of the chaos which followed the Ōnin war, for the Japanese were too vigorous and too sane a people to tolerate indefinite anarchy, and their country too small to hold two masters. Indeed, as we shall presently see, the warfare and the political turmoil of the sixteenth century, degrading and destructive as they were, did not spell institutional decay. But, although the restoration of a stable central government may have been the resultant of natural forces, they worked through the agency of great men, whose several talents were those which the times demanded. Chief among them were Oda Nobunaga, Toyotomi Hideyoshi, and Tokugawa Ieyasu; and brief biographies of these three will serve, while recording their achievements, as a convenient summary of the history of the period of reconstruction which culminated in the undisputed dominance of the Tokugawa Shōgunate after 1615.

Oda Nobunaga (1534-1582) was the son of a feudal chieftain of obscure antecedents in the province of Owari who in the early sixteenth century had made a position for himself at the expense of neighbouring landholders, and had acquired tolerable wealth and military strength. Nobunaga, building on this foundation, by brave and skilful strategy was able to defeat some powerful enemies, and thus raising himself to a level with the great barons could aspire to the prize coveted by them all, the imperial commission as Shōgun, or at least the office of deputy. It might be supposed that a soldier strong enough to be offered this commission would already be in so dominant a position that the title would be a mere ornament. But the office of Shōgun still carried with it great prestige, and it conferred at least theoretical command over all the armed forces of the empire. Consequently any baron who resisted the Shōgun was technically a rebel, and this fact, though it might not deter his boldest adversaries, would give them pause before attacking a delegate of the throne. It would afford to the holder of the title a balance of advantage over an otherwise well-matched rival. Therefore Nobunaga, as he consolidated his position in the provinces of Owari, Mikawa and Mino by fighting, and secured his flank and rear by matrimonial and other alliances with his neighbours, attracted the attention of the then emperor (Ōgimachi). He, in his sore straits, remembered that Nobunaga's father had come to the aid of the needy court during a previous reign. In 1562 and again in 1567 he appealed secretly for help to Nobunaga, who in the interval, despite certain reverses, had further extended his influence and was now within striking distance of Kyōto. The Ashikaga Shōgun of the day (Yoshiteru) had committed suicide in his palace as it went down in flames after an attack by rebellious barons. Yoshiaki, his brother and putative successor, was a refugee. Nobunaga, after due precautions, advanced upon Kyōto, occupied the city and set up Yoshiaki as Shōgun. Before long he himself was the *de facto* Shōgun, and the Ashikaga house ruled no more.* Yet he had by no means subdued all his enemies. North, east, south and west lay hostile barons who were even singly his match in military strength. He had however the definite, if hazardous, benefit of a central situation and of the imperial commission, and he was extremely fortunate in his associates, since both Hideyoshi, his trusted general, and Tokugawa Ieyasu, his ally, were men of genius. Hideyoshi, himself the son of an *ashigaru* employed by the Oda family, joined Nobunaga's army as a common soldier but soon rose from the ranks. Ieyasu was a small vassal of the Imagawa who, when his lord was defeated by

* Technically Yoshiaki remained the titular Shōgun till his death in 1597.

Nobunaga, went over to the Oda side, married his son to Nobunaga's daughter, and remained Nobunaga's lieutenant throughout his campaigns.

The task before these three was to conquer or win over their most powerful enemies, and though we cannot here recite their victories we may mention that by 1573 they had defeated barons in Echizen and Ōmi who threatened their rear and their flank, and were masters in the home provinces. But their hold was precarious, and that they kept it was due more to Nobunaga's luck than his talents, for his two most dangerous and capable enemies died in their prime, Takeda Shingen of Kai, aged 53, in 1573 and Uesugi Kenshin of Echigo, aged 49, in 1578. It is a noteworthy fact that Nobunaga, though he still had other powerful enemies to deal with, now concentrated all his efforts upon subduing the Buddhist church. Not only the monks of Hieizan, whose militant habits we have already noted, but other monasteries also had taken sides with Nobunaga's rivals, and had caused him great embarrassment from time to time. It has sometimes been said that at the close of the fifteenth century the Buddhist church came near to gaining the secular empire of Japan, but there is not sufficient ground for such a high estimate of its power. It was as much a prey to schism as the feudal warriors were prone to factions, and none of the monasteries was strong enough to tackle single-handed a baron of more than moderate estate. Several of them were situated in excellent defensive positions, but they were not organised for distant campaigns, and even had they gone a long way towards securing military dominance it is hardly conceivable that the feudal lords would have given to the Buddhist church an allegiance which they paid only grudgingly to the Shōgun himself. Though there is very little record of persecution in Japan on grounds of doctrine alone, the whole of her mediæval history shows that her feudal leaders would never permit interference by religious institutions in major political issues. In matters of belief they were tolerant and catholic even to the point of absurdity, and no doubt gifted churchmen indirectly exercised great influence over them; but we have only to examine the record of such politically-minded ecclesiasts as Nichiren to see that they were promptly suppressed when their activities clashed with feudal interests. It is true that the Bakufu would stand

a great deal from the Hieizan monasteries, largely out of superstitious dread; but the descents of the monks upon the capital were
of only local importance, and as soon as they began to take a part in
the conflict for feudal supremacy the rising military leaders turned
ruthlessly upon the church and crushed it for ever as a political
power. Nobunaga in 1571 sent a force to deal with some recalcitrant monasteries in Settsu, which had given him trouble a year or
so before, and as for Hieizan, though some of his adherents
scrupled to take extreme measures against such a holy place, he en-
circled all its three thousand buildings, and destroyed them by fire.
Hardly any of its inmates escaped death by flame or sword, its
lands were confiscated, and on the lower flanks of the mountain he
built a strong castle to guard against its revival. Though this was
perhaps an extreme example of Nobunaga's drastic methods, he
displayed throughout his career an unabated hostility towards all
the great Buddhist sects, except that he was on tolerably good
terms with certain Zen monks. In 1581, for instance, he burned
down a temple in Idzumi which had resisted a survey of its lands,
and in the same year he threatened to destroy the great Shingon
monastery of Kōyasan for harbouring some of his enemies. His
most stubborn opponents, however, were the so-called Monto or
Ikkō sects, which we have seen firmly installed in the Ishiyama
Hongwanji of Ōsaka and in the provinces defying the secular
authority in frequent risings during the fifteenth century. In the
sixteenth century these Ikkō stalwarts much hampered Nobunaga
in the subjugation of his enemies, with whom they were often in
league. He overcame them at length, though they resisted stubbornly. In Mikawa they were very strong, and for some years after
1560 gave Ieyasu many hard knocks before he could reduce them
with the help of their sectarian rivals. Nobunaga in his own province of Owari was routed by Ikkō forces in 1571, thrice attacked
them again unsuccessfully in the following year, and finally only
defeated them by one of the disgusting stratagems so common in
those days. He lured them out of their stronghold under pretence
of a truce, and massacred them all in an ambush. He then (1572)
marched into the provinces of Kaga and Echizen, where he at last
destroyed the power of the Ikkō fraternities which they had maintained, from the time of their victory over the feudal lord Togashi,

for nearly one hundred years. Even then he had not mastered this stubborn sect, for they held out against him in the fortified Monastery of the Original Vow, the great Ishiyama Hongwanji which, since the Kyōto Hongwanji had been destroyed (1465) by monks from Hieizan, was their headquarters. Nobunaga first attempted to reduce their stronghold in 1573, but it baffled his generals, and he was never able completely to reduce it by assault or by trickery, though he tried both methods persistently for over ten years, and at one time, it is said, invested it with an army of 60,000 men. In the end a compromise was reached and the Hongwanji was transferred to another district.

It may be objected that, since the Ikkō sect was able to resist such strong military pressure, one can scarcely argue that the Buddhist church did not at this time threaten to usurp the secular power. But it must be remembered that the military success of the great monasteries depended largely upon their association with feudal lords who welcomed any help in their private quarrels and were equally ready to turn upon an ally once he had served their purpose. The Hongwanji owed its power of survival to its strong defensive position, but also to support which it received from Nobunaga's great antagonists, notably the Mōri family in the west and the Takeda family in the east.* Moreover the Ikkō sect, which came the nearest to defeating feudal power, was in some respects hardly a religious body at all by the middle of the sixteenth century. Its abbots and monks kept no rule, they did not fast, they married, they took the same part in affairs as any layman, and it was in the measure of their assimilation to the type of a feudal landholder that they were able to compete in the feudal truggle. No doubt some of the great churchmen, such as Kōsa (Kennyo), the Hongwanji abbot, aimed at temporal sovereignty, but the fact remains that they never achieved it and this, in the circumstances, goes a long way towards proving that they never could have done.

With the resistance of the church stemmed, if not entirely broken, it remained for Nobunaga and his lieutenants to subdue the great

---

* Mōri for example sent 700 boatloads of rice into the beleaguered Hongwanji monastery in the summer of 1576. He was well content to keep Nobunaga occupied, and so to stave off an attack on his own domains.

chieftains in the midlands and the west of Japan. His military head-quarters were now at the fortress of Adzuchi in the province of Ōmi, and he could the more easily leave his base near the capital as this was a strong new castle, built between 1576 and 1579, the first of its kind in Japan. It was, like all buildings in Japan up to that date, a wooden structure, but it stood upon a massive stone base over seventy feet high. It showed a great advance in solidity upon all previous defensive works in Japan, and it was probably influenced by western models, for by that time firearms had been known in Japan for more than a generation, and some knowledge of European methods of warfare had been acquired since the first arrival of the Portuguese in 1542. A biography of Nobunaga is not complete without some account of his dealings with these strangers, Jesuit missionaries who played an important part in the Japan of his day: but we will first pursue the record of his military undertakings. The campaign against the Mōri family was entrusted chiefly to Hideyoshi, who set out from Adzuchi in 1577 with a strong force of picked men. Within the next five years he had driven Mōri out of seven central provinces and was holding him at a disadvantage, when in 1582 Nobunaga perished at the hands of a discontented general. At his death he was master of more than half the provinces of Japan—those which, being centrally grouped round the capital, were strategically the most important. But his position, though strong, was not inexpugnable. Much fighting, much diplomacy was needed before Japan could be unified once more.

For a time Hideyoshi was in danger, both from his enemies and his former allies. There was a breach with Ieyasu, but after some manœuvring the two came to terms and together completed the task begun by Nobunaga. In 1584 Hideyoshi was made regent (*kwampaku*) though he would have preferred to become Shōgun. That the powerless and penniless court was still the source of the most coveted honours is shown by the fact that, only a year before, he had gratefully accepted from the emperor the fourth rank, which was that usually held by minor state councillors. He now began to remove the obstacles which still stood in his path to complete military domination of Japan. He suppressed the troublesome Shingon monastery at Negoro in Kii, whose monks were armed

with arquebuses, and threatened but spared Kōyasan. He entered
into an alliance with certain barons in the North, and then set out
to reduce the great Shimadzu family of Satsuma in Kyūshū. Such
was the pride and power of this house (risen from a steward of the
manor of a court noble in the twelfth century), and so long and
difficult was the route, that he called upon all his provinces to
assist him in getting together a force of 250,000 men and supplies to
last a whole year.* Hideyoshi first made generous offers to Shimadzu, which were rejected. He then put his great army in motion,
and with little difficulty forced the Satsuma leaders to surrender
and pay him homage. He exacted hostages and divided Kyūshū
among local chieftains and his vassals, but he treated the Shimadzu
lords with liberality, restoring to them a great portion of their
holdings as new grants in fief. This was in 1587.

There now remained to conquer only two powerful chieftains
who had not yet submitted to the emperor, or rather to his regent.
These were Date, in the fastnesses of Mutsu and Dewa, and Hōjō
in Idzu, Sagami and adjacent regions. This latter family was distinct from the Hōjō regents, though remotely of the same ancestry,
and had risen to eminence from about 1500. Hideyoshi, as was his
custom, at first made friendly overtures to them, but these being
rejected he set about the business of reducing them with great
deliberation and thoroughness. Three columns (to the total number of 200,000 men) advanced from Kyōto by different routes
upon the Hōjō stronghold at Odawara. The castle was strong and
stoutly defended, so that Hideyoshi was obliged to sit down before
it for a prolonged siege. There has been preserved in the monastery
called Kōdaiji in Kyōto a letter which Hideyoshi, then in camp,
wrote to his wife. It runs in part as follows:—

> "Now we have got the enemy like birds in a cage and there
> is no danger, so please set your mind at rest. I long for the
> Young Lord (i.e. his infant son Tsurumatsu) but I feel that
> for the sake of the future, and because I want to have the
> country at peace, I must give up my longing. So please set
> your mind at rest. I am looking after my health and even hav-

---

* These numbers seem enormous, but they are not exceptional. The Shimadzu archives show that in 1581 Shimadzu besieged the stronghold of a rival
baron with an army of 115,000 men.

ing the cautery. So there is nothing to worry about. I have sent orders to all the daimyō and told them we shall hold on before Odawara, and they are to send for their wives. Since as I have thus declared it will be a long siege, I wish to send for Yodo (Yodo-gimi, his concubine and the mother of Tsuru-matsu). I wish you to tell her and make arrangements for her journey, and tell her that next to you she is the one who pleases me best. . . . I was very glad to get your messages. We have got up to within two or three hundred yards and put a double fosse round Odawara and shall not let a single man escape. All the men of the eight Eastern Provinces are shut up inside, and if we destroy Odawara the way is clear to Dewa and Mutsu. That means one-third of all Japan, and though I am getting old, I must think of the future and do what is best for the country. So now I mean to do glorious deeds and I am ready for a long siege, with provisions and gold and silver in plenty, so as to return in triumph and leave a great name behind me. I desire you to understand this and to tell it to everybody." (17th May, 1590.)

The fortress fell in July, and Date hearing the news decided to swear fealty to Hideyoshi. Japan was now at peace for the first time for more than a century. But it was not long before Hide-yoshi began to think of fighting again. Within a year or two he re-vived a project which he seems to have conceived during his cam-paign against Mōri in 1577, namely the conquest of China.[1]

There is much doubt as to his motives. Ambition predominated, we may be sure; and, since feudal armies were easier to assemble than to disband, perhaps he felt that he had better employ the great fighting force which he had constructed on some new enter-prise, lest the feudatories should fall to squabbling again. It must also be remembered that from the time of the Ashikaga Shōguns the Japanese had taken kindly to overseas adventure, not always of a pacific kind. The corsairs who terrorised the maritime pro-vinces of China and Korea in the fifteenth and sixteenth centuries, and constrained the Ming emperor to fortify his coasts against them, were not mere casual marauders, but organised bodies under the control of various feudal chieftains whose domains fringed the shores of the coastal provinces of Western Japan. The

Ōuchi family in particular used to arrange and sometimes to command raids on a large scale in China and Korea. Chinese accounts of attacks in the years about 1550 say that ten or twenty Japanese ships would appear off their shores, each carrying a crew of from 50 to 300 men, who would land and plunder one town after another. Piracy in those days was a respectable profession, which a nobleman's son might properly follow. Legitimate trade was also eagerly pursued. Hideyoshi gave licences to a number of vessels for an annual voyage to Annam and Cambodia, and the great feudatories were, as we have noticed, extremely anxious to extend their commercial intercourse with China. They would go to considerable lengths to obtain some kind of monopoly. It might even be said that, once the territorial possessions of the feudal families had been approximately fixed as a result of Hideyoshi's supremacy, the struggle for land was converted into a struggle for wealth in other forms, and they naturally looked overseas for new sources of gain. In any case Hideyoshi had no difficulty in assembling a large army for an expedition to China. He demanded of the king of Korea that his troops should pass through Korean territory, but the king would not consent, for the emperor of China was his suzerain. After elaborate preparations at a base in Kyūshū a force of nearly 200,000 men was transported across the Straits of Tsushima in 1592, and fought its way north, one contingent reaching Pyöngyang (the ancient capital of Rakurō) and another the extreme northeastern frontier, at a point on the river Tumen. This was a truly remarkable achievement, and the Chinese began to feel alarmed. With that engaging disdain which marked all their dealings with foreigners, they despatched a force of only 5,000 men to deal with the Japanese invaders. It was promptly wiped out, but by this time the Japanese had realised that they were in a tight place. They withdrew before a much larger army which the Chinese now sent against them, and almost exactly a year after their landing began to evacuate Korea, leaving only one division in occupation of the southern littoral. Chinese envoys came to Japan in 1593 to arrange a peace which was not finally concluded until 1596. But when the Chinese mission arrived at the Castle of Ōsaka, they produced a letter from the Ming emperor, investing Hideyoshi with the dignity of King of Japan, which was couched in such patronising

language that he burst into a rage and sent the ambassadors away
without an answer. But his anger soon seems to have been transferred to the unhappy Koreans, and in 1597 he sent a second army
to Korea. It met with strong opposition from Korean and Chinese
forces, and had serious commissariat troubles. Towards the end of
1598 the Japanese won some pitched battles, and slaughtered
thousands of Chinese and Korean soldiers: but both sides were

FIG. 48. *Honda Tadakatsu* (*1548-1610*). *A comrade of
Ieyasu in his campaigns.* (*After a contemporary portrait.*)

tired of the struggle and had begun to discuss peace, when news
came of the death (in September, 1598) of Hideyoshi. Shortly
afterwards the invaders withdrew, and from then until modern
times Japan abandoned hopes of foreign conquest, as well she
might, since this one overseas adventure had lasted six years and
had cost her in vain many lives and much treasure.

Upon the death of Hideyoshi there ensued, as may be imagined, a hot dispute as to who should succeed him. The political history of the next few years is complicated and in part obscure, but it resolves itself into a trial of strength between Tokugawa Ieyasu and his allies on the one side and a group of recalcitrant barons on the other. The enemies of Ieyasu included such powerful families as the Mōri, the Shimadzu and the Uesugi, who though they had been subdued by Hideyoshi had never been thoroughly broken. A decisive trial of strength was made at the great battle of Sekigahara in October, 1600. Ieyasu was victorious, and he at once set about a redistribution of fiefs which should secure him against further insubordination. In this process he met with some stubborn opposition, and it was not until 1615 that, by destroying at the siege of Ōsaka the party which still held out in support of the claims of Hideyoshi's family, he won for the Tokugawa family a dominance over Japan which lasted for two hundred and fifty years.

2. FIRST CONTACTS WITH THE WEST

Such were the main political events of the century of civil war. We may now return and review some important aspects of its social and institutional development. Nobunaga's career was mostly taken up with destructive work, clearing the site for a new edifice, which Hideyoshi was to commence and Ieyasu to complete. But during his lifetime there began movements which had an important bearing on later history. In 1542—the date is not quite certain —three Portuguese who had taken passage in a Chinese junk for Liampo were driven north by a typhoon and landed on Tanegashima, a small island off the coast of Ōsumi, then part of the Shimadzu domains. They were hospitably welcomed, and the arquebuses which they carried caused the greatest excitement. The Japanese, who had never seen firearms, at once set about copying them; and for centuries after the name for a musket in Japan was "Tanegshima." News of the coming of these strangers and of their weapons and other marvellous possessions soon spread to neighbouring fiefs, while the Portuguese in settlements along the China coast and in Malaysia on hearing of the discovery of Japan at once fitted out expeditions to trade in this new market. Within two or three years—certainly before 1549—not only had several

Portuguese ships visited harbours in Kyūshū, but Portuguese traders had reached Kyōto, which they described as a city of 96,000 houses—an interesting confirmation of other evidence that the population of the capital, even after the dreadful Ōnin war which had reduced it to ruins, was over half a million, and therefore considerably greater than that of any European city of the day.

Within a few years the traders were followed by Jesuit priests from the missions at Macao and Goa. The traders were all Portuguese and the missionaries were all Jesuits for, it will be remembered, Portugal had at this time been confirmed by the Pope in a monopoly of both spiritual and commercial undertakings in the East, and the company of Jesus, formed in 1540, had founded in Portuguese territory its first seminaries. These two facts have important sequels in the history of Japan's relations with the West, since thus her early contacts with European traders revealed to her international commercial rivalry in a phase of armed aggression, and her first knowledge of Christianity was gained from the most militant and uncompromising of its orders.

In 1549 Francis Xavier with two other Spanish Jesuits landed at Kagoshima, where they began to preach with the full permission of the lord of Satsuma. It says a great deal for the tolerance of the Japanese that a stranger, preaching a strange doctrine, was not molested but was even encouraged by all classes, including a number of Buddhist priests who listened respectfully to such expositions of the Catholic faith as the Portuguese were able to give. Soon Xavier had baptised 150 converts, but their understanding of the new religion must have been very vague, for Japanese is a difficult language and Christianity is hard to explain.[2] Perhaps it was because these early converts did not fully understand what their creed entailed that the Jesuits made such rapid progress in the first years of their labours. In at least one early official document they are described as propagating the Law of Buddha. Their ritual was not unlike that of Buddhism, and their teaching may have seemed like some new form of the comfort of Amidism, or the worship of a merciful goddess akin to Kwannon. But there were other and more potent reasons for the early success of Christianity in Japan. First in point of time, and some think in importance, was the desire of the great feudatories to derive profit from foreign trade. We have already seen how powerful this motive had become and it is quite clear from the early records, both Japanese and Portuguese, that a number of the barons in Kyūshū gave special facilities to the missionaries because, having noticed the deference paid by the traders to the priests, they hoped thus to attract merchant ships to harbours in their own fiefs. Within a few years of Xavier's arrival we find one chieftain after another ordering his people to treat the Jesuits with respect, or even to adopt Christianity *en masse*. In particular those barons who held the harbours of Kyūshū—Kagoshima, Hirado, Ōmura, Funai—competed for the patronage of the foreign traders, sometimes to the extent of persecuting Buddhists; but more than once, when they found that no ship came, they drove the missionaries away and ordered their subjects to revert to their former faiths. They were not always without justification for this sudden change of mind, for the Jesuits did not study the feelings of others, and their zeal easily took the form of an aggressive bigotry, though it must be granted that they displayed a splendid courage which undoubtedly gained them the respect of the military class. Xavier himself was in 1550 ordered to leave Satsuma, then a home of devout Buddhism, largely because his intolerance at length offended the Buddhist monks; and in Yamaguchi, the capital of the Ōuchi domains, he made the bad mistake of insisting that all the dead who had not been Christians during their lifetime would burn for ever. To a people who had never believed seriously in the flames of hell, and who paid to the memory of their ancestors a most reverent devotion, this was revolting doctrine; and it is not surprising that his disputations caused an uproar in a city where many learned monks resided, and that Christianity was proscribed in the Ōuchi domains.

But Xavier and his friends learned one valuable lesson from their stay among the western feudatories, for they discovered that in Japan the favour of princes would almost work miracles. They therefore went up to Kyōto, with the intention of gaining the protection of the emperor, but the city was in the throes of war, and they could see no one in authority. Xavier left Japan in 1552, and for some years the Jesuits had only moderate success, gaining converts in some localities and arousing dangerous antagonism in others. Their voluntary converts were for the most part people of low condition to whom they gave medical care. A missionary report of 1576 admits that no man of position would dare to accept the gospel, and in one fief during twenty years the only gentleman who became a Christian was one whom they had cured of the French evil. But soon afterwards the fortunes of the Jesuits improved, for they were able to convert certain barons, who forced their vassals to follow suit. Almost all their converts were in western Japan, in the domains of small rulers who, whether out of fanaticism or desire for trade, did not hesitate to persecute the Buddhists. Presently, however, the Jesuits had some success in the neighbourhood of Kyōto, where a Jesuit named Vilela had gone in 1559 at the invitation of a Tendai abbot of Mount Hiei, who was anxious to learn about the new sect. In the capital the question of trade did not immediately arise and they were judged on their personal characters and on the merits of the doctrine which they preached. Gradually, after a discouraging beginning in which they met great opposition from the Hieizan monasteries, traditionally haters of new sects, a small group of Jesuits, never more than a dozen or so, began to make modest headway among the upper classes and, though they were detested in some circles, worked themselves into a position of esteem in high quarters. They were received by the Shōgun, converted a number of small barons, who became most ardent Christians and whose family connections proved of great value to the missionaries. More than once, in the years of their sojourn in Kyōto and the home provinces, in times when bloodshed was constant and life was cheap, they were saved from peril by loyal friends not all of whom were Christians. At last, in 1568 they were received by Nobunaga, then almost at the zenith of his power, and treated by him with an affability which astounded those Japanese who knew him only as an unbending, callous master. From that time until his death he befriended the missionaries, and they prospered under his favour, for it mattered little that the emperor had in deference to the Tendai monks proscribed the Christian faith. Nobunaga was the most powerful ruler in Japan, and the Jesuits had easy access to him, sometimes dining with him in private or receiving him unattended

at their seminary for noble youths. There could hardly be a more
deeply interesting story than the record (as it can be pieced together from the Jesuits' letters and Japanese sources) of the life of
these strangers in the exotic surroundings of a foreign court, admitted to intimacy with a powerful autocrat, closely observing and
even taking a part in stirring events.

Yet numerically their gains were not imposing. Their report to
Rome of 1582 puts the total number of converts in the whole of
Japan at 150,000, and most of these were the inhabitants of
Kyūshū fiefs whose rulers had obliged them to adopt Christianity.

There has been much speculation as to the motives which led
Nobunaga and powerful war lords to tolerate and even to encourage these foreign preachers. Each historian tends to select one
reason and neglect others. Of the economic motive we have already treated, and it is quite certain that the Jesuits would not
have got far without the inducements of trade offered by their
compatriots. But this is not enough to explain why Nobunaga
should have shown himself not merely tolerant but positively gracious and friendly. Yet if we consider his position his sentiments
become fairly clear. In the first place he was an autocrat who could
afford no intimacy with his vassals and probably welcomed intercourse with men of strong character and high attainments from
whom he had nothing to fear. There is ample proof that he admired their courage. Cruelly intolerant these Jesuits may have
been, but they kept a severe rule, they had breeding and learning
and a touch of haughtiness—all qualities that were admired in
feudal Japan. For these reasons, and maybe because there is something in the Japanese character which responds to the Latin temperament, it is likely that no European of that day could have
made so favourable an impression as a Spanish Jesuit.* Certainly
one reason why Nobunaga liked Christians was that he hated
Buddhists. During all the time that he was in relations with the

---

* Even on mere grounds of physical appearance they would perhaps be less
startling than Northerners. Many centuries before, the Chinese had peopled the
unseen world with demons whom they imagined as creatures only remotely
resembling humans, having vermilion faces, red hair, and protruding blue
eyes; so that when they first saw Nordic men they naturally exclaimed: "Here
are the Foreign Devils."

Jesuits he was engaged in suppressing rebellious sects, destroying Hiyeizan in 1571, then attacking the Ikkō forces in Osaka.

Though Nobunaga had in common with the Jesuits a hatred of Buddhist monks, and though Buddhism in his day showed clear signs of degradation, this is not to say that he actively furthered Christianity as a faith. He listened to sermons now and then and as a ruler he was well disposed to any religion that promoted good behaviour and obedience. But he favoured the missionaries because they were useful and agreeable to him, and he was far more interested in their profane learning than in their dogma. He liked to talk to them about western matters, and he was, of course, pleased by their gifts of western things. His war helmet which is still preserved has a frontlet ornamented with crimson cloth of Portuguese or Flemish make. Altogether, though Christianity found in Japan both saints and martyrs, it left but little mark upon the national life, and it certainly had a less enduring effect upon Japanese thought and sentiment than did the philosophy of Chu Hsi. Of certain material benefits of Western culture the Japanese were not slow to avail themselves. Perhaps it is true to say that potatoes and tobacco, blessings which were introduced by Europeans, were better appreciated than their doctrines.* Such articles as clocks, globes, maps and musical instruments seem to have aroused great curiosity, and certain scholars were interested to learn about Western notions of natural science, but it can hardly be said that the Japanese were as eager to adopt European ways of thought as they had been in the seventh century to take over Chinese culture wholesale. They do not appear to have had any taste for speculative philosophy, which, as a European observer (Kaempfer) at the end of the seventeenth century said, they thought an amusement proper for lazy monks, though for what he calls the "moral part" of philosophy they had a great esteem. The crowning triumph of the Western intellect, the great gift which at that time Europe might have made to them, they were either unprepared or unwilling to receive, for, to quote the same authority, they knew "nothing of mathematicks, more especially of its deeper and speculative parts."[3]

* Potatoes seem to have been introduced from Java by the English in 1615, and tobacco by the Portuguese about 1590.

It is sometimes said that the introduction of firearms revolutionised warfare in Japan, and it certainly helped to establish a class of foot-soldier of the Ashigaru type, modified strategy, and promoted the building of massive castles with metal-protected casemates, doors and bridges. But the arquebus and the cannon did not have the same effect as in the West upon the structure of society, for they did not accelerate the break-up of feudalism. The professional fighting man, the samurai whose weapon was the sword, retained his high position and was not displaced, as had already been the mounted knight in Europe, by infantry armed first with the long bow and later with the gun.* The dominating idea of the rulers of Japan from the close of the sixteenth century was, having achieved stable institutions, to see that they were not changed. They therefore resisted, consciously or unconsciously, any innovation which tended to alter their existing arrangements, finally taking the extreme step of closing the country completely so as to exclude all alien influences. But this was not until they had ample and ominous experience of Europeans, both priests and laymen.

Hideyoshi, on succeeding Nobunaga, made no change in the treatment of the Jesuits. For some years he was more than cordial towards them. The prospects of the missionaries were very fair. Then without warning he issued in 1587 an edict banishing them all from Japan, though he was careful to explain that Portuguese merchants might continue to trade. His chief reason for this sudden change of front was undoubtedly political. The Jesuit leaders, under his favour, had of late made good progress in their deliberate policy of gaining adherents in high places, and they had al-

---

* In the well equipped and warlike fief of Satsuma, according to a roster of 1636, there was less than one gun to twenty males of the population. The military contingents which the Tokugawa Shōguns called upon their greater vassals to furnish varied slightly from time to time, but about 1650 they were in the proportions of two matchlock men, one bowman, and three spearmen in every twenty-three men, the remainder being swordsmen, of whom about one in ten was mounted. Those small direct retainers (*hatamoto*) of the Shōgun whose fiefs were worth 1,000 *koku* of rice per annum at this period furnished twenty-three men, including one bowman, one match-lock man and two spearmen.

Not only were firearms scarce, but the Shogunate discouraged their use by the vassals, and tried, though not with complete success, to control their manufacture and sale.

ready made converts of certain of his strongest barons and ablest commanders. This seems to have caused him some misgiving lest Christianity should form a bond to unite his vassals against him, but he did not take serious steps to enforce his edict, and winked at the continued presence in Japan of a number of fathers, who took care to go about their business without ostentation. They continued to have a success so amazing that, though a number of their converts were beyond all doubt genuine to the point of fanaticism* and adhered to their new faith in the face of great danger, one cannot but suspect that it had, by one of those crazes which have often swept over Japan, become the fashion to ape the customs of foreigners, including their religion. We know that rosaries and crucifixes were eagerly bought and worn by many who were not Christians, even, it is said, by Hideyoshi himself; and it was modish to wear foreign clothes and to be able to recite a Latin prayer. For ten years after his edict Hideyoshi forbore to enforce it, and meanwhile the Jesuits were discreet; but as time went on many things occurred to confirm his view that Christianity was a political danger. Spanish Franciscan monks and traders came to Japan, and intrigued against the Portuguese, till in the end the sectarian quarrels of the missionaries and the boasting of the pilot of a Spanish galleon convinced Hideyoshi that the foreign missionaries were merely forerunners of political aggression. He had by this time been pretty well posted as to the methods of the Spanish and the Portuguese priesthood, as assistants in colonial enterprise, and he determined to be rid of them all. There then ensued a proscription of Christianity, accompanied by an outbreak of persecution, in 1597. Six Spanish Franciscans and three Jesuits and seventeen Japanese converts were executed. A number of devoted Jesuits still remained in Japan, mostly in hiding, but a few with Hideyoshi's tacit permission. On the whole the edict was enforced with severity but not ferociously, and the behaviour of Hideyoshi seems enlightened and tolerant in comparison with the cruelty of contemporary Europe. Those were the days of the Inquisition, of the massacre of St. Bartholomew, of Alva's torture of the Nether-

---

* Such as Ōtomo, Lord of Bungo, "who went to the chase of the Bonzes (Buddhist monks) as to that of wild beasts, and made it his singular pleasure to exterminate them."

lands and of the merciless slave trade. If Hideyoshi had sniffed the faintest perfume of all these flowers of the Renaissance—as no doubt he had, for Japanese had by now travelled to India and Rome and had reported upon European civilisation—he could hardly be blamed for concluding that his native institutions were more benevolent.

The reasons for his moderation after the martyrdoms of 1597 were various. He probably did not care to press too hard some of his Western feudatories, who were well disposed towards the Jesuits. Towards Christianity as a religion he bore no kind of animosity, and after his first outburst he would probably have been satisfied had the missionaries only gone quietly about their holy business, since he could put his hand on them at any moment, and the Japanese like the English used to have a convenient if illogical habit of winking at disobedience of laws, so long as it was not too flagrant. Moreover he was not quite certain that if he kept out the Portuguese priests he would not lose the Portuguese traders, and since Ashikaga days foreign trade had assumed a great importance in the eyes of the Japanese. It must not be supposed that this trade was confined to European products. On the contrary it consisted at this time largely of goods of Asiatic origin. The most important item in the cargoes was silk yarn, which was far superior in quality to what the Japanese, whose industries had suffered during the civil wars, could then produce. Chinese textiles, books, pictures and porcelains, together with drugs, spices, gums and perfumes from China and the Indies, were luxuries which a wealthy Japanese deemed indispensable. There was also at this time a considerable import of gold in exchange for copper and silver.* Hideyoshi, before his projected conquest of China, had attempted to conclude a commercial treaty with China but the negotiations fell through, and the Portuguese profited by this situation, since they became not only the carriers but also the intermediaries in Japan's trade with China. Perhaps this alone is sufficient to explain why Hideyoshi hesitated to enforce his edict.

* This is a difficult question, for there was a movement of precious metal both ways. But it seems to be established that at this time the balance was in favour of Japan. Hideyoshi had ideas about metallic currency, was against copper coinage, and made efforts to attract gold to Japan. The subject is complicated by a fluctuating ratio of value between gold and silver.

Could he have found a substitute for the Portuguese he might have expelled all the fathers, but after 1597 he was occupied with other matters, and he died in 1598, thus affording a respite to the missionaries in Japan.

Ieyasu, on succeeding to Hideyoshi's power, at first displayed a similar tolerance, and for similar reasons. His policy was to encourage the growth of Japan's merchant marine, but meanwhile her foreign trade must not be allowed to diminish. Through a Spanish Franciscan he got into touch with the Spanish authorities in the Philippine Islands and offered to open the ports of Eastern Japan to Spanish ships, at the same time making it clear that he would not enforce the edicts against Christianity. It is significant that he proposed reciprocal freedom of commerce, and asked that experts in shipbuilding should be sent to Japan. Clearly he had at that time no idea of excluding foreigners and even wished his own countrymen to engage in overseas traffic. But before long, finding that the Spaniards while eager enough to send missionaries seemed lukewarm about commerce with Eastern Japan, he began to grow suspicious, kept a strict watch on the Christians in his new capital at Yedo, and looked round for other channels of foreign trade. This was in 1605. For some years already the Dutch had begun to challenge the Portuguese monopoly of trade in the Orient, and had sent merchant ships to Japan. One of these, detached from its unlucky consorts, arrived in a harbour in Bungo in 1600. It happened to carry the pilot-major of the squadron, an Englishman named Will Adams, who was taken into Ieyasu's favour and acted as his adviser on matters connected with trade and navigation. Ieyasu, it is to be noted, was much interested in maps and "some points of jeometry" which Adams was able to explain. He also learned some points about the Dutch and the English, and Adams informed him of the attitude of Protestant states towards the church of Rome. Naturally he began to feel it preferable and possible to have foreign trade without foreign priests. He still treated the missionaries with forbearance and even with liberality, but his suspicions were growing the while, and in 1612 he resolved to have done with them.

A close examination of the facts, as presented by both Christian and Japanese records, makes it clear that as ruler of Japan he could not reasonably have come to any other decision. He had seen the Jesuits intriguing to have the Spaniards expelled, the Spaniards pressing for the exclusion of the Dutch. He had learned of bitter quarrels between Franciscans and Dominicans. On more than one occasion the conduct or the language of both Spaniards and Portuguese had given him reason to fear that they would like to see his government overthrown and even harboured designs upon the sovereignty of Japan. The Spaniards or the Portuguese can scarcely have supposed that they could conquer Japan by force of arms, but the missionaries certainly hoped that the then government might be overthrown and replaced by a party favourable to Christianity. Such an event was by no means out of the question, seeing the success of the Jesuits among the ruling classes, and both Hideyoshi and Ieyasu felt that here was a real danger. And when Ieyasu found one of his officials guilty of misfeasance in the interests of a Christian feudatory, lighted on a conspiracy against himself between certain of his vassals and some of the foreigners, heard of a fleet of Spanish ships of war based on Manila, and learned from spies who had been sent to Europe something of the ambitions of Christian monarchs and the pride of the Roman church, then he decided that he must act without delay. By this time he had little reason to fear the loss of foreign trade, for he knew that Dutch and English merchantmen were anxious to visit his ports, and though there was still no authorised traffic with China, Japanese junks had of late gone far afield to bring back Chinese produce from entrepôts in Cochin-China and elsewhere.

Yet even now he did not proceed to extreme measures against the Christians. There had been perfunctory bans in 1606, 1607 and 1611; and in 1612 and again in 1613 he issued further edicts prohibiting Christianity. These were not drastically enforced, but were rather in the nature of warnings. The blow fell at first gently. In some fiefs Christians were imprisoned, tortured or killed, in others the rulers or their officials, whether out of sympathy with Christian doctrines or out of common humanity, only ostensibly carried out the orders of Ieyasu. It is remarkable, too, that in the capital and in the direct Tokugawa domains neither foreign nor Japanese Christians had been molested by Ieyasu before 1612, and even after that date he and his officers, though they pulled down some churches and took vigorous measures against Japanese converts of the military class, especially those of high rank, did not deny to the members of the lower classes freedom of religious belief. It is important to understand that this was, and for centuries had been, the attitude of the rulers of Japan. They did not interfere with religion so long as religion did not interfere with government.

This policy, though it may be ascribed to indifferentism or to tolerance according to taste, was, it must be allowed, extremely enlightened. In the same way the Japanese, who have always given a hospitable welcome to foreign visitors, on the whole treated the missionaries with great respect and forbearance, though nobody can deny that they were often irritating and meddlesome guests. The Jesuits and other priests who conceived it their duty to remain at their posts were, despite this flouting of his edicts, not maltreated by Ieyasu, and it is clear that he was reluctant to shed the blood of foreigners. It may be that he feared retaliation from Spain or Portugal, but the fact remains that the first execution of a foreign priest took place in 1617, after Ieyasu's death, though one brave Jesuit suffered indescribable hardship in gaol in 1615. Meanwhile, however, the native converts had fared ill. The official Martyrology (of Delplace) records in the years 1612 and 1613 a number of banishments, the destruction of some sanctuaries, and not more than fifty executions throughout Japan. When early in 1614 Ieyasu issued another edict, in some districts the persecution became more intense. In and near Nagasaki it was conducted with such cruel atrocity that the best of the Kyūshū samurai when called in to help merely feigned to carry out their orders. On the whole sympathy was with the Christians and the edict was only partially and mildly enforced, both in the capital and in the territories of most of the great vassals. From the close of 1615 Ieyasu was occupied with his great struggle against the party which under Hideyoshi's son, Hideyori, held out against him in the fortress of Ōsaka; and both priests and converts had a respite until after this campaign. It was not until Ieyasu, having established the dominance of the Tokugawa family, died in June, 1616, and was succeeded by his son Hidetada that the contact of

native institutions with foreign civilisation produced an antagonism
so widespread and so bitter that it culminated in a persecution,
which, as a modern Japanese writer has observed, in its ferocity
"equalled if it did not exceed" any such horror as has been
perpetrated in the West.

NOTES TO CHAPTER XIX

[1] Page 413. Hideyoshi's designs on China. It seems likely that Hideyoshi inherited the idea of conquering China from Nobunaga, who
had talked about it to the Jesuits. Frois, writing to the General of the
Jesuits in 1582, says that Nobunaga "determined that when he should
have finished subjugating Mōri and be master of all the sixty-six
provinces of Japan, he would prepare a great Armada to go and conquer
China and take it by force of arms."

[2] Page 417. The linguistic difficulties confronting the missionaries
were in the beginning almost too much for them. It appears that in
his first sermons St. Francis Xavier unknowingly exhorted the Japanese
to worship Dainichi, thinking that Dainichi (the Buddha Vairocana)
was the Japanese word for a supreme deity. The problem of the translation of the word "God" was to prove a serious stumbling block to the
propagation of Christianity, since neither Chinese nor Japanese contained a word exactly expressing the monotheistic Christian conception.
In China there was acute dissension among the missionaries as to the
proper equivalent for Deus, until Clement XI gave a ruling in the Bull
Ex illa die of 1715. But the arguments used did not meet with the approval of the Emperor K'anghsi, who wrote in the margin of a Chinese
translation of the Bull: "After reading this Decree, I can only say that
foreigners are small-minded people."

In considering the development of foreign philosophies and religions
in Japan, we should always bear in mind this problem of language.

[3] Page 421. Mathematics in Japan. The Chinese had done some work
of distinction in mathematics in the twelfth and thirteenth centuries,
but do not appear to have made any advances subsequently, since they
were no match for the Jesuit astronomers in China after 1600. The
Japanese worked out an original method of the differential calculus
from hints coming through the Dutch, and in general they appear to
have displayed remarkable ingenuity in application of a limited
knowledge; but Kaempfer's judgment as to their backwardness in
theory seems to have been correct.

Chapter XX

ADZUCHI AND MOMOYAMA

1. NEW FEUDAL INSTITUTIONS

HAVING seen the results of the first impact of Western civilisation upon Japanese institutions, we may now return and trace the growth of those institutions during the century and more of fighting that terminated in the capture of the castle at Ōsaka (1615). We have noticed before that in Japan the most destructive warfare, though it may have impeded, never entirely checked cultural progress; and indeed there is much to be said for the view that the excitement of conflict, the emulation among rival chieftains, and perhaps more than anything the removal of barriers between classes, gave a movement and a variety to the age which it lost as peace returned.

The gradual collapse of the Ashikaga government meant the failure of its laws, but the great feudal houses had for centuries past observed their own codes rather than injunctions from the capital. To conserve their own strength in times of anarchy they were obliged to govern in their own fiefs with a firm hand, and therefore during the wars law flourished rather than decayed. Each powerful family compiled or amended its house-law, and it is probably true to say that there was more legislation, and more enforcement, during the sixteenth century than there had ever been before. Among the oldest of these codes then in force is that of the Ōuchi family, known as the "Ōuchi Wall-writing." Some 50 articles are still extant, the earliest going back to 1440, the latest to 1495. The most comprehensive is the code of the Date family which was entitled the Dust Heap, not because it is composed of rubbish but because its contents are so various. Its articles number 171 and most of them were drafted with extreme care by the (13th) Date who ruled over a great part of Northern Japan about 1550 and whose descendant sent an embassy to the Pope in 1613. It includes very detailed regulations dealing, for instance, with such matters as loans and mortgages. Some of the codes, on the other hand, embody merely the moral principles and the political ideas traditional in a family, as for instance the Satomi House

Law, which bears an epigraph stating that these are the rules of conduct laid down by the four previous heads of the house. They were supplemented by written instructions issued from time to time and placed in the hands of the members of the family and its principal retainers. Other codes deal only with the duties of vassals. Such were the Injunctions (*okite*) of the Mōri family, drawn up in 1572 in the form of an oath to which the vassals subscribed.

All these different codes were framed to meet the personal and local requirements of the barons, and therefore present wide variations in detail. But in spirit they are fairly uniform, because they are all based on the same conception of society, namely that of a regional lord striving to safeguard his domains. Consequently they are concerned with duties, and pay no attention to rights. The earliest, like the Ōuchi Wall-writing and the Date Dust-heap, are modelled upon the feudal laws of the thirteenth century, such as the Jōei Formulary and its supplements. In general there was a tendency among the daimyō to ape the Shōgunate, and to reproduce in their fiefs on a smaller scale the hierarchy of regents, counsellors, "house-men" and stewards. This kind of vanity contributed to the uniformity of feudal legislation. Another feature which these laws had in common was their oppressiveness. Thus they carried to extremes the principle of joint responsibility by punishing for the offence of an individual not only his family, but also his neighbours, and sometimes a whole village or even a whole district. All these laws had as their object the preservation of order as conceived by the lawgiver, and the judge was not concerned with abstract justice. So we find, as early as 1445, such a proclamation as, "All quarrels and disputes are strictly forbidden. If this is disobeyed, both sides will be put to death, without inquiry into right and wrong." This simplified procedure, like many other arbitrary acts, is clearly an outgrowth of martial law, based on the notion that internal dissension is a source of weakness. The military liking for prompt rather than correct solutions ran riot during the period of wars, when it was free from the restraint of civil opinion. Punishments became exceedingly barbarous, in contrast to the relative leniency of the penal system evolved during the Heian period. From the close of Muro-

machi we find frequent mention of methods of killing and tor-
turing whose very names cause a shudder. Such were crucifixion
head-downwards, sawing off limbs with bamboo saws, trans-
fixing with stakes, roasting, boiling and slicing; but it does not
appear that this fiendish repertory contained anything that had
been overlooked in Europe. These torments were as a rule reserved for the lower orders, and samurai of above a certain
rank were ceremoniously decapitated or allowed to commit
suicide. This latter practice, there can be no doubt, owed its prevalence not so much to disregard of death as to a sensible desire to
avoid something more painful and degrading. Priests, it may be
noted, were not put to death, but were "exposed," or banished to
remote inhospitable places, so that if they should unfortunately
die their judges could not be blamed for transgressing the law of
the Buddha by taking life.

If the control of a feudal lord over his subjects was rigorous, his
attitude towards strangers from other fiefs was extremely hostile.
Some codes forbade all communications with persons in other
domains, and even where strangers were admitted they were
closely supervised. In general the feudal lord kept a close watch
over the movements of his subjects, and dictated their private
arrangements in an astonishing way, not allowing them to marry,
to adopt a child, to employ a servant, or to make a journey, without his consent. It can readily be imagined that a system so
founded on mistrust and interference proved unbearable to men of
spirit, and was no doubt partly to blame for many of the acts of
rebellion and treason which mar the record of later feudalism. To
supplement their legislation the ruling class continued to foster, as
we have seen them doing in the past, certain ethical sentiments
which tended to secure for them loyal and continuous service.
The new feudal aristocracy, who for the most part had risen to
power by disregarding all the laws, written and unwritten, of
fealty and gratitude, now set themselves to inculcate in their
dependents those very ideals of filial piety and knightly faith to
which they themselves had so often been untrue.

The careers of Nobunaga and Hideyoshi were so filled with
fighting and intrigue that they had small leisure for constructive
legislation. Nobunaga left behind him little but some injunctions

such as any feudal chieftain might issue to his vassals. Hideyoshi,
though he had more definite ideas of government, preferred to act
as emergencies arose and not to be bound by precedents. Most of
his enactments took the form of edicts under his vermilion seal.
They were couched in simple language, but they were when he
chose most rigorously enforced, and they overrode the traditional
code of the Shōgunate. They were as a rule respected by Ieyasu,
and had an important influence upon legislation in the Tokugawa
period. We may cite one or two specimens, to give some idea of
their nature:

　　　(1581). Fixing the rate of land tax, and the proportion in
which the crop is to be shared by farmer and steward.

　　　(1586). When a quarrel occurs at Nagasaki between a
foreigner and a Japanese, and one wounds the other, the
officials shall inquire into the circumstances, and if it is five
each out of ten (i.e. if both parties are equally at fault) the
Japanese shall be punished.

　　　(1587). A set of 19 articles regulating transport by sea,
which seems to have been drawn up in response to sugges-
tions from the merchants of Sakai. It is the second authentic
merchant shipping law in Japan, and contains provisions as
to charters, bills of lading, demurrage and responsibility for
loss and damage. The first law of this type is of uncertain
date, but seems to belong to the late Kamakura period.

It was as proclamations under the vermilion seal that the edicts
against Christianity were issued. Apart from the tragic interest of
those documents perhaps the most significant of Hideyoshi's lawgiving is to be found in three short ordinances which deserve
attention because they lay down the cardinal rules of feudal institutions that survived until well into the nineteenth century. The
first is an order issued in 1585 and repeated in the following year,
which prescribes that no persons in service, from samurai down to
farmer, may leave their employment without the permission of
their overlord, and that persons engaging a man who has so left his
employment shall be punished. Here we have an early enuncia-
tion of the policy of Hideyoshi, Ieyasu and their successors, which
may be shortly defined as a determination, once they had by
their efforts brought feudal society to a certain point of order and

stability, to guard against its disruption by fixing its organisation and permitting no further change. The first essential was to see that no man left that station in life to which he was born.

The above edict merely forbade a samurai to transfer his services from one chief to another, and was the legal expression of the feudal principle that a man must be true to one master, just as a wife must be faithful to one husband, in life and in death. A later edict goes further and is intended to establish a rigid division of classes. It is dated 1586, and decrees that a samurai may not become a townsman, that a farmer may not leave his land and work for hire, and that no landowner may give protection to vagrants and men who do not cultivate the soil. We have already seen that there was an extremely free intermingling, almost a reversal, of classes from the Muromachi period onwards, and Hideyoshi himself, who promulgated this edict, would never have risen to power had it been in force in his youth, for he was the humblest of menials as a boy. But now that he had conquered and organised the empire, he wanted in the name of stability to revert to the old order of rigid class distinctions, as did all those who had profited by its breakdown in the age of wars. This short-sighted but not unnatural conservatism gained ground during the following century, and was responsible for the almost fossilised condition of all but certain urban layers of society throughout the Yedo period. One other enactment is worth attention for the light which it throws on current ideas of social economy. In 1587 Hideyoshi proclaimed that all farmers were to hand in their weapons. This measure, known as the Taikō's Sword Hunt, had a double purpose. It was intended not only to remove a source of danger but also to emphasise the class distinction between soldiers and farmers, and to make the wearing of the sword a badge of rank. It should be noted that it thus officially marks the end of that stage of feudalism in which the soldier in times of peace farmed his own land. This stage, indeed, had vanished long ago, and had been replaced by an order in which the class of samurai or professional soldiers was supplemented by peasants who from choice or necessity would take a hand at fighting. The armed peasant had become a danger to the feudal lords in religious and agrarian riots, such as the Ikkō risings of the Muromachi period; and other feudal lords had deemed it necessary to disarm him before Hideyoshi did so on a national scale. The language of the edict is engagingly ingenuous. It announces that all the arms confiscated will be melted down and turned into nails and bolts for use in building a hall to contain the Great Buddha which Hideyoshi was then about to erect at Kyōto. Freed from the danger of these weapons and conscious of their holy use, the peasants can feel safe, he says, not only in this world but the next!

While thus dealing with the commoners, Hideyoshi strove continuously, even when mortally ill, to perpetuate the balanced system of feudal power which he had built up. He forbade marriages and all other engagements between families of his vassals unless they were approved by him; he enacted a number of sumptuary laws regulating the behaviour of the daimyō; and he made his great officers swear on oath that they would not alter his house-law. In these and many other ways he commenced that policy, which his successors extended, of legislation against change. But he forgot that in decay institutions have an enemy more relentless than reform.

2. THE CULTURAL SCENE

NOBUNAGA's castle at Adzuchi on the shore of Lake Biwa may serve as a symbol of his times, for it was new and large and lavishly decorated with gold. It was probably the first to be built under the influence of European ideas of fortification and it at once superseded all previous feudal strongholds, which had been merely wooden barracks protected by earthworks, ditches and stockades. Within a few years castles of this type had been built in most fiefs. The greatest of all was the castle of Ōsaka, built in 1583-85 by Hideyoshi. This was a colossal edifice of immense granite blocks, surrounded by deep moats and steep escarpments. In dimensions and solidity it far outstripped any building that had ever been erected in Japan, though the Hall of the Great Buddha at Nara remained probably the largest wooden building under one roof in the world. The castle of Adzuchi, commenced in 1576 and completed in 1579, was not conceived on such an immense scale, yet it was for those days a great undertaking, and its cost was so enormous that all the provinces under Nobunaga's sway were laid under contribution. It was a well-protected structure, but it does not seem to have been equipped with any special defence against artillery. At that time firearms though in use throughout Japan were still neither numerous nor effective at a long range, so that moats and walls would be sufficient to cope with musket-fire; while of artillery there was practically none. Adzuchi was intended not only as a strong citadel but as a lordly residence. Some of the material and the interior decoration was brought from the Kyōto palace of the deposed Ashikaga Shōgun. In all the living apartments walls, ceilings and pillars were coated with gold or with black or red lacquer, or on the panels were painted pictures by great artists like Kanō Eitoku. This was not the first time that a feudal chief risen from obscurity had indulged in vulgar display and poured out his new wealth on buildings and entertainments; but hitherto the successful captains had sooner or later deferred to Kyōto standards, which were lavish enough when there was money to spend, but saved from mere wanton profusion by a long habit of restrained elegance. The Ashikaga Shōguns, we have seen, developed a form of luxury so far the opposite of rich and cloying that it is termed by the Japanese *shibui* or "astringent," an idea which can perhaps best be understood by comparing a sweet fruit with one of slightly acid flavour. From Nobunaga's time, largely because Kyōto was in ruins and the members of its old society were now scattered or lived an indigent, secluded life, the old courtly influence waned, and a new criterion tended to replace the severe canons of Zen æsthetics. There began a time in which gold glittered, colour came back into pictures, and the arts veered towards those Japanese equivalents of the rococo and the baroque which distinguish the period called Momoyama, after Hideyoshi's palace of that name.

We are often told that the East is unchanging, but there is very little in the history of Japan to support that very dubious dictum. Nowhere have men more eagerly, nay recklessly, leaped to welcome new things and new notions. It is true that in the record of government we can trace a deep respect for ancient institutions; and successive rulers of Japan have often endeavoured to fix immutably the order of society. But doubtless they have so acted in part because they well knew the mercurial habit of their own people—a people which, from its very isolation, was peculiarly open to the charm of novelty. We have seen Japan from the dawn of her history submitting to wave after wave of foreign influence and as the art of navigation progressed establishing contacts with more and more distant cultures. The sea-rovers of Ashikaga times began to make long voyages and by 1600 there were few places in the East that Japanese travellers had not visited, while (whether as pirates or mercenaries) a decade later they were trading or fighting in considerable numbers in the Philippines, Malaya, Siam, and Indo-China. Sir Edward Michelborne, on a privateering cruise in 1604, suffered heavy loss in a sea-fight with Japanese corsairs off Singapore, when his pilot-major, the Arctic explorer Davys, fell a victim to a Japanese sword. Most of these adventurers were men of a desperate type, who preferred not to risk returning home, but others came back, bringing with them strange objects and stranger tales, not always flattering to the West. Their cargoes, and those of the Portuguese, wrought certain changes in Japan. We have already suggested that Christian doctrine, stupendous as was its first effect, did not in the long run leave much mark upon Japanese life, and we shall return to this question presently; but there can be no doubt as to the influence of certain material importations which took place at this time.

Guns we have mentioned, and tobacco,* and potatoes. Other foreign goods which, from being fashionable luxuries, soon became almost necessities were the water-melon; the pumpkin (still called *kabocha*) from Cambodia; incense sticks from Fukien; mosquito nets; and for a time among the wealthy there was a rage for Portuguese costume, just as in former times the courtiers had loved to dress like Chinese. Pictures are extant showing Japanese exquisites parading in tunics and balloon-like trousers, long

---

* Tobacco was welcomed and adopted with an almost frenzied enthusiasm. It was also condemned by moralists, such as that stern Confucian scholar Hayashi Razan, who, however, admitted that he could not break himself of the habit. Smoking became so popular that it was regarded as a public danger, until in 1609 (ten years before James I's "counterblast" against ignoble Tabagie) it was forbidden by an edict which however had no effect, though repeated three or four times in ensuing years. Its only result was to create the crime of smuggling, and for a time tobacco was sold under the name of Life-prolonging Tea.

cloaks and high-crowned hats. We learn also from a Japanese grammarian of the time that it was the fashion—which he much disliked—to use scraps of Portuguese in conversation. In the modern language there is still an echo from those days, in such words of Portuguese origin as *kappa*, a cape; *pan*, bread; *karuta*, playing cards; *casteira* (Castille), a kind of sponge cake; *biidoro*, (vitro), glass; *furasoko*, flask; *juban* (gibão), a shirt; *birōdo* (velludo), velvet; and a number of religious terms.

Of European sciences which came to Japan at this early date, apart from a knowledge of firearms, we may mention printing. Hideyoshi's destruction of Christian churches in Kyōto in 1588 drove the missionaries to Kyūshū, and there they set up a college and a printing press, on the island of Amakusa. Foreign works were translated into colloquial Japanese and printed in the Latin alphabet. One of the earliest, apart from religious books, was "*Esopo no Fabulas*," Æsop's Fables, translated by a Japanese convert, a leper who had previously been a Zen monk, and printed in 1593.* Printing, of course, was not by any means new in Japan. Wood block printing was known in the eighth century if not before, and there were printed books in the tenth. Movable types (of cast metal) were first used by the Koreans, very soon after 1400, and knowledge of this process came to Japan first from Korea and not from Europe.[1] It did not find much favour and the Japanese soon reverted to block-printing.

On the whole it cannot be said that the intellectual influence of Europe upon Japan in the sixteenth and early seventeenth centuries was either profound or lasting. To judge from subsequent history, it was the applied sciences that made the most permanent impression—astronomy, cartography, shipbuilding, mining and metallurgy; and it seems as if until recent times the East has always welcomed our mechanical devices and been cold to our philosophy. The changes that took place in Japan after the middle ages were as much the result of internal growth as of external stimulus. At

---

* There was also a press in Kyōto, managed by one "Antonius" Harada, from which issued (in 1610) a book entitled *Contemptus Mundi*. This was the *Imitation of Christ*, which had already been printed in Japan in the Latin alphabet, but was now translated into Japanese and printed with movable types.

first, when we read of century after century of war, it seems as if
the country must have been a waste of trampled fields and
ruined cities; but on looking closer it appears that wealth and
productive power increased rather than diminished. There is perhaps as yet not enough evidence to support such a view entirely,
but certainly most of the known facts point that way, and in the
records there is very little trace of permanent destruction. For one
thing there was, except in Kyōto and one or two other cities, not
much to destroy. Most towns and villages consisted only of flimsy
wooden buildings, easily burned but easily rebuilt. Rice-fields,
which were not very suitable terrain for fighting, appear to have
been generally respected, and since Japan is not a pastoral country
there was no loss of flocks and herds through the foraging of enemies. Monasteries, which were among the chief local repositories
of treasure, as a rule escaped. The damage suffered by agriculture
seems to have been caused chiefly by levies of men and produce
made by the competing armies, and such damage, though serious
enough, could be made good within a few years.* Meanwhile the
fighting, except in certain important pitched battles, does not
seem to have been very deadly, if we may judge from the numbers
of killed in engagements of which there is a full record. On the
other hand from the Ashikaga period onwards several causes operated to increase wealth. As the struggle for power, and even for
existence, developed among the feudal barons, each of them was
obliged not only to husband but to expand his resources. Thus we
observe them competing for foreign trade, or protecting their
peasantry, or encouraging local industries, such as mining; and all
the time communications by land and sea were being improved,
while commerce developed in specially favoured centres such as
Sakai and later Ōsaka. Even the depredations of the armies sometimes indirectly contributed to the growth of trade, since supplies
from China were called upon to meet a shortage of domestic production due to the removal of men from their work, as we have
already seen from the example of raw silk.

---

* The area under cultivation *circa* 1450 is said to have been about 3,000,000
acres and by 1500 it had diminished by 5 per cent. These figures are doubtful,
but anyhow they do not indicate any more serious loss than might come from a
bad harvest, although this period includes the destructive Onin war.

Altogether, if we make an exception of the particularly ruinous Ōnin war—say for a generation or so after 1467—it appears that the period of mediæval warfare in Japan cannot properly be dismissed as a Dark Age. It was, allowing for fluctuations, a period of expanding culture and growing productivity. Perhaps one of the most beneficent effects of the feudal struggle was to spread over the whole country wealth, influence and learning hitherto concentrated in and around the capital, for by this diffusion the danger of wholesale destruction was practically removed.

By the time of Hideyoshi Japan had reached a stage of prosperity such as she had hardly known before. It does not, of course, follow that its foundations were secure, and indeed her subsequent history reveals one weakness after another in her economic structure; but superficially the so-called Momoyama period is one of flourishing activity in the arts of peace. Hideyoshi's undertakings were all conceived on a grand scale. He caused to be made a complete land survey of Japan, he erected in 1583 the castle of Ōsaka, in 1586 the Great Buddha at Kyōto, in 1587 the Jūrakudai or Mansion of Pleasures, and in 1594 the Momoyama Palace. All these, like his campaigns and his ambitions, were imposing projects, and the writers of his day had at their command hardly enough superlatives for the description of his magnificence. The castle of Ōsaka could not compare as an architectural monument with, let us say, one of the great cathedrals of the middle ages in Europe, but in sheer size, in the effort required to transport and assemble its massive materials of stone and timber, it probably rivalled any building in the West, especially in point of the speed with which it was erected.* As to its beauty there is no room for comparison, for there is no exact counterpart in the West to the scheme of decoration depending upon elaborate wood-carvings, usually polychromatic, and the free use of pigment and gold foil on partitions and large folding screens, which characterises the castles and palaces of this period. It is perhaps the screens and the wall paintings which best figure the ideals of Momoyama art. Not much of the original structures now remains, but some portions, including paintings, have been preserved and from them one can

* If we may believe temporary records tens, even hundreds of thousands of men were engaged in the building of Ōsaka, Momoyama and Jūrakudai.

gain an idea of the splendour of the whole.* Great screen painters
flourished at this time, notably Eitoku (1543-90) and Sanraku
(1557-1635) of the Kanō school. They worked on a large scale,
covering great panels of silk or paper with decorative compositions. On the walls, mostly of bright gold, there are blue-eyed
tigers prowling through groves of bamboo, or multi-coloured
shishi—mythical beasts like lions, but amiable and curly-haired—
that gambol among peonies against a golden background. There
are gorgeous landscapes, thick with old pines and blossoming
plum-trees, where bright birds perch on fantastic rocks or float
amid ripples of deep blue. There are groves and banks and gardens, rich with brilliant leaves and flowers; bearded and sinuous
dragons winding their complicated length through sepia clouds;
gaggles of wild geese sweeping across the moon; and scenes of the
Chinese court peopled with ancient worthies. As a rule these
apartments display, suite after suite, such profusion of colour and
detail, such a deliberate effort to overwhelm the eye with splendour, that they come perilously near to vulgarity. But from this
danger they are generally saved by a certain bravery, a boldness
of stroke and a brilliance of design. Their full mastery can only be
appreciated through comparison with less competent works of
the same school. The usual effect is one of size and richness, far
remote from the pensive simplicity of Ashikaga ink drawings,
whose artists hinted where the Momoyama painters spoke em-
phatically aloud. The carvings, too, leave nothing unsaid. There
is a gate from Momoyama called *Higurashi*, "Livelong Day,"
because a whole day may be spent in studying its amazing detail.
As for the fittings and utensils in the castle of Ōsaka, we know
that they were all of the most costly materials, and lavish to the
point of absurdity. Hideyoshi liked to show them off to visitors,
one of whom records that all the ceilings and pillars were plas-
tered with pure gold, that kettles, bowls, tea-cups, medicine
chests, almost every kind of vessel in fact, were of pure gold, as
were the locks, bolts, hinges and ornaments of shelves and ward-
robes, doors and windows. Another writer (in 1589) describing
Hideyoshi's land survey, and his new assessment of land tax,

---

* Thus some of the apartments of the present Western Hongwanji Temple in
Kyōto appear to have been transferred from the destroyed Jūrakudai.

points out that this is the source of his wealth, and concludes, "As for its use, the very privies are decorated with gold and silver, and paintings in fine colours. All these precious things are used as if they were dirt. Ah! Ah!"

Hideyoshi well understood the uses of hospitality. He made it a practice to give immense entertainments, which served to display his wealth and power; and there is good reason to suppose that, quite apart from mere ostentation, which was his weakness, he purposely encouraged his barons to compete among themselves in luxury, hoping by this means to weaken them financially and so to render them less dangerous to himself. His celebrated Kitano Tea Party aptly illustrates his own megalomania and the contemporary lapse from the high æsthetic standards of Muromachi. In October, 1587, he announced publicly in Kyōto, Ōsaka and other cities that he would hold a great tea ceremony in the next month. Everybody was invited to attend, from his richest vassals down to the humblest peasants, who were told that they need bring only a kettle and a cup and a mat to sit upon. The fête lasted ten days, there were plays and music and dancing. Hideyoshi exhibited his art treasures, as did other great collectors of the day. He had evidently a taste for monster gatherings, for we hear also of flower-viewing parties and similar feasts on a prodigious scale. One of these, indeed, was conceived so lavishly that an ancient temple (the Sambō-in) was restored and enlarged to accommodate his numerous guests, with the happy result that there now remains in the outskirts of Kyōto a group of fine buildings in gardens of great charm. On another occasion he gave a party at which trays piled with gold and silver were handed to the guests, some of whom received thousands of large gold pieces. Doubtless this unheard of extravagance was largely the fruit of Hideyoshi's megalomania, but it seems to have accorded with the spirit of his times. Those were the spacious days of Japan, and they show few signs of that littleness, that lack of copious plan and bold execution which is sometimes said to be the weakness of the national character. It is instructive to follow the growth of the tea ceremonial from the time of the first Ashikaga Shōguns. Under them it was an aristocratic cult, expensive no doubt, but essentially belonging to a restrained æstheticism. Under Nobunaga and Hideyoshi it be-

comes a means of ostentation, almost a parody. The rich daimyō
compete madly for bowls and tea-jars and such-like adjuncts of the
ritual of tea-drinking. Prices soar, and fantastic sums are paid for
things that may be beautiful but must be rare. Matsunaga Danjō,
one of Nobunaga's constables, before committing suicide, smashes
to atoms a precious tea-kettle rather than let it fall into the hands
of a rival collector. Takigawa Kadzumasa, one of Nobunaga's
boldest captains, appointed to an important but remote province,
writes to a friend in the capital: "I have fallen unawares into
hell," and explains that he is in a desperate state because he is far
away from cultured society and has no crony versed in tea ceremonial to whom he can talk æsthetics. The successful men in these
energetic days were immoderate even in their polite accomplishments. Yet this lapse from the fastidious standards of the Muromachi æsthetics was only temporary, and while the feudal mag-
nificos were indulging in proud display severer canons were
being formed. To these, it is interesting to observe, they in time
submitted. Among the most important figures of the Momoyama
period was Sen Rikyū, an expert in the arrangement of flowers,
a tea-master, and an arbiter of taste. He stood in the same relation to Hideyoshi and his court as had done Seami to the Shōgun
Yoshimitsu. Under his influence styles of severe beauty were encouraged in the arts, notably in ceramics, for tea-bowls and jars
and other utensils of special quality were needed to suit the
exacting taste of the tea cult. These were the days of famous
potters, such as Shonzui, Chōyu and Rokubei, artists who displayed a great virtuosity in devising shapes and controlling the
colours of their glaze.* Their work had to please fastidious
patrons, who shuddered at the least hint of floridity, so that the
beauty of their wares is often sombre if it is not even factitious. But
there were other potters, whose work had a more popular appeal.
On the expedition to Korea the Japanese were struck by the excellence of Korean porcelain and faience, and a number of Hideyoshi's commanders took back to Japan with them Korean arti-

---

* Shonzui brought back fine specimens from China in 1513; Chōyu (Chōjirō)
made the celebrated Rakuyaki, a ware (*yaki*) named after Hideyoshi's mansion, Jūrakudai; and Rokubei *circa* 1580 developed the hitherto rustic pottery
of Bizen.

sans and set up kilns in their domains. It is to these beginnings that we owe such celebrated wares as Satsuma, Nabeshima, Yatsu-shiro, Imari and so forth, which unlike the strict "tea" utensils display a marvellous range of shape and colour and pictorial design. Though it is generally admitted that they rarely attain the sublimity of Chinese masterpieces, it has to be remembered that most Japanese potters had to contend against technical difficulties, chiefly in the supply of materials, by which the Chinese were not hampered. Yet this deficiency alone is not enough to explain the curious fact that the Japanese, always so eager to emulate the arts of China, should in the progress of ceramics have lagged centuries behind her, at least until Hideyoshi's day. Before then, vessels of lacquer or plain earthenware had usually sufficed for domestic and religious uses; but after his time, with settled conditions, safer transport and above all the growth of prosperous urban communities, there was an increasing demand for fine porcelains. Perhaps this tardy advance in the potter's craft is to be looked upon as a herald of years of peace in which fragile and beautiful things might escape destruction.

TABLE OF MAIN POLITICAL EVENTS IN "SENGOKU" PERIOD

A.D. 1534 Oda Nobunaga born (d. 1582).
1542 Portuguese discover Japan. Firearms introduced.
1549 St. Francis Xavier reaches Japan.
1568 Nobunaga is *de facto* Shōgun.
1571 Nobunaga destroys Hieizan monasteries and in general wages war on the Buddhist Church.
1576 The new castle at Adzuchi.
1577 Campaign against feudatories of western Japan (Mōri and Shimadzu), by Hideyoshi on behalf of Nobunaga.
1582 Hideyoshi succeeds to Nobunaga's power.
1587 First Christian Persecution.
1590 Hideyoshi subdues remaining adversaries by successful siege of Odawara. Yedo founded.
1592 Hideyoshi sends an army against Korea, which is unsuccessful and withdraws.
1597 Second Korean expedition, broken off in 1598.
1598 Hideyoshi dies. Succeeded by Ieyasu.
1600 Battle of Sekigahara won by Ieyasu.
1603 Ieyasu appointed Shōgun.
1615 Siege of Ōsaka. Ieyasu victorious, and now supreme ruler in Japan.

NOTE TO CHAPTER XX

[1] Page 437. There is evidence of printing from metal types in the Nara period.

PART SEVEN—YEDO

Chapter XXI—THE TOKUGAWA RÉGIME

1. THE NATIONAL POLICY OF EXCLUSION[1]

WE have seen how throughout her history the feudal rulers of Japan attempted to arrest the processes of change by legislating in perpetuity and by fostering a morality that seemed to them to fix an order in which they were supreme. Ieyasu and his immediate successors pursued this foredoomed policy in a most thorough-going manner; but signs of failure are visible from the very outset and the history of the Tokugawa may be read as a lesson in the futility of all such attempts to resist powerful and uncomprehended forces.

Ieyasu had at Hideyoshi's advice settled upon Yedo as his military headquarters, and here in course of time there grew up the greatest stronghold and the greatest city in Japan.* Ieyasu took up residence at Yedo in 1590, but it was not until after the battle of Sekigahara that he finally selected this place as his capital. His decision was an important one. It meant that he was thenceforth to cut loose from Kyōto and to rule Japan from the centre of his military power. Long before, Yoritomo had deliberately established himself at a distance from Kyōto, and the decay of Shōgunates in succeeding centuries could be explained in part by the failure of his descendants to keep clear of the seductions of Court life and the dangers of Court intrigue. Ieyasu was determined to avoid their mistakes. Kamakura had been the headquarters of feudal power when feudalism was immature and a civilian government in Kyōto still exercised, however feebly, its authority. But Ieyasu's policy was such as to make of Yedo not only a military and administrative capital, but also the economic and indeed the cultural centre of Japan. Large tracts of land were reclaimed, and sites were allotted for the mansions of the feud-

---

* Yedo, though at that date merely a village in a swamp, had a respectable record. In its vicinity neolithic sites are scattered more thickly than in any other part of Japan. Its position at the head of a bay, with terrain difficult of passage in its rear, gave it strategical value for a soldier who wished to dominate the eastern provinces; and this was early perceived by a warrior of Ashikaga times, one Ōta Dokwan, who built there a castle in 1456.

atories, while provision was made for merchants and shopkeepers, who were naturally attracted from Kyōto and Ōsaka by the creation of this new metropolis. An immense castle was built, more imposing even than the great fortress of Ōsaka, and for assistance in such undertakings Ieyasu called upon his barons, whose resources he strained by this and similar levies, which they dared not resist. It was his chief preoccupation to ensure that no single feudatory should remain rich or strong enough to challenge him, and to guard against combinations which might endanger his position. To these ends he took very decided steps, which are worth describing, because they are at the very foundation not only of the feudal policy of the Tokugawa, but of many of the most characteristic institutions of the Yedo period.

Shortly after the battle of Sekigahara (in 1601) he obliged the feudatories to sign a written oath of loyalty, by which they swore to obey all orders from Yedo, and not to give protection or shelter to the enemies of the Shōgunate. This was a most important document, and the fact that it was signed shows how complete was Ieyasu's mastery over his vassals, for despite many sad lapses from earlier feudal standards of integrity the Japanese warrior did still as a rule observe the letter of his bond. Consequently, when Ieyasu had by the siege of Ōsaka (1615) subdued his remaining enemies, he was in a stronger position than any previous Shōgun, and he proceeded to consolidate it by all the means in his power. He himself died in 1616, but his policy was continued by his successors, the second Tokugawa Shōgun, Hidetada (1616-1622), and the third, Iemitsu (1622-1651). Their enactments we may describe without special reference to persons, for they were the work of the Bakufu machine, expressing not merely the sentiment of individual rulers but the prevailing feudal conception of society. It is convenient to point out here that, whereas by this date feudal institutions in Europe had collapsed and been replaced by centralised monarchical government, in Japan feudalism had only just reached maturity, and though government was more centralised and more autocratic than ever before it was exercised by a paramount feudal chieftain and the monarchy was in abeyance.

One of the first steps taken by the Shōgunate was to draw up

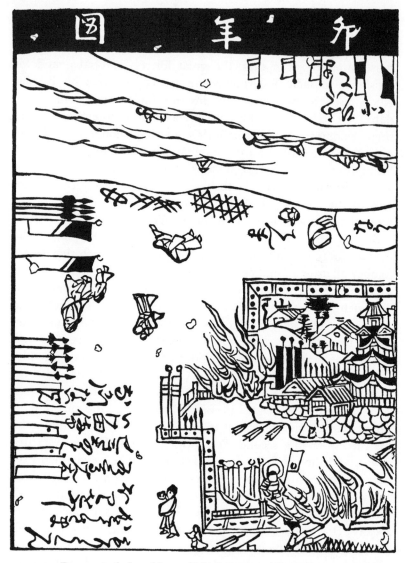

FIG. 49. *Fragment of a broadsheet sold in the streets of Yedo in 1615, announcing the fall of Ōsaka Castle.*

regulations governing the functions and behaviour of the Emperor and the Court. Ieyasu was fairly generous to the imperial family, and assigned them adequate revenues, yet all but the pettiest daimyō were richer than the sovereign and his nobles, who, moreover, received their incomes in kind, and were not permitted to own land. No administrative function whatever was left to the Throne. Powerful Bakufu officials resided at the Court to supervise and indeed to command the emperor, whose sole remaining prerogatives were the appointment of the Shōgun and certain other officers of state. These were purely formal, and the Imperial office, though still invested with its ancient dignity, was entirely ceremonial.

To guard against insubordination on the part of their vassals, the Tokugawa Shōguns took very careful measures. In their treatment of the barons they made a distinction between those who had from the days when the Tokugawa were merely local lordlings fought on their side, and those who had submitted to them only after the battle of Sekigahara. The former were known as the *fudai* or hereditary vassals, the latter as the *tozama* or Outside Lords. The Outside Lords were individually the richest and ostensibly the most elevated of the vassals. They were, until the Shōgunate felt firmly seated, ceremonially treated by the Shōgun almost as equals, which indeed they were, for he himself was by origin insignificant in comparison with the heads of such lordly houses as Maeda, Shimadzu and Date. But, at the same time, everything possible was done to reduce their offensive power. They were obliged, as we have seen, to contribute heavily to great public undertakings; and so that they should not hatch mischief in their domains there was evolved a system of hostages, ultimately taking the form known as *sankin kōtai*, or "alternate attendance" at the Shōgun's Court, under which each important daimyō was compelled to spend several months every year at Yedo, and to leave his wife and family behind when he returned to his fief. The hereditary vassals, though not so rich in estates as the great *tozama*, were assigned lands at points of strategical importance, commanding the main highways and towns, or so situated with relation to the domains of possible enemies of the Shōgun as to threaten their flank or their rear should they ever venture to march upon Yedo.

The Bakufu strictly limited the building and even the minor repairs of feudal castles. Whereas in Europe great cities like Venice
or the Hansa towns tended to maintain or increase their special
privileges, in Japan the process was now reversed and trade centres like Ōsaka, Sakai and Nagasaki, together with places of
special importance from a political point of view, such as Yamada
in Ise, the home of the worship of the imperial ancestors, were
placed under the direct control of Bakufu officials. Barriers were
maintained on the principal traffic routes so as to keep a check on
the goings and comings of travellers,* and the Government
deliberately refrained from building bridges and otherwise
facilitating communications on the main lines of approach to
Yedo. They even so far extended their policy of weakening their
potential enemies as to interfere in religion, by obliging the Hongwanji sect of Buddhism to split up into two branches, thus halving
the danger which, judging from its previous record, they might
not unreasonably fear from that powerful descendant of Shinran's
congregation of mild believers in the compassion of Amida.

By these and similar devices the Tokugawa Shōguns planned to
secure the continuance of their rule; but they were careful to
reinforce what we may call the physical features of their supremacy by what in modern terminology would be described as
cultural propaganda, both widespread and intensive. Though
there was almost unbroken peace after the fall of Ōsaka in 1615,
for some generations the temper of the rulers of Japan was warlike, they conducted their administration practically upon a war
footing, and the law that prevailed was in essence martial law.
The Bakufu, true to its name, was essentially a military dictatorship under which the military class was supreme and all other
classes, whether farmer or artisan or merchant or labourer, were
held to subserve its interests. This was their duty and their discipline. All that was exacted of them was obedience, but for the
dominant samurai class a special law and a special morality were

---

* Passports were closely scrutinised. The examining officers had to guard in
particular against "outward women and inward guns" (de-onna iri-deppō), because any vassal planning mischief was likely first to get his hostages out of the
Tokugawa domains and firearms into them. But in general traffic between fiefs
was discouraged, because each wished to remain a self-contained unit, to lose
none of its produce and to admit no possible spies.

thought desirable. These existed already, of course, in the tradition which we have seen slowly forming during the strife of the
clans in the eleventh century, suffering degradation under the
strain of anarchy during the long civil wars, but always persisting
in some degree and gradually regaining strength as order was restored to society. It was the business of the Shōgunate to give definite shape and authority to this tradition; and they soon began
to legislate with great thoroughness on points affecting the duties
and conduct of samurai. We shall examine some details of their
lawgiving presently, but here it is sufficient to say that the Bakufu
enacted on various occasions rules for the behaviour of members
of the military class, from the daimyō down to the *ashigaru*. They
were in essence an extension of the house-law of the Tokugawa
lords of Mikawa, and therefore similar in kind to those which we
have already described when dealing with feudal legislation under
Nobunaga and Hideyoshi. But under the Tokugawa not only
were they more detailed and explicit, but they were effective
throughout Japan, and they have been aptly described as the
Constitution of Japan under the Tokugawa. This Constitution,
it is worth repeating once more, was regarded by the Shōgunate as
fundamentally unchangeable. It was reaffirmed by each Shōgun
on his succession, in a solemn ceremony attended by all his vassals,
and though circumstances sometimes forced them to alter it in
detail, they never admitted or even contemplated any deviation
from its essential principles, and they punished without mercy
any breach of its commands.

It is only in the light of this determination to preserve unchanged the feudal régime over which they presided that we can
understand many seemingly irrational acts of Ieyasu's successors.
The first of these to attract a student's attention, and one which
was fraught with tremendous consequences in the later development of Japan, was the final enforcement of the edicts against
Christianity and the thorough-going exclusionist policy by which
it was crowned.

At the time of Ieyasu's death (1616) the persecution had been
suspended at a point where, though converts in certain localities had
suffered cruel martyrdom, there was no popular animus against
Christianity and in some high quarters even an active sympathy

with it. The law might easily have become a dead letter and Christians been allowed that liberty of faith which other sects had usually enjoyed. The Bakufu was now firmly enough entrenched to cope with subversive political movements and cared little what religion the people held so long as they were tractable. Moreover, once the supremacy of the Tokugawa was established, they made it their policy not to interfere in the internal administration of any fief outside their direct domains. A daimyō had the fullest jurisdiction over his people, he could oppress them or cherish them as he liked, provided that his conduct did not seem to imperil the major policy of the Shōgunate, which was the maintenance of stability and order. But it was precisely such a danger which the second Shōgun, Hidetada, thought he discerned in the presence, if not of Christians, then of Europeans, in his realm. At this time the Portuguese, the Spaniards, the Dutch and the English were all competing for trade privileges, each group only too ready to slander the countrymen of others and to hint to the Shōgun's officers, what was true enough, that European nations harboured aggressive designs on Eastern lands. The Spaniards had the Philippines, the Portuguese had Macao, the Dutch had Formosa, the English had a footing in Malaysia, and not all their navigators held very strict views about the rights of property on land or at sea. The English merchant Cocks describes in one of his letters how he in 1616 at Yedo "cried quittance with the Spaniards" by suggesting that they were counting on the insurrection of some Christian daimyō, to whose standard all the "papisticall" Japanese would flock, and seize some stronghold which they could keep until reinforcements came from overseas. The Spaniards, he pointed out, had ships available for this purpose, laden with soldiers and treasure, so that they wanted neither "money nor men for thackomplishing such a strattgim."

Doubtless this statement strengthened misgivings that were already in Hidetada's mind, for no sooner was it made than a new anti-Christian edict was issued. It exiled all priests without exception, and it forbade the Japanese under pain of death to connect themselves with Christianity in any way whatever. There was a brief delay pending the funeral of Ieyasu, and then in 1617 the persecution recommenced, to be continued with increasing severity as the officers charged with enforcement of the edict found that ordinary penal measures utterly failed to deter the priests from preaching or their converts from clinging to the faith. The ensuing record of sickening tortures and cruel martyrdoms is too gruesome to be repeated here. It is sufficient to say that, if it bears witness to the foul depths to which humanity can sink in the name of law and order, it is a sad yet stirring testimony to the heroism to which men will rise in defence of an ideal. There could be no finer tribute to the bravery of the Augustins, the Dominicans, the Franciscans and the Jesuits than the touching steadfastness of their converts, mostly untutored peasants, who faced diabolical cruelties and death with as great and calm a courage as any samurai schooled in fortitude from infancy. Women and men, they went to the rack, the stake, the cross and the pit in their thousands, often singing hymns of praise and exhorting their comrades never to recant. For years the persecution went on with unabated cruelty, until at last it began to tell upon the numbers of the Christians. It is significant that even during this terrible phase the authorities were reluctant to inflict the death penalty on foreign missionaries. They were deported wherever possible, or thrown into prison, and it was only when they proved utterly recalcitrant that the extremest measures were taken. Towards 1622, however, the Shōgun had some reason to suspect the complicity of the Roman Catholic Church in Spanish plots to invade Japan, and from about that time he treated the priests more harshly and re-enacted the anti-Christian edicts; so that the persecution, which had slackened somewhat, was now revived and from western Japan extended to the direct Tokugawa domains. In 1624 he ordered the deportation of all Spaniards in the realm, both priests and laymen, and decreed that no Japanese Christian should travel overseas. Yet missionaries continued to arrive and seek martyrdom, making converts in the brief space between their landing and their execution. There is disagreement as to the number of Christians in Japan at this time, and the Church historians are not entirely reliable, but it seems probable that at their most numerous they reached about 300,000. How many of these were martyred it is hard to say; for a large proportion must have embraced Christianity without deep conviction, if not merely at the command of their overlords, and it is likely that such easy converts soon earned their pardon by apostasy. Yet there can be no doubt that an imposing number of Japanese clung to their faith with a stubbornness which has puzzled later observers, who were misled perhaps by the light-hearted devotions of crowds upon a holiday into supposing that here was no deep-seated religious fervour but only a pagan frivolity. Yet gloom is not a necessary ingredient of faith; and we have already seen in the record of Buddhism in Japan many occasions when, for instance, both soldiers and peasants happily met a violent end in the belief that they would enter Amida's paradise, or fought valiantly in defence of the scripture of the Lotus. These people did not fear death. It may be that life was not sweet to them, because of some underlying pessimism in their temperament, or even because of poverty and despair; but the fact remains that they suffered and perished for their creeds.

It is sometimes difficult to disentangle the spiritual from the economic factor in certain religious movements in Japan. Thus it is hard to say to what extent the Fanatic (Ikkō) risings of the fifteenth century can be accounted for by agrarian unrest, and this is true also of the so-called Christian Rebellion of Shimabara, which broke out in 1637 and was among the immediate causes of Japan's cessation of intercourse with the outside world. From about the year 1626 the vigour of the persecution was on the wane. Christianity seems to have been either eradicated or driven underground.* But in some districts which were remote enough from close official scrutiny it was still practised stealthily by converts who resorted to pathetic frauds in order to escape detection. They would worship small statuettes of the Virgin made to resemble, say, a Kwannon and secreted in their household Buddhist shrine or Shintō "god-shelf" (kamidana); or again they would keep in the dark recesses of their farmhouse kitchens some utensil bearing an incised sacred emblem. The places where the Christian faith lingered longest were usually those where it had first been

---

* One authority states that down to 1635 as many as 280,000 Japanese had been "punished for accepting Christianity." But the official martyrologies record only a few thousand deaths, exclusive of those who perished at Shimabara (37,000).

introduced, and chief among these were the regions adjacent to Nagasaki. It was hereabouts that persecutions became most intense. Towards the end of the year 1637 there was an uprising among the people inhabiting the island of Amakusa and the Shimabara peninsula, which attracted Christians from neighbouring districts. It is very likely, as some chroniclers allege, that they were rendered desperate by the oppression of their feudal lord, for in common with peasants in many parts of Japan they were taxed to the very limit of endurance; but it seems that what gave them courage to revolt was their Christian faith, for they knew that in any event death or misery was their portion, and they believed in future happiness. Early in 1638 several thousands of them, men, women and children, joined forces and took possession of a dilapidated feudal castle on a steep headland in Shimabara. They were led by five samurai, disaffected men who had fought under Christian generals in the feudal campaigns but were now without a master; and many of the insurgents likewise were not simple peasants but veterans whom the fortunes of the civil war had left stranded and without prospects. They held out for more than two months against the considerable forces despatched to quell them, and their banners, inscribed with such legends as *JESUS, MARIA, ST. IAGO* and *LOUVADO SEIA O SÁCTISSIMO SACRAMENTO*, fell only when their food and munitions were exhausted. Nearly all were put to the sword,* and by this massacre Christianity was virtually exterminated in Japan, though it survived secretly in a few rustic communities, to come to light in the middle of the 19th century.

There can be little doubt that it was dread of such uprisings as these that gave the last impetus to the exclusionist movement which had been gradually gaining strength among the rulers of Japan. In their minds the Christian faith was now linked with foreign aggression, and they determined to avoid the dangers of both by cutting themselves off from all contact with the West. It is to be noted that they came very slowly to this conclusion. In their treatment of foreigners, both priests and merchants, they had shown from the beginning a most creditable liberality. This absence of

---

* According to one credible account, the investing forces numbered as many as 125,000 men, and the besieged Christians about 37,000. Of these only 105 are said to have been spared.

racial and national animus can be explained in part by their anxiety to obtain material benefits; but it certainly arose also from an ingrained habit of friendliness towards strangers, and a strong sense of hospitable duty. What in the end led them to lapses from their high standards was that baleful source of evils, fear. They had expelled the Spaniards in 1624, and now in 1638 the Portuguese (largely, it appears, because they were suspected of complicity in the Shimabara rising) were also driven out. Once the exclusionist movement began in earnest, once it was supposed that the safety of the realm was at stake, the treatment of foreigners became harsh. Certain Portuguese envoys who came in 1640 to press for the reopening of trade relations were summarily beheaded, thus meeting the same fate as befell the luckless Mongol ambassadors in 1280 and for a similar reason, namely to make it clear that the determination of the Japanese was not to be shaken. It must be added that, even when applying their harshest measures against the foreigners, the Japanese officials displayed a strong feeling for the correct and seemly. Thus condemned priests, until their stubborn flouting of the law drove the administration to extremes, were executed, one might almost say respectfully, in the ceremonial manner reserved for Japanese of high rank; ample notice of the expulsion edicts was given; and both the persons and the property of those who obeyed were treated with meticulous care. The English and the Dutch did not come within the scope of these edicts, but the English trading station had, through bad management, been closed in 1623, so that by 1640 there were no foreigners in Japan except certain authorised Chinese and a handful of Dutchmen, who were confined, almost imprisoned, in a small settlement at Nagasaki. Hither came annually a few trading ships, strictly limited and closely watched. This trickle of foreign goods and foreign ideas was for over two hundred years Japan's only* communication with the world at large, for in 1637 the Bakufu had decreed that no Japanese subject should leave the country or, having left it, should return. In each case death was the penalty for an attempt, and to

---

* Except for an abortive Portuguese mission in 1647, one English ship in 1673, and a few Russian and American vessels at intervals afterwards. All these were sent away after a brief parley. The English ship was refused entry on the ground that the King of England was married to a Roman Catholic Portuguese princess.

ensure the full enforcement of this law the building of any ship of more than 500 *koku* capacity, that is any ship of a size sufficient to make a voyage overseas, was forbidden.

By these enactments the Japanese chose to deny themselves all the gifts which the West then had to offer. It is not unprofitable to speculate as to what they lost by this decision, since their culture becomes easier to understand if we remember what elements it lacked. Looking at the condition of Europe in the sixteenth century, when the Portuguese first arrived, a dispassionate critic can scarcely pretend that the Japanese had at that time anything to learn from the West in practical morality, private or public. Their ethical code and their theories of government had the sanction of immense antiquity and had stood tolerably well the test of time. Their religion, they might not unreasonably argue, was surpassed by Christianity neither in the sublimity of its conceptions nor in the comfort of its dogma; and had they been able to peruse the writings of some Christian Fathers they, an ancestor-worshipping people, would have shuddered with horror at pictures of a paradise in which one of the chief pleasures of the elect was to gloat over the agonies of the damned. In the arts they were heirs to a superb tradition, and in æsthetic cultivation they had reached refinements hardly dreamed of by their European contemporaries. Even in the science of slaughter, which might well have been Europe's proud boast at that day, they needed little teaching, as may be judged from Michelborne's report of 1605 which said: "The Japanese are not allowed to land in any part of India with weapons, being a people so desperate and daring that they are feared in all places where they come." At this rate, it might be supposed, Europe had nothing to teach Japan but variations on the theme of iniquity. Yet this would be a very false and partial view, neglecting all the great victories of heart and brain that culminated in the splendours of the Renaissance. We may leave out the vexed question of religion, observing merely that the essence of Christian teaching, the doctrine of love and humility, does not seem to have struck a responsive chord in the minds of the Japanese, or perhaps it was imperfectly presented to them. Eager as were their minds, in general they were unwilling or unready to receive the intellectual treasures of Europe. By 1600, when many missionaries to Japan had come and gone, the Renaissance was in full swing all over Europe, stimulated largely by the knowledge and the gold gained on just such voyages as took the Portuguese to the East. Such wide horizons were opening out to Japan, and she was on the verge of acquiring wealth that would have radically altered her own economy, when of her own will she shut herself off from all these prospects. Those were the days when Leonardo da Vinci had laid the foundations of the experimental method and therefore of modern scientific inquiry; Copernicus had taught a new theory of the Universe; Harvey had lighted on the circulation of the blood; and Gilbert had commenced the study of electricity. But since these discoveries were unpalatable to the Inquisition, which burned Bruno at the stake and imprisoned Galileo, it is unlikely that the Japanese gained any inkling of them from the missionaries.[2] It is true that a cosmology which displaced man from the centre of the universe would have made little stir among priests and scholars familiar with Buddhist thought; but certainly there seems to be no trace in Japan up to the time of the exclusion edicts of any knowledge of the movements that were then changing the intellectual life of Europe. The Japanese welcomed, as we have remarked, certain inventions in applied science, in particular those which bore upon war, shipbuilding and navigation, but of the spirit and the method of scientific inquiry which produced them they can have had only the haziest notion. Therefore when after 1640 they were cut off from the source of new learning, it is not surprising that their minds turned in upon themselves and evolved nothing but elaborations and refinements of their own culture, a culture withal so remarkable and unique that in itself it almost provides an answer to the common allegation that the Japanese as a people are wanting in inventive genius. For what could be a better testimony to originality than to have created a civilisation unlike any other? There is no need, however, to resort to such dubious entities as racial character for an explanation of the course taken by Japanese civilisation after the sixteenth century, its failure to expand and flower. It can be accounted for quite simply on other grounds. There came into operation in Japan few of the remote and hardly any of the proximate causes which in Europe brought about the Renaissance. The culture of mediæval European countries was not borrowed, as Japanese culture had been borrowed from China, but was inherited in direct succession from the ancient world: and allowing for pauses due to war and pestilence the intellectual development of western Europe was continuous. The passage from Scholasticism to Humanism was made easy in the first place by the diffusion over a wide area of one common medium of speech and writing, the Latin tongue. It is hard to overestimate the importance of this factor in making available to the whole of western Europe the wisdom of men who might otherwise have remained silent in its remotest corners. As a matter of sheer arithmetic the chances of progress were improved as more minds were brought to bear on the same problems, and this advantage was increased by the interplay and the competition of nationalities. An astonishing variety of ingredients went to the formation of Western learning, from Greek, Roman, Byzantine, Hebrew and Arabian to elements out of all the national categories of modern Europe; and in examining the great names in the intellectual history of Europe one is struck by the diversity of their origin. Avicenna was a native of Bokhara; Averroes, a Cordovan; Copernicus, a Pole; Tycho Brahe, a Dane; Galileo, an Italian; Newton, an Englishman; and Descartes, a Frenchman who worked in Holland and died in Sweden. In striking contrast was the position of the Japanese, so placed that they could draw direct inspiration only from the almost static and uniform culture of China. Even the religion and the art which they acquired from other parts of Asia were not handed on to them until they had received a Chinese imprint.

Nor were these the only causes that arrested the cultural development of Japan. Perhaps her most serious handicap was the check which she imposed upon her own economic expansion. One of the chief factors promoting the Renaissance was the wealth that poured into European countries as foreign trade developed: for invention in its widest sense is the child not of necessity but of leisure and riches. The Japanese were dimly conscious of this when from Ashikaga times they took eagerly to overseas adventure; and it is a striking fact that there then began, in spite of internal disorders, a period of great cultural activity. All this activity ceased, or was confined to well-worn channels, when Japan lapsed into isolation. Her problem now was not how to obtain and utilise wealth and wisdom from abroad, but how to conserve and increase her own resources. It is to this problem, complicated by the transfer from an agricultural to a mercantile economy, that we must look for a key to her history under the Tokugawa.

2. ADMINISTRATION AND LAW

BEFORE proceeding to a survey of economic changes in the Yedo period, and their effect upon social institutions, it will be convenient to complete the picture of those institutions as they existed in the seventeenth century. We have already seen what steps were taken in turn by Nobunaga, Hideyoshi and Ieyasu to establish firmly their administrative and social hierarchy. The efforts of their successors, say, to the middle of the seventeenth century, were devoted to perfecting its organisation. It was especially in the period of the third Shōgun, Iemitsu (1622-1651), that feudal institutions reached their zenith. We need not enter into the intricate detail of their machinery of government, but some knowledge of its general principles is necessary if we are to understand how it functioned and why it ultimately broke down.

The central government under the Tokugawa began, and for some decades continued, as an extension into times of peace of the supreme command in times of war. It was not based upon any theory of the State, as had been the system adopted in 645 from China. It made use of existing arrangements, and was in essence little more than the application to a whole country of the methods used by a feudal baron in a single fief for the control of his vassals and subjects, and the maintenance of his armed strength. This is clear even from the titles of the great officers of the Shōgun, which all have a homely flavour, as if the Tokugawa, to use the words of a writer of their day, managed their affairs "after the fashion of a village headman." There was a kind of Council of State composed of from four to five Elders (*toshiyori*) and presided over by one of their number, styled the Great Elder (*Ō-doshiyori*). They were concerned with matters of high policy, which included the relations of the Bakufu with the Imperial Court, and its control over the daimyō. Beneath them were from four to six Junior Elders (*Waka-doshiyori*), whose functions were miscellaneous but had to do principally with supervision of direct vassals of the Shōgun below the rank of daimyō, namely the *hatamoto* or banner knights and the *go-kenin*, or household retainers, who included the majority of the unfieffed samurai in the service of the Tokugawa, down to those of the lowest grade. Attached to the boards of elders were officials styled *metsuke*, whose functions have been frequently misunderstood. They have been described as "spies" but their title may be better rendered as "censor." Their functions were in origin military. In war-time the *toshiyori* formed a kind of General Staff, and the *metsuke* acted as their intelligence officers. Spying played a great part in feudal warfare, and the military classics, both Chinese and Japanese, which were widely studied by soldiers, paid much attention to this question and recommended most dubious methods of gaining an enemy's confidence or investigating his affairs. In peace-time the duties of the *metsuke* resolved themselves into surveillance of the conduct of the vassals, great and small. They had to keep the central government posted in the doings of the barons and the people, so that it should be prepared to deal with any subversive movement; and since that government was based upon repression and not upon consent, it was natural that this system should develop into a network of espionage, with all the apparatus of secret services, black cabinets, informers and *agents provocateurs* that characterise an uneasy autocracy.

Subordinate to the Council of Elders were numerous administrative, executive and judicial officers called *bugyō*, an elastic term which may be rendered as "commissioners," but was a general appellation for such diverse functionaries as ministers and secretaries of state and local and municipal administrators and judges. There were *kanjō-bugyō* who administered the finances of the Bakufu; *machi-bugyō* who were the chief city magistrates and police authorities; *jisha-bugyō* who controlled the affairs of shrines and temples and settled their disputes; and revenue and other officials of various grades, all bearing the title of *bugyō*. The Tokugawa administration, especially in its early stages, was by no means logical and systematic. It grew up in a somewhat haphazard fashion in response to practical requirements, and has been likened to the old city of Yedo, an irregular maze of streets, in contrast with the symmetrical plan of the ancient capital. The functions of its various officers were ill-defined. Moreover it had the serious defect of being so devised as to discourage initiative, for its high offices were duplicated or their functions were discharged not by individuals but by councils, because it was thought necessary to guard against the monopoly of power by one person. Further, its operations were hampered by a system of rotation, under which the elders and the highest commissioners took turns of duty for a month, and were therefore apt to muddle or procrastinate; and this fault tended to throw real power into the hands of persons behind the scenes, such as chamberlains, masters of ceremonies, or even officials in the women's apartments. Altogether, in studying the workings of the Tokugawa régime, one cannot help feeling that it was conducted in an atmosphere of suspicion and mistrust. It should be added that, since the cardinal principle of all Tokugawa administration was to conserve the power and the wealth of the Tokugawa and their associates, high offices were only by exception open to members of the families of Outside Lords (*Tozama*) but tended to become hereditary in the families of direct vassals, while rigid class distinctions sadly limited the talent available for all posts. Under these conditions government, however enlightened in theory, could not in practice fail to be partial and to neglect the interests of the nation at large.

Local government on the whole followed the pattern of central government. Within their own fiefs the barons enjoyed a very full measure of autonomy. Bakufu officials were stationed only in certain large cities or in the direct Tokugawa domains, which were situated mostly in eastern Japan and at points of strategical importance in other regions. But the Shōgunate, without interfering, used to keep a sharp watch on the conduct of the feudatories, and it was one of the chief duties of the censors (*metsuke*) and their travelling inspectors to report upon affairs in the fiefs. For this and similar reasons there was a general tendency among the daimyō to assimilate their administrative and judicial methods to those of the central authority, and the legislation in which the Shōguns freely indulged soon began to displace the house-laws of the fiefs where it did not clash with local sentiment and habit. Partly because the Shōgunate was only the replica on a grand scale of a feudatory's government, and partly because the smaller lords liked to ape the greater, even in petty fiefs the baron would be served by

his Council of Elders and other officers bearing grand titles. Therefore legislation gradually approximated to uniformity throughout
Japan, particularly as the Bakufu had early decreed that "laws
like those of Yedo" should be observed "in all matters and in all
provinces and places." Only such great houses as Shimadzu and
Maeda were strong enough to resist this tendency, and even they
as a rule used their autonomy with discretion, so as not flagrantly
to oppose the policies of the Bakufu. Similarly, though in the
beginning the Yedo authorities did not interfere with the internal
arrangements of such self-governing bodies as religious sects, trade-
guilds and even village communities, they were later inclined to
override all private jurisdiction or at least to confine it within
narrow limits. The following outline of the legislative and judicial
system of the Tokugawa may therefore be taken as applying in
general to the whole of Japan, and in increasing detail as the
seventeenth century progressed.

In its main feature the law was minatory and repressive, because
in origin and early growth it was nothing but the expression of the
will of a dominant chieftain in a state of war. Though, as order was
established and his supremacy was secured, it grew in many respects more lenient, it was in essence martial law continued into
times of peace. Its fundamental assumptions are to be found in
Hideyoshi's Sword Hunt, which fixed a rigid division of classes
headed by the soldier, and in the laws of the Military Houses
(*Buke-Hatto*) which Ieyasu promulgated in 1615, immediately
after the fall of Ōsaka. It is a document which, like the Formularies
and House-Laws of earlier times, is not so much a systematic
collection of specific injunctions and prohibitions as a group of
maxims, in somewhat vague language, supported by learned extracts from the Chinese and Japanese classics. The first two of its
thirteen articles lay down rules for the conduct of the military
class, who must devote themselves earnestly both to literature and
arms, and must abstain from debauchery. The next three articles
(3-5) deal with the maintenance of order in feudal domains and
the relations between one domain and another. The next three
(6-8) are directed against combinations between daimyō, or other
activities likely to endanger the Shōgunate. One form of combination much practised in Japan for political reasons was, of course,

marriage; and article 8 reads: "Marriages must not be contracted at private convenience." It is followed by the explanation, backed by citations from the Book of Changes and the Book of Odes, that marriage depends upon the harmonious blending of *yin* and *yang*, and must therefore not be lightly undertaken. The next three articles (9-11) prescribe the retinues, costumes, vehicles, and so forth, proper to each class. The last enjoin frugality upon the samurai and recommend the daimyō to eschew favouritism and to employ retainers according to merit. These two exhortations had been repeated by rulers from ancient times, and their echo can still be heard. It seems that those in authority were always a little anxious because they were aware that their people were given to liberal spending and loved to do kindness to relatives and friends.

It will be seen at once that these were not statutory enactments or codes, as we understand them. They were merely statements in writing of the principles underlying customary laws, which they did not replace but only supplemented. From the middle of the Tokugawa period there was an extremely prolific output of laws and regulations in writing, but it mostly took the form of commentaries or compilations of precedents, and though it gradually became systematised it was entirely different in character from modern laws. Perhaps it would be fair to say that, whereas an English judge may have to decide the intention of a law from its text, a Japanese judge was told only the intention of the law and then had to give it effect at his own discretion. This contrast, though no doubt exaggerated by being so expressed, is probably what accounts for one of those picturesque but inaccurate statements which are so frequently made about Japanese institutions. It has often been said that the Yedo Government was so obscurantist as even to conceal its laws from the public, who therefore never knew whether they were offending or not. There is a little but not much truth in this statement. It is good Confucian doctrine that the common people should do what they are told, without asking why; and certainly no Japanese ruler went out of his way to explain his commands to his humblest subjects. Thus the so-called Code of a Hundred Articles (*O-Sadame-gaki Hyakkajō*) bore the following endorsement: "These provisions have been submitted to the Shōgun and approved. They are not to be seen by others than magistrates (*bugyō*)." But this does not mean that the whole code was secret. Each article consisted of a prohibitive and a penal clause. The prohibitions were made public by oral proclamations and notice-boards. It was only clauses intended for the guidance of judges which were not disclosed, such as, for example, those stating the discretion which they were allowed in awarding punishments; and naturally the penalties, being customary, were matters of common knowledge. Obviously they must become increasingly familiar with the lapse of time, and by the close of the Tokugawa period editions of this code were on sale in bookshops, bound in yellow covers like the novels of the day.

In general the Tokugawa rulers did not regard it as part of their function to compile and enforce a coherent and specific body of laws, civil or criminal. They were even opposed in principle to detailed legislation based upon a theory of jurisprudence. They seem to have preferred to work upon empiric lines, promulgating laws to meet occasions as they arose but not anticipating them. The rationalising element in their legislation is rather to be found in certain ethical principles which they held or professed. Chief among these, as we have noticed in describing conditions throughout the feudal period, was the principle of loyalty, the bond of duty subsisting between master and man. In origin this kind of loyalty was a feudal virtue, an almost exclusively military relationship; but in the Yedo period, during the years of peace, it became the common ideal of all classes, and was regarded as the touchstone of conduct not only as between lord and vassal, but also as between farmer and labourer, merchant and clerk, artisan and apprentice, and even gambler and pupil. On one occasion, some peasants whom the Bakufu proposed to move from one fief to another made a demonstration with banners on which was inscribed "Even a farmer does not serve two lords," an ironical application of the boast that had once led the samurai to follow their master in death. But the relationship between master and man was now much closer, much more concrete and much less ideal than the bond that united the old-style feudal chieftain with his vassals or retainers. They, at the call to arms, would leave their rice-fields and hasten to the front with patched armour, a rusty halberd, and a bony horse. But the Tokugawa samurai, living in a

garrison town, was a professional soldier, well equipped and receiving regular pay or sustenance in return for which his life was
at the disposal of his lord. It was thought proper to invest this
contract with an ethical character, and the rulers of Japan, finding,
it must be admitted, ready pupils in a people always disposed to
view problems from an ethical standpoint, spared no pains to inculcate the doctrine of loyal service. They succeeded to such a
point that law and literature and art, to say nothing of social and
family relationships, were dominated by this feudal conception. It
might fairly be said that they elevated to the summit of the scale of
morality the obligation of service, so that the one time paramount
virtue of filial piety became only a single aspect of loyalty to a
master and benefactor.

Since the Tokugawa administrators took the view that the conduct of a citizen should be based not upon rules of law but upon
rules of ethics, such legislation as they made public very often
took the form of admonitory placards (*satsu* or *fuda*), attached to
high posts in conspicuous places throughout the towns and villages.*
One of the most celebrated of these is known as the Parents and
Children Placard (*Oyako-kyōdai-fuda*) because it recommended the
members of a family to preserve harmonious relations. It went on
to say that servants should be faithful, masters just; that everybody
should be frugal and industrious and should keep to his station in
life; and in general that conduct should be virtuous. Such placards
were very common, particularly about the year 1700, when the
earlier repressive, purely feudal government had begun to
transform itself into a somewhat more lenient bureaucracy. But
until that time the law as applied to specific offences remained
harsh in nature and entirely deterrent in intention. Both in popular
language and contemporary legal treatises this aspect was freely
recognised. The punishments for criminal offences were admittedly
devised so as to strike terror into the hearts of the citizens. There
was not only plain decapitation and exposure of the head and
trunk in public, but drawing and quartering, stabbing with spears,
and many other painful forms of death. Some criminals were
buried up to the waist, and any spectator allowed to carve them

* And hence called *kōsatsu*, high placards. The modern Tokyo street name
Fuda-no-tsuji means the "placard cross-roads."

PORTION OF A CELEBRATED LANDSCAPE SCROLL PAINTED BY SESSHŪ

ANOTHER PORTION OF A CELEBRATED LANDSCAPE SCROLL PAINTED BY SESSHŪ

with a bamboo saw before they were finally despatched. The corpses were often placed at the disposal of samurai, for testing their swords. Burning was reserved for those guilty of arson, a good example of punishment to fit the crime. Criminals under examination were regularly tortured, and the sufferings of prisoners were cruel. For further horrible particulars of this nature the reader may be referred to the late J. C. Hall's papers on feudal law in Japan, but he would do well at the same time to look up some account of penal methods in England in the seventeenth century, and even later.

It was characteristic of both civil and penal legislation of the Tokugawa that it followed the class distinctions of their régime. The samurai and the commoner were punished for different crimes and in a different manner. In the early Yedo period it is definitely understood that if "persons of low degree such as townsmen and farmers be guilty of insulting speech or rude behaviour they may, should it be unavoidable, be cut down." This rule, popularly known as *kirisute gomen*, or "permission to cut down and leave" (without further to-do), was interpreted more strictly as time progressed, but it shows clearly how the feudal governors viewed the position of the soldier in the state. In matters of marriage and succession there were two laws, one for the samurai and one for the commoner. The same offence was described as an "excess" when committed by a samurai, as a "crime" when committed by a commoner. An official collection of Tokugawa laws says: "All offences are to be punished in accordance with social status," and an examination of the penalties enforced under the Tokugawa shows that this principle was observed. A samurai was often let off lightly for an offence which in a peasant was punished even with death, while on the other hand he might be condemned to suicide or banishment for an act which would be venial in a commoner. The law applied the social theory that farmers and townsmen existed for the benefit of the military class.

3. ECONOMIC CONDITIONS

It will be clear from the foregoing outline that when the Tokugawa Shōguns decided to perpetuate the military organisation of the country in times of peace, they were setting themselves an economic problem of considerable magnitude. They had to

ensure the maintenance of a very numerous privileged class, which
was not only unproductive, but in addition must be furnished with
arms as well as dwellings, food and clothing on a scale suitable to
its dignity. As they had chosen by the exclusion edicts to cut
themselves off from outside sources of supply, they were dependent
upon the produce of their own territory, and with this they had
to meet a growing demand, since the restoration of peace brought
not only an increase of population but also a rise in the standard
of living. They were therefore confronted with two difficulties, that
of supply and that of distribution. These were primarily different
aspects of one problem, and it will be sufficient for our purpose
to consider them together.

The dangers of the situation did not become threatening until
the eighteenth century was well on its way. The successful barons
and their retainers settled down after the wars to enjoy their lands
and their privileges, and there seemed to be no reason why the
farmers should not continue humbly to grow crops for their
betters to consume, and the tradesmen respectfully to furnish other
commodities. For a time, even, there was considerable prosperity
at first real and later only apparent. At the opening of the century
the revenue of Japan was estimated at 28 million *koku* (say 140
million bushels) of rice. Wealth was measured in terms of rice,
because it was the most important medium of exchange as well as
the staple foodstuff. For this reason, and because the sense of
ownership of land has always been feeble in Japan, the revenues
not only of landowners but of all classes were assessed in measures
of the standard crop. Of the above 28 million *koku* some 8 million
belonged to the Shōgun, and the remainder (except for some
40,000 *koku* allotted to the imperial court) belonged to the 270
daimyō among whom the country was divided.* A daimyō was in
fact a vassal who had been granted or confirmed in a holding of
land assessed at over 10,000 koku. Among them were such powerful
Outside Lords (*tozama*) as Maeda, with an annual income of over
one million koku, followed closely by Shimadzu, Date, and several
others, while the average revenue of the hereditary vassals (*fudai*),
who numbered some 150, was about 100,000 *koku* each. All these

* The number varied as families became extinct or fiefs were amalgamated or
divided by the Shōgun.

barons, from the Shōgun downwards, kept a considerable state, and had to support a large number of retainers of every grade, from the Elders on their Council to the lowest foot-soldier. Thus the leading samurai in an important barony would often receive as much as 10,000 *koku*, while even the *ashigaru* was usually allotted rations which permitted him to live on the same scale as a well-to-do peasant. Below the daimyō came other vassals of the Shōgun. There were some 5,000 *hatamoto*, or Banner Knights, who received less than 10,000 *koku*, and some 15,000 *go-kenin*, or House-Men, who received only a hundred *koku* or so. It will be seen that what may be politely called the leisured or rentier class was extremely numerous, and caused a great drain upon the country's resources. Their sustenance was derived almost exclusively from the labours of the peasants. All the land in a domain was carefully surveyed by officials of the overlord, and its yield was estimated in accordance with its position, the nature of its soil, the number to its cultivators, and in certain cases the harvest obtained from a test area. The overlord then took his share of the crop, which was divided in a customary ratio, generally "*shi-kō roku-min*" or "four to the prince and six to the people," but sometimes even two to the prince and one to the people. In the surveying, the assessment and the sharing there was ample room for abuses, and in many fiefs the oppression of corrupt or over-zealous officials goaded the farmers into revolt. Their lot was wretched enough at the best of times. By the novels, plays and prints of the Yedo period one is led to fancy that country life in Japan in those days had a simple idyllic charm. One sees a picture of rustic communities, where happy peasants in rude health sing their folk-songs as they plant out the young rice, throng in their best clothes to their temples on feast days, or between seedtime and harvest trudge sturdily on pilgrimages to distant shrines. Doubtless they had their simple pleasures, and one should not accept without reserve the statements to be found in economic treatises which had a case to prove. Yet altogether the evidence is too strong to be denied. In the first place the attitude of the ruling classes towards the producers was unmistakable. They paid lip service to the theory that agriculture was the foundation of the state. The farmer ranked next below the samurai and above the artisan and the merchant. In Tokugawa literature one often comes across such sayings as "A farmer is worth two samurai and three beggars are worth four townsmen." But these were mere vestiges of ancient theory, and in reality the peasant was regarded, and was treated, as a machine to produce rice for the samurai to swallow. Statesmen thought highly of agriculture, but not of agriculturalists. Early Tokugawa edicts relating to agriculture usually open with the preamble, "Since peasants are stupid people" or "Since peasants are people without sense or forethought." It was held that the proper way to govern was to see that the farmers "had just enough to keep alive on and no more"—to cite a dictum ascribed to Ieyasu by a political writer of his day. The rulers, moreover, constantly interfered in the private life of the peasants. A notorious proclamation of 1649 orders them to rise early, to work at night, not to eat rice, but to be content with coarser fare, to abstain from tea and tobacco, and if their wives are flighty and like visiting temples or rambling in the hills to divorce them at once. If this was the situation of a great mass of the population in normal times, it is easy to imagine their misery in seasons of storm, drought and pestilence; and it speaks nobly for their character as a class that they came through centuries of such trial gentle, kindly, courteous and no more parsimonious than peasants the world over. It should be added that there were some fiefs whose rulers were enlightened enough to study the interests of the farmers, and others where the samurai retained their old simplicity, and did not disdain to till the soil.

But on the whole it is true to say that the peasants were heavily oppressed by members of the knightly order, who soon in their turn were exploited by the rising class of merchants. Then, as the daimyō and the samurai attempted to transfer their burden of debt to the already overladen shoulders of the farmers, the agricultural economy broke down, and was replaced by a mercantile economy which Japan was unable to support without calling upon the outside world. Her history for more than two hundred years is summarised in that brief statement, which we may now slightly expand.

The first tolerably exact census of Japan dates from 1726. It is imperfect, by reason of both omissions and duplications, but it is exact enough to allow us to estimate the population with reasonable certainty at from 28 to 30 million early in the latter half of the Tokugawa period; and subsequent records show that it remained almost stationary at that level between 1725 and 1850. We do not know the movement of population in the first half of the period, but such fragmentary data as exist bear out the *a priori* assumption that there was between 1600 and 1725 a moderate increase. In these years there was peace, there was leisure, there was a continuous development of industry and commerce, a somewhat freer circulation of goods, all of which favoured a rise in the standard of living and therefore a high excess of births over deaths. But these movements could not progress beyond a certain limit, for a variety of reasons. In the first place the constitution of the population underwent after 1615 an important change. Yedo, the capital of the Shōgun, and the castle towns of some two hundred to three hundred daimyō now became the permanent homes of the barons, of their important vassals and of the majority of their soldiers. Consequently even the smallest fief had to support a numerous population of unproductive persons, including not only the samurai themselves but their personal retainers and domestic servants, who, it should be noted, were now withdrawn from agricultural pursuits. To meet the needs of this community there grew up a class of merchants, artisans and labourers, which in the larger cities reached important dimensions. Ōsaka, Sakai, Nagasaki and a few other places already had a history as trade centres, and they naturally prospered in an era of peace, developing under direct jurisdiction of the Shōgun as almost exclusively industrial and commercial cities. But it was Yedo which grew in the most astonishing way. Before 1600 a wretched straggling village, under the Tokugawa administration it became not only the centre of government containing the offices and residences of all the Bakufu officials, but also the home of the daimyō, who were obliged to spend a great part of the year in attendance at the Shōgun's court. They, with their soldiers and servants in thousands, poured into Yedo, and in a very short time their mansions, the barracks of their troops, and the shops and houses of merchants and tradesmen made of it an extensive city. Exact records are not available, but we know that in 1723 the population of Yedo was over 500,000, and this figure excluded the samurai class, who did not come upon the registers. Towards 1800 the population is thought to have far exceeded 1,000,000. Merely to feed these great numbers required transport facilities on an important scale, and though the Shōgunate still clung to its policy of obstructing traffic improvements on the approaches to Yedo, the main highways were now thronged with the retinues of daimyō passing to and from their fiefs, officials and messengers travelling to Ōsaka, Kyōto or other places under Bakufu control, and a heterogeneous crowd of merchants, pedlars, pilgrims, players and other itinerants. Strung out along these main roads was a succession of townships, composed chiefly of shops and inns, eating-houses and less seemly establishments to meet the needs of travellers, scenes of that bustling many-coloured life which was later to be recorded by Hokusai and Hiroshige in such series of colour prints as the familiar Fifty-three Stages of the Tōkaidō. There was also a rapid growth in water transport, by coastal vessels which carried merchandise to Yedo from other parts of Japan and brought immense wealth to the chartered guilds of shipowners, who could virtually hold the city at ransom since it depended almost entirely upon them for regular supplies of food.

It is easy to see that all these factors combined to increase not only the numbers of townspeople, but also their wealth and influence; and as communications improved and town life grew in complexity more kinds of townspeople, different merchants, different shopkeepers, different artisans, came into being to fulfil the now manifold demands of consumers. But even more significant than their growing number and variety was the gradual and inevitable change in their methods. City life and long-distance transport are incompatible with mere barter or payment in kind. They demand some less cumbrous medium of exchange, and consequently it was not long before money began to displace rice in business transactions. There had been silver and copper money as far back as the seventh century, but its circulation was very limited and it was not until the fifteenth and sixteenth centuries that it obtained even a moderately wide currency. Its further use was much stimulated by the growth of foreign trade, for what the Portuguese and Spanish, and later the English and Dutch merchants, mostly wanted from Japan was precious metals, gold and silver. Both Hideyoshi and Ieyasu, as well as several daimyō, minted gold and silver coins, and promoted mining, so that by about 1600 Japan was tolerably well supplied with metal currency —gold, silver, and copper—though its use was still restricted and its value uncertain. Thenceforward, for the reasons which we have given, "as metal money permeated the economic life of the people, rice lost its function as a medium of exchange, until by the end of the seventeenth century it was completely disregarded" (Takizawa).

It is unnecessary to trace here in detail the effect upon social and political institutions of the penetration of money economy in Japan, but it may without hesitation be said that it caused a slow but irresistible revolution, culminating in the breakdown of feudal government and the resumption of intercourse with foreign countries after more than two hundred years of seclusion. What opened the doors was not a summons from without but an explosion from within. Here we need concern ourselves only with the more immediate results of the new economic forces. One of their first effects was an increase in the wealth of the townspeople, gained at the expense of the samurai and also of the peasants, if anything more could be extorted from that down-trodden class. The daimyō and their retainers spent their money on luxuries produced by the artisans and sold by the tradesmen, so that by about the year 1700, it is said, nearly all their gold and silver had passed into the hands of the townspeople. They then began to buy goods on credit. Before long they were deeply indebted to the merchant class, and were obliged to pledge or to make forced sales of their tax-rice. One reputable scholar of the day asserted that by about 1700 the debts of the daimyō alone amounted to a hundred times the total of money in the country; and though we need not suppose this estimate to have been more than a bold guess there can be no doubt that the expansion of credit was immense. Abuses and disaster followed thick and fast. The merchants took to rice-broking, and then to speculating, so that sometimes the price of rice was driven down, to the distress of the peasants and the dismay of the barons, since both had incomes fixed in units of rice and not of money; and sometimes it was driven up, and other prices followed, so that people who lived on a money wage were thrown into distress. The government tried to mend matters by recoinage,

which generally spelled debasement, or by controlling the rice
market by decree, which was merely futile. The truth is that
nobody understood the new phenomenon, neither statesmen nor
people.[3] More eloquent than volumes of economic history is the
following diagram* of fluctuations in the price of rice. Its crazy
graph shows how lost they all were in this strange environment.

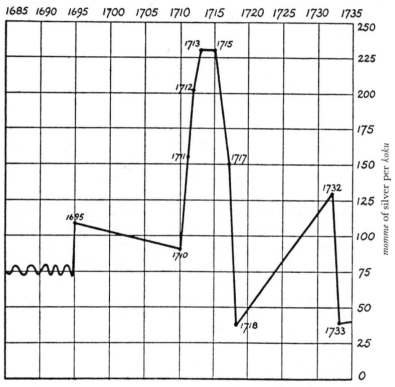

FIG. 50. *Graph of rice prices in terms of silver.*

It was the members of one class only, and not all of them, who
profited by these conditions. These were the merchants, in
particular the brokers and money-lenders, despised *chōnin* or
townsmen, who in theory might be killed with impunity by any
samurai for mere disrespectful language. Their social status still

* Approximate. Based upon data in the works of Professor K. Nakamura and
Professor Eijirō Honjō.

remained low, but they held the purse, and they were in the ascendant. By the year 1700 they were already one of the strongest and most enterprising elements in the state, and the military caste was slowly losing its influence. Economic and social disintegration were to proceed much further, and to gain increasing momentum; but we will leave a description of those later movements to a final chapter, and attempt a survey of the cultural scene at the opening of the eighteenth century.

NOTES TO CHAPTER XXI

[1] Page 444. In considering the causes which brought about the national policy of seclusion, it is important, I think, to recollect that there were strong reasons of domestic policy why the Tokugawa rulers should wish to close the country. They had only recently, after years of feudal struggle, imposed their authority upon their great feudal rivals. They saw that if those rivals, especially the great feudatories in Western Japan, could secure the help of foreigners and trade with them for fire-arms, technical assistance in making ordnance and building ships, and perhaps even for actual military support, then the ruling house might easily fall victim to an alliance between domestic uprising and foreign intervention. These facts tend to show that the compelling reason for closing the country was not entirely an isolationist habit of mind. It is true that throughout their history the Japanese have desired to preserve their native institutions unchanged and uncontaminated. But this has never prevented them from following aggressive and expansionist policies, as is witnessed by their record of overseas adventure, from the almost prehistoric raids on Korea to the voyages in the Pacific which, as traders or as pirates, they continued on an increasing scale until the very moment of the edicts by which overseas navigation was forbidden.

[2] Page 456. Some readers have objected to my account of the attitude of the Roman Catholic Church towards scientific discovery, but I see no reason to change it. I am aware that Pope Clement VII approved of Copernicus' treatise in 1530, that Leonardo was liberally treated by the Church, that Galileo was only technically imprisoned, and so on; but it cannot be denied, I think, that by about 1550 the Church had become reactionary and defended anthropocentric philosophies against the new cosmology, with occasional persecutions.

[3] Page 472. It is an exaggeration to say that nobody understood the economic phenomena of the times. Scholars like Arai Hakuseki, Miura Baien and Ogyu Sorai had a grasp of certain basic points of economic theory, and their economic writings are of considerable interest.

Chapter XXII

GENROKU

GENROKU is the era-name of a very short period, from 1688 to 1703, but it stands also for a definite cultural phase which reached its peak at the turn of the century. By this time the various economic changes just described had brought the commoners to a position of real importance, which the military class no longer enjoyed. The samurai still had their dignity, the consciousness of high social standing; but the commoners had most of the money and most of the fun. By commoners, it should be understood, is here meant not the farmers, but the *chōnin* or people of the towns, for the merchants profited as much as did the soldiers by exploiting the peasantry. The difference in the official attitude towards countryman and townsman respectively is brought out very clearly by comparing the oppressive edicts issued to the peasants with the mild proclamations by which the Bakufu attempted to guide the tradespeople into frugal paths. "Townsmen and servants should not wear silk," and "Townsmen should not wear cloth mantles," and "Townsmen should not live extravagantly," and "Townsmen should not give lavish entertainments." But that is precisely what the townsmen chose to do, and all the Shōgun's edicts failed to stop them from enjoying the pleasures which their money could procure. Now and then a too ostentatious merchant or usurer would shock the Bakufu into confiscating his wealth, and there were times when the Shōgun's officers tried to enforce the letter of his sumptuary laws by arresting richly-dressed shopkeepers. But the habit of luxury was far too deeply rooted to be checked, and the townsmen, when external display was forbidden, merely spent their money on less obvious but even more costly splendours. Thus a young man about town would wear a sober-looking robe, but its lining would be of rich material; or his sister might seem to be clad like a servant-maid, but her under-clothing would be of the brightest and most expensive silks. There are traces in modern Japanese costume of this enforced modesty, which was, it should be added, in keeping with an old tradition of restraint.

Restraint, however, was certainly not the note of Genroku

society in those quarters of Yedo and Ōsaka which were not under
the influence of severe military standards. As always in Japanese
history, one perceives at this period a stern, frugal sentiment
struggling, and usually struggling in vain, against a strain of frivolity and extravagance. It cannot even be said that the ruling
classes were uniformly patterns of simplicity. For all their virtuous
protestations, it was they who spent their gold and silver feverishly,
and they who set the pace which the townsmen gladly followed. It
was the money which they circulated that later paid for the clothes
and the entertainments of the merchants and created in Japan a
new aristocracy. Nothing, indeed, could be further from the truth
than to suppose that the popular arts of Genroku and succeeding
periods were those of a vulgar and ignorant class. A natural
reaction has followed the early vogue of Japanese colour prints
and decorated porcelains among European collectors, and some
are now inclined to condemn these things as mere proletarian
rubbish, unworthy of a connoisseur's attention. But this haughty
view is surely mistaken. From Tempyō statues down to Ashikaga
drawings, art in Japan had mostly "smelt of China." The perfume
was not necessarily undesirable, and it is true that in time it grew
fainter; yet the plastic arts, and for that matter the arts in general,
had rarely escaped from Chinese influence, chiefly because they
were in the hands of a limited class the foundation of whose learning was Chinese. But in and about the Genroku era the artistic
impulse was more widely diffused, less hampered by convention,
possibly even more vital than it had been for many generations,
and it certainly expressed a most truly native spirit. Its patrons,
moreover, were well-to-do and sophisticated, not the men to be
satisfied with a feeble pattern on a dress, a clumsy shape in a tea-
pot, a careless theatrical broadsheet, or a badly acted play.
Yodoya, the great rice merchant of the period in Ōsaka, whose
wealth annoyed the Shōgun and was confiscated, had fifty pairs of
gold screens, three hundred and sixty carpets, innumerable precious stones, mansions, granaries and storehouses everywhere, and
gold pieces by the hundred thousand. He, of course, was excep-
tionally rich, but there were many who ran him close, and the
general standard of living among the traders and skilled artisans
was extremely high, while for cheap unskilled labour and domestic

service they could draw freely upon the peasants, who were only too anxious, so the government thought, to escape from the hardships of country life, to enjoy the delights of the city, and get regular meals of the rice which at home they grew but might not eat.

There is no need to elaborate this theme. It may be taken for granted that by the year 1700 the townspeople had reached a high stage of affluence and culture; and, though the samurai might pretend that the *chōnin* were people of base origin, disreputable occupation and low tastes, the *chōnin* had very definite and strict ideas of their own as to a good book, a good play, a good picture, and, it should not be forgotten, as to good behaviour. By 1700, too, there had been time for them to establish an almost venerable tradition, since Ōsaka and Sakai had now a long history as commercial centres which had grown up tolerably free from military interference, and were therefore able to develop a culture of their own, while Kyōto, though the scene of much fighting and the frequent prey of military factions, had always kept some remnant, however faded, of its ancient civilian prestige, and its populace had a certain metropolitan elegance reflected from the Court. Therefore the early Yedo culture was, so far as the townsmen were concerned, transplanted from the western part of Japan, and was not entirely an indigenous growth. However, it soon developed a special character, the product of its physical and social environment, for Yedo differed in climate and surroundings from Ōsaka and after the earlier migration of merchants from the western cities was inhabited by a medley of enterprising people from all parts of Japan, among whom there was a strong element of tough and quarrelsome men from the eastern provinces. Thus by the Genroku period there was already a marked difference of temper between the western cities and Yedo. The people of Ōsaka and in particular of Kyōto were more polished, more gentle and perhaps more original, those of Yedo were inclined to be rough, quicker, and more argumentative, so that from them there later descended the typical *Yedokko*, a kind of Cockney, sharp, critical, slangy and cheeky. These distinctions may seem unimportant—and they are of course mere generalised comparisons—but they serve to show that the plain citizens had now begun to develop a strong class character and a class consciousness which set them in contrast, verging on antagonism, with the military caste. These latter still carried the swords, and the townsmen still had to pay them external deference; but from the close of the seventeenth century the interests of the classes clashed, and there was continuous conflict, moderated by a gradual decline in the economic power of the samurai, and by a mingling of the two elements which ended in the nineteenth century in a complete fusion. In the Genroku period, however, the samurai clung desperately to his privileges, and endeavoured to preserve his own traditions, while the *chōnin*, fettered by a less restrictive ethical and social code and with no prestige to uphold, could afford to be spontaneous and experimental. At this time, therefore, we find two separate cultures, the old, which was a perpetuation of, so to speak, classical standards; the new, which was popular and unrestrained.

The culture of the townspeople was essentially the culture of a prosperous bourgeoisie devoted to amusement. Their arts centred round what was called in the current language of the day *Ukiyo* or the "Floating World." This is the world of fugitive pleasures, of theatres and restaurants, wrestling-booths and houses of assignation, with their permanent population of actors, dancers, singers, story-tellers, jesters, courtesans, bath-girls and itinerant purveyors, among whom mingled the profligate sons of rich merchants, dissolute samurai and naughty apprentices. It is chiefly the life of these gay quarters and their denizens which is depicted in the popular novels and paintings of the day, the *ukiyo-sōshi* and the *ukiyo-e*, the sketch books and the pictures of the floating world; while acting and all the ancillary arts of the stage developed in harmony with the taste of this lively society. It is easy to see that such an irresponsible way of life, such frank indulgence in pleasures, was repugnant to the sterner sort of samurai and in general distasteful to the ruling class, the more so when they realised that the amusements of the townsmen were being paid for with money extracted from themselves. They therefore endeavoured, by such sumptuary edicts as we have mentioned, to stem the tide of luxury among the commoners; and they were inclined to wrap themselves in their own dignity and follow their traditional pursuits, as if the pastimes of the vulgar were beneath their notice. They failed in the long run, and had to give way to strong economic and social forces beyond their control; but we owe to their conservatism the survival of certain of their traditional arts—in a somewhat fossilised form, it is true—and of very important elements in their code of morality. It is desirable to pay some attention to these before studying the popular movements which had gathered force by the Genroku period.

In the arts alone there is not much to record. The old forms continued, rather lifelessly, in building, painting and poetry, and it was only on its ethical side that the culture of the samurai showed some signs of vitality.

It is curious that the growth of a great city like Yedo should have failed to stimulate architecture, yet certainly there is nothing in either early or late Tokugawa times which calls for high praise. The most important palaces and mansions were uninspired copies of Momoyama types, and in shrines and temples there was a preference for *gongen-dzukuri*, an uninteresting style exemplified in such buildings as the Zenkōji of Nagano. The most celebrated architectural monuments of the Yedo period are the great mausolea of the Shōguns at Nikko. Technically these are debased forms of *gongen-dzukuri*, and though gorgeous in colour and marvellous in detail, they are fiddling and æsthetically ill-conceived; but they are saved from vulgarity by a noble setting among giant trees and a certain impressive profusion. It is possible that the decline of domestic architecture was due to the rapidity with which Yedo grew, and the frequent fires which laid great areas waste. Its population is said to have increased from 150,000 in 1624 to 350,000 in 1693 and 500,000 in 1700. In 1657 it was almost completely destroyed by fire and there was a further conflagration a year later. The city was subsequently rebuilt on a more regular plan than before, but with attention to convenience rather than to beauty.

Religious sculpture fell on evil days, and apart from a few second-rate images there is nothing worthy of notice except the progress of ornamental wood carving which, it must be granted, reached an almost incredible point of dexterity. Its intricate detail gave only an unseemly fussiness to sacred edifices, and was best suited to the dolls and the little personal ornaments of the

"Floating World," so that it was in a secular atmosphere that sculpture now thrived. Painting of the old schools followed the same road as architecture and sculpture, tending to dull repetitions of the themes and treatment of the painters who had prospered in the Momoyama period. But it was saved from decay by such artists as Honami Kwōetsu (d. 1637), "Tawaraya" Sōtatsu (d. 1643) and Tosa Mitsuoki (1617-1691), incomparable painters of flowers and birds; while Sanraku (d. 1635), of the Kanō school, turned to figures, which were more in the traditions of Yamato-e, the old genre painting, than his own. We need not continue this list; but it is worth while to notice that, though Sanraku, and later another Kanō pupil, Hanabusa Itchō (d. 1724), were perhaps strictly speaking the leaders of a revival of the Yamato school and kept a saving classic grace, it was in the measure of their departure from old conventions and their approach to the lively, topical realism of the Ukiyo-e that their painting was admired. In the same way the work of such masters of design as Ōgata Kwōrin (d. 1716), who was also a great artist in lacquer, was freshened by breezes from the Floating World.

Perhaps the last refuge and stronghold of the æsthetics of the samurai was the Nō. It had been patronised by Ieyasu, who had invited companies from the four leading schools* to perform in his Kyōto palace, and from that time Nō performances had been a regular part of Bakufu ceremonial on grand occasions, such as the New Year Banquet or the reception of Korean envoys. Some later Shōguns carried their addiction to extremes. They took part in the plays themselves or gave samurai rank to their favourite actors, who were even allowed to haunt the innermost apartments of the castle. Soon after 1700 the great Confucian scholar, Arai Hakuseki, who was a kind of official moralist to the Shōgunate, advised his master (in three memorials, one of which comprised some 50 fascicules) that the Nō was a danger to the State, and the Shōgun reluctantly agreed to substitute for it, at a Court banquet in 1711, certain ancient music which Hakuseki thought more edifying. Thenceforward the Nō seems to have lost its official prestige, and to have survived only in conservative corners, partly because it conferred a certain distinction as an upper class amuse-

* Kwanze, Komparu, Hōshō and Kongō.

ment, and partly because of its genuine æsthetic appeal. Though it was historically rather a patrician than a popular entertainment, the texts of the plays and the technique of their presentation had by now become familiar in most circles with any pretence to education, so that a number of amateurs among the commoners took pleasure in learning the chants and the dances, thereby providing professional teachers with a living and ensuring the continuance of a tradition which might otherwise have perished. The Nō in this way not only survived as a separate form of art, but also exercised an important influence upon the development of the popular drama. As for the tea-ceremony, which thrives in the same æsthetic climate as the Nō, it cannot be said to have prospered. It lost its never very conspicuous virtues of purity and elegance, and tended to degenerate into an empty ritual, far too intricate and nice for the commoners, who preferred a heartier kind of recreation.

A similar fate seems to have overtaken most of the cultural prerogatives of the former dominant class. They lapsed into formalism and kept their vitality only in so far as they were enlivened by contact with the commoners' activities. Classical poetry was dead, and even the once fashionable *renga* or linked verses were replaced by still more irregular modes, which would have made Tsurayuki shudder. As for Buddhism, it seems to vanish from the historical scene in the Yedo period, and there is no sign of any activity in religious literature, or indeed of any cultural contribution from the Church. Nobunaga and Hideyoshi having broken its power, Ieyasu, by his legislation, had ensured its impotence, and from his day we hear of no distinguished prelate and no great religious reformer. This sudden collapse of Buddhism is extremely hard to understand. It is not a question into which we can enter here, beyond observing that, although certain Buddhist conceptions had by now entered deeply into the national consciousness and certain Buddhist observances had become part of every-day life, the Buddhist church as an institution seems to have been unsuited to the temper of the times. Contemporary literature contains many slighting references from which it is clear that the clergy were disliked among the commoners and despised by men of learning.

Though Buddhism, once the nurse of scholarship in Japan, was now eclipsed, there was on the other hand a strong revival of Chinese studies, particularly in the philosophical field, which in the Far East usually means the field of political and social ethics. As peace followed centuries of war, the leaders of thought in Japan turned their attention to questions of government, endeavouring to discover right principles of conduct for rulers and subjects. Most of them were so imbued with feudal ideology that they did not get very near to a solution of these grave problems; but they did their best to promote a coherent and precise doctrine of morality, which dominated the minds of serious members of the military caste and had a considerable effect upon standards of behaviour through all the social classes. These philosophical currents influenced profoundly later political trends and must therefore presently be discussed; but for the moment we need allude only to those features which have a special bearing upon Genroku manners, that period being taken as representative of the early Yedo culture. The intellectual movements in question may be conveniently described as a return to Confucianism. They included many elements which Confucius would not have recognised, and there was considerable divergence of views, not to say bitter antagonism, among the professors of various schools; but they exhibited in common a conception of public and private morality based on the duties of loyalty and service. They differed among themselves in their definition of virtue, but they were at one in pronouncing that a man's chief concern should be not his own welfare but that of the group to which he belonged. We need not suppose that this cult was able to abolish human frailty, and it is easy to see that, leaving undecided what was the true interest of the community, it tended merely to promote acquiescence in the existing order; but it did set a standard of disciplined, unselfish conduct. For this there was a traditional sanction, and the doctrines of the philosophers found acceptance in common life. They were drilled into the samurai, they were cited in edicts, and they were explained in simple language to the people. So we find late in the eighteenth century a popular dissemination of Shingaku or Heart Learning, which consisted of easy instruction in ethics, based on the philosophy of Wang Yang-ming but utilising also

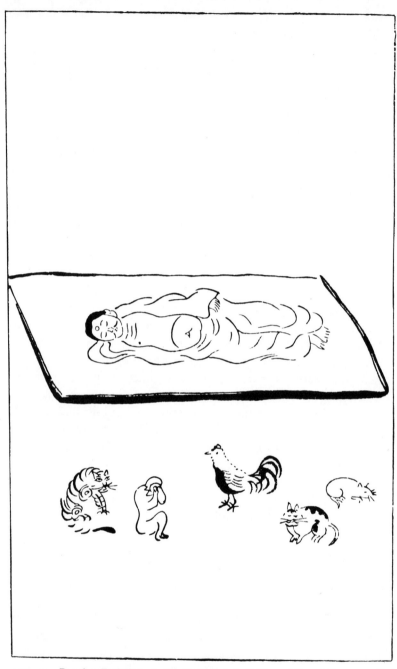

FIG. 51. *Popular Buddhism in the Yedo period. A cheap print of the type called Ōtsu-ye. It represents the Entry into Nirvana.*

Buddhist and Taoist doctrine, and emphasising above all the virtues of obedience and filial piety. There were Shingaku schools in Yedo and Kyōto, and public discourses in the streets. Before this Kaibara Ekken, a distinguished Confucianist (1630-1714), though addressing himself principally to the samurai class, wrote in simple language a great number of popular treatises on education and practical morality which were widely read; while even the works of Chikamatsu, the great playwright (1653-1724) and sometimes those of Saikaku, the novelist (d. 1693), which were admired in the gayest quarters, were imbued with Confucian sentiment. Altogether, therefore, it may be said that the ethics of the Chinese sages, systematised and modified by the Japanese to suit their own peculiar society, had by the opening of the eighteenth century begun to permeate all classes in Japan. The ruling orders, if only to mark themselves off from the plebeian mass, set themselves a more unrelenting ideal than the peasant and the shopkeeper; but the conduct of the commoners was governed, when it was governed at all, by much the same notions of right and wrong.

The life of the townspeople, especially in the Genroku period, judged if not by European practice at least by European standards, appears to have been extremely dissolute; though it must be remembered that their numbers were few in comparison with the industrious millions of peasants, and also that we learn from books and pictures chiefly of their more extravagant amusements. Further, their morality was not based upon religious emotion, nor was it conditioned by fear of divine retribution. In the history of Japanese thought little part is played by the personal sense of sin, which in Western men has engendered puritanical complexes and driven them to extremes of restless inquiry and despair.[1] The Japanese have cared little for abstract ideas of Good and Evil, but they have always been concerned with problems of behaviour, as questions of a man's duty not so much to himself as to the society of which he is a member. It is therefore not surprising that the most influential moralists of the period, notably Yamaga Sokō and Ogyū (Butsu) Sorai, held authoritarian views which might have been stated by Hobbes in his *Leviathan*. In general Chinese and Japanese philosophers have tended to the belief that man's disposition is innately good. They have agreed that he needs guidance, and they

have set great store by decorum, but they have mostly reprobated
only such actions as entail direct evil consequences to society.

One should bear these considerations in mind when studying
the life of the Floating World in Yedo, for—the deplorable fact
cannot be concealed—its principal figures were the courtesan and
the actor, while among its supernumeraries were the disreputable
crowd of panders and procurers who haunted the gay quarters.
There had been since the early days of Yedo, at a place on its
outskirts called Yoshiwara (Reedy Plain), a pleasure haunt where
the citizens gathered to see plays and dancing; and here prosti-
tutes plied their trade until they were suppressed by the Bakufu.
In 1617 an enterprising townsman obtained a licence from the
authorities, set up the business again, and succeeded in attracting
large numbers of citizens to the quarter. Its name, by a change of
ideograph, he had altered to mean Happy Fields; but they were
soon deserted owing to the competition of a class of female bath-
attendants who came into fashion at this time. The bath-houses
became gay resorts, whose stylishly dressed clients, both townsmen
and the lower orders of samurai, were entertained by the much
bedizened bath-girls. One of the most celebrated of these establishments was in front of the mansion of a great daimyō, and this
open flaunting of illicit prostitution caused the Bakufu to suppress
the bath-girls in 1650. After the great fires of 1657-1658 the Yoshiwara was removed to a different district, where the bath-girls and
others assembled. By Genroku it was exceedingly flourishing, and
is said to have contained some two thousand courtesans. Known
as *Fuyajō* or the Nightless City, it was almost self-contained,
since it harboured as well as those ladies a numerous population
of their attendants, of dancing and singing girls, jesters and other
entertainers, together with a most varied collection of tradespeople to supply their needs. Hither resorted not only the young
townsmen, but also samurai in disguise, and even high officers of
the Shōgun or his vassals, while rich merchants were known to
give costly, fantastic entertainments within its walls. There thus
grew up a distinct town, with its own customs, its own standards
of behaviour, and even its own language. In this world of licence
and disorder, everything was highly regulated. There was a
formal etiquette between a house and its clients. There was a

strict hierarchy among the courtesans, whose ranks and appellations were solemnly observed. They were treated with forms of great respect, attended by richly-dressed waiting maids and hedged about by an elaborate ritual. From time to time they made public progress through the streets of the quarter, in stately processions which were eagerly witnessed by thousands of spectators from all parts of the city. Everything seems to have been done to make patrons feel that they were sojourning among people of discreet and delicate sentiments. It was, of course, an essentially sordid business, but it does seem to have been invested with glamour and even a certain elegance. The social side of family life was, probably owing to the subordination of women, undeveloped except in its formal aspects, and the townspeople were debarred from public functions: so that it is perhaps not unnatural that they should have flocked to places where they found light and colour and feminine society in luxurious surroundings. However that may be, the pleasure quarters were a conspicuous feature of city life, not only in Yedo, but in Kyōto, where there was the famous district of Shimabara, in Ōsaka, which boasted of its Shin-machi, and in many smaller towns, such as the more important stages on the main highways. Many of them were founded in much earlier times, but it was in Genroku, that, to quote from an eighteenth century work, "their splendour was by day like Paradise and by night like the Palace of the Dragon King." Their prosperity encouraged all the crafts of the entertainer, such as instrumental music, dancing and singing, to say nothing of juggling and buffoonery, while their variegated life attracted artists of a Bohemian temperament. The pleasure quarter offered the most tempting models to a painter, in the movement of crowds, the colour of costumes, and the shapes of women who lived by their beauty; the playwright and the novelist could find there all the tragedy and all the comedy they desired; and since the great courtesans and the leading rakes, their patrons, were known by name to all the gossips in the city, books and pictures which depicted their amours or their adventures had a ready sale.

The theatre attracted numerous and similar patrons, with the exception that its audiences were in part composed of the wives and daughters of townspeople. If one may judge by the number of plays written in and shortly after the Genroku period the stage at this time had reached amazing popularity. The beginnings of the *kabuki* or popular drama are obscure. Its earlier developments were worked out in Kyōto and Ōsaka, where it consisted of open-air performances of dancing and singing, with a more or less coherent motif. Farcical pieces called *kyōgen* or "mad words" were frequent, and the *kabuki* seems to have been a poor relation of the Nō, descended like it from the *sarugaku* but departing from its strict canons and growing more realistic and more familiar in its appeal, to satisfy the taste of audiences who wanted something downright and lively. The growth of the *kabuki* is closely bound up with the development of a form of metrical romance called *jōruri* after an early piece describing the life of a legendary princess of that name. There were *jōruri* already in the Muromachi period, tales chanted to a measure, as had been the old military romances like the *Heike Monogatari;* and with the introduction of a new instrument (the three-stringed *samisen*) these gained a more musical character, and soon found a considerable vogue. Their further popularity was assured by the improvement in puppet shows. The manipulators of the dolls attained such expertness that they were able—as they still are—to produce an astonishing dramatic illusion. To a modern spectator the little figures, handled by men in black robes and cowls, strut and prance as if they were indeed the playthings of destiny. The orchestral and vocal accompaniment, though as music sometimes to Western ears excruciating, is stirring and significant. It is therefore easy to understand why the puppets had such success, and why the *jōruri* became important as an adjunct to the puppet plays. The marionette theatres owed some of their prosperity also to the lax conduct of actors and actresses. Actresses were forbidden by edict and boy actors got into trouble with the authorities more than once because of their vicious habits, so that wooden dolls were a safer investment for theatrical managers. By Genroku both puppets and *jōruri* had reached tremendous popularity in Yedo as well as in Kyōto and Ōsaka. Great advances were made in technique; the dolls could roll their eyes, raise their eyebrows and waggle their fingers; the musicians endeavoured to perfect the chants and the instrumental accompaniment; while men of letters devoted themselves to writing plays for the puppet theatres. Of these the most celebrated was at Dōtonbori in Ōsaka. It was chiefly for this theatre that Chikamatsu Monzaemon, Japan's greatest playwright, worked for over thirty years. He wrote in particular for a *jōruri* singer named Takemoto Gidayū, the most celebrated performer of his day, who gave his name to the style of chant still called *gidayū* and still practised.

No description of Genroku society would be complete without some account of the theatre by which it was mirrored. The plays demand attention first. It is a remarkable fact that the best and the most celebrated were written for puppet performances, and this accounts for certain peculiarities in their construction and text. They naturally contain for instance a great proportion of recitative, needed to eke out the gestures of the puppets, and their emphasis is dictated by the needs of their mechanical, dumb performers. Since many of the plays written for marionettes were adapted for the ordinary stage, the technique of acting in Japan shows traces of marionette influence. These facts should always be borne in mind when studying the Japanese theatre, and they should be allowed for when considering the literary value of the plays. European students are disappointed when they read the texts of plays which the Japanese admire, perhaps because they look for the things which they would expect to find in European literature. These they do not find. But the plays of Chikamatsu have great merits. They are full of the kind of incident that his audiences adored, they skilfully embody material from his vast store of learning, and they display at times a torrential eloquence. He was most prolific and versatile, as can be seen from these titles taken at random from a volume of his works: *Kokusenya Kassen*, adventures of Coxinga, a pirate chief; *Ikudama Shinjū*, the love affair of O Saga, a courtesan, and Kaheiji, the son of a porcelain merchant, which ends in their suicide; *Nihon Furisode-hajime*, a curious play recounting the myth of the Age of the Gods and the origins of poetry and dancing, and ending with a dance by the dragon-quelling deity Susanowo; *Tai-shoku-kwan*, episodes of court life in the Fujiwara period, in which the regent Kamatari figures; and the famous *Chūshin-gura* or Treasury of Loyal Retainers, which takes as its theme the vendetta of the Forty-seven

Rōnin, a contemporary incident. The language and the structure of these plays show clearly that their writers were influenced by the Nō texts. The "books" of Chikamatsu's plays* contain many passages which, taken alone, might be extracts from a Nō play, and the stage directions use Nō terminology; but the resemblance

FIG. 52. *A doll representing the actor Danjuro I. Such dolls were popular in the Genroku period.*

is only superficial and even when the *kabuki* plays deal with classical themes they treat them in a florid, verbose way which Seami would not have tolerated. In the *kabuki* no effect is missed

---

* We may call them plays for convenience, but strictly speaking they are *jōruri*. The stage versions were usually the work of managers and actors, based upon the *jōruri*, which they cut or expanded or re-arranged. Many well-known Japanese plays were not written works, but excursions on some popular theme, worked up by actors and musicians and transmitted for the most part by verbal tradition in the leading families of actors. Several of these families have maintained an unbroken line since the early eighteenth century, by resorting to adoption where hereditary talent failed.

for want of underlining. There is no difficult symbolism, no im-
passive mask, no mere shadow of a gesture, but red blood flows
and the actors declaim, grimace and posture with admirable
energy. The Yedo audiences in particular demanded noise, movement and thrill, so that the most applauded actor in Genroku was
Ichikawa Danjurō, famous for his *aragoto* or "rough business."
This was partly because Yedo, being the military capital, had a
taste for historical drama with a great deal of action, sword-play
and heroics, while Kyōto and Ōsaka like to have their tender
emotions roused and favoured such actors as Sakata Tōjurō,
a master of *nuregoto*, or "moist business." But it should not be
supposed that in any of these places the theatre-goers put up
with mere barnstorming. The standard of acting rose rapidly.
Audiences became critical and players developed an extremely
subtle technique which could be mastered only after long and
painful training. Thus when the Bakufu forbade women to appear
on the stage, female parts were taken by men, some of whom subjected themselves to the severest preparation, living even in
private like women, modelling their speech and deportment
upon women, and wearing women's clothes, so that when they
appeared on the stage their movements were spontaneously
feminine. Their artistic conscience was highly developed, and
within the limits imposed by their peculiar convention they
achieved a trained but easy finish which is rare in Europe and is
perhaps matched only by a few ballet dancers and actors who
have undergone a rigorous discipline since childhood. Indeed the
popular stage in Japan shows in a striking fashion how a seemingly irrational convention in art, if competently managed, far
from impeding expression, assists it by falling into place as an
unmistakable framework.

We have noticed the theatre at some length because of its significance in æsthetic history, but it has a further importance as a
social phenomenon which should not be overlooked. A number of
jōruri were devoted to erotic themes, which they treated with considerable licence; and they were sometimes suppressed on that
account. But the plays of Chikamatsu are all highly edifying.
Virtue is always triumphant, or if by chance the plot will not permit a happy issue then the moral or the social code is vindicated

by the suicide of offenders. The strictest principles of contemporary Confucian ethics are inculcated throughout—in the historical plays the code now called *Bushidō*, in the domestic dramas the obligations of loyalty or filial piety. In fact it may be said that the typical crisis in tragedy arises always out of the conflict of a natural emotion, whether friendship or love or passion, with the claims of society. That is why almost all the plays deal either with the clash between feudal loyalty and family affection, or with elopements and double suicides. The former was a popular theme with the townspeople, because it took them into high social circles, giving scope for splendid costume and panache; the latter because it came near to their own daily life. A handsome young tradesman, though his marriage is arranged, falls in love with a fascinating Yoshiwara girl, whom a rich merchant protects. To pay for his pleasures, or to buy her out of servitude, he embezzles his employer's money, fears discovery, and then decides that he cannot reconcile *ninjō*, human feelings, with *giri*, moral duty. The lovers therefore, agree to die together. He "takes up his dagger and stabs her, crying *Namu Amida Butsu*. She falls back with a groan, and he twists the weapon till her limbs squirm. Another thrust, and the agony is upon her. Again he twists and twists the dagger. Her eyes grow dim, she draws her last earthly breath, and enters the Dark Road." (*Ikudama Shinjū*.)

It is to be noted that there is no religious problem here. The governing motive is one of social ethics. In the play just quoted the unhappy young man, having despatched his sweetheart, takes up the dagger to wipe it before plunging it into his own body. Then he remembers that this blade was given to him by his parents as a keepsake. To use it on himself would be a crowning offence against filial piety, and he therefore takes the girl's girdle and hangs himself. Yet though he thus acts under the compulsion of Confucian principles, his resolve is strengthened by a sentiment which is profoundly Buddhist: he believes that he and the girl have done some wrong in a previous existence, for which they must now suffer; but in their future lives they will be husband and wife. This is the Buddhist doctrine of *in-gwa*, the chain of causation, which in its popular, unphilosophical form, was widely accepted in Japan, and has entered deeply into common sentiment.

Often such tales, as in *Umegawa Chūbei or Post-Haste to Hell*, were merely idealised versions of contemporary incidents, topics of current gossip. Conversely they acted so powerfully upon the minds of the suggestible public that the number of love suicides, embezzlements and elopements grew at an alarming rate, till the Shōgun Yoshimune, a martinet fearing for the morals of his samurai, prohibited (1739) certain of the more inflammatory styles of *jōruri*. But there is no doubt that these were what popular taste demanded, and also that the *kabuki*, though in theory beneath the notice of the samurai, soon began to attract members of all classes.* Even some of the grave Confucian scholars approved of certain plays by Chikamatsu, which they thought had an educative value. Yet what the populace liked was not the moral lessons of the drama, but its excitement. The influence of the theatre upon life in Japan in the eighteenth century is evident at all points. Not only did the plots and language of the plays affect contemporary behaviour and speech, but the dress and conduct of the actors, followed with the closest interest, dictated the fashions of the day. Designs of fabrics, modes of hair-dressing, styles of cloak and hat were brought into favour by popular actors or courtesans, and by their names are still known. The charming patterns of bold stripes or checks now known as *genroku* are revivals of the gaudy costumes of the theatres or the pleasure quarters in those times, while all the world knows that the early masters of the colour-print found their models on the stage or in the Yoshiwara. These artists and their works are too familiar to need description here. We need only mention that it was in the Genroku period that the characteristic *ukiyoe* style was evolved, by such painters as Hishigawa Moronobu (1645-1715). They may be said to have led a popular revolt against the old-fashioned schools, particularly those which aped the Chinese. They prefixed to their signatures the words "Japanese Painter" (*Yamato Eshi*), and their aim was to depict not imaginary Chinese scenes but the life passing before their own eyes. Consequently they painted mostly actors and frail ladies, or notorious frequenters of the gay world. One of the most conspicuous triumphs of Yedo art is its loving portrayal of cos-

* There is a well-known print by Moronobu showing a samurai brawling in a theatre, and samurai with their families are shown in others.

FIG. 53. *A street scene in Yedo in the eighteenth century. The entrance to a theatre.*

tume. It was not a new discovery, for Fujiwara artists had delighted in the line and colour of court robes. Later, in the Muromachi period, when the Portuguese came to Japan, painters,
lacquer workers and potters seized on the pictorial value of their
strange dress, and made delightful designs by exaggerating the

FIG. 54. *The Green Room of a Puppet Theatre (Genroku Period), showing a
joruri singer.*

length of their limbs, the swell of their baggy breeches and the
haughty curve of their noses. Now in Genroku not only the painting of costume, but costume itself, becomes one of the fine arts,
attracting to its service all the talents. Naturally it was in such
haunts of extravagance as the green-room and the Yoshiwara that
the Ukiyo painters found the most seductive models. Their tastes,
or the lively temper of the times, had some effect upon the con-

ventional schools, which now produced such artists as Hanabusa Itchō, whom we have already mentioned as a painter trained in the Kanō manner but converted to the Yamato style. He retained the old humorous Yamato-e outlook, but devoted himself to topical subjects, using a delicate, faithful touch sharpened with satirical insight. His street scenes, with their rowdy apprentices, blind shampooers, and strolling singers, his ferry-boats crammed with passengers of a hundred types, are delightful pendants to any written description of his period. It was characteristic of the new movement in art that he should be an intimate of the great profligates of his day. He spent much of his time at the Yoshiwara in the company of celebrated spendthrifts and certain dissolute daimyō: and at the same time he was a poet of distinction. He may be looked upon as a symbol of the intermingling of classes and the formation of a middle layer worked upon by influences from above and from beneath. It was this layer which leavened society throughout the subsequent centuries. It produced a cultivated bourgeoisie, patrons of the arts. They were popular, sometimes a little vulgar, arts, but they were for the enjoyment of a public many of whose members were prosperous and discerning. The colour-print artists were not mere ignorant craftsmen, but men of some education, who profited moreover by being heirs to an ancient æsthetic civilisation. Their work, posters and broadsheets, sold in the streets of Yedo for a few cash apiece, opened new vistas of pictorial treatment to the de Goncourts and to Whistler, but to a Japanese artist it was a perfectly natural mode of expression, based on principles discovered centuries ago and merely given a slight shift to meet the mood of their time.

That mood was lively, comic and rather impatient of old habits and restraints. It is revealed in literature as well as painting. The typical men of letters of the day were Bashō the poet and Saikaku the novelist. Bashō developed the *haikai* and the *hokku*, short epigrammatic verses which need not observe any of the severe canons of classical poetry. These could be thrown off by anybody with good native wit and an ordinary vocabulary, and on the most familiar subjects. In ordinary hands they made a pleasant parlour game, but under the magic touch of a master like Bashō they became little drops of the essence of poetry. Bashō himself preferred nature as a theme, but some of his followers found their material in the Floating World, and composed sharp-pointed epigrams on its manners. They were not always nice in their language or their topics, and in that way too they were products of their age. Saikaku the novelist could moralise on occasion, and he wrote such edifying works as *Giri Monogatari*, Tales of Virtuous Conduct, and *Nijū Fukō*, Twenty Examples of Unfilial Behaviour. He was more at home, however, in novels describing the depredations of merchants and the amours of loose livers, and it is for these that he is remembered. He was a skilful though unlearned writer, who handled his medium well; but he had many imitators whose only gift was their lubricity, and they prospered exceedingly. Prudery in those days had not been discovered. Publishers and printers thrived on the sales of erotic books and pictures, while entertainers were expected to flavour their performances copiously with spice. A popular street-corner story-teller was much applauded when he took to beating the measure of his recitations with a large wooden phallus, and in amorous passages on the stage both talk and gesture were extremely unrestrained. The Bakufu, fearing as usual for the morals of their samurai, tried again and again to suppress these abuses. They confiscated pornographic prints, elegantly called Spring Pictures, and in 1723 they seized several thousand indecent books, though in many cases they were unable to discover either publisher or printer. But their efforts were not too successful and their anxiety was perhaps superfluous. It was true that the samurai and even the daimyō were taking to vulgar pastimes, visiting the theatres, composing irregular verses and singing popular songs. Their wives, old-fashioned people said, were better acquainted with the names and ages of popular actors than with the use of the needle. Even in the august precincts of the Imperial Palace the strains of new-fangled ballad-music might be heard, to the dismay of noble lords, one of whom in his diary (1718) laments in these words: ". . . His Highness sings songs called *nagebushi*. These are licentious tunes. It is extremely improper that a descendant of the revered Sun Goddess should do such things . . . which even a right-thinking shopkeeper would not do." It was all very sad and degenerate to lovers of the decorous past; but the fact was that, after centuries of repression, the ordinary man was now able to taste some of the delights of freedom and prosperity. The experience went to his head, and he broke out into excesses. Yet what his rulers mistook for decadence was merely high spirits. This was a rare phenomenon in Japanese history, and one that they mistrusted: so they set about destroying all the gay, instinctive things which came to the surface in Genroku, *sharé*, the sense of fun, *sui*, the feeling for "chic" or elegance, and other amiable qualities not compatible with feudal discipline. It is the conflict of absolutism with these and other subversive growths which makes the political history of the later Yedo period.

NOTE TO CHAPTER XXII

[1] Page 483 (see also p. 53). The sense of sin. I am afraid that this passage has been misunderstood, and even interpreted as meaning that the Japanese do not distinguish between right and wrong! That, of course, would be an absurd proposition. What I tried to suggest was that, although they have very definite and firm ideas as to right conduct, they do not usually seem to think in terms of individual moral judgment and responsibility. They have a plentiful vocabulary to denote specific virtues like piety, faithfulness, loyalty, benevolence, and so on; but their language is deficient in words to express such ideas as are represented by sin, conscience, repentance, forgiveness or atonement, in the sense in which they figure in Christian doctrinal and devotional works. It would be difficult to translate into Japanese intelligible to a person without previous knowledge of Christian thought such a sentence as "Lord, have mercy upon us, miserable sinners!" and he would find the symbolism of washing away sin by the blood of the Lamb most difficult of comprehension, if not even distasteful. The Buddhist rite of baptism (abisheka), it should be noticed, is not a rite of cleansing, but of initiation into an order, and it is not essential for an ordinary believer. The washing and sprinkling so common in Shintō ceremonies are acts of ritual purification, to remove not the stain of original sin but the defilement of unclean things. It is, I think, significant in this connection that in Japanese mental institutions cases of religious melancholia are almost unknown, whereas other forms of melancholia are frequent.

It is probable that the doctrine of Karma, as it is understood in popular Japanese Buddhism, has stood in the way of the development of a personal sense of sin, because a man's nature is thought of as conditioned by his previous existences, and he is therefore not to be regarded as the wholly responsible agent of his deeds.

A FEUDAL CASTLE OF THE YEDO PERIOD

"THREE SAINTS", BY KANŌ MASANOBU

It is true, however, that this is not strict Buddhist teaching, for the Buddha is recorded to have dismissed the dilemma of Free Will and Predestination, saying that there was no conflict to be resolved. It is indeed remarkable that in the history of Japanese thought and, I believe, of Far Eastern thought in general, the problem rarely if ever arises. Japanese thinkers would no doubt agree with Locke, though perhaps on different grounds, in feeling that to ask whether man's will be free is "like asking whether sleep be swift or virtue square," This is not the approach of popular Buddhism, but it may perhaps be argued that where there is no controversy as to the freedom of man's will there is little interest in the problem of moral responsibility for his acts.

Chapter XXIII

THE BREAKDOWN OF FEUDALISM

1. INTELLECTUAL CURRENTS

IT is a curious fact that the ruling classes at all times and in all countries, while showing a deep concern for the moral welfare of their subjects and labouring to promote such virtues as industry, sobriety and obedience, have been only spasmodically alive to economic necessity. Japan in the seventeenth century presents this spectacle, of administrators endeavouring to solve an economic question on moral lines. They saw developing a prosperous class of townspeople who were not only absorbing the wealth of the military class but were, as they understood it, corrupting feudal manners and thus undermining the foundations of the State. This problem they attacked by what we may call the Confucian method. They suppressed, or tried to suppress, all new habits which seemed to them pernicious. They directed an inky cloud of sumptuary edicts against extravagance of every kind, refusing to believe that the luxury of one age is the necessity of the next. The so-called Tokugawa Constitution—the Laws of the Military Houses (*Buke Hatto*) and similar enactments, promulgated in 1615 and confirmed by each new Shōgun—was in fact one comprehensive sumptuary code. It was reinforced by numerous measures of frugality introduced under the eighth Shōgun, Yoshimune (1716-1745). In the time of the eleventh Shōgun, Ienari (1786-1837), his prime minister, Matsudaira Sadanobu, a conscientious and, it would appear, benevolent statesman, issued an astonishing series of restrictive edicts forbidding almost every form of expenditure by almost every kind of person. He decreed, for instance, that those with an income of less than 10,000 *koku* should buy nothing new; and, ordering women to dress their own hair, he enjoined professional coiffeurs to become washermen. In conformity with the spirit of these laws he awarded prizes for chastity, piety, and similar virtues.

Such enactments, it is true, were usually evoked by some critical situation. Sadanobu's edicts were issued in the hope of repairing the effects of natural calamities, floods, famines and fires, which had swept the country bare between 1783 and 1786, and they may perhaps be justified as emergency measures equivalent to taxation. Nevertheless they show how the official mind was pervaded by ideas of government by precept; and there is something admirable, if pathetic, in this trust in human reasonableness. The feudal rulers had abandoned religion as a statesman's instrument. They were therefore obliged to fall back upon some code of secular morality: and it is for this reason that we observe, particularly from the beginning of the eighteenth century, a deliberate policy of ethical propaganda. Its most obvious result is to be found in the formation of the cult known as *Bushidō* or the Way of the Warrior. It is a difficult subject, apt to lead to fruitless controversy, and it is complicated by its relation to various conflicting schools of Chinese philosophy; but no account of the culture of the Yedo period would be complete without some reference to this phenomenon, and we must accordingly try to describe its main features.

The first point to be noted about *Bushidō* is that its name is comparatively new. The word itself was in use in the eighteenth century, but it seems not to have had any wide currency or exact connotation until quite recent times; while the creed or cult which it stands for has certainly varied from age to age, and cannot properly be discussed as a static group of ideas. Its beginnings can be traced far back, to those conceptions of a soldier's duty which inspired members of the great military houses in the Fujiwara period, or even to the traditions of the Ōtomo, the ancient imperial guard. From those times onward, the ideals of the military class began to take shape as a more or less coherent body of ethical teaching incorporating new elements and rejecting old ones as the progress of events revealed them unnecessary or inexpedient. Various factors contributed to its growth—the need for some assured fidelities in an age of bloodshed and treachery; Chinese notions of virtue operating upon a native hierarchical sentiment; a certain æsthetic sensibility; the self-discipline of Zen Buddhism; and in general the demands of a society that depended for its security upon organised domestic and social relationships. This cult subsisted throughout the Middle Ages rather as a set of ideals guiding the conduct of the better class of warrior than as a precisely formulated doctrine. Though it has contributed to Japanese culture some of its most admirable features it is idle to suggest, as some dithyrambic writers have done, that it has ever been widely practised in any degree of perfection, any more, let us say, than the teachings of the Sermon on the Mount have been closely followed in Europe. Noble, if somewhat ill-balanced because it was rooted in class-consciousness, it was more than once forsworn on a grand scale, as can be seen in the record of the Ashikaga period; and when in the seventeenth century it came to be systematised, preached, discussed and dissected, it began to lose vitality, to grow self-conscious, and tended to degenerate into mere punctilio.

Probably we should regard the feudal House Laws as the first considered formulation in writing of the principles of *Bushidō*, but roughly speaking it may be said to date, as a codified instrument of policy, from the establishment of the Tokugawa Shōgunate, and the *Buke Hatto* may be regarded as its canonical authority. From the beginning of the seventeenth century its character begins to change. It is no longer what it was in Kamakura days, a sentiment rather than a creed, and a sentiment growing out of the intimate relationship between lord and vassal, founded on direct personal service in battle. It now has a definite philosophical basis, and depends upon abstract conceptions of loyalty. It may even be argued that the growth of systematised *Bushidō* was hastened by the decline of the older spontaneous military virtues. The very fact that Hideyoshi and Ieyasu were able to win over many of the adherents of their enemies testified to a collapse of loyalty; and the frequent armistices during the Korean campaign show that death was no longer the alternative to victory. Moreover the behaviour of the samurai for some decades after the establishment of the Tokugawa Shōgunate caused the authorities grave concern. Their unruly qualities were not suited to times of peace, and even those who displayed the traditional disregard of death were merely a nuisance, with their vendettas and their brawls and their duels on fantastic points of honour, to say nothing of their murderous attacks upon unarmed citizens. They were mostly *rōnin*, masterless samurai whose occupation was now gone; and far from being romantic knights-errant they were often simply an unfortunate class of unemployed, doing mischief under cover of an outworn

FIG. 55. *A street scene in Yedo in the eighteenth century. Samurai brawling outside a theatre.*

creed. Until about 1650 they were extremely troublesome, and once or twice they led risings against the Bakufu. These were suppressed, but the administration began to perceive that it was unwise to encourage the military spirit in times of peace, unless it were tempered by a regard for civil practice. There were indeed certain great scholars and moralists (like Ogyū Sorai and Satō Naokata) who attacked the old feudal morality, arguing that it was inconsistent with good government, should be demolished and replaced by pure Confucian ethics. The Shōgunate, depending as it did upon armed force, could not go to such lengths; but from the middle of the seventeenth century its policy (even allowing for a certain revival movement under Yoshimune, *circa* 1720) veered away from militarism and, though the feudal framework was preserved, became progressively bureaucratic. The transition can be observed most clearly in the circumstances attending the famous vendetta of the Forty-seven *Rōnin*. It is now a hackneyed tale, and we may pass over its dramatic aspects, which have been amply chronicled; but it has a most interesting political and social significance. About the year 1700 Asano, a daimyō of moderate standing, while rehearsing the etiquette of a state ceremony in the Shōgun's palace at Yedo, was insulted by his instructor, Kira, a high Bakufu official, who, it is said, had not received a sufficient present from Asano's steward. Asano drew his sword and wounded Kira. To bare a weapon in the palace, quite apart from attacking an officer of the Shōgun, was a grave offence. Asano was ordered to commit suicide, and his fief was confiscated. Here we have an excellent example of the severity of the Tokugawa towards their feudatories. Asano having obeyed, forty-seven of his principal retainers, now *rōnin*, pledged themselves to avenge their master. They scattered to avoid observation, for they knew that Kira would be on his guard; and it was only after two years of patience and hardship that, his caution relaxed, they found their opportunity. They forced their way into Kira's mansion on a snowy morning in February, 1703, and took his life. They then surrendered themselves to justice, fully expecting death, because they had committed a capital crime by accomplishing their purpose within the direct domain of the supreme overlord. The Bakufu did not expressly forbid the vendetta, which had a strong traditional sanction; but they had come to regard private vengeance, especially if it was wrought under their noses, as an affront to their prerogative of justice, and it was therefore difficult for them to overlook this offence, the more so as it could be read as a protest against the application of their own law to the case of Asano. At the same time, they could not but approve the act of the *rōnin*, since it was in full accord with Confucian principles which they upheld. A vassal must not remain "under the same heaven" as the murderer of his lord, and Kira, by his insulting conduct, was virtually the assassin of Asano. There was, accordingly, prolonged discussion as to the proper treatment of the avengers. High authorities, including the Shōgun himself, thought that they ought to be pardoned, and popular sympathy was with them. Certain strict Confucianists held the same view; but other scholars argued very strongly that the men must die. Chief among these were Sato Naokata and Ogyū Sorai, whom we have just noticed as opponents of traditional *Bushidō*. They believed in loyalty, but they took the strictly logical line that Confucian principles must be observed in the light of the law, and not interpreted by individuals at their own fancy. Both Asano and his retainers had offended against the code of the Bakufu and it was proper that they should perish. After a year's delay the *rōnin* were ordered to commit suicide. This they did, and became almost national deities, in their own times and ever since. To this day the celebrated play of Chikamatsu, *Chūshin-Gura*, draws crowds to the theatre, moving audiences to tears and excitement as it develops the theme of sacrifice. A magnificent drama, with forty-seven heroes, it must have worked powerfully upon the emotions of the citizens of Yedo.

Yet in real life there was no true unanimity as to the principles of *Bushidō*. There was a conflict between sentiment and theory, and, more than this, there were splits among theorists. Ōishi Yoshio, the leader of the forty-seven, was a follower of Yamaga Sokō and had sat at the feet of Itō Jinsai, both eminent philosophers of the "Ancient" school of philosophy (*Kogaku-ha*) which, despite its name, was a protestant school; and the fact is that *Bushidō* in the eighteenth century was no longer what it had been before, a customary code developed among soldiers under the stress of war, but a system of practical ethics evolved out of the disagreements of philosophers and in process of adaptation to the needs of peaceful society. To call it the Way of the Warrior is to give a wrong impression of its scope. It was a code which set high ideals before all good citizens, and it gained its military-sounding name only because it originated among the ruling classes, who being for the most part of samurai origin were naturally disposed to regard it as a mark of their own caste—though it was in fact by no means their monopoly. Yet careful study leads one to believe that it was not the somewhat bombastic dogma or the sanguinary practice of the soldiers that inspired the best thought and the finest conduct in Japan, but the teachings of her high-minded, peppery philosophers. Some knowledge of the main philosophical currents of the period is therefore needed for an understanding of the course of events in the eighteenth century and after.

The first article of the Tokugawa "Constitution" had decreed that the vassals and their men should devote themselves equally to learning and military exercises. This seemed a rational policy, since the object of the rulers of Japan was to safeguard the existing order, which depended upon the dominance of an arm-bearing class, but also to ensure peace, which depended upon the encouragement of civilian pursuits. The Bakufu had embarked upon an interesting but perilous experiment, for they must, if it was to succeed, keep a just balance between martial enthusiasm and literary ardour. Perhaps these qualities are not fundamentally irreconcilable; but in practice the Bakufu, rather timid of fostering a too warlike spirit, since it might one day be directed against themselves, gradually came down on the pacific side. From the days of Ieyasu they encouraged learning, and though they were hostile to new ideas and tried to keep men's studies within approved channels, they insensibly nourished a spirit of inquiry which in the end brought about their own downfall.

The learning which the rulers officially patronised and promoted was almost exclusively Chinese learning. They employed as advisers Confucian scholars, who assisted them in drafting laws and in formulating those ethical principles on which their administration was based. It was largely due to the labours of the scholars and the support which the Bakufu gave them that Japan was indebted for the peace which she enjoyed for over 200 years; and it is also to their researches and their controversies that were due the political developments which culminated in the breakdown of feudalism. It is therefore convenient to complete the foregoing account of intellectual movements of the Tokugawa period by a brief reference to its leading philosophers.

The official philosophy in Japan in the early Tokugawa period was that of Chu Hsi (1130-1200), a leading figure of the important philosophical renaissance which took place in China under the Sung dynasty. The canon of this school was Chu Hsi's commentary on the works of the Chinese sages, entitled in Japanese *Shisho Shinchū*, or a New Commentary on the Four Classics. The teaching of Chu Hsi, it will be remembered, had been studied in the Muromachi period by a small number of learned monks of the Five Monasteries, but it was not until the late sixteenth century that his philosophy became more widely known, through the efforts of a scholar named Fujiwara Seigwa (1561-1619), who, it is interesting to note, was a Buddhist priest. Under the Tokugawa régime the Chu Hsi philosophy* was virtually adopted as the official school of thought, and Hayashi Razan, its chief exponent, was appointed adviser to the government. From his time, it is said, Confucian scholars let their hair grow long. This curious item of history is highly significant. Hitherto learning had been associated with the Church, and scholars had shaved their heads like priests; but now Confucian studies were no longer the recreation of learned monks. The Confucian philosophy had an official status, and it may almost be regarded as having achieved the position of an established religion. Confucianism in one form or another displaced Buddhism in the esteem of the educated classes, and Buddhism seems to have surrendered without a struggle. Buddhist observances were not generally abandoned,† but the strictest Confucianists were as bitterly opposed to Buddhism as to Christianity and they followed a strict Confucian ritual which included ceremonial reverence to the

---

* It is usually described in Japan as the Tei-shu system, after the Japanese names of Chinese masters, Tei standing for Ch'eng and Shu for Chu Hsi.

† Under the third Shōgun (Iemitsu, 1622-1651) the vassals were obliged to declare their adherence to one or other of the Buddhist sects, and the people had to register as parishioners of a church. But this measure was not intended to promote religion. It was part of the anti-Christian policy.

memory of the Chinese sages and obeisance at a shrine of Confucius. Such shrines were erected at official expense and even visited officially for worship by the Shōguns themselves. In other ways the administration was at great pains to promote Confucian studies. An academy had been founded in 1633, and this became in 1690 the college named Shōhei-kō (after the birthplace of Confucius, which is called in Japanese Shō-hei), the University of Yedo. The office of Rector of this college was always held by a member of the Hayashi family, who thus became, so to speak, hereditary philosophers to the Shōgunate, and were official advisers on ethics and education. They were all uncompromising adherents of the Chu Hsi system. We shall see that other systems were studied in Japan, but it was the Chu Hsi philosophy which enjoyed the widest acceptance and the monopoly of official patronage. It was the orthodox school, and despite extremely strong counter-currents it remained the most influential throughout the eighteenth and even the nineteenth century. There is good ground for thinking that no single body of doctrine has had such a powerful effect in Japan upon thought and behaviour among the educated class. Buddhism, of course, was an important vehicle of culture for a thousand years, and has left a deep mark on popular sentiment, but when one considers how venerable was its tradition and how widespread its beliefs, it is surprising to find how few traces of its direct influence are visible in the culture of the Yedo period. As for Christianity, despite its one time prosperity, it vanished from the scene, and among the ruling classes survived only as the bitter memory of a pernicious faith.*

It will be asked why a mere system of philosophy, borrowed from a neighbouring country, should have gained such a hold on the minds of the Japanese as did the teaching of Chu Hsi. The explanation is not far to seek. The Japanese have always been more interested in practical ethics than in abstract speculation. This is clear enough to anybody who will study their intellectual history, and has been generally admitted by their own philosophers who (to use the words of an eminent modern scholar, Dr. T.

---

* There was an anti-Christian edict as late as 1868 decreeing capital punishment for those who would not recant. But from 1873 complete religious freedom was allowed.

Inouye) feel that "in Western ethics the dominant principle is intellectual inquiry and not the cultivation of virtue." Chu Hsi's philosophy was not without an interesting cosmology. Indeed the Sung philosophers may in a general way be said to have transformed the ancient Confucian ethics by fitting the unsystematised precepts of the Sages into a metaphysical framework of their own construction; and further in composing their ontology they made free use of Buddhist and Taoist ideas, though they would have been extremely annoyed at such an imputation. But it was upon the ethical doctrines of Chu Hsi that the Japanese fixed their attention. We need not enter into details of his philosophy. It is enough to point out that he preached the importance of self-culture. He held that man is innately disposed to right conduct, just as all nature is animated by a beneficent principle,* but that it is necessary for him to study the laws of the universe, so as to comprehend virtue. By induction from those laws he will discover that the relationships of natural phenomena have their counterpart in the relationships between individuals, supreme among which are those of sovereign and subject, parent and child, husband and wife. It will be seen that, in effect, Chu Hsi does little more than recommend those virtues that had always been honoured by the Japanese; but the old Confucian morality had hitherto been generally applied in a dogmatic way. Now it was rationalised, far beyond the dreams of Confucius, and given a kind of metaphysical sanction. Chu Hsi's ethical system therefore seemed particularly suited to the needs of the rulers of Japan. Its central point was loyalty, and though it insisted upon the importance of learning it set great store on orthodoxy, being in essence moderate, practical and conservative. Its very definition of evil is "disarrangement" or "confusion," which can conveniently be taken to mean disturbance of ancient order.

The Tokugawa Government consequently gave all possible encouragement to followers of Chu Hsi, and they supported teachers like Hayashi Razan, who most violently denounced all other creeds, not Buddhism and Christianity alone but any variation from orthodox Confucianism as stated by its official expositors. In

---

* Strictly speaking Chu Hsi was not a monist, but his dualism was very queer, and most of his Japanese followers discarded it.

other words the Bakufu, while showing a commendable desire to
promote learning, endeavoured to suppress the spirit of free inquiry. At first they met with some measure of success, and during
most of the seventeenth and eighteenth centuries the Chu Hsi
school was supreme in Japan, producing a number of learned
moralists; and although it presently encountered hostile currents
of thought and languished for a short time it did not lose its vitality
until it was, in common with other ancient philosophies, shaken by
contact with Western thought in the eighteen-fifties. Some idea of
its influence can be best gained from a glance at the careers of its
leading exponents. Hayashi Razan was followed by Kinoshita
Junan (1621-1698), who had three celebrated pupils, Amamori
Hōshū (1611-1708), Murō Kyūsō (1658-1734) and Arai Hakuseki
(1656-1726). Amamori is remarkable chiefly as an exponent of
that syncretic principle so common in Japanese history, by which
Buddhism, Confucianism and Taoism were regarded as different
expressions of one truth, the three legs of a philosophical tripod.
To this extent he was heretical, since no strict Confucianist could
be so eclectic, but his views were perhaps an entering wedge, which
helped to split the traditional school.

Arai Hakuseki is a more conspicuous figure in his country's
chronicles. He may be looked upon as a fine example of that remarkable apparition in Oriental history, the philosopher-states-
man. During his few years of office he was fully trusted by the
Shōgun, and he endeavoured to apply to problems of administration the principles of Confucian philosophy. He held the classical
view that government should be conducted by means of Music and
Rites. Stated so baldly, it seems a fantastic theory; but Hakuseki
was, though bigoted and perhaps reactionary, an earnest, practical-
minded man. He knew the refining influence of the arts, and he
was aware that manners are easier to establish than morals. The
Chinese had long ago discovered the social and political value of
etiquette and decorum, and it was, he thought, neglect of their
uses which brought about all those so deplorable features of the
Genroku age, its frivolity, its extravagance, its taste for gay pleasures and its disrespect for old standards. That was why he pressed
the Shōgun to substitute ancient music for Nō performances, and
why he travelled to Kyōto to make a special study of Court eti-

quette. He paid great attention to all matters of ceremony at the Shōgun's palace, and drew up regulations governing the dress to be worn on official and private occasions. Such matters were not his only concern, for he advised the Shōgun on matters of finance and trade, took a hand in currency reform, and fought hard against corruption and the waste of public money. But he carried so far his principles of government on purely civil lines that there was a certain militaristic reaction on the accession of the eighth Shōgun, Yoshimune (1716), who led a kind of "Back to Ieyasu" movement, endeavouring to revive the feudal regimentation of society; encouraging military exercises, to the consternation of many samurai now set in comfortable habits, but paradoxically enough relaxing the interdict upon Western learning. Yoshimune's policy is a little hard to understand, for it seems to be composed of conflicting elements. But he appears to have been a man of considerable talents and some originality of mind. Certain of his measures show that, while he approved of good old fashions, he was by no means reactionary but progressive and liberal by the standards of his day. He respected the orthodox Confucianism, but he was not prepared to deprive himself of wisdom from other sources. He therefore encouraged scholarship of every complexion, with results which he can scarcely have contemplated. He bestowed his patronage impartially upon Confucianists of various schools, thus setting up philosophical currents which were in course of time to engulf the Bakufu; and his attitude towards Western learning revived an interest in studies which had lapsed under the exclusion policy but in time were to be among the chief instruments of its reversal.

The chief adviser to the new Shōgun on matters of administration as well as philosophy was the celebrated Muro Kyūsō (1658-1734), who replaced Arai Hakuseki in his position. The presidency of the official college (Shōheikō) was still a preserve of the Hayashi family, and Chu Hsi's philosophy remained the orthodox teaching. But influences were at work which tended to undermine its authority. Kyūsō, though belonging to the Chu Hsi school, gave to its doctrines a very individual flavour. In his hands they came to differ from the cold dogmatics of his predecessors, who held rather harsh views about virtue, and gained a warmth and an immediate interest which made them welcome to average thinking men. He was strictly orthodox in intention, and a fierce enemy of schism, but while he was stern on points of duty and loyalty as foundations of the military creed, he differed from most of its exponents in preaching pity and humility, which are hardly explicit in the code called *Bushidō*. In that sense perhaps he departed from orthodoxy, though he would not have admitted it. Certain of his older contemporaries, moreover, had already moved away from the strictest Chinese doctrines. Kaibara Ekken has already been mentioned as a scholar interested in education, who expounded philosophy in simple language. He wrote a great deal about Happiness, which he identified with Virtue, and he was by no means an unswerving advocate of Chinese practice. Yamazaki Anzai (1618-1682), though a follower of Chu Hsi, went many steps further in his disapproval of Chinese institutions. In his later years he came under the influence of students of the native religion and the annals which traced the descent of the emperors from the gods; and he evolved a curious compromise between the doctrines of Chu Hsi and the principles of nationalism. The strict Confucianists of his day were aghast, and one of them (Hattori) said: "This is a funny kind of Chu Hsi." But Anzai had started a movement that was later to have a profound influence upon political, if not philosophical opinion in Japan. It was he, and his followers, who gave an impetus to the anti-Chinese school which, by restoring the ancient literature of Japan and delving into her ancient chronicles, gave new life to the Shintō cult over which the imperial line presided. They thus made it clear that the Shōgun was, if not a usurper, at least a mere delegate of the throne, and so furnished the enemies of the Bakufu with the political weapon by which it was ultimately despatched.

It has been necessary to describe this reaction against pure Confucianism at some length, because it is important to observe that it set in very soon after the establishment of the Tokugawa régime. Once the prestige of Buddhism had vanished, Shintō could begin to raise its head; and once men began to question the interpretations of Virtue given by the official philosophers of the Shōgunate, it was open to doubt whether loyalty to the throne did not transcend loyalty to a feudal overlord. It is interesting to observe to what extremes even a Confucian scholar could be carried by his nationalism. Anzai is stated to have cried that if Confucius or Mencius ever came interfering with Japan he and his followers would don their armour, grasp their swords and destroy the enemy!

There were other powerful rivals of the Chu Hsi school, of which the most important were the followers of the Chinese philosopher Wang Yang-ming, called in Japan Ō-Yōmei (1472-1529). He may be briefly described as an idealist whose teaching was directly opposed to that of Chu Hsi in that he held self-knowledge to be the highest kind of learning, and self-culture man's highest duty. The professors of the Chu Hsi school insisted on the necessity of knowledge as a preparation for right conduct. The Ō-Yōmei school, though not opposed to learning, believed in the rule of conscience and attached the greatest importance to introspection. They did not make much headway at first, being frowned upon by the authorities, but they later gained many adherents, including some of the most remarkable men and finest characters of the age. It is interesting to speculate upon the reasons for this success. They seem tolerably clear, if we look back for an analogy to the record of Zen Buddhism in Japan. Like Zen, the Ō-Yōmei philosophy rejected the authority of written works, recommended a practical subjective morality, and insisted upon the intuitive perception of truth to be reached by self-study and self-command. Such doctrines, because they were free from traditionalism and pedantry, had always appealed to the most vigorous and most thoughtful type of Japanese of the upper classes, and it is perhaps because they were dimly aware of this that the Bakufu opposed the Ō-Yōmei school, since independence of mind was not a quality they could safely encourage. The most celebrated Japanese followers of Ō-Yōmei were resolute men, of a reforming spirit, and it is noteworthy that the list includes, as well as great scholars, leaders of revolutionary movements like Ōshio, who attacked Ōsaka at the head of a hungry mob in 1837, and Yoshida Shōin,* who broke the exclusion edicts in 1859. We cannot stop to study the work of these men, but we must mention the name of Nakae Tōjū (1608-1648), who founded the Ō-Yōmei school in Japan and thus sowed the seed of opposition to the authority of official Confucianism. His teachings, as they were handed down, were subjected to changes and accre-

* There is an account of his life by R. L. Stevenson.

tions. Like Yamazaki Anzai's views, they were combined with Shintō, or applied to the principles of government, usually in a manner unfavourable to the Tokugawa interests. Indeed it is most noticeable that Confucian philosophy throughout the Yedo period tended, in the hands of Japanese scholars, to identify itself with movements for the restoration of Shintō and the Monarchy. Perhaps this was to be expected, since the Japanese throughout their history had always been more interested in politics than in philosophy; but it is none the less worthy of remark. Fujiwara, the first great exponent of Chu Hsi, said: "Shintō and Confucianism are the same truth under different names." Hayashi Razan said: "Shintō is Ōdō (Loyalty to the Sovereign) and Ōdō is Confucianism";[1] and as scholars all over Japan continued their researches into the history and literature of their own country, it became evident that the Tokugawa Shōguns, by usurping the Imperial power, had committed an offence against all those codes. It may therefore fairly be said that by attempting to found its rule upon Confucian ethics the Bakufu contributed to its own destruction. Even the so-called Ancient School (Kogakuha) of philosophy, though it claimed to revive the doctrines of antiquity and went back to Confucius and Mencius, placed entirely new interpretations on the words of those sages. All its early leaders were opposed to the orthodox Chu Hsi school. Yamaga Sokō (1622-1685) was a student of military science, and is regarded as one of the founders of *Bushidō*. Yet he was rusticated for his intransigeance, lived in Asano's fief and, as we have seen, inspired the forty-seven *rōnin*. Itō Jinsai (1627-1705) was a leader in Kyōto of the revival of ancient Japanese literature, and the first systematic opponent of Chu Hsi. Ogyū Sorai (1666-1728) was an original and powerful thinker, who believed in absolutism and served the Bakufu faithfully, but he also was heterodox as a philosopher, and his influence contributed to the weakening of the official school.

Though these philosophers differed among themselves most violently, and were given to using the most unrestrained language about one another, they were on the whole unanimous in approving existing social institutions. They disagreed on points of political theory, but it does not appear that any of them, except perhaps some extreme followers of Ō-Yōmei, were against existing class

divisions and prevailing conceptions of social duty. Yet it is probable that here they might have found a worthy outlet for their
reforming zeal. It is one of the most conspicuous features of the
morality of those times that it was a class morality, or to be more
accurate a group morality. The authorities liked dealing with
groups, and thus discouraged individual responsibility. The system
of boards and councils and duplicated offices which characterised
the higher administration had its replicas right through the scale,
down to the small *kumi* or group of five peasants which formed the
unit of rural organisation. This arrangement, while it fostered
mutual obligations within a group, tended to promote if not
hostility between groups at least a neglect of the duty of one
individual to another and to society at large. It will be apparent
that such a limited conception of morality must have promoted
discipline at the expense of a wider integrity: and though we need
not labour this point, it may assist the reader, if he will bear it in
mind, to understand some puzzling aspects of the culture of Japan
under a feudal régime. Perhaps the most characteristic example
of contemporary ethical practice was to be found in the commercial
class. Certain prescribed obligations between employer and servant, or master and apprentice, seem to have been most scrupulously observed, and solidarity was secured by a strict mutual
faithfulness among the members of a trade guild. But this high
standard of corporate morality was offset by a ruthless unconcern
for the rights of persons outside the group, amounting sometimes
to grossly anti-social conduct. It is perhaps for some reason such as
this that when Japan was thrown open to foreign trade, and organised upon a new mercantile basis, it was not the members of the old
commercial class who became leaders of new enterprise in finance
and industry. Their outlook was too narrow, they had thrived
under protection, and with a few exceptions they fell back to
huckstering, while ambitious samurai of low and middle rank
became bankers, merchants and manufacturers. Their standard,
too, was a class standard, but they had a broader horizon.

Individualism is not the whole of wisdom; and nobody will deny
that, in spite of its shortcomings, the creed embodied in *Bushido*
was of the greatest value to Japan in trying periods of transition.
The moral life which it fostered fitted the social framework of

feudal times, but as the feudal constitution disintegrated under economic stress then the principles which supported it were bound to be called in question. One challenge came from within, as new philosophical ideas and political sentiments gained acceptance. Another came from without, when Yoshimune while Shōgun (1716-1745) opened the door again to occidental learning. Since the exclusion edicts, the only channel of communication with the West had been the little Dutch settlement at Nagasaki, and the Japanese could learn of the outside world only through merchants and shipmasters and, on rare occasions, some learned man like Kaempfer, attached to the regular Dutch embassy to Yedo in 1690, or a surgeon belonging to the Dutch East India Company. Now that the Shōgun allowed the importation of foreign books (except those relating to Christianity) the Japanese very naturally first turned their attention to those branches of western science that seemed immediately useful, such as medicine and astronomy. Of surgery they had gained some empiric knowledge from Portuguese and Dutch visitors more than a century before, but for further progress they must be able to read Dutch books. They encountered at first the most heartbreaking difficulties, for even the official interpreters to the factory at Deshima knew only a few common phrases, which they had noted down in *kana** and learned by heart, while scholars in Yedo had, after many years, painfully acquired from them the alphabet and a small vocabulary of words like Sun, Moon, Earth, Man, Tiger, Dragon, and Bamboo. Even such meagre accomplishment was frowned upon by the Bakufu in unauthorised scholars, and there is a story that the writer of a work called *Tales of the Red-Hairs* (1765) was reprimanded because as an illustration of foreign customs he reproduced the alphabet. Gradually, by feats of almost incredible patience, dictionaries were compiled and works on anatomy, geography, and other sciences were slowly translated. A manuscript Dutch-Japanese dictionary was made for the Government by Aoki Bunzō, an official Confucianist, in 1745. A book of anatomical drawings with explanatory text was, after years of labour, translated by a physician named Sugita Gempaku in 1774, and by the opening of

---

* Almost the least suitable script in the world for phonetic notation of this kind.

the nineteenth century there had been acquired in Japan a fair knowledge of some western sciences and, it should be added, of western politics.

More than one cause contributed to swell the enthusiasm for this new learning. The mid-eighteenth century in Japan was in some respects a prosperous period. Yoshimune's economic policies benefited at least certain classes, and there ensued one of those extravagant periods when people look round for new amusements and new ways of spending money. This gave a fillip to the import of curiosities from Europe, and there was a great demand for glass-ware, watches, woollens and velvets, as well as things like telescopes, magic-lanterns, Leyden jars, thermometers, barometers and so on. All these (fashionable at a time when we were beginning to admire China teacups and the inscrutable wisdom of the East) stimulated the interest of thoughtful men, and led to further inquiries. Later, when times were bad, as after the great famine of 1783-1787, many grew restless, and some became dimly conscious that all was not well with their country's institutions. Typical of this class, tired of their own civilisation and eager to learn about the West, was Hiraga Gennai (1732-1779), who sold all his possessions to buy a Dutch book on natural history, made a deep study of medical botany, formed a commercial company, constructed electrical apparatus, wove a fire-proof cloth by using asbestos, and in the intervals of his researches threw off extremely popular *joruri* plays and sketches as a means of livelihood. After 1790 more than one attempt was made by Russian and American ships to open relations with Japan, and as early as 1787 some patriots had grown alarmed at her defenceless state, while others had declared that she had much to learn and had better bring her seclusion to an end. Some scholars, of whom one was Sugita Gempaku who translated the Anatomy, would have liked to import foreign learning and then close the country again, so that they could digest it in a realm of peace; but Sugita observed scornfully that the modern samurai were so miserably effeminate that they could not be trusted to keep out invaders. Perhaps the wisest were men like Honda Rimei (Toshiaki) who saw the weakness of Japan's economic situation, and wrote (*circa* 1798) that her culture was at a standstill. The only solution of her difficulties, he said, was for her ships to sail the seas and earn wealth in foreign trade. It was even suggested that, since a series of good harvests had followed the famine after 1790, the export of rice would benefit the samurai.

It was not merely practical benefits that were foreseen from intercourse with the West, for there were a few who felt that China was not the only home of wisdom. It cannot be said that Japan then turned to Europe for the sublimer sorts of knowledge. Confucian philosophy of one kind or another remained supreme, and perhaps it was unfortunate that, when at last the Japanese had time to consider the nobler efforts of the western mind, it was the dreary ratiocinations of Herbert Spencer or the homiletic of men like Benjamin Franklin and Samuel Smiles which seemed best to stay their intellectual pangs. In the arts they had as much to teach as to learn, and it was not long before their colour-prints, their lacquer and their porcelains began to provide us with a somewhat astonished delight. The mysteries of their æsthetics, the beauties of their ancient painting and sculpture, had to wait some generations before they could be understood. But meanwhile Japanese artists turned to the study of western methods. Their own schools were flourishing enough, for there are great names in the later Yedo period: Ito Jakuchū (1713-1800), Tani Bunchō (1765-1842), Maruyama Ōkyo (1733-1795), and many celebrated masters of *ukiyoe* and of the humorous or eccentric school known as *Bunjingwa* (Literary Men's Pictures).[2] Naturally therefore the Japanese were interested in questions of technique rather than of æsthetic theory, and they studied carefully Western principles of perspective and chiaroscuro. These were not entirely new to them, for there are Japanese paintings of European kings on horseback, which look like copies of tapestry and date from the early seventeenth century; and a painter named Yamada Uemon, who was involved in the Shimabara Rebellion of 1637, was known for his pictures in foreign style. But the anti-Christian edicts made men chary of showing an interest in western art, in which religious motives were so common, and it was not until the time of Shiba Kōkan (1737-1818) that the study was resumed. He painted a great number of rather bad pictures, both oils and water colours, which were widely distributed, and brought him a considerable reputation in his day. But he is more deservedly known for his all-round, insatiable interest in western things—geography, history, inoculation, engraving, all the natural sciences he could learn anything about and particularly those which had a strong spectacular element, requiring the use of globes and other exciting instruments. In their restless curiosity he and his friend Hiraga Gennai were but slightly abnormal specimens of a now numerous type, men who wanted something new, they did not know exactly what, but certainly nothing that was offered by the culture of the East.

All these intellectual forces which we have attempted to describe—the decline of orthodox Confucianism, the revival of national history, literature and religion, the loyalist movement and the steady penetration of western ideas—combined with powerful economic tendencies to break down the exclusion policy, and in 1868 to restore the imperial dynasty to its ancient supremacy.[3]

2. ECONOMIC MOVEMENTS

THE Tokugawa Government, calling in the aid of philosophers, attempted to solve their numerous difficulties by treating them as if they were mainly ethical problems, and most of their efforts were directed towards preserving unchanged the existing class divisions. But they were in reality faced with economic conditions which could not be remedied on such lines. Fundamentally their problem was an economic problem, the perennial problem of food supply; and this they could never solve so long as they refused to change the social institutions over which they presided. During the years from 1600 to 1725 the population of Japan increased, agriculture taken as a whole prospered, industry made moderate advances, and methods of distribution were improved; so that the country was able to support a general rise in the standard of living. But further progress was checked by a number of obstacles. The most important of these we have already enumerated, when tracing the first results of the transition from agricultural to mercantile economy. The substitution of money for rice as a medium of exchange, while it caused a decline in the power of the samurai which was disturbing to the Bakufu, had an even more serious effect in that it reduced the productive power of the farmers. A mere transfer of wealth from one unproductive class to another, from soldiers to merchants,

would doubtless have caused an unpleasant derangement of the
social order; but this might have been adjusted without much
difficulty, particularly as many of the *chōnin* rendered services to
the community in the carriage of goods, the investment of capital,
and the manufacture of essential commodities. The sufferings of
the farmers, however, their poverty and their tenancy troubles, in
a word the agrarian problem, struck at the foundation of the State.

The agrarian problem in Japan under the Tokugawa régime,
though complicated in its details, can at very little expense of
accuracy be stated in the following terms. The life of the peasant,
wretched at the best of times, was rendered almost unbearable by
fluctuating prices of rice and by the rising standard of living among
all classes but his own. Since no surplus was left to him by the tax
collector, he could profit little by a good crop, while a bad crop
left him on the verge of starvation. These misfortunes affected the
farming class in various ways, but nearly always to their increasing
disadvantage. Some got into debt* to the few slightly more prosperous cultivators than themselves or to usurious townspeople; and
for a peasant to get into debt was to be on a steep road down to
destruction. Some migrated to other districts, in the hope of
making a fresh start. Some absconded and became vagrants. Some
made their way to the towns in search of employment as domestic
servants or day-labourers. Those who remained on the land found
themselves short of workers for their fields, and unable to support
their families. And meanwhile the daimyō and their retainers,
pressed by the merchants and money-lenders, turned the screw on
the already tortured peasants, so that (to quote from a work written
before 1750) the farmers were treated by officials and tax-gatherers
"as a cruel driver treats an ox or a horse, when he puts a heavy
burden on the beast, and lashes it mercilessly, getting all the
angrier when it stumbles and whipping more violently than ever,
with loud curses." Peasants were often compared to seeds, like

---

* Because farmers now began to need money for a variety of purposes, where
they had previously bartered with rice. Owing to intensive culture, which the
increased demand for foodstuffs brought about, they had to buy manure. And
they had to pay with money for agricultural implements, horses, and oddments
of clothing, &c., which rose steadily in price in terms of silver. The feudal landholders, moreover, tended to exact taxes in money instead of rice, of course, at
a rate favourable to themselves.

sesame, which were pressed for their oil, because "the harder you press the more you squeeze out." Such testimony to the misery of farmers is to be found throughout Tokugawa literature; naturally, since the position of agriculture was so desperate that it could not escape the notice of the most callous observer. Nor can it be said that the rulers of Japan were blind to these abuses. They tried to remedy them, and to understand them within the limits of their knowledge. Indeed it is one of the most striking features of the intellectual activity of the age that its leading scholars concerned themselves with economic problems, and its learned literature consists largely of treatises on agriculture, currency and similar topics. The greatest Confucian scholars paid the closest attention to such problems. Arai Hakuseki wrote on currency reform; Dazai Shun wrote a treatise on Political Economy; and other well-known philosophers in the eighteenth century, of whom we need mention only Ogyū Sorai, Muro Kyūsō, and Kumazawa Banzan, composed important essays or memorials on similar subjects.* It is remarkable that, at least until the early part of the nineteenth century even the most penetrating minds among them failed as a rule to grasp the truth, that the wealth of Japan was adequate neither in amount nor in distribution to the needs of her society. Some of them saw it dimly, but most of them proposed only neat ethical solutions of the terrible equation of supply and demand. Peasants must work hard and respect their betters, merchants must be honest and content with small profits, and samurai must not be extravagant.

Meanwhile the decrease in the farming population, which may be looked upon as having set in from about 1725, reacted further upon the condition of the peasants, accentuating their already severe distress and giving still greater speed to movements that tended to diminish food supply or to cause disastrous fluctuations in prices. These movements cannot be described fully here, but some idea of their nature can be gained from the following disconnected account of the more spectacular features of agrarian

* There was moreover a considerable body of popular writing of the same kind. Thus the *Tsūzoku Keizai Bunkō*, or Library of Popular Economics (Tokyo, 1916), consists of twelve volumes of reprints of popular works belonging to this period, dealing with money, trade, agriculture, &c., and this is only a selection of typical books.

distress. It should be premised that not all farmers were impoverished. There were a few who prospered, usually by getting a hold
on the land of other men, and working them like slaves, so that a
writer on social topics (*circa* 1800) could say: "For one man who
makes a fortune there are twenty or thirty reduced to penury."
Such impoverishment made it impossible for the peasants to support children, and they resorted freely to abortion and infanticide.
There are traces of these practices before Tokugawa times. Then
they seem to have been sporadic and to have followed natural
calamities like famine and plague; but by the middle of the eighteenth century they were prevalent throughout Japan, and had
reached such alarming dimensions that they were prohibited by
official edict in 1767. Naturally such decrees had no success. Infanticide was regarded as a quite proper process, and was known as
mabiki,* which is the word used of thinning a row of vegetables by
uprooting. Conversely, in order to secure a supply of children for
work in the fields without the expense of bringing them up,
farmers were known to buy children kidnapped in the large towns
by regular traffickers known as "child merchants."

While infanticide and abortion kept down the numbers of the
agricultural population, there was also a constant drain upon
farm labour owing to the influx of peasants into the towns. City
life offered a refuge from the endless struggle on the land, to the
young a delightful prospect of pleasures and excitements, to their
parents a relief from oppression, for as *chōnin* they were untaxed
and received a money wage which they could spend as they chose.
Even as early as 1712 the decrease of the rural population began to
cause concern, and the Tokugawa government decreed that all
peasants must return to their native villages. Decrees of this kind
were repeated at intervals until as late as 1843, when forcible
measures were taken to send migrators back to their provinces
from Yedo. Nothing, however, could stop men from deserting their
farms, since hardly any punishment could be worse than the life
they had to lead in the country. There is no means of knowing
exactly the movements of population during this period, but it may
be safely assumed that the number of agricultural workers re-

---

* More euphemistic terms were *kaeshi* and *modoshi*, which mean "sending
back."

mained almost stationary even if it did not actually decrease. It appears that there was, generally speaking, an increase in the area of land under cultivation, thanks to reclamation in certain parts of Japan, and methods of cultivation tended to improve, if only to meet the exactions of landlords. But most of this advantage was offset by abuses. In northern and eastern Japan large tracts were abandoned by farmers because the land would not produce enough to satisfy the tax-gatherer. At the other extreme there were good farms which were so productive that the officials marked them down for absurdly high assessment, with the fantastic result that their owners relinquished them to poor peasants, who even in some cases had to be given a sum of money to induce them to accept the gift. Into the question of tenancy we need not enter here, but it is worth observing that the poverty of the peasants forced them, in many instances, to surrender their land by sale or pledge to creditors, and there were thus brought into existence two new classes, one of persons who owned land which they did not farm, the other of persons who farmed land which they did not own. This created new hardships for agriculturalists and a clash of interests between tenant farmers and landowners (other than feudal lords). The most curious anomalies arose, as for example when a landowner reproved his tenant for producing too much rice, because taxation increased in proportion to the yield, while the tenant objected that unless the yield were high there was no surplus for his own subsistence. Tenant disputes continued throughout the eighteenth and nineteenth centuries and in some parts of Japan they have recurred in quite recent years.

As if the peasantry were not sufficiently oppressed by human greed and stupidity, Nature took a hand in completing the tale of their miseries. There were frequent epidemics of pestilence, while famine raged from 1732 to 1733 and again from 1783 to 1787. The loss of life through plain starvation, and the lowering of the power of resistance of the ill-fed classes, reduced the population by over 1,000,000 in the years between 1780 and 1786. It may be imagined that those peasants who had any spirit left revolted against their hardships in such ways as were open to them. Accordingly we find that during the latter half of the Tokugawa régime there were frequent agrarian risings. Sometimes they were demonstrations in force made by small tenant farmers goaded to desperate action by the oppression of their creditors, but often they were blind, angry rushes against the local authorities, which generally ended in the cruel death of the ringleaders. Bitter tenancy disputes are recorded early after 1700. In these, though on the whole the landowners were in a strong position, a compromise was usually reached because the tenants in the last resort could—and occasionally did—merely abandon their farms. More serious were the farmers' riots, which as time progressed took on an increasingly political complexion. As far back as the Kamakura period there had been agrarian risings (known as *tsuchi-ikki*), some of which we have already mentioned with reference to the Virtuous Administration (*Tokusei*) edicts of the fourteenth and fifteenth centuries. They were not always purely agrarian riots, for at times they were complicated by religious fervour, as in the *Ikkō Ikki* or Fanatic Risings, and at times they were stimulated by class hatred, as when peasants banded together, crying "Down with the samurai," to resist the depredations of military factions. In the Tokugawa period the motive was at first purely economic, and the action taken by the peasants varied from a humble petition to an armed demonstration. The classical instance is that of Sakura Sōgorō, a poor farmer who on behalf of 300 of his fellows oppressed by their lord presented a memorial to the Shōgun himself, in 1651. The guilty baron was punished by the Bakufu for his misrule, but Sōgorō and his wife were crucified, having first seen their children beheaded. From about 1750 peasant uprisings became more frequent.* Sometimes they were mere peaceful demonstrations, sometimes they were angry revolts by armed mobs in their thousands. Generally the leaders were punished by death because such combinations were illegal, but their demands were mostly accepted; and it is significant that towards the year 1800 the rioters became bolder and the samurai less inclined to resist.

To this account of agrarian troubles it is only fair to add that not all feudal barons were tyrannical and not all tax-gatherers corrupt. Despite the horrors that we have depicted, there were territories, notably those of "Outside Lords," in which the peas-

---

* More than fifty are mentioned in published historical works after 1714, and there are MS. accounts of hundreds more.

ants were well enough treated, allowed a fair measure of self-government, and secured against usury and eviction. Thus certain enlightened daimyō gave allowances to peasants to enable them to bring up children, and in other ways improved conditions in the villages, while in certain fiefs there still survived a class of well-to-do self-reliant farmer descended from the mediæval warrior who had tilled his land between campaigns. Thanks largely to this combination of paternalism and autonomy, the Japanese peasant (to quote the words of an authority* whose learning and judgment are beyond question) "emerged from the feudal period with little or no active interest and training in the conduct of the larger affairs of the country, but with the sterling virtue of industry, with a remarkable capacity for discipline, and with a secure though diminutive holding in land."

If we now turn from the country to the town we see an entirely different picture. The superficial aspects of city life we have attempted to portray in an account of the culture of Genroku, and there can be no doubt that the gaiety and extravagance of that period betokened a prosperous society in which money came as easily as it went. Yet the prosperity of the merchants was built upon the misfortunes of other classes. The wealth which the daimyō extracted from the peasants was passed on to the samurai, but it soon left their purses. By the opening years of the eighteenth century the military class were feeling acutely the pinch of poverty and the power of the townspeople. The immediate cause of their decline was the breakdown of rice economy. The revenues of the daimyō and the stipends of their retainers were fixed in terms of rice. But most of them lived in towns, at least for a great part of the year. There they needed money for their daily needs; needs which, moreover, increased as the standard of living in cities rose owing to the lavish ways of the daimyō and the prosperous habits of the bourgeoisie. They could convert their rice into money only at rates fixed by the merchants, and somehow they always found themselves the losers. Either the price of rice was low, or the coinage was debased, and in any case they scorned to inquire into vulgar questions of money, since anything that savoured of bargaining was beneath their dignity. Many powerful barons were in

*Asakawa. *Contributions of Feudal Japan to New Japan*—1912.

the hands of money-lenders and one writer said: "The anger of
the wealthy merchants of Ōsaka can strike terror into the hearts
of the daimyō." Deeply involved in debt, the daimyō looked
round for means of making or saving money. A few encouraged
industries in their fiefs, such as cotton-spinning and the production of special kinds of silk textiles, and gradually it became clear
to many members of the military class that they could get out of
the grip of the merchants only by following the merchants' example. But the higher their rank, the less inclined were they to
step down from their pedestal; and anyhow there were natural
limits to such industrial expansion. For the most part the feudal
lords attempted less scientific methods of relieving their own distress. They borrowed money from their samurai, by the simple
device of reducing their stipends. Nominally a certain proportion,
from one-tenth to six-tenths of the annual grant of rice, was held
back, to be issued at a later, unspecified date; but in practice this
was a forced loan, at no interest, in perpetuity. No wonder, then,
that the samurai class fell into even more serious indigence than
before, and that their loyalty was strained. Their growing distress
gradually ate into their idealism and consumed their pride. As
early as 1700 we learn of sad lapses from military virtue. They dispensed with their hereditary retainers, who should have carried
their spear or led their horse in wartime, and hired townsmen as
servants, often first exacting a money payment. They thus began
to destroy the old lifelong feudal relationship between master and
man, which had been based on loyalty and not on cash. The most
needy of them even resorted to infanticide when they found their
families growing too numerous. Others would sometimes, displacing their natural heirs, adopt the son of a rich commoner if
they could induce his father to pay handsomely enough for the
privilege. This was extremely significant of impending social
changes, for it meant that the samurai class no longer prided
themselves, to the exclusion of all other sentiments, on the purity
of their blood and the dignity of their ancestral name. The practice grew in frequency, and towards the end of the Tokugawa
régime it was quite usual for a commoner to purchase the rank of
samurai. Such transactions are recorded as early as 1710, when
decrees were promulgated calling attention to the love of money

and the decay of honesty in the military class. But these measures could not right the economic situation of the samurai, and contemporary literature contains many passages which show that often their integrity declined with their fortunes, and this double collapse brought them slowly but surely down in the esteem of the commoners. They could no longer slash the commoners with their swords for fancied insults. Sometimes their swords were in pawn, with their armour and their ceremonial robes, and mostly they dared not resent affronts from their creditors. Their situation can be expressed, if we may be pardoned a feeble play upon words, by saying that they could no longer cut down merchants because they were obliged to cut down expenses. Their distress as individuals was serious enough, but the decline in their prestige as a class caused the government grave misgivings. Various remedies were tried for the benefit of the daimyō and samurai. The unsuccessful attempts of the Bakufu to regulate the price of rice have already been mentioned, as also their disastrous currency measures. They tried of course the old policy of government by exhortation, and issued edicts on thrift at intervals from the seventeenth to the nineteenth century, but it was idle to prescribe saving to those who had no money to spare. They endeavoured to fix rates of interest, with no real effect; and they resorted to the extreme measure of repudiation, that certain symptom of a changing social order. As early as 1716 certain obligations previously incurred by samurai were declared void. In 1730 townspeople were forbidden to assemble outside samurai houses to collect debts. In 1789 a celebrated edict decreed that all debts incurred before 1785 by *hatamoto* and other direct retainers of the Shōgun should be cancelled, and all debts incurred in 1785 and after were to be repaid in instalments so small that the creditors lost most of their capital.

All these causes contributed to a fusion of classes, or at least to a blurring of that distinction between classes upon which the feudal régime was based. Farmers, we have seen, became townsmen. Townsmen bought farms. Commoners and some farmers entered the ranks of samurai by adoption or purchase. And it was not uncommon for samurai to surrender their social privileges and become *chōnin*, generally to their financial advantage. By about 1850

if not before, there was a regular tariff for the entry of a commoner
into a samurai family, and many men of humble antecedents thus
obtained samurai status, including (in the words of a writer in
1816): "Sons of low-class commoners; relatives of usurers; sons of
blind men;* criminals who had fled to Yedo from their native
towns; people expelled by their daimyō or master; excommuni-
cated priests; sons of monks who had broken their vows, and even
members of the pariah class." But the new samurai were not all so
disreputable as this notice would have one believe, and it was often
the most ambitious or worthy of the commoners who, as a first step
in their careers, bought positions as low grade samurai. Some of
these rose to important positions towards the end of the Shōgunate,
becoming dependable officials, particularly in posts where they
were concerned with financial problems or city administration.
Indeed it may be said that the organisation of Japan at and
following the Restoration of 1868 was in a great measure the work
of samurai of the lower grades. Prince Itō, one of the most famous
of these, was the son of a respectable farmer who had purchased
the position of samurai from a retainer of the Mōri family in
western Japan.

This growing confusion of classes, with its redistribution of
wealth and power, though it brought the townsmen to a new
position of importance in society, naturally did not operate in
favour of every inhabitant of the towns. The mercantile organisation of the *chōnin* was almost as stiff and minutely regulated as the
feudal hierarchy, while their charters and their guild privileges
were so jealously guarded that free competition was almost unknown. It therefore resulted that they were often able to hold the
community at ransom, whether by putting prices up against consumers or by keeping wages down against workmen. Their financial control was such that the uncertainty of money values in the
long run worked out to their advantage while it impoverished
almost every other class. The usurers and the rice brokers and the
great wholesale dealers in particular grew fat, and though the
Shōgunate tried to reduce their corpulence by levies called *goyō-
kin* or "money for government use" it usually came back to them

---

* Because blind men were specially protected and their debtors forced to pay
them, so that as usurers they became rich.

in another form. It was the plain citizens, the small shopkeepers and the day-labourers who suffered, and they constituted the mass of the townspeople. Official attempts to stabilise rice prices at a high level in the interest of the samurai time after time brought the populace to the verge of starvation. Then the Bakufu would grow alarmed and prohibit rice-hoarding or try to fix the price at a lower figure. All their interference only made matters worse, and food riots, of the type known as *uchikowashi*, or "smashing up," occurred repeatedly. The rioters raided shops and the houses of rich men, looting food and wrecking buildings. These risings occurred throughout the eighteenth century, and into the nineteenth, but the most serious was that of 1787. This was at the end of a long famine. The price of rice, 61 *momme* in 1785, rose to 101 in 1786 and 187 in 1787. There were raids not only in Yedo, but throughout the country, from Kyūshū in the west to Mutsu in the north-east. In 1837 there was a pitiful uprising led by one Ōshio, a scholar and a leading Ō-Yōmei philosopher, who had already sold his books to help the hungry poor. The rebels attacked Ōsaka, and tried to set fire to the city, but they were put down by government troops and Ōshio took his own life. It is an ironical commentary on the position of the samurai under the Tokugawa règime that on most of the rare occasions when they were called to arms it was to suppress a mob of starving indigents. They themselves were, it is true, victims of circumstances; but no panegyric can cleanse the feudal record of such stains as the murder of Sōgorō, typical of the pitiless oppression of the weak by a class whose rule was founded upon violence. It was high time that it came to an end.

Such were the economic conditions which the feudal government had to face in the first decades of the nineteenth century: and there is no doubt that they were ill at ease. The strongest rivals of the Shōgunate, the great *tozama* or Outside Lords, like Satsuma, Chōshū (Mōri), Tosa and Hizen, had always held aloof from the Tokugawa. They had governed their fiefs in their own way, kept clear of most of the financial embarrassments which were weakening the Shōgunate, encouraged industry and commerce in their domains without falling into the clutches of usurers, and, perhaps most important of all, had preserved among their people the old feudal virtues of discipline and frugality. The Bakufu, even in its most enlightened phases, had always governed in the interest of the Tokugawa family and their close adherents. Consequently there was little in the Tokugawa policy, or its execution, to command the allegiance of these great barons or of the discontented samurai—not only masterless men but also retainers of the Shōgun and his hereditary vassals—whose numbers were constantly swollen by financial distress, and whose loyalty was breaking under the strain of misrule. The country was full of restless spirits, dissatisfied with their condition and thirsting for activity. There were nobles who wanted independence and foreign trade, to develop the resources of their domains; samurai who wanted opportunities to use their talents, whether as soldiers or as officials; merchants who wanted to break the monopolies of the guilds; scholars who wanted to draw knowledge from new springs; humble peasants and townsmen who wanted just a little freedom from tax and tyranny. Every force but conservatism was pressing from within at the closed doors: so that when a summons came from without they were flung wide open, and all these imprisoned energies were released.

TABLE OF MAIN POLITICAL EVENTS IN YEDO PERIOD

A.D. 1615 Ieyasu promulgates the "Laws of Military Houses" (*Buke Hatto.*)
1616 Death of Ieyasu. Hidetada, Second Shōgun.
1617 Renewed persecution of Christians.
1622 Iemitsu, Third Shōgun (d. 1651).
1624 Expulsion of Spaniards.
1637-1638 Shimabara Rebellion. Japanese forbidden to travel abroad.
1639 Expulsion of Portuguese.
1640 Other Europeans excluded. Portuguese envoys from Macao beheaded.
1641 Dutch moved from Hirado and confined in Deshima.
1651 Ietsuna, Fourth Shōgun.
1657 Great fire in Yedo.
1660 Beginnings of Mito school of historians, under Tokugawa Mitsukuni. They promoted study of national literature and religion, thus setting on foot a revival movement which tended later to undermine the Shōgunate and to restore the imperial house to its legitimate supremacy.
1673 English attempt to renew trade relations fails.
1680 Tsunayoshi, Fifth Shōgun. Corrupt administration, great freedom of manners. "Genroku Period," 1688-1703.
1709 Ienobu, Sixth Shōgun. Advised by Confucian Arai Hakuseki.

Reaction against laxity of Tsunayoshi's régime. Attempted financial reforms.

1713 Ietsugu, Seventh Shōgun.

1715 Completion of "Great History of Japan" (*Dai-Nihonshi*) commenced by Mitsukuni.

1716 Yoshimune, Eighth Shōgun. Attempt to stiffen administration. Relaxation of edicts against western learning.

1745 Ieshige, Ninth Shōgun.

1760 Ieharu, Tenth Shōgun.

1786 Ienari, Eleventh Shōgun. Serious famines and epidemics.

1783-1787 Rice riots. Matsudaira Sadanobu, prime minister, attempts economic and social reform. Growing feeling against Shōgunate, owing largely to study of ancient history, literature and religion by scholars like Kamo Mabuchi (1697-1769), and Motoori (1730-1801), who published the *Kojiki* with a full commentary, and thus called attention to the claims of the imperial dynasty. Shintō revival movements.

1791-1792 American and Russian ships visit Japan but are sent away. Decrees against foreign shipping reissued.

1797 American ship (Eliza) calling at Nagasaki is treated as Dutch ship and allowed to trade. Slight relaxation of the edicts for a few years, and then strict enforcement.

1837 American vessel "Morrison" driven away from Yedo Bay.

1838 Ieyoshi, Twelfth Shōgun. Famines. Financial embarrassment of Shōgunate.

1846 U.S. warships at Uraga invite Japan to sanction foreign trade. Refused.

1853 Iesada, Thirteenth Shōgun.
Commander of U.S. squadron (Perry) repeats invitation and states he will return for an answer next year.

1854 Perry returns and treaty is concluded between Japan and U.S., followed shortly by treaties with other Powers.

1858 Iemochi, Fourteenth Shōgun.

1866 Yoshinobu (Keiki), Fifteenth Shōgun.

1867-1868 Resignation of Shōgun. Armed conflict between Shōgunate party and loyalists. Feudalism abolished and Monarchy restored.

NOTES TO CHAPTER XXIII

[1] Page 512. Strictly speaking Odō is not merely loyalty to the sovereign. Odō, the "Kingly Way" (in Chinese, Wangtao), is a Confucian ideal of government, an early version of philosophic anarchism according to which perfection of wisdom and benevolence in the ruler evokes perfection of conduct and loyalty in the people, so that laws and sanctions become unnecessary. It is, of course, easy and tempting for advocates of despotic rule to start from an assumption that the ruler is fully equipped with wisdom and benevolence, and thus to exact unquestioning trust from the people. In that sense it is correct to say that feudal philosophers like Hayashi Razan thought of Odō in terms

of loyalty to the sovereign, whose virtue they had already postulated. Their successors in modern times have perverted the classical doctrine of Wangtao so as to justify the extremest kind of totalitarianism, in which the ruler is infallible and the subject has no function but obedience.

² Page 516. For want of space, I could do no more than merely mention here the names of leading painters, but students of art history will find interesting material in this period, for it shows very clearly, parallel with other cultural developments, a revolt against old standards in art, and a revival in painting leading to the growth of new and original schools, mostly with a naturalistic outlook. I mentioned Tani Bunchō because, though not of the first rank, he was characteristic of the times in his eclecticism. He could paint in many styles and he also made some use of Western technique.

The Bunjingwa is an interesting phenomenon in Japanese æsthetics, which is not well understood by Western students. It provides a link between literature and painting and it furnishes a medium of expression for the man of taste and culture who is not necessarily a proficient artist. It has a dilettante flavour, but it is something more than the diversion of an amateur painter in water-colours, though I should hesitate to say where the difference lies. I can only suggest that the Bunjingwa would repay more careful study than it has hitherto received from students of Far Eastern art.

³ Page 517. In describing the intellectual forces which, in combination with economic trends, paved the way for the Restoration of 1868, attention should be paid to the revival of Japanese studies by the school of Wagakusha, that is to say scholars devoted to native learning in contrast to classical Chinese and Buddhist studies. Movements which conspired to bring about the surprising transformation of Japan in the latter part of the nineteenth century had already begun to make themselves felt in the eighteenth century. One of these was a movement in favour of Pure Shinto, as distinct from Chinese philosophical systems. This was favoured by the decline of Japanese Buddhism, which faced by the hostility of the official Confucianists had never recovered from the attacks of Nobunaga and Hideyoshi and the restrictive measures of Ieyasu. The Shinto movement, destined to play an important part in the downfall of the Tokugawa, stemmed from the literary activities of Mitsukuni (1628-1700), head of the Mito branch of the Tokugawa family, who with the help of a band of scholars composed the *Dai Nihonshi*, a general history of Japan down to 1413. It brought out clearly the nature of the forces which had caused the decline of imperial authority and the decay of the native creed. In the next century followed such distinguished exponents of Shinto and of the national language and literature as the great Wagakusha Mabuchi

(1697-1769), Motoori (1730-1801) and Hirata (1778-1843). Although the movement embodied in their works seems to be literary and philosophic, even sometimes purely philological, it had a most important political effect. It was intensely Japanese, and anti-Chinese and anti-Buddhist. But in exalting everything that was purely Japanese it had to fall back on the Kojiki, the Nihongi and other ancient writings which deal with the history of the imperial house. Here it found itself in conflict with doctrines acceptable at Yedo, since all its researches tended to glorify the Emperor and by implication to condemn the Shōguns as usurpers. Although the labours of the Wagakusha undoubtedly contributed to the overthrow of the feudal régime and the consequent opening of the country, it may be argued that the exaggerated nationalism of latter-day Japan, with its emphasis upon the "Japanese spirit" and its claim to peculiar racial virtues, was a lineal descendant of their antagonism to all foreign elements in Japanese culture.

INDEX

For the greater convenience of users of this index who are unfamiliar with the Japanese language, the given and family names of persons, both actual and mythological, appear in the index in small capitals. Titles of books, names of temples and specific names of statues and other works of art appear in the index in italics.